Tobacco Counterpoints

Jean Stubbs first went to Cuba in 1968 to conduct research for her PhD (University of London, 1975). She married there, had two children, and lived and worked in Havana until 1987. On her return to London, she was drawn into Caribbean and Latin American Studies, and served as chair of both the UK Society for Caribbean Studies and the regional Caribbean Studies Association. In 2009, she was awarded the UNESCO Toussaint Louverture Medal for combatting racism in political, literary and artistic fields, and in 2012 was elected a member of the Cuban Academy of History.

She has published widely on Cuba, with a specialist interest in tobacco, class, race, gender, nation and migration. In 1985, *Tobacco on the Periphery* (Cambridge University Press, republished by Amaurea Press, 2023) established her place as a pre-eminent historian of Cuban tobacco; and her work in particular on the Havana cigar has led her to trace cultivation, trade, manufacture, labour and consumption on a regional and global scale, linking commodity and migration histories, drawing on sociological, anthropological and agronomic approaches, as well as archival and oral history. Her work on contemporary Cuban migration built on this to explore how commodities and nation-branding have shaped new Cuban diasporic mobilities; and her interest in commodity frontiers and environmental history led her to co-produce the documentary *Cuba: Living Between Hurricanes* (2019).

Her most recent publications include the *Handbook of Commodity History* (Oxford University Press, 2024) and *Tobacco in Global Perspective: Trade, Knowledge and Labour, 1780-1960* (Palgrave Macmillan, 2024).

Jean is Professor Emerita of London Metropolitan University, and Associate Fellow of the Centre for Latin American and Caribbean Studies, University of London.

Tobacco Counterpoints

Cuba and the Global Habano

Jean Stubbs

Copyright © 2024 Jean Stubbs

The moral right of Jean Stubbs to be identified as author of this work has been asserted by her in accordance with the Copyright, Designs and Patents Act 1988

All rights reserved. Apart from any fair dealing for the purposes of criticism or review, as permitted under the Copyright Acts, no part of this book may be reproduced, copied or transmitted in any form or by any electronic or mechanical means, including information storage and retrieval systems, without permission in writing from the publisher.

ISBN 9781914278730 (hardback)
ISBN 9781914278693 (paperback)
ISBN 9781914278716 (ebook edition)

This edition © 2024 Amaurea Press

British Library Catalogue in Publishing Data
A catalogue record for this book is available from the British Library

Cover, book design & typesetting by Albarrojo
Published in the United Kingdom by Amaurea Press

Amaurea Press is an imprint of Amaurea Creative Productions Ltd.
London, United Kingdom
www.amaureapress.com

Printed and bound by CPI Group (UK) Ltd., Croydon, CR0 4YY

*To all who wittingly or unwittingly
became part of my tobacco journey*

Contents

Preface	xi
Acknowledgments	xvi
Editor's Note	xviii

Part One: Class, Race, Gender and Nation

1. Dandy or Rake? Cigar Makers in Cuba, 1860-1958	3
2. Labour and Economy in Cuban Tobacco, 1860-1958	14
3. Women on the Agenda: The Cooperative Movement in Rural Cuba	31
4. Gender Issues in Contemporary Cuban Tobacco Farming	48
5. Gender Constructs of Labour in Pre-revolutionary Cuban Tobacco	81
6. Women and Cuban Smallholder Agriculture in Transition	104

Part Two: Nation and Migration

7. Political Idealism and Commodity Production: Cuban Tobacco in Jamaica, 1870-1930	121
8. Turning Over a New Leaf? The Havana Cigar Revisited	150
9. Tobacco in the Contrapunteo: Ortiz and the Havana Cigar	170
10. Havana Cigars and the West's Imagination	188
11. Reflections on Class, Race, Gender and Nation in Cuban Tobacco, 1850-2000	196
12. Reinventing Mecca: Tobacco in the Dominican Republic, 1763-2007	211

Part Three: Transnation

13. *El Habano* and the World it has Shaped:
    Cuba, Connecticut and Indonesia ... 255

14. Beyond the Black Atlantic: Understanding Race, Gender
    and Labour in the Global Havana Cigar ... 284

15. *El Habano*: The Global Luxury Smoke ... 307

16. Transnationalism and the Havana Cigar:
    Commodity Chains, Networks, and Knowledge Circulation ... 329

17. Beyond Iberian Atlantic Spaces:
    Trans-imperial & Trans-territorial Entanglements
    in Havana Cigar History (1756-1924) ... 344

18. Cuba-Canaries Havana Cigar Connections:
    A Hemispheric, Transatlantic and Global History ... 381

19. Dominican, Puerto Rican and Cuban tobacco
    in the Long Shadow of Monopoly (1717-1930) ... 411

Select Bibliography ... 435

Index ... 451

Tables

1: Peasant sector by form of organisation, 1979-1985	33
2: Size of farms & value of production, 1945	51
3: Land tenure of farms & value of production, 1945	52
4: Tobacco farms according to size and territory	52
5: Area worked under various kinds of land tenure, 1945	53
6: Value of farm production according to territory, 1945	54
7: Farms according to territory, income, workers & wages, 1945	55
8: Tobacco by farming system, San Luis and Cabaiguán, 1984	57
9: Tobacco agricultural production cooperatives (CPA), 1979-84	57
10: Agricultural production cooperatives, 1984	61
11a: Private sector composition, CPA, San Luis, 1984	67
11b: Private sector composition, CPA, Cabaiguán, 1984	68
12a: Private sector composition, CCS, Cabaiguán, 1984	69-70
12b: Private sector composition, CCS, San Luis, 1984	71
13: Tobacco CPAs, 1984-85 partial balance	77
14: Difference in production costs, Havana & Trenton	84
15: Tobacco factory workers, 1899-1943	89
16: Selected tobacco occupations by gender and race, 1943	90-1
17: Unemployment in Cuban tobacco, December 1945	93
18: Unemployment amongst stemmers, December 1945	93
19: Underemployment in La Corona cigar factory, 1949	94
20: Census returns, tobacco factory operatives, 1899	95
21: Census returns, tobacco factory operatives, , 1907	98
22: Gender literacy in the tobacco industry, 1899-1907	99
23: Unionisation in the Cuban tobacco industry, 1944	100
24: Unionisation among stemmers according to province, 1944	100
25: Tobacco imports from Jamaica, for export, 1865	135
26: General tobacco exports and re-exports from Jamaica, 1865	136
27: Tobacco acreage in Jamaica, 1878-1911	137
28: Cuban-born population in Jamaica, 1878-1921	137
29: Tobacco planters in Jamaica, 1881-1921	138
30: Cigar makers in Jamaica, 1881-1921	138

Preface

LOOKING BACK over the years, as this volume has compelled me to do, it has become evident to me how much my work on tobacco falls into three phases, each linked to changes in both my professional and personal life. This is reflected in the chronological approach to the volume and its three parts.

The first part includes six early publications that draw on research conducted during the years I was living and working in Cuba. They further develop themes that today are more widely understood as the intersectionality of class, race and gender – themes I had signalled but not delved into fully in my 1975 University of London PhD thesis on the Cuban tobacco sector and its workers before the 1959 Revolution. The thesis was the basis for my subsequent book, published in the United Kingdom in 1985 by Cambridge University Press and in Cuba, in Spanish, in 1989 by Ciencias Sociales, and in new UK English and Spanish editions in 2023 by Amaurea Press.

Three of the six draw entirely on my early research on the pre-revolutionary period and were facilitated by a two-year stay in the United Kingdom in the early 1980s, with short fellowships at the then Institute of Latin American Studies, University of London, and St Anthony's College, University of Oxford. My involvement in the UK Society for Caribbean Studies and Society for Latin American Studies began then, and subsequently, when I was back in Cuba, my links with the regional Association of Caribbean Historians and Latin American Studies Association, all of which enabled me to expand my horizons.

The three publications on women and gender in agriculture address the revolutionary period against the backdrop of tobacco's pre-revolutionary history. They draw on detailed statistical analysis, participant observation, and in-depth interviewing in two key tobacco-growing areas of Cuba, conducted on my return to Cuba. That research would not have been possible without the collaboration of Mavis Álvarez at the National Association of Small Farmers (ANAP), and her co-authorship of the first of the three, 'Women on the Agenda'.

Drawing out the more conceptual implications of the in-depth research entailed some inevitable overlap in the publications. It was also this, however, that enabled me to analyse for broader audiences issues facing Cuba from a development perspective, such as state and grass-roots strategies for rural democratisation among the peasantry, social equity and agrarian transition, and provided the grounding for more general work on women and gender, as well as race, in Caribbean and Latin American context, which is beyond the scope of the present volume. The challenges posed, I would argue, not only remain, but are arguably heightened today

The six publications included in the second part date from my latter years in Cuba and when I was back in the United Kingdom, living and working in London, and they transcend the island borders of Cuba. An early reader of my work had signalled the need for a study of the whole Cuban tobacco universe. At the time anonymous, that reader was Louis Pérez Jr., then based at the University of South Florida, in Tampa, who had helped spearhead not only historical research on Tampa's late nineteenth- and early twentieth-century émigré Cuban tobacco history, but also safeguarding what remained of its architectural heritage. His comment and my later visit to Tampa, hosted by him, marked the beginnings of my own wider Cuban tobacco journey.

Not long after, an invitation to present on my work at the University of the West Indies, in Mona, Jamaica, provided me with the opportunity to conduct research on Cuban tobacco émigrés in Jamaica in the same late nineteenth and early twentieth centuries. The findings of that research constitute the first of the publications included in this second section, exploring connections between Cuba and Jamaica linked to tobacco, parallel to those of Tampa.

Amidst all the global health concerns surrounding tobacco, the 1990s were years of a veritable global cigar boom, in no small part engineered by the glossy *Cigar Aficionado*, which launched in New York in 1992 and contained a mine of journalistic information that fuelled my quest. This caused me to reflect on how developments in Cuba's tobacco sector were not only fundamental to Cuba's strategy in confronting the crisis 1990s – triggered by the implosion of the Soviet Union, by then its major trading partner – but also intricately linked to wider developments outside Cuba creating new offshore sites rivalling *El Habano*, the Havana cigar, much as they had in the past.

I returned to the work of Cuban ethnographer Fernando Ortiz and his 1940 classic *Cuban Counterpoint: Tobacco and Sugar*, to fashion a new Cuban counterpoint between tobacco in and beyond island Cuba. I mused on the West's imaginary conjured up by the Havana cigar and Cuba as a nation, and my earlier thinking on class, race and gender in Cuba's tobacco history broadened to encompass nation and migration. I also had the opportunity to research Cuba's new offshore rival cigar epicentre, the Dominican Republic, discovering the work of Pedro Francisco Bonó, whose nineteenth-century contrapuntal vision of Dominican tobacco and sugar predated by almost a century that of Ortiz for Cuba.

Through fellowships, funding, and collegial hospitality enabling my research in the United States (Connecticut, Florida, Georgia and New York) and Puerto

Rico, the Netherlands and Indonesia, Spain (especially the Canary Islands) and Germany, I began to feel what those Cuban cigar makers of old must have felt when they travelled around with their *chaveta*; and I found myself almost serendipitously, as the twentieth century came to an end and the twenty-first began to unfold, exploring new twists and turns to that nineteenth- and twentieth-century Havana cigar history with which I was familiar.

New transnational connections laid the foundations for the publications included in the third and final part, which start with those in Connecticut (and its Caribbean and Puerto Rican tobacco history) and Indonesia, taking my work in new directions. My incursion into Indonesia was occasioned by an invitation to present on my work at the University of Yogyakarta, Java, collaborating with a Dutch team based at the International Institute of Social History in Amsterdam researching indigo, sugar, and tobacco in India and Indonesia.

This marked the start of a longer collaboration with the Institute, bolstered by the global historical reach of the Commodities of Empire British Academy Research Project, which I helped found, and a subsequent invitation from colleagues in Germany to interrogate the concept of the Black Atlantic in my work led me to draw on my Connecticut and Indonesia research to conceptualise a critique along global class, race and ethnic lines.

My later involvement with a group of Iberian tobacco historians catapulted me to think more conceptually about the longue-durée of *El Habano* becoming the luxury global smoke it is today. I began to link migratory movements of people, networks and knowledge circuits, and to situate trans-imperial and trans-territorial connections in hemispheric, transatlantic and global context. I also returned to the wealth of primary and secondary sources I had amassed over the years – more than I have been able to do justice to in my published work thus far – to delve more deeply into comparative history at the intersection of empires in the case of Cuba and the Canary Islands, and more recently Dominican-Puerto Rican-Cuban tobacco history in the long shadow of monopoly.

As in Part One, so in Parts Two and Three there is duplication of material, in no small measure due to publications having been written for different audiences unfamiliar with the detailed empirical research on which they were based. Read together, however, they show how my thinking and approach have evolved. At the time of writing my thesis, publishing my early monograph and other early work, while my entrée was Cuban labour history, I was drawn into the history of Cuban tobacco agriculture and industry in the context of world capitalism. I was very much influenced by the core/periphery approach, which led me to categorise nineteenth- and twentieth-century prerevolutionary developments in Cuba as a deforming process of de-industrialisation on the periphery of developed capitalist countries and their giant tobacco conglomerations. I concluded this, and resistance to it, had left pre-revolutionary Cuba's tobacco sector with an archaic mode of capitalist agricultural and industrial production, in the form of small farming and the hand-rolled cigar.

I have since been proved so wrong in conceiving of it in that way. In the reforms of the early revolutionary years, tobacco manufacturing was nationalised, and after the early 1970s 'tobacco recuperation' programme small farmers were encouraged to join agricultural production cooperatives. The 1990s, however – again described as a period of 'tobacco recuperation' – unfolded with an emphasis away from collective agriculture and on the smallholder farm, as also, within the industry, on the hand-rolled Havana cigar. This revival of both small farming and hand-rolling proved key in enabling Cuba to ride the crisis years ever since, becoming a mainstay in an otherwise very fragile Cuban economy, with a viable and highly prestigious export sector, emblematic of national pride.

The work of Ortiz, foundational for his invaluable conceptualisation of transculturation and yet flawed in historical detail, has been an inevitable springboard for much of my work and for the title of this volume – tobacco counterpoints. The counterpoints are not only of tobacco with sugar but within tobacco itself, in Cuba and abroad, as the Havana leaf and the craft of hand-rolling *El Habano*, against all the odds, established and defended itself to become the yardstick by which to judge a good cigar, sought after, imitated and counterfeited the world over.

At the time of writing this Preface, the high-end Habanos World Days in London just concluded with a gala dinner at the Victoria & Albert Museum, where five exclusive humidors were auctioned, raising €5,150,000, and the proceeds are to be donated to Cuba's public health system. The occasion was the world premier launch of Trinidad Cabildos Edición Limitada 2024. Named after the old colonial city in central Cuba, Trinidad the cigar was initially, like the Cohíba, rolled specially for then President Fidel Castro to smoke (until he stopped on health grounds) and gift to visiting dignitaries. Today it is coveted by cigar connoisseurs the world over, including the United States, whose over sixty-year embargo on trade with Cuba renders the island Havana cigar a forbidden smoke. Throughout history, tobacco prohibitions have never lasted, and the odds are that this one eventually won't either. When it might end is hard to predict, yet for all that, and perhaps today in part because of it, *El Habano*'s mystique is riding high.

I am deeply indebted to all those who have accompanied me on my tobacco journey, many more than perhaps realise, and many of whom became close friends as well as colleagues, all testimony to how much the personal and the professional can be interwoven; to the institutions and funding bodies from whom I received financial support; to the publishers who granted permission to reprint my work in this volume; and especially to Jonathan Curry-Machado, whose historian's eye first singled out my initial monograph, based on my

PhD thesis, for new editions in both English and Spanish, and then nurtured this compilation for Amaurea Press. The responsibility for their veracity, of course, remains mine.

Jean Stubbs
London, June 2024

Acknowledgments

I BEGAN MY Cuba research in 1967 having received a UK Department of Education and Science Parry Studentship, which fully funded my University of London PhD, including all research and travel. In my early postgraduate research, I was assisted by a grant from the US Social Science Research Council and American Council of Learned Societies. From the University of North London, I received a 1993 semester sabbatical, which I spent as a Rockefeller Scholar at the Center for Latin American and Caribbean Studies and Center for African Studies, University of Florida, and a 1996 semester sabbatical, when I returned to Florida. I was the recipient of a 1997 British Academy small research grant; two further Rockefeller Scholarships in 1998 – on the Caribbean 2000 Program, at the University of Puerto Rico, and at the Cuban Research Institute, Florida International University; and a Visiting Fellowship in the Netherlands, in the Department of Caribbean Studies, Royal Institute of Linguistics and Anthropology, in Leiden.

In 2002, by which time the University of North London had merged with London Guildhall to become London Metropolitan University and the Caribbean Studies Centre was established, attached to the International Institute of Culture, Tourism and Development, I received Institute funding to conduct research in the Canary Islands, and travel grants and project funding have since aided my research, notably in 2011 as the Bacardi Scholar at the University of Florida, and through my involvement in the Commodities of Empire British Academy Research Project, and sister collaborative projects: Plants, People and Work, at the International Institute of Social History (IISH), in Amsterdam; Global Commodity Chains, at the University of Konstanz; and Commodity Frontiers Initiative, headed by colleagues in the US at Brown University and Harvard University and in the Netherlands at Ghent and IISH. I also have a debt of gratitude to the Iberia tobacco historians' group. They, and many others who have assisted me along my extended journey, are duly thanked in specific chapters.

I am grateful to the editors and publishers of the articles and book chapters for granting permission for them to be included in this volume: *Institute of Commonwealth Studies Collected Seminar Papers* (1982); *Historical Reflections*

(1985); Carmen Diana Deere & Magdalena León de Leál (eds), *Rural Women and State Policy* (Westview Press, 1987); *World Development* (1987); *Social and Economic Studies* (1988); Janet Momsen (ed), *Women and Change in the Caribbean* (James Currey/Indiana Press/Ian Randle, 1993); *Cuban Studies* (1995); *New West Indian Guide* (2000); Mauricio A. Font & Alfonso W. Quiroz (eds), *Counterpoints: The Legacy of Fernando Ortiz*, (Lexington, 2004); Sander Gilman & Zhou Xun (eds), *Smoke: A Global History of Smoking* (Reaktion Books, 2004); Constance Sutton (ed), *Revisiting Caribbean Labor: Essays in Honor of O. Nigel Bolland* (Ian Randle, 2005); *Commodities of Empire Working Papers* (2007); *Cuban Studies* (2010); *Comparativ* (2012); Jonathan Curry-Machado (ed), *Global Histories, Imperial Connections, Local Interactions* (Palgrave Macmillan, 2013); Catherine Krull (ed), *Cuba in Global Context: International Relations, Internationalism, and Transnationalism* (University of Florida Press, 2014); Santiago de Luxán Meléndez & João Figueiroa-Rego (eds), *El tabaco y la esclavitud en la rearticulación imperial ibérica (s.XVI-XX)* (Universidad de Evora, 2018); Santiago de Luxán Meléndez, João Figueiroa-Rego & Vicent Sanz Rozalén (eds), *Grandes vicios, grandes ingresos: el monopolio del tabaco en los imperios ibéricos, siglos XVI-XX* (Centro de Estudios Políticos y Constitucionales, 2019); Santiago de Luxán Meléndez (ed.), *La transición del monopolio al libre mercado del tabaco en Cuba, Canarias y Filipinas y otros espacios americanos. Experiencias comparadas* (Servicio de Publicaciones del Cabildo de Gran Canaria, 2024).

Editor's Note

THE CHAPTERS in this book have all been previously published. As a result, their original versions employed a wide range of referencing and linguistic styles. In order to ensure consistency within this volume, all references have been standardised, and language changed to British usage.

Having been written over a span of more than forty years, some comments within the individual articles have become dated. While the substantive text of each has been maintained essentially as originally published, some of the more date-specific endnotes have been revised so as to continue to be relevant for a contemporary readership.

Full citations are given upon first occurrence within each chapter, and abbreviated subsequently. The bibliography at the end has been limited to published texts that are either of particular importance for tobacco history, or which are referred to on several occasions through the book. The intention is that this would serve as a useful resource as suggested further reading.

All quotations have been translated into English. Where the translation was included in the original source material, then this has been maintained; but where the original source was non-English, the author has provided English translations. In some cases, the author's original published article included quotations in Spanish. These have all been translated into English for the present edition.

Part One

Class, Race, Gender and Nation

1

DANDY OR RAKE?
CIGAR MAKERS IN CUBA, 1860-1958*

A CERTAIN AURA of myth and legend has grown up around cigar manufacturing in Cuba and pervaded even its more serious historiography. The very mention of it somehow conjures up a thriving second major industry. La Corona, H. Upmann, Partagás, Montecristo, were those household words for the nineteenth century aristocracy of Europe and the United States, and cigar makers were that strong elite of workers hand-fashioning from a particularly strong, fragrant leaf a quality product that carved a lasting niche on the luxury world market. Or did it? Was it such a thriving industry and were those cigar makers all they have been made out to be? This paper argues not, and intends to dispel some of the myth and legend, about both cigar making and cigar makers.

A Legacy to Past Prosperity

There is no doubt but that cigar manufacturing was Cuba's nineteenth-century industry par excellence. Although there are few serialised production figures available, those that are, plus more descriptive material for the period, allow for a fairly accurate picture to be built up. Catering to a rapidly growing export market from the early century on was a rapidly growing industry, and some rapidly growing concerns. Thus, subject to yearly fluctuations, exports increased from just over 140,000 units in 1840 to nearly 360,000 in the peak year of

---

* Originally published in *Collected Seminar Papers* 29, Caribbean Studies, Vol.1, Institute of Commonwealth Studies, University of London, 1982, pp.17-25.

1855, during which period some of the major cigar factories were founded, largely with Spanish though also some German capital. H. Upmann's La Madama (1844) and La Corona (1845) are cases in point. Of the others, some, like Cabañas (1810) and Partagás (1827), dated back to the initial expansion years and some to the subsequent prosperity of the '60s (Bock's Águila de Oro) and '80s (Henry Clay and Bock). According to a statistical report of 1861,[1] of a total of 1,217 cigar-rolling shops throughout the island, 516 were situated in Havana and 158 classified as 1st class, i.e. with over 50 workers. In some, numbers were already into their hundreds, the Cabañas factory in 1862 having 300 workers. By 1890, the Cabañas, Henry Clay and La Corona factories were employing 1,000 to 2,000 workers and their greatness was such as to be described as "palaces of great architectural splendour, setting the tone of building for the period."[2]

This, however, was the great zenith of Cuban cigar manufacturing. Three major developments in the world tobacco industry, one of which was already becoming evident during the latter half of the nineteenth century, were to conspire to ensure this should be so. Firstly, tobacco manufacturing, protected by tariff barriers, developed at such a rapid pace in Europe and later the United States that these once major importers of manufactured tobacco became major importers of leaf, themselves re-exporting the finished product. The die was cast for the growing division between the advanced tobacco manufacturing centres and the primary producers of leaf. Second, the discovery of mild Virginia tobacco and the advent of the cigarette machine initiated the age of twentieth-century mass monopoly mild cigarette production, undercutting all other kinds of smoke and leaf at company and country level, changing what had been a largely mercantile relationship between the fast-consolidating manufacturing centres and primary producers to one of direct penetration and control by monopoly capital. Third, the advent of the cigar machine and monopoly mass production of cheaper cigars from the 1920s on cornered what was left of a particularly hard-hit market.[3]

In Cuba, these developments in turn had a threefold effect. They meant, first, a falling cigar export market against a parallel increase in leaf exports from the mid-1850s on; second, direct capital penetration by the single largest US tobacco concern, American Tobacco, over the 1890s and 1900s, consolidating this trend; and, third, a post-1920s period when the bottom had really fallen out of the market.

The first and second of these developments have gone largely ignored; the third and last, while patently obvious, has consequently never been fully understood.

Two factors helped obscure the first: namely, the very prosperity of those great nineteenth-century concerns to which I have referred, and a rapidly growing US market for cigars up until the 1890s (due largely to late industrial take-off after the War of Secession). However, in the years 1859-70, for example, Cuba's major cigar markets of Germany and France cut imports by two-thirds and a half, respectively. And when US imports began to fall off in the 1890s, at a time when the United States handled by far the greater part of the market, total export figures stood at approximately half the 1850s level. Moreover, while prior to the 1850s cigar exports had risen roughly proportionate to the level of leaf, from 1855 to 1890 there was, as against a drop in cigar exports, a 30 percent increase in leaf exports to Germany and other European countries and to the United States.[4] The value of exports was consequently inverted; in 1859, the value of cigar exports was twice that of leaf; in 1890, leaf twice that of cigar.

This trend did not go ignored by the more intelligent of the Havana manufacturing oligarchy of the time and was reflected in both the press and some unsuccessful demands for the prohibition or reduction of leaf exports, or export duties to be levied. Thus, in 1862, it was lamented that "it was not impossible to see . . . what we need for our own production leave the ports of this country to be re-introduced through them in the form of what we need for our consumption, after having been worked abroad".[5] As the century progressed, each new tariff, especially US tariff, caused a renewed slump in manufacturing; and, by the 1870s, this was constant cause for comment in British consular reports documenting British investment possibilities in this field. More commonly documented was the resulting trend of Cuban manufacturers to transfer their concerns to the United States, which was aggravated during the 1868-78 War of Independence. Tariffs were so high by this time that one manufacturer calculated émigrés' production costs to be around three-fifths of Havana costs.[6] The extra paradox of this in the relative prosperity of the inter-war period of the 1880s was that, while smaller Havana manufacturers were ruined, there was equally a concentration of capital in the industry on an unprecedented scale: hence, the magnificence of those 1890 factories.

US protectionism reached its height in the 1890 McKinley Tariff, coinciding with great resistance on the part of the Spanish authorities to any attempted renegotiations of either internal taxes or other terms of the US tariff. Particularly eloquent manufacturers' reports of 1890-94 to this effect fell on stony ground.[7] As a result, again tobacco was a major factor in the second, 1895-98 Independence war, from which it was also to suffer such dire consequences.

American Tobacco speculated on the crisis years of the war to effect the earliest and most complete onslaught of monopoly capital on any one sector of the Cuban economy. Backed by an agreement with earlier British interests,[8] it bought up land and businesses, including some of the major cigar and cigarette factories, operating them under two subsidiaries, Cuban Land & Leaf and Havana Tobacco. It successfully exported the best leaf and, after half-hearted attempts to modernise plant in Havana, started to transfer export production to the more profitable United States. In 1902, the Trust, as it was called, handled 90 percent of cigar exports; in 1904, only 52 percent. By 1905, it had reduced its factories to 7, by the late 1920s to one (aptly nicknamed the Pantheon), and its workers, from some 5,000 to 500. In 1932, it withdrew all that was left of its cigar export trade, leaving some 200 workers for domestic manufacturing.[9]

Its strategy clearly fitted in with a world situation it and other tobacco monopolies like it had helped foster, and with which even major manufacturers who had managed to hold out at the turn of the century were hardly equipped to cope. Fiercely proud of their past and their quality brands, the 'independents', as they were called, plunged into head-on rivalry with the Trust[10] and were to spend the next fifty years on the defensive, fighting for piecemeal measures to keep the old industry going. In 1900, during the time of the first American occupation, they likened their lot to "one who builds castles in the air that get swept away by a heavy North wind" and clamoured for preferential US duties.[11] In 1909, they complained especially of competing imitation Havanas abroad;[12] in 1925, they set up the National Commission for the Defense and Propaganda of the Havana Cigar, arguing for its uniqueness and basing much of their case against mechanisation on just that, seeing it as the 'De Profundis' of quality cigar manufacturing;[13] in 1936, they called for a form of New Deal for tobacco and from then on there was increasing "national concern" over the whole "tobacco question".[14]

Their concern should not be overestimated. Again, while by the 1920s leaf exports had almost doubled their post turn-of-the-century level, cigar exports had dropped to roughly one-third, and their 1920s value was little over one-third that of leaf. From then on, this proportion was roughly maintained but the level of both greatly reduced. Thus, on the whole, the only period in which the 1920s level was regained were the late Second World War years of artificially created demand and the boom of the late 1950s.

Interestingly enough, subject to fluctuations of both a seasonal and cyclical nature – overall twentieth-century cigar output remained fairly constant. This was because there was an increase in the home market for a growing population, but this was by no means a market for expensive cigars, such as those made for export, and continued to be largely catered to by small, second-rate, local concerns and even private home rollers scattered throughout the island, as it had been in the nineteenth century.[15] Thus, on the one hand, there were the large 'independents', few of whom were ever able to expand greatly in the face of twentieth-century foreign competition[16] and who, on the strength of this, developed their own reluctance to change. On the other hand, there was a proliferation of small sweatshop production, often ephemeral in nature.[17] It stood to reason that overwhelming numbers of both, for very good if historically outmoded reasons, should resist any attempt to introduce the cigar machine, successfully opposing it in the 1920s, and even in the 1950s, after a six-year-long struggle, still managing to ensure government limitation on its use.[18]

The overall effect in terms of industrial structure was a certain process of de-industrialisation which reinforced an archaic mode of production. The total figure of 'factories' for 1945[19] was not all that different from the 1862 figure: 1,050 as against 1,302. As against those 158 factories with over 50 workers in 1862, some 98 in Havana alone by 1890, there were in 1945 only 9 with over 200 workers, the largest of which was the H. Upmann factory with 800. With the sole exception of the Trust, they were all old family firms, many of which had been passed down from generation to generation, their glory waning in the process. And yet they were trapped as such in an economy with few other investment possibilities.

Cuba might have retained its image of 'land of the best cigars in the world' but, producing as it was an item for a very special, luxury market, it was no longer either a major or a thriving cigar manufacturer.

A Force on the Wane

What were the consequences of this for the labour force in the industry? Several points emerge from the previous discussion.

In the context of Cuba's development, those colossal factories of the nineteenth century meant that tobacco was the one industry to produce a class of salaried labour on anything like a large scale, and did so on a scale unparalleled in that same industry in the twentieth century. That they should have remained one of the largest sectors of the Cuban working class right up until the 1940s and 1950s was an indictment of the development of Cuban industry as a whole and not a measure of progress in the tobacco industry itself.[20]

The very fact that Cuba's manufacturing potential for quality cigars was cut short inevitably meant a considerable decrease in the number of cigar makers, its most predominant industrial grouping. This was especially marked in Havana, where the large export factories were concentrated. At the same time, the backwardness of the industry as a whole meant that the overall number of workers did remain relatively high, with a large sector scattered throughout the island and a continued high proportion of home and small shop workers to factory workers as such. Thus, whereas figures for the 1860s point to some 15,000 cigar rollers in Havana, 20,000 in the island as a whole, the 1899 figure for Havana had dropped to 10,000, although still 20,000 in all. In 1919, only 3,500 (60 percent less) were given for Havana; and this drop largely accounted for the drop in the industry as a whole to 14,000, given that figures in certain other tobacco provinces doubled over that same period.

According to 1945 statistics, the overall figure was just over 12,000, of whom one-third were out of work, and the Havana figure was just over 5,000, with two-fifths out of work.[21] The 1943 census corroborated these figures to a large extent and also gave the breakdown of 30 percent self-employed, 30 percent not known. Added together, this would coincide with O'Connor's figure of 60 percent of the industry in the 1950s being in the home and outwork sector.[22]

Bearing these figures in mind alone, the much-touted aristocracy-of-labour-in-cigar-rolling theory has to be looked at more carefully. Accepting the validity of the term as applying to a distinctive upper stratum of the working class, better paid, better treated and generally more respected than the mass of the proletariat, it is a term that has been quite misused as far as Cuban cigar makers go. Cigar-rolling is skilled work, but there is little to indicate that it was originally treated as such in nineteenth-century Cuba. While producing significant concentrations of salaried labour, it was also peculiar in that working alongside free labourers were considerably large numbers of slaves, much larger probably than established opinion would have it. Piecing together scant figures for the 1860s, for example, it is possible that one third of the island's, one half of Havana's, cigar makers were at the time slaves, and a further 13 percent and 18 percent, respectively, free coloureds.[23] That amounts to the astonishing figure of 63 percent of Havana's work force, 55 percent of the island's, as non-white, when whites far outnumbered blacks in the population at large.

By 1899 that percentage had dropped to 30 percent and 37 percent, respectively. Clearly, it was to be expected that, against the backdrop of war turmoil and abolition, blacks would be hit most, especially in Havana where the work force was declining. But it is equally clear that a class of white, skilled workers grew up, swelled by an influx of Spanish immigrants to the better Havana factory jobs. Thus, in the 1899 census, one in five of Havana's cigar factory operatives was classified as foreign white, and it is possible to assume that a further one in five at least was only first-generation Cuban-born.

It must be remembered in the context of this racial make-up of cigar rollers that shortage of labour had been a constant concern for much of the nineteenth century, and a rapidly expanding industry meant operatives were scarce. Indeed, this was one of the main reasons given in 1851 for introducing the cigar makers' *libreta*, a compulsory card in which was noted the name of the employer and any money owing him. As long as there was money owing, the worker could not leave the factory, nor any other manufacturer employ him unless he liquidated his debt. Its effectiveness clearly inferred that wages were, if not always at least sufficiently often, inadequate. Certainly average 1852 rates quoted in the order of 1 to 3 pesos a day were not substantially higher than the 1 to 1.50 for day labourers.[24]

From the late 1850s and 1860s on, however, there were definitely growing wage differentials. The 1861 figure gave 4 pesos a day for a master cigar maker, as against the 1 to 3 peso average cigar makers' pay.[25] De la Sagra's 1862 figure set this somewhat lower, as 2 pesos to one.[26] By 1890, however, top cigar makers were quoted as earning 10 pesos a day against the average cigar makers' 2, a differential of 5:1.[27]

This would help account for the widely varying descriptive accounts of these years. Rivero Muñiz writes of the early "wage labourers" living in, side by side with slaves and contracted Chinese,[28] in overcrowded, insanitary conditions in badly ventilated galleries over the rolling shops, receiving only part of their pay in money form and having leave of absence only once a week. Their movement was obviously restricted by the *libreta*, and, he records, long apprenticeships were also common in return for 20 percent or less of going wages. He also makes the point that, after abolition, conditions did not change all that greatly. This contrasted greatly with the 1890 description of La Corona factory in Aldama Palace, where cigar makers worked "below the rich, panelled ceilings, excellent paintings, notable water colours and frescoes . . . on marble shining clean . . . [where] only the fragrance of cedar-wood prevails."[29]

Clearly, the small elite in the latter were worlds apart from the majority of cigar makers and the common labourers. Indeed, a sizeable number were creamed off into professional or managerial rank. Suffice it here to mention Rafael García Marqués, cigar maker turned manufacturer; José Aguirre, cigar maker turned manufacturer, leaf broker and editor; Fernando Alonso, who became company president; José Rivero Muñiz, Gaspar Jorge García Galló and José Luciano Franco, who later followed in this tradition, to become prominent tobacco historians.

The very prominence of such men was what helped propagate the wider myth of the artisan "suave and slick / and spruced to the nines . . . a toff cheery and gay / And in fine clothes apt to strut . . . cigar makers who are confounded / With the doctors and merchants with whom they're surrounded / Because of the fine figures they cut."

In terrific hats
And spiffy shoes
With a heavy watch on a gold chain.
They stand on the corner of High and Main
Shooting the breeze and swapping the news.[30]

"Those intelligent men," it was said of them at the turn of the century, "have reached such a state of perfection that they have a good job assured them for the rest of their lives."[31] But, it was also said, "illusion is here today and gone tomorrow."[32]

For the repatriate cigar makers to independent Cuba, there was little work to be had in the large factories. And for those entrenched in them, these were to be years of cut-backs in production and costs. In the initial years, this was manifest in less direct ways, such as expecting first-rate workmanship from second-rate leaf, payment in Spanish currency which was worth less than American money, according to which most goods were priced, etc. Later, when there were increasing numbers of unemployed, more direct methods were to be used, such as demanding very substantial wage cuts and transferring factories to cheap labour areas, especially in depression years.

Over the first two decades, wages in the Havana factories still probably remained among the highest of all industrial wages. There were, however, some very considerable cuts. In 1915, the Trust, reputed to pay the highest wages, reduced wage rates by 50 percent because of "war difficulties". By the end of the war, there was a record of average wages for cigar makers of 2 to 6 pesos a day. Increases in the order of 10 percent were registered in Havana factories during the 1920s but the outstanding salaries for which the industry was earlier renowned were rare because there was limited work available and often few days of the week were worked. In 1932, manufacturers succeeded in making even top cigar makers accept reductions which put them back to 1917-18 rates.[33] Wages outside Havana were estimated to be some 1 to 1.50 pesos a day. In the post-depression years, wages were no higher. In 1936, it was reckoned that a top cigar maker would find it difficult to earn more than 2.50 pesos a day, and average factory wages were quoted as around 1.10 pesos.[34]

The cigar maker of the 1930s was, then, to have little in common with the image of his nineteenth-century predecessor. This was reflected in the literature of the time. "No vestiges are left of that romantic figure who used to grace the street corners," wrote García Galló in 1936. "There remains only a washed-out caricature that has degenerated so much that it can no longer be considered a cigar maker. What remains is the rake hanging out on street corners, given to vulgar language, and effeminate gestures who, out of sarcasm, smokes American cigarettes, if not marijuana."[35]

García Galló might have been a bit hard on the poor cigar maker, but such caricatures of the 1930s compared to those of the 1890s and early 1900s sum up the situation only too eloquently. By the late 1930s, the semi- and non-factory worker was predominant. Cigar makers laid off from the factories turned to making a living as best they could, even if this meant rolling the cheap *tabaquitos a kilo* – the one-cent cigars – and hawking them on the streets. In so doing, the cigar maker entered that vast under-paid reserve army which the manufacturers could tap whenever they wanted to put pressure on the remaining, relatively well-off factory workers. In 1930, this cigar maker might be earning no more than 40 to 50 cents a day against the average factory worker's 1.10 pesos. The odds were that this worker would also find it difficult to get back into the factories again on a permanent basis.

During the 1940s, along with much legislation and a pension and insurance scheme for the industry, industrial wage rates were introduced for cigar makers and increases to the tune of 50 percent or so. This in itself meant that wages were only being brought into line with those prevailing during the second and third decades, and there is little evidence to indicate, with the exception of the large factories, that the official rates were ever paid. Small, ephemeral rolling shops, where "workers were left rotting in terrible conditions," could, and did, easily evade legislator controls.[36]

This, added to the unstable, seasonal nature of the work, meant that if the numbers of workers in the factories were at all maintained this was often at the expense of a shorter working week. Time sheets for La Corona factory in the early 1950s, for example, show individual variations of between 1 and 26 days worked, according to the time of year.[37] Take-home wages, then, could fluctuate enormously, against a general 60 percent drop in real wages against the purchasing power of foodstuffs, say.[38]

This made for a situation of great flux in the labour force in this sector. Interviews conducted in the late 1960s confirmed that only a tiny few of the cigar makers had held down factory jobs all their working lives. The great majority had at times worked in factories, at times in small shops and at times at home on their own. Outside Havana, many worked on the land during harvest time.[39]

Cigar makers who had once shared the prosperity of their industry had seen their position being slowly but surely eroded away. How they were affected by this, the sort of feelings aroused in them and the ways in which they tried to fight against what was happening to them, must, regrettably, be left to a follow-up paper.

Notes

1. Valentín Pardo y Betancourt, *Informe ilustrado y estadístico* (Havana, 1863).
2. Texifonte Gallego y García, *Cuba por fuera* (Havana, 1890).
3. Although there are some informative straight histories of tobacco and the tobacco business in the United Kingdom, United States, Germany and some other countries, to my knowledge there has been no serious work done on the changing nature of the world structure of production with the advent of imperialism.
4. 'Half-Spanish' was what American cigar manufacturing was called from the mid-century on. A US-made 'Havana' with some Cuban leaf retailed at 4 to 5 times the price of other domestic cigars.
5. Ramón de la Sagra, *Cuba 1860* (Havana, 1903). De la Sagra was commenting on two articles published in *Diario de la Marina* on 11 & 12 December, 1861, in which the author refers to the problem of increasing leaf exports and declining cigar exports. These viewpoints contrast with those of a decade before on the stable future augured by the conditions in the tobacco industry.
6. Quoted in the *Revista Económica* (Havana, 1878), p.237.
7. The Cigar Manfacturers' Union's *Memoria de los trabajos más importante realizados*

por la corporación desde 18 de septiembre de 1890 hasta 5 de febrero de 1894 en defensa de los intereses generales de la industria que representa (Havana, 1894).
8   There was British capital invested in Cuba in the 1880s and 1890s, but by 1901 an agreement was reached between American Tobacco and the British Imperial Tobacco to leave Cuba and Puerto Rico as ATC domain.
9   The full story of this move can be pieced together from the Fondo de la Comisión Nacional de Propaganda y Defensa del Tabaco Habano in the Cuban National Archives (ANC). The US magazine *Fortune* (Vol. I, No.2, and Vol. III, No. 13) ran wry accounts of this move.
10 Particularly hostile clashes can be ascertained from José Aguirre's *La verdad sobre la industria tabacalera* (1905), an independent manufacturer's reply to a pamphlet of the same title by the Trust's Gustavo Bock in 1904.
11 Rafael García Marqués, president of the Cigar and Cigarette Manufacturers' Union, in *An account of the grave situation of the tobacco industries, the causes of their decadence, and measures which are considered necessary to save them from the ruin that menaces them* (Havana, 1900).
12 *Cuestionario relativo a la producción, elaboración y exportación del tabaco en Cuba* (Havana, 1909). This was followed by another report, *Trabajo presentado al Hon. Señor Presidente de la República por la Comisión nominada que le informara al Gobierno acerca de la actual situación del cultivo, y de la industria del tabaco* (January 1910), contained in ANC, Fondo Donativos, Caja 84.
13 The setting up of the Commission was followed by several manufacturers' reports. One very interesting one was published in full in the daily *El Mundo* of 11 October 1926, under the lead: 'De la Unión de Fabricantes de Tabaco y Cigarros de la Isla de Cuba: Exposición al Señor Presidente de la República'.
14 A very good picture of these years can be built up from major economic magazines of the period, such as the *Cuban Foodstuff Record* (1926-7), whose title was changed to *Cuba Importadora e Industrial* (1928-44), and *Cuba Económica y Financiera* (1944-56), the *Revista Económica*, plus more specialised magazines such as *Habano*, the journal of the Cigar Manufacturers' Union.
15 A cursory glance through the Havana Trade Register alone confirms an astoundingly large number of small concerns registered for a few years and then folding up, and many more must never have been registered.
16 Romeo y Julieta seems to have been the one big exception to this, increasing output from 2 to 18 million units from 1902 to 1918.
17 There is much testimony to the problem of sweatshop production in magazines and reports of the larger manufacturers who saw the proliferation of this side of production as yet another thorn in the flesh.
18 Mechanisation of Cuban cigar manufacturing is a whole subject unto itself, from both the manufacturers' and the workers' angle, and can be closely documented in Jean Stubbs' doctoral thesis on 'The History of the Tobacco Industry and its Workers, 1860-1958' (University of London, 1975), and subsequent book, *Tobacco on the Periphery: A Case Study in Cuban Labour History, 1860-1958* (London: Amaurea Press, 2023 [1985]).
19 *Primer censo de obreros de la industria tabacalera* (Havana, 1947).
20 As in most underdeveloped countries, there was in Cuba, in addition to the predominance of agriculture, an imbalance toward the trade and service sectors and away from manufacturing.
21 Figures taken from Pardo y Betancourt, *Informe ilustrado* (1863), the 1899 national census and the 1947 tobacco workers' census.
22 See O'Connor, 'Industrial organisation in the old and the new Cuba', *Science and Society* (1966).
23 There are no direct figures for slave labour. Different sources, however, quote such varying figures for the number of cigar rollers in the same number of 'factories' that the only feasible explanation is slave labour not having been included.

24 José García de Arboleya, *Manual de la Isla de Cuba: compendio de su historia, geografía, estadística y administración* (Havana, 1852).
25 Pardo y Betancourt, *Informe ilustrado* (1863).
26 De la Sagra, *Cuba 1860* (1903).
27 Gallego y García, *Cuba por fuera* (1890).
28 José Rivero Muñiz, *Tabaco: su historia en Cuba*, 2 vols. (Havana: Instituto de Historia, 1965). There are no figures available for Chinese in the industry. They may either, as indentured labour, have been excluded like slaves, or included among the whites as opposed to 'free coloureds'.
29 *Album de la Corona: Obsequio a sus favorecedores* (Havana: Tipográfico O'Reilly, 1888).
30 Quoted by Jorge Gaspar García Galló, *El tabaquero cubano: psicología de las profesiones* (Havana 1936).
31 Undated, untitled pamphlet on the government of Estrada Palma and social and political institutions, thought to have been written around 1904-05.
32 Felipe Zapata, 'Esquemas y notas para la historia de la organización obrera', *Unidad Gastronómica* (Havana, 1948-51).
33 Included in papers of the unclassified records of the American Tobacco subsidiary Tabacalera Cubana SA (1932-58) in the Fondo de la Comisión Nacional de Propaganda y Defensa del Tabaco Habano.
34 These and other wage figures have been pieced together from company and other reports in the archives and the press.
35 García Galló, *Tabaquero cubano* (1936).
36 The issue of evasion in the 1940s was well documented in the economic magazines quoted above and the journal of the Cigar Makers' Union, *El Tabacalero*.
37 1950-60 time sheets have been kept in La Corona factory.
38 No cost of living index has been calculated for either nineteenth- or twentieth-century Cuba. From the 1900s on, however, strong evidence points to a heavy inflationary pressure on prices and corresponding deflationary pressure on money. From the 1930s on, there is an index for basic foodstuffs, which indicates that the purchasing power of the peso in this regard dropped to 42.5 in 1949 (1937 = 100).
39 For greater detail on this, see Stubbs, *Tobacco on the Periphery* (2023 [1985]).

2

Labour and Economy in Cuban Tobacco, 1860-1958[*]

THE SPIRALLING nineteenth-century development of Cuban tobacco, catering initially to opening European and US markets for quality cigars – and to a lesser extent cigarettes – but far more, as the century wore on, to the raw-material needs of incipient manufacturing industries in those self-same areas, fast made tobacco Cuba's second major agro-industry and export product. By the same token, the growth of European and US monopoly tobacco corporations fast cemented protectionist tariff structures which placed the Cuban manufactured product out of the mass market, while those corporations imported increasingly large quantities of Cuban leaf to blend in their own quality cigars.

While Cuba's quality cigar exporting continued, the outcome was the transformation of Cuba from a cigar-exporting to raw leaf-exporting country, a process which was consolidated with direct monopoly capital investment around the turn of the century. In 1901, two giant tobacco corporations of the West – namely, the American Tobacco Company (ATC) and its British rival Imperial Tobacco (ITC) – reached an international agreement whereby Cuba and Puerto Rico were ceded as ATC domain. Effectively, American Tobacco cornered the better part of quality tobacco lands and manufacturing enterprises, leaving lesser lands and businesses (known as the 'independents'), especially the greater part of the domestic market, to cope as best they could with a monopoly structure of world tobacco cultivation, production and distribution pitted increasingly against them.

By the 1930s, the technical revolution in cigarette manufacturing, coupled with the discovery of mild Virginia tobacco, had made mild cigarettes the

[*] Originally published in *Historical Reflections* (December 1985), pp.449-67.

twentieth-century world's mass tobacco product, undercutting all other forms of smoke and the stronger, darker tobaccos of many small tobacco-producing countries. For a country like Cuba, over-production became a key problem in both agriculture and industry, and a further blow was dealt with the US invention and monopoly of the cigar machine.

As a result, Cuba's industry and agriculture were held back, and an archaic mode of production was maintained, a mode of production that might have resembled an earlier phase of capitalist development but was essentially the product of a deforming process of de-industrialisation on the periphery of the developed capitalist countries and their big tobacco companies. The consequences of this in terms of labour and economy are what I shall be addressing here.

The Quasi-Plantation Economy

Unlike Cuba's first product, sugar, tobacco did not develop along the lines of a plantation economy in any classical sense. Nineteenth-century capitalist development did, however, incorporate into it elements of feudalism and slavery; and there was a marked fusion of merchant, manufacturer and grower capital, especially in the quality western tobacco regions of Pinar del Río.

Fernando Ortiz,[1] pinning his work as he did on the essential contrast between sugar and tobacco, would seem to have completely underestimated this and other tobacco trends and to have coloured other accounts, such as those of Klein and Knight.[2] The result has been a concentration of the literature on the small farm, individually cultivated, and the largely free-labour crop. And yet small growers, many of whom are said to have been attracted to Cuba from the Canary Islands by the tobacco boom, were soon at the mercy of buying and credit mechanisms controlled by middlemen. Friendländer wrote of the 1820-1840s:

> A certain number of Havana merchants (some of whom probably had warehouses) bought tobacco direct from the suppliers, the price being set more or less arbitrarily, related more to the debts the tobacco growers had run up in the shop than to the worth of the plant.[3]

Both Rivero Muñiz and Arredondo describe how increasing tobacco cultivation to satisfy both home and foreign market was accompanied by latifundism.[4] Neither go into detail, but agricultural statistics available would corroborate a large increase in not only the number but size of holdings. In the Western Department's Partidos area, between 1800 and 1862, the number of tobacco *vegas* or farms increased sixfold and capital invested increased two-hundred-fold, as average capital per farm increased from 11 to 400 pesos.

Rapid development, plus the overall nineteenth-century shortage of labour would seem to have made for more slave labour than is usually accredited to tobacco. In 1827, a figure of 7,297 slaves was quoted for tobacco farms over the island and by 1862 – technically well after the slave trade, though not slavery, was abolished – the number had more than doubled. The total number of slaves recorded that year was 17,675, with a further 28,527 free coloureds, out of a total of 75,058 engaged in cultivation. By far the greatest single concentration of slaves was in Pinar del Río: a total of 20,174, alongside 9,024 free coloured out of a total of 36,766.[5] This would corroborate other accounts of major tobacco manufacturers (Partagás was one) operating large tobacco plantations in Pinar del Río based largely on slave labour.

In the period 1862-1877, when Havana export manufacturing concerns such as H. Upmann, Henry Clay and Bock, Murias and Gener consolidated tobacco lands for their thriving export concerns, a 40 percent drop in the number of tobacco farms was registered. This corresponded to new sophisticated systems of land-leasing which made poor tenant farmers and sharecroppers out of growers. Initially, most were still able to have oxen, livestock, and a small subsistence plot, but an increasingly large part had to be given over to the cash crop as landholders took their substantial cut.

The tremendous increase in the demand for Cuban leaf on the US market from the 1870s on, together with abolition, help account for the reason why sharecropping would seem to have developed with a vengeance in the 1880s. The press of the time was full of articles on the plight of growers, whose subsistence farming dwindled as the pressure for cash crop production increased.

Earlier Spanish, German and British capital in manufacturing – and by extension growing – was in the 1880s fast overtaken by large-scale US capital investment, speculating on the crisis years leading up to, during and after the Second War of Independence (1895-1898). Henry Clay and Bock, Cabañas and Partagás were some whose land and manufacturing businesses were absorbed over these years, to the extent that in quality areas of Pinar del Río like Vuelta Abajo almost the only lands kept under plough during the war years were those with foreign capital backing.

As both domestic and foreign capital consolidated, the stage was set for a land scramble that reached its peak in the war years and their aftermath. In 1898, the Honourable Robert Porter could write, "A tobacco plantation or *vega* as it is known, with its kitchen garden, its *platanos* for feeding the hands, its flowering and fruit trees, its stone walls, its entrance gates and pretty houses, is the most charming agricultural sight."[6] However, direct buying, and price and credit fixing, was creating very different overall conditions, especially after a monopolistic agreement between the newly dominant American Tobacco, through its subsidiaries Cuban Land & Leaf and Havana Tobacco, and the so-called 'independents'. As Arredondo vividly describes it:

> The dealer had to sell or go under. And even though he might have had great economic power and a great capacity to stockpile tobacco, in the long run he would fall, bound hand and foot before the formidable might of the manufacturer. As is obvious, the burden which the dealer bore he immediately passed on to the grower. In this case, the latter became the most exploited element in the whole process.... If trader and industrialist possessed the means to evade the crisis, the grower was alone, defenceless against the brutal determinism of economic reality.[7]

In the early decades of the twentieth century, it was leaf-trader capital that became particularly predominant, with the growth of prosperous leaf concerns. Between 1899 and 1929, total tobacco land area remained roughly unchanged, while output was more than doubled and the number of farms almost halved (from 9,500 to 4,000 in Pinar del Río and from 15,000 to 9,000 in the central lesser-quality tobacco-growing area of Santa Clara province). Land ownership, however, was quoted in the region of 25 percent for the whole period.[8] This again corresponded to some large-scale plantation agriculture with administration land that could produce a substantial annual payroll of 400,000 pesos for the Cuban Land & Leaf in 1935, but also sharecropping taken, in Arredondo's words, "to the limits of extraordinary cruelty and the sharp rhythm of monocultivation."

As the 1930s depression set in, general concern over the leaf sector also focussed public attention on the lack of trade ethics, unscrupulous buying agents and illegal practices. This was particularly the case for the central region where domestic and foreign capital interests (General Cigar was one) preferred on the whole to operate through monopoly credit and price-fixing arrangements through landowners and middlemen; but neither did Pinar del Río escape such practices: "The grower was at the mercy of speculators and the landowners to whom he paid rents that were exaggeratedly high"; "The methods used for buying leaf from the *vegas* can be defined as gangster-like, as the weight and quality of leaf were tampered with...."[9]

Subletting of land became common and almost certainly accounts for the wide discrepancy in statistics in the 1940s. In 1942, Raggi y Ageo put the total number of tobacco farms at 4,417.[10] Alienes y Urosa claimed 3,852 in 1943 and 5,732 in 1945 (the increase being attributed to abnormally high wartime demand).[11] The National Commission for the Defence of the Havana Cigar (CNPDTH) quoted 22,750 in 1945;[12] and the agricultural census of that year 34,437.[13] Land ownership was set at around 20 percent.

More descriptive accounts of the period throw these figures into relief.[14]

Cuban Land & Leaf, with the largest expanse of administration land, was quoted as having, in addition to 3,300 wage labourers, *partidarios* who would keep for themselves only one half of their shade crop, three quarters of sun tobacco. A 405-hectare farm, El Corojo, near San Luis in Pinar del Río, had 500 wage labourers plus *partidarios*. *Tercedarios* and *cuartidarios* in the Remedios area of central Cuba paid rent to absentee landowners and sub-rented to *partidarios* who paid half of their crop. In such cases, the *cuartidario* furnished a place to sleep and board, and the *partidario* was essentially a farm labourer paid in kind.

It was this subletting and sharecropping system that made the tobacco grower all the more vulnerable to market gluts of the kind memorialised in this popular rural refrain of the 1940s:

Once it has been harvested
And stocked up high
Comes the eternal cry
That tobacco's nigh
Down in Havana stockpiled.
No-one wants to buy
And wait we must
In our fate trust
For all comes to dust
After a hard year's try.[15]

Many were the tobacco growers who for part of the year at least had to sell their labour power – or that of their family – in local sorting, stemming and rolling shops, or in sugar. Some were forced off the land altogether; others, while never completely landless, came to swell the ranks of the rural proletariat.

Manufacturing Held Back

Intensified sharecropping had its industrial corollary in outwork and small sweatshop production. There was a period in the mid-to-late nineteenth century when large-scale factory manufacturing, centred mainly in Havana for the export business, truly came into its own. Somewhat paradoxically, given that cigar and cigar tobacco were the motive force behind Cuba's boom in tobacco, it was the cigarette that was *the* Cuban smoke, and the cause for early innovation and concentration of production. By 1863 Susini's La Honradez factory employed some 2,500 workers in all on a daily output of 3,000,000 cigarettes, accounting for one twentieth of the island's production and supplying the Royal Houses of Europe. In 1867, a first elaborate Susini cigarette machine was on display at the Paris Trade Fair and the factory heralded as "an establishment of the first order, the most important perhaps of the Spanish overseas possessions and one of the greatest in the manufacturing world."[16]

Rapidly overtaken by US and European cigarette giants, cigarette manufacture was at home rapidly overshadowed by, and merged with, the manufacture of cigars, which was to become the nineteenth-century industry of Cuba. There were, by the 1860s, several Havana factories with workers running into the hundreds and, by the late 1880s, into the thousands. Five great Havana palaces, with "rich, panelled ceilings . . . frescoes . . . and marble floors," setting the tone of late nineteenth-century splendour, were in fact tobacco factories.

This was when manufacturing for export was at its zenith, and not characteristic of the period before or since. Much of the early nineteenth-century cigar and cigarette rolling was done in the prisons and the barracks, or in the home. In cigarette production, there is reference to no more than 45 workers in rolling shops in 1848; to only 65 'factories' registered throughout the island in 1862, only 6 or which employed 50 or more workers.

Larger cigarette factory owners like Susini made a point of claiming not to use slave labour but had no compunction in using indentured labour, complaining they could not get the women out of the homes into the factories. In addition to 300 indentured Chinese, Susini has been recorded as distributing material to some 500 soldiers in the Havana barracks who, in their moments of leisure, took to rolling cigarettes, and to "*femmes délaissées*" with small children to keep, and several poor families of the surrounding area. He also asked the governor for 50 orphans "to feed, clothe, educate, and teach them a craft."

The technical revolution in cigarette manufacturing slowly began to change this, but even in the 1890s, outwork in the cigarette industry was common enough to produce the rather unusual poetic introduction to an 1898 album of Henry Clay and Bock's La Corona factory:

> In this land in all truth
> So poor is it oft sold
> But lung and life it doth
> Destroy . . . be I so bold!
> Who in white paper pair
> Shredded tobacco with hair,
> Nails, cockroaches and the such!
> They send tobacco to prison
> Where convicts fashion
> Cigarettes oh so slimy
> With their hands all grimy.
> To the hospital of St Lazarus
> Yet much fouler still
> Whence comes a large fill

Of contagion and illness
And a stench so loathsome
As the smoke arrives from them.
La Corona is different:
Its building is spacious,
Its machines prodigious,
Its halls well airy
Where in two-hours barely
Are made 20,000 a cigarette:
Graceful clean women
And decent workingmen
Who care for each sheaf
Of Vuelta Abajo leaf.[17]

In none of the 36 cigarette factories recorded in 1890 had hand labour been completely eliminated. A case in point was La Legitimidad which employed a total of 700 workers, and only 12 on the 6 machines in use.

The relatively little plant modernisation in the cigarette sector after the American Tobacco onslaught at the turn of the century – company policy proved to be centred more on cigars and even then on the gradual transfer of production to the United States – meant that other tobacco interests were able to build up without great competition. They did not, however, dispose of large quantities of capital to invest in extensive plant equipment.

This in turn meant there were other small factories that sprang up both in Havana and in the provinces, especially during the 1920s. Almost all catered for a strictly local market and were never significant in size; many eventually faded out of existence. The great exception was Trinidad y H'nos of Ranchuelo, in the heart of the central tobacco region, which, from the time of its founding in 1922, gained such a rapid hold on the surrounding market that in 1930 output was superior to that of any other Cuban factory.

Nonetheless, a great majority of the small factories were able to survive for a surprisingly long period of time. There were 29 factories in 1930. Two, Havana Tobacco's Henry Clay and Bock and Trinidad y H'nos, accounted for 50 percent of total production, but the other 50 percent was still fairly well shared between the 27 small- and medium-sized factories.[18] The 1945 tobacco workers' census still listed 24, although by 1958 there were only 12, 3 of which accounted for some 60 percent of production.

Outwork and small sweatshop production had a much longer lifespan in cigar manufacturing where the technical revolution was much delayed and where those late nineteenth-century concerns had no twentieth-century parallel.[19] A combination of economic factors in the form of protectionist tariff barriers and political factors in the form of Spanish colonial restrictions, and persecution of any opposition to them, produced a particularly marked migration of whole factories plus workers to the United States, especially against the backdrop of the First (1868-1878) and Second (1895-1898) Wars of Independence. After independence, major political considerations may have been removed but twentieth-century world tobacco monopoly production only consolidated further tight protectionist controls. One effect was that it was much cheaper to produce quality 'Havanas' in the United States with imported Cuban leaf than it was in Havana, which is why after buying up a lot of Cuban industry, this is precisely what American Tobacco did. The gradual transfer of company export manufacturing was finally consolidated in 1932, leaving only domestic manufacturers in the hands of a newly formed Tabacalera Cubana SA. Other cigar manufacturers carried on, but on a much depressed scale and under much depressed conditions. As against 158 factories with over 50 workers in 1862, some 98 in Havana alone by 1890, there were in 1945 only 60. As against factories of 1,000 to 2,000 workers in 1890, there were in 1945 only 9 with over 200 workers, the largest of all with 800.

Subject to both seasonal and cyclical fluctuations, total twentieth-century cigar output remained fairly constant. This was because there was an increase in the home market for a growing population, but not a market for expensive cigars, such as those made for export, a market largely catered to by small, second-rate, local concerns and private-home rollers scattered throughout the island, as it had been in the nineteenth century. Hence the striking comparison between figures for the industry over the span of a century. In 1862, a total of 498 cigar 'factories' were recorded in Havana, 1,302 for the island as a whole. These averaged eight to ten workers, in Oriente province three, and in Pinar del Río one to two. In 1945, there was a total of 1,050 'factories, 701 of which were small shops of less than twenty-five workers, a further 289 with no wage labour at all, and 1,382 were private rollers. In Las Villas, the average shop employed not more than six workers, in Oriente province, one to two.

It was this local and outwork sector that was producing what a 1910 report on the cigar industry referred to as the problem of "inferior quality cigars marketed in boxes of accredited trademarks."[20] Over the next twenty years an estimated 80 percent of total domestic output came from this sector. From the 1930s on there was constant reference to sweatshop production. "Few are the rolling shops with the exception of Havana [and surrounding area] where the number of workers passes 50," commented a *Tabaco* editorial of August 1939. "The majority are small shops of *chinchales* in which a dozen or half dozen rollers rot under terrible conditions." Twenty years later CHPDTH estimated that of 1,092 'factories', over half were on the margin of all tobacco legislation.

On the one hand, there was a handful of larger 'independents' few of whom were ever able to expand greatly in the face of twentieth-century foreign competition and who, on the strength of this, developed their own reluctance to change. On the other hand, there was a proliferation of often ephemeral small sweatshops and of home production. It stood to reason that overwhelming numbers in both, for very good, if historically outmoded reasons, should join with the workers in resisting any attempt to introduce the cigar machine. It was successfully opposed in the 1920s and even in the 1950s, after a six-year-long battle, government limitation was still ensured on its use for export alone. Only eight 'independents' installed machinery, and by 1958 only six continued machine production. In only two did output top pre-1920 levels. Combined, all six accounted for less than 20 percent of official estimated cigar output, possibly more like 10 percent of the real total.

By the late 1950s, while cigarette manufacturing could be classed as one of the more advanced sectors of the Cuban economy (which says more about the general state of the economy than about the cigarette industry in itself), cigar manufacturing was one of the most backward.[21]

Rural and Urban Labour

It goes without saying that a very considerable proportion of Cuba's population was involved in tobacco growing and manufacturing. Rivero Muñiz claims about half the total population of the island to have been dependent on this one crop around the 1850s; reports of the 1890s claim one-third; and by the mid-twentieth century there were still whole areas and towns in Pinar del Río, Las Villas and Havana provinces for which this still held. Because this was so, the particular mode of production in tobacco was to have profound and far-reaching consequences.

Overall decrease in numbers, radically changing composition, increasing fluidity among sectors, general beating down of conditions all further complicated the make-up of what was already one of the most heterogeneous and complex sectors of the Cuban peasantry and proletariat by virtue of the many different stages in the processing of tobacco from the leaf to the finished product.

Sharecropping and outwork, which came to be prevalent in the tobacco sector, is characteristically done by the family unit as a whole and thereby involves much hidden labour on the part of women and children. In nineteenth-century Cuba, this was compounded by slave, indentured and tied labour, plus a much-abused system of apprenticeship and living-in, features of which were carried over to the twentieth century. These more nebulous aspects of work in tobacco have yet to be explored in depth. However, in both agriculture and industry, certain trends can be postulated.

First, those involved in tobacco growing comprised numerically the largest sector by far, even if numbers dwindled into the twentieth century. A total of 120,000 were reported as engaged in cultivating the tobacco leaf in official 1862 statistics, some 58,000 (out of a total population of 69,000) in Pinar del Río alone. Clearly this figure implied virtually every man and woman, and many a child too. By the same count, there were relatively few in jurisdictions of what was later to become Las Villas province, less it would seem in the Eastern Department. As the demand for inferior-quality tobacco filler from the tobacco-growing areas grew, so also did the numbers in the tobacco-growing sector.

Any growth in numbers was, however, relative. Despite increasing output, the very nature of capitalist development in agriculture, producing as it did some large plantations with scientific farming but also sharecropping in its most exploitative form, meant that the numbers declined considerably in comparison with mid-nineteenth-century figures. This was becoming evident in the latter part of the nineteenth century, but for the most part was a process which took place over the early decades of the twentieth. The 1899 figure of 80,000 was almost certainly a reflection of the state of agriculture by the end of the war, especially in Pinar del Río province. By the 1940s, however, the figure was not much higher: in the region of 80,000 to 90,000 – some 33,000 in Pinar del Río and 49,000 in Las Villas.[22]

Large plantation agriculture and more intensified sharecropping also meant that the small peasant grower class disintegrated to a large extent, giving way to a new semi-peasantry semi-proletariat which spilled over into other tobacco sectors, especially the swelling leaf-sorting and stemming[23] sectors for the export market. This vast, largely seasonal and rural work force grew to such proportions that by 1944 there were, in addition to the 88,000 reported in growing, some 51,000 sorters and 20,000 stemmers.

Of the 51,000 sorters, 19,000 and 28,000 (38 percent and 56 percent) were to be found in the major tobacco-growing areas of Pinar del Río and Las Villas provinces. At the height of the harvest, hundreds could be found in a single sorting shed in some of the provincial tobacco towns – 400 in the General Cigar Company shed in Cabaiguán, Las Villas, in July 1945. Of the 20,000 stemmers, over 8,000 worked in stemming sheds in Las Villas, over 5,000 in Pinar del Río. While the greater part of stemming came to be carried out for the leaf export market, with stemming sheds in small provincial tobacco towns, many stemmeries were also located in the larger towns and especially Havana. Moreover, all the large cigar and cigarette factories had their own stemming departments, often in the main factory building. Thus, the 1944 figure for stemmers in Havana alone was 5,000 (one-quarter of the total), and there were almost 4,000 (one-fifth) in factories. This meant that, as a sector, stemmers straddled the rural and industrial sector.

As to the industrial work force proper, tobacco was the one nineteenth-century industry to have produced a class of urban industrial wage labourers on anything like a large scale. It also did so on a scale completely unparalleled in the twentieth century. That the tobacco workers remained one of the largest sectors of the Cuban working class right up until the 1940s and 1950s was again an indictment of the development of Cuban industry in general, not a measure of progress in the tobacco industry itself.

Certain sectors of tobacco workers were hit harder than others. The very fact that Cuba's manufacturing potential for quality cigars was cut short inevitably meant a considerable decrease in the number of cigar makers, the industry's most predominant industrial grouping. This was especially marked in Havana, where the large export factories were concentrated. At the same time, the backwardness of the industry as a whole meant that the overall number of workers did remain relatively high, with a large sector scattered throughout the island and a continued high proportion of home and small-shop workers to factory workers as such.[24] Thus, whereas figures for the 1860s point to some 15,000 cigar rollers in Havana, 20,000 in the island as a whole, the 1899 figure for Havana had dropped to 10,000, although still 20,000 in all. In 1919, only 3,500 (60 percent less) were given for Havana, and this drop largely accounted for the drop in the industry as a whole to 14,000, given that figures in other tobacco provinces doubled over that same period. According to 1944-45 statistics, the overall figure was just over 12,000 cigar rollers and the Havana figure, just over 5,000.

These figures compare with an approximate overall twentieth-century figure of 2,000 to 3,000 cigar sorters and ringers, box decorators, general employees, warehousemen and the like, and a further 2,000 to 3,000 in the manufacture of cigarettes. It should be said here that, while grossly inadequate, mid-nineteenth-century estimated production figures would point to something in the order of 7,000 to 10,000 cigarette rollers. The 2,500 in Havana's factories throughout the early twentieth century were probably the only significant labour force, as hand and outwork labour was completely beaten down across the island.

Computing overall occupational figures on a percentage basis, it can be seen that by the mid-twentieth century over 50 percent of those involved in tobacco were in growing, some 30 percent in sorting and 10 percent in stemming, while only around 6 percent were in cigar rolling and a tiny 1 percent in the manufacture of cigarettes.

Race, Gender and Skill

The fact that the 6 percent and 1 percent of the tobacco proletariat retained a particular importance in both Cuban tobacco and the Cuban economy and society as a whole merits attention on many counts. Not least is the particular interlacing of race, gender and skill in the industry.

Cigar rolling is skilled work but there is little to indicate it was originally considered as such in nineteenth-century Cuba, as cigar makers were found in barracks, prisons and people's homes and as considerable numbers of slaves. Chinese and free coloureds were brought into rolling shops alongside white wage labour, often under quite appalling conditions. In this, the early cigar industry differs little from the cigarette industry.

Rivero Muñiz mentions Chinese in the tobacco industry from the beginning of the nineteenth century, and numbers almost certainly increased after 1847 when the first indentured Chinese were brought over. Although the Chinese in tobacco were considered to be among the most dextrous of workers and better off than the majority of their fellow countrymen, they were also reputed to be among the hardest worked and lowest paid. In occupational statistics, they would seem to have been classified as whites, and no overall figures have been handed down. But perhaps the most eloquent portrait is Hazard's in the 1860s, referring to those rolling cigarettes for Susini:

> It is curious to see those Asiatics, with their blue uniforms like the ones prisoners wear . . . scrupulously clean in body and apparel, in compliance with the rules of the establishment. . . . All the workers have to wear a special cap, with the name of the factory affixed. The whole establishment is subject to a notable degree of precision and military order. For the Chinese indentured labour, there is a punishment system based on fines. . . .[25]

Rivero Muñiz writes of early "wage labourers" living in, side by side with slaves and contracted Chinese in badly ventilated galleries over the rolling shops, receiving only part of their pay in money, having leave of absence only once a week, and having to hold down a cigar maker's *libreta* or identification card in which debts were recorded, restricting workers from freely transferring their labour from one factory to another. Graphic illustrations of the period testify to this, if occupational figures do not.

Whereas 1836 returns have a breakdown of 1,622 free labourers and 612 slaves out of a total of 2,234 cigar makers, from that point on slavery disappears. Of an estimated 14,000 cigar makers quoted for 1846, there were over 9,000 whites and just under 4,000 free coloureds, but no slaves.[26] Nonetheless, an 1857 *Diario de la Marina* advertised: "A negro of repute and good appearance, creole, 30 years of age, good cigar roller of Londres, earns one peso a day, has known no owner but the one for whom he was born and the present, for the price of $1,000 for the seller, healthy, with no taints and no debts."[27] Moreover, widely varying figures for the 1860s for a like number of cigar-rolling shops point to the possible existence of over 7,000 slaves and outworkers of a total of 15,000 cigar makers in Havana, and a similar figure out of a total of 20,000 for the island as a whole.[28]

There was also in the 1860s a significant percentage of free coloureds among cigar makers: 13 percent in Havana and some 18 percent throughout the island. In all, this would seem to point to over 60 percent of Havana's work force, 55 percent of the island's, as non-white, when whites far outnumbered blacks in the population at large.

By 1899, that percentage had dropped to 30 percent and 37 percent respectively. Clearly, it was to be expected that, against the backdrop of 1880s abolition and 1890s depression and war turmoil, black workers would be hit hardest, especially in Havana where the work force was fast on the decline. But it is equally clear that there had been an entrenchment of white workers in the rolling and sorting of quality export cigars, swelled in numbers by an influx of Spanish immigrants to the better Havana factory jobs. Thus, in the 1899 census – the first to distinguish between native and foreign-born – one in five of Havana's cigar factory operatives was classified as foreign white, the majority Spanish-born. And, of the further two out of every five who were white native-born, it is reasonable to assume that one at least was first generation only.

Martínez-Alier makes the point that considerable numbers of free coloureds in the crafts in nineteenth-century Cuba served to make the whites in them that much more inferior,[29] and there is certainly this factor in the racial make-up of cigar rollers. Conversely, white entrenchment served to consolidate white superiority and enforce strict demarcation lines as to skill levels. Stringent requirements needed to be met to become a master cigar maker, sorter, or box decorator, as entry into the cream of the cigar trades became restricted along race and craft lines, as much by the white workers as by manufacturers.[30] Correspondingly, this was when the 'skill' of cigar rolling most came into its own. One description of the classic artisan was:

> In Cuba, if his hands are quick,
> The cigar maker is one of those
> Artisans who, history shows,
> Can, if he wishes, make quite a lick
> Of money. Suave and slick
> And spruced up to the nines . . .
> . . . Such a toff is cheery, gay,
> And in fine clothes is apt to strut
> So much that there are cases, what,
> Of cigar makers who are confounded
> With the doctors and merchants with whom they're surrounded
> Because of the fine figures they cut.

Throughout the declining twentieth-century cigar industry, the quality rolling skill was maintained in theory but not always in practice, and its national and racial component was thereby broken down. The ratio of 1:5 foreign- against native-born in 1899 had dropped to 1:10 in 1907, 1:15 in 1919 and 1:50 in 1943.[31] Despite the new wave of Spanish immigrants into Cuba after independence, few were attracted to tobacco and this, together with the fact that many Spaniards already resident opted for Cuban citizenship, helps account for the initial drop. Other factors were the returning Cuban-born cigar makers from Tampa, Florida and Key West (though by no means all were able to find work), and the proliferation of local rolling. Between 1899 and 1907, there was an increase from 30 percent to 38 percent in the proportion of black workers in Havana. In the relatively prosperous years between 1907 and 1919 this dropped back to 30 percent, to increase over the depressed 1919-43 period to reach 40 percent.

Throughout the industry, the percentage of black workers was higher in the provinces. This held for the 'blacker' cigar makers, as well as for the more exclusive factory trades where there were significantly higher percentages of white workers: cigar sorters, for example, registered 19 percent black in the island, 11.5 percent in Havana.

Clearly a racially differentiated industry, manufacturing was also gender-differentiated. There is little reference in either nineteenth-or twentieth-century Cuba to women cigar rollers, although a preponderant outwork industry would suggest the contrary. Interestingly, not a few women interviewed in the late 1960s certainly spoke of being taught particularly by their fathers to roll cigars in the home and of being sporadically employed in cigar rolling in smaller local concerns. There seems to have been no attempt to employ women in the newly mechanised factories of the 1950s, as was very much the case in other countries with the advent of the machine, especially the United States. The particularly volatile nature of the whole mechanisation issue against a backdrop of unemployment and underemployment clearly ruled this out at the time.

More interesting still in this respect is the cigarette industry. While, to all accounts, many women were involved in home cigarette rolling in the nineteenth century, mid-century complaints to the effect that women could not be brought into the factories compare with one reference to "a shop exclusively for women cigarette rollers under the supervision of a lady of known repute."[32] However, the continuing reluctance of women to go into the factories and the continuing predominance of outwork up to the turn of the century may explain how men came to dominate the factory jobs and continue to do so even after mechanisation. The twentieth-century Havana cigarette machinists were an overwhelmingly white, male work force who, like cigar makers before them, hastened to ensure control over their 'skill'. They were doing so when, in the cigarette manufacturing countries of the United States and the United Kingdom, the male work force had already been considerably beaten down and replaced by cheap female labour. A similar process of white male entrenchment was to be observed in later years in the only major cigarette sector outside Havana, namely Trinidad y H'nos of Ranchuelo.

Women were, of course, drawn into the factory over time. They were employed as cigarette packers, as well as to place the bands and cellophane and metal tubes on the cigars. More significantly, they accounted for the vast majority of that considerable sector of stemmers. The first signs of female factory labour on anything like a large scale came after the 1868-78 War of Independence, and it came in stemming. The shortage of labour produced by the war and the exodus of cigar makers to Tampa and Key West may also have occasioned male factory stemmers to move up to the more prestigious work, causing a particularly acute shortage in a newly expanding sector for both export and manufacturing. Over the years, stemming came to be seen as a woman's job in Cuba, such that by the mid-nineteenth century, 90 percent of stemmers were women. Straddling the industrial and rural proletariat and employing considerable numbers of black women (30 percent in Havana, 40 percent in Las Villas in 1943), stemming was far from recognised as the skill it clearly entailed.

A poignant poem published in a 1936 issue of *Tabaco* magazine ran:

The stemmer:
Her beauty untrammelled, come what may,
In her home-made dress to work did fly
At six in the morning, nimble, fey,
The stemming shop worker in times gone by.
The rose of her beauty – delicate, shy –
The frenzied work robs its blush away
Just as the gold wings of the butterfly
Lose their dust in the light of day.
In front of the barrel, for ten hours she
Toiled in the dirt and humidity
That on her meagre strength did pall.
She did this back-breaking work – for shame! –
For a pittance – Yet there are those who claim
That Cuban women don't work at all!

Inevitably tied up with the particular historical configuration of Cuban tobacco, race and gender differentials were further factors complicating labour demarcation in what was on the surface a considerably integrated industry.

Notes

1. Fernando Ortiz, *Cuban Counterpoint: Tobacco and Sugar* (Durham & London: Duke University Press, 1995 [1940]).
2. Herbert S. Klein, *Slavery in the Americas: A Comparative Study of Cuban and Virginia* (Chicago: University of Chicago Press, 1967); Franklin W. Knight, *Slave Society in Cuba during the Nineteenth Century* (Madison: University of Wisconsin Press, 1970).
3. Heinrich Friedländer, *Historia económica de Cuba* (Havana: Jesús Montero, 1944).
4. José Rivero Muñiz, *Tabaco: su historia en Cuba*, 2 vols (Havana: Instituto de Historia, 1965); Alberto Arredondo, *Cuba: tierra indefensa* (Havana: Editorial Lex, 1945).
5. *Noticias estadísticas de la Isla de Cuba en 1862* (Havana: Imprenta del Gobierno, 1864).
6. Robert P. Porter, *Industrial Cuba* (New York & London: G. P. Putnam's Sons, 1899).
7. Arredondo, *Cuba* (1945).
8. See *Report on the Census of Cuba, 1899* (Washington: US War Department, 1900) and *Estadística agropecuaria* (Havana, 1929).
9. Manuel Fabian Quesada, 'La crisis del tabaco, causas y soluciones', *Carteles* (27 October 1935).
10. Carlos M. Raggi y Ageo, *Condiciones económicas y sociales de la República de Cuba* (Havana: Lex, 1944).
11. Julian Alienes y Urosa, *Características fundamentales de la economía cubana* (Havana: Banco Nacional de Cuba, 1950).
12. Comisión Nacional de Propaganda y Defensa del Tabaco Habano (CNPDTH), *Primer censo de obreros de la industria tabacalera* (Havana: CNPDTH, 1947).
13. *Memoria del censo agrícola de 1946* (Havana: Ministerio de Agricultura, 1947).
14. Lowry Nelson, *Rural Cuba* (Minneapolis: University of Minnesota Press, 1950).
15. José Rivero Muñiz, 'El tabaco en la poesía', unpublished manuscript (1946) in the Havana Institute of History Library.
16. *Projet définitif d'une fabrique de cigarettes (genre Havanais). Etablie à St Sebastien (frontière d'espagne) avec la marque* LA HONRADEZ *(L'Honorabilité) de la Havane et funcionant avec les* MACHINES SUSINI *brevetées* (Paris: Imprimerie A.-E. Rochette,).
17. *Album de la Corona: Obsequio a sus favorecedores* (Havana: Tipográfico O'Reilly, 1888).
18. Archivo Nacional de Cuba, CNPDTH, TCSA unclassified files.
19. For a fuller discussion of cigar manufacturing and workers, see Jean Stubbs, 'Dandy or Rake? Cigar makers in Cuba, 1860-1958', *Collected Seminar Papers* 29, Caribbean Studies, Vol.1, Institute of Commonwealth Studies, University of London (1982), pp.17-25 – Chapter 1 of the present volume.
20. *Trabajo presentado al Honorable Señor Presidente de la República por la Comisión nominada para que le informará al Gobierno acerca de la actual situación del cultivo y de la industria del tabaco* (Havana, 1910).
21. In this I would agree with James O'Connor, 'Industrial Organisation in the old and new Cuba', *Science and Society* (1966).
22. These and subsequent figures are taken from Felipe Zapata, 'Esquemas y notas para la historia de la organización obrera', *Unidad Gastronómica* (Havana, 1948-51).
23. A process whereby the central stem is taken out of the leaf prior to export (thereby reducing the dutiable weight) and manufacture.
24. Gaspar Jorge García Galló, *El tabaquero cubano: psicología de las profesiones* (Havana: Imprenta El Siglo XX, 1936), makes the point that there was little in common between the cigar maker of the 1890s and the 1930s.
25. Samuel Hazard, *Cuba: a pluma y lápiz, 1871* (Havana: Cultural SA, 1928).
26. *Cuadro estadístico de la siempre fiel Isla de Cuba correspondiente al año de 1846* (Havana: Imprenta del Gobierno, 1847).
27. Quoted in Rivero Muñiz, *Tabaco* (1965), p.280.

28 Compare for instance *Noticias estadísticas* (1864) with Valentín Pardo y Betancourt, *Informe ilustrado y estadístico* (Havana: Imprenta del Tiempo, 1863).
29 Verena Martínez-Alier, *Marriage, Class and Colour in Nineteenth-Century Cuba* (Cambridge: Cambridge University Press, 1974).
30 Early craft unions were particularly exclusive. This only began to break down in the 1880s along colour lines and in wider trade union terms in the 1920s along gender lines.
31 See the official censuses for these years.
32 Quoted in Antonio Gordon y Acosta, *El tabaco en Cuba* (Havana: La Propaganda Literaria, 1897), p.5.

3

Women on the Agenda: The Cooperative Movement in Rural Cuba*

Cuba embarked on a cooperative movement almost a decade ago in response to the need for modernisation in the fragmented private agricultural sector. The cooperative movement also stemmed from the national need to produce an agricultural surplus for export and home consumption and to generate an infrastructural base and financial surplus for further rural investment.

Rural women were among the more ardent supporters of voluntary collectivisation. The reasons women gave for joining the new agricultural production cooperatives (Cooperativas de Producción Agrícola, CPAs) included the possibility of gaining amenities in the new cooperative villages, the relative ease of working collectively as opposed to individually, and a measure of economic independence from fathers and husbands.

Under the initial agrarian reform policies of 1959, female heads of household were accorded land titles. But in practice, such awards proved to be the exception rather than the rule. Even when a woman secured a land title, a man would take on farm production responsibilities. Rural women did benefit from the numerous state development initiatives over the subsequent fifteen years.

---
* Co-authored with Mavis Álvarez, and originally published in Spanish as 'La mujer campesina y la cooperativización agraria en Cuba', in Magdalena León & Carmen Diana Deere (eds), *La situación de la mujer rural en América Latina y el Caribe y las políticas del estado* (Mexico City: Siglo XXI-ACEP, 1986); and in English in Carmen Diana Deere & Magdalena León (eds), *Rural Women and State Policy* (Boulder & London: Westview Press, 1987), pp.142-61.

With the new cooperatives, however, for the first time in Cuban agrarian history a specific agricultural policy was spelled out encouraging women to join cooperatives and ensuring them the identical statutory rights that men had.

That such a policy was implemented testifies to the qualitative changes in the fabric of Cuban rural society that have taken place over the course of the Revolution. It also reflects a major national campaign of the Federation of Cuban Women (FMC) and the revolutionary government to redress continuing inequalities in the position of women. Increasingly under scrutiny are job and training possibilities for women and other aspects included in the Family Code of 1975 and the Family Education Campaign of the late 1970s.

The results of this concerted mobilisation effort were that in 1979 over a third of cooperative farmers were women (see Table 1). In 1983, a peak year for the cooperative movement, the figure dropped to 28 percent, although in absolute terms the number of women had more than quadrupled. By 1985, both absolute and relative figures had dropped slightly: women represented 25 percent of cooperative members and 42 percent of the members of cooperative executive committees.[1] The sudden visibility of women in the cooperative sector has fast outstripped the state agricultural sector; women only account for 14 percent of that sector's workforce and 6 percent of executive posts.[2]

What do these figures mean? In this chapter we consider why women were singled out for special policy attention within the cooperatives and what the subsequent impact was on the position of women.

Rural Versus Urban: The Development Context

Cuba is perhaps exceptional in the Third World in that although the country is still characterised as an agro-export economy, the majority of women are not defined as rural. Over the intercensal period of 1970-81 the proportion of the total female population defined as rural dropped from 70 percent to 31 percent. More recent figures quote 29 percent. In effect, the proportion of Cuba's population defined as rural has been falling steadily over the last few decades.

This fact is partly the result of census definitions: Cuba classifies as urban any town of 2,000 inhabitants or more; towns of 500 to 2,000 with electricity, running water, education and health services; and also the new towns of 200 to 500 people with those amenities. This lower number of rural women, however, is much more a question of development. Since 1959, Cuba has embarked on a policy of agricultural development with marked emphasis on upgrading rural standards of living, providing sources of employment, and improving overall rural work, housing, education and health conditions. The notion of rural urbanisation was understood to cover a whole range of economic, social, and cultural amenities as the benefits of the city were transferred to small

Table 1: Peasant sector by form of organisation, 1979-1985, Cuba

Organisation	1979				1981				1983				1985			
	Total	M	F	F % Total	Total	M	F	F % Total	Total	M	F	F % Total	Total	M	F	F % Total
CPA Members	14,696	9,594	5,102	34.7	16,900	11,202	5,704	30.4	82,515	60,013	22,502	27.7	71,246	53,181	18,065	25.4
CCS Members	152,794	142,473	10,321	6.8	141,376	132,176	9,200	6.5	107,972	105,276	6,696	6.2	101,193	94,632	6,561	6.5
– Titleholders	111,711	105,254	5,957	5.4	101,706	96,002	5,704	5.6	81,158	76,616	4,542	5.9	72,392	67,862	4,530	6.3
– Relatives	41,583	37,219	4,304	10.4	39,670	36,174	3,496	8.8	30,814	28,660	2,154	7.0	28,801	26,770	7,931	7.1
AC Members	12,885	11,784	1,071	8.2	11,643	10,507	1,136	9.8	11,064	9,816	1,248	11.3	10,129	8,943	1,186	11.7
– Titleholders	10,249	9,520	729	7.1	7,987	7,253	734	9.2	8,017	7,145	872	10.9	8,602	7,593	1,009	11.7
– Relatives	2,606	2,264	342	13.1	3,656	3,254	402	11.0	3,047	2,671	376	12.3	1,527	1,350	177	11.6
TOTAL	180,145	163,851	16,494	9.2	189,919	168,381	21,538	11.0	201,551	171,105	30,446	15.1	182,568	156,756	25,812	16.5

Notes: CPA (Cooperativa de Producción Agrícola) is an agricultural production cooperative in which land is owned and worked collectively; CCS (Cooperativa de Crédito y Servicio) is a credit and service cooperative that brings together independent private farmers in order to acquire credit or technical assistance from the state; AC (Asociación Campesina) is a farmer association that primarily serves to coorindate independent peasant production plans with the state.

Source: Compiled from ANAP figures for the relevant years.

rural communities.³ By 1975, a total of 282 new communities had been built by the state as a direct product of integrated socioeconomic projects, whether around sugar cane, livestock, or other crop plans. The promotion of production cooperatives among small private farmers was an extension of this policy of rural urbanisation; it placed greater emphasis on self-reliance and self-help in the building of similar local communities.

Two major land reforms initially paved the way for such sweeping rural change. The 1959 Agrarian Reform Law set a ceiling on the size of private farms of approximately 400 hectares; land exceeding that limit was expropriated by the state and plots of up to 67 hectares were given to tenants and sharecroppers. Decapitalisation as well as overt political hostility on the part of the middle agrarian bourgeoisie largely motivated the second Agrarian Reform Law of 1963, which lowered the ceiling on all private holdings to 67 hectares.

Land reform, coupled with nationalisation of all foreign enterprise (1960), and the large-scale expropriation of domestic enterprise (1961) paved the way for ambitious – and at times overambitious – state development plans with agriculture as the lynchpin. In effect, rural development was inserted into a wider process of planned socialist development. Its salient feature, sugar production, was from 1963 defined as the springboard to generate the resources for the diversification of both agriculture and industry, thus encouraging import substitution and self-sufficiency. The process was assisted by negotiated index-linked prices and markets in the socialist bloc, which today accounts for 85 percent of external trade.

In the early postrevolutionary years an attempt was made to immediately diversify the sugar-dependent economy. This attempt proved costly, however, for diversification was impossible to finance because of the relative collapse of sugar production. To restore export capacity, sugar was again accorded priority. The sugar plantations had been converted to state farms shortly after their nationalisation, and subsequently state farms were seen as the model of socialist agriculture. It was assumed that they would allow for the more rapid introduction of modern technology and mechanisation. State enterprises were subsequently developed in cattle, dairy, poultry, citrus, banana and plantain production. In the 1970s the new schools in the countryside and the combined study/work programme were fostered in conjunction with the expansion of the state farm sector.⁴

The attention given to the development of the state sector was inevitably felt in the nonstate sector. An all-out effort for a record sugar harvest in 1970 channeled major resources into sugar production, to the detriment of other branches of agriculture where the private sector was much larger. The 1969-70 tobacco harvest, for example, was only 44 percent of the level of the 1965-66 harvest, and similar, if less drastic, declines in production were recorded for other crops. These declines pointed to the need for a reevaluation of the role of small private farming; such an initiative was begun at the 1971 Congress of National Association of Small Farmers (ANAP).[5]

From the start of the Revolution the private sector had benefited from a positive state agricultural policy including improved credits, pricing and agricultural extension work. In the 1970s, more agricultural research stations and technical institutes were built, and greater attention was paid to soil improvement, irrigation and the use of fertiliser and pesticides. In addition to the Ministry of Agriculture, ANAP had its own agricultural extension team that catered exclusively to the private sector. The application of technical know-how was facilitated by generally improved educational standards in rural areas (all ANAP farmers today have a ninth-grade education) and a phytosanitary activist movement.

The costs of such natural disasters as hurricanes, flooding and drought were absorbed by the state over the years through the cancellation of farmers' debts on loans and material and financial assistance for reconstruction. A more recent development has been the introduction of an extensive low-cost agricultural insurance scheme.

Since the land reform, the private sector accounted for an increasingly smaller proportion of total agricultural land (initially 30 percent, today 15 percent). However, the crops produced by the private sector continued to be either important export items (in the mid-1980s tobacco growing is still 75 percent private because of the prerevolutionary predominance of sharecropping, tenant and subtenant farming) or items crucial to internal consumption (the private sector accounts for 82 percent of bean production, 66 percent of vegetables, 54 percent of coffee, 53 percent of fruit and 34 percent of tubular production). Although private production was lucrative – profiting from high prices on first a black market and then a provisionally legalised free peasant market[6] – small farm production as a whole was left behind in development terms. It was fragmented, little mechanised and labour intensive, although private farmers themselves were hard working and productive.

The key to change was seen in encouraging this dispersed private sector to pool land and resources on a gradual, voluntary and autonomous basis. With land concentration and technification, it was hoped that productivity would increase, thereby augmenting agricultural output and undercutting high market prices. Moreover, through the formation of cooperative villages, it was hoped it would be economically feasible to further break down the social isolation of the poorer peasant household and extend the state's rural urbanisation policy. The whole cooperative idea was an extension of earlier farmer's associations (ACs) and credit and service cooperatives (CCS) in line with the new state economic management and planning system which, in the state farm sector, encouraged decentralised decision-making and local initiative.[7] The goal was to attain agricultural self-sufficiency. As a result of these policies rural Cuba, like Cuba as a whole, has been buffered to a large extent from the current world economic crisis and external debt problems. In fact, its socioeconomic indices in some respects put it more on par with the developed than the underdeveloped world.[8] It has achieved greater social equity, which has meant a significant narrowing of the urban-rural gap.[9]

Women were defined as an integral part of Cuba's development policy from the outset of the Revolution.[10] They were afforded equality before the law, employment on the basis of equal pay for equal work, and training schemes. As a result, women have begun to make inroads into new and more skilled occupations although most women are employed in health and education services in both urban and rural areas. Although agriculture is still today a major source of full-time paid employment for men, it only accounts for 10 percent of women in full-time paid occupations; a significant proportion of that 10 percent are in clerical and technical jobs.

Over the years it has become clear that the gender-based division of labour and social conceptions of male and female roles are very difficult to change, which points to the complexities and dimension of women's subordination. And studies have shown that the more rural the area, the more resistant it is to change and the more traditional the gender roles. This aspect is seen in educational differences, the low percentage of women defined as economically active, higher fertility rates, early marriages, multiple teenage pregnancies, and larger families.[11] It was hoped that the cooperative movement would bring about fundamental changes in the position of women, particularly in the more rural areas.

Women in Agriculture

The pitfalls of trying to quantify, let alone evaluate, the work of women in the rural sector include the straightforward statistical problem of whether women's labour is defined as "labour force participation." The very definition of the economically active population (EAP) is unwieldy enough in the agrarian context because of the prevalence of seasonal and unwaged labour, but it is particularly difficult to apply in the case of female family labour.[12]

Cuban statistics prove to be most deficient when it comes to data on women. The 1946 Agricultural Census gives a total of over 800,000 people working in agriculture – 41.5 percent of the economically active population of 14 years and over. Supposedly included in this estimate are farmers, agricultural labourers, and unremunerated family labour; yet women constitute only 1.5 percent of the estimated agricultural EAP.

These figures have generally been interpreted as showing the minimal involvement of Cuban women in prerevolutionary agriculture, and they are explained in terms of the disruption of traditional peasant farming at the hands of foreign and local sugar cane plantation agriculture, land extensive cattle ranching, and, to a lesser degree, tobacco and other capitalist production. This process of capitalist development was held to have created a large class of landless labourers,[13] generating a labour surplus and minimising subsistence agriculture and the agricultural work of women.

In recent studies, Pollitt argues that these census categories were oversimplified and obscured the existence of a sizable semiproletariat, or semipeasantry, that sold its labour power and farmed small plots.[14] Agricultural modernisation had certainly not been homogeneous. On the contrary, forms of production such as sharecropping proliferated, and agricultural capital accumulation was based on the visible seasonal exploitation of male wage labour. In maleheaded households, women participated in seasonal cash-crop harvest and processing activities, subsistence production and family reproduction – all crucial to family survival. Though mitigated, this area of women's work and its invisibility continued after the Revolution.

In the small farm sector, women's participation continued to go unrecorded and hence largely unheeded, though women did respond in large numbers to the FMC-ANAP (National Association of Small Producers) volunteer agricultural brigades.[15] Women were found in the (remunerated) casual and seasonal workforce, the (often unremunerated) volunteer brigades, and as an integral part of (unremunerated) small farmer family labour, much of which escaped census and yearbook statistics. For example, over the 1970-81 intercensal period, unremunerated female family labour dropped from 1.2 percent to 0.0 percent of the EAP.

According to the 1984 yearbook, women constituted 20 percent of the rural EAP. Of the 70,000 women employed in agriculture, slightly over 60,000 worked in the state sector and some 5,000 were women cooperative farmers, whereas 607 worked as hired labour in the private sector, 505 were self-employed and 220 were reported as unpaid family labour. ANAP's own figures for 1981 show a total of some 11,202 cooperative farm women and 10,336 women members of CCSs and ACs; in 1985 these figures stood at 18,065 and 7,747, respectively (see Table 1).

The discrepancy in the number of women enumerated as cooperative members by the yearbook and by ANAP is largely the result of differences in the definition of membership and conceptualisation of economic activity. Membership in a cooperative does not automatically imply that a woman performs agricultural field work. Moreover, membership criteria vary from cooperative to cooperative. Some cooperatives automatically include women who contribute land (either in their own right or jointly with their husbands), whether they work in the fields or not. Nevertheless, whether one takes the lower or upper estimate of female cooperative membership, Cuban women clearly represent a much higher share of cooperative members than in other Latin American countries.

The data reported for CCS and AC membership are even more arbitrary. Since the vast majority of women are family members of male small farmers, many express little need for registering as a member when they consider they can be adequately represented by the men. The CCS and AC women registered are often those who have become activists in ANAP. Thus the reported data capture political if not economic participation.

Women and the Cooperative Movement

A particular combination of social and economic factors of the cooperative movement proved the greatest attraction for Cuban women and engendered their support for cooperativisation. Though male peasant farmers spoke of how wrenching it was to stop farming the land individually, women viewed the formation of production cooperatives and cooperative villages more in terms of access to running water, electricity and amenities such as stores and schools, especially in the remote areas.[16] In this sense, women were perhaps motivated for reasons of reproduction more than production, but in the process they became part of a socioeconomic unit where individual well-being depended directly on collective economic success. Women's participation was recognised as both integral and important. The extent to which women were incorporated into production, however, varied considerably and was inevitably coloured by traditional farming practices, development planning strategies, and subjective as well as objective factors at the local cooperative level.

The new agricultural production cooperatives were a more carefully organised variant of earlier moves in the 1960s to pool private holdings into collective production units owned and managed by farmers themselves. The remaining few such cooperatives provided the example, and the ACs and CCSs out of which the new CPAs grew were already versed in acting collectively on behalf of individual farmers.[17] In these 'lower form' cooperatives, land was worked individually, but the cooperatives negotiated agreements on state quotas for production, inputs and credits.

In the CPAs, land and other basic means of production are collectively owned, and each individual farmer's contribution is valued and paid off over a period of time from funds set aside by the cooperative. The cooperative is farmed and run collectively as an autonomous enterprise within the constraints of national and regional planning. It receives low interest credits from the state and preferential treatment in the allocation of certain resources. A percentage of profits goes to the state in return for services; a percentage is ploughed back into production and amenities. The rest is divided between members according to their labour contribution. The cooperative elects its own president and executive committee and meets monthly as a whole. At a major end-of-the-year meeting, the members decide upon production plans, investment programmes, and consumption requirements and discuss such issues as advance pay, profit sharing, and the admittance of new members.

Individual farmers not wishing to join a cooperative in a given region are not pressured.[18] However, agricultural labourers – and in exceptional cases even industrial workers – can join the cooperatives. These groups of workers make no material contribution other than labour and hence receive no compensation for means of production, although such members do have statutory rights identical to those of other cooperative farmers. The same applies to landless wives and grown children of male household heads.

Planners envisioned that once the cooperatives were under way their greater social and economic advantages would be widely recognised and others would be formed following the initial examples. They also expected that, given encouragement, women would participate in cooperative life.

The cooperative movement did mushroom beyond all expectations.[19] The peak year in the number of cooperatives and membership was 1983, and a less marked growth is expected over coming years. The number of CPAs has dropped because of fusions, and hence the average size of CPA land has increased. Membership, which rose to over 82,000 in 1983, has fallen to 71,000, largely as a reflection of the age structure of cooperative membership and the new social security laws, whereby for the first time cooperative farmers can take paid vacation and retire on a pension, the men at 60 and the women at 55.[20] Figures for women's membership have dropped from a high of 22,000 (27 percent of the total membership) to today's figure of 18,000 (25 percent) (see Table 1). Age and the fact that current cooperative membership more accurately reflects women farm workers account for this drop. Even so, the figures on women's participation vary considerably from province to province according to the predominant crop, with tobacco and coffee provinces in the lead.

The current level of cooperativisation generally varies from province to province and crop to crop. It is at its height in sugar production, where the CPAs account for 73 percent of nonstate land. In tobacco, cooperatives account for some 50 percent of the nonstate land, in coffee 39 percent, and tubers 34 percent. Cane and coffee-producing cooperatives account for 30 percent and 28 percent, respectively, of the total number of CPAs.

The hopes pinned on cooperative production, with technical and advisory services from both the state and ANAP, in terms of output in key crops were not disappointed. Yields increased significantly and cooperative members themselves reaped the benefits of improved socioeconomic conditions. However, the rapid growth of the cooperative movement has not been without problems, especially in crops like tobacco and coffee, which allow for little mechanisation and are highly labour-intensive.[21] Economies of scale in coffee production are particularly difficult to secure because of the particularly fragmented mountain terrain in which coffee is grown. Only in the area of Pinar del Río has lowland tobacco production been spatially concentrated to a minimal extent necessary to reap economies of scale.

Both tobacco and coffee are traditional small-farm products, whose production uses a high input of seasonal female labour and high family labour component in general. This labour structure has meant that the transition from the household farm to the cooperative farm unit, in which all labour time is computed and remunerated with guaranteed minimum wages and benefits, has significantly raised labour costs and affected the potential profitability of the cooperative sector.

Gender Patterns in Tobacco Cooperatives

Research conducted in two major tobacco-growing areas, San Luis (western Pinar del Río province) and Cabaiguán (central Sancti Spíritus province), revealed that women have played a central role in small-scale tobacco production. Nevertheless, their participation in decision-making was minimal. The household division of labour was based on male responsibility for agricultural production; men rarely took on any major aspect of domestic labour, such as washing, cooking, cleaning, caring for the children, fetching and carrying water, picking tubers, grinding corn, or feeding the chickens and pigs.

Although census enumerators may not have considered such servicing tasks to be work, peasant families, including both men and women, certainly did. Women's work was recognised as crucial to family survival and reproduction, although within socially defined categories of what constituted women's work. The more this unpaid labour could be squeezed under capitalist productive forms, the greater was the surplus that could be extracted from sharecropping families and male wage labour alike. The same applied to child labour, which helps explain why large families were prevalent.

The general pattern before the Revolution was that girls and boys started their working lives around age seven, the boys in the field with their fathers and the girls around the house with their mothers. At the height of the harvest when extra labour was essential, women and girls also cooked for the field hands. The poorer the peasant family, the greater was the need to fall back on family labour by using women and girls in the field to plant, weed, prune and harvest the tobacco.

The type of tobacco determined to a large extent the kind and amount of work the women did. The cigar wrapper of San Luis, for example, was traditionally harvested by leaf, and the leaves were then threaded together to be strung on poles to dry. This work came to be almost exclusively women's work. It was considered particularly well suited for women because threading was carried out in the shade, with needle and thread. In contrast, the dark filler tobacco of Cabaiguán was stickier because of the black resin, and it was tougher to harvest. It was traditionally harvested by knife, on stalks of four leaves that were strung over the outstretched arm and then transferred to poles. This heavy work, along with field labour in general, was traditionally considered unsuitable for women. Also this tobacco did not need to be threaded because it was hung straight on the poles in the barns.

Regional variations were also evident in the tobacco sorting practices carried out before the harvest. In both municipalities, sorting provided temporary employment for thousands of women. The better quality wrapper tobacco of San Luis demanded greater classification into grades and therefore more skilled and better paid personnel. On average, 100 to 300 women were employed in each sorting shed in peak periods. The more select the farm, the better were the conditions of employment in this, the almost only rural paid labour for women outside the fields.[22] But because of economic necessity many women and girls from the age of ten were forced to accept pittance wages for long hours of work in the less select sheds. In Cabaiguán, conditions of work and pay in the sorting sheds were on the whole worse. Moreover, given the lesser intensity of tobacco production in the province, larger sorting sheds employing up to 1,000 women were located only in towns, and women had to travel extensive distances, often on foot, to find wage employment.

Through the agrarian reform and rural development policies, peasant families received title to their land, family income was effectively increased, and children were placed in school. But – despite explicit government policies to the contrary – the old societal definition of women servicing the home and family was to a certain extent reinforced, especially in tobacco areas. This outcome was in part linked to the decline in production in the 1960s and the reduced demand for female labour in both the fields and sheds. The 'tobacco recuperation' of the 1970s, in concert with the FMC-ANAP brigades and regularised employment for women in harvesting and sorting in the Cubatabaco state enterprise, has since helped bring women out of the home, as have the cooperatives.

Currently all tobacco farmers belong to either CCSs or CPAs. Within the CPAs, there has been a marked increased in the visibility of women and also a generally heightened awareness of women's role in production and of women's subordination even when women do not necessarily participate in either production or the day-to-day management of the cooperative. On the whole, neither the men nor the women expressed the view that women should not be working outside the home for the cooperative but rather spoke of how women's domestic responsibilities are an obstacle to their increased participation. Their dual role is by and large where the problem lies.

In the San Luis area, women constitute 31 percent of the CPA membership, compared with 1.6 percent of CCS membership and 21 percent of the workers on state farms. In the Cabaiguán area, they make up 38 percent of CPA membership, compared with 25 percent of CCS membership. As of 1983, there were no tobacco state farms in the municipality. In all three organisational forms, the figures exclude the seasonal labour participation of women, which at the height of the harvest is considerable; it runs to over a hundred on a typical large tobacco cooperative and over a thousand on a state farm. This seasonal female labour force includes women contracted from Cubatabaco, recruited among local nonworking women and from other sectors of production.

Criteria for membership differed enormously in the tobacco regions studied. On one of the older cooperatives both men and women had automatically been made members upon pooling their land, and thus membership numbers were fairly equal for the sexes. Among landless members, the application of strict criteria regarding stability of employment in agriculture often went against the incorporation of women as members. There were anomalous cases of landed women members who neither worked in the fields nor were active in cooperative business, and women who worked substantially in agricultural production, but whose membership was not recognised because they did not bring land into the cooperative. One working woman member lost her membership status upon divorcing because the man was considered the landed member.

In not one of the cooperatives studied was there any concept of household servicing being a part of the collective accumulation of wealth. At most, it was a semiconscious concept in discussions on such issues as eating facilities. Few cooperatives organised collective lunches for members, only for outside seasonal workers when these were employed. Women who cooked lunch on such occasions were remunerated as paid labour; those cooking for family members were not. One male accountant ventured to say that collective lunch facilities were "costly" to the cooperative, while at the same time lamenting that women's responsibilities in the home worked against their stability in field labour. On that cooperative, women constituted 50 percent of the members. Of the women members, only 19 percent actually worked in the fields; only 7 percent worked on a regular basis. Correspondingly, women worked only 11 percent of the total number of days worked by all cooperative members in the year and took a corresponding 11 percent of annual profits.

The slightly lower percentage of women members in San Luis (31 percent as against 38 percent in Cabaiguán), despite their longstanding work in tobacco, is explained in terms of its more urbanised nature; it provides other job possibilities for women. One recently formed cooperative found that the only potential woman member was the new young accountant from the area.

Some wives of the cooperative farmers already worked for Cubatabaco as paid labour and would only be hired back by the cooperative during the harvest time. Other wives were older or with young children and would only work during peak harvest periods. Grown daughters were often employees of the state sector in education and health, at least until marrige, when small children interrupted work. Even then, San Luis differed from Cabaiguán in having more accessible day-care facilities. "Women in these parts don't like the fields," was the general comment about hard agricultural work there under the hot sun. In the Cabaiguán area, women often took in sewing from a nearby garment factory that could be done in the home as a 'soft' option to field work.

Women's field work also varied considerably by region. In the dark filler tobacco area of Cabaiguán, where women had traditionally been less involved in tobacco production, women were organised into support brigades in such non-tobacco activities as the production of roots and other vegetables for local consumption and sale to the state. This work was by no means obligatory for women, and some women took pride in working in tobacco rather than in these side-line activities. In San Luis, there was less production of other crops, women traditionally worked more in tobacco, and the division of field labour by gender was not marked.

One way in which younger women are integrated as cooperative members has to do with their studies: They may come back as the accountant or agronomist.[23] This trend can also be seen among younger men who may return as the qualified technician or tractor, truck, or combine harvest operator rather than as a field hand. Hope for the future is closely allied with technification.

Paradoxically, tobacco and coffee production, while mobilising large numbers of seasonal women workers, has the least participation of women on cooperative executive committees, and to date no tobacco cooperative has had a woman president. Yet there are several women presidents of sugar cooperatives, even though women have not traditionally been heavily involved in that crop.

Over the last few years a concerted political effort has been made to ensure that at least one woman is a member of each cooperative executive committee. When one is a member, she still tends to be charged with the accounts or educational and recreational work while the men handle production.

One complaint from men in the Cabaiguán area was that women members not only worked in the fields less but also took less interest in day-to-day cooperative business. For example, some would not show up for the meetings. The women's complaint was that the men were going to have to change and carry their weight around the home for women to be able to participate more.

Although women's agricultural role may not have changed greatly, there is a growing questioning of gender roles. Generational change, especially between the women, is very marked and much talked about on the CPAs. 'Machismo' is a current topic of conversation. The older generations feel that things are a lot easier than in their time and that new horizons are opening for women but that older women are too old to change now. The younger generations, schooled away from home, are beginning to challenge certain taboos. For example, Nena, now retired in her mid-sixties, remembers how from her early teens she had to help her mother by carrying food to the field hands and fetching water. Later she worked in the sorting sheds and took in washing and ironing. Now, she virtually runs her own household as well as her daughter's next door. Although her daughter, who works in the new local store, grew up in the early years of the Revolution, she was quite restricted as a girl and married at seventeen. The granddaughters now have opportunities denied their mother. Nena's son, who became a college professor, continued to live with his mother in the cooperative village and did some housework even after marrying. In contrast, her daughter's husband, as president of the cooperative, has little or no time for the home. The granddaughters expressed resentment at being expected to help in the home much more than their brother did. The older granddaughter, in particular, was critical of the old-fashioned small community gossip which limits girls' mobility, such as being out at night with boys.

Although few men currently perform housework, their participation is at least on the agenda. The women making the greatest demands on the men tend to be those who hold down jobs and political or social responsibilities. They might also be involved in the recently formed women's militia so that they are working a double or triple shift. These women are gaining confidence and questioning established mores, including the gender division of labour, male authority, and dual sexual standards.

Among the women's complaints was that men still felt that they had a right to have affairs whereas women did not. When the men in question held posts of authority, such behavior could be cause for collective action. In the case of a married couple on one executive committee, the husband went out with a younger woman member to the embarrassment of his wife and other committee women; as a result the man was suspended from his duties. Male-female tensions of this kind, both at a cooperative and personal level, cannot be resolved in the near future; however, they can be handled supportively if there is raised consciousness.

A New Crossroads in a Decade of Transition

It has been argued here that women's work was a key component to traditional peasant agriculture. As the work and the development context in which it was placed changed, so did the nature and extent of women's work and lives. As economic pressures lessened and educational and job possibilities opened up, three marked trends appeared in women's work: (1) to seek work other than in agriculture; (2) to work on a casual, paid or unpaid basis in agriculture; and (3) to shake off field work and run the home. As a result, in a typical farm household, some peasant women show greater and others lesser degrees of agricultural participation and some engage in both agricultural and non-agricultural labour for the state. These same trends apply to the new cooperative sector but with the difference that women show a greater sense of commitment to the cooperative as such, both as a production unit and community in its own right, even if this commitment is not immediately manifest in quantitative ways.

We have attempted to show how integral women's labour is to peasant production as an economic form and the economic problems that are raised in the transition from the household to the cooperative farm. In the tobacco areas studied, the extent to which women became involved in both work and cooperative life, and the resulting changes in collective and personal gender patterns, depended often on technical questions such as the kind of tobacco and the way it had been traditionally harvested and on overall development factors of the region concerned. The two areas varied on both counts, and this variation, within general policy precepts and campaigns for women's equality, coloured the kind of advances made.

The dichotomy between the small amount of full-time employment for women and the larger proportion of female casual and seasonal labour has meant that: (1) the actual running of the cooperative fell more logically into male hands; and (2) the payment of formerly 'family' labour has become an increasingly costly problem, limiting cooperative profit margins.

We argued that, with strong policies and support for women at this juncture, cooperatives provide the productive structure best suited to catering to peasant women's needs in the productive and reproductive processes, ameliorating their subordinate position in both. At the last ANAP congress, in 1982, cooperative women delegates raised the issue of the obstacles limiting women's participation, the need for attention on this front, and the difference it makes once women are involved in the cooperative decision-making process.

Notes

1. ANAP keeps detailed statistics at the national, provincial, and municipal level, and many of the private sector statistics have been taken from its records.
2. 1981 Census.
3. Iliana Rojas, Mariana Ravenet & Jorge Hernández, 'Desarrollo y relaciones de clases en la estructura agraria en Cuba', in *Estudios sobre la estructura de clases y el desarrollo rural en Cuba* (Havana: Universdad de La Habana, 1983); José Acosta, 'La estructura agraria y el sector agropecuario al triunfo de la revolución', *Economía y*

Desarrollo 9 (1972), and 'La revolución agraria en Cuba y el desarrollo económico', *Economía y Desarrollo* 17 (1973).
4 Shortage of labour was a constant throughout the 1960s and 1970s, and state agricultural enterprises relied heavily for their workforce on students from such schools spending half a day in agriculture and half a day in the classroom and from the school-to-the countryside programme, whereby urban students spent from four to six weeks a year in agricultural camps. Aside from solving a labour problem, this arrangement allowed students (boys and girls) to benefit from experiencing the value of productive work.
5 Adelfo Martín Barrios, *La ANAP, 20 años de trabajo* (Havana: Editora Política, 1982).
6 Parallel state markets were introduced to sell produce at a higher price than on the rationing system but at prices that undercut the small farmer free-market prices, especially as produce became more plentiful from the cooperatives. Most cooperatives took the eminently political decision to sell only to the state market and not on the free market, although they were under no obligation to do so. Free markets were finally eliminated at the request of the cooperatives after the May 1986 second national meeting of the CPAs.
7 In a sense, there has been a convergence between state farms and cooperatives. By the late-1980s both enterprises rely heavily on self-management, and a direct percentage of end-of-year profits are plowed back for enterprise and local development. State farms or enterprises were still seen as a 'higher form' of production. The rule of thumb generally was that in areas where there was a need for development plans with high investment, there was a preference for peasant land to pass into the state sector. Where there was no need for high investment but there was peasant specialisation, then the best solution was the union of peasants into cooperatives.
8 According to Ministry of Health figures, hunger, malnutrition and poverty had been effectively eliminated. In 1983, child malnutrition was down to 4.6 percent under the age of one, 0.7 percent for ages one to four. Infant mortality was down from 38.8 per 1,000 live births in 1970 to 17 per 1,000 in 1982, 15 per 1,000 in 1985.
9 Recent annual growth rates of around 5 percent were unquestionably more equitably distributed over society. According to official yearbook and census figures, in the 1980s there was a 48 percent increase in agricultural salaries compared with an 18 percent increase for wages in industry. In 1953, Cuba had an illiteracy rate of 10 percent, but the rate was 40 percent in the countryside, and only 34 percent of rural children aged six to sixteen were in school, contrasting with 67.7 percent of urban children. The Literacy Campaign of the early 1960s and its subsequent boost to education meant that by 1981, 94 percent of urban children and 88 percent of rural children in that age group were in school. In 1958, there was one rural hospital; by 1983, there were 54 general hospitals, 163 medical posts and 55 maternity homes in the countryside, not counting the many community polyclinics and the new family doctor plan.
10 Isabel Larguía & John Dumoulin, *Hacia una ciencia de la liberación de la mujer* (Havana: Ciencias Sociales, 1984), and 'La mujer en el desarrollo: estrategia y experiencia de la Revolución', *Casa* 149 (1985).
11 Alfonso Morejón Farnos, Fernando González & Paul Hernández, *Las mujeres trabajadoras y los cambios demográficos en Cuba* (Havana: Universidad de la Habana, 1982); Niurka Pérez Rojas, *Características socio-demográficas de la familia cubana, 1953-70* (Havana: Ciencias Sociales, 1979); Jean Stubbs, 'Cuba: The Sexual Revolution', *Latin American Women Minority Groups Report* 7 (1983); Sonia Catsús, 'Características de los núcleos familiares en dos áreas de estudio: Plaza de la Revolución y Yateras', *Serie Monográfica* 2 (Havana: Universidad de la Habana 1984); Lidia Elizabeth Cruz Vera, 'Composición de la familia rural cubana', unpublished dissertation, Centro de Estudios Demográficos, Unviersidad de la Habana, 1985.

12 Carmen Deere & Magdalena León de Leal, 'Medición del trabajo de la mujer rural y su posición de clase', *Estudios de Población* 5 (1980).
13 Juan Martínez-Alier, 'The Peasantry and the Cuban Revolution from the Spring of 1959 to the End of 1960', *Latin American Affairs* (1970).
14 Brian Pollitt, 'Some problems in enumerating the "peasantry" in Cuba', *Journal of Peasant Studies*, 4:2 (1977), 'Agrarian reform and the "agricultural proletariat" in Cuba, 1958-66: further notes and some second thoughts', University of Glasgow, Institute of Latin American Studies, Occasional Paper 30 (1980), 'Revolution and the mode of production in the sugar-cane sector of the Cuban economy, 1959-80: some preliminary findings', University of Glasgow, Institute of Latin American Studies, Occasional Paper 35 (1981), and 'The Transition to Socialist Agriculture in Cuba: Some Salient Features', *IDS Bulletin* (1982).
15 FMC-ANAP brigades were organised in the 1960s to mobilise women in agricultural work, especially when men were mobilised for the military for distant work in the sugar harvest. By the late 1970s, with work more regularised, women pushed for their work to be remunerated, and regular production brigades of women were formed. Now, almost all work is remunerated and the brigades are virtually in abeyance.
16 This view came out strongly in the media at the time, The press ran features and interviews, and documentaries were shown such as the National Film Institute's twenty-minute documentary *Tierra sin cerca*, made by Idelfonso Ramos in 1977.
17 ACs grew originally out of prerevolutionary struggles against peasant eviction. CCSs emerged in tobacco areas where small growers needed collective access to certain resources, credits and services. Agricultural societies went a step further by actually pooling land in the early 1960s. Some of Cuba's oldest cooperatives started out as agricultural societies. After an initial flourish, many of them disintegrated, partly because they received little expressed state support in comparison with the state enterprises. From as many as 346, there were only 41 left at the start of the current cooperative movement.
18 A study by Niurka Pérez Rojas, 'Análisis comparativo de las relaciones político-económicas del campesinado en dos complejos agroindustriales azucareros en la provincia de La Habana', Centro de Estudios Demográficos, Universidad de la Habana, n.d., mimeo, shows how individual (male) farmers still worry about losing their private farm and independence, being told what to do, and having to depend on others. On their own, they can make good sales on the free market and can set their own work pace. The study was conducted in a prosperous area, and individual small farmers were waiting to see if their cooperative counterparts were really better off.
19 Orlando Gómez, *De la finca individual a la cooperativa agropecuaria* (Havana: Editora Politica, 1983); Oscar Trinchet Vera, *La cooperativa de la tierra en el agro cubano* (Havana: Editora Política, 1984).
20 Given that the private sector is an aging sector, cooperatives found substantial numbers of farmers retiring on pensions. A case can be made that with the age factor, migratory and generational patterns will of their own accord disintegrate the peasant economy. This is yet another reason to boost cooperativisation and technification.
21 The problems (not dealt with here) include structural issues of cooperative organisation, stale-cooperative relations, 'illicit' extra-agricultural activities of cooperatives, and the negative impact on the cooperative movement of lucrative individual farmer speculation – all of which were critically analysed at the May 1986 second national meeting of the CPAs.
22 *Cuba Contemporanea* (Havana: Editorial Panamericano, 1942).
23 Ministry of Education figures for 1983 show women in the majority (51 percent) in higher agricultural studies for the 20-24 age group; the figure is significantly lower (15 percent) for the 40-49 age group.

4

GENDER ISSUES IN CONTEMPORARY CUBAN TOBACCO FARMING[*]

IN THE market economy of twentieth-century prerevolutionary Cuba, much traditional farming had been disrupted by large-scale foreign and local capital investment. This was particularly true of sugar plantation agriculture and land-extensive cattle ranching and held to a lesser degree for tobacco and other branches of agriculture. Nowhere, however, had it ushered in any uniform agricultural modernisation. On the contrary, it had often served to strengthen archaic forms of production. There were significant variations from sector to sector; operating alongside modern farming units with salaried labourers, was a particularly intensive form of small-scale labour-intensive, small-tenant and subtenant farming and sharecropping. This produced a semi-peasantry/semi-proletariat which farmed small plots of land according to an intricate system of land tenure and rent-in-kind, was highly dependent on unpaid family labour and was forced, at certain times of the year, to sell its labour.

This was particularly true of tobacco, once Cuba's second major industry and crop.[1] Nineteenth- and twentieth-century local and foreign capital – with some notable exceptions – preferred to use credit and buying mechanisms rather than to farm the land directly. The drive to accumulate capital was attempted through local landlords renting and subrenting their land and complex systems of sharecropping, which usually required sharecroppers to hand over one-third, one-quarter, or one-fifth of the crop. A visibly exploitative form of male labour in male-headed households was accompanied by intensi-

---

[*] Originally published in *World Development* 5:1 (1987), pp.41-65, and Andrew Zimbalist (ed.), *Cuba's Socialist Economy Toward the 1990s* (Boulder & London: Lynne Rienner Publishers, 1988), pp.43-68.

fied women's participation in subsistence production and family reproduction crucial to family survival, plus the seasonal harvesting and sorting of tobacco.[2]

The inner workings of this essentially subcapitalist system of production and the nature of the post-1959 transition to new farming systems under the socialist-oriented agricultural development policies, are explored in this paper. The paper examines gender issues in the context of farming policies and systems, especially the new cooperative farms, in two predominantly tobacco-growing areas: San Luis (Vuelta Abajo) in Pinar del Río province and Cabaiguán (Vuelta Arriba) in Sancti Spíritus province. It attempts to highlight significant differences between the two provinces in history, land structure and organisation, and type of tobacco grown – all factors which have had a bearing on past and present gender patterns. The paper also attempts to show how overall policy has been successful in opening up new avenues for women but has at the same time thrown up new challenges which will demand future policy action if women are to consolidate their gains.

Developments in Tobacco Agriculture

It has been pointed out that the exceptional speed of the transition to socialist forms of postrevolutionary agrarian organisation reflected in large measure an earlier process of agricultural development characterised by specialised commercial farming, in which the production of cash crops (especially sugar cane) for export was predominant. Cuba's highly differentiated agrarian class structure, with a large wage-earning proletariat, distinguished its prerevolutionary agrarian system from most, if not all, other agrarian societies which would subsequently experience transitions to socialist agriculture. Of those considered 'economically active' in agriculture, forestry and fishing in the 1953 census in Cuba, less than 30 percent were classified as farmers and livestock breeders and some 60 percent were classified as agricultural wage workers. This has to be qualified in that the census procedures yielded statistically simplified rural occupational structures which made any clear-cut classification problematical.[3] Even in sugar, Cuba's most modernised crop, a significant semiproletarianisation combined wage and non-wage labour in agriculture with a diversity of nonagricultural work; this, along with intensive cheap labour and little technology, served to hold back the successful later development of state farms.

In tobacco, the fluidity between non-wage or peasant and predominantly wage forms of agricultural organisation was accentuated. Tables 2 and 3 compare the 1945 size of farms, value of production and land-tenure system in tobacco to sugar and cattle. Tables 4 and 5 reflect the patterns for tobacco broken down to the provincial and municipal levels. Table 6 reflects the predominance of tobacco in San Luis and Cabaiguán, and Table 7 shows unpaid and seasonal labour on tobacco farms.

Several points become obvious from the comparison between San Luis and Cabaiguán. From Table 4 it can be seen that in San Luis the size of farms was clustered fairly evenly in the 1.0-4.9, 5.0-9.9 and 10.0-24.9 hectare brackets, whereas in Cabaiguán the balance tilted toward the larger farms, more in line proportionally with the provincial figures for both Pinar del Río and Las Villas.[4] Table 5 shows that in San Luis the greatest number of farms were sharecropped and were very small.

Farms in San Luis, however, were more lucrative than in Cabaiguán. Land yields and the superior quality of the export cigar wrapper tobacco grown there made for farms of double the value and income of those in Cabaiguán (as can be seen from Tables 6 and 7). Table 6 also shows how cattle and sugar were proportionately more important in Cabaiguán. Table 7 shows the large proportion of unpaid labour, especially in San Luis, where there was much greater crop intensity.

By catering specially to export and manufacturing interests from the nineteenth century on, both areas produced strong tobacco interests. San Luis, in particular, had respected tobacco-growing families that made up an influential agrarian bourgeoisie, which worked fertile land on a patriarchal system of local benefits. Major farms, including the American Tobacco subsidiary Cuban Land & Leaf and the Rodríguez family El Corojo estate, operated through several farms in the area, almost all with sharecropping families and wage labourers and their own sorting sheds.[5] Owners and dealers exerted exclusive buying and selling rights over the crop and were able to turn the National Tobacco Growers' Association (founded 1942) into a powerful instrument of their own; a counter organisation was the Sharecroppers' and Tenant Farmers' Association (1952), which attempted to protect members against the abuses of patron dependent relationships.[6]

The letting, subletting and sharecropping of land is crucial to any understanding of labour in the tobacco sector. Depending on the land-tenure system, growers could be particularly vulnerable to landowners, creditors, buyers and the many middlemen and speculators. In Cabaiguán many landowners were absentee or managed far-removed parts of their cattle estates and let or sharecropped out the tobacco land. In San Luis, landowners characteristically oversaw part of their tobacco land and let or sharecropped out the rest. They often called on paid or unpaid tenant farmer or sharecropper labour for other services and had their own local stores, which functioned on credit and pay chits. In this way, owners and managers bore little of the risk of what was a highly delicate and seasonal crop. In San Luis, where little else was grown, tobacco families were particularly susceptible to market changes. Wage labourers, even at peak harvest times, faced an influx of migrant labour from sur-

Table 2: Size of farms and value of production for tobacco, sugar and cattle, 1945

Size of farms (hectares)	Total value of farm production $	Source of income					
		Tobacco		Sugar		Cattle	
		Farms reported	Value $	Farms reported	Value $	Farms reported	Value $
All sizes	331,885,242	34,437	33,844,244	42,470	138,167,239	97,573	69,476,465
Up to 0.4	56,156	17	4,458	8	3,066	626	78,185
From 0.5 to 0.9	214,286	102	25,514	60	6,644	884	50,286
From 1.0 to 4.9	12,012,328	6,376	4,559,694	2,797	514,497	14,177	1,204,391
From 5.0 to 9.9	21,482,401	9,163	6,701,860	5,711	1,969,218	17,596	2,408,087
From 10.0 to 24.9	56,933,281	13,274	13,319,116	14,622	11,202,785	30,987	8,239,698
From 25.0 to 49.9	47,723,801	3,609	5,349,377	9,322	17,208,615	16,083	8,316,374
From 50.0 to 74.9	22,456,907	867	1,589,571	3,199	8,391,029	5,620	5,157,800
From 75.0 to 99.9	13,585,467	327	773,420	1,483	5,753,088	2,691	3,424,663
From 100.0 to 499.9	82,097,403	605	1,200,118	4,380	46,193,023	7,294	20,812,640
From 500.0 to 999.9	31,981,846	57	212,249	600	18,159,772	1,023	10,413,747
From 1,000.0 to 4,999.9	34,357,156	32	92,730	262	22,586,586	518	7,820,023
5,000.0 or more	8,978,210	8	16,157	26	6,178,916	74	1,598,571

Source: Taken from Ministerio de Agricultura, *Memoria del censo agrícola nacional, 1946* (Havana: Editora Política, 1951), Table 47

Table 3: Land tenure of farms and value of production for tobacco, sugar and cattle, 1945

Type of land tenure	Total value of farm production $	Source of income					
		Tobacco		Sugar		Cattle	
		Farms reported	Value $	Farms reported	Value $	Farms reported	Value $
All kinds of tenure	331,885,242	34,437	33,844,244	42,470	138,167,239	97,573	69,476,465
Landowner	85,843,376	6,730	6,457,255	10,508	22,307,752	29,605	28,469,077
Manager	50,777,150	726	1,080,951	2,418	26,030,487	5,668	14,139,164
Tenant farmer	126,564,089	8,895	7,672,979	20,973	72,125,463	30,940	20,222,477
Subtenant farmer	13,891,384	1,547	967,396	3,266	7,399,205	4,980	1,799,347
Sharecropper	45,627,290	15,820	17,353,101	4,358	8,635,651	18,755	3,736,856
Squatter	6,520,472	553	152,781	501	186,399	6,622	756,752
Others	2,660,851	166	159,781	346	1,482,282	1,003	352,795

Source: Taken from Ministerio de Agricultura (1951), Table 48

Table 4: Tobacco farms according to size and territory

	Total no. of farms	Number of farms of each size (hectares)										
		Up to 0.4	0.5- 0.9	1.0- 4.9	5.0- 9.9	10.0- 24.9	25.0- 49.9	50.0- 74.9	75.0- 99.9	100.0- 499.9	500.0- 999.9	1000.0- 4999.9	5,000+
Cuba	159,958	1,148	1,877	29,170	30,335	48,778	23,901	8,517	3,853	10,433	1,442	780	114
Pinar del Rio prov.	23,030	117	68	3,997	6,149	8,667	2,303	575	258	647	121	108	20
San Luis mun.	981	5	7	297	262	298	67	18	1	22	2	1	1
Las Villas prov.	40,182	361	375	6,504	7,296	12,895	6,604	2,268	1,065	2,552	313	130	19
Cabaiguán mun.	2,073	–	5	558	367	701	264	60	23	61	3	1	–

Source: Compiled using figures from Table VIII, Ministerio de Agricultura (1951)

Table 5: No. of tobacco farms and area worked under various kinds of land tenure, 1945

	Total no. of farms	Total land area (hectares)	Farms worked by							
			Landowner		Manager		Tenant farmer		Subtenant farmer	
			No. farms	Total area	No. farms	Total area	No. farms	Total area	No. farms	Total area
Cuba	159,958	9,077,086	48,792	2,958,964	9,342	2,320,445	46,048	2,713,130	6,987	21,521
Pinar del Río prov.	23,030	968,853	3,373	208,114	616	200,452	4,942	225,804	1,048	21,410
San Luis mun.	981	25,109	141	3,382	24	4,491	99	10,554	31	562
Las Villas prov.	40,182	2,033,190	11,546	693,986	1,949	3,375,636	15,860	972,794	2,676	64,730
Cabaiguán mun.	2,073	43,969	504	13,110	25	4,647	656	18,509	109	1,430

	Farms worked by					
	Sharecropper		Squatter		Others		Idle	
	No. farms	Total area	No. farms	Total area	No. farms	Total area	No. farms	Total area
Cuba	33,064	552,079	13,718	244,589	2,007	72,134	636	25,210
Pinar del Río prov.	12,559	189,209	393	2,536	99	21,328	99	2,628
San Luis mun.	617	5,871	52	212	17	37	1	54
Las Villas prov.	7,166	110,692	632	7,136	349	8,218	107	10,857
Cabaiguán mun.	772	6,240	3	26	4	185	1	20

Source: Compiled using figures from Table IX, Ministerio de Agricultura (1951)

Table 6: Value of farm production for tobacco, sugar and cattle according to territory, 1945

	Total value of farm production	Source of income					
		Tobacco		Sugar		Cattle	
		Farms reported	Value $	Farms reported	Value $	Farms reported	Value $
Cuba	331,885,242	34,437	33,844,214	42,470	138,167,239	97,573	69,476,465
Pinar del Rio prov.	37,510,845	17,387	18,833,844	1,322	4,377,146	14,458	3,784,949
San Luis mun.	4,175,069	1,387	4,574,512	472	97,496	312	84,739
Las Villas prov.	77,479,694	11,833	11,031,142	16,916	32,726,832	29,379	16,392,066
Cabaiguán mun.	4,472,944	1,380	2,197,199	614	280,979	1,384	976,015

Source: Taken from Ministerio de Agricultura (1951)

GENDER ISSUES

Table 7: All farms and predominantly tobacco farms according to territory, income, number of workers and wages paid, 1945

		No. of farms	Total income	Percentage of total farm income	Number of workers					Total wages
					Unpaid		Paid			
					All year	Part year	All year	Part year		
Cuba	All farms	159,958	331,885,247	–	331,724	20,561	53,693	423,690		109,443,834
	Tobacco	22,750	40,755,323	86.6	64,395	4,994	24,965	279,155		71,503,935
Pinar del Río	All farms	23,030	37,510,845	–	67,885	969	4,919	35,198		7,296,130
	Tobacco	12,116	21,653,249	81.4	27,572	561	1,072	15,936		2,051,235
San Luis	All farms	931	4,175,069	–	2,499	59	259	3,421		678,831
	Tobacco	816	3,936,466	94.8	2,181	57	205	3,194		636,335
Las Villas	All farms	40,182	77,479,694	–	83,999	5,914	11,500	78,789		21,362,236
	Tobacco	8,032	14,227,421	69.6	20,348	772	901	3,056		916,936
Cabaiguán	All farms	2,073	4,247,944	–	4,172	125	325	2,230		416,063
	Tobacco	1,154	2,703,314	78.8	2,582	23	202	897		201,359

Source: Taken from Ministerio de Agricultura (1951), Table 54

rounding areas, which undercut already low casual wage rates. In Cabaiguán, there was a greater chance of other agricultural and nonagricultural work, but the area as a whole was less prosperous.⁷

The fluidity of labour patterns emerged over and over again in life histories of tobacco farmers in the two areas, and this was carried over in the revolutionary period. If land reform and the transition to socialist agriculture in sugar had its complexities, in tobacco it had even more.

The First Agrarian Reform Law of May 1959, substantially implemented by summer 1960, set a ceiling of approximately 400 hectares on the size of private farms. Generally speaking, land from plantations above this size was taken over by the state, while land that had been parcelled out under the various farming systems was turned over to tenant and subtenant farmers and sharecroppers. These then became private farmers in their own right and were grouped together under the National Association of Small Farmers (ANAP) in May 1961. The Second Agrarian Reform Law of 1963, which limited private farms to 67 hectares, was largely motivated by a stepped up depreciation of property, capital and services, as well as an overt hostility to what was already a clearly defined socialist process on the part of the middle agrarian bourgeoisie.⁸

Roughly speaking, the first law affected 70 percent of agricultural land, of which 40 percent became state controlled and 30 percent was placed in the hands of a small peasantry, leaving the remaining 30 percent in the hands of a middle peasantry. This last bit of private land was for all intents and purposes eliminated under the Second Agrarian Reform Law. In the late 1960s, the sale or rental of private land to the state resulted in an 80 to 20 percent ratio of state to private agricultural land; these figures roughly hold true today. In the late 1960s there were 400,000 labourers working in agriculture on state farms in the region and some 250,000 ANAP members; today the comparable figures are 700,000 and 180,000.

In practice, just as before the Revolution, the categories of state farm worker and small farmer have never been as neat as may have appeared. Many small farmers were, from the very early years, involved in mutual aid organisations that were given explicit support through ANAP. Peasant associations (ACs) were the most loosely organised variant, emerging originally out of prerevolutionary struggles against peasant eviction. Credit and service cooperatives (CCSs) were a more structured attempt to collectively organise agricultural inputs and services. Agricultural societies (SAs) were a further step toward actually pooling the land in the early 1960s. All helped modify traditional peasant relations of production. Conversely, state farm workers privately tended small siphoned-off plots for subsistence production. There were also constant mobilisations of casual and seasonal labour, both paid and voluntary, from state to non-state sectors and vice-versa, making for a continued, if different, fluidity of labour.⁹

GENDER ISSUES 57

Table 8: Tobacco according to farming systems. San Luis and Cabaiguán, 1984

	Land area (cab)*	CPA membership				CCS membership				State farm membership		
		Total	M	F	%F	(cab)	Total	M	F	%F	(cab)	Total	M	F	%F
San Luis	154	681	520	161	23.6	189	1,410	1,388	22	1.6	192	1,260	—	—	—
Cabaiguán	906	1,899	1,172	727	38.3	1,385	2,775	2,097	678	24.4	—	956	204	16

* One caballería = 13.46 hectares

Source: Compiled from local research data

Table 9: Tobacco agricultural production cooperatives (CPA), 1979-84

	Unit	1979	1981	1983	1984
No. CPAs	Unit	220	233	230	220
Land area	'000s hects	28.8	55.6	116.5	128.4
Membership	Unit	6,315	9,384	15,347	12,836
Av. CPA area	'000s hects	130.8	238.9	506.6	507.0
Av. CPA members	Unit	29	40	67	58

Source: CEE (1984)

CPA land area according to main crop (1984)

[Bar chart showing percentages for Cane, Coffee, Tobacco, Veg., Beans, Citrus, Cattle, Fruit, Other — with Total and Main crop bars]

The vast proportion of state land was in the sugar sector, which had been overwhelmingly a plantation economy. In other branches of agriculture, where this had been less so, the proportion of state land was markedly less. State land was at its lowest in tobacco, almost the inverse of national figures, with 25 percent state and 75 percent private land; this is explained by the prerevolutionary agrarian structure in tobacco. Table 9 shows how predominant the non-state sector has been in tobacco, up to the present day.

Again, there were variations in the two areas under study. In San Luis, a substantial part of quality leaf production fell into state hands when Cuban Land & Leaf and El Corojo lands were merged to become the new Santiago Rodríguez state tobacco farm. Also, the Patricio Lumumba experimental tobacco farm was set up on what was previously scrub land, but with good soils and nearby water. In Cabaiguán, the tobacco that fell into state hands was much more dispersed, often by default rather than because it had been farmed by any large-scale enterprise before. The contrast between the San Luis and Cabaiguán experience is an interesting one and points to the question of continuity and break in land patterns and farming practices. Whereas state farms in San Luis continued the large company farming tradition, in Cabaiguán traditional growers remained in the private sector and state farms were left to grow tobacco with less experienced labourers and no such company tradition. Although various state farms grew tobacco over the years, it was never very successful, and in 1983 was left entirely to the private sector.[10] Table 8 shows the 1984 distribution between private and state sectors among tobacco farms in San Luis and Cabaiguán.

As the prime beneficiaries of land redistribution in the private sector, tobacco growers were the pioneers in peasant societies and credit and service cooperatives in the early years. They contributed substantially to the 346 agricultural societies and 587 credit and service cooperatives set up in 1963, grouping together farmers for the collective use of curing sheds, irrigation and machinery, credit and supplies. The overall number of societies had dropped to 136 by 1967, and 41 by 1971, although the number of credit and service cooperatives in general had grown to 1,119 by 1971.[11]

The drop in the number of societies has to be seen in the context of an initial flight from sugar and tobacco, because of the market dependency they had signified in the past. In sugar, this trend was reversed in 1963, as sugar was redefined as a necessary foreign-exchange earner for future economic investment and diversification. The resulting prioritisation of sugar and its state farm model affected policy and resources in other areas of production and the larger private sectors within them. The all-out effort for a record 1970 sugar harvest particularly highlighted this: the 1969-70 tobacco harvest, for example, was only 44 percent of the 1965-66 harvest and dramatically indicated the need for a re-evaluation of agricultural policy and small farming.

Both the 1971 and 1977 ANAP Congresses were instrumental in this respect. The 1971 Congress initiated a period of greater state attention to branches of agriculture other than sugar. The years 1971-76 were defined as a period of "tobacco recuperation," as both private and state sectors brought tobacco production back up to previous levels.[12] In these and subsequent years, much attention has been paid to crop costing and pricing and tobacco agrotechnology.

An initial price reform acted as a major impetus toward increased tobacco production. Private small farmers had previously found it more remunerative to harvest staple crops than tobacco; these were often in short supply and could be marketed both to the state and a highly lucrative black market.[13] Farm research stations (San Luis and Cabaiguán both have one in their area) and technological institutions specialising in tobacco placed an emphasis on new, improved Cuban strains of tobacco, soil improvement, irrigation, fertiliser and pesticides, new methods of curing, and technification where possible, all of which was made available to both the state and private sectors. Today. there are ongoing cooperation projects with Canada, Mexico and Bulgaria, though none grows such specialised cigar tobacco as Cuba, and this has proved a major drawback to the introduction of modern technology.

The application of technical know-how has been facilitated by generally improved educational standards in rural areas (a recent major adult education drive encouraged all state agricultural workers and ANAP members to complete a ninth-grade education). In addition to the Ministry of Agriculture's extension workers, ANAP has its own team of agronomists and local para-professionals, through whom there has evolved a whole technical activist movement. The extension agents encourage farmers and farm workers to come forward with improvements and innovations and to be on the phytosanitary alert. This last effect has ensured that blights such as the blue mould, which decimated the 1979-80 tobacco harvest, have been kept under strict control, and the volume and quality of leaf in recent years in both the state and private sectors have been excellent. Over the years the cost of natural disasters such as hurricanes, flooding and drought were absorbed by the state, through a cancellation of debts on credits, and material and financial assistance for reconstruction. A more recent development has been the introduction of an extensive low-cost agricultural insurance scheme. And, since the 1977 ANAP Congress announced support for a pronounced pooling of private land and resources in agricultural production cooperatives (CPAs), these have received a strong boost from the state.[14]

The underlying rationale for the new CPAs, which, it was emphasised, were to be formed on a gradual, voluntary and autonomous basis, was to modernise a dispersed, labour-intensive private sector through land concentration and technification. It was hoped that productivity would increase, thereby augmenting output and undercutting first black and later free-market prices on certain products.[15] At the same time, the new economic management and planning system[16] was to encourage greater decentralisation of decision-making, local initiative and agricultural self-sufficiency in the state sector. In a sense, this brought about a convergence between state and private sectors, with both state farms and cooperatives in effect functioning as enterprises which rely on self-management and utilise a direct percentage of end-of-year performance for enterprise and local development.[17]

The new agricultural production cooperatives were a more carefully organised variant of attempts in the 1960s to pool private holdings to form agricultural societies (SAs). The remaining few such societies set the example by becoming CPAs; the ACs and CCSs out of which other CPAs grew were already versed in acting collectively on behalf of individual farmers: the land might still have been worked individually, but ACs and CCSs negotiated agreements on state quotas for production, inputs and credits.

In the CPAs, land and other basic means of production are collectively owned and each individual farmer's land contribution is valued and paid off over a period of time from funds set aside by the cooperatives expressly for this purpose. The cooperative is farmed and run collectively as an autonomous enterprise within the constraints of national and regional planning. It receives low interest credits from the state and preferential treatment in the allocation of certain resources. A percentage of profits goes to the state in return for services, a percentage is turned back for production and amenities, and the rest is divided among members, according to their labour contribution. The cooperative elects its own president and executive committee and meets in full once a month. At a major end-of-year meeting, production plans, investment programmes, and consumption requirements are decided upon, as well as such issues as advance pay, profit sharing and the admittance of new members.

Individual farmers not wishing to join a cooperative formed in a given region are not pressured to do so. Conversely, agricultural labourers – and in exceptional cases even industrial workers – may join the cooperatives. In such cases, there is no material contribution other than labour and hence no compensation for means of production, although these members do have statutory rights identical to those of other cooperative farmers. The same applies to landless wives and grown children of male household heads.

It was envisioned that once the first few cooperatives were organised, their greater social and economic advantages would be widely recognised and others would soon be formed. The cooperative movement did, in fact, mushroom beyond all expectations, and agricultural output doubled and in many cases tripled. The number of cooperatives and membership in cooperatives peaked in 1983, and a less marked growth is expected in coming years. The number of CPAs has dropped since 1983 because of fusions, hence the average CPA land size has increased. Membership, which rose to over 82,000 in 1983, has

GENDER ISSUES 61

Table 10: Agricultural production cooperatives (CPA) in tobacco, sugar and cattle, 1984

Region		No. CPAs	Total no. of members	Total land area (cab)*	Av. CPA land area (cab)*	Land area per member (cab)*	Area given to main activity (%)	Av. CPA membership
Tobacco	Cuba	220	12,836	8,311.12	37.78	0.65	12.85	58
	Pinar del Río prov.	139	7,404	4,670.47	33.60	0.63	15.21	53
	Sancti Spíritus prov.	29	2,602	1,572.81	54.23	0.60	11.30	90
Sugar	Cuba	433	31,449	29,431.81	67.97	0.94	52.54	73
	Pinar del Río prov.	12	683	542.85	45.24	0.79	54.05	57
	Sancti Spíritus prov.	26	2,931	2,013.79	77.45	0.99	44.42	78
Cattle	Cuba	192	6,020	9,944.12	51.79	1.35	66.68	31
	Pinar del Río prov.	10	330	898.50	89.85	2.72	22.54	33
	Sancti Spíritus prov.	3	121	206.31	68.77	1.71	91.29	40

* One *caballería* = 13.46 hectares

Source: Compiled with data from CEE (1984)

fallen back to 71,000: in large part this reflects the age structure of cooperative membership and the new social security laws, whereby cooperative farmers may, for the first time, take paid vacation and retire on a pension.[18] The drop is also due to members leaving the cooperatives, a point touched on in the last section of this article.

Today tobacco CPAs account for some 50 percent of privately held land; they have in many cases increased their yields but are also running into problems. The cooperative movement as a whole faces problems ranging from organisation, state-cooperative relations, 'illicit' extra-agricultural activities and the negative impact of lucrative farmer and middleman speculation, all of which were critically analysed at the May 1983 Second National Meeting of CPAs. In tobacco, there is also the problem of continued sharecropping in the individual farm sector, although on a much less exploitative scale, and the very key question of economies of scale.

CPAs stood to gain the most from land concentration through technification and resulting economies of scale. Given the kind of tobacco grown in Cuba, however, the introduction of technology on cooperatives, as on state farms, is generally limited. Moreover, following the general cooperative trend, the problem of increasing land size has been compounded by the problem of falling membership. Table 9 shows that, in the case of tobacco, the number of cooperatives reached a peak in 1981 and then fell back to the 1979 level by 1985, though the land area had more than quadrupled. Membership was at a peak in 1983 but had fallen such that in 1985 for four times the land area, there are only twice as many farmers.

Interestingly, the structural and financial constraints facing the cooperatives are very similar to those facing the state farms which, even when highly successful in terms of the volume and quality of the tobacco grown, are running at a considerable loss. Observation shows that the more tobacco-intensive the farm, the greater the financial loss. Of a total of 138 tobacco CPAs whose 1985 financial standing has been analysed, 51 – the majority of which were in Pinar del Río province, where the cooperatives relied much less on mixed farming and were much more tobacco-intensive – reported net losses. One core problem for both the cooperative and the state farm that helps explain these losses is the relative shortage of and high cost of labour.

One San Luis state farm manager cited as major outlays: (1) labour costs; (2) fertilisers and pesticides; and (3) cheesecloth (the farm grew shade tobacco) – in that order. The labour costs included bringing in temporary labour from other areas, transport, accommodation and food costs, and higher salaries for non-agricultural workers. Cooperative farm presidents expressed similar concern over labour costs, especially finding and bringing in outside labour. The great shortage of agricultural labour is rooted in the rapid development of other sectors the economy which compete too favorably with agriculture.

It is also, however, very much related to the transition from household to collective (whether state or cooperative) farming in that household farming has traditionally had a high family labour component.

Women's Labour in Tobacco

The otherwise very complete 1946 Agricultural Census has virtually no separate figures on women and is symptomatic of Cuban statistics in general, as far as information on women's work is concerned. The Census recorded over 800,000 people as working in agriculture, or 41.5 percent of the economically active population of 14 years and over. Supposedly included in this were farmers, agricultural labourers and unremunerated family labour, and yet women constituted only 1.5 percent of the estimated economically active population working in agriculture. According to the 1953 Population Census, less than 2 percent of those working in agriculture were women, the vast majority of whom worked as wage labourers rather than unwaged family labourers.

Figures such as these have been used to show the low involvement of Cuban women in prerevolutionary agriculture: they have been explained in terms of the prerevolutionary market economy and the disruption of traditional farming, which generated a surplus of rural labour and kept subsistence farming and the work of women to a minimum. Just as it is more accurate to look at a semi-peasantry/semi-proletariat, so it is important to probe women's intensified participation in subsistence production and family survival, as well as seasonal harvesting and sorting. In tobacco, for example, while there was no gender breakdown by crop in the 1946 Agricultural Census, it can be deduced that a sizable part of the substantial returns on permanent unpaid and temporary paid labour in Table 7 came from women, and that a great many more women were not included in census returns.

While mitigated, it is clear that women's work not only continued after the Revolution but continued not to be recognised, least of all in official statistics. Hence, over the intercensal period of 1970-81, unpaid family labour supposedly dropped from 3.9 percent to 0.2 percent of the total economically active population and from 1.2 percent to 0.0 percent for women. By the 1980s, less than 10 percent of the economically active population working in agriculture were women.

In the small farm sector, women's participation continued to go unrecorded and hence largely unheeded, though women did respond in large numbers to the volunteer agricultural brigades organised jointly by ANAP, and the Federation of Cuban Women (FMC).[19] In the state farm sector, factors such as increasing technification and mechanisation changed the requirements demanded of labour: new skills, that for social reasons were not always easy for women to acquire, were needed. An initial separation of agricultural work from the domestic unit posed the classical break between 'work' and the home; improved rural living standards as a result of overall development policy often meant less economic pressure on women to supplement family income – and when women did choose to work, openings in such expanding nonagricultural spheres as health and education often proved far more attractive. As a result, women were to be found most in the (unremunerated) casual and seasonal work force, the (often unremunerated) volunteer brigades, and as an integral part of (unremunerated) small farmer family labour.

A breakdown of state and private sectors in the 1984 *Statistical Yearbook*, shows that, of 70,000 women active in agriculture in 1984, slightly over 60,000 worked in the state sector, some 5,000 were members of cooperatives, 607 worked as hired labour in the private sector, 505 were self-employed and 220 performed unpaid family labour. ANAP returns for that same year seemed to contradict the private sector figures, showing a total of some 11,000 cooperative farmwomen and just over 10,000 women members of CCSs and ACs.

In 'straight' economic terms, ANAP figures are largely inflated. Membership in a cooperative did not automatically imply that a woman performed agricultural field work, and membership criteria varied from cooperative to cooperative. Some cooperatives automatically included women who contributed land (either in their own right or jointly with their husbands) whether they worked in the fields or not, and were hesitant to admit women who did work but contributed no land. CCS and AC data are even more tricky to handle, since women members of small farm families expressed little need to register as members when they could be represented by their men. Those women who did register had usually become active in the local organisation and this was more of a determinant than their labour.

Given the inadequacy of the general data available and the almost total absence of any gender breakdown by crop (beyond cane and non-cane agriculture), plus the fact that the conceptualisation of women's economic activity was highly coloured by traditional definitions, it was essential to build up some good local disaggregated data, incorporating life history techniques. In the case of tobacco, from the research conducted in San Luis and Cabaiguán,[20] it became clear that women had, indeed, been central to what was mainly small-scale tobacco production.

Historically, the domestic division of labour had been fairly complete; men oversaw agricultural production in the broader sense and rarely took part in servicing the family and household, whether it be washing, cooking, cleaning, caring for the children, fetching and carrying water, picking tubers, grinding corn, or feeding the chickens and pigs.

If this was not considered work by the census enumerators, it certainly was by peasant families, both men and women alike. The wider societal view of women in the home was very much tempered by the recognition that women's work was crucial, although within socially defined categories of what that work was. The more women's unpaid labour could be exploited, the greater the surplus that could be extracted from sharecropping families and male wage labour. The same applied to child labour, which helps explain why large families were prevalent.

The general pattern was that girls and boys started working at age seven, the boys in the fields with their fathers and the girls around the house with their mothers. At the height of the harvest, when extra labour was essential, girls' and women's work also involved cooking for the field hands. The poorer the peasant family, the greater the need to fall back on family labour, in which case women and girls would also be out in the fields planting, seeding, pruning and harvesting the tobacco.

The type of tobacco determined to a large extent the kind and amount of work the women did. The cigar wrapper tobacco of San Luis, for example, has traditionally been harvested by leaf in baskets and the leaves then threaded together to be strung on poles to dry. This was seen almost exclusively as women's work; the drying, in particular, was done in the shade, with needle and thread. The dark filler tobacco of Cabaiguán was stickier (from the black resin) and tougher. It was traditionally harvested by knife in stalks of four leaves at a time, hung over the outstretched arm, and then transferred to poles. Heavy work such as this, and field labour in general, were traditionally considered unsuitable for women. In any case. the Cabaiguán tobacco did not need to be threaded, as it was hung straight on poles in the barns.

There were also variations in the seasonal sorting of tobacco in the initial months after harvesting, during which both municipalities provided temporary employment for thousands of women. The better quality wrapper tobacco of San Luis demanded greater classification into grades and therefore more skilled and better paid personnel; on average 100-300 people were employed in each sorting shed in peak periods. The more select the farm, the more select this, one of the few forms of paid labour for rural women. But there were many sorting sheds where the economic necessity of tobacco families was such that women and girls from age 10 would accept pittance rates for long hours of work. In Cabaiguán, conditions and pay in the sorting sheds were on the whole worse and, given the lesser intensity of tobacco growing and the concentration of larger sorting sheds (holding up to 1,000) in towns, extensive distances had to be travelled to reach the work.

With the agrarian reform and rural development policies, the land peasant families worked was made their own, the family wage was effectively upped, children were sent to school, and, despite explicit government policies to the contrary, the old societal definition of women servicing the home and family was to a certain extent reinforced, especially with the fall in tobacco production in the 1960s and the decreased labour needed in the fields and the sheds. The 'tobacco recuperation' of the 1970s, including improved wages and working conditions for both men and women, the FMC-ANAP brigades, and regularised payroll work for women in harvesting and sorting through Cubatabaco, the umbrella state tobacco-handling enterprise,[21] and the production cooperatives, have helped to redress this disadvantageous position of women in the labour market.

The cooperatives marked a definite policy departure as far as women were concerned. Under the initial agrarian reform of 1959, female heads of household had been accorded land titles, but they were the exception rather than the rule and often the title had meaning only on paper and not in practice, as a man would take on farm production responsibilities. In the long run, the Revolution's wider educational and agricultural development policy opened up new horizons for farm women.[22] It was not until the new CPAs, however, that a specific agricultural policy prescription for women was spelled out, and women were encouraged to join cooperatives in their own right and have statutory rights identical to those of any other cooperative member.

The result, in less than a decade, has been quite startling. Following the initial flurry of cooperative formation, by 1979, over a third of all CPA members were women. In 1983, a peak year for the cooperative movement, the figure had dropped to 27 percent, although in absolute terms the number of women had more than quadrupled. Today, both absolute and relative figures have dropped, again partly because of the age factor, partly because recent figures apply more strictly to working women members, that is, active rather than passive ones. According to 1985 figures, women accounted for 25 percent of total CPA members and 12 percent of executive committee members. While moderate in scale, this sudden visibility of women has outstripped the state agricultural sector, in which, in 1985, women accounted for only 14.4 percent of the work force and 6 percent of executive posts.

Tobacco areas have been among those to show higher percentages of women coop farmers. The CPAs have brought with them a marked increase in the visibility of women as compared to the rest of the private sector. In the San Luis and Cabaiguán areas, all tobacco farmers are now in CPAs or CCSs; in San Luis women comprise 24 percent of the membership in CPAs and 1.6 percent in the CCSs; in Cabaiguán the figures are 38 percent and 25 percent respectively. For the state farms in San Luis, women make up 16 percent of the workforce, still lower than the CPAs. In all three, the figures exclude the considerable seasonal labour of women, which at the height of the harvest can run into hundreds. For this, local non-working women and women from other sectors of production work on a contract basis through Cubatabaco.

Despite overall policy prescriptions, membership criteria differed enormously from CPA to CPA in tobacco. At one of the older cooperatives in

Table 11a: Private sector composition. Agricultural production cooperatives (CPA), San Luis, 1984

	Land area (cab)*	Membership				Land contributors				Labour force			FMC members
		Total	Men	Women	Women % total	Total	Men	Women	Women % total	Total	Men	Women	Women % total	
San Luis														
Menelao Mora	7.4	42	30	12	28.6	13	13	–	–	ng	ng	ng	ng	ng
José Martí	11.5	52	32	20	38.5	26	26	–	–	ng	ng	ng	ng	ng
José A. Echeverría	19.7	73	51	22	30.1	28	28	–	–	ng	ng	ng	ng	ng
Frank País	8.7	42	33	9	21.4	28	28	–	–	ng	ng	ng	ng	ng
Isidro de Armas	6.1	49	43	6	12.2	31	31	–	–	ng	ng	ng	ng	ng
Niceto Pérez	10.1	52	49	3	6.1	27	27	–	–	ng	ng	ng	ng	ng
Lenin	2.9	23	22	1	4.5	11	11	–	–	ng	ng	ng	ng	ng
Leopoldo Trocha	4.4	28	23	5	2.2	15	15	–	–	ng	ng	ng	ng	ng
Alfonso Valdéz	9.0	30	27	3	10.0	34	24	–	–	ng	ng	ng	ng	ng
Hnos Venas	16.2	83	54	29	35.0	18	18	–	–	ng	ng	ng	ng	ng
17 de Mayo	10.2	28	22	6	21.4	15	15	–	–	ng	ng	ng	ng	ng
Carlos Lóriga	20.5	66	49	17	25.8	27	27	–	–	ng	ng	ng	ng	ng
Antonio Guiteras	11.0	52	45	7	13.5	17	17	–	–	ng	ng	ng	ng	ng
General Antonio	13.0	49	34	15	30.6	16	16	–	–	ng	ng	ng	ng	ng
Renato Guitart	2.8	22	16	6	37.5	11	11	–	–	ng	ng	ng	ng	ng

* One *caballería* = 13.46 hectares

Source: Compiled with data from local ANAP returns for 1984.

Table 11b: *Private sector composition. Agricultural production cooperatives (CPA), Cabaiguán, 1984*

	Land area (cab)*	Membership				Land contributors				Labour force				FMC members
		Total	Men	Women	Women % total	Total	Men	Women	Women % total	Total	Men	Women	Women % total	
Cabaiguán														
La Nueva Cuba	51.6	191	112	79	41.4	58	33	25	43.1	114	74	40	35.1	84
Juna González	135.8	324	176	148	45.7	98	44	54	55.1	156	128	28	17.9	148
10 de Octubre	118.2	289	177	112	38.8	104	62	42	40.4	193	125	68	35.2	110
13 de Marzo	58.1	122	82	40	32.8	37	15	22	59.5	68	52	16	23.5	40
Aramis Pérez	62.8	170	100	70	41.2	66	50	16	24.2	117	87	30	25.6	65
21 Aniversario	34.8	65	42	23	35.4	24	13	11	45.8	53	40	13	24.5	23
6ta Cumbre	30.5	66	40	26	39.4	27	19	8	29.6	31	27	4	12.9	26
Victoria de Angola	29.9	82	51	31	37.8	32	16	16	50.0	56	45	11	19.6	31
Victoria de Girón	85.9	50	32	18	36.0	30	30	–	–	43	31	12	27.9	18
La Victoria	22.4	28	23	5	17.9	18	10	8	44.4	24	20	4	16.6	–
Noel Sancho Valladaares	50.0	60	43	17	28.3	23	16	7	30.4	34	27	7	20.6	17
Mártires de Cabaiguán	32.3	73	53	20	27.4	30	21	9	30.0	43	36	7	16.3	40
Romanico Cordero	28.1	78	53	25	32.1	36	24	12	33.3	72	61	11	15.3	30
Eduardo G. Lavandero	41.5	111	66	45	40.5	48	18	30	62.5	65	52	13	20.0	45
Camilo Cienfuegos	58.8	54	33	21	38.8	36	20	16	44.4	45	35	10	22.2	8
1ro de Enero	45.4	75	49	26	34.7	40	14	26	65.0	52	42	10	19.2	80
Mártires de Neiva	20.0	61	40	21	34.4	17	3	14	82.4	44	36	8	18.2	21

* One *caballería* = 13.46 hectares

Table 12a: Private sector composition. Credit and service cooperatives (CCS), Cabaiguán, 1984

CCS	Land area (cab)*	Membership				Titleholders				Landless members			
		Total	Men	Women	Women % total	Total	Men	Women	Women % total	Total	Men	Women	Women % total
Cabaiguán													
Alfredo López Brito	28.7	81	54	27	33.3	38	36	2	5.3	43	18	25	58.1
Emilio R. Capestany	51.4	110	84	26	23.6	60	50	10	16.6	40	34	16	40.0
Nieves Morejón	62.5	130	84	46	35.4	63	49	14	22.2	67	35	32	47.8
Niceto Pérez	53.7	118	101	17	14.4	73	68	5	6.8	45	33	12	26.7
Arturo Cabrera	53.6	101	70	31	30.7	55	50	5	9.1	46	20	26	56.5
Ciro Redondo	52.6	61	50	11	18.0	37	33	4	10.8	24	17	7	29.2
Francisco Rivas	40.0	63	47	16	25.4	35	29	6	17.1	28	18	10	35.7
Patria o Muerte	46.2	96	59	37	38.5	36	32	4	11.1	60	27	33	52.4
Jerónimo Ramírez	73.7	94	81	13	13.8	67	62	5	7.5	27	19	8	29.6
Julio Piñero Lorenzo	33.0	82	49	33	35.1	32	30	2	6.3	50	19	31	62.0
Rogelio Rojas	60.9	118	77	41	34.7	55	47	8	14.5	63	30	33	52.4
Horacio González	20.0	57	34	23	40.4	22	20	2	9.1	35	14	21	60.0
Sergio Soto	72.8	148	104	44	29.7	62	56	6	9.7	86	48	38	44.2
Gerardo Abreu Fontán	25.2	64	43	21	32.8	23	22	1	4.3	41	21	20	48.9
Alfredo Ferrer López	59.4	111	78	33	29.7	61	55	6	9.8	50	23	27	54.0
Beremundo Paz	50.6	96	69	27	28.1	48	45	3	6.3	48	24	24	50.0

* One *caballería* = 13.46 hectares

Table 12a (cont.): Private sector composition. Credit and service cooperatives (CCS), Cabaiguán, 1984

CCS	Land area (cab)*	Membership				Titleholders				Landless members			
		Total	Men	Women	Women % total	Total	Men	Women	Women % total	Total	Men	Women	Women % total
26 de Julio	40.0	55	36	19	34.5	25	23	2	8.0	30	13	17	56.7
Hnos Calera	50.6	90	66	24	26.6	56	51	5	8.9	34	15	19	55.9
Jorge Austiny	33.1	70	45	25	35.7	39	32	7	17.9	31	13	18	58.1
Eloises Pérez	37.8	88	70	18	20.5	66	59	7	10.6	22	11	11	50.0
Marino Rodríguez	17.4	38	32	6	15.8	25	22	3	12.0	13	10	3	23.1
Jesús Menéndez	16.5	32	27	5	15.6	24	19	5	20.8	8	8	–	–
Armando González	34.3	97	87	10	10.3	55	48	7	12.7	42	39	3	7.1
Julio Careaga	38.0	76	71	5	6.6	42	40	2	4.8	34	31	3	8.8
Frank País	54.8	103	92	11	10.7	58	56	2	3.4	45	36	9	20.0
Abel Santamaría	49.8	76	66	10	13.2	54	49	4	7.5	23	17	6	26.1
Mártires de Taguasco	95.6	140	120	20	14.3	104	94	10	9.6	36	26	10	27.8
Luis Turcios Lima	90.0	140	122	18	12.9	99	84	15	15.2	41	38	3	7.3
José Martí	51.3	79	70	9	11.4	29	22	7	24.1	50	48	2	4.0
Fernando Conde	41.0	95	68	27	28.4	58	47	11	19.0	37	21	16	43.2
Ramón Balboa	40.0	66	41	25	37.9	34	27	7	20.6	32	14	18	56.3

* One *caballería* = 13.46 hectares

Source: Compiled with data from local ANAP returns for 1984

Table 12b: Private sector composition. Credit and service cooperatives (CCS), San Luis, 1984

CCS	Land area (cab)*	Membership				Titleholders				Landless members			
		Total	Men	Women	Women % total	Total	Men	Women	Women % total	Total	Men	Women	Women % total
San Luis													
Luis Ferrer	16.0	91	91	–	–	54	54	–	–	37	37	–	–
Jesús Menéndez	11.0	137	132	5	3.6	103	102	1	0.9	34	30	4	11.8
Calixto Sánchez	10.0	39	39	–	–	21	21	–	–	18	18	–	–
Cuco Barceló	18.0	126	115	11	8.7	101	100	1	0.1	25	15	10	40.0
Viet Nam Heróico	18.0	75	75	–	–	45	45	–	–	30	30	–	–
Sergio González	5.0	33	33	–	–	20	20	–	–	13	13	–	–
Mariana Grajales	7.0	75	75	–	–	48	48	–	–	27	27	–	–
José Maceo	13.0	122	120	2	1.6	55	55	–	–	67	65	2	3.0
Cmdte Acanda	9.0	85	85	–	–	45	45	–	–	40	40	–	–
26 de Julio	9.0	71	71	–	–	40	40	–	–	31	31	–	–
Ignacio Agramonte	7.0	48	48	–	–	29	29	–	–	19	19	–	–
José A. Labrador	19.0	122	122	–	–	61	61	–	–	61	61	–	–
Pedro Ortiz	17.0	132	130	2	1.5	68	68	–	–	64	62	2	3.1
Ramón L. Peña	4.5	32	32	–	–	25	25	–	–	77	77	–	–
Francisco Barrios	5.0	62	62	–	–	50	50	–	–	12	12	–	–
Camilo Cienfuegos	20.0	160	158	2	1.3	108	108	–	–	52	50	2	4.0

* One *caballería* = 13.46 hectares

Source: Compiled with data from local ANAP returns for 1984

Cabaiguán, it was found that both men and women were automatically made members upon pooling their land and membership numbers were fairly equal for the sexes. In San Luis this was not the case, as no women were quoted as land contributors. Among the women who were not considered land contributors, strict rules regarding stability in agriculture often worked against them. In all cooperatives, there were both active and non-active members of both sexes. Among the men, the non-active were usually retired. Among the women, there were found anomalous cases of 'landed' women members, who neither worked in the fields nor were active in cooperative business, and women who worked substantially in agricultural production but were not landed and whose membership had not been recognised.

The lower percentage of women in cooperative members in San Luis can largely be explained by the urban setting, which provides other job opportunities, in tobacco and in general. One recently formed cooperative found that there were simply no women who could join, except a young graduate accountant. Wives of cooperative farmers were already on the Cubatabaco payroll as paid workers and would be hired back out to the cooperative during the harvest time. Other wives were older or had young children and could only work during peak harvest periods. Grown daughters were often working for the state sector in education, health and the like, at least until marriage and small children interrupted work. Even then, San Luis differed from Cabaiguán in that it offered more accessible daycare facilities.

Women's work on the cooperative varied considerably. In the dark filler tobacco area of Cabaiguán, where women had traditionally been less involved in tobacco, women might be organised into support brigades in non-tobacco activities: producing root and other vegetables for local consumption and sale to the state – although this was by no means obligatory and some women took a pride in working the tobacco. In San Luis, other crops were produced less, women had traditionally worked more in tobacco, and this division of field labour was not marked. Interestingly, when Cabaiguán cooperatives last year experimented with Burley tobacco, the women were particularly pleased to be able to pick and thread the leaves. One cooperative even took the tobacco to the women in their homes to be threaded on their front porches. Women who had retired from the fields or had other family commitments were all able to help out and earn some money.

So far, household servicing is still only dimly perceived as part of the collective process of accumulation of wealth, except in a semiconscious sense over issues such as meals. Few cooperatives organised collective lunch for their members, only for outside seasonal workers. Cooking lunch for outside workers was recognised as paid labour, cooking for family members was not. One male accountant ventured to say that collective lunch facilities were "costly" to the cooperative, while at the same time, he lamented that women's responsibilities in the home worked against their stability in field labour. At that cooperative, almost half of all members were women. Of that 50 percent only 19 percent actually worked in the fields, and of that 19 percent, only 38 percent (or 7 percent of the total reported female membership) worked at all regularly. Correspondingly, women worked only 11 percent of the total number of days worked in the year and took a corresponding 11 percent of annual profits.

This was an extreme case. A nearby cooperative reported only 15 percent of members were women, but almost all worked on a regular basis and took a more proportionate share of annual profits. Nonetheless, the general comment was that women did not like the field work, which was clearly hard agricultural labour under a hot sun. In the Cabaiguán area, women took on sewing from a nearby garment factory as a softer option.

Younger women are increasingly coming back to work on the cooperatives, in a technical capacity – as the accountant or agronomist – a trend which is noticeable generally in the tobacco areas, where almost a third of such technical personnel are women.[23]

Gender Issues in Focus

It was a particular combination of social and economic factors of the cooperative movement which proved most attractive to Cuban women, engendering their support for cooperativisation. While male peasant farmers spoke of cooperativisation as a wrench to stop individual farming of the land, women, especially those in the remote areas, viewed the formation of production cooperatives and cooperative villages more in terms of access to running water, electricity and amenities such as stores and schools.[24] In this sense, women were perhaps motivated more for reasons of reproduction than production, but in the process they became part of a socio-economic unit in which individual well-being depended directly on collective economic success. Women's participation was recognised as both integral and important. The extent to which women were incorporated into production, however, varied considerably and was inevitably coloured by traditional farming practices, development planning strategies, and subjective as well as objective factors at the local cooperative level.

In the tobacco areas studied, there had been a marked increase in the visibility of women and also a generally heightened awareness of women's role in production and women's subordination, even when women did not necessarily participate in either production or the day-to-day management of the cooperative. On the whole, neither the men nor the women expressed the view that women should not work outside the home for the cooperative, but spoke rather of how women's domestic responsibilities are an obstacle to their increased participation.

This is reflected in the high number of women labourers at the casual and seasonal level and the relatively low number of women at the executive level. Over the years, the FMC and the government have made a concerted political effort to probe the problems women face in taking on regular employment and securing job promotions. Over the last decade, this effort has ranged from political education work aimed at passing the new 1975 Family Code, which challenged an established gender division of labour, to campaigns against on-the-job and promotion discrimination against women.

The complexities and dimensions of women's subordination have, however, proven highly resistant to change, especially in the less developed rural areas. In the CPAs, for example, an attempt has been made to ensure that at least one woman member sits on the executive committee. Even so, women members still tend to be charged with the accounts or educational and recreational work, while the men handle production.

In the Cabaiguán areas men complained about women members because not only did they work in the fields less, they also took less of an interest in day-to-day cooperative business. For example, they claimed, some would not show up for meetings. The women had their own complaint: the men would have to change and begin to carry their weight around the home in order for women to be able to participate more.

Generational change, especially among the women, is very marked and much talked about on the CPAs. While much has still not changed, there is a growing questioning of gender roles. 'Machismo' is a current topic of conversation. The older generations feel that things are a lot easier today than in their time and that new doors are opening for women but that it is too late for them to change. The younger generations, schooled away from home, are beginning to challenge certain taboos.

Nena, for instance, now retired and in her mid-sixties, remembers how from her early teens she had to help her mother carry food to the field hands and fetch and carry water. Later, she worked in the sorting sheds while also taking in washing and ironing. Now, she virtually runs her own household, as well as her daughter's next door.

Her daughter, who works in the new local store, grew up in the early years of the Revolution. She, nonetheless, was quite restricted as a girl and married at 17. The granddaughters now have opportunities denied their mother. Nena's son, who did study and become a college professor, continued to live with his mother in the cooperative village and was one of the men who did housework, even after marrying. In contrast, her daughter's husband, as president of the cooperative, has little or no time for the home. The granddaughters expressed a certain resentment at being expected to help in the home much more than their brother. The oldest granddaughter in particular was critical of old-fashioned small community gossip which limits girls' mobility.

While few men currently participate in housework, it is at least on the agenda. The women who make the greatest demands on men tend to be those who hold down jobs or have political and social responsibilities. They might also be involved in the recently formed women's militia, making theirs a double or triple shift. These women are gaining confidence and questioning established mores, including the gender division of labour, male authority and dual sexual standards.

Women expressed resentment that men still thought it their right to have affairs while expecting that women should not. When the men in question held posts of authority, this could be cause for collective action. In the case of one married couple, both on the executive committee, in which the husband went with a younger woman member, the situation was such an embarrassment for the wife and other committee women, that the man was suspended from his duties. Clearly, male-female tensions of this kind, both at a cooperative and personal level, will not be resolved in the near future. They can, however, be handled supportively when consciousness has been raised and crucial space created for women.

Special technical and advisory services from the state to the tobacco sector, both state and private, plus the recent land concentration in the form of cooperatives, with a centralisation of resources and production, have reaped bumper harvests in recent years. Similarly, tobacco areas have reaped the benefits of a state investment programme in social as much as economic spheres, with a considerable injection of self-help.

However, several policy imperatives related to tobacco production are now emerging. One is greater land concentration, so as to avoid further dispersal of land. In the more tobacco-intensive areas of San Luis, where there is a veritable mosaic of state, cooperative and individual private farms, all interspersed, an exchange of plots is essential for any further advance. A second policy imperative is a greater attempt to select maximum productivity work brigades and organise smaller, more manageable plots on a piece-rate basis.[25] A third is a revision of crop pricing.

All three are felt to be crucial if tobacco growing is to be made more profitable again. In the case of the cooperatives, other factors are important: the inevitable outlays required of any new investment, and the inefficiencies in organising and managing a new kind of production unit that requires technification and new skills, yet is susceptible to over-ambitious production targets. This is especially likely as the cooperative grows in land size and the number of cooperative farmers drops, as has been the trend over the last few years. And yet. it was state farm managers, whose farms had been going much longer, who most strongly argued for a price review if profitability were to be achieved, especially when the exporting and manufacturing of tobacco were particularly profitable.

Perhaps a fourth policy imperative should be added: a reconsideration of the labour question in gender terms. This would imply recognising the effect on labour costs and end-of-year profits in a crop like tobacco, a traditionally small-farm product with a high unpaid family labour component, of the transition from a household to cooperative or state farm unit, in which all crop labour is economically computed and remunerated under a socialist rather than a capitalist system, whereby there are applied minimum guarantees and wages for workers.

Interestingly, bank statistics show a much lower positive end-of-year balance on credits for the cooperative tobacco farmer than for the individual tobacco farmer (140 pesos against 1,510 on average, a ratio of less than 1:10, for the 1983-84 harvest).[26] The only approximate indicator available that can serve as a point of comparison between the cooperative and individual farm, this bank statistic is in itself highly problematical, precisely because it conceals the real distribution of income in each type of economy. In the individual small farm, all income is registered under the farm owner or representative: the work of family members and others in the production process is not taken into account. In the case of the cooperative, the farmer's income is that which is received for work done individually, as well as advance daily pay, social security, paid maternity leave for women, sickness and other similar benefits (and there may be two or more cooperative farmers in a single family).

It is to be noted that, in the case of sugar, which is much less a small farm product, has a much lower female labour input, and admits mechanisation and economies of scale, the figures for cooperative and individual farmers are much closer (734 pesos against 886, a ratio of some 9:10, for 1983-84). In coffee, which shows much greater similarity to tobacco, the figures are again very uneven (40 pesos against 532, less than 1:12, for the same harvest).

To pursue the point further, it is important to note that today, Cabaiguán cooperatives are more profitable than San Luis cooperatives. Table 13 shows average land size, membership and profit margins for tobacco areas. In Sancti Spíritus, coops are less dependent on tobacco, and the profitability edge comes from the more extensively farmed and more mechanised cattle and sugar estates; whereas Pinar del Río relies much more exclusively on highly labour-intensive and specialised tobacco.

In the case of the cooperatives, which are conceived not only as an economic but also as a social form of organisation, such factors can be crucial. They are seen as another step forward in the humanisation of work in rural Cuba, and as coming from a more rational and equitable social system, as much as from straight technical advance. Cooperatives have to prove themselves from both a productive and social point of view and, while some of the older (male) farmers might be a little disheartened with the process and even desist (again Pinar del Río is proving to have the highest desertion rate – 6 percent

Table 13: Tobacco agricultural production cooperatives (CPA), 1984-85 partial balance ('000s pesos)

Region	No. CPAs*	No. of members	Value of production	Cost per peso of production	Advance pay	Salary	Net profits	Profits shared out
Cuba	138	7,559	20,532.2	0.87	8,491.8	2,492.6	3,066.3	2,270.9
Pinar del Río (dark tob.)	76	3,333	10,206.3	0.91	3,734.1	1,113.5	740.4	859.0
Pinar del Río (mild tob.)	9	688	1,472.3	1.08	819.6	267.3	-29.4	26.2†
Villa Clara	20	1,536	4,053.2	0.84	1,661.2	409.6	622.7	303.7
Sancti Spíritus	23	1,667	4,321.4	0.70	2,016.5	576.3	1,767.2	1,072.6
Granma	10	335	479.0	1.04	260.4	125.9	-34.6	9.4‡

* Figures refer to the CPAs for which returns had been computed. †Figure refers to the three out of the nine CPAs that were profitable. ‡Figure refers to the four out of the ten CPAs that were profitable.

Source: Compiled with data from ANAP returns for 1985

of membership in 1985, as against only 1 percent in Sancti Spíritus and a national average of 3 percent), women and younger generations in particular want to hold onto the wider benefits and not turn back the clock. The crucial problem of retention in agriculture so necessary to the country depends now on the level of attraction to rural areas and that in turn involves a challenge to many traditional areas of life.

With strong policies and support for women at this juncture, it can be argued that cooperatives provide the structure best suited to rural women's needs in the productive and reproductive processes, helping them out of a subordinate and hence underestimated position in both. While there has been a certain dropping off of female membership, women in cooperatives are now coming forward and questioning more. At the 1982 ANAP Congress, it was cooperative farm women delegates who raised the issue of obstacles women face in the cooperatives and called for greater attention on this front. They also highlighted the positive benefits of women's active participation in production and the decision-making process. Their voice at a congress of what has traditionally been a male farmers' organisation was both a testimony to change and a challenge for the future.

Notes

1. See Jean Stubbs, *Tobacco on the Periphery* (London: Amaurea Press, 2023 [1985]).
2. My thoughts on this have been stimulated by the now considerable body of research on Third World, especially Caribbean and Latin American women, the work of Carmen Diana Deere and Magdalena León, in particular, although I have seen little on women in tobacco. My research was facilitated by ANAP, with support from: the Ministry of Agriculture; the Institute of Physical Planning; the state tobacco enterprise, Cubatabaco; national and local archives, libraries and museums; and most of all the tobacco-growing families who opened up their lives and homes to me on my field trips.
3. Brian Pollitt's work in this respect is interesting. See, for example, 'The Transition to Socialist Agriculture in Cuba: Some Salient Features', *IDS Bulletin* (1982).
4. Tables for 1945 include Las Villas province, to which Cabaiguán belonged. Under the new 1975 political administration division of the country, Las Villas was divided into several provinces, one of which was Sancti Spíritus, which include Cabaiguán. Tables for the post-1975 period quote Sancti Spíritus province, but there is clearly no point of comparison. Pinar del Río province was left unchanged.
5. A considerable body of information on the two areas can be found in *Cuba Contemporánea* (Havana: Editorial Panamericano, 1944).
6. The history of struggle can be found in Antero Regalado, *La lucha campesina en Cuba* (Havana: Editora Política, 1979), and Mayo, *Dos décadas de lucha contra el latifundismo* (Havana: Editora Política, 1980).
7. Rogelio Concepción Pérez, *Historia de Cabaiguán*, 3 vols, unpublished (1970) provided much background information, as did his *Pinar del Río* (Havana: Oriente, 1978), and *Sancti Spíritus* (Havana: Oriente, 1978).
8. A good overview of agrarian reform can be found in Acosta, 'La revolución agraria en Cuba y el desarrollo económico', *Economía y Desarrollo* 17 (1973) and Ileana Rojas, Mariana Ravanet & Jorge Hernández, 'Desarrollo y relaciones de clases en la estructura agraria en Cuba', in *Estudios sobre la estructura de clases y el desarrollo rural en Cuba* (Havana: Universidad de La Habana, 1983).
9. Shortage of labour was a constant throughout the 1960s and 1970s, and voluntary temporary brigades would be mobilised for stints in agriculture. In the 1970s, the new schools in the countryside and combined study/work programmes were fostered in conjunction with the expansion of the farm sector. In tobacco, student labour is highly seasonal and used for weeding and harvesting.
10. The tobacco growing was particularly dispersed. The agreement reached between private and state sectors was that the latter would take on more of other crops, such as tubers, which required less specialised attention, and private tobacco growers would concentrate more on what was their specialised crop.
11. This point comes out clearly in a highly informative work by Adelfo Martín Barrios, *LA ANAP, 20 años de trabajo* (Havana: Editora Política, 1982), himself once a Pinar del Río tobacco grower and now a key ANAP figure. ANAP also has many internal studies of its own.
12. Attention was paid to tobacco as a traditionally important industry and crop, both as a potential foreign exchange earner and major domestic product in a nation of tobacco producers and smokers. In a situation of greater demand than supply, tobacco has been heavily rationed at state-subsidised prices and sold on the free market at much higher prices. The health hazard posed by smoking is an anomaly that was only faced fully from the 1980s, with a major nationwide anti-smoking campaign.
13. Tobacco farmers interviewed referred to the disincentives to growing tobacco. They also grew rice, beans, vegetables, etc., which they marketed locally.

14 Policy on this was spelled out in theses and resolutions at the First and Second Party Congresses (1975 & 1980). A good overview of policy and progress is to be found in Fidel Castro's speeches at the close of the Fifth and Sixth ANAP Congresses of 1977 and 1982. Since then, several studies have charted the progress of the cooperative movement. Orlando Gómez, *De la finca individual a la cooperativa agropecuaria* (Havana: Editora Política, 1983) is a journalistic account. Oscar Trinchet Vera, *La cooperativa de la tierra en el agro cubano* (Havana: Editora Política, 1984) is quite comprehensive, although it has no breakdown by crop or on women. A good introductory cross-country analysis including Cuba can be found in Carmen Diana Deere, 'Rural women and state policy: The Latin American agrarian reform experience', *World Development*, 13:9 (1985).

15 Free farmers' markets were legalised in the late 1970s, to sell private farm surplus directly to the consumer. The hope was to boost production and undercut any black-market prices. In turn, parallel state markets were introduced, marketing farm surplus on produce in shorter national supply at a higher price to undercut the free-market prices. especially as produce from the CPAs became more plentiful. Most CPAs took the eminently political decision to sell only to the state market and not the free market, although they were under no obligation to do so. Free markets were finally eliminated at the request of the cooperatives after the May 1986 Second National Meeting of the CPAs. Tobacco was not such a market crop, rather, it was bought almost exclusively by the state, but both private growers and cooperatives did grow other staple produce that could be marketed in this way.

16 The economic management and planning system came in the mid-1970s and was an attempt to introduce greater decentralisation and flexibility within central planning requirements, as well as a programme of material and moral incentives.

17 State farms or enterprises are still as a 'higher form' of production. Generally speaking, the rule of thumb is that in areas where there is a need for development plans with high investment, there is a preference for peasant land to pass into the state sector. Where there is no need for high investment but peasant specialisation. then the best solution is the union of peasants into cooperatives.

18 Given that the private sector is an aging sector, cooperatives found substantial numbers of farmers retiring on pensions. There is a case to be made that, with the age factor, migratory and generational patterns will of their own accord disintegrate the peasant economy. This is yet another reason to boost cooperativisation and technification.

19 Founded in 1961, the FMC mobilised around job and training opportunities for women. The FMC-ANAP brigades were organised for sporadic and temporary work during the years when many men were mobilised militarily or for harvest periods. By the 1970s, their work was more regularised and the women formed remunerated production brigades. By the 1980s, the volunteer brigades were almost in abeyance.

20 Participant observation and open-ended interviews were complemented by the compilation of statistical data from the individual state farm, CPA and CCS.

21 At the time of writing, women were employed year-round, either in sorting or other stages of tobacco production. If for any reason work was not available, they were guaranteed 40 percent of salary. Cubatabaco has also invested in improving conditions in the sorting sheds and has upped piece-rates for women's work.

22 Little has been written on rural Cuban women as such, although there is a wide literature on women in general. Readers might refer more particularly to Isabel Larguía & John Dumoulin, *Hacia una ciencia de la liberación de la mujer* (Havana: Ciencias Sociales, 1984), and 'La mujer en el desarrollo: estrategia y experiencia de la Revolucion cubana', *Casa* 149 (1985). The FMC has detailed Congress documents and reports, working papers and studies of its own, in which reference can be found to the early schools and brigades.

23 Women are in the majority (51.6 percent) in higher agricultural studies for the 20-24 age group.
24 This came out strongly in the media at the time. The press ran features and interviews, and documentaries such as the National Film Institute's 20-minute *Tierra sin cerca* (Idelfonso Ramos, 1977) were made. This was also clear from my own interviewing in tobacco areas.
25 This was a national drive. Experienced former workers in crops such as sugar and tobacco were brought in temporarily for the harvest in an attempt to guarantee work productivity. Piece-rates rather than flat rates were also used as an incentive to increase productivity. The smaller plot applies particularly to a crop like tobacco, where each plot was the responsibility of a foreman.
26 This was the balance of money reimbursed to the farmer on sales against repayment of bank loans, as quoted by the Banco Nacional de Cuba, *Crédito al sector campesino y cooperativo* (Havana, 1984).

5

GENDER CONSTRUCTS OF LABOUR IN PRE-REVOLUTIONARY CUBAN TOBACCO[*]

THE CURRENT interdisciplinary gender critique of the theory and methodology, objectives and findings of research has been particularly intense where women's history is concerned. It has meant looking not only at women's lives, labour, struggles and perceptions but also the gender constructs which played their part in shaping such forces of history as domestic and capital accumulation, the social division of labour and labour's response to it. It has meant rethinking the questions that have to be asked and the methods and source material that can be used. The aim of this paper is to reflect on some of the complexities of this thrown up in recent historical research on tobacco workers in Cuba.[1]

Initially conceived as a labour history project on urban cigar makers over the period 1914-58, the research soon extended in both time and scope. A more comprehensive study of the tobacco sector linked the history of factory to non-factory work, and that of urban industrial labour to the rural and semi-rural proletariat and peasantry, in the wider national and international context of tobacco growing and manufacturing. The study was still largely on socio-economic and political aspects of formal labour history. This meant a bias toward the more structured, better documented, largely male sector of the cigar makers, by far the largest single industrial grouping; but pointers were raised as to other less documented sectors, especially those involving large numbers of women and children, and the particular interaction of gender, race and class.[2]

---
[*] Originally published in *Social and Economic Studies* 37:1 & 2 (March & June 1988), pp.241-69.

The fact that many documents, especially those relating to the twentieth century, had not been kept, had disappeared or been destroyed (especially over the insurrection period), and that many more were unclassified and hence difficult to work with, turned out to have its advantages as well as its disadvantages. Although it made for the laborious task of ploughing through much documentation when never sure of its relevance, there was often an unsuspected wealth of information to be obtained from unlikely sources. The careful cross-checking of statistics which were at first sight poor, very contradictory and therefore treacherous to handle, in conjunction with a confrontation of various sources of information such as mainstream press and trade journals with worker publications, proved to be edifying. Finally, it was, the many open-ended interviews with tobacco workers and their families, building up a wider oral history and individual life stories that proved most useful in filling in gaps and directing research along new paths. In effect, the research came to demand a certain resourcefulness and flexibility, taking cues and leads from the written to the oral sources and vice versa.

The lie was given to many previously held assumptions about the tobacco industry and the tobacco workers in Cuba that had pervaded even the more serious historiography. The very mention of tobacco somehow conjured up a man's world. La Corona, H. Upmann, Partagás and Montecristo were the cigars of the nineteenth and twentieth century elite smokers of Europe and the United States, from kings to statesmen, and cigar makers were those Cuban male aristocrats of labour fashioning their quality product from a particularly strong, fragrant leaf.

Symbolically, it was the myth and legend surrounding the prestigious cigar export industry and the master cigar maker that had gone down in history. Perhaps the most familiar icon of Cuban cigar makers was – and still is – a (male) group being addressed by Cuba's late nineteenth century national independence leader José Martí (not in Cuba but Tampa's Ybor City). The second most familiar must surely be that of the (equally male) cigar reader in the cigar rolling shops. Both stood for solid labour, political idealism and militancy. The single most obvious iconography of women was, by contrast, the passive sales image of seductive embossed ladies on the bands and box labels of luxury cigars. Reality, as always, lay somewhere in between.

What follows is an attempt to explore the gender in-between of labour in the processing of tobacco,[3] structured around certain key thematic areas: the international and national division of labour, technology and skill; and the gender challenge in the interfacing of economic, social and political history.

Juggling Technology and Gender:
International and National Division of Labour

The year 1932 came as a major jolt to the Cuban tobacco industry. It was when the American Tobacco Company (ATC) consolidated one of the most radical twentieth century changes in the prerevolutionary manufacturing history of fine Cuban cigars, with the transfer of the rolling of La Corona and its related brands from Havana, Cuba, to Trenton, New Jersey.

Ostensibly riding the wave of the 1930s depression, claiming the need to cut Havana production costs, ATC was out to test the strength of labour. ATC's George W. Hill wanted and secured Cuban manufacturers' support in delivering an ultimatum to Havana workers: they would have to accept a 12 percent wage cut and a strict limitation on the traditional cigar allowance per worker per day, or face factory closures. Should the unions prove too strong – as they had in the past – Hill's trump card was to do away with Cuban (male) cigar rolling for export and put newly trained Trenton 'girls' into full production.

For five months, not a cigar was made in Havana as the Cuban Cigar Makers' Union was out on strike. Meantime, as the February 1933 issue of *Fortune* magazine put it: "In New York and London, silk-hatted smokers were getting their Coronas as usual – from the stock of 13,000,000 left over from 1931."[4] On 1 June, the cigar city of Havana learned that it had lost most of its major cigar factories. The workers accepted a renegotiated cut too late: all but two large manufacturers moved out of the capital, and American Tobacco was pulling right out of the country. *Fortune* magazine further wrote:

> The American Cigar Co., which had for many years manufactured its *Antonio y Cleopatra* and *Flor de Cuba* cigars with Cuban labour in bonded factories in Tampa, Florida, had already met with labour difficulties there and moved the rolling plant to Trenton, New Jersey, employing women to do the work for which male Cubans had previously been considered essential. Now, in this Trenton plant, New Jersey girls, instructed in the art by Veteran Cigar Man Albert Gold (forty years in the business and manager of the *Henry Clay and Bock* plant) began practising on *La Corona*, using the identical Vuelta Abajo tobacco which had once been familiar to the fingers of Havana's Federación Nacional.
>
> In three months, 200 apprentice girls had made a million cigars, some good, some bad, some indifferent. These practice *Coronas* were packed into boxes and sold anonymously at fifty cents per hundred. Mr. Gold from his sunny desk in Trenton then announced that he was ready to produce *La Corona* for the trade.

It was a new twist to an old story: the way in which capital could and did manipulate labour, in this case along national and gender lines. By moving rolling to the custom-built, tropicalised Trenton plant, ATC cut the price of what were long considered the finest cigars available to American smokers by 50 percent through: 1) importing the cured leaf (on which duties were anything up to 100 percent); 2) consolidating the rolling activities of several companies under one management and one roof planned with the utmost regard for economy; and 3) lowering the cost of production by changing from the Havana-style piece-rate system to time rates in Trenton, and substituting cheaper females who didn't smoke even one cigar a day for males who used to smoke as many as twelve. *Fortune's* calculated difference in production costs was as follows:

Table 14: Difference in production costs, Havana & Trenton

Costs	Havana	Trenton
Wholesale per thousand	$476	$240
Retail price	$600	$333
Labour	$54	$49
Material	$87	$95
Leaf, factory expenses, etc.	68	30
Duty, taxes	$127-90	$35

Source: *Fortune*

Hill hit hard with "Trenton girls can make cigars better and cleaner and more rapidly than Cuban *hombres*." To drive home the point, *Fortune* captions read:

> In Havana, men ... used to roll the 262 shapes and sizes of the famous *La Corona* cigars. They got from $16 to $188 a thousand and smoked from eight to twelve cigars per day – which cost $25,000 a month, or $1,000 per working day. They stopped work whenever they felt like it.
>
> In Trenton, girls ... in trim uniforms, taught *La Corona* practices by Don Emilio Rivas and Master Cigar Man Albert Gold, roll the new *La Corona*. They get good wages, roll the imported leaf, leave no waste, smoke no cigars. Net result: greater productivity, a saving of at least $5 per thousand.
>
> An old Spanish custom ... which has been slightly modified in the fine new rolling plant in Trenton, New Jersey, where 60,000,000 *La Corona* cigars will be made in 1933. In the old days (1931 and earlier) the 1,500 rolled in the *Havana La Corona* plant were entertained as they worked by a reader, selected and paid for by themselves, who regaled them with the latest news, adventure stories, jokes and general comment. The trouble was that the general comment too often ran to industrial radicalism. When it did, the workers were likely to put down their tobacco and stand around on street

corners for a while indulging in the Latin American equivalent of a strike, coming back to work only to ask for (and often get) higher wages. Girls in the Trenton plant will be entertained by piano playing only.

The move came in the wake of some very significant developments in the US cigar manufacturing industry. The 1920s were witness to the introduction of the first really reliable cigar machine and were the threshold to a complete restructuring of the industry, similar to that which had taken place earlier in cigarette manufacturing. Mechanisation brought corporate expansion in the wake of reduced production costs and the beating down of labour, which often included substitute cheaper female workers.

In Cuba, the technical revolution was held back and gender patterns in manufacturing proper were reinforced rather than broken down. The development of the cigarette industry resembled that of its much larger northern counterpart but was also rapidly overtaken by it internationally, and equally rapidly overshadowed by and merged with cigar manufacturing at home. In cigar manufacturing, the technical revolution was almost completely delayed. A combination of economic factors in the form of protectionist tariffs, especially where its major US market was concerned, and political factors in the form of Spanish colonial restrictions, plus the persecution of any opposition to them, produced a particularly marked late-nineteenth century migration of whole factories and workers to the United States, especially against the backdrop of the First (1868-78) and Second (1895-98) Independence Wars. After independence, major political considerations may have been removed but twentieth century world tobacco monopoly production only consolidated further tight protectionist controls.

One effect was that it was much cheaper to produce quality Havana cigars in the United States with the imported Cuban leaf than it was to import them from Havana, which is why, after buying up a lot of industry, this is what American Tobacco did. Other cigar manufacturers, known as Independents, carried on, but on a much depressed scale and under much depressed conditions.

Subject to both seasonal and cyclical fluctuations, total twentieth century cigar output remained fairly constant. This was because there was an increase in the home market for a growing population, not of expensive cigars such as those made for export, but of an inferior cheaper kind, again largely catered to by a host of small, second-rate local concerns and private rollers scattered throughout the island.

On the one hand there was a handful of larger independent family businesses, few of whom were ever able to expand greatly in the face of foreign competition and who, on the strength of this, developed their own reluctance to change. On the other, there was a proliferation of often ephemeral small sweatshop and home production. It was logical then that overwhelming numbers of both, for very good, if historically outmoded reasons, should join with the workers and public opinion at large in resisting any attempt to introduce the cigar machine. The machine became a major national issue on which was seen to rest the survival of an important sector of an ailing economy and population. It was successfully opposed in the 1920s, in the build-up to the Depression, when only one other factory besides the ATC subsidiary could possibly afford to mechanise; and even in the 1950s, after a six-year-long battle against a handful of Havana export manufacturers, a government limitation was still secured on its use for export alone and machines were only introduced in a small number of Havana factories.

The beating down of labour in the tobacco industry was not, however, a result of the technical revolution. Mid-nineteenth century estimated production figures for cigarettes would point to 7,000-10,000 cigarette rollers. The 2,500 in Havana's factories throughout the early twentieth century were probably only meaningful in global terms as hand and outwork labour was completely beaten down across the island. There was a marked decrease in the recorded number of cigar makers in Havana, where the large export factories were concentrated. At the same time, the backwardness of the industry as a whole meant that the overall number of workers did remain relatively high, with a large section scattered throughout the island and a continued high proportion of home and small shop workers to factory workers.

From the statistics, it can be seen that the 15,000 cigar rollers of Havana in the 1860s had steadily dropped to some 5,000 in the 1940s, while out-of-Havana figures increased from some 5,000 to 14,000 in the early twentieth century, continuing to fluctuate around that figure. Almost certainly, many of the more casual home workers never even made it into the statistics.

This particularly puts into question the figures for women's labour in the industry. Characteristically, it is the outwork sector that relies heavily on women's and child labour, and this was by far the major sector. Not surprisingly, oral history work conducted in the 1960s went to corroborate how women interviewees, in their own lifespan had rolled cigars at home and at times entered small local concerns. What the figures reflect is a continued male predominance in the cigar and cigarette *factory* sector.

An example of how spurious the figures can be is an 1862 listing of women cigar and cigarette workers in only 4 out of 32 towns: Bahía Honda – 4, Bejucal – 23, Sancti Spíritus – 226, and Jiguaní – 97, making for a total of 756 women out of an overall total of 13,209 (5.7 percent).[5] The total absence of figures for women in Havana (and low figures for Havana in general) is telling when there were references from 1860 to Pablo González's La Africana, "A shop exclusively for women cigarette rollers under the supervision of a lady of known repute,"[6] and reports of the Susini factory not being able to get the women into the factory but having to send out to "femmes délaissées."[7] In the 1890s, La Corona factory boasted its "graceful clean women / and decent workingmen / who never manhandle[8] / the Vuelta Abajo leaf."[9]

In the growing late nineteenth century division of labour in the factories, women came to be employed mainly as cigarette packers, to place the bands and later cellophane wraps and metal tubes on the cigars, and more significantly in stemming the cigar leaf. Characteristically perhaps, it was the ATC forerunner – the Henry Clay and Bock factory – that was first recorded as employing women stemmers in 1879. The end of the First Independence War and the exodus of workers to Tampa and Key West may well have caused a conjunctural shortage for stemming, a newly expanding sector for both manufacturing and export, as Cuba was fast becoming a leaf, rather than cigar, exporting country.

By the onset of the depression of the 1890s, shortage of labour would no longer have been the issue for tobacco, especially in Havana, from where the British Consul was to write: "Havana, into which one-seventh of the whole population of the island has flocked, is filled with men and women for whom work cannot be found; so great is social pressure that what is regarded as women's work is here usurped by men."[10] And yet, the 1899 post-independence census quotes 1,580 women "tobacco factory operatives," 6.5 percent of the total census work force. Even with a wave of Cuban tobacco workers returning from the United States, stemming was fast coming to be defined as a woman's job in the industry.

Table 15 shows a gender breakdown of serialised census statistics that group together "tobacco factory operatives" for 1899-1919, and "cigar and cigarette workers" for 1943. From them it can be seen how both the numerical and percentage figures of women grew over the period 1899-1919. The figures were particularly marked for Pinar del Río, Havana and Las Villas, where the 1919 percentage of women in the work force was 36.6 percent, 27.8 percent and 19.6 percent respectively, in comparison with a national average of 19.3 percent. Census parameters change for 1943 and 1953, which makes comparison more difficult. The figure included in Table 15, which was at a Second World War low, refers to actual employment, whereas Table 16 gives a much higher occupational figure.

The 1945 tobacco workers' census gives a more accurate idea of the total number of tobacco workers. It unfortunately has no gender breakdown, but from Tables 17 and 18 it can be seen there was a total of 37,701, including 12,286 cigar makers and 20,208 stemmers. Of the stemmers, 9,898 were in Las Villas province alone. The figures need to be qualified in that only 30,470 were in the active labour force – 8,510 cigar makers and 17,272 stemmers. Even so, that figure is significantly higher than the subsequent 1953 population census, which gives no occupational figures but an overall industrial total of 20,302, of whom 16,666 were women.

A closer look at Table 16 shows that a mere 6.2 percent of cigar and cigarette workers were women, in comparison with 94 percent of stemmers, 63.3 percent of ringers and 52.4 percent of sorters. The Havana figure for stemmers was even higher (96.2 percent), as was that of cigar and cigarette workers. The percentage of women cigar and cigarette workers was low for all provinces, although in Pinar del Río the figure was a relatively high 14.8 percent. Interestingly, while only 6.5 percent of ringers and 20.3 percent of sorters were listed for Havana, the figure was much higher for Pinar del Río (95.8 percent and 89.2 percent, respectively) and significantly higher in Las Villas (44.4 percent and 52.9 percent). However, ringers and sorters together accounted for less than 4.6 percent of the total workforce, as against the stemmers' over 30 percent. On 1945 figures, stemmers accounted for over 50 percent, and on 1953 figures could well have neared 75 percent.

Cuba's Carmens

Carmen may have immortalised Seville's women cigar rollers, but clearly Cuba's Carmens were overwhelmingly the stemmers. As Cuba's role in the international division of labour became that of prime exporter of the raw leaf rather than the manufactured product, so twentieth-century monopoly capital found its female undercutting of male labour in Cuba through the stemming of leaf for export, to be rolled, by hand and later by machine, by equally female labour in the United States. Insofar as this was the case, Cuba's women stemmers were in a much disadvantaged position over time vis-à-vis their male Cuban and female US industrial counterparts.

Originally introduced in the factories as part of the cigar manufacturing process, stemming had become particularly important in the rapidly growing leaf-export business, as by taking out the central stem of the leaf, weighable duties and taxes were significantly reduced. Large export stemmeries in Havana, Las Villas and Pinar del Río, many of them belonging to foreign export companies and grouping together hundreds of women at the height of the stemming season, were to make particular use of female and often black female labour, in what was the major expanding tobacco sector where labour was concerned.

Urban and rural stemmeries, along with stemming departments in factories, made for a workforce that straddled the urban and rural proletariat, the latter being highly seasonal and scattered through small tobacco towns. The 1945 tobacco workers' census gives a total of 20,000 stemmers, broken down into only one-fifth in the factories, one-third in Havana and one-half in Las Villas. Seasonal and cyclical fluctuations to which the non-factory sector was highly vulnerable, but which factory stemmers did not escape altogether

GENDER CONSTRUCTS OF LABOUR 89

Table 15: Tobacco factory workers, 1899-1943

Province	1899				1907				1919				1943			
	Total	Male	Fem.	% Fem.	Total	Male	Fem.	% Fem.	Total	Male	Fem.	% Fem.	Total	Male	Fem.	% Fem.
Havana Province	16,647	15,390	1,257	7.6	18,983	15,860	3,234	17.3	11,862	11,528	3,234	27.3	7,612	7,096	516	6.8
Havana City	12,128	11,312	816	6.7	13,540	11,299	2,241	16.6	6,191	4,478	1,716	27.7	–	–	–	–
Matanzas	1,123	1,030	93	8.3	958	951	7	0.7	895	846	49	5.5	600	579	21	3.5
Pinar del Rio	889	820	69	7.8	1,036	1,036	39	3.6	1,588	1,026	582	36.6	1,511	1,389	124	8.2
Camagüey	238	237	1	0.4	290	286	4	1.4	395	377	18	4.6	1,082	1,045	37	3.4
Las Villas	2,598	2,460	138	5.3	2,681	2,533	148	5.5	4,629	3,722	907	19.6	4,504	4,174	330	7.3
Oriente	2,674	2,652	22	0.8	3,516	3,495	21	0.6	3,100	2,985	115	3.7	4,708	4,601	107	2.3
CUBA	24,269	22,589	1,580	6.5	27,503	24,161	3,342	12.2	25,389	20,484	4,905	19.3	10,049	8,814	1,235	12.3

Source: Report on the Census of Cuba, 1899; Censo de la República de Cuba

Table 16: Selected tobacco occupations by gender and race, 1943

Province	General total	MALE					FEMALE			
		Total	% gen. total	White	Black	% Black	Total	% gen. total	White	Black	% Black
Pinar del Río											
Ringers	118	7	5.9	6	1	14.3	111	94.1	84	27	24.3
Sorters	268	29	10.8	25	4	13.8	239	89.2	194	45	18.8
Cigar & cigarette workers	1,513	1,289	85.2	748	541	42.0	224	14.8	170	54	24.1
Stemmers	1,829	135	7.4	87	48	35.5	1,694	92.6	1,128	566	33.4
Havana											
Ringers	62	58	93.5	53	5	8.6	4	6.5	2	2	50.0
Sorters	286	227	79.4	198	29	12.8	59	20.6	55	4	6.8
Cigar & cigarette workers	7,612	7,096	93.2	4,331	2,765	39.0	516	6.8	401	115	22.3
Stemmers	4,773	180	3.8	155	25	13.8	4,593	96.2	3,599	994	21.7
Matanzas											
Ringers	3	3	100.0	3	–	–	–	–	–	–	–
Sorters	5	3	60.0	–	3	100.0	2	40.0	–	2	100.0
Cigar & cigarette workers	600	579	96.5	297	282	48.7	21	35.0	15	6	28.6
Stemmers	10	6	60.0	2	4	66.6	4	40.0	2	2	50.0
Las Villas											
Ringers	18	10	55.6	9	1	10.0	8	44.4	7	1	12.5
Sorters	631	297	47.1	236	61	20.5	334	52.9	258	76	22.8
Cigar & cigarette workers	4,504	4,174	92.7	2,549	1,625	38.9	330	7.3	267	63	19.1
Stemmers	2,613	179	6.9	139	40	22.4	2,432	93.1	1,462	970	39.9

Source: Censo de la República de Cuba

Table 16 (cont.): Selected tobacco occupations by gender and race, 1943

Province	General total	MALE					FEMALE				
		Total	% gen. total	White	Black	% Black	Total	% gen. total	White	Black	% Black
Camagüey											
Ringers	1	–	–	–	–	–	1	100.0	1	–	–
Sorters	7	3	42.9	2	1	33.3	4	57.1	3	1	25.0
Cigar & cigarette workers	1,082	1,045	96.6	648	397	38.9	37	3.4	23	14	37.8
Stemmers	25	11	44.0	10	1	9.1	14	56.0	11	3	21.4
Oriente											
Ringers	8	8	100.0	5	3	37.5	–	–	–	–	–
Sorters	4	3	75.0	1	2	66.6	1	25.0	1	–	–
Cigar & cigarette workers	4,738	4,631	97.7	1,566	3,065	64.7	107	2.3	36	71	66.4
Stemmers	95	41	43.2	28	13	31.7	54	56.8	42	12	22.2
CUBA											
Ringers	210	87	41.4	76	11	12.7	123	58.6	93	30	24.4
Sorters	1,201	563	46.9	462	101	17.9	638	53.1	510	128	20.1
Cigar & cigarette workers	20,049	18,814	93.8	10,139	8,675	46.1	1,235	6.2	912	323	26.2
Stemmers	9,345	552	5.9	421	131	23.7	8,793	94.1	6,246	2,547	29.3

Source: Censo de la República de Cuba

either, contributed to an unstable labour situation and high unemployment and underemployment figures.

Table 17 shows how unemployment was endemic to the industry in general as a result of abnormal Second World War years. Table 18 shows this reflected in the case of the stemmers. Table 19 shows how, while employed, there were very few stemmers – as indeed any other labour group – working every day of the month, even in a top Havana export factory in the year 1949. Again oral interviewing would corroborate this as a general pattern. A consistently important labour issue of this period was the sharing out of work to ensure that everyone was kept on the books, although doing less. At this, the women stemmers would seem to have been very assiduous, and only in extreme cases would they agree to workers being laid off, with a strict respect for seniority.

Tables 20 and 21 show how the numerical and percentage figures for black women grew over the period 1899-1907: an 11.5 percent increase in the total female work force, in comparison with an only 1.7 percent increase of black males in the total male work force, although the overall figures for men were higher. The very high figure for Oriente province was probably a reflection of the predominantly black population of that part of the island, and did not change substantially over the period in question. It can be seen from Table 16 that the overall percentage of black women ringers, sorters, cigar and cigarette workers, and stemmers ranged from 20 percent to 29 percent. It was significantly higher in Pinar del Río and Las Villas provinces – 33.4 percent and 39.9 percent, respectively. The fact that they were women, many of them black, went to compound endemic seasonal and cyclical factors, and helped 'deskill' stemming, causing stemmers to become among the worst paid and least considered groups in the industry.

This had not always been the case. There is little evidence of late-nineteenth century stemmers being particularly low paid. "It's true they don't make as much as the cigar makers, but this doesn't mean they don't get a good day's wage," wrote Estrada y Morales in 1892.[11] In 1905, however, former (male) stemmer Manuel Rodríguez Ramos was writing that stemmers were accorded "the same treatment as the lowest workers in the factory and yet they had to do their work well to get a day's wage that barely sufficed to meet the most pressing of their needs."[12] He claimed that, because of the size of the hands they had to work, stemmers were able to earn little more than the equivalent of 50-60 cents a day, when the average unskilled labourer's wage was $1.00 a day.

Wages in the order of a peso a day increased only by some 10 percent during the 1920s, at a time when cigar makers were getting 2-6 pesos a day and cigarette workers more. Even this 10 percent increase was to be lost at the height of the Depression years, when a major strike in the industry was unsuccessful and both stemmers and cigar makers were put back onto 1917-18 pay scales. It should be noted that this was in the Havana factories, where

Table 17: Unemployment in the Cuban tobacco industry, December 1945

Sector	Total	Active	Inactive	
			No.	%
Cigar makers	12,286	8,510	3,776	30.7
Ringers	734	524	210	28.6
Box decorators	221	156	65	29.4
Cigar sorters	161	110	51	31.7
Leaf selecters	137	102	35	25.6
Stemmers	20.208	17,274	2,934	14.5
General employees	907	788	119	13.1
Warehousemen	300	288	12	4.0
Cigarette workers	2,476	2,476	–	–
Others	271	242	29	10.7
TOTAL	37,701	30,470	7,231	19.2

Source: CNPDTH

Table 18: Unemployment amongst stemmers, December 1945

	Total	Active	Inactive	
			No.	%
Race				
White	12,018	11,284	734	6.1
Brown	2.304	1,955	349	15.2
Black	1,649	1,440	209	12.7
Civil status				
Single	8,512	7,834	678	8.0
Married	6,461	5,914	547	8.5
Divorced	156	146	10	6.4
Widowed	842	785	57	6.8
Age				
16-25	4,948	4,608	340	6.9
26-35	4,975	4,513	462	9.3
36-45	3,893	3,562	331	8.5
46-55	1,330	1,226	104	7.8
56-65	677	628	49	7.3
Over 65	148	142	6	4.1
TOTAL	15,971	14,679	1,292	8.8

Note: Only 79% stemmers included in the census were further censused in this way, disproportionately more of those active.
Source: CNPDTH

Table 19: Underemployment in La Corona cigar factory, 1949

Month	Cigar makers		Leaf selectors		Cigar sorters		Box decorators		Ringers		Stemmers	
	No.	Days worked	No.	Days worked	No.	Days worked	No.	Days worked	No.	Days worked	No.	Days worked
January	206	13	8	13	18	15	14	15	16	14	136	19
February	124	24	8	18	18	20	14	20	14	20	110	24
March	107	30	7	–	18	25	14	24	15	24	114	30
April	207	21	7	–	18	18	14	16	14	17	115	16
May	211	20	7	20	19	17	14	16	15	18	114	13
June	206	25	7	25	17	20	13	20	16	19	115	17
July	204	–	7	–	19	15	14	16	15	15	116	20
August	200	25	7	25	18	18	12	20	15	19	115	25
September	200	21	6	21	19	14	11	17	15	15	113	21
October	204	20	6	20	21	14	12	14	15	16	110	19
November	200	26	6	–	20	16	20	21	15	21	100	–
December	84	31	8	–	19	–	13	–	14	–	122	–

– Left blank because the number of days varied so much per worker that to have calculated mean would have been misleading.

Source: Archivo de Seguridad Social, Ministerio del Trabajo, Havana

Table 20: Census returns on tobacco factory operatives by gender and race, 1899

Province	Total work force	MALE				FEMALE			
		Total	White	Black	% Black	Total	White	Black	% Black
Havana Province	16,647	15,390	10,888	4,502	29.3	1,257	980	268	21.3
Havana City	12,128	11,312	7,737	3,575	31.6	816	643	173	21.2
Matanzas	1,123	1,030	649	381	37.0	93	87	6	6.5
Pinar del Río	589	520	528	292	35.6	69	50	19	27.5
Puerto Príncipe *	238	237	170	67	28.3	1	1	–	–
Santa Clara	2,598	2,460	1,676	784	31.9	138	116	22	15.9
Santiago de Cuba *	2,674	2,652	612	2,040	76.9	22	7	15	68.2
CUBA	24,269	22,589	14,523	8,066	35.7	1,580	1,850	330	20.9

* Puerto Príncipe and Santiago de Cuba became Camagüey and Oriente provinces.

Source: *Censo de Cuba*, 1899

pay scales were both on paper and in practice considerably higher than in provincial tobacco towns.

The 1930s were perhaps an all-time low for tobacco, and stemmers paid the price as much if not more than other groups of the industry's workers, as there was an oversaturation of Cuban leaf on the market. From 1934 on, general social and labour legislation was introduced, including the eight-hour day, labour contracts, equal pay, 15 days' paid vacation, maternity benefits as well as in the case of stemming, for example, some very elaborate official tariffs for Havana and the provinces, according to the type of tobacco worked. Labour's battle was that any of this be enforced. In straight wage terms, the 1943 census (which was carried out in July before the seasonal stemming was over) quoted 60 percent of all stemmers as earning less than 30 pesos a month (in comparison with only 21 percent of cigar and cigarette workers) and a further 38 percent from 30 to 59 pesos. Much depended on the number of days worked. In the Las Villas stemmeries of the General Cigar Company, the average monthly wage quoted during the late 1940s and early 1950s fluctuated from 3 to 5 pesos in February to 20-30 pesos in March and April when the tobacco stemming was in full swing. A similar situation existed in the large factories where the number of days worked and, correspondingly, the wages received, could vary tremendously, from as little as 3 to 26 days and from a few to 17 pesos for the month, as seen in Table 19.

La Corona might have had its smiling women stemmers posing in full uniform[13] – the nearest sensual image to a Carmen rolling cigars on thighs was one stemming tobacco in such a way. But for the vast majority what more poignant reflection of their lot than the poem written in the 1930s:

> Her beauty untrammelled, come what may,
> In her home-made dress to work did fly
> At six in the morning, nimble, fey,
> The stemming shop workers in times gone by.
> The rose of her beauty – delicate, shy –
> The frenzied work robs of its blush away
> Just as the old wings of the butterfly
> Lose their dust in the light of day.
> In front of the barrel!, for ten hours she
> Toiled in the dirt and humidity
> That on her meagre strength did pall.
> She did this back-breaking work – for shame! –
> For a pittance . . . Yet there are those who claim
> That Cuban women don't work at all![14]

Labour's Gender Challenge

Skill, as an all-encompassing concept of what is recognised and treated as such, is relative; it is not only technically but socially defined. What in Cuba went into defining master cigar rolling as skilled and stemming as unskilled falls as much into the latter as into the former category.

It was only in the mid- to late-nineteenth century, at the height of Cuba's fine cigar manufacturing history, that Cuba's master cigar makers established themselves as an aristocracy of labour and their trade as an exclusive skill. They did so on the strength of an increasing division of labour within the large factories and the distinctions of their handcraft, with the aid of highly restrictionist early guilds for exclusively white male workers that gained considerable control over entry into the cream of the trade.

The first major challenge to the exclusiveness and control of the trade came in the 1880s, from cigar makers in the less prestigious and well-paid factories working on inferior-type cigars who were not unionised, at a time when a large concentration of production and workers coincided with the abolition of slavery and a potential influx of newly freed labour. It was compounded by the fact that, in the turbulent inter-independence war years, often newly immigrant Spaniards had come to dominate the better jobs.

The challenge came in the form of an explosion of labour militancy and strikes with marked racial and nationalist overtones to straight class interests. These could scarcely be channelled into any alternate form of labour organisation before the onset of the Second War of Independence and its equally turbulent aftermath of US military occupation of the island, when American investment secured the greater part of the Havana industry.

A second major challenge came in the 1920s, when a semblance of national craft unions had been consolidated, again amidst hard economic times, as the 1930s Depression loomed near and the question of mechanisation hovered over the industry, and as the right-wing Machado dictatorship stepped up its anti-labour repression. Again militancy and strikes went far beyond the confines of existing unions and this time involved women stemmers in the industry whose work had never been recognised as a skill and for whom unionisation was still in its infancy.

The cyclical, seasonal and gender base to stemming undoubtedly ran counter to any continuous solid form of labour organisation. There is reference to a short-lived Gremio de Despalilladores (the original masculine word for stemmers) in 1878 and no other recorded attempt until the 1917 Gremio de Despalilladoras (the word by then feminine in ending). Nonetheless, the cigar makers' tradition of militancy and emphasis on worker education, and that time-honoured institution of the reader, inevitably carried over. Like their male counterparts, women in the industry showed surprisingly high turn-of-

Table 21: Census returns on tobacco factory operatives by gender and race, 1907

Province	Total work force	MALE				FEMALE			
		Total	White	Black	% Black	Total	White	Black	% Black
Havana Province	18,247	15,124	10,062	5,062	33.5	3,123	2,102	1,021	32.7
Havana City	13,540	11,299	6,348	3,951	35.0	2,241	1,495	746	33.3
Matanzas	958	951	554	397	41.7	7	5	2	28.6
Pinar del Río	1,075	1,036	687	349	33.7	39	27	12	30.8
Camagüey	290	286	202	84	29.4	4	4	–	–
Santa Clara	2,681	2,533	1,713	820	32.4	148	114	34	23.0
Oriente	3,516	3,495	805	2,690	77.0	21	7	14	66.6
CUBA	27,503	23,425	14,759	9,042	37.4	3,342	2,269	1,083	32.4

Source: Censo de la República de Cuba, 1907

the-century literacy rates, as can be seen from Table 22. The fact is that by the 1940s, cigar makers and stemmers were working together to guarantee minimum conditions in the industry and create a strong labour challenge. Moreover, through their sheer strength of numbers (female stemmers far outstripped their male cigar making counterparts) and their militancy, the women would seem to have held their own in terms of their craft union organisation and leadership.

There are various references to the 1917-20 stemmers' strikes over tariffs, and their continued strikes of the late 1920s and 1930s were cause for the cigar workers' press to take up the stemmers' struggle, as did the wider women's movement of those years for social emancipation, and vice versa. In the late 1930s, the first truly national general trade union confederation had its forerunner not only in the Federación Nacional de Tabaqueros but also in the Federación Nacional de Despalilladoras. Tables 23 and 24 show stemmers to have had by the 1940s one of the highest unionisation rates for the industry. This applied also to industry in general: textile workers, for example showed only 27 percent unionisation. The figures were high for the provinces as well as for the capital, Havana. As Cuba's majority female labour grouping (domestics and textile workers were the only other comparable sectors), women stemmers came to be a force to be reckoned with on issues vital to the very fabric of industry, economy and society.

Mechanisation of the industry was one such issue. The women stemmers were solidly behind the men cigar makers in opposing the machine in both the 1920s and the 1940s, in the knowledge that the cigar machine would be the floodgate for subsequent stemming machines also. The joint worker state-

Table 22: Gender literacy in the tobacco industry, 1899-1907

Province	% males able to read & write		% females able to read & write	
	1899	1907	1899	1907
Havana Province	79.3	89.6	51.9	78.1
Havana City	80.9	91.7	60.5	79.3
Matanzas	66.4	71.5	62.4	85.7
Pinar del Río	64.5	81.1	59.4	64.1
Puerto Príncipe	20.0	85.3	100.0	100.0
Santa Clara	70.0	80.7	50.0	75.7
Santiago de Cuba	69.3	84.8	72.7	68.2
CUBA	75.9	87.1	53.0	77.8

* Very few women were reported but all could read and write.

Source: Census of Cuba, 1899; Censo de la República de Cuba, 1907

Table 23: Unionisation in the Cuban tobacco industry, 1944

Sector	No. workers	No. unions	Unionised workers		Workers paying dues	
			No.	% total	No.	% total
Cigar makers	10,159	69	10,159	100.0	5,187	51.1
Cigarette workers	2,650	4	1,523	57.5	1,306	85.8
Growers	87,828	8	5,180	5.9	841	16.2
Leaf sorters	50,675	23	33,234	65.6	14,847	44.7
Stemmers	16,453	15	15,609	94.5	9,400	60.2

Source: Felipe Zapata, 1948-51

Table 24: Unionisation among stemmers according to province, 1944

Province	No. workers	No. unions	Unionised workers		Workers paying dues	
			No.	% total	No.	% total
Pinar del Río	4,194	2	4,194	100.0	1,338	32.1
Havana	4,314	5	4,314	100.0	3,510	81.4
Matanzas	-	-	-	-	-	-
Las Villas	7,101	8	7,101	100.0	4,552	64.1
Camagüey	573	-	-	-	-	-
Oriente	271	-	-	-	-	-
CUBA	16,453	15	15,609	94.5	9,400	60.2

Source: Felipe Zapata, 1948-51

ments on the question contained sophisticated analyses of the significance of foreign-controlled machinery in a dependent economy and of how doubly disadvantageous it could be to labour.

From the turn of the century, militant (largely male) unionised labour in the US industry had hardly sat back and accepted the machines and redundancy. There were many head-on confrontations of capital and labour before a generalised corporate response to move to a different area and employ new, often female labour. These confrontations might be engineered along 'side' issues. In the 'Cuban' Florida factories (which had, apparently, employed immigrant Cuban women alongside Cuban men in cigar rolling almost from the start),[15] one of the struggles of the late 1920s had been precisely over the reader. Manufacturers argued they had a right to screen what was to be read, clearly alluding to the militant choice of reading material. It was part of a build-up to that final move north of fine 'Cuban' cigars which left West Tampa, Ybor City and Key West as crumbling, yet still proud relics of a cigar past.

In Cuba, aside from the intrinsic threat of the machine to a mainstay of the economy and thousands of tobacco workers and their families, the two attempts at mechanisation coincided with two significant national anti-labour periods in twentieth century Cuban history: the Machado period referred to earlier and the Grau government's cold war union bashing of the late 1940s. This made the issue volatile and ensured broad solidarity among tobacco and non-tobacco sectors alike for the anti-machine movement.

There were similar 'side' confrontations around that central issue of mechanisation, over wage cuts, cigar allowances, etc. (although, after an initial prohibition in the 1860s, the institution of the reader would seem to have been left alone). The 1932 ATC/Independents ultimatum to labour, with which this paper started, had come in the aftermath of a mechanisation attempt that had failed precisely because of the broad internal anti-machine movement. According to *Fortune,* ATC's G. W. Hill was still bent on persuading the world "that even that great luxury, the Havana handmade cigar, is better and more sanitary when made by machine," on which day, "the picturesque Cuban will have lost finally and forever."[16]

That ultimatum, coming as it did at the height of the Depression, found workers in a vulnerable situation that manufacturers and government were able to maximise. Their ultimate success in implementing the cuts was due to a neat transfer of industry rather than any lack of worker mobilisation. After a five-month strike, stemmers' president Amparo Lara could still shout to fellow workers, "Let the factories close. I prefer that to working for 10 hours at a starvation rate of 50 cents."[17] Inocencia Valdés, another long-time stemmers' leader, later to become general secretary of the stemmers' federation, declared that unless the need for cuts was proved, the women "would be the last back."[18]

Such militancy was to be evidenced over and over again but came to a head in La Corona's Siboney stemmery in 1948. Government wanted an end to communist-led unions, a handful of Havana manufacturers wanted the machine, and both coincided in the usefulness of ousting the old trade union leadership in favour of a government-supported counter-union structure. This move coincided with the Siboney stemmery announcing it would close down for a few months because of lack of work. With little support, not even the new leaders could accept closure and asked that it at least be postponed. After many discussions, agreement was reached whereby the stemmeries would work four weeks in March, two in April and two in May, at the rate of four days a week. Company lawyer Felipe Silva wrote: "That was neither what the Company needed, nor what the labourers demanded, but only a practical compromise . . . the untoward attitude was more in keeping with the labour element of 20 years ago."[19] Stemmery manager Isaac Muniains (dubbed by the workers Von Muniains) was reported in the press as angrily claiming "the need for a bloody purge, a need to put a stop to these nigger women, to have a death as in La Corona cigar factory."[20]

Telegrams of solidarity flooded in from all over the country for the Siboney stemmers. Their case symbolised every possible facet of labour oppression: a foreign company, controlling market and labour conditions in keeping with a twentieth century international division of labour it had helped establish, it could exploit an international and national political climate to its own end, and show itself highly insensitive to labour in national, class, race and gender terms.

The ultimate response of labour in the Cuban situation was to be channelled into general insurrection, to change socio-economic and political structures. Interestingly, gender was one early issue in the post-revolutionary industry: stemming might not have been questioned as a woman's job but in the overall restructuring of production women began to be trained for that previously coveted master cigar making craft.

The ultimate historical irony is that Trenton, New Jersey, like its earlier Florida counterparts, would have stood derelict today, had not urban developers moved in to convert the beautiful old stucco structure into a luxury apartment building.[21] Not even the piano played eternal. By way of contrast, in Cuba, after major upheavals in the 1960s, and early 1970s there has been a cigar revival for newly diversified markets;[22] many of the cigars are now made by women on equal terms to men, and with those labour benefits so often denied in the past. To parody *Fortune's* 1930s judgement: the picturesque Cubans had *not* lost forever.

Notes

1 See Jean Stubbs, *Tobacco on the Periphery* (London: Amaurea Press, 2023 [1985]).
2 Some of these pointers are further raised in Jean Stubbs, 'Labour and Economy in Cuban Tobacco, 1860-1958', *Historical Reflections* (1985), pp.449-67 – Chapter 2 in the present volume.
3 No attempt has been made here to include women in agriculture. This is referred to in Stubbs, 'Labour and Economy' (1985), and *Tobacco on the Periphery* (2023 [1985]; and dealt with more extensively in 'Gender Issues in Contemporary Cuban Tobacco Farming', *World Development* 5:1 (1987), pp.41-65 – Chapter 4 in the present volume.
4 This and following quotes are taken from 'La Corona', *Fortune* 7:3 (February 1933) and 'Notes on Cuban Revolution', *Fortune*, 1:2 (June 1930).
5 *Noticias estadísticas de la Isla de Cuba en 1862* (Havana: Imprenta del Gobierno, 1864).
6 Mentioned in José Rivero Muñiz, *Tabaco: su historia en Cuba*, 2 vols. (Havana: Instituto de Historia, 1965).
7 Referred to as part of the charitable patronage of Susini. See *Projet définitif d'une fabrique de cigarettes (genre Havanais). Etablie à St Sebastien (frontière d'espagne) avec la marque* LA HONRADEZ *(L'Honorabilité) de la Havane et funcionant avec les* MACHINES SUSINI *brevetées* (Paris: Imprimerie A.-E. Rochette,).
8 The verb *maltratar* in Spanish means *'to ill-treat'* or *'mis-/manhandle'!*
9 *Album de La Corona: Obsequio a sus favorecedores (*Havana: Tipográfico O'Reilly, 1888).
10 *British Parliamentary Papers, Blue Books*, Cuban Consular Commercial Reports, London-Havana Trade and Shipping, 1890, London, p.13.

11 Benjamin Estrada y Morales, *Obreros distinguidos (tabaqueros)* (Havana: La Prensa, 1892).
12 Manuel Rodríguez Ramos, *Siembra, fabricación e historia* (Havana: Librería e Imprenta, 1905).
13 A company photo of the time was found in Archivo Nactional de Cuba (ANC), Comisión Nacional de Propaganda en Defensa del Tabaco Habano (CNPDTH).
14 Taken from *Tabaco* (November 1936), p.29.
15 On the Florida 'Cuban' tobacco industry, see Stubbs, 'Labour & Economy' (1985); *Tampa Bay History (A Centennial History of Ybor City)* (Tampa: University of South Florida, 1985); Glenn L. Westfall, *Key West: Cigar City USA* (Key West: Historic Key West Preservation Board, 1984); and Gerald E. Poyo, 'Cuban émigré communities in the United States and the independence of their homeland, 1852-1895', PhD thesis, University of Florida, 1983. Current research by Stubbs on the Cuban tobacco migration to Jamaica is showing (not published until later, in 1995 – Chapter 7 in the present volume) similar patterns and, interestingly, that women were also employed in what in Cuba was a traditionally male factory job.
16 'La Corona' (1933).
17 There was a collection of press clippings on the 1932 strike in ANC, CNPDTH, unclassified files.
18 Inocencia Valdés was a particularly central figure to Cuban tobacco labour history. She went to Key West in 1871 with her parents at the age of four and became the first stemmer at the Villamil factory there, as well as president of the Revolutionary Aid Club and secretary of the Mariana Grajales Society. She went back to Cuba in 1917 and subsequently became active in the stemmers' guild. She also belonged to the Radical Union of Women and the Popular Socialist Party in the 1940s. It would be interesting to pursue the development of her ideas first in the US Cuban tobacco émigré community and later back in Cuba.
19 Felipe Silva's report was included in ANC, CNPDTH, unclassified files.
20 ANC, CNPDTH, unclassified files.
21 Sally Lane, 'Trenton's Old Caribbean Air', *Sunday Times Magazine* (7 October 1984), p.3.
22 The conversion of Trenton was due, among other reasons, to the demise of tobacco in the developed world on health grounds. Indeed, one big question for the future of world (and Cuban) tobacco is that of health. In the 1980s, Cuba embarked on an anti-smoking campaign and it was publicly said that ultimately this must affect the tobacco industry. In such a strong tobacco country as Cuba, this will no doubt take time and is certainly outside the scope of this paper. Cigars and cigar tobacco may be less damaging to health than the chemically processed mild cigarette tobaccos. Even so, as a non-smoker of the female sex, among whom smoking and related diseases are on the up, I am all for it and for labour to be channelled into some more positive area!

6

WOMEN AND CUBAN SMALLHOLDER AGRICULTURE IN TRANSITION*

THE 1990S opened with the Cuban government declaring a 'special period' in which food self-sufficiency was to be crucial. Export crop (especially sugar) lands were to be turned over to domestic production and there was to be a return to the plough. For a country that had, for three decades, followed an increasingly technically oriented, agriculturally based, export-led development model, this was a dramatic shift. It came as a two-pronged response to both a stepping-up of the threat from the United States and to the speed of events in Eastern Europe, which had resulted in the breakdown of established trading patterns.[1] If carried through, the 'special period' could have some highly significant ramifications for agricultural policy and agrarian relations, not least in smallholder agriculture.

Currently facing one of its toughest periods since the 1959 Revolution and having embarked on a 'rectification' process heading in a diametrically opposite direction from that of Eastern bloc market reforms,[2] Cuba is under more pressure than ever before to reevaluate smallholder production and the centrality of women to that production. External events have only compounded significant internal factors that had already occasioned considerable rethinking along these lines.

This chapter takes a new look at some of these factors.[3] It draws extensively on an earlier study of cooperatives to explore linkages between gender, household and agrarian policy. In the context of a national women's movement

---

* Originally published in Janet Momsen (ed.), *Women and Change in the Caribbean*, London/Indianapolis/Kingston: James Currey/Indiana Press/Ian Randle, 1993, pp.219-31.

centred on the Federation of Cuban Women (FMC), which has taken up women and development issues[4] and is now focusing more closely on gender and patriarchy within the socialist development experience,[5] it suggests the existence of a gender-sensitised, pre-collective voice among Cuba's women farmers.[6]

Rethinking Smallholder Agriculture

Cuba was an anomaly among the post-Second World War wave of Third World 'peripheral' countries embarked on socialist transformation, in that collective forms of agriculture quickly came to predominate over private. In addition, there continued to be an explicit preference for large state farms, even after the recognition in the mid-1970s that agricultural production cooperatives were a transitional form.[7]

The reason for this lay primarily in Cuba's pre-revolutionary agro-exporting economy with foreign and local capital investment. The 1959 and 1963 land reforms placed 70 percent of farm land in state hands.[8] Formerly private US and Cuban-owned sugar estates were to become the technologically advanced state farms of socialist agriculture.[9] US reprisals in the form of a trade embargo were met with a 1963 Soviet-Cuban trade agreement whereby the USSR would replace the United States as Cuba's major sugar market. This was seen by many as the 'new dependency'.[10]

Throughout the 1960s, state enterprises were similarly promoted in cattle, dairy, poultry, citrus, banana, plantain and other areas of production. In the 1970s, these were fostered in conjunction with 'technification', integral development plans and schools in the countryside that could provide labour. The external link came from relatively favourable trading with the West (the United States excluded) and increasing integration into the Eastern European trading bloc.

Given the predominance of large-scale agriculture, a commonly held myth about Cuban smallholder agriculture is that it was insignificant, both before and after the Revolution. The disruption of traditional farming was argued to have generated a surplus of rural labour and to have kept subsistence farming to a minimum. However, agricultural modernisation also strengthened archaic forms of production, as capital accumulation was sought through credit, buying and land-leasing operations. Large-scale modern farming units coexisted with small-scale tenant and subtenant farms and sharecropped holdings.

The smallholder sector was actually strengthened under the 1959 agrarian reform through land entitlement.[11] The sector has declined since, both in terms of the number of smallholders, and as a proportion of total agricultural land. In the late 1960s, when there were 400,000 state farm workers, there were 250,000 farmers in the National Association of Small Farmers (ANAP) on some 30 percent of the agricultural land. By the mid-1980s, comparable figures were 600,000 state farm workers but only 180,000 ANAP farmers on 15 percent of the land. However, among the crops produced by this sector were important export items, especially tobacco which continues to be 75 percent nonstate produced, and a significant proportion of food crops for domestic consumption including 32 percent of the bean crop, 66 percent of vegetables, 54 percent of coffee, 53 percent of fruit and 34 percent of tubers. This in itself proved reason enough for greater attention to be paid to smallholder production.

Since 1970, there have been four turning points in attitudes to smallholders. The first came after the 1971 ANAP Congress, which resulted in a revitalisation of the small farming sector. It occurred in the wake of the disastrous effects of the all-out drive by the state for the ten million ton sugar harvest, which had led to the halving of output of other export crops such as tobacco and a critical shortfall in production for domestic consumption.[12] The second was in 1977, when the ANAP Congress endorsed an agrarian policy favouring a voluntary, autonomous cooperative movement within the small farm sector. The aim was to encourage smallholders already grouped together in credit and service cooperatives (CCSs) or peasant associations (ACs) to pool their land and other means of production to form agricultural production cooperatives (CPAs). It was hoped that these would boost agricultural output and generate resources for cooperative village services and amenities, thereby attracting people, especially the young, to stay on the land.[13]

The third occurred in 1985, after the Second National Meeting of Cooperative Farmers, with the closing down of the famers' market and the tightening up of the smallholder, cooperative and state agricultural sectors. These measures were a response to tense agrarian relations because of the enrichment of the middle-sized farmers from the market and a fall in domestic production to meet export commitments, especially sugar.[14]

The fourth turning point came in 1990, with the call for intensified food production, involving switching some sugar lands back into domestic food crop production in the state, cooperative and smallholder sectors. This development also involves increased irrigation and streamlining of the food distribution network.[15]

Women in Smallholder Agriculture

Closely tied in with the view that Cuban smallholder agriculture has been insignificant is the notion that there was a low involvement of women in the pre-revolutionary period. This was supported by the disaggregated figure for women in the 1959 agricultural census, which indicated that they comprised only 1.5 percent of the economically active agricultural population. The figure in the 1953 census was similar at 2 percent. There was little change in the post-revolutionary period. By the 1930s women made up less than 10 percent of the economically active agricultural population.

The figures reflect statistical information gathering and notions of what is defined as economically active rather than the realities of women's agricultural labour.[16] In the Cuban case there was a school of thought that saw pre-1939 capitalist development as having created a large class of landless labourers.[17] Another view pointed to the prevalence of small tenant and subtenant farms and sharecropped holdings,[18] which supported a large semi-peasantry/semi-proletariat that paid rent in kind (a quarter to half the crop) and was highly dependent on family labour and forced at different times of year to employ or sell labour. Neither approach took into account the fact that visible exploitation of male labour in male-headed households was accompanied by intensified child and female participation in seasonal harvesting and in the subsistence production and family reproduction crucial to survival.

After the Revolution, child labour virtually ceased and there was a certain withdrawal of women's labour.[19] In the state farm sector, increasing 'technification' and mechanisation demanded new skills that for social reasons were not always easy for women to acquire. An initial separation of agricultural work from the domestic unit posed the classical break between work and home. Improved rural living standards, as a result of overall development policy and changing family structures,[20] often meant less economic pressure on women to supplement family income and when women did choose to work, openings in such expanding non-agricultural spheres as health and education often proved far more attractive. As a result, in agriculture proper, women were to be found mostly in the unremunerated casual and seasonal workforce, the often unremunerated volunteer brigades organised by ANAP and the Federation of Cuban Women (FMC) and as an integral part of unremunerated small farm family labour.[21]

Some of these points began to be highlighted when women in smallholder agriculture proved to be strong supporters of Cuba's agricultural cooperative movement of the late 1970s. Whereas men expressed doubts about giving up their private plot of land and having to adapt to working with others, women liked working in the fields collectively as opposed to individually, economic independence from fathers and husbands through paid labour, and the new cooperative amenities.

Under the 1959 land entitlement programme, land security had been given to male heads of households for the most part, reflecting an agrarian pattern more characteristic of contemporary Hispanic America than that of the Caribbean. Some female heads of household had been granted land titles but they were the exception rather than the rule. Even when a woman secured a land title, a man in the family would, in most cases, take on farm production responsibilities.

For the first time in Cuban agrarian history, with the cooperatives (CPAs) women were encouraged to become farmers in their own right, on an equal basis with men. The result of a concerted mobilisation effort was that in 1979 over a third of the cooperative farmers were women.[22] This sudden 'visibility' of women in the CPAs had fast outstripped the state agricultural sector, where in 1981 women accounted for only 14 percent of that sector's work force and 6 percent of the executive posts.

In 1983, a peak year for the cooperative movement in many respects, the indicators for women went into reverse. They made up only 23 percent of total cooperative farmers, although in absolute terms they had more than quadrupled in number. In 1985, when CPA figures in general were worsening, women represented 25 percent of cooperative members and 12 percent of cooperative executive committees. A concerted effort to consolidate the cooperative farm movement as of 1986 has so far failed to stem the downward trend, including that of women. In 1987 the figure stood at 22 percent when 81 percent of women were considered fit for work. That same year, women accounted for only 13 percent of executive committee members, and there were only six women presidents as opposed to twelve in 1983. When the 1987 work figures are broken down further, women accounted for less than 12 percent of the total work time. Partly because women on the whole worked shorter hours but also because they often did different kinds of work, average daily pay for women was $4.87, whilst for men it was $5.75.[23] In effect, a withdrawal of women from field labour was taking place, similar to that which had occurred in the 1960s on the state farms. We shall now turn to consideration of some of the factors involved in one particular case study.

Cooperative Smallholder Tobacco

A study of women in tobacco cooperatives[24] was conducted in 1984 to collect some local disaggregated data on what was at the time seen as a national success story. The indicators for both women and cooperative farming were, as it transpired, just beginning to change and the gender approach to the study illuminated some of the problem areas.

Tobacco was chosen on the strength of prior historical knowledge of the sector[25] and because it continued to be a crop characterised by smallholders, women's labour and a burgeoning cooperative movement. The two areas of study – San Luis (Vuelta Abajo) in western Pinar del Río province and Cabaiguán (Vuelta Arriba) in central Sancti Spíritus, formerly part of Las Villas province – were both famed for their tobacco but differed as to the kind of tobacco grown, land tenancy and several other variables, which could then be seen in relation to gender patterns. A 1940s to 1980s time span was taken to see points of continuity and rupture over pre- and post-revolutionary periods within the life experience of farm people.

On 1945 agricultural census figures, San Luis farms were smaller, more intensely sharecropped and more lucrative than those of Cabaiguán. High yields and the superior quality of its export cigar wrapper tobacco gave San Luis farms double the value and income of those in Cabaiguán, where, in terms of income, cattle and sugar were more important. The largest proportion of unpaid labour was in San Luis, where there was much greater crop specialisation and an influential agrarian bourgeoisie in tobacco. Fertile company land was worked on a waged labour, tenanted and sharecropped basis, through a patriarchal system of local benefits, calling on family labour for services and operating local stores on credits and chits. Owners and managers bore little of the risk of what was a highly delicate and seasonal crop and, since little else was grown, tobacco families were particularly susceptible to market changes, using cheap migrant labour from surrounding areas at peak harvest time. In Cabaiguán many landowners were absentee or managed far removed parts of their cattle estates and let or sharecropped out the tobacco land. There was a greater chance of other agricultural and non-agricultural work but the area as a whole was less prosperous.

The revolutionary land reforms wrought significantly different changes in the two regions. In each they provided security for smallholders. In San Luis, however, an effort was made to keep a substantial part of former company land under state control and tenants and smallholders were encouraged to become part of new state farms that proved to be successful in growing quality tobacco but less so at being cost-effective ventures. In Cabaiguán, the tobacco that fell into state hands from the large estates, often by default, was much more dispersed. Cabaiguán growers became smallholders and state farms were left to grow tobacco with less experienced labour. Although various state farms grew tobacco over the years, it was never very successful and in 1983 was turned over entirely to the smallholder sector.

As prime smallholder beneficiaries of land redistribution, tobacco growers were pioneers in grouping together farmers for the collective use of curing sheds, irrigation and machinery, credit and supplies, such that tobacco ACs and CCSs numbered over 1,000 by 1971. If they suffered from the emphasis on sugar in the late 1960s, they benefited from the 'tobacco recuperation' period of 1971-75, with special emphasis on crop costing and pricing and tobacco agrotechnology. Strong support for the cooperative movement of the late 1970s came from the tobacco sector, but tobacco cooperatives were also among the first to run into difficulties.

Major CPA stumbling blocks detected in the 1984 study concerned economies of scale, costing and profits. In line with the cooperative movement in general, mergers caused the number of tobacco CPAs to start declining in 1983. Membership dropped back that same year after new social security laws provided retirement pensions for cooperative farmers, a good many of whom were already of an eligible age. This compounded an already observable pattern of increasing CPA land size, such that by 1985 land area had more than quadrupled in contrast to only a doubling of the number of farmers. The resulting structural strains and financial losses in labour-intensive tobacco were such that, by 1985, almost a third of tobacco CPAs, a good many of them in San Luis where farms were the most tobacco-intensive, recorded net losses.

Tobacco CPAs, like state farms, reported that their principle outlays were labour costs, fertilisers, pesticides and (if growing shade tobacco) cheese-cloth, in that order. The labour costs included bringing in temporary labour from other areas and other sectors, paying the often considerably higher salaries that labour would earn otherwise, and also providing transport, accommodation and food. The shortage of agricultural labour was rooted in the rapid development of other sectors of the economy which competed too favourably for an increasingly educated work force.

It was also, however, related to the transition to collective farming systems (whether state or cooperative) from smallholder farming with its high family labour component.

Gender & Household in Tobacco

Prior to 1959, according to the life stories of San Luis and Cabaiguán farm families, it is clear that the gender division of labour was such that men were broadly responsible for agricultural production but rarely undertook domestic chores, whether washing clothes, cooking, cleaning, caring for the children, fetching and carrying water, picking tubers, grinding corn or feeding the chickens and pigs. The pattern was for boys and girls to be working by the age of seven: the boys in the fields with their fathers and the girls around the farmhouse with their mothers. At the height of the harvest, when extra labour was essential, girls' and women's work also involved cooking for the field hands. The poorer the tobacco family, the greater the need to fall back on family labour and in this situation women and girls would also be out in the fields planting, weeding, pruning and harvesting the tobacco.

The type of tobacco determined to a large extent the kind and amount of work the women did. The cigar wrapper tobacco of San Luis was traditionally harvested by leaf in baskets and the leaves were then threaded together to be strung on poles to dry. This was seen almost exclusively as women's work, done in the shade, with needle and thread. The dark filler tobacco of Cabaiguán was tougher and stickier because of the black resin it contained. It was traditionally harvested by knife in stalks of four leaves at a time, hung over the outstretched arm and then transferred to poles. Heavy work such as this, and field labour in general, were traditionally considered unsuitable for women. The Cabaiguán tobacco did not need to be threaded, as it was hung straight onto poles in the barns.

There were also variations in the seasonal sorting of tobacco in the initial months after harvesting, during which both municipalities provided temporary employment for thousands of women. The better-quality wrapper tobacco of San Luis demanded greater classification into grades and therefore more skilled and better paid personnel; on average 100-300 people were employed in each sorting shed in peak periods. The more select the farm, the better the pay and conditions in this, one of the few forms of paid labour available to rural women. But there were many sorting sheds where the economic necessity of tobacco families was such that women and girls from the age of ten would accept pittance rates for long hours of work. In Cabaiguán, conditions and pay in the sorting sheds were on the whole worse and, given the lower intensity of tobacco growing and the concentration in towns of large sorting sheds employing up to 1,000 workers, considerable distances had to be travelled to reach the work.

With the agrarian reform and rural development, the land peasant families worked was made their own, the family wage was effectively raised, children were sent to school and, as tobacco production fell in the 1960s, less labour was needed in the fields and sheds. However, the 'tobacco recuperation' of the 1970s involved women in FMC-ANAP brigades doing regular salaried work in harvesting and sorting. A more stable labour market was created, organised at first through Cubatabaco, the umbrella state tobacco-handling enterprise, and later by the production cooperatives.

Tobacco areas were among those to show higher percentages of women cooperative farmers but again San Luis and Cabaiguán differed quite markedly. In San Luis women comprised 24 percent of the membership in CPAs and 1.6 percent in the CCSs; in Cabaiguán, the figures were 38 percent and 25 percent respectively. Membership criteria could differ enormously from one CPA to another. At one of the older cooperatives in Cabaiguán, it was found that both men and women were automatically made members on pooling their land and membership numbers were fairly equal for the sexes. In San Luis, on the other hand, no women were listed as land contributors and strict rules regarding stability in agriculture often worked against them. In all cooperatives, there were active and non-active members of both sexes. Given the ageing demographic structure of tobacco growers, many of the 'non-active' had retired. This was especially true for women. Also among the women, there would be 'land-contributory' members who neither worked in the fields nor were active in cooperative business, and also women who did substantial work in agricultural production but had not contributed land and whose membership had not been recognised.

The lower proportion of women cooperative members in San Luis may also be explained by the small town location which offered a greater variety of job opportunities. One cooperative found no women who would join except a young graduate accountant. Wives of male cooperative farmers were already on the Cubatabaco pay-roll as salaried workers and would be hired back by the cooperative during harvest time. Other women were older or had young children and only worked during peak harvest periods. Grown daughters were often working for the state sector in education or health, at least until marriage and children interrupted work. Even then San Luis differed from Cabaiguán in that it offered more accessible child-care facilities.

Women's work on the cooperative varied considerably. In the dark filler tobacco area of Cabaiguán, where women had traditionally been less involved in tobacco, they were often organised into non-tobacco agricultural work, producing root crops and vegetables for local consumption and sale to the state, though this division of labour was by no means obligatory and some women took pride in working the tobacco. This pattern was less marked in San Luis, where other crops were produced less frequently and women had traditionally done more work in tobacco. When Cabaiguán cooperatives experimented with Burley tobacco, the women were particularly pleased to be able to pick and thread the leaves. One cooperative took the tobacco to the women in their homes to be threaded on their front porches. Women who had retired from the fields or who had other family commitments were able to help out and earn some money. In both areas, women predominated in cultivating produce and lending livestock for family consumption, organised either collectively (when it was recognised as cooperative labour) or around the individual household (when it was not).

Household servicing was only dimly perceived as part of the collective process of accumulation of wealth, over issues such as meals. Few cooperatives organised collective lunch for their members and then only for outside seasonal workers. Cooking lunch for outside workers was recognised as paid labour, cooking for family members was not. One male accountant ventured to say that collective lunch facilities were 'costly' to the cooperative, while at the same time he lamented that women's responsibilities in the home worked against their stability in field labour. At that cooperative, half the members were women, of whom only 19 percent actually worked in the fields and only 7 percent worked regularly. Women accounted for only 11 percent of the total number of days worked during the year and took a corresponding 11 percent of the profits.

Another cooperative reported only 15 percent of members were women but almost all worked on a regular basis and took a more proportionate share of annual profits. None the less, the general comment was that women much preferred not to have to do the hot and hard field work. In the Cabaiguán area there were women who took in home sewing from a nearby garment factory as a softer option.

The marked increase in the visibility of women had produced a generally heightened awareness of women's role in production. Neither men nor women expressed the view that women should stay at home and not work for the cooperative, but rather saw women's domestic responsibilities as an obstacle to their increased participation. This was reflected in the high number of women in casual and seasonal work and the poor representation of women at the executive level of the cooperative.

In the Cabaiguán area, men complained about women members because they worked less than men in the fields and took less of an interest in day-to-day cooperative business. Women had their own complaint: they wanted the men to change and begin to carry their weight around the home so that women could participate more in the cooperative.

Generational change was very marked and talked about. Machismo was very much a topic of conversation. Older women felt that things were a lot easier than previously and that new doors were opening for younger women, even if it was too late for them. Younger women schooled away from home returned challenging taboos.

The mother-in-law of one cooperative president, retired and in her sixties, remembered how from her early teens she had had to help her mother carry food to the field hands and fetch and carry water. Later, she worked in the tobacco sorting sheds while also taking in washing and ironing. She was at the time virtually running her own household as well as that of her daughter next door. Her daughter, who worked in the cooperative store, grew up in the early years of the Revolution. Quite restricted as a girl, she married at 17. The granddaughters had had opportunities denied their mother. The son, unlike the daughter, had been allowed to go away and study. He was a school teacher but had come back to live with his mother in the village. He was one of the few men who did housework, even after marrying. In contrast, the daughter's husband, as president of the cooperative, had little or no time for the home. The granddaughters expressed a certain resentment at being expected to help at home much more than their brother. The eldest granddaughter, in particular, was critical of old-fashioned small community gossip which restricted the freedom of girls.

Few of the men did much around the house, but the women making the greatest demands on them tended to be those who were working, gaining confidence in themselves and questioning established mores such as the gender division of labour, male authority and dual sexual standards. Women expressed a lot of resentment that men still thought they had the right to have affairs but that their women did not. When the men in question held posts of authority, this could be cause for collective action. In the case of one married couple, both on the executive committee, when the husband had an affair with a younger cooperative member, the situation was judged lo be such an embarrassment for the wife and other committee women that the man was suspended from his duties.

Cooperative & Gender Challenges for the 1990s

By definition, cooperatives are socio-economic units in which individual wellbeing depends on collective success. In the San Luis and Cabaiguán tobacco areas, by the mid-1980s economic success was in doubt and several policy imperatives were proposed. One was land consolidation. In San Luis, in particular, the haphazard way in which land tenure patterns had changed had created a veritable mosaic of state, cooperative and smallholder farms. A second proposal was to break up the biggest and most unwieldy of the cooperatives into more manageable plots and, in some instances, to dismantle them as cooperatives per se by introducing a system of piece-rate labour. A third option, given the ample profit margins on tobacco manufacture and trade compared to losses in cultivation, was a revision of crop pricing. A fourth was to review the labour question in gender terms.

Bank statistics for the 1983-84 tobacco harvest showed a much lower positive end-of-year balance on credits for the cooperative than for the smallholder Canner (140 pesos against 1,510 on average, a ratio of less than 1:10). As an approximate comparative indicator, this figure is highly misleading, precisely because it conceals real distribution of income. For the smallholder sector, all income is registered under the farm owner or representative and the work of family members and others in the production process is not taken into account. In the case of the cooperative, the farmer's income from work done individually is supplemented by advance daily pay, social security, paid maternity leave for women, and sickness and other related benefits. In addition, some families may have more than one cooperative farmer. Cooperatives in Cabaiguán were more profitable than in San Luis because they were both less dependent on tobacco and had income from cattle and sugar.

Figures for cooperative and individual farmer incomes were much closer for sugar (734 pesos against 835, a ratio of 9:10), which is much less of a small farmer crop, has a lower female labour input and admits mechanisation and economies of scale. In coffee, which is more like tobacco, the statistics were again uneven (40 pesos against 512, a ratio of less than 1:12). Coffee has the added dimension of being grown in mountain areas which had seen an exodus of population to lowland development zones. Special measures were taken vis-à-vis this crop in the late 1980s, with debt cancellation, crop price increases and the organisation of special work brigades. The area was also helped by the creation of a special mountain infrastructure including village mini-dams and solar energy plants, road and home building efforts and the first family doctor programmes.

Since 1984, awareness of the complexities of the rural household in transition and of the life cycle and generational factors in accounting for women's labour input has been significantly heightened. As household economic pressures eased, women in many of the farm households joining the cooperatives, especially older women and women with small children, found it a great relief to be able to give up field labour, but by so doing they jeopardised the successful running of the cooperative. Cooperatives needed women's involvement if they were to succeed. But for this to happen, attitudinal changes were needed among men and women and men needed to become more involved in the household.

By the late 1980s, women made up over a third of all extension workers in the cooperatives and frequently reported encountering incomprehension from male farmers. In company with women doctors, nurses and farmers on the cooperatives, they began to be more vocal within the cooperative movement. In 1988, a first National Women Farmers' Meeting was held with 300 delegates drawn from all levels of agriculture. The meeting raised a new voice within the farm movement, challenging the overwhelmingly male face of ANAP and calling for a re-evaluation of the role of women farmers.

They were arguing not to turn the clock back but to overcome newfound obstacles. As women, they wanted to strengthen the cooperatives with more training and job possibilities and less job segregation. They wanted a break with traditional canons of women's work, especially with a view to attracting and keeping young women coming out of agricultural schools and institutes. While the urban-rural gap had narrowed considerably and the rural population in general, including women, had benefited from many of the revolutionary state's development initiatives, certain gender patterns had emerged. Rural women had lower educational and work attainments, higher rates of fertility, earlier marriages, multiple teenage pregnancies and larger families than urban women. As the rural household was perceived less as an economic than as a social unit, so it had in some ways been reinforced as the woman's 'domain', especially given the relative lack of change in gender relations in rural areas and the concomitant lack of socialised facilities such as rural daycare centres and dining rooms. The women demanded priority for such facilities, along with the schools and doctor/nurse clinics, whose proximity has particular ramifications where the gender division of labour is concerned. Their demands were in tune with the wider societal concerns raised in the post-1985 national campaign of 'rectification' endorsed by ANAP and the FMC, for, despite the still telling slogan of *atención al hombre* (literally: attention to men), rectification looked to less economic and more socio-political concerns, a return to a more collective approach rather than the individual enrichment and the free-marketing solutions that had been under experimentation.

As Cuba moves into the 1990s, cooperatives will have to prove themselves from both a productive and a social point of view. The post-1985 effort to consolidate them has so far only been tentative. There would seem little incentive for remaining smallholders to pool their land on straight economic grounds, since their overall productivity and profit margins continue to surpass those of the cooperatives.[26] Socially, the response of smallholders remains to be seen as the ageing individual smallholder is not being replaced and women are questioning their subordinate role in this sector.

However, success at this juncture arguably lies less with internal than with external factors. When the cooperative movement started Cuba had favourable trade relations with both West and East. In the early 1980s the tide in the West turned with the collapse of prices for Cuba's major exports and rising interest rates, which caused Cuba to default on its foreign debt repayments. The buffer was trade with Eastern Europe and with the Soviet Union in particular. When economic restructuring *(perestroika)* began in the Eastern bloc in the mid-1980s, the Cuban government had embarked on its 'rectification' in a radically different direction. The drawbacks of the 'new dependency' on Eastern bloc models, whether pre- or post-*perestroika*, became more obvious.

Cuba has found itself having to administer its own 'structural adjustment' and attempt more autochtonous, cost effective, less technical, basic needs approaches in its 'special period'. This has involved mass labour mobilisations in the state sector. Greater strain has also been placed on the already more labour-intensive, non-state, cooperative and individual smallholder sector, with new pressures on the rural household. Yet, out of an overall panorama that is currently bleak, could come something positive. If handled well, the emphasis on food self-sufficiency has the potential of rendering the domestic table less bare. And there would seem to be women ready to try to shape things to come in ways that will further not hinder their own as well as their families' position.

Notes

1 The 'special period' was announced in spring 1990, in the wake of aggressive US policy in the area: military invasion of Panama, drug enforcement policies in Colombia, electoral policies in Nicaragua, attack on a Cuban merchant vessel, large-scale naval exercises in the Gulf of Mexico and increased troop presence on the US Guantánamo naval base in south-eastern Cuba. It outlined absolute priorities in industry and agriculture in the worst possible scenario of invasion and total blockade. The United States continues to operate its trade embargo with Cuba

and this single factor is considered Cuba's major development obstacle, perhaps more so than ever before given present levels of global integration. US pressures on other advanced Western countries to follow suit also take their toll. In the rest of the Western hemisphere, trading with Latin American countries is slowly on the increase but there is little with the Caribbean area, except for Guyana. In 1993, the Third World as a whole accounted for less than 10 percent of Cuba's overseas trade. Major uncertainties lay with the Eastern bloc. Trade with countries like Hungary and Czechoslovakia was drastically affected, and the collapse of the Soviet Union with whom 70 percent of Cuba's total overseas trade was index-linked on terms highly advantageous to Cuba, spelled major dislocation throughout 1991 and 1992. In the former Soviet bloc, there was a body of opinion to the effect that trading was as important to the Soviet bloc as it was to Cuba, and the 1990 Russia-Cuba trade agreement even exceeded that of previous years. However, there followed dramatic shortfalls, not least of the oil that used to drive the Cuban energy system, factory and farm equipment included.

2   Carmelo Mesa Lago, 'Cuba's Counter Reform (Rectification): Causes, Policies and Effects', in Sergio Roca (ed.), *Socialist Cuba Past Interpretations and Future Challenges* (Boulder: Westview Press, 1988); Sergio G. Roca, 'Reflections on Economic Policy: Cuba's Food Program', in Jorge F. Perez-Lopez (ed.), *Cuba at a Crossroads: Politics and Economics after the Fourth Party Congress* (Gainesville: University Press of Florida, 1988); Andrew Zimbalist & Claes Brundenius, *The Cuban Economy: Measurement and Analysis of Socialist Performance* (Baltimore: Johns Hopkins University Press, 1989); Carmen Diana Deere & Mieke Meurs, 'Markets, Markets Everywhere? Understanding the Cuban Anomaly', *World Development*, 20:6 (1992), pp.825-39.

3   This is a revised and updated version of earlier articles based on research conducted by the author in conjunction with Mavis Álvarez, agricultural economist of the National Association of Small Farmers of Cuba (Jean Stubbs & Mavis Álvarez, 'Women on the Agenda: The Cooperative Movement in Rural Cuba', in Carmen Diana Deere and Magdalena Leon (eds), *Rural Women and State Policy: Feminist Perspectives on Latin American Agricultural Development* (Boulder: Westview Press, 1987), pp.142-61 – Chapter 3 in the present volume; Jean Stubbs, 'Gender Issues in Contemporary Cuban Tobacco Farming', *World Development* 5:1 (1987), pp.41-65 – Chapter 4 in the present volume.

4   Isabel Larguía & John DuMoulin, 'Women's Equality and the Cuban Revolution', in June Nash & Helen Safa (eds), *Women and Change in Latin America* (South Hadley: Bergin & Garvey, 1986).

5   Rita Pereira, 'La mujer en Cuba: Realidades y desafíos', paper presented at Conference '30 Years of the Cuban Revolution', Halifax, 1989; Federación de Mujeres Cubanas (FMC), 'Proyecto de Tesis', 5th Congress, Havana, 1990.

6   Over its 30-year history, the FMC has been active at a national policy-making as well as grassroots level, rural areas included. However, issues of gender and patriarchy tended to be subsumed under assumed benefits for women of overall socialist development, and relatively little attention was paid to farm workers *per se*.

7   José Acosta, 'La estructura agraria y el sector agropecuario al triunfo de la revolución', *Economía y Desarrollo* 9 (1972), and 'La revolución agraria en Cuba y el desarrollo económico', *Economía y Desarrollo* 17 (1973); Arthur MacEwan, 'Cuban Agriculture and Development: Contradictions and Progress', in D. Ghai, A. R. Khan, E. Lee and S. Radwan (eds), *Agrarian Systems and Rural Development* (London: Macmillan, 1979), pp.331-65; David Lehmann, 'Agrarian Structure, Migration and the State in Cuba', in P. Peek and G. Standing (eds), *State Policies and Migration in Latin America and the Caribbean* (London: Croom Helm, 1982); José Luis Rodríguez, 'Agricultural Policy and Development in Cuba', *World Development*, 15:1 (1987), pp.25-39.

8 Acosta, 'La estructura agraria' (1972), and 'La revolución agraria' (1973); Rodríguez, 'Agricultural Policy' (1987).
9 Brian Pollitt, 'Revolution and the mode of production in the sugar-cane sector of the Cuban economy, 1959-80: some preliminary findings', University of Glasgow, Institute of Latin American Studies, *Occasional Paper* 35 (1981), and 'The Transition to Socialist Agriculture in Cuba: Some Salient Features', *IDS Bulletin* 13:4 (1982), pp.12-22.
10 Brian Pollitt, 'Sugar, "Dependency" and the Cuban Revolution', *Institute of Latin American Studies Occasional Paper* 43 (University of Glasgow, 1985).
11 Juan Martínez-Alier, 'The Peasantry and the Cuban Revolution from the Spring of 1959 to the End of 1960', *Latin American Affairs* (1970); David Lehmann, 'Smallholding Agriculture in Revolutionary Cuba: A Case of Under-Exploitation?' *Development and Change* 16:2 (1985), pp.251-70.
12 MacEwan, 'Cuban Agriculture' (1979); Lehmann, 'Smallholding Agriculture' (1981); Adelfo Martín Barrios, *LA ANAP, 20 años de trabajo* (Havana: Editora Política, 1982).
13 Peter Peek, *Collectivizing the Peasantry: the Cuban Experience* (ILO, 1984); Oscar Trinchet Vera, *La cooperativa de la tierra en el agro cubano* (Havana: Editora Política, 1984); Cristobal Kay, 'New Developments in Cuban Agriculture: Economic Reforms and Collectivisation', *Occasional Paper* 1, University of Glasgow, Centre for Development Studies, (1987); Stubbs & Alvarez, 'Women on the Agenda' (1987).
14 Mieke Meurs, 'Agricultural Production Cooperatives in Cuban Socialism: New Approaches to Agricultural Development', in Sandor Halebsky and John Kirk (eds), *Transformation and Struggle: Cuba Faces the 1990s* (New York: Praeger, 1990), pp.115-30; Jean Stubbs, *Cuba: the Test of Time* (London: Latin America Bureau, 1989).
15 Carmen Diana Deere & Mieke Meurs, 'Markets, Markets Everywhere? Understanding the Cuban Anomaly', *World Development*, 20:6 (1992), pp.825-39.
16 Carmen Diana Deere & Magdalena León de Leal, 'Medicion del trabajo de la mujer rural y su posición de clase', *Estudios de Población* 5 (1980).
17 Martínez-Alier, 'The Peasantry' (1970).
18 Lowry Nelson, *Rural Cuba* (Minneapolis: University of Minnesota Press, 1950); Brian Pollitt, 'Some problems in enumerating the "peasantry" in Cuba', *Journal of Peasant Studies* 4:2 (1977), pp.162-80, and 'Agrarian reform and the "agricultural proletariat" in Cuba, 1958-66: further notes and some second thoughts', University of Glasgow, Institute of Latin American Studies, *Occasional Paper* 30 (1980).
19 Historical parallels might be drawn between women's withdrawal from field labour in the aftermath of slavery in the late nineteenth century, in the state farm sector in the early revolutionary period and on the cooperatives in the 1980s.
20 Mavis Álvarez, 'Experiencia cubana en la promoción del rol de la mujer en la economía campesina', paper presented to the FAO/ECLA panel on 'Peasant Economy Strategies: The Role of Women' (Bogotá, 1983); Iliana Rojas, Mariana Ravanet & Jorge Hernández, 'Desarrollo y relaciones de clases en la estructura agraria en Cuba', in *Estudios sobre la estructura de clases y el desarrollo rural en Cuba* (Havana: Universidad de La Habana, 1983); Lidia Cruz Vera, 'Composición de la familia rural cubana', unpublished dissertation, Universidad de La Habana (1985).
21 Stubbs & Alvarez, 'Women on the Agenda' (1987).
22 Carmen Diana Deere, 'Rural women and state policy: The Latin American agrarian reform experience', *World Development*, 13:9 (1985), pp.1037-53; Stubbs & Alvarez, 'Women on the Agenda' (1987).
23 Mavis Alvarez & Niurka Pérez, 'La mujer campesina en Cuba: respuesta a las estrategias de Nairobi: avances, obstáculos y recomendaciones', manuscript (1989).
24 Stubbs, 'Gender Issues' (1987).
25 Jean Stubbs, 'Labour & Economy in Cuban Tobacco, 1860-1958', *Historical Reflections* (1985), pp.449-67 – Chapter 2 in the present volume.
26 Deere & Meurs, 'Markets, Markets Everywhere?' (1992).

Part Two

Nation and Migration

7

Political Idealism and Commodity Production: Cuban Tobacco in Jamaica, 1870-1930*

THE ICONOGRAPHY of Cuba's nineteenth-century independence struggles and the Cuban tobacco universe boasts two photographs of singular interest-paradoxically, both taken outside Cuba. They are of Cuban independence leader José Martí, in exile, in the early 1890s. One shows Martí at the center of a group of Cuban tobacco workers on the steps of the Vicente Martínez Ybor cigar factory in Ybor City, Tampa, Florida. The other is of Martí with a group of Cuban tobacco growers on the Temple Hall Estate, in the foothills north of Kingston, Jamaica. On each occasion, Martí was visiting émigré Cubans in the area to rally support for his newly founded Cuban Revolutionary Party. He and the party succeeded in bringing cohesion to disparate Cuban forces, on the island and elsewhere, and paved the way for the outbreak of Cuba's Second War of Independence, 1895-98.

The better-known photograph is the first, just as tobacco migration north-primarily to Florida – and the US-based Cuban independence movement have been best recorded to date. However, as the second might suggest, the two photos together are icons of a wider phenomenon of tobacco migration and independence, involving other areas of the Caribbean and Central America, notably Jamaica, Costa Rica, Dominican Republic, Honduras and Mexico. In each place, Cuban tobacco interests united to build a new economic reality in the settler country. Tobacco – either on its own or combined with Cuba's other two main crops, sugar and coffee – provided a familiar means of livelihood

---
* Originally published in *Cuban Studies* 25 (1995), pp.51-81.

for the displaced migrant community and became an economic and political mainstay for the continuing independence struggle back home. Over time, rival economic and political interests built up, with trading and other advantages over a weakened home country in the wake of turmoil.

The migratory phenomenon was to reemerge over sixty years later, with the 1959 Revolution. Nicaragua and Puerto Rico were among those added to the list of Cuban tobacco 'host' countries. Smaller manufacturers, dealers and growers proved to be as astute as larger monopoly capital in finding fertile ground for overseas business. They profited from the post-1959 internal economic upheaval that was the product of insurrection, agrarian reform, and nationalisation, and the tight trade blockade that was the area's political response to revolution.

This latter-day rerun of an older lesson in political economy renders historical analysis all the more relevant and enlightening. What follows is an initial incursion along the Cuba-Jamaica tobacco road between 1870 and 1930, before and after Cuba's independence from Spain. The period opens and closes the 'Cuban era' of Jamaican tobacco. I will focus on links between political idealism and commodity flows in the 'push-pull' phenomenon of migration from Cuba, the sender, to Jamaica, the receiver, and on the long-term impact of that migration on Jamaica.[1]

Outward Push, Inward Pull: Cuba, Spain, and the United States

The early nineteenth century, with the abolition in 1817 of Spain's monopoly on tobacco manufacturing, saw the beginnings of a spiralling Cuban tobacco economy with Spanish, British and German capital. Overseas nineteenth-century markets began to open up with the technical and industrial transformation of Europe, and by mid-century the Havana cigar was a much coveted luxury product for Europe's elite. An early cigarette industry, producing in the 1860s what was perhaps a first in the world, the Susini cigarette machine, was fast overshadowed by and merged with cigar manufacturing at home, before both were overshadowed by an industrial tobacco takeoff in Europe and the United States in the latter part of the century. A turning point came with the 1850s European trade depression, as German imports dropped by two-thirds and French by one-half, although the English market was maintained. The United States became Cuba's only fast-growing market, handling virtually all Cuba's cigar exports. Even so, by the 1890s, total export figures were at half the 1850s level. Over that same period, leaf exports to those same countries increased by one-third. Whereas in 1859 the value of cigar exports had been twice that of leaf, by 1890 the value of leaf exports was twice that of cigars.

By the 1850s, 'half-Spanish' was true of the high-quality US cigar industry.

In the 1840s and 1850s, great warehouses had been built in Havana for the export of Cuban leaf, especially to the United States. A strong Havana tobacco oligarchy expressed growing concern over the future of Cuban manufacturing and the extent to which tariffs, especially US tariffs, could hit the industry. The 1856 US tariff, brought in to protect the United States' domestic tobacco industry, was a case in point: Cuba's tobacco exports dropped by one-third overnight. Foreign competition, overseas tariffs, and heavy Spanish-imposed taxes and export duties placed Cuba in the anomalous position of political dependence on Spain – whose interests lay in protecting its own manufacturing interests – and economic dependence on non-Spanish markets, especially the United States – with its own incipient industry embarking along the same protectionist path as its earlier European counterparts.

This duality generated widely varying political responses in Cuba, from loyalty to Spain, to US annexation, to independence – the last cause finding among cigar manufacturers and workers some of its more loyal supporters. Parallel to this, there was a considerable migration by manufacturers, workers and their families to the United States, especially after the outbreak of the first War of Independence (1868-78), for an amalgam of economic and political motives. For the workers in particular, the pattern was not altogether unidirectional, but often one of circulatory relief and return migration. However, many Cubans remained in the Florida tobacco industry, and those on the island were left lamenting the fierce competition from émigré manufacturing.

Manufacturers stood to benefit in the United States by importing the leaf and by-passing high Cuban export duties and US import tariffs on manufactured tobacco products. Cuban workers had a sought-after skill. They arrived initially in Key West – a small island at the southernmost tip of the United States, only ninety miles from Cuba, with a climate similarly suited to handling tobacco – just as enterprising northern US manufacturers were either relocating there or opening up branch factories and building model worker homes. Within a matter of years, Key West was transformed into a Cuban outpost, with estimates of 2,000-8,000 cigar makers in the early 1870s, who not only introduced Spanish cigar brand names and their tradition of readers while they worked in the factory, but also brought Spanish and Cuban customs and cuisine to a hitherto Anglo community. A return exodus at the end of the war in 1878 was short-lived; 57 factories had an estimated 3,000 workers in 1880, and in 1888 there were 129 cigar factories.[2]

As in Cuba, so in Key West, the 1880s saw manufacturers and workers divided among themselves along national lines and pitted against each other along class lines. Revolutionists called for unity around the cause of independence, while anarchists argued against workers supporting the party of their exploitative employers. A major strike in 1885 caused some 600 workers to leave for Havana and elsewhere. When a fire left the wooden buildings of

Key West's entire industrial downtown in ashes in 1886, Spanish agents were implicated in arson and labour inducements-including support for the anarchists and boats providing free transport out-in attempts to undermine Key West backing for Cuban separatism. Veteran independence generals Máximo Gómez and Antonio Maceo visited Key West in the 1880s to raise funds and mobilise political support, as did the new civilian leader José Martí in the 1890s, forging revolutionary unity and winning over the anarchists to the independence cause.[3] Key West and its mainstay cigar industry were obvious targets when Spain prohibited Cuban tobacco exports in 1896.

Spanish-Cuban hostilities on the key, the 1885 strike, and the 1886 fire caused leading manufacturer Vicente Martínez Ybor to move further north and build the model community Ybor City, near Tampa. This grew as a major rival to Key West and was followed by Martí City, West Ocala, in 1889, West Tampa in 1892, and smaller cigarette-manufacturing communities in St Augustine, Palatka, St Petersburg, Pensacola and Tallahassee. By 1900, Florida was the leading industrial state of the South, thanks to the cigar industry.[4]

Marti City and West Tampa were unique in being 'exclusively Cuban' experiments. Forward-thinking Ocala and West Tampa authorities and entrepreneurs offered tax and other incentives only to Cuban manufacturers and their workers (not Spaniards). The aim was to create conditions in which the industry could thrive without conflict and to support the liberty of Cuba. Marti City remained small but thriving until 1896, when it became a ghost town almost overnight as leaf supplies dried up. West Tampa and Ybor City were less vulnerable and their industries continued up to the 1920s and 1930s, when a combination of the Depression, the mass cigarette market, and the advent of the cigar machine finally undercut worker militancy as manufacturing moved north to New Jersey. Key West itself saw a cigar revival in the early 1900s, when there were seventy-four factories, and after 1912 with the Florida Keys Railroad. But it was rent apart by a strike in 1905 and devastated by hurricanes in 1909, 1910 and 1919, followed by fire in 1920.

Today, only a handful of Key West buildings remain to testify to that past. Marti City has been completely erased. Derelict factories and warehouses stand in West Tampa. Only Ybor City boasts a museum, complete with restored cigar makers' cottages.[5] The museum is unique in tobacco history and immensely symbolic, yet it masks more problematic areas of the past: the struggles of Cuban women, for example, who held out against the separation of male and female unions in the industry.[6] And the picture painted is that of an overwhelmingly white Hispanic Cuban presence, when the Cuban community cut across and actively resisted the racially segregated boundaries of the US South. The Martí-Maceo Club, founded by Afro-Cubans around the turn of the century, stands as eloquent testimony to this resistance.[7]

Sister Islands: Cuba and Jamaica

Historical imagery, and indeed historiography, are often created within very specific contexts. Our knowledge of the migration to the United States by Cuban tobacco workers in the late nineteenth century comes from four main sources: first, contemporary economic and political documentation and accounts, including the voluminous work of José Martí; second, the spate of biographical work on Cuban independence figures, not least Maceo and Martí, produced in Cuba in their centennial 1940s (Maceo, 1945) and 1950s (Martí, 1953); third, standard Cuban tobacco histories, which, with notable exceptions, contain only passing reference to the US migratory phenomenon;[8] and, finally, archival and oral history conducted by Florida social and labour historians to recapture not only a local lost Cuban presence but also one very different from the newer postrevolutionary Cuban-American influx in its social, economic and political base.[9]

The Cuban migration to Jamaica is richly documented by solid contemporary accounts[10] and in biographies such as those of Martí and Maceo.[11] Cuban tobacco histories totally ignore Jamaica; and no oral histories or research by social and labour historians have so far been attempted. Before the island's independence from Britain, there was in Jamaica renewed political interest in Cuba, in part fuelled by Bustamante. In 1952, for example, a statue of Antonio Maceo was erected in Heroes Park, Kingston.[12] Jamaican historian, William Adolphe Roberts, quotes lines from a poem by Tom Redcam describing Jamaica and Cuba, at the outbreak of the 1895-98 second War of Independence, as sisters with hands locked beneath the sea "whose love is unknown/ but may not yet be shown."[13] Perhaps it was Redcam who inspired Adolphe Roberts to write a historical novel, *The Single Star,* a love story set in the late nineteenth-century about gun-running operations and expeditions from the north coast of Jamaica to eastern Cuba.[14]

It is an unpublicised fact that Jamaica, strategically close to Cuba, had been an important route for such operations and expeditions. The Cuban struggle was viewed sympathetically in more progressive circles in Jamaica, but the struggle and its supporters were also watched closely by Spanish consular authorities with British backing. There were affluent Cubans in Jamaica who came with financial backing and were mainly of white Hispanic origin, and others who had arrived destitute and were often brown and black.

Not all émigrés were committed to Cuba's independence cause. However, Jamaica did provide refuge for some of Cuba's leading independence leaders, activists and their families. Among them was the veteran brown general of the first war, Antonio Maceo, and his family, including his mother, Mariana Grajales, and wife, María Cabrales, both of whom were staunch *independentistas* in their own right.[15] Maceo headed the Baraguá Protest against capitulation to

Spain under the 1878 Zanjón Truce that year, and accepted leaving Cuba with his family only when entrusted by the revolutionary government to muster much-needed support for the cause among Cuban communities abroad. The Maceo family was given a Spanish amnesty and escort aboard a Spanish frigate from Santiago to Kingston.

José Luciano Franco recounts how Maceo arrived in Kingston in May 1878, with Brigadiers Leyte Vidal and Rius Rivera and Lieutenant Colonels Santa Cruz Pacheco and Lacret Morlot. He describes their reception by the Cuban émigré community, under the protection of the English flag, as one of marked hostility. In August 1879 General Calixto García met with Maceo in Kingston to communicate the Cuban Revolutionary Committee's decision to relieve him of the Eastern Command, saying, "The Spanish are saying that this is a race war and here in Kingston, the white Cuban émigrés have their fears."[16] It was a bitter pill for Maceo to swallow, but from 1878 until his return to Cuba to fight in the 1895-98 war, he was in and out of Jamaica, constantly on the move in North and Central America and the Caribbean, rallying support, collecting money, and organising expeditionary ventures. Family members remained in Jamaica up until the early 1900s.

After Maceo's highly successful 1885 fund-raising visit to Key West, a group of expeditionaries were on a coal ship to Jamaica, bound for Cuba. A contemporary account by Eusebio Hernández describes how they almost all arrived in Kingston with fever and, after a few hours rest in Kingston, were billeted in Temple Hall with Cuban families "lacking the money to feed and clothe them."[17] Hernández himself went barefoot and ate cassava, eddo, plantain and whatever else he could find. He preferred to be with his would-be comrades-in-arms despite, on his own admission, having some of the best homes of Kingston at his disposal. Among those at Temple Hall were Martín Morua Delgado, Rafael Serra, Achille Duverger, Captains Lao and Rojas, Elizardo Maceo Rizo, Colonels Agustín Cebreco and José Maceo, Brigadier Flor Crombet and General Antonio Maceo. The explanation they gave to any who asked was that they were hardening themselves for the return to Cuba.

The Temple Hall photo referred to at the beginning of this essay was taken in 1892, on the first of José Martí's two short visits to Jamaica (the second was in 1894). It was taken by Cuban photographer Valdés Acosta, originally from Bayamo and resident in Kingston. It is to Valdés that we also owe one of the few full-length photos of Martí, taken in Bond Hall, as well as photos of the Maceos, Grajales, Cabrales and the Kingston-based José Martí Women's Revolutionary Club. In the most complete account we have of the story behind the photos, Gonzalo Quesada y Miranda described Jamaica as "a hospitable land for many Cuban émigrés co-operating generously and nobly in our struggles for independence."[18]

Martí's visit to the Cuban émigré community was part of the same whirlwind political and fund-raising tour that took him to Florida in 1892. Jamaica was considered to be a strategic location, given its proximity to Cuba. In a letter to General Ramón Leocardio Bonachea in 1890, Martí had written of Carlos Roloff and Colonel José María Aguirre going to Jamaica as a stepping stone to Cuba. He also commented on the internal dissention among the Cubans there. In 1892, however, revolutionary associations on the island fused into five clubs of the Cuban Revolutionary Party, inspiring Martí to write in that year's 18 June issue of *Patria:* "There, where continual setbacks and defective plans, untoward expeditions, close knowledge of the uglier and vicious side of nature that besets revolution, could cloud thought and patriotism, the émigrés in Jamaica persist of clear mind, declaring their constant faith in the revolutionary strength of Cuba."[19]

In early October 1893, midway between Martí's first and second visits, the *Daily Gleaner* reported that the Spanish consul, Sr. Almirana, was shot while staying at Park Lodge, an event "shrouded in mystery" and announced a Grand Cuban Concert to aid orphans and widows of Cubans. On 14 October, the paper ran an article drawing attention to Jamaica as a retreat for exiles from Cuba as well as from Haiti. Cubans were described as having "surface reticence and quietude," as opposed to the "noisier and shallower procedures" of Haitians. The article referred to the "unbearable yoke of Spain" and "despotic Spanish monopoly on public office" and the undue burden of taxation, detailing the frequent uprisings of nineteenth-century Cuba, from the 1829 Black Eagle Conspiracy to the independence wars and patriots in the East. It concluded that Spain was unlikely to give up Cuba, but to prosper Cuba needed a better and more liberal government. An item on 19 October quoted J. Guerra, treasurer of the Cuban Revolutionary Party in Kingston, as saying that José Martí was well and in South America organising for revolution, that Cuba was now ready for war all over the island, and that there were revolutionary Clubs in Cuba, Jamaica, Haiti, and in ten localities in the United States. On 27 November a small feature, "Cubans Confident of Success," quoted Martí that the movement was growing on the island.

The Temple Hall photo, writes Guillermo de Zendequi, was "as Martí wanted to see all Cubans: united, with no distinction of race or rank, bearing the flag as if ready for battle, with himself in front, representing the party of the Revolution." The distinctions were nonetheless evident: from the top-hatted white Hispanic gentleman to the more humbly clad white and black field hands. Martí himself referred to Cubans in Jamaica "respected for their moral standing and public service," among them Don Benito Machado, founder-owner of the prestigious Kingston Machado cigar factory, and also "the grey-haired veteran of the Ten Years War, his children around him, rolling cigars on his Sunday of rest to further the contribution to the homeland."[20]

Cubans in Jamaica were engaged in tobacco, marble and tile production.

They were also among the best barbers in town – at a time when barbers were quasi-doctors, known in Jamaica as tonsorial artists.[21] But it was tobacco and tobacco money that seems to have been instrumental in the independence effort. As a corollary, from the 1870s on, it was Cubans who gave a crucial boost to the Jamaican tobacco economy. They were responsible for guaranteeing the early cultivation of Cuban leaf and the manufacture of quality cigars, which also inaugurated Jamaica's industrialisation process.

By the 1890s, the Benito and Juan Machado factory in Kingston was unparalleled, but was not alone. The *Jamaica Post* and *Daily Gleaner* of those years ran regular advertisements for Leonte Quesada, G. J. de Cordova, M. Delgado, Lascelles de Mercado, L. Chacón, S. V. Durán and C. A. López. (Durán and López later married into and merged with the Machado family.) Brand names for their products included 'Elegantes', 'La Flor de Habana', 'Especiales de Quesada', 'La Amalia'. All the Cuban companies were early entries in the official Jamaican Register of Incorporated Companies and Societies, kept after 1889, along with Colbeck's Cigar Company, the Cooperative Tobacco Company Ltd., Desnoes & Geddes, Jamaica Tobacco Company, Black Horse Tobacco Co. Ltd., BAT Co. (Panama) Ltd. and Gore Ltd.[22] Later, strikes by cigar makers were among the first to rock the Kingston labour scene, attributed in part to the Cuban tradition of readers in the factories. Old Kingstonites still remember the voice of the reader wafting through the open windows of the Machado factory, as also the sound of cheering workers if they approved the reading.[23]

Pioneer Cuban Migrants to Jamaica

The Machado Story (1982) charts the history of the family business and tells the romantic story of how the two Machados (Benito and Juan, cousins according to this version, brothers according to others) were of an established Santa Clara landowning family. Caught up in the 1868-78 war against Spain, they fled to the United States when they were in their early twenties. Their Cuban property was confiscated, but having money with them, they went to Jamaica, where they married two Cuban sisters, each with her own fortune. According to company history, Benito learned about the cigar business in the United States. There is no mention of whether the Machado land in Cuba was given over to tobacco, though this would be quite possible since Santa Clara lies at the heart of the central Vuelta Arriba tobacco area. In New York, since they were of delicate health, Martí is said to have suggested that they go to Jamaica, which was climatically more akin to Cuba, and take up tobacco there.

The Machados arrived in Jamaica in 1874. They imported tobacco from Cuba's western Vuelta Abajo area, famed for its fine cigar wrapper tobacco; contracted experts at Temple Hall (St Andrew) and Colbeck (Clarendon), with land, soil and climate similar to Vuelta Abajo and within fairly easy reach of the capital city and port of Kingston; and employed refugee tobacco growers and cigar makers from Cuba. Prior to this, tobacco had been grown in Jamaica in the form of rope tobacco, lengths of which were cut and sold at a modest price in markets and by the roadside. This changed with the advent of the Cuban leaf. "The Machados travelled throughout Jamaica encouraging farmers to grow the tobacco leaf, advising on the best methods of cultivation and curing, and advancing money."[24] In 1874, they set up the initial firm, "a small affair, no larger than a reasonable sized drawing room, and employing only about twenty-five workers, who were all ex-Cubans skilled in the art of making fine cigars." Within a few years, they had gone to three hundred workers, moved to new premises and registered their first trademarks, the first in Jamaica: 'Fantasia Habanera Cigarros Superiores' and 'La Tropical'. By the turn of the century, tobacco seed had become native to Jamaican soil and Cuban cigar makers "had passed on their knowledge and skills to Jamaicans among whom they lived and with whom they had intermarried, and they were by now true citizens of Jamaica."

An equally romantic, if undocumented and less fortunate, story is that of the Palominos and the Blanchets. According to family history, Lorenzo Palomino escaped wounded from fighting in Cuba early in the first War of Independence and arrived in Jamaica penniless in a fourteen-foot rowboat. He and a fellow Cuban worked their way across the island, cutting sugar cane and doing any other work that came their way, heading for Spanish Town, where they had heard there was a community of Cubans. There, Lorenzo married a Jamaican and settled, growing tobacco in Colbeck for the Machados.[25] A family close to them was that of José Blanchet and Margarita Rojas, two Cuban refugees who married and settled in Jamaica. Blanchet is thought to have grown tobacco in central Cuba before fleeing to Jamaica and undertaking tobacco cultivation for the Machados. The Palominos and the Blanchets belonged to a small but tight-knit Cuban community that later became dispersed.[26]

All these families were phenotypically white, of primarily Hispanic-Cuban descent, though the Blanchets were of possibly French-Haitian and Cuban descent; they all had black Cuban tobacco families working with them. However, we know much less about the Afro-Cuban community in Jamaica, with the exception of the Maceos, the Grajales and the Cabrales, who are known to have had a small house in Kingston and a small farm for tobacco and market gardening just outside Kingston, possibly at Corbet or Temple Hall.[27] The Temple Hall community is thought to have comprised twenty families, some hundred people in all, on the remaining 1,500 acres of a much larger sugar estate that had been divided and auctioned off at mid-century after the decline in sugar. A substantial part of the property had been first rented and then bought by Middle East-born, American-naturalised Simon Soutar.[28]

Family history has it that when Simon Soutar and his brother were on their way to Australia, they had to leave the ship in Havana because of the brother's serious illness and subsequent death. Unwilling to distance himself too much from the place of his brother's death, Soutar went from Havana to Jamaica, taking a knowledge of Cuban tobacco with him, and bought several properties, including one in Richmond, Temple Hall, and a wharf downtown.[29] Soutar himself left a businesslike account of how, in Havana in 1863, he was "struck with the great prosperity of the tobacco industry and the influence it had on the commerce and prosperity of that port."[30] In Jamaica, his first attempt to get seed failed, and the seed he secured later did not germinate; finally he procured seed through Hope Gardens. He subsequently experimented in three different areas, finally settling on some 100 acres of the Temple Hall area which he cultivated with Vuelta Abajo planter José Pita. In 1872, it yielded a leaf similar to the celebrated Vega Pilotos in Vuelta Abajo belonging to the Partagás tobacco company. He explained:

> In that year I got about twenty of the best Havana cigar makers, revolutionists who came to Jamaica as refugees – Sestrero, Badell, Pino, and others, all celebrated workers from the factories of Partagás, Cabañas, and 'La Honradez'. They made the cigars I exhibited at the Vienna Exhibition in 1873, which gained the highest Medal and Diploma, and secured orders from Prince Milan (afterwards King of Serbia), the Sultan of Turkey, and a number of other notables who considered them better than the usual run of the Havana cigars of that day.[31]

Soutar's cigars took prizes in Jamaica in 1872 and in Philadelphia in 1876. He was employing 100 cigar and cigarette workers in his Kingston factory. But, he complained,

> a number of people had by this time gone in for cultivation of tobacco and manufacture of cigars and were flooding the foreign markets with questionable Jamaica cigars to my prejudice, so I gave up the factory in favour of the Machados, renting the lands to Cubans.
> The system of cultivation pursued now, is that of Vuelta Ariba [sic] which can never produce a high-class tobacco.[32]

In 1882, Simon Soutar is recorded in the *Blue Book for Jamaica* serving as consul to Denmark, from September 1880, and as acting consul to Sweden and Norway.

Jamaica's Pull: Early Cuban Tobacco Cultivation

In 1873, a treatise on the growth, culture and manufacture of tobacco by Guillermo González was published in Kingston "for no personal gain." González prefaced his work as follows:

> Since his residence in the Island of Jamaica, the writer of it has seen large quantities of native Tobacco of admirable quality and equal in their original state to any grown in Cuba. But through ignorance of the manner of planting it, in the first instance and by reason of even less experience in its proper treatment while growing, and subsequent process of curing, the value of the product was essentially diminished, while the labour bestowed on it, if it had but been properly directed, would have made it in every respect most valuable to the producer, and fully equal to plant of Cuban growth. He therefore, as matter of instruction to the Island at large, and in grateful idea towards a country in which his compatriots have found genial shelter, has written the work.[33]

Before the decade was out, the *Jamaica Handbooks, Blue Book Departmental Reports* and *Governor's Reports* were all commenting favourably on the island's tobacco. The 1880-81 governor's report thus refers to increasing tobacco cultivation and export:

> Cigars of native manufacture were exported to the extent of 25,928 lbs, as against 8,826 lbs in 1879-80, being the largest exporter in any year since the experience of tobacco cultivation. . . . The Jamaican cigars of certain brands have now made a name for themselves in the English market. In the Colony, they are almost universally smoked and their manufacture in Kingston alone gives employment to a large number of men, foreigners and natives.[34]

Attention was drawn to the Cuban origins of the new tobacco expansion, and the special benefits of growing Cuban tobacco. In this, Jamaica had an obvious edge over Florida. The 1883-84 departmental report refers to "General Vijegas *[sic]*, formerly of Cuba but now an extensive cultivator of Havana tobacco at Colbeck's plantation" whose judgment was "that there are in Jamaica many thousands of acres well adapted for the cultivation of Havana tobacco and that, contrary to common opinion, the drier parts of the island, provided suitable soil be selected, are quite well-adapted to tobacco."[35] That same year, the *Public Gardens and Plantation* report commented with concern on "the want of success in properly curing and preparing the crop for the market."

In many parts of the island, however, tobacco growing in small patches is being extended and new applications are made for the best qualities of Havana Tobacco Seed.... The Cubans settled on the island are apparently the only persons who can cure tobacco properly but unfortunately their numbers are decreasing and in many cases they take up other industries which appear to them to offer better returns for their labours.[36]

A complete section followed on "this great secret of curing tobacco for cigars properly and for which we are indebted to the people of Cuba, who certainly understand the mode of curing this kind of tobacco better than any other people. It is to them the source of great wealth, and may be made equally so to others."[37]

In 1891-92, the governor's report stated, "An increase in cigars exported of 7,966 lbs quantity and £3,985 value appears to indicate the development of a taste for Jamaican-made cigars, most of which were, it seems, shipped to order." The director of public gardens and plantations similarly pointed out, "The export of cigars has increased considerably, and it is understood that it is capable of much greater extension, if the cigars were pushed by merchants in Europe."[38] In 1892-93, the customs and internal revenue report read: "Tobacco is only cultivated on any scale in St Andrews with 183 acres and St Catherine, 66 acres, and in this item also there is a falling off of 15 acres in the aggregate, and of 30 in St Andrew, attributed by the collector to the withdrawal from the parish of many Cubans who had been engaged in the cultivation of this article."[39] An entry for 1893-94 ran: "The cultivation of tobacco is practically confined to the parishes of St Andrew and St Catherine, where it is in the hands of the Cubans."[40]

Quantities of the best Cuban seed were brought in through the offices of the British consul in Havana and Hope Gardens in Kingston and offered free of charge to potential growers, along with the help of visiting experts. The aim was to obviate the need to import wrapper tobacco for cigars, and to export any surplus at a good price on the European market. Such hopes had been fired after Jamaica (in the form of the Machado Company) shared a London Chamber of Commerce prize for its tobacco with British North Borneo. The 1896-97 Agricultural Society Report on new settlers on the island stated:

> The Board recognises the advantages that have accrued to the island and will continue to accrue from the settlement here of large numbers of experienced orange growers from Florida and of tobacco planters from Cuba and further views the recent introduction of a considerable amount of capital for the development of our agricultural industries as a matter for cordial congratulations.[41]

By 1898-99, the customs and internal revenue report noted increased revenue from tobacco. The collector of taxes' report that same year for St James noted "the cultivation on a large scale of tobacco at Montpelier in his Parish,"[42] while the chief of Manchester Collectorate spoke "of improved methods of cultivation" and entertained "hopeful anticipation of the results to accrue from the establishment of a fast steam service between the Colony and the UK."[43] The public gardens and plantations report corroborated the increase in growing at Montpelier where, "at the Hon. Evelyn Ellis' estate, 60 acres were planted out exactly with seedlings raised from Vuelta Abajo seed and the tobacco which was cured on the spot, was sold to a New York buyer, realizing high prices."[44]

The Heyday of Cuba-Jamaica Tobacco

The Hon. W. Fawcett, director of public gardens and plantations in Jamaica, in an 1907 article, 'Tobacco in Jamaica', articulated two crucial points: first, that the British, through Kew Gardens in London and Hope Gardens in Kingston, guaranteed the quality of tobacco seed from Cuba; and second, that Cubans provided the tobacco growing and curing, and cigar-manufacturing expertise. A corollary, given the intensive, delicate work of raising this crop, was that only small Cuban growers were really able to grow tobacco cost-effectively. The expertise required for larger plantations was expensive, which reduced profit margins, especially after the turn-of-the-century tobacco tax laws – one factor that encouraged planters to change their growing regime.

In Fawcett's words: "The history of economic plants in Jamaica is part of the history of the efforts made by the British Government to aid the colonies.... The history of the tobacco industry in Jamaica is a good illustration."[45] In the time of Jamaica's Governor Grant (1866-74), it was "a scandal that with the East and West Indies in our possession we had not a good cigar from either" and it was suggested that Jamaica should be "getting seeds, together with histories of their manufactures, of various kinds from Cuba, Manila, etc., through our Consuls, and . . . some enlightened Jamaica proprietors to commence the cultivation."[46] These efforts started in 1868-69. By the mid-1870s, several smaller manufactories, principally worked by Cuban refugees, were using more locally grown tobacco. Two large Kingston establishments, one of them being Messrs. Soutar, were using entirely Jamaica-grown leaf.

Fawcett mentions several Cubans in connection with tobacco in Jamaica. Among them were Count José Duaney, owner of the Hall Head estate; O. M. Feurtado [sic], owner of Bellevue; Pedro Cisneros (from Manzanilla), a grower at Cherry Garden; General Vijegas [sic], an extensive grower at Colbeck's plantation; J. C. Espin, who published a treatise on tobacco in the 1889 Jamaica

Bulletin; and Antonio León, a planter who advised Hope Gardens on cutting and curing. They all contributed to the dramatic transformation of the late nineteenth-century Jamaican tobacco economy.

Table 25 shows that in 1865 Jamaica imported, for reexport, substantial quantities of leaf from the Spanish West Indies and the United States, and manufactured tobacco from South America. Table 26, for the same year, reflects how little locally produced tobacco was being exported from Jamaica; rather it was coming from British, foreign and other colonial possessions, for reexport primarily to the United Kingdom, in the case of leaf; to the British West Indies in the case of the manufactured product.

Through the 1870s, Jamaica was growing more of its own leaf, though this fell off in the 1880s, picking up again around the turn of the century. By the late 1870s, Jamaica had been transformed from a net importer to net exporter of cigars, and by the turn of the century was exporting other tobacco manufactures. Bremen, Germany, was a major destination. However, tobacco promoters also had the advantage of local backing and preferential status with Britain, when London was a major European market, and by extension with other British colonies. In this, Jamaican manufacturers and dealers had a potential edge over those in Cuba, much as manufacturers in Florida enjoyed in the US market.

The fluctuating amounts of acreage devoted to tobacco referred to in official reports for 1878-1911 are set out in Table 27.

Machado's early twentieth-century rival, the Jamaica Tobacco Company, seems to have courted Cuban growers. José Blanchet, a Cuban, went over to cultivate Jamaica tobacco land in Morgan's Valley, Clarendon.[47] In the latter years of the nineteenth century, Evelyn Ellis built up a cigar manufacturing concern with cigar tobacco grown on his Montpelier estate, St James. In time, members of the Cuban Palomino family also went into manufacturing, but produced cigars of lesser quality than the Machados.[48] Census figures in Table 28 indicate a generally growing Cuban population in Jamaica, 1861-81, but their numbers were reduced to half by 1891, were halved yet again by 1911, then redoubled in the 1920s. These trends reflect the influx caused by Cuba's first War of Independence, a falling off during the interwar years, then a period of arms shipments and organising insurgent expeditions for return to Cuba, and the postindependence era. The largest concentrations of Cubans were in Kingston, St Catherine, Clarendon and St Andrew, where tobacco was important, although it is impossible to know how many Cubans were connected with tobacco, growth and manufacture.

Tables 29 and 30 show the distribution of planters and cigar makers in Jamaica. Planters scattered among island parishes may also have been rolling cigars for a local market or other cigar concerns, but these persons are not broken down by country of origin. It is likely that census figures underesti-

Table 25: Tobacco imports from Jamaica, for export, in 1865

Country imported from	Quantity imported (lbs)	Quantity for home consumption (lbs)	Value of total imports (£)	Duty (£)
Cavendish				
Great Britain	80	597	28	–
United States	335	4,370	311	–
Spanish West Indies	15	15	5	–
TOTAL	430	4,982	344	208
Leaf				
Great Britain	3,576	–	–	–
British West Indies	–	418	12	–
United States	52,413	55,735	2,374	–
Foreign states, South America	3,409	529	25	–
Spanish West Indies	59,488	37,791	766	–
TOTAL	118,886	94,473	3,177	2,173
Manufactured				
Great Britain	2,170	264	19	–
British North American colonies	236	236	24	–
British West Indies	–	120	8	–
Foreign states, South America	59,461	38,076	3,172	–
Spanish West Indies	3	3	5	–
TOTAL	61,894	38,725	3,228	1,614

Source: Compiled from the *Bluebook for the Island of Jamaica*, 1865, 1026-29

Table 26: General tobacco exports and re-exports from Jamaica in 1865

Countries exported to	Produced in Jamaica		Produced in British Foreign, and other colonies		Total	
	Exports (lbs)	Value (£)	Exports (lbs)	Value (£)	Exports (lbs)	Value (£)
Amount exported (lbs)						
Leaf						
Great Britain	–	–	31,256	4		
Hanse Town	–	–	3,589	180		
Foreign states, South America	–	–	2,634	108		
Spanish West Indies	–	–	1,436	65		
TOTAL	–	–	38,915	427	38,915	427
Manufactured						
Great Britain	–	–	120	6		
British West Indies	–	–	1,638	36		
United States	–	–	883	30		
Foreign states, South America	–	–	915	205		
TOTAL	–	–	3,556	277	3,556	277
Cigars						
Great Britain	–	–	60	20		
British West Indies	90	40	10	8		
Foreign states, South America	–	–	160	58		
Spanish West Indies	–	–	10	4		
Republic of Haiti	–	–	120	25		
TOTAL	90	40	360	115	450	155
Snuff						
Foreign states, South America	200	7	–	–	200	7

Source: Compiled from the *Bluebook for the Island of Jamaica*, 1865, 1020-23

Table 27: Tobacco acreage in Jamaica, 1878-1911

Parish	1878	1883	1888	1893	1898	1903	1911
Kingston	–	–	–	–	–	–	–
St Andrew	17	24	97	166	47	–	–
St Thomas	92	24	–	2	10	52	362
Portland	24	1	1	1	2	1	–
St Mary	–	–	3	–	–	1	–
St Ann	2	–	4	1	–	–	–
Trelawny	16	–	–	1	6	1	1
St James	11	6	3	4	–	–	–
Hanover	1	1	–	2	2	–	–
Westmoreland	6	–	–	–	1	–	–
St Elizabeth	11	5	4	6	1	19	138
Manchester	8	2	22	–	2	–	–
Clarendon	152	108	4	3	66	56	2
St Catherine	50	57	32	60	59	128	398
TOTAL	390	227	170	246	196	258	901

Source: Compiled from the *Bluebook for the Island of Jamaica*, various years.

Table 28: Cuban-born population in Jamaica, 1878-1921

Parish	1871			1881	1891	1911	1921
	Male	Female	Total				
Kingston	296	366	662	471	295	158	201
St Andrew	17	4	21	41	32	20	83
St Thomas	–	1	1	41	5	5	13
Portland	6	–	6	33	2	8	36
St Mary	3	–	3	–	12	2	8
St Ann	1	–	1	–	1	1	38
Trelawny	–	–	–	17	1	–	16
St James	–	–	–	6	–	–	33
Hanover	–	–	–	–	–	2	18
Westmoreland	1	–	1	–	–	1	18
St Elizabeth	–	–	–	–	–	3	29
Manchester	2	1	3	1	3	–	37
Clarendon	–	–	–	101	2	7	28
St Catherine	35	17	52	264	106	38	32
TOTAL	361	389	750	975	459	245	590

Source: Compiled from the *The Jamaican Censuses*, various years

Table 29: Tobacco planters in Jamaica, 1881-1921

Parish	1871	1881	1891			1911			1921		
			M	F	Total	M	F	Total	M	F	Total
Kingston	-	-	-	-	-	-	-	-	-	-	-
St Andrew	2	5	-	-	-	41	10	51	52	13	65
St Thomas	-	-	1	-	1	3	1	4	10	5	15
Portland	3	-	-	-	-	-	-	-	-	-	-
St Mary	-	-	1	-	1	6	-	6	7	2	9
St Ann	-	-	-	-	-	8	3	11	9	-	9
Trelawny	3	-	-	-	-	46	6	52	21	3	24
St James	3	-	4	-	4	16	1	17	5	2	7
Hanover	-	1	-	-	-	5	1	6	13	7	20
Westmoreland	-	1	1	-	1	54	9	63	53	12	65
St Elizabeth	-	-	-	-	-	205	69	274	62	26	88
Manchester	-	-	-	-	-	64	23	87	37	5	42
Clarendon	1	10	-	-	-	53	5	58	51	33	84
St Catherine	3	-	8	2	11	64	5	69	31	7	38
TOTAL	15	17	15	3	18	565	133	698	351	115	466

Source: Compiled from the *The Jamaican Censuses*, various years

Table 30: Cigar makers in Jamaica, 1881-1921

Parish	1871	1881	1891			1911			1921		
			M	F	Total	M	F	Total	M	F	Total
Kingston	131	230	256	-	256	292	33	325	287	66	353
St Andrew	12	1	5	-	5	36	4	40	43	9	52
St Thomas	-	2	7	-	7	1	1	51	3	2	5
Portland	4	10	6	-	6	33	-	33	7	-	7
St Mary	4	-	10	-	10	6	-	6	2	-	2
St Ann	3	-	5	-	5	1	-	1	2	-	2
Trelawny	10	12	15	-	15	5	-	5	2	-	2
St James	14	7	7	-	7	3	-	3	-	-	-
Hanover	-	-	-	-	-	1	-	1	-	-	-
Westmoreland	1	-	1	-	1	1	1	2	5	-	5
St Elizabeth	12	-	3	-	3	7	3	10	1	-	1
Manchester	-	1	8	-	8	-	-	-	-	-	-
Clarendon	-	-	1	-	1	1	-	-	-	-	-
St Catherine	11	-	25	-	25	7	-	7	5	1	6
TOTAL	202	263	349	-	349	394	41	435	360	78	438

Source: Compiled from the *The Jamaican Censuses*, various years

mated the number of Cubans in Jamaica: the 1881 census peak falls far short of the 5,000 quoted in the Machado Company history. Their numbers probably fluctuated widely from year to year and parish to parish, and while such fluctuation is explained by return migration, the reduced numbers may indicate that many Cubans became citizens through intermarriage and naturalisation in Jamaica.[49]

Twentieth-Century Takeoff

Jamaican historian Veront Satchell describes the disintegration of the large sugar estates during the 1860s, when small settlers acquired private and public land and much acreage was farmed by squatters.[50] The 1870s saw the repossession of properties by the government and by private owners, as well as many land purchases by foreigners, including Cubans. During the 1880s, landownership grew more concentrated, as companies bought property to cultivate bananas and other fruits, with the United Fruit Company in the lead. There was also some smaller-scale experimentation with potentially profitable crops, like tobacco. In the 1890s, the banana plantations in particular came into their own, with a concentration of acreage owned by a few large landholders. During these years large tobacco plantations were being consolidated by Evelyn Ellis and the Jamaica Tobacco Company, a development that continued into the early decades of the twentieth century with the backing of British and then US capital. Cubans who stayed in Jamaica found themselves being dispossessed, much as they were being ousted in their own country on a much larger scale. Nonetheless, a Cuban presence remained in Jamaica.

In 1907, examples of Jamaica's best tobacco were taken to London's Crystal Palace Tobacco Exhibition. Machado's award-winning 'La Tropical' cigars were a firm favorite, along with 'Flor de Machado', 'Exquisitos', and many others. El Caribbean Cigar & Tobacco Company, successors to S. V. Durán and Company, were represented by their agent Charles de Cordova; among their award-winning cigars 'Flor de Norbrook' and 'Londres'. The Jamaica Tobacco Company was also there with its brand 'Golofina'. An article about Jamaica's tobacco, on the occasion of the exhibition, began:

> In 1905-6 there was an increase of seventy-four acres in tobacco; but again, it is incomprehensible why the island would rather import leaf and manufactured tobacco . . . than cultivate a crop closely approaching in quality that of Cuba's best. It is piecemeal production of this sort that has caused Jamaica to be lightly considered in the world's tobacco markets, notwithstanding the cigars manufactured by Messrs. B. and J. B. Machado, the Jamaica Tobacco Company, and in the El Caribbean Factory have the 'body' and 'bouquet' of better-class Havanas. . . . It was the judgment of

this expert that tobacco similar in quality could be marketed in England in quantity at remunerative prices, and yet Jamaica has a balance of trade in tobacco adverse to itself – in face, too, of the further fact that Cuba had one of its recurring rebellions on the tapis seriously affecting its tobacco crop. Why this island should not supply the United Kingdom with leaf tobacco and cigars is inexplicable.[51]

The exhibition was "a unique opportunity for colonial manufacturers and tobacco growers to impress the British trade and the British public." The author drew special attention to the Machado factory:

It is most unfortunate that this factory was destroyed, and that fatalities attended the destruction, because the 115 workmen employed there were turning out a finished article to suit the exacting smoker. Of these employés, fifty were Cubans when I visited the factory twenty-four days before the earthquake, and the specimens of 'Gentlemen' and 'Flor de Machado' cigars inspected on that occasion are proofs in themselves of excellent workmanship with the choicest tobaccos grown on the island and blended by expert Cubans.[52]

The cigar department of the Jamaica Tobacco Company, with ties to the British companies Wills & Wills, Lambert & Butler, John Player & Son and others, was highlighted as having a Cuban-born manager, Miguel Founaris [sic], and skilled Cuban cigar makers in its employ.

If Froude had reason to admire "the good cultivation of tobacco by immigrant Cubans at Temple Hall," 'Vaquero' in *Life and Adventure in the West Indies* (1914) included the following reference to a tobacco farm in the Temple Hall area:

At the door of the house was an elderly man, apparently of white race, from whom I asked permission to walk through the field, but instead of answering me, he inquired in Spanish from a girl at his side, "What does he say?" When, however, I spoke to him in his own language, he readily gave consent, with the result that I walked about the field which was under cultivation of tobacco with two lads who were probably his sons and one or two negro labourers. It was evidently the family of one of those Cuban refugees who have introduced this industry so successfully that the best brands . . . such as those of Machado, can hardly be distinguished from Cuban production, and are largely exported into the other British islands.[53]

If the early Machados reputedly had benign paternalistic relations with their farmers, Jamaica Tobacco did not. A no doubt overstated case was made out by the Machado Company:

When the crop failed or when, for some other reason, farmers could not pay back what they owed, the Machados were patient and waiting. There is no record of the Machados ever foreclosing or seizing a farmer's land because be owed money and could not pay. Thus, the relationship between the farmers and the Company and its officials flourished in an atmosphere of friendship, trust, and cooperation.[54]

By contrast, the Spanish Town Island Register Office in 1918-19 recorded cases of planters trapped into agreeing to advances on mortgages of livestock and other property to the Jamaica Tobacco Company in the event of crop failure. The terms of the typical advance would be: "for the purpose of tobacco cultivation in such sums as the mortgagees may from time to time see fit," up to the quantity seen fit according to the mortgage value of livestock. Thus, Marcelino Muñoz, in Clarendon, mortgaged two steers Clarín and Rosado; Joseph Blanchet, of Colbeck, St Catherine, mortgaged eight cows, five calves, two heifers, three bulkins, one young steer and nine work steers, and a further nine cows, one bull, one mule and six steers, with names such as Arogante, Chiquito, Benado, Pajarito, Marinero, Negrito and Valiente.[55] For some, this was but a first step in the descent from planter to labourer.

It was a time when James B. Duke and the American Tobacco Company were carving out markets in the Caribbean – Cuba, Puerto Rico, Jamaica – with the backing of a turn-of-the-century agreement between American Tobacco and Britain's Imperial Tobacco Company and the subsequent formation of British American Tobacco. British American bought into Jamaica Tobacco. In 1912, a total of seventy manufactories were registered, mostly connected with tobacco and tanning. The largest tobacco enterprise was the Jamaica Tobacco Company (JTC), employing about 120 men and 90 women. It was followed by Machado Tobacco Company. The two were on a par in terms of cigar production, each producing about 30,000 cigars a day, but JTC turned out some 600,000 cigarettes a day, as against Machado's 10,000.[56] In 1922, the two companies merged, retaining the Machado name.

The British American-Jamaican Tobacco takeover was not trouble-free, as attested from cigar workers' strikes that made the press: in 1908 and 1917, JTC production was paralysed, in each instance over attempts to take away the traditional 'free smoke'; and in the turbulent 1920s, strikes spread to the Machado factory in 1920 (over pay rates) and 1927 (sparked by 'faulty' work due to substandard tobacco). It is worth looking at these strikes in some detail. Few of the workers' leaders had Cuban-sounding names, though some may well have been of Cuban descent. However, in their timing, the issues raised, and sequence of events bear close correlation to those of cigar workers' strikes in Havana and the United States; moreover, cigar makers were at the heart of early attempts at industrial unionisation.[57]

On 1 July 1908, the *Jamaica Daily Telegraph and Anglo-American Herald* reported on a strike of seventy JTC cigar workers over management's attempts to abolish the time-worn tradition of giving workers their 'smoke' of five cigars each afternoon. The workers contended these were worth at least one shilling and would not take less in recompense. When JTC's president, Mr. S. Delisser attributed the move to a government increase in excise duties on cigars and refused to restore the concession, the striking workers formed the Cigar Makers' Union, in affiliation with US cigar makers. The *Jamaica Times* of 4 July recounted:

> The sixty-five men employed by the Jamaica Tobacco Co., Kingston, were out on strike Tuesday. It had been the custom to let each man have five cigars every afternoon. The Company decided to stop this but offered instead one penny per hundred more than the price hitherto paid for the cigars made. The men refused to accept this offer and at 12 o'clock held up work and left the factory. Each of these men can make 200 cigars a day. They projected a public meeting for Wednesday evening and will appeal to the Labour Unions abroad to help them.[58]

The *Jamaica Times* of 9 April 1910 reported that A. Bain Alves, leader of the cigar makers, led a deputation asking the governor to repeal or revise the excise duties on cigars. Alves described himself as an employee of the Jamaica Tobacco Company, but with twenty-five years of experience as a cigar maker and superintendent of a large factory. The executive officers of the Cigar Makers' Union in 1912 were A. Bain Alves, N. George Hylton, John Hunt, J. S. Clarke, M. Gregoire, C. C. Brent, and T. Robinson.

The 1917 strike erupted over withdrawal of the daily three to four free cigars for apprentices. *The Gleaner* reported that 172 workers walked out, 40 of them 'juniors'; that the company had decided to withdraw free smokes from all employees (claimed by management to amount to 200,000 cigars, and by workers to only £170, a year); that Alves declared at a public meeting: "I think it is the duty of every workingman to assist the cigar makers financially and otherwise to fight this strike in an orderly manner to a finish, as Jamaica has not yet formed part of the USA."[59] The *Jamaica Times* on 22 September complimented the cigar makers on the orderly strike and referred to a company claim that cigar makers were the best paid workers in Jamaica; and the *Gleaner* noted that fifty women workers were staging a sympathy strike. A mass meeting held in Convent Gardens was an unqualified success, with a capacity crowd of supporters that included the mayor, Mr. Bryant, who was said to be sympathetic. The strikers' committee was headed by A. Marques. The *Daily Chronicle* editorial declared: "The bottom reason why this country is free in the main from such agitations is that the work people are so poorly paid for their labours that they cannot afford to risk even a week's wages on which their very lives depend." It ended on a plea for "enlightened self-interests."[60] The next day, the paper ran a poem:[61]

> You should have heard the fine speeches on Capital and Labour,
> And why everyone should help his poorest neighbour,
> Thrown to the winds was colour, class or creed
> All showed that Jamaican can unite, where there's need.
>
> Jamaicans will surely benefit by the Cigar-Makers' strike
> Sweating employers will be cautious, when on retrenchment they like,
> Our people have shown that they've a solid backbone,
> Bosses no more to try on their ungentlemanly tone.
>
> Some people thought the movement would end like a child's soap bubble,
> But it has brought the JTCo some unexpected trouble.
> How sympathetic and wise – the women have stood by the men
> One pictures life on earth – an Eden again.
>
> The Craft claim the return of the apprentices' ancient smoke.
> President will find their stand is no little joke,
> 'Jamaica's Red Letter Event' – will be this cool-headed campaign.
> The world shall see the strike had not been a movement in vain.
>
> We are pleased to see the interest of the public and press.
> And Machado and his men – may God forever bless.
> The position now, is 'United we stand – Divided we fall –
> And whoever unjustly come between us must go to the wall.'
>
> It is their intention to form a Big Trade Union
> And keep their craft protected against any further confusion.
> No more will the 'Bosses' try with them to bluff and fight,
> For their Union will stand up for 'Right against Might.'
>
> It is a thing now to be everywhere understood,
> That the strikers now hold out for Jamaica's good.
> (More than three cigars now's in it) it must not be told
> That to unitedly stand for any cause we cannot hold.
>
> [by] PROGRESS

A strike settlement was reached after three weeks: JTC would recognise the Committee of Cigar Makers, the committee would consult with management over disputed matters, there would be a new scheme for apprenticeship training, there would be no reprisals against workers, and free smokes would be reinstated. British American Tobacco had sent in one of its men, Mr. J. H. Busey, to help reach a settlement. The *Daily Chronicle* reported: "Let it go on record that Messrs. B. and J. B. Machado not only provided work for a number of men; but the employees of the oldest cigar factory in the island, which is now located at Park Lodge, subscribed as much as £40 one week to the strike fund."[62]

The strike was viewed as the precursor to trade unions on the island, with over 300 men and women signing up as members of the newly created Cigar Makers' Union. In 1920, Alves was president of the union and of the Jamaica Federation of Labour. In January 1920, both JTC and Machado cigar makers came out on a short-lived strike when the workers' demand for a 50 percent increase was rejected. Within the week, workers were back with no increase in pay. Machado workers were out again for twenty weeks, from November 1926 to May 1927. The strike was sparked by Machado firing a worker for 'bad work', whereupon other employees challenged the decision, expressed dissatisfaction with rates of pay, and asked for a 3 percent increase. The Cigar Makers' Strike Committee, chaired by T. Aitcheson, comprised H. R. Hibbert, S. A. Smith, N. Edwards, R. Philips, W. J. Kennedy, T. Desouza, and J. Francis. By February 1927, it was suggested that machines might replace men in the cigar factory. The Cigar Makers' Committee responded that such machines ought to be banned from the island. More than half the strikers reportedly rolled cigars at home, selling them for less than factory prices to an appreciative market. When workers went back in May, it was with only marginal gains.

Postscript: Tobacco, Independence and Revolution

In 1954, Machado brought its cigar operations to a close. Cigarettes were the big expansion sector, and B. & J. B. Machado Tobacco Company became the Cigarette Company of Jamaica Ltd. Machado marked Jamaica's independence from Britain in 1962 by describing the company as "a part of Jamaica and a memorial to its founders who came seeking a home where they could live in peace and freedom and who in exchange gave Jamaica its modern tobacco industry. This is the Machado story and now the company looks forward to contributing to the life and prosperity of the independent nation of Jamaica."[63]

Ironically, Machado lost interest after Jamaica's independence in 1977, when Carreras of the United Kingdom (part of the Imperial Tobacco-British American group) bought out the company. The old Machado factory still stands, under its new name, Cigarette Corporation of Jamaica, Ltd., Carreras

Group. Carreras had since 1962 been growing Virginia tobacco on a big scale in Jamaica, through contract farming in St Thomas and Clarenden.[64] Today the company produces mainly mild cigarettes, in keeping with the major twentieth-century mass demand for this cheaper, more standardised product.

Until the 1940s, Temple Hall was maintained as one estate, growing tobacco for Machado's Churchill cigars and also Virginia cigarette tobacco farmed by about 500 tenants on the level lands. It has since been subdivided over the years. While one family of Soutar descendants still owns a small farm, the rest have died or left for the United States. Today the area no longer supports tobacco cultivation. The only hint of the past lies in a part still called Cuba Mount. However, a new chapter in Cuban-Jamaican cigar manufacturing, after Cuba's 1959 Revolution, opened in 1965 when leading Havana cigar manufacturer Ramón Cifuentes left Cuba and set up the General Cigar Company of Jamaica, renamed Cifuentes y Cía in 1976. That is but one of the stories yet to be told.

Notes

1   The ideas for this article originated from research for Jean Stubbs, *Tobacco on the Periphery* (London: Amaurea Press, 2023 [1985]). The article is based on research carried out in Jamaica in 1986. I am grateful to Barry and Merle Higman, Patrick Bryan, Mark Figueroa, Joy Lumsden, Veront Satchell, Karl Watson, and students at the University of the West Indies (Mona); to the Jamaican Archives, Spanish Town; the National Library of Jamaica, Kingston, and the West Indies Library at UWI (Mona); and for their life stories to Eliose-Marie and Imelda Palomino, Blanca Blanchet, Dudley Soutar, and Spencer Soulette. The ideas are shaped by knowledge of Cuban tobacco in Florida and passing reference to Cuban tobacco in other countries. Perhaps my research and that of other historians will generate interest in forgotten connections among overseas Cuban tobacco communities. Thus, Severo Rijo, 'Máximo Gómez, veguero', *Revista Tabaco* 9 (1941): "At the end of the first War of Independence in 1878, veteran Dominican-born General Máximo Gómez left Cuba to join his family in Jamaica and was offered money by Manuel Codina to grow tobacco in Corbet." In 1883, Gómez was back in Honduras with Antonio Maceo, with a project for a Cuban tobacco-growing colony. At Monte Cristi in the Dominican Republic, in 1888, Gómez discussed with Alejandro Grullón and Rafael Rodríguez the possibility of money for tobacco. In his *Campaign Diary* Gómez wrote of his aim. Gómez went to Jamaica to farm 'La Reforma', Laguna Salado, in Guayacanes (Dominican Republic), dubbed 'La Meca Insurrecta'. See Patrick Bryan, 'The Transformation of the Economy of the Dominican Republic, 1870-1916', PhD thesis, University of London (1977), p.140: "In 1890, a number of Cuban farmers were introduced (from Jamaica) to plant tobacco at Guayacanes, employing Cuban skill, experience, and expertise. The Cubans who fled to Santo Domingo during and after the Ten Year struggle for independence from Spain had since the 1870s contributed their knowledge to the growing of tobacco in Santo Domingo. A number of these Cubans assumed managerial positions in the manufacture of cigars and cigarettes, which took place both in the north and south of the Republic". In 1891, Gómez founded with Antonio Maceo and others a settler colony of 100 Cubans farming sugar, tobacco and coffee in Nicoya, on the Pacific coast of Costa Rica. For Dominican tobacco history, see Chapters 12 and 17 in the present volume.

2   See Glenn L. Westfall, *Key West: Cigar City USA* (Key West: Historic Key West Preservation Board, 1984).
3   See Westfall, *Key West* (1984); and for José Martí's campaigning and support among the Cuban tobacco workers, Gerald E. Poyo, *With All and for the Good of All: The Emergence of Popular Nationalism in the Cuban Communities of the United States, 1848-1898* (Durham: Duke University Press, 1989); and Luis Alpizar Leal (ed.), *Documentos Inéditos de José Martí a José D. Poyo* (Havana: Editorial de Ciencias Sociales, 1992); Eusebio Hernández, 'El periódo revolucionario de 1879 a 1895', in *Maceo: Dos Conferencias Historicas* (Havana: Instituto del Libro, 1968), p.155.
4   See Glenn L. Westfall, *Don Vicente Martínez Ybor: the Man and His Empire: Development of the Clear Havana Industry in Cuba and Florida in the Ninteenth Century* (New York: Garland, 1987); 'Hugh Macfarlane, West Tampa Pioneer', *Sunland Tribune* 5 (1979); and *The Mystique of Marti City, Florida's Short-lived Cuban Industrial Community, 1889-1896*, unpublished (n.d.).
5   Historic Ybor City was saved from 'urban renewal' by local historians, including Westfall, who became the first curator of the museum.
6   The history of Cuban tobacco women's struggles is charted in Nancy A. Hewitt, '"The Voice of Virile Labor": Labor Militancy, Community Solidarity, and Gender Identity among Tampa's Latin Workers, 1880-1921', in Ava Baron (ed.), *Work Engendered: Toward a New History of American Labor* (Ithaca: Cornell University Press, 1991), pp.142-67.
7   See Susan D. Greenbaum, *Afro-Cubans in Ybor City: a centennial history* (Tampa: University of South Florida, 1986). Martí spoke out strongly on the question of racial unity and made a point of staying in Ybor City at the home of black Cubans Paulina and Ruperto Pedroso. (The land on which their home stood was purchased by the Cuban Government in the early twentieth century and technically still belongs to Cuba.) The pervasive belief that the Cuban heritage is Hispanic and white raises questions as to the exclusion of nonwhites, who presumably merged into the local Afro-American community.
8   See José Rivero Muñiz, 'Los cubanos en Tampa', *Revista Cubana* 74 (1958).
9   The nineteenth-century Cuban émigré community in Florida, as documented in the work of Glenfall, Poyo, Greenbaum and Hewitt, is much more radical, black, and working-class than the postrevolutionary twentieth-century community.
10 See *Handbook of Jamaica: Comprising Historical, Statistical and General Information Concerning the Island Compiled from Official and Other Reliable Records* (Kingston; Government Printing Establishment, 1883-1911); *Jamaica Departmental Reports* (Kingston: Government Printing Establishment, various years); *Census of Jamaica* (Kingston: GPO, various years); *Island Records Law* (Kingston: Island Record Office, 1879); and, for various years, *Register of Letters Patent for Inventors Under Law 15 of 1891*, Kingston; *Register of Incorporated Companies and Societies*, Kingston; *Register of Incorporated Societies*, Kingston; *Register of Trademarks (Tobacco)*, Kingston; and the Jamaica National Library Maps Collection.
11 See José Martí, *Collected Works*, vols. 1-3, 5, 20; Gonzalo de Quesada y Miranda, 'Martí en Jamaica', *Anuario Martiano* 5 (1974); *Antonio Maceo, Ideología Política, Cartas y Otros Documentos*, 2 vols. (Havana: Sociedad Cubana de Estudios Históricos e Internationales, 1950-52); and *Antonio Maceo, Documentos para su Vida* (Havana: Publicaciones del Archivo Nacional de Cuba, 1945); José Luciano Franco, *Antonio Maceo: Apuntes para una Historia de su Vida*, 3 vols. (Havana: Ciencias Sociales, 1975), and *La ruta de Antonio Maceo en el Caribe* (Havana: Oficina del Historiador de la Ciudad, 1961).
12 The statue of Antonio Maceo stands almost forgotten today. Bustamante had been a cop in Cuba.
13 Walter Adolphe Roberts, *Jamaica: The Portrait of An Island* (New York, 1955).
14 Walter Adolphe Roberts, *The Single Star* (Kingston: Pioneer Press, 1956). The book

opens with a dirty sloop rounding the coast, with the description "the cut of the dark sails had a rakish Latin air."

15 See Nydia Sarabia, *Historia de una familia mambisa: Mariana Grajales* (Havana: Editorial Orbe, 1975). See also Jean Stubbs, 'Mariana Grajales Cuello: Social and Political Motherhood in Cuba', in Bridget Brereton & Verene Shepherd (eds), *Engendering History: Caribbean Women in Historical Perspective* (Kingston: Ian Randle, 1995), pp.296-317; 'Race, Gender and National Identity in Nineteenth-Century Cuba: Mariana Grajales Cuello and the Revolutionary Free Browns of Cuba', in Nancy Naro (ed.), *Blacks & Coloureds in the Formation of National Identity in Nineteenth-Century Latin America* (London: ILAS/Palgrave, 2003), pp.95-122; 'Mariana Grajales Cuello', in Colin Palmer et al. (eds), *Encyclopedia of African American Culture and History* (New York: Macmillan Reference, 2006), pp.937-8; 'Grajales Cuello (Coello)', in Franklyn W. Knight & Henry Louis Gates Jr. (eds), *Dictionary of Caribbean & Afro-Latin American Biography* (New York: Oxford University Press, 2016); 'En busca de Mariana: raza y género en la nación', in Damaris Amparo Torres Elers & Israel Escalona Chadez, *Mariana Grajales Cuello: Doscientos años en la historia y la memoria* (Santiago de Cuba: Ediciones Santiago, 2015), pp.63-72.
16 Franco, *Ruta de Antonio Maceo* (1978). See also Philip Foner, *Antonio Maceo: The Bronze Titan of Cuba's Struggle for Independence* (New York & London: Monthly Review Press, 1977). In Jamaica, as in Cuba and the United States, Maceo was accused of fomenting a black Haiti. In Haiti, he was accused of being a traitor to his race for staying in a movement itself fearing black promotion. In an 1880 letter to *El Yara*, the journal edited by José Dolores Poyo in Key West, Maceo declared: "I have never been affiliated with any political party. I have always been a soldier of the national freedom which I desire for Cuba, and I reject nothing with as much indignation as the pretentious ideas of a race war.... I love all things and all men, because I see more of the essences than the accidents of life, for that reason I have above the interests of race, whatever that may be, the interest of Humanity." *(Antonio Maceo,* 2:200-01).
17 Hernández, *Maceo* (1968), p.157.
18 Quesada, 'Martí en Jamaica' (1974).
19 José Martí, *Patria (18* June 1892). While in Jamaica, Martí visited Maceo's wife María Cabrales and mother Mariana Grajales, shortly before the latter's death, and actively sought unity with Maceo, whom he saw as "indispensable for Cuba." He wrote, "To me you are, and I say it sincerely, one of the most complete, magnificent, strong, and useful men of Cuba. You are too great, Maceo. I must say that I feel such a deep and intimate affection for you that, believe it or not, it is as though I were conceived in the same womb with you. Doesn't María love me like a brother? Didn't your mother caress me as she would her own son? Didn't she publicly call me her son? Rest assured that while I have a hand in the matter you will be fully recognized" (*Patria,* 20 April 1894, in *Epistolario de Héroes, Cartas y Documentos Históricos,* ed. Gonzalo Cabrales, Havana: Imprenta El Siglo, 1922, pp.30-1).
20 Guillermo de Zéndegui, *Ambito de Martí* (Havana: Fernández y Cia, 1954). José Martí is said to have stayed at the Machado home during his ten days in Jamaica.
21 Interview with Spencer Soulette. Martínez was said to be the best barber in Kingston, the most aristocratic, on King Street, then Harbour Street, then Church Street (where the Maceo-Grajales had their house). Cubans were infamous on other counts, some best overlooked. According to Lord Sydney Olivier, *Jamaica: The Blessed Island* (New York, 1936), commenting on the number of fatherless children in the city, Cubans, along with Mexicans, "had a reputation for corrupting young girls in Kingston." This is perhaps reflected in '*The Spanish Sonnet:* A Corollary':

>   A swellish young dude about town
>   Once pined after wealth and reknown,
>   And thinking it mannish,

> He made love in Spanish,
> Just to polish his creole off brown.
> He made a miscue, I am told,
> Which left him "way out in the cold."
> For her papa got "on it"
> And wrote a mad sonnet,
> Then shipped to Colón all his gold.
>
> (Sympathy. *Jamaica Post*, 7 September 1892.)

22 See *Register of Incorporated Companies and Societies*. no. 1. Similarly, the cigar entries featured prominently in the early years of the *Register of Trademarks* (Tobacco 45) and *Register of Letters Patent for Inventors under Law 15 of 1891*. See also Gisela Eisner, *Jamaica, 1830-1930* (Manchester: Manchester University Press, 1961).

23 Interview with Spencer Soulette. His father John Soulette, a jeweler and advocate of home rule, was involved in gun-running for Cuba in grandfather clocks, and had articles he wrote for *The Daily Gleaner* read to cheering workers by the 9 a.m. reader.

24 This and the following quotes are taken from *The Machado Story: A Pioneer Industry in Jamaica 1874-1962* (Kingston: B. & J. B. Machado Co., Ltd., n.d.).

25 Interview with Sisters Eloise-Marie and Imelda Palomino, daughters of Lorenzo Palomino.

26 Interview with Blanca Blanchet, dauaghter of José Blanchet and Margarita Rojas.

27 Reference can be found in several sources, including Franco, *Ruta de Antonio Maceo* (1978) and Sarabia, *Historia de una familia mambisa* (1975). Again, the historical question of ethnicity in Cuban heritage has to be raised in the Jamaican context. To this day, the Cuban heritage as passed down in Jamaica is predominantly Hispanic and white – Martí is better than known than Maceo. Why? Did the Afro-Cubans merge into the Jamaican population?

28 Simon Soutar bought Temple Hall through the Encumbered Estates Court on 27 July 1881, for £2,240: 1,433 acres, together with buildings, fixtures, and machinery, and wharf at Kingston. According to information contained in the Maps Collection, STA 1058, National Library, Institute of Jamaica, Kingston: "There is an ample supply of labour settled on the Estate. . . . The Estate is in the occupation of Simon Soutar Esq, a tenant from year to year, at the yearly rate of £160. The same will be made subject to the rights of Mr. Soutar. as such tenant. . . . The Estate is in good cultivation by small occupiers, holding under the said Simon Soutar, and produces sugar, tobacco, coffee and ground provisions." He also leased from the Government of Jamaica 280 acres at Rose Mount, St Andrew, for six years at £13 per annum. See Veront M. Satchell, *From Plots to Plantations: Land Transactions in Jamaica, 1866-1900* (Mona: University of the West Indies, 1990).

29 Interview with Dudley Soutar, Simon Soutar's great-grandson.

30 Quoted in Hon. W. Fawcett. 'Tobacco in Jamaica', *West Indian Bulletin* 8:2 (1907), p.214. I am grateful to Juan José Baldrich for suggesting this article to me.

31 Ibid., p.215.

32 Ibid.

33 Guillermo P. González, *Tobacco Culture: As Practiced in Cuba* (Port Royal: De Cordova, McDougall, 1873).

34 'Governor's Report on Blue Book of 1881', *Jamaica Departmental Reports* (Kingston: Government Printing Establishment), p.xv.

35 'Governor's Report on Blue Book of 1884', *Jamaica Departmental Reports*.

36 'Departmental Reports: Public Gardens and Plantations, 1883-84', *Jamaica Departmental Reports*, pp.43-4.

37 Ibid.

38 'Governor's Report on Blue Book of 1891-92' and 'Director of Public Gardens and Plantations', *Jamaica Departmental Reports*, pp.xvii, 31.

39 'Collector-General's Customs and Internal Revenue Report, 1892-93', *Jamaica Departmental Reports*, p.143.
40 'Collector-General's Customs and Internal Revenue Report, 1893-94', *Jamaica Departmental Reports*, p.102.
41 'Agricultural Society Report for 1897', *Jamaica Departmental Reports*, p.341.
42 'Collector General's Customs and Internal Revenue Report, 1898-99', *Jamaica Departmental Reports*, p.151.
43 'Collector of Taxes, 1898-99', *Jamaica Departmental Reports*, p.152
44 'Public Gardens and Plantations, 1898-99', *Jamaica Departmental Reports*, p.319.
45 Fawcett, 'Tobacco in Jamaica' (1907), p.209.
46 Ibid.
47 Interview with Blanca Blanchet.
48 Interview with Sisters Eloise-Marie and Imelda Palomino, corroborated in interview with Spencer Soulette, that Palomino's property was on Orange Street, Kingston, and under Entry 1540 in the Jamaica Register of Companies.
49 Naturalisation of Cubans is mentioned in *Handbook of Jamaica 1884-5*, p.265: "The provisions of this Act have frequently been had recourse to, and this was especially the case in the years during which emigration to a large extent from Cuba and Hayti took place in consequence of the disturbances in those countries".
50 Satchell, *From Plots to Plantations* (1990). See also Eisner, *Jamaica (1961)*.
51 Alexander Gray, 'Jamaica's Tobacco', *Jamaica in 1907, Supplement to the African World* (9 Mar 1907), p.43.
52 Ibid, pp.44-5.
53 'Vaquero', *Life and Adventures in the West Indies* (London: Bale and Danielsson, 1914).
54 *The Machado Story*.
55 For examples of mortgage on livestock, see Jamaican Archives, Spanish Town, Island Record Office: Jamaica Tobacco Company, Liber 227, 107 (Marcelino Muñoz), 108, 109 (Miguel Muñoz), 112, 114 (Joseph Blanchet), 385, 386 (Lorenzo Palomino). The Island Record Office is a rich source of detailed information, including patents, inventories, crop accounts, slave registers and manumissions, parish registers, court records, letters of administration and testament, maps, and such like.
56 See A. F. Aspinall, *The BWI: Their History, Resources and Progress*, pp.240-41.
57 See Stubbs, *Tobacco on the Periphery* (2023 [1985]).
58 *Jamaica Times* (9 April 1910), p.20. I am grateful to Richard Lobdell for information on tobacco workers' strikes.
59 *Gleaner* (18, 19, 20 September 1917).
60 *Daily Chronicle* (6 October 1917), p.1.
61 *Daily Chronicle* (3 October 1917), p.4.
62 *Daily Chronicle* (9 October 1917), p.1.
63 *The Machado Story*.
64 Raymond A. Reid, *Contract Farming in Jamaica: The Carreras Experience* (1985); *Carreras of Jamaica Ltd, Prospectus* (Kingston, 1963). The Virginia tobacco expansion in Jamaica in the 1960s and 1970s mirrors the experience of 1950s Cuba, so also the kind of prerevolutionary Cuban contract farming. The farmer was to produce Virginia tobacco in accordance with company field officers, with company methods and equipment for growing, harvesting and curing. The farmer was responsible for the labour of growing, harvesting, and curing, was to deliver the final graded tobacco at times agreed, and was not permitted to sell to other persons.

8

Turning Over a New Leaf? The Havana Cigar Revisited*

THE YEAR 1993 marked the most significant turning point for Cuban agricultural policy since the sweeping agrarian reforms following the country's 1959 Revolution. Most striking of all was the transformation of state farms into Basic Units of Cooperative Production (UBPC). As a result, the proportion of state-run agricultural land was radically reduced, from 75 percent in 1992 to 30 percent in 1995. Simultaneously, individual plots of land were given either for food self-sufficiency (*autoconsumo*) or smaller-scale cash crops such as tobacco. The restructuring of land tenure patterns and the regeneration of the peasantry (*recampezinación*) were seen as essential to stimulate production to meet the domestic food crisis and to boost quality export crops such as tobacco. The emphasis was on a combined package of market mechanisms and social regulation to increase yields, profitability and food self-sufficiency. Production was now linked to a defined area of land (*la vinculación del hombre al área*), thereby reining in the 'bigger is better' syndrome (*gigantomanía*) and simulating the conditions of the smallholder plot within larger productive forms.

This was a remarkable, if understated, policy switch from previous agrarian reforms, when early massive land appropriations were made by the state, and subsequently, in the late 1970s, the shrinking peasant sector was given a strong incentives package to move beyond the loosely organised Credit and Service Cooperatives (CCS) to Agricultural Production Cooperatives (CPA). The ideology underpinning policy equated modernisation with large, mechanised units of production and saw state farms as the superior form of production,

---

* Originally published in *New West Indian Guide* 74:3 & 4 (Dec 2000), pp.235-55.

cooperatives as next best, and smallholder peasant farming as backward, inefficient and destined to disappear.

The tobacco sector arguably helped usher in this *volte face*. Tobacco, always an anomaly in revolutionary agrarian history, still accounted for some 70 percent in the smallholder sector and cooperative sector. In the latter, tobacco CPAs were among the first to experience problems with profitability and diseconomies of scale in the early 1980s and among the first to experience de-collectivisation in the late 1980s.[1] Toward the end of the 1990s, the trend was quite clear and moving away from state farm to UBPC and, in 1998, in tobacco in particular, from CPA to CCS *fortalecido* (strengthened CCS).

What further differentiated cigar leaf from other tobacco and agricultural sectors as of 1994 was that it was a pioneer in attracting joint venture capital from overseas marketing companies, including crop pre-financing and dollar-incentive payments to growers and workers to improve quality and productivity. In the process of what was described as a "tobacco recuperation" programme, yielding increased output of quality leaf, some of the old tobacco growers on family farms began to reap relative, and in some cases quite substantial, financial and other gains. Octogenarian Alejandro Robaina, whose farm is in the heartland of Pinar del Río's famed Vuelta Abajo region, is one who now travels the world with his tobacco. Declared 1999 *Habano* man of the year, he netted US$15,000 (a small fortune in Cuba) and has Vegas Robaina cigars, made from his leaf, named after him.

In effect, reforms in the cigar sector not only turned around a severe cigar crisis; they also pioneered wider policy responses to a crisis triggered by the post-1989 demise of the Eastern European socialist bloc, a crisis of dramatic proportions hitting all sectors of the economy. Such radical internal developments in cigar tobacco growing, I argue here, can only be understood in their wider context, both historical and contemporary. Thus, what follows provides first a brief historical backdrop and then a detailed account culled from specialised journalistic coverage of the crucial three-year period, 1992-94, when Cuba sank to, and pulled out of, the depths of its post-1989 crisis. This was precisely when competition from the post-1992 boom of what I have come to call the 'offshore Havana cigar', made with Havana seed leaf grown outside Cuba, became particularly fierce. I conclude by considering scholarly interpretations of the 1990s agrarian reforms in Cuba and emphasise the need to foreground the interplay between external and internal factors. Without reference to this interaction, I contend, it is impossible to understand how and why Cuba is 'turning over a new leaf'.

The Offshore Connection

Cuba's tobacco product par excellence, the cigar, considered since the mid-nineteenth century to be the best in the world, has been long imitated elsewhere.[2] This was a process fostered by Cuba's own political history of nineteenth- and twentieth-century political upheavals and emigration, creating émigré communities and rival economies. The cigar was one of the products manufactured by the émigré Cubans thus creating an 'offshore' next to the island Havana cigar, for non-US and US markets.

After the 1959 Revolution, émigré Cuban cigar tobacco communities grew up in Nicaragua, Honduras and Costa Rica, joining older ones in the Caribbean – Jamaica, Puerto Rico and the Dominican Republic – Mexico and the United States – Florida, New Jersey and Connecticut. Smaller manufacturers, dealers, growers and workers profited from the post-1959 internal economic upheaval in Cuba that was the product of insurrection, agrarian reform and nationalisation, plus the tight trade embargo that was the political response of the United States (and for a while the whole area) to the Cuban Revolution. While Eastern European bloc and Third World countries emerged as Havana cigar partners, Western European markets became a battleground for disputed Havana cigar brands.

Thirty years on, a new chapter opened when the demise of the Eastern European socialist bloc in 1989 signalled the end of Cuba's special trade and aid relationship. At the same time, the United States took steps to tighten and extra-territorialise the embargo in the form of the 1991 Torricelli and 1996 Helms-Burton Acts. As external geopolitical realities compounded internal weaknesses, both economic and political, the Cuban revolutionary government devised a short-, mid- and long-term structural adjustment strategy, courting non-US trade and investment. The Havana cigar became a key player, as Cuban production plummeted, and battles fought in international courts over market brand names were but the more visible tip of a cigar war. A US cigar revival was gaining momentum, involving the two US cigar giants – Connecticut-based General Cigar and Consolidated Cigar in Fort Lauderdale – along with émigré Cuban tobacco interests, in the Dominican Republic especially, followed by Honduras, Nicaragua, Mexico and Connecticut, in all-out competition with island Cuba.

This was the backdrop to the 1993 land reforms and the 1994 introduction of part-dollar payments as an incentives package for the tobacco sector, along with the setting up of a new holding company, Habanos SA, to handle overseas marketing ventures. Both measures followed fast in the wake of two landmark 'credit for tobacco swap' deals struck between the Cuban state tobacco enterprise, Cubatabaco, and its French and Spanish parastatal tobacco counterparts – Societé Nationale des Tabacs (SEITA) and Tabacalera Española

SA. A European cigar-marketing joint venture was set up in Britain, with Hunters & Frankau. In 1996, a further venture was created with British-American Tobacco Company's Brazilian subsidiary, Souza Cruz, and Cuba was investing heavily in tobacco to help meet a world market demand in excess of supply. Heightened US-European rivalry in the contemporary world of the Americas' cigar politics was mirrored by that within the Havana cigar universe, though there are signs this is already abating, national policies notwithstanding. In 1999, Tabacalera Española and SEITA formed Altadis (Alianza de Tabacos y Distribución), which bought 50 percent shares in Habanos SA; Tabacalera Española had earlier in the year bought Consolidated Cigar Co. and was thereby heavily involved in both the Havana and clone Havana cigar business.

The Cigar Boom in the 1990s

The post-1992 US hand-made cigar revival was well orchestrated. It has been attributed to aggressive marketing, more recently on internet, and most especially to the New York-based glossy *Cigar Aficionado*. Started in 1992, and by the late 1990s with a circulation of some half million, *Cigar Aficionado* caters primarily, though not exclusively, to an upmarket, male, cigar smoking readership. Its features on cigar companies and personalities, combined with other accounts, provide an invaluable source of information on the years in which Cuba devised a strategy to rise out of the depths of its post-1989 crisis in a climate of fierce cigar competition.

In summer 1994, the French SEITA and the Spanish Tabacalera each agreed to finance inputs to help raise Cuban tobacco productivity – offsetting shortages of fuel, fertilisers and pesticides that had most affected production (compounded by the 1993 hurricane in which about 60 percent of the tobacco crop was lost) – in exchange for guaranteed tobacco supplies.[3] In 1992, Spain, Cuba's largest tobacco buyer, accounted for some 57 million cigars of Cuba's cigar exports.[4] In 1994, the figure had dropped to 27 million cigars.

France was the second largest market after Spain. Tobacco was France's second main import from Cuba, after sugar, and has been since pre-Revolutionary days. However, disputed brands represented 53 percent of Cuba's cigar exports to France. This explains the importance attached to a July 1992 Paris court ruling to the effect that Montecristo, Partagás, H. Upmann and Por Larrañaga belonged not to the Cuban state but to a Curaçao-based subsidiary of the US company Cuban Cigar Brands, which had bought the brands in 1976 and 1977 from the original owners who had left Cuba after 1959. Cuban Cigar Brands then sold to Tabacalera, which inherited the lawsuit. The brand names continued to be Tabacalera property and a restraining order was served on Cubatabaco to prevent sales in Spain and France.[5]

The 1994 Tabacalera deal was crucial in ending a long-smouldering dispute. Since early 1993, Cubatabaco had been attempting to shake Tabacalera's hold over a total of nine famous Havana cigar brands bought from their former owners on Cuba's behalf. In late 1990, incoming Tabacalera general manager German Calvillo went back on Tabacalera's agreement to act as intermediary in purchasing the brands. In April 1993, Cubatabaco ceded ownership of trademarks but also announced a marketing offensive in Spain involving an end of leaf tobacco sales to Tabacalera. This led to the virtual disappearance of Cuban cigars from the Spanish market, though Cuba's export revenues were also hit as unfavorable weather caused multi-million dollar damage in prime tobacco areas already affected by fuel, pesticide and fertiliser shortages. The 1994 agreement with Tabacalera outlined a twenty-year cooperation framework. Recognising Cuba's crucial supply shortages, Tabacalera provided up to US$25 million a year in gasoline, pesticides, fertiliser and water pumps to resource-starved Cuban tobacco growers to help increase production. In return, Tabacalera would be buying 70 to 80 percent Cuban leaf and 40 percent Cuban cigars, and would have first preference in the event of a Cuban shortfall in meeting market demand. By 1996 Tabacalera expected to be selling 36 million Cuban cigars.[6]

The gravity of the Cuban situation at the time should not be underestimated. In the 1980s, Cuba exported some 120 million cigars a year, 90 percent of which were handmade. In 1990 exports were down to 80 million, 75 percent of them handmade; in 1991, 77 million; in 1992, 67 million; in 1993, 57 million, while the world demand for quality Cuban cigars could easily top 100 million. (This figure excluded the US market, although it was estimated that some six to eight million cigars a year were taken in illegally.) In 1993, tobacco planting covered only one third of the projected acreage. Then, internal measures fast ensued for a 'tobacco recuperation' programme; and, in October, Habanos SA was set up as the international marketing company for Cuban cigars in all international markets except France, where it continued to be Cubatabaco. By 1994 cigar sales were up 26 percent over 1993, and the cigar recovery was being attributed to giving priority to production and the agreement with Tabacalera. Given the serious deterioration of production, Cuban Minister of Agriculture Alfredo Jordan in November announced a US$3.5 million dollar allocation for part-payment to farmers, workers and managers in tobacco agriculture, industry, distribution and marketing. "Rapid tobacco recuperation is vital for the country to acquire the foreign exchange it needs," Minister Jordan declared.[7]

This was the first such measure in Cuban agriculture, though similar payment was introduced in fisheries and electricity, and was already operative in tourism. The part-payment consisted of a voucher-incentive plan, with vouchers to purchase consumer goods in hard-currency stores. The aim was for a 1996 production back to the 1985 level of US$115 million cigar exports, and a return to more direct links between retailer, manufacturer and grower. Such links included new taste tests and the launch of new cigars. Hunters & Frankau, one-time owner of the hundred-and fifty-year-old Havana H. Upmann factory (1922-38) and presently joint Anglo-Cuban London importer of Havana cigars, held taste tests with a social conscience. At one in September 1994, in Havana's Las Ruinas Restaurant, exclusive cigars were auctioned off at a value of US$ 16,000, which was donated by H. Upmann to the González Coro Hospital in Havana. A second was a US$ 1,000 per head meal in Paris for 160 persons (including US citizens) selling cigars for a donation to UNICEF. By 1994, the Havana cigar was being sold in ninety countries, and *Casas del Habano* (Havana Cigar Houses) had been opened in various cities.

The Cohíba brand was especially suited to new lines. Cohíba was first made in 1968, in the newly created El Laguito factory, which was started in 1961 as a cigar-rolling school for women at a time when prestigious cigar rolling for export was the preserve of male rollers. It was originally made exclusively for President Fidel Castro (organised by a former bodyguard), and as the gift only he gave to visiting dignatories. Made with the most select Vuelta Abajo leaf, since its commercialisation in the early 1980s, it fast became the most coveted of Havana cigars. A new Cohíba Linea 1492 was presented in Seville in 1992, to mark the five hundred years of Columbus's discovery of Cuba with five cigars called Siglo I, Siglo II, Siglo III, Siglo IV and Siglo V. When Cuba released five hundred limited edition humidors with fifty Línea 1492 cigars in autumn 1992, Hong Kong sold its eighty boxes in a few weeks; London's seventy boxes and Canada's twenty went within the month. London retailers said they could have sold twice the amount.[8] In November 1993, a box of Cohíba cigars signed by President Castro sold at a London auction for £12,500, to raise money for medical aid to Cuba.[9] In July 1994, news leaked that Pierre Cardin was planning to launch a new cigar called Maxim's.[10]

A New Epicentre: The Dominican Republic

The 1994 SEITA and Tabacalera deals ended a European deadlock on Havana cigars that had existed since 1989 when Zino Davidoff broke with Cuba. From the mid-1960s, Davidoff had a whole range of Havana cigars bearing his name, making him the leading world supplier of hand-rolled Havanas. In 1989, complaining about the poor quality of the Cuban product, Davidoff ended his business partnership and switched to Dominican suppliers.

The Dominican connection was not fortuitous but part of the wider Cuban exile story. The Dominican Republic was not historically considered a producer of quality cigar leaf.[11] In 1962, however, an émigré Cuban tobacco agronomist, Napoleón Padilla, was part of the Washington reconstruction plan after the fall of Trujillo and helped found the Institute of Tobacco in Santiago de los Caballeros in the Cibao.[12] Thirty years later, when Cuba was facing the depths of its post-1989 crisis and dislocation, long years of major investments and effort in the Cibao were bearing quality Havana seed leaf and cigar. The full story involved not only disputed brands, legal and counterfeit, rolled by Cuban hands in exile, but also 'Cuban seed' tobacco wrapper from Connecticut and Cameroon, and filler from Jamaica, Mexico and Honduras, as well as the Dominican Republic.

Arturo Sosa, originally from the Canary Islands,[13] was a producer of leaf filler in Remedios until 1960, left for Key West, built up a factory from scratch in Miami's Little Havana, and wound up manufacturing cigars in the Dominican Republic rolled with Cameroon wrappers, exporting to Fox's of London. Similarly, Cuban-born Benjamín Menéndez, whose family once owned H. Upmann factory and the Montecristo brand, left Cuba in 1959 and, as the mid-1990s vice-president of General Cigar's operation in the Dominican Republic, was overseeing production of Partagás (with wrapper from Cameroon) and Macanudo (with Connecticut wrapper).

The Dominican Republic had become a home of operations to major cigar manufacturers outside of Cuba such as General Cigar and Consolidated Cigar, along with Arturo Fuente, Tabacos Dominicanos and MATASA, among others. These produced a range of premium brands for the US market, including Partagás, Macanudo, H. Upmann, Arturo Fuente and Davidoff. "For most, the journey was a simple choice based on business necessity – a place to make cigars after Fidel Castro took control of the Cuban cigar industry and the US trade embargo closed the doors on Cuba in 1962."[14] The Quesada family of MATASA, which started out in Cuban tobacco in the 1880s, manufactured Fonseca, Romeo y Julieta, Licenciados, Sosa, Casa Blanca, José Benito and the new Cubita. In the 1930s, one uncle brokered tobacco in the Dominican Republic, creating a permanent family foothold there. The Quesadas left Cuba in 1960, and, with a 1961 Royal Bank of Canada £200,000 loan (no collateral), they bought warehouse facilities in the Dominican Republic. In 1972, MATASA was born, and was producing some four million cigars in 1994.

Best known in the Dominican Republic was Carlos Fuente, of Arturo Fuente & Cía. Four Fuente factories of pre-Dominican times were damaged by fire: two in Tampa – one in 1921 and another in 1948 – one in Nicaragua in 1977, and one in Honduras in 1979. After a failed effort in Tampa in 1979, with Cuban and Vietnamese labour, Fuente almost abandoned the business:

"We were left with two choices. Sell out or go to a foreign country again", said Fuente Sr.

> Civil wars or political instability in Central America argued against returning there. Mexico's strict foreign investment laws at the time dampened

expectations of a reasonable profit. And Cuba was out of bounds. In a sense, the Dominican Republic was the only option left. . . . The government was seeking investment and jobs, and the rapidly expanding free trade zones offered a plentiful labor pool, a satisfactory infrastructure and duty-free import and export.[15]

In 1992 Fuente claimed to be the largest handmade cigar factory in the world, with four hundred rollers making 18 million cigars a year, including a new Hemingway brand. Fuente's arrival coincided with a turning point in the Dominican cigar industry. In 1976, only five million cigars were exported to the United States; in 1979, that figure had risen to eleven million, a leading player being General Cigar. Between 1979 and 1981, when Consolidated Cigar moved its operations from the Canary Islands to La Romana under Tabacalera de García, exports tripled to 33 million. In 1990, 52 million cigars were shipped to the United States, accounting for 47 percent of the US premium cigar market. All wrapper leaf was imported but filler was produced in the Cibao valley, where all manufacturers but Consolidated Cigar were located. The five major manufacturers represented contrasting worlds of the corporate, large, and small family firms – Consolidated Cigar, General Cigar, Fuente, MATASA and Tabacos Dominicanos, where, since 1988, Davidoffs have been made. In 1992, the latter two each employed sixty to seventy rollers making some five million cigars (3.5 million of which were Davidoffs).

Nearly all export quality cigars were made in free trade zones, which facilitated not only export of the finished cigar but also import and holding of leaf. In 1992, Consolidated employed four hundred workers producing H. Upmann, Henry Clay, Don Diego, Primo del Rey and Royal Jamaica, and had warehouses for twenty-four different tobacco leaves: filler from Brazil, Java and the Dominican Republic; binder from Indonesia and Mexico; wrapper from Cameroon, Connecticut, Mexico, Nicaragua and Brazil. In Santiago de Caballero's free trade zone, General Cigar, in 1992, employing sixty sorters and leaf graders and 120 rollers, had warehouse inventories of leaf, including their famed Connecticut shade wrapper, valued at US$20 million. By spring 1994, Fuente was looking to a breakthrough wrapper from his El Caribe farm.

Connecticut and General Cigar

In the 1990s, Northern Connecticut produced the US cigar industry's most sought-after, and expensive, wrapper leaf for premium hand-rolled cigars, most of which was shipped down to the Dominican Republic for manufacture. The wrapper was grown in the Connecticut River valley. Tobacco farming in Connecticut dates back to the 1630s, but it was in the 1820s that cigar wrapper tobacco was developed, and by the 1920s, some 15,000 acres were under cultivation. This had dropped back to 1,300 acres in the 1980s, only 200 acres in 1992, with the overall decline in the cigar business, but it then began to creep back up with the cigar revival.

Cullbro Tobacco, a subsidiary of Cullbro Corporation, the parent company of General Cigar, was the leading producer of Connecticut wrapper. The fortunes of Cullbro and the Cullman factory date back to when Joseph Cullmann, the son of a German immigrant, started buying tobacco in Ohio in the latter part of the nineteenth century. In 1906-07, his son Joseph started to grow Cuban seed, brought from Havana. Connecticut tobacco acreage increased to a peak of 18,000 acres, and, with 1,800 acres of wrapper, Cullbro became one of the world's largest wrapper growers, on a par with American Sumatra. Grandson Edgar Cullman, today chairman of Cullbro, tells how he went to learn all about the cigar business with H. Anton Bock in New York in the 1940s. Moving into cigars, a family consortium bought up General Cigar in 1961 and the Temple Hall factory in Jamaica in 1969.[16] Temple Hall was small but had made Macanudo and Montecristo during the Second World War, when Havana couldn't meet demand, and made export cigars for British American Tobacco. Their own brands were Temple Hall and Crème de Jamaica. With Connecticut wrapper and filler from Jamaica, the Dominican Republic and Mexico, Cullbro launched a high-class advertising push for Macanudo as 'the ultimate cigar'.

In 1963-64, Ramón Cifuentes, owner of the Partagás brand who had left Cuba for the United States, went to work for General Cigar, as did Benjamín Menéndez and other Cubans. For the first ten years, Cifuentes thought Castro would be ousted and he would get his Havana factory back, but he was gradually becoming disillusioned. In the words of Edgar Cullman:

> So, around 1974 I said, what do you think about selling the brand? That's not a bad idea, he said. So we discussed the selling of the brand, and I talked to his uncle, his brothers and his nephews in Spain. Then I had a talk with the people who worked at General Cigar. They said, you can't do that, we are going to do business with Castro tomorrow. We are going to recognize Cuba. And I said, it's not going to happen that fast. I made my bet that we could own the Partagás brand, make it a brand and nothing would happen in Cuba ...
>
> The packaging is the same as in Cuba. We marketed it. We spent money advertising it with Ramón Cifuentes in the ads. It started to grow so fast that we had to decide whether we could expand in Jamaica or whether it was wise to have another place to make these cigars. At that point, we had our shade operation in Connecticut and our tobacco-sorting operation in the Dominican Republic. So we spoke to the officials in the Dominican Republic's free zone and they welcomed us.[17]

That was in the late 1970s. In February 1981 General Cigars also registered Cohíba and began marketing in a limited way. On this Cullbro was more cautious: "We have no big plans at the moment. We are looking over what we should do. We are very conscious of the fact that should Cuba open, we want to have a position with Cohíba. What that would be we are not sure today."[18]

Cuban Americans Head South

Meanwhile, in southern Miami's Little Havana, a few dozen immigrant Cuban rollers, one-time workers in top Havana factories, made about one million La Gloria Cubana, La Hoja Selecta, El Rico Habano and Dos Gonzales cigars for Ernesto Carillo's El Crédito factory. Some were as inexpensive as one-third the price of cigars from well-known companies, but they were good, made from a mixture of Connecticut shade and a Sumatra-seed tobacco from Ecuador, with blends from Nicaragua, Brazil and Mexico. The Carillo family had purchased El Crédito cigars in 1928 in San Antonio de los Baños, Cuba, and also owned several Pinar del Río tobacco plantations. The family left for Miami in 1959. In Miami and Tampa, Florida, as well as Union City, New Jersey, freshly rolled Cuban cigars could be picked up for US $1 apiece. They were made in small sweatshops – *'chinchales'* in Spanish, known locally as 'buckeyes' – where production depended on the availability of tobacco, the local smokers' market, and hiring and keeping cigar makers. In Little Havana, Arnaldo Laurencio employed about fifteen rollers making Antelo cigars, while four to six rollers could be found at Orlando Rodríguez's El Canelo.

Tampa, especially around Ybor City, was a cigar-industry ghost town.[19] The few that remained were small, like the Vincent & Tampa Cigar Co. and Rodríguez and Menéndez. Tampa was home in name only to M & N Cigar's Cuesta-Rey brand – it was made exclusively by Tabacalera A. Fuente in the Dominican Republic, as was La Única, while other M & N cigars were hand-rolled at Nestor Placencia's factory in Honduras. M & N's founding Newman family, whose tobacco interests date back one hundred years and who bought Cuesta-Rey in 1958, struck a 1986 deal with Fuente: the Newmans would manufacture machine-made cigars for Fuente at the Tampa factory, and Fuente would make the hand-rolled Cuesta-Rey for Newman.

New Jersey's cigar community dates back to the 1920s and 1930s when American Tobacco shifted production from Cuba to Trenton and Union City. Decades later, they would relocate back to the Caribbean, but the Cuban community stayed behind making cigars for their own consumption. Small-scale examples were Berto Ale's La Isla and José Suárez's Boquilla. Rolando Reyes's Aliados (former Cuba Aliados of Sancti Spíritus subcontracted to Partagás, Por Larrañaga, El Rey del Mundo and H. Upmann – Reyes left Cuba in 1968) was larger, with operations in Miami, the Dominican Republic and Honduras – where tobacco was grown and labour was plentiful. According to the Cigar Association of America, more than 40 million Honduran cigars were imported into the United States in 1992, up from 34 million in 1991. That put Honduras in solid second place, behind the Dominican Republic. After the Central American wars in the 1980s, cigar producers of the 1990s pushed ahead from the hot coastal plains of San Pedro Sula to the cool mountains of Santa Rosa de Copán and Danlí in the Nicaraguan border region. Among those who have been called the new tobacco 'godfathers' are many Cubans:

> Through these men, the shadow of Cuba and its legendary tobacco looms large in Honduras. They stand guard over the process and the tradition of making premium cigars. Antonio 'Nico' Fernández (once manager of H. Upmann in Havana) and Nestor Placencia (whose family owned a 200-acre farm in Vuelta Abajo before leaving for Nicaragua) at Tabacos Placencia, Estela Padrón and Frank Llaneza at Honduras American Tobacco, Julio Eiroa at Tabacos Rancho Jamaestran, José Quesada at US Tobacco's Danlí operation known as CACSA, or Central American Cigars. Even the Honduran patriarch, Dr. Jorge Bueso, at Tabacos Flor de Copán, remembers Cuban tobacco as the standard, and today he extols the heritage of his Cuban seed leaves. Above all, these men know what they like: They like the cigars they make. They know how to make excellent products year after year. They are men who understand cigars.... "In the cigar industry, if you don't talk Cuban, no one believes you anyway," says Dr. Bueso ...
>
> The Honduras-Cuban connection reads like a spy versus spy novel. Dr. Bueso tells the story of a high-ranking Cuban agricultural official, Jacinto Argudín, who sent a letter to him citing Honduras's history of high-quality tobacco and suggested he ask the new Cuban government for help in setting up a cigar tobacco operation. When no help was forthcoming, Argudín, who had been Dr. Bueso's college roommate at Louisiana State University in 1941, circumvented restrictions on the export of Cuban cigar tobacco seed and sent five pounds of seed through a diplomatic pouch to Honduras. That was the first Cuban seed planted in Central America, according to Dr. Bueso.[20]

Honduran manufacturers bought wrapper tobacco from the northern Estelí and Jalapa area of Nicaragua, a war-ravaged part during the *contra* war. John Oliva, son of Cuban Angel Oliva, who ran the Oliva Tobacco Company in Danli, entered into negotiations with the Tabacalera Independiente Nicaraguense SA (TAINSA) group, which included three former cooperatives formed under the Sandinista government and the cigar factory in Estelí, to begin farming in the Jalapa region again. But the tensions inevitably remained: the manager of Consolidated Cigar's Tabacos San Andrés factory in Danlí was Indalecio Rodríguez, former director of the *contra* organisation, the Nicaraguan Democratic Front. Workers here were newcomers to cigar rolling, often young and women.

The Mexico connection was less developed and less fraught, yet in a not altogether dissimilar vein. San Andrés Valley is the home of Mexico's finest cigar tobacco and cigar exports. While tobacco has Mayan origins, legend has it that today's cigar business has been shaped by three revolutions: the Mexican Revolution of 1910-17 broke up many great cigar estates; the Sukarno takeover in Indonesia in 1949 caused Dutch cigar interests to move to Mexico with Sumatra seed; and the 1959 Cuban Revolution brought the Cubans. In fact, the Cubans in Mexico dated further back than that.[21] "We learned a lot from the Cubans. . . . A lot of them came to Veracruz and they helped change the way we presented cigars to the world", explained Jorge Ortiz Álvarez.[22] Cuban-born Pedro Gómez, production manager of Matacapan Tabacos cigar factory, home of Te Amo cigar, started out as a roller in H. Upmann, in Havana, in the 1930s. He went to Spain, the Canary Islands, Tampa, the Dominican Republic and finally Mexico: "His ports of call included only places where fine cigars were produced and savored as he worked to become a master in his own right. His passport reads like a guidebook to the history of cigars in the twentieth century."[23]

Brand Wars

In 1994, in Cuba, six key factories produced the quality export cigars: H. Upmann, Partagás, Romeo y Julieta, La Corona, El Laguito and El Rey del Mundo. El Laguito was the exception because it was set up after the Revolution. The other five were the traditional Havana factories of old. In the words of Romeo y Julieta manager José Fabelo:

> Here in Havana we make our cigars not only with great skill but also with a lot of love. Other places may be able to make very good cigars, but nowhere has the tradition of Havana. Thus, we have the quality tobacco from Vuelta Abajo, which as a growing area can't be duplicated.[24]

Each of the five Havana export factories could make four to five million cigars a year, yet in 1994 each was lamenting how production could be increased 50 to 100 percent to meet demand, if only more quality wrapper tobacco could be produced. Meanwhile, retailers round the world were facing supply shortfalls. Simon Chase, marketing director for Hunters & Frankau, declared:

> We could have easily sold more than 3,000 boxes of Hoyo Double Coronas

last year if we had had them. . . . If everyone had Hoyo Double Coronas, it might be different, but I could pick up the phone today and sell 40,000 of them with very little trouble at all. And that might be to just one person.[25]

Counterfeiting and brand wars were (and still are) major problems facing the industry of island Cuba, but cigar connoisseurs, especially in Europe, still say a Havana cigar is a Havana cigar, that what makes the difference is the Cuban-grown tobacco. They see the Dominican and other cigars as a different, lesser product, no matter how much the aggressive marketing of major US and Cuban-American cigar companies has been striving to convince otherwise, as in the following *Cigar Aficionado* ads:

"When A Cigar Can Make You Forget Havana, That's One-Upmannship" (Spring 1993).

"Before 1976, Ramón Allones cigars were made in Havana by Cuba's most respected cigar-maker. Since 1978, they have been made by the same Cuban cigar-maker in the Dominican Republic in their rich Cameroon wrapper leaves." (Spring 1993).

"Guess Who's Coming To Dinner? El Rey del Mundo, Coming To America in 1994" (Winter 1993/94).

"The Rebirth of A Legend, the new Romeo y Julieta Vintage Cigar: From its Cuban origins in 1875 to its heralded rebirth in the Dominican Republic, the Romeo y Julieta has always been the connoisseur's choice" (Winter 1993/94).

"Cuba Aliados, Premium Quality Cuban Style Cigars: Rediscover the Art & Mystery of Pre-Embargo Havana" (Spring 1994).

"So good they should be illegal! Casa Blanca (Dominican Republic) Aliados and El Rey del Mundo (Honduras)" (Spring 1994).

"Ever Wonder What The Great Cuban Cigar Makers Did After Leaving Cuba?" (Summer 1994).

"'Fidel Castro thought I had left Cuba with only the clothes on my back. But my secrets were locked in my heart.' Ramón Cifuentes and Partagás. The cigar that knew Cuban when." (Summer 1994).

Cigar Aficionado commented:

Americans, of course, are not permitted legal access to the Cuban cigar, so only a percentage of US smokers can decide for themselves which country makes their favorite cigar. But nothing lasts forever. The Cuban trade embargo will fall someday. The debate over where the best cigars are made will only get more intense. Cigar smokers will relish the search.[26]

In Europe, *El Habano* was in business. After Spain and France, key 1992 Cuban cigar export markets were the United Kingdom (5 million), Switzerland (3 million), Belgium (1.2 million) and Germany (1 million). Montecristo was the number one selling cigar brand, accounting for some thirty million cigars, close to half all exports. But, in summer 1993, Tabacalera and Cubatabaco were locked in confidential talks about the future of Montecristo and other brands, including H. Upmann, Partagás and La Gloria Cubana. In September 1991, Tabacalera had bought the world rights – excluding Cuba, the United States and the Dominican Republic – for US$10 million from Cuban Cigar Brands, a partnership formed by the American tobacco giant Consolidated Cigar and Spain's Internacional Cifuentes. Court cases in Spain and France subsequently supported Tabacalera's ownership of the brands over Cuba. High stakes were created in the battle for Montecristo. Spain had the trademarks but didn't have the cigars. Cuba had the cigars but couldn't sell them because Spain had the trademarks. In 1993, the Cubans were not easily won over: "We are dealing with the problem at the moment," maintained [then Cubatabaco director] Francisco Padrón:

> Some things are more complicated than they seem. . . . If we cannot solve our problem with Tabacalera, we are going to launch a new brand name as a substitute for Montecristo. We would then withdraw the brand [Montecristo] from Spain. No problem.[27]

A year previously, *Cigar Aficionado* had commented:

> The big question is when the United States will begin trading with Cuba. Presumably, the big US tobacco companies have their lawsuits ready for the first shipments of Cuban cigars to the States. One company based in New York even has the US trademark for Cuba's most prestigious brand, Cohíba. "It is not that important the US opens," said Cubatabaco's Padrón. "I will not take a single cigar from the European market and sell it to the States if it opens. I want to remain loyal to my customers in Europe."[28]

Asking a tobacco grower in the Vuelta Abajo about such intricacies of international trade is generally answered by a shrug of the shoulders. Cubans say that in their plantations hatred cannot exist as long as the tobacco grows well. "It is just a pity that Americans cannot smoke Cuban cigars," said Rafael Guerra, assistant manager of El Laguito factory, where the famous Cohíba brand is made. "It is all a question of politics. I really hope that one day it all changes."[29]

In spring 1994, Padrón declared to *Cigar Aficionado:* "I am not a politician. Things are moving. As José Martí said, 'the most important thing in politics is what you don't see.'"[30] In summer 1994, this was followed by an exclusive *Cigar Aficionado* interview with Fidel Castro, who talked about how eight years earlier he had given up smoking as a matter of principle on health grounds but who also extolled the virtues of the Havana cigar.

Over a million Cuban Americans, centered in the key electoral state of Florida and to a lesser extent New Jersey, formed a strong lobby in Washington. Many were diametrically opposed to both Castro and the Revolution – a 'no deals with Castro' position. In his 1992 electoral Democrat bid, William Clinton courted the hitherto loyally Republican Cuban American National Foundation lobby, endorsing the Cuban Democracy Act, introducing extraterritoriality into the thirty-year-old US trade embargo on Cuba. This created a foreign policy problem, as it was contested by major trading partners of both the United States and Cuba: Canada and Mexico (both in NAFTA) and Spain, France and the United Kingdom, in the European Union. After the Cuban rafters crisis in the summer of 1994, the heat was on domestically in the United States over the Cuban immigration issue. When in 1996 the Helms-Burton bill, designed to tighten extraterritorial sanctions, became law overseas allies were further antagonised.

By no means all the US and Cuban-American tobacco interests featured here shared the anti-Castro lobby. In the words of Lionel Melendi, manager of New York's De La Concha tobacco store, himself the grandson of a Cuban tobacco grower and cigar manufacturer: "If the embargo were ever lifted, there would be a tremendous demand for Cuban cigars in the US. They'd be lined up around the block."[31] Cullbro/General Cigar chairman Edgar Cullman adopted a similar line:

> I think that the taste of a Cuban cigar is a very rare taste, a beautiful taste, and people who like that taste will do anything to get a Cuban cigar . . . such as bring them in illegally and smoke them illegally. . . . If we ever could find a way to deal with Cuba. it would be a great boon for the cigar business. But I'm not a politician. . . . There could very well be a revival of the cigar business when people want to taste Cuban tobacco. . . . I think [the end of the embargo] is going to come, but I don't know when. . . . The best-case scenario will be: the embargo ends and the American government says that until we can buy enough tobacco to satisfy the American demand by the US-owned manufacturers to make whatever cigars they want with

Cuban tobacco, it will hold up allowing Cuban cigars in. That was the understanding we had with the State Department way back in the 1970s when we thought we were going to have some rapprochement.[32]

Clearly, the best scenario for General Cigar would not be the best for Habanos SA.

Turning Over a New Leaf?

Whether Cuba's ongoing reform process is conjunctural or structural – that is, driven by primarily external or internal considerations – has thus far been debated at the macro rather than a micro level, and often solely in the realm of policy. With some notable exceptions, Cuban scholars have tended to lend primacy to the crisis caused by the post-1989 demise of the Eastern European socialist bloc, while foreign scholars have argued the crisis of a whole economic model.

Where agriculture is concerned, the picture is less clear-cut. Key areas highlighted in the early 1990s reforms were the quest for greater food self-sufficiency[33] and ecological agriculture.[34] From research conducted since in Cuba, we now have a clearer understanding of the CPA and UBPC, and issues of local autonomy, participation, land and market reforms.[35] Scholars agree that non-state farms are performing better in volume and quality than state farms, and within non-state farms, CCS better than CPA and CPA better than UBPC. This is despite inverse unequal access to factors of production and other resources, with UBPC receiving more state-allocated inputs than CPA and CPA more than CCS.

Here certain departures come into play on how to interpret this. One study characterises this as peasantisation, depeasantisation, repeasantisation.[36] Other authors conclude that post-1959 revolutionary policy has been a failure, because it was premised on the state farm as the ideal form of agricultural organisation; their corollary argument is that a lessening of state intervention in the agricultural sector could bring about considerable improvements.[37] In 1991 the CPA was still being described in Cuba as a "superior form of collective production" and the CCS as a "primary organisation of a collective nature," backward and slow to adapt to modern technology; and yet the former was being out-performed by the latter. The creation of the UBPC in 1993, Álvarez and Puerta argue, is a massive turnaround in economic thinking and demonstrates that the Cuban leadership has finally come to terms with these realities. It not only denotes recognition of the failure of a policy implemented for more than three decades, it should also induce the leadership to extend the privatisation process throughout the economy.

Likewise, certain conclusions have been drawn from foreign agribusiness investment. Thus the 1994 pre-financing agreements with Tabacalera and SEITA, while tying up a large part of Cuba's cigar leaf and cigar exports to Spain and France, are held to go a long way toward explaining the overall increased tobacco output from 25,000 metric tons in 1995 to 33,100 in 1996 and 50,000 in 1997, and the quadrupled manufacture of cigars from 60 million in 1995 to 193 million in 1996 and 250 million in 1997.[38]

As described in this paper, however, the situation in tobacco is complex and, if anything, demonstrates that no simplistic conclusions can, or should, be reached. This has been corroborated in case studies conducted in Cuba.[39] My own earlier studies of the tobacco sector in the 1970s and 1980s[40] homed in on internal factors such as crop specificity in tobacco history, land size, diseconomies of scale, household and gender. My research in the tobacco areas of Vuelta Abajo and Vuelta Arriba in 1999 pointed to diverse experiences, but to an overall growing awareness of the possibilities and the pitfalls of both internal and overseas markets, as well as individual and collective autonomy, plus a desire to retain perceived social benefits. Concerns were expressed regarding the drive to meet unrealistically high tobacco harvest targets (some even likened this in kind to the 1970 drive for the ten million ton sugar harvest). In Vuelta Abajo, the push to tobacco monoculture was taking its toll on food self-sufficiency and contrasted markedly with the more mixed economy of Vuelta Arriba. One highly successful CPA from Vuelta Arriba is La Nueva Cuba, in Cabaiguán, which has continued to grow in land area and membership, produces quality tobacco, is food self-sufficient and markets a surplus, and return profits are used for social betterment as well as re-investment in production. Even so, there, as elsewhere, questions are being raised concerning the impact of the 1990s reforms on social equity, household and gender, all of which remain to be studied.

And yet, the fact is that the strategy of the 1990s agrarian reform dovetailed with the courting of non-US investment, enabled island Cuba to ride an internal tobacco crisis of unprecedented proportions, in the process 'turning over a new leaf.' Both the output and quality of production and export increased, outstripping fierce overseas brand competition and helping subsidise other sectors of the economy and society. As a result, the "proud cigar band," to borrow the words of Fernando Ortiz,[41] helped propel Cuba into the twenty-first century.

Notes

1   In 1992, only 32 percent of tobacco land was in state hands, 22 percent in CPA, and 43 percent in CCS, leaving a residual 3 percent in other plots. By late 1996, the

cooperative sector comprised 54 percent of tobacco land, but made up largely of UBPC (43 percent), with CPA trailing behind (11 percent).
2. This I noted, but did not develop, in my monograph on nineteenth- and twentieth-century Cuban tobacco history, Jean Stubbs, *Tobacco on the Periphery* (London: Amaurea Press, 2023 [1985]).
3. *Cuba Business* (July-August/September 1994).
4. Spain had not always figured so prominently. In 1961, political tensions between Spain and Cuba were at a height and for a whole year Spain refused to import tobacco, until the new Cuban government paid compensation to Spanish owners of tobacco firms expropriated after the Revolution. Following negotiations, a compromise was reached and Cuban exports to Spain were resumed.
5. *Economist Intelligence Report*, 4 (1992).
6. *Washington Post* (17 June 1994).
7. *Granma* (19 October 1993).
8. *Cigar Aficionado* (Spring 1993).
9. *CubaInfo*, 5:15 (1993).
10. See Spanish press agency *EFE* (26 July 1994).
11. While not considered quality leaf, the Dominican Republic does, however, have a strong tobacco history. See Michiel Baud, *Peasants and Tobacco in the Dominican Republic, 1870-1930* (Knoxville: University of Tennessee Press, 1996).
12. Napoleón S. Padilla, *Cultivo del tabaco negro: sol y tapado* (Santo Domingo: Instituto del Tabaco de la República Dominicana, 1982), and *Memorias de un cubano sin importancia* (Hialeah: A. C. Graphics, 1998).
13. For the involvement of Canary Islander migration in Cuban tobacco, see Mario Luis López Isla (ed.), *La aventura del tabaco* (Santa Cruz de Tenerife: Centro de la Cultura Popular Canaria, 1998).
14. *Cigar Aficionado* (Autumn 1992).
15. Ibid.
16. For the Cuban tobacco history of Temple Hall, see Jean Stubbs, 'Political Idealism and Commodity Production: Cuban Tobacco in Jamaica, 1870-1930', *Cuban Studies*, 25 (1995), pp.51-81 – Chapter 7 in the present volume.
17. *Cigar Aficionado* (Autumn 1994).
18. *Cigar Aficionado* (Spring 1993).
19. For the Cuban tobacco history of Tampa and Ybor City, see Louis A. Pérez, Jr., 'Cubans in Tampa: From Exiles to Immigrants, 1892-1901', *Florida Historical Quarterly* 57:2 (1978), pp.129-40; Glenn L. Westfall, *Key West: Cigar City USA* (Key West: Historic Key West Preservation Board, 1984); Gerald E. Poyo, *With All and for the Good of All: The Emergence of Popular Nationalism in the Cuban Communities of the United States, 1848-1898* (Durham: Duke University Press, 1989); and Armando Méndez, *Ciudad de Cigars: West Tampa* (Tampa: Florida Historical Society, 1994).
20. *Cigar Aficionado* (Spring 1993).
21. For the broader tobacco history, see José González Sierra, *Monopolio del humo: Elementos de la historia del tabaco en México y algunos conflictos de tabaqueros veracruzanos: 1915-1930* (Xalapa: Veracruz University, 1987).
22. *Cigar Aficionado* (Winter 1994).
23. *Cigar Afiicionado* (Winter 1994).
24. *Cigar Aficionado* (Autumn 1994).
25. *Cigar Aficionado* (Autumn 1994).
26. *Cigar Aficionado* (Autumn 1992).
27. *Cigar Aficionado* (Summer 1993).
28. *Cigar Aficionado* (Winter 1992-93).
29. *Cigar Aficionado* (Winter 1992-93).
30. *Cigar Aficionado* (Spring 1994).
31. *Cigar Aficionado* (Spring 1993).
32. *Cigar Aficionado* (Autumn 1994).

33 Carmen Diana Deere, 'Cuba's National Food Program and its Prospects for Food Security', *Agricultural and Human Values*, 20:3 (1993), pp.35-51; Sergio G. Roca, 'Reflections on Economic Policy: Cuba's Food Program', in Jorge F. Pérez-López (ed.), *Cuba at a Crossroads: Politics and Economics after the Fourth Party Congress* (Gainesville: University Press of Florida, 1994), pp.94-117.
34 Richard Levins, 'The Ecological Transformation of Cuba', *Agriculture & Human Values*, 10:3 (1990), pp.52-60; Peter Rosset & Medea Benjamin (eds), *The Greening of the Revolution: Cuba's Experiment with Organic Agriculture* (Melbourne: Ocean Press, 1994).
35 Carmen Diana Deere & Mieke Meurs, 'Markets, Markets Everywhere? Understanding the Cuban Anomaly', *World Development*, 20:6 (1992), pp.825-39; Carmen Deere et al., 'Toward a Periodization of the Cuban Collectivization Process: Changing Incentives and Peasant Response', *Cuban Studies*, 22 (1992), pp.115-49; George Carriazo Moreno, 'Cambios estructurales en la agricultura cubana: La cooperativización', *Economía Cubana - Boletín Informativo*, 18 (1994), pp.14-29; Carmen Deere et al., 'The View from Below: Cuban Agriculture in the Special Period in Peacetime', *Journal of Peace Studies*, 21 (1994), pp.194-234; 'Household Incomes in Cuban Agriculture: A Comparison of the State, Cooperative, and Peasant Sectors', *Development and Change*, 26:2 (1995), pp.209-34; Carmen Deere, 'The New Agrarian Reform', *NACLA Report on the Americas* 29:2 (1995), pp.13-17, Evolution of Cuba's Agricultural Sector (1996); Angel Bu Wong, 'Las UBPC y su necesario perreccionamiento', *Cuba: Investigación Económica*, 2 (1996), pp.15-43; Armando Nova González, 'El Mercado agropecuario cubano: Practica y teoria', *Economía y Desarrollo* 3-4 (1996), pp.41-50, *Economía Agropecuaria* (Havana: Ministerio de Economía y Planificación, 1997); Victor Figueroa Albelo, 'El nuevo modelo agrario en Cuba bajo los marcos de la reforma económica', in Niurka Pérez Rojas et al. (eds), *UBPC: Desarrollo rural y participación* (Havana: Universidad de La Habana, 1996), pp.1-45, 'Cooperativización del campesinado en Cuba: Evolución y expectativas', in Niurka Pérez Rojas, *Cooperativismo rural* (1998), pp.1-22; Niurka Pérez Rojas & Dayma Echeverría León, 'Políticas diferenciales para la promoción campesina en Cuba: La vinculación del hombre al área en el cultivo del tabaco', in Niurka Pérez Rojas, Emel González Mastrapa & Miriam García Aguiar (eds), *Campesinado y participación social* (Havana: Universidad de La Habana, 1998), pp.113-24; Pérez Rojas et al., *UBPC* (1996), *Cooperativismo rural y participación social* (1998), *Campesinado y participación social* (Havana: Universidad de la Habana, 1998); Juan Valdés Paz, *Procesos agrarios en Cuba, 1959-1995* (Havana: Ciencias Sociales, 1997); Carmen Deere et al., *Güines, Santo Domingo, Majabacoa* (Havana: Ciencias Sociales, 1998); Santiago Rodríguez Castellón, 'Evolución del sector agropecuario en los noventa', in *Balance de la economía cubana a finales de los 90* (Havana: Centro de Estudios de la Economía Cubana, 1999); ; Hans-Jürgen Burchardt, *La última reforma agraria del siglo: La agricultura cubana entre el cambio o estancamiento* (Caracas: Nueva Sociedad, 2000), pp.169-94; Nora Cárdenas Toledo, 'La cooperación agropecuaria como medio de desarrollo', unpublished paper, 22nd Annual Conference of the Latin American Studies Association, Miami (2000).
36 Deborah Bryceson, Cristobal Kay & Jos Mooij (eds), *Disappearing Peasantries? Rural Labour in Africa, Asia and Latin America* (London: Intermediate Technology Publications, 1999).
37 Ricardo Puerta & José Álvarez, *Organization and Performance of Cuban Agriculture at Different Levels of State Intervention* (Gainesville: University of Florida Food and Resource Economics Department, 1993); José Álvarez & Ricardo A. Puerta, 'State Intervention in Cuban Agriculture: Impact on Organization and Performance', *World Development* 22:11 (1994), pp.1663-75.
38 María Antonia Fernández Mayo & James E. Ross, *Cuba: Foreign Agribusiness, Financing & Investment* (Gainesville: University of Florida, 1998). It is unfortunate that tobacco was not included in a study of Cuba's current transition and Florida's

agricultural economy: José Álvarez & William A. Messina, Jr., 'Potential Cuban Agricultural Export Profile under Open Trade Between the US and Cuba', *Agricultural and Human Values*, 10:3 (1993), pp.61-74; José Álvarez, *Cuba's Current Transition and its Implications for Florida's Agricultural Economy* (Gainesville: University of Florida Cooperative Extension Service, Institute of Food and Agricultural Sciences, 1997).

39 Grizel Donéstevez Sánchez et al., 'La finca cooperativa: Una nueva contribución al proceso de socialización de la CPA "La Nueva Cuba"', in Pérez Rojas et al., *UBPC* (1996), pp.165-76; Dayma Echeverría León, 'Relaciones de las UBPC tabacaleras con sus miembros y con la empresa estatal', in Pérez Rojas et al., *Cooperativismo* (1998), pp.87-98; Pérez Rojas & Echeverría León, 'Políticas diferenciales' (1998); Belkis Rojas Hernández, 'Análisis comparativo de las UBPC y las CPA tabacaleras en el municipio de San Luis', trabajo de diploma, Universidad de la Habana, 1999. New courses have been run to train tobacco agronomists, and new texts brought out: see Instituto de Investigaciones para el Cultivo del Tabaco, *Instructivo técnico para el cultivo del tabaco* (Havana: Ministerio de Agricultura, 1998).

40 Jean Stubbs, 'Gender Issues in Contemporary Cuban Tobacco Farming', *World Development*, 5:1 (1987), pp.41-65 – Chapter 4 in the present volume; 'State versus Grass-Roots Strategies for Rural Democratization: Recent Developments among the Cuban peasantry', *Cuban Studies*, 21 (1993), pp.149-68; 'Social Equity, Agrarian Transition and Development in Cuba, 1945-1988', in Christopher Abel & Colin Lewis (eds), *Welfare, Poverty and Development in Latin America* (Basingstoke: Macmillan, 1993), pp.281-95; 'Women and Cuban Smallholder Agriculture in Transition', in Janet H. Momsen (ed.). *Women and Change in the Caribbean* (Kingston: Ian Randle; Bloomington: Indiana University Press; London: James Currey, 1993), pp.219-31 – Chapter 6 in the present volume; Jean Stubbs & Mavis Álvarez, 'Women on the Agenda: The Cooperative Movement in Rural Cuba', in Carmen Diana Deere & Magdalena Leon (eds), *Rural Women and State Policy: Feminist Perspectives on Latin American Agricultural Development* (Boulder: Westview Press, 1987), pp.142-61 – Chapter 3 in the present volume.

41 Fernando Ortiz, *Cuban Counterpoint: Tobacco and Sugar* (Durham & London: Duke University Press, 1995 [1940]). My research has led me to return to the thinking of Fernando Ortiz and develop a new Cuban counterpoint between the offshore and the island Havana cigar: Jean Stubbs, 'Tobacco in the Contrapunteo: Ortiz and the Havana Cigar', in Mauricio A. Font & Alfonso W. Quiroz (eds), *Cuban Counterpoints: The Legacy of Fernando Ortiz* (Lanham: Lexington, 2004) – Chapter 9 in the present volume.

9

Tobacco in the Contrapunteo: Ortiz and the Havana Cigar[*]

THE LAST decade of the twentieth century was one in which the island of Cuba was catapulted once more onto the international cultural arena. In the late 1990s, the *son* stole back the show from *salsa* through the octogenarian Buena Vista Social Club.[1] The revival of the *son* was predated by other Cuban revivals, two of which are of concern here: Fernando Ortiz and the Havana cigar. The Ortiz revival, and its contrapuntal critique of postcoloniality, modernity and postmodernity, was largely literary and anthropological. Tobacco, like sugar, was relegated to a secondary plane. Yet Ortiz, in developing the *Contrapunteo*,[2] dwelt on tobacco, even more than sugar, and especially on the cigar, to construct his counterpoint and concept of transculturation, which have been at the heart of the Ortiz revival.

I look first at the Ortiz revival and the *Contrapunteo*. I then chart the history behind the Havana cigar revival, recentering Cuba's tobacco product par excellence in the *Contrapunteo*. My story is of a new Cuban counterpoint, within tobacco itself – more precisely, between what I have come to call the 'offshore' and the island Havana cigar, involving island and émigré Cubans, for non-US and US markets. It is contrapuntal with the work of Ortiz and my own earlier work.[3] In centrifugal fashion, there is the main story and two complementary essays. The first spans a century (1895-1995) of Florida *Habano* history and is framed by two tobacco embargoes. The second functions as a representational play, which raises key questions for our understanding of Cuba's 'national'

---

[*] Originally published in Mauricio A. Font & Alfonso W. Quiroz (eds), *Cuban Counterpoints: The Legacy of Fernando Ortiz*, Lanham: Lexington, 2004, pp.105-23.

history. I conclude by posing a hypothetical question: What would Ortiz, in true contrapuntal fashion, have made of these latter-day developments?

The Ortiz revival began among the Cuban-American academic community in the United States with the work of Gustavo Pérez-Firmat and Antonio Benítez-Rojo.[4] Both drew on postmodernism, and, while in historical and anthropological context, their analyses were linguistic and literary.

Pérez-Firmat argued that Cuban national identity is translational not foundational, highlighting how the Ortiz metaphor of the *ajiaco*, a stew of Amerindian origin, the culinary emblem of Cuba, was not so much *fusión* (a melting pot fusion) but *cocción* (an incessant simmering concoction). It is not difficult to see how powerful current of thinking this might be for Cuban émigrés, like Pérez-Firmat. It legitimised their *cubanía*, in the Ortiz sense of the term (the spiritual or desired condition, the "conscious, ethical identification" with what is Cuban), as opposed to their *cubanidad* (the civil status, or "generic condition", of being Cuban).

Benítez-Rojo interpreted transculturation through chaos theory, whereby in nature order and disorder are not the antithesis of each other but rather mutually generative phenomena to argue that, within the sociocultural fluidity and the apparent disorder of the Caribbean, seen largely through the prism of Cuba, there emerges an 'island' of order. This repeats itself, in the paradoxical sense it appears in the discourse of chaos, whereby every repetition entails the unpredictable flux of transformative change, transition, and return. He characterised the Caribbean above all as a region of performance, whose coherence is that of *mestizaje*, understood as both cultural and racial mixing, not as a synthesis but as a "concentration of differences," "generalized promiscuity," and the "impossibility of a stable identity."

In his preface to the new English-language edition of *Counterpoint*,[5] Fernando Coronil heralded Ortiz as a thinker ahead of his times; in tune with the fluidity of the contemporary world, fashioning binary opposites as metaphors or tropes, for events, ideas and interpretations that were in constant flux. Coronil applied the postmodernist maxim that each reading of the book opens up a different book. Ortiz, he argued, would have welcomed a perspective that "recognizes its provisionality and inconclusiveness, the contrapuntal play of text against text and of reader against author."[6] He paid tribute to Ortiz "by engaging in this transcultural exchange, as Ortiz's book does, in counterpoint with the historical conditions of its own making."[7] For him, *Contrapunteo* was written in times of international and domestic upheaval, which frame its concerns and help explain its allegorical character. Yet, *Counterpoint* proposed neither unambiguous solutions nor a blueprint for the future.[8] This was precisely its attraction over half a century later, in a much-changed world, "in which globalizing forms of capital accumulation and communication are met both with transnationalizing and reconfigured nationalist responses, have unsettled certainties associated with the belief in modernity."9

One interesting dimension of the revival has been the extent to which Ortiz is interpreted as giving primacy to harmony over conflict, especially that of the races, a highly charged notion in Cuba's crisis 1990s, as discussed in Pérez Sarduy and Stubbs.[10] As we enter the new millennium, this message is a sobering one, wherein what emerges uppermost is a less harmonious and more conflictual and contended terrain of racial paradigms facing Cuba (and the world). Nonetheless, while interpretations of Ortiz's work vary widely, on and off the island, his utopian vision remains a beacon to many, as does his notion of the *Contrapunteo*.

Pérez-Firmat values *Contrapunteo* for its conceptual, "textual" counterpoint. Ortiz, he declares, was not a good "scientist," in that many of his conclusions were based on incomplete data or erroneous assumptions. In the impact of tobacco and sugar on the history of Cuba:

> Ortiz found a subject on which he could exercise his relational talent to best advantage. The contrasts between tobacco and sugar are both determining and representative. They are determining inasmuch as the peculiarities of the two industries have done much to shape the course of Cuban history; and they are representative because the counterpoint of the two products symbolizes many of the defining features of the Cuban character.[11]

The literary precedent, the dispute between Carnival and Lent, sets up an allegorical drama in which *Don Tabaco* and *Doña Azucar* enact a long sequence of literal and figurative contrasts. Not least among them is sugar as a centripetal, centralising force reproducing the relationship between the exploitative metropolis and the exploited colonies, and tobacco as a centrifugal, decentralising force signifying autonomy, freedom and independence. Tobacco is quality and distinctiveness, "the best," as opposed to "the most" for sugar.

Benítez-Rojo begins his discussion of Ortiz and the *Contrapunteo* with a latter-day quote from French historian Fernand Braudel: "Interdisciplinarity is the legal marriage of two neighboring sciences. But as for me, I am for generalized promiscuity."[12] Benítez-Rojo sees this in tune with the new history and multidisciplinary pluralism of today. His preferred reading of *Contrapunteo* is "not only as a socio-economic study of tobacco and sugar, but rather as a text that tries to speak to us about Cuban, and by extension Caribbean, experience."[13] In drawing attention to the structure of *Contrapunteo*, he signals its two parts. The first sets up the binary opposition; the second treats it as a discursive strategy, since tobacco and sugar do not in fact inhabit such extremes. *Contrapunteo* evades the canon of "for or against," "true or false" that characterise the analytical models modernity uses most: "When Ortiz says that 'to study

Cuban history is fundamentally to study the history of sugar and tobacco as the visceral systems of its economy,'14 he is suggesting to us 'another' mode of investigation whose prototype would be that of the *Contrapunteo*."15

Tobacco, Coronil reiterates, functions as the counterpoint to the socio-economic power of the sugar mill accumulated under capitalist production. When Ortiz speaks of tobacco, he discards all allusions to capitalist power and evokes an indigenous, primitive mode of production that has mystery and rite of passage, religion and magic, harmony and sacred dance: "The proud cigar band as against the lowly sack."16 The counter-contrast to capital's growing domination of Cuban society is a utopian solution to the fairy tale, because "there never was any enmity between sugar and tobacco," a fruitful marriage, compromise and fusion, rather than conflict or transformation, "the intermeshed transmigrations of people":

> The more Ortiz tells about tobacco and sugar, the more the reader learns about Cubans, their culture, musicality, humor, uprootedness, baroque manner of refashioning their identities by integrating the fractured meanings of multiple cultures. The two commodities become highly complex metaphorical constructs that represent at once material things and human actors, or, Ortiz "uses the fetish power of commodities as a poetic means to understand the society that produces them" presenting "a counterfetishistic interpretation that challenges essentialist understandings of Cuban history."17

A New Cuban Counterpoint

It has been over thirty years since I embarked on the research for my own tobacco monograph. As a British historian, I was influenced by the British Marxist school of history and by empiricism – the need for empirical evidence. My London-based reading of the English-language *Cuban Counterpoint* was for background documentation. As my research progressed, the text, wonderful though it is, jarred with what I was discovering. Primarily concerned with twentieth-century tobacco history, I began to delve into the nineteenth century in an attempt to understand phenomena that presented themselves as significantly other than the 'accepted truths.' Only now, as I return to Ortiz, having espoused a more relativist, dare I say almost postmodern, approach to Caribbean and Cuban history, do I realise the extent to which those 'truths' derived from Ortiz, when Ortiz himself never posited them as such. When I wrote the book, it seemed fitting to take my opening quote from Ortiz:18

> Out of the agricultural and industrial development of these amazing plants

were to come those economic interests that foreign traders would twist and weave for centuries to form the web of our country's history, the motives of its leaders, and, at one and the same time, the shackles and the support of its people. Tobacco and sugar are the two most important figures in the history of Cuba.[19]

I titled chapter one 'Don Tabaco: 1817-1888', as it covered the period on which the classic Ortiz counterpoint most held sway. In reflection, the rest of the book was structured in such a way as to challenge the Ortiz position, though overtly only once, in chapter 6, 'The Peripheral Mode of Production'. The target of my attack was Ortiz's insistence on the delicate process of tobacco agriculture and industry, which made it less lucrative to foreign capital and therefore more Cuban: tobacco signified freedom and national sovereignty in opposition to the slavery and colonising influence of sugar.

At the time of writing my book, dependency theory had given way to core/periphery thinking, and *Tobacco on the Periphery* seemed an obvious title for what I was observing.[20] I charted what now appears to me an almost linear approach of the inevitability of foreign domination over an industry in decline. That line was broken with the 1959 Revolution, but it has also been fragmented, both before and since, in multiple directions, perhaps none so dramatic as in the 1990s.

When the book manuscript was read for publication, I was struck by one reader's comment: that what we needed was the full story of the 'Havana Cigar Universe'. The reader was Cuba's historian Louis Pérez, and his comment was grounded on the Havana cigar history of Key West and Tampa. Haunted by his comment, I embarked on a larger on- and off-island cigar history, which became compelling with the 1990s cigar revival: behind the 1990s cigar cool lay a swashbuckling, godfather-type history of fires, hurricanes and revolutions, but also a subtext of a more harmonious kind. This led me to rethink received wisdom on Cuba's 'national' history, as well as my own earlier work and that of Ortiz.

If we take the classic Ortiz counterpoint of tobacco symbolising all that sugar was not, in particular nationalism, freedom and independence, the picture I paint is somewhat different. It is one in which the Havana cigar has long been at the heart of political and economic rivalries, linked with foreign and local capital and labour, and with out-migration at key turning points in Cuban history. The synopsis of my story runs as follows. Late nineteenth-century independence and the 1959 Revolution created Cuban communities and economies abroad, centered around products like tobacco. These in turn came to constitute serious competition for, while also being interlocked with, island production. Today, as in the past, parallel production and marketing systems of identical or similar brands, and the cultural and labour practices associated with them, raise issues of identity and reconciliation in the context of both political nationalism and economic pragmatism.

Cuban tobacco was developed with Spanish, German, British and French capital, for European, North American and world markets. It formed part of a nineteenth-century world cigar tobacco economy whose tobacco blends were produced as far afield as Cameroon, Turkey, Java and Sumatra, and whose key retail outlets were London, Amsterdam, Bremen and New York. The backdrop to Cuba's First and Second Wars of Independence from Spain (1868-78 and 1895-98) was an out-migration to the United States, the Caribbean and Central America. Cuban tobacco interests came together in the settler countries, providing a familiar means of livelihood for the displaced migrant community and an economic and political mainstay for the independence struggle at home. Over time, rival economic and political interests built up, with trading and other advantages over a home country in turmoil. US capital investment came fast in Cuban tobacco, swallowing up tracts of Cuban tobacco land and major manufacturing companies. There were 'independents' who held out, but the industry as a whole never regained its former glory. Thirty years later, the 1930s depression and labour unrest culminated a process whereby US-owned manufacturing withdrew from Cuba to the United Stares.

The mass migratory phenomenon reemerged with the 1959 Revolution. Newer Cuban tobacco 'host communities' grew up in the Dominican Republic, Nicaragua, Honduras, Costa Rica and Ecuador, joining older established ones in Jamaica, Mexico and the United States – Florida, New Jersey and Connecticut.[21] Smaller manufacturers, dealers, growers and workers proved to be as astute as larger monopoly capital in finding fertile ground for overseas business. They profited from the post-1959 internal economic upheaval in Cuba that was the product of insurrection, agrarian reform, and nationalisation, plus the tight trade embargo that was the political response of the United States (and for a while the whole area) to the Cuban Revolution, Western European markets became a battleground for disputed Havana cigar brands. At the same time, the Eastern European bloc and key Third World countries emerged as Havana cigar partners.

Thirty years on, a new chapter opened when the demise of the Eastern European socialist bloc in 1989 signaled the end of Cuba's special trade and aid. At the same time, the United States took steps to tighten and extraterritorialise the embargo in the form of the 1991 Torricelli and 1996 Helms-Burton Acts. As external geopolitical realities compounded internal weaknesses, the Cuban revolutionary government devised a structural adjustment strategy, courting non-US trade and investment. The Havana cigar became a key player in the Cuban strategy for the 1990s, as Cuban production plummeted, and battles fought in international courts over market brand names were but the more visible tip of a cigar war. A US cigar revival was gaining momentum, involving the two US cigar giants – Connecticut-based General Cigar and Fort Lauderdale-based Consolidated Cigar – along with émigré Cuban tobacco interests, in the Dominican Republic, followed by Honduras, Nicaragua, Mexico and Connecticut, in all-out competition with Cuba.

As of the late 1980s, the state-owned Cuban tobacco sector blazed the internal adjustment trail with the disaggregation of tobacco land from cooperatives back into private smallholdings. In 1994, part-dollar payments were introduced as an incentives package for the tobacco sector, and a new holding company, Habanos SA, was set up to handle overseas marketing ventures. Both measures followed fast in the wake of two landmark 'credit for tobacco swap' deals struck between the Cuban state tobacco enterprise, Cubatabaco, and its French and Spanish parastatal tobacco counterparts, Societé Nationale des Tabacs (SEITA) and Tabacalera Española SA. A European cigar-marketing deal was struck in Britain with Hunters & Frankau. By 1997, Cuba was investing heavily in tobacco to help meet a world market demand in excess of supply. Heightened US-Europe rivalry in the contemporary world of American cigar politics was mirrored by that within the Havana cigar universe, though with global capital mergers, national policies notwithstanding. A new twist came in 1999 when Tabacalera Española and SEITA formed Altadis (Alianza de Tabacos y Distribución), which bought 50 percent of shares in Habanos SA. Tabacalera Española had earlier that year bought Consolidated Cigar Co. and was thereby heavily involved in both the Havana and clone Havana cigar business.

A Tale of Two Embargoes (1895-1995)

The Havana cigar counterpoint of island and offshore production is graphically illustrated by Florida cigar history, framed by two US embargoes on Cuban tobacco imports: the lesser-known embargo of the early 1890s and the current forty-year embargo dating back to the 1960s. The first helped establish Florida as a major Havana cigar tobacco-growing, manufacturing and retail state. The second culminated in Florida's deagriculturalisation and deindustrialisation in the cigar sector. The century as a whole, from the 1890s to the 1990s, was one of successive boom-bust processes. These were initially in Florida itself, in Gadsden County (1890s-1970s), the Tampa Bay area (1890s-1990s), and Miami (1960s-90s). Then, as growing and manufacturing that had come from Cuba once again moved offshore, they were transplanted to the Caribbean and Central America (Nicaragua, Honduras, Mexico, Dominican Republic, Jamaica, Costa Rica and Ecuador) as part of wider processes of regionalisation and globalisation, controlled mainly from the United States and for the lucrative US market.[22]

If cigar tobacco growing was short-lived around the Tampa area, it was to remain in northern Florida up until the 1970s. Cuban tobacco was first introduced there in 1828, but it was later in the nineteenth century that a hybrid Havana-Sumatra seed, shade-grown, Georgia-Florida wrapper was developed, paving the way for 1880s-90s expansion. Alongside the better-known manufacturing histories of Key West, Tampa and Marti City, today Ocala,[23] is the untold growing history of Gadsden County, with its tobacco towns of Havana, Sumatra, Amsterdam and Quincy, linked to machine manufacturing in Jacksonville and Tampa,[24] the latter becoming the 1950s cigar smoke capital of the world.[25] The corollary to this agricultural development was a state infrastructure of tobacco agricultural research and extension.[26]

In 1960, the United States broke diplomatic ties with Cuba and, in 1962, declared an embargo on tobacco imports from the island. Before then, steps were being taken to prepare for such a contingency. In January 1961, the US Department of Agriculture's Tobacco Research and Marketing Advisory Committee recommended that a study be conducted to determine the effect on the cigar industry and tobacco farmers if supplies of Cuban tobacco were no longer available and also the effect of a change in duty rates. High priority was given to the project, and a study group sought the views of growers, manufacturers and dealers in compiling a seventy-one-page *Special Study on Cigar Tobacco* in November of that year.

According to the report, all except about 0.5 percent of cigars sold in the United States were produced in factories in the United States and Puerto Rico. Cuba was the source of nearly one-fourth of cigar tobacco (31 million pounds out of a total of 135 million pounds). Of the 7 billion cigars sold in a typical recent year, 4.7 billion – some two-thirds – contained Cuban tobacco. Around 670 million were made entirely of Cuban or predominantly Cuban tobacco: the 'clear Havanas' (100 percent) and the 'Havana filler' cigars (100 or near 100 percent Cuban filler but not the binder and wrapper). These predominantly 'Cuban tobacco cigars' used about 45 percent of all Cuban imported tobacco. The other 55 percent was used in 'blended filler' cigars in varying proportions, which varied from 20 to 50 percent Cuban tobacco. If imports were to cease, 'clear Havana' manufacturers saw their problems as "extremely difficult and probably insurmountable."[27]

A February 1962 University of Florida Circular from Cooperative Extension Work in Agriculture and Home Economics to All County Agents and Assistants (9 February 1962) referred to the fact that "Small scale tests have been made in the Quincy area to produce a wrapper similar to that produced in Cuba, through modification of curing techniques." This was also reflected in a May 1962 article in the *Tampa Tribune* titled 'Specialists Eye Growing Cuban Tobacco in Florida'. It reported that Florida agricultural experiment stations at Quincy and Gainesville were experimenting with Cuban seed that had been obtained.[28]

In the 1950s, Tampa was again a source of overseas support for Cuban revolutionary organisations (the 26th of July movement was a case in point), and the Havana cigar industry was still the largest single employer in the city, with thousands working in cigar manufacturing and related fields (box making, label printing, etc.). This changed dramatically as the industry relocated. In May 1962, the *Tampa Tribune* ran articles titled 'Cigar Firms Hope for Survival but Workers Despair-Manufacturers Feel They Have Chance to Hold onto Market; Employees See No Place to Turn' and 'Future Bleak for Jobless Unwanted Ex-Cigar Workers'.[29] More than six thousand cigar makers lost their jobs, and, by 1971, the cigar industry was disappearing as a factor in the economic life of Tampa Bay. A few small *chinchales* had opened in the intervening years, but most of these were for the tourists and not considered an integral part of the industry. Villazón was more typical, having opened two factories in Honduras for the manufacture of handmade Havanas: Hoyo de Monterrey and Punch. The Armenia Avenue factory stayed in West Tampa, but to produce only machine-made cigars. By the 1980s, it was increasingly the newly developed homogenised leaf that was being used, driving yet another nail in the coffin of the quality handmade cigar and craft cigar maker.[30]

The outcome was that, as recorded in the 1992 US census, there were only 27 US cigar companies, making primarily machine-made cigars with a total employment of 2,600. By the late 1990s, companies fell into two broad categories. The first comprised the two major US players. One was Consolidated Cigar, which in the 1970s acquired rights to the Cuban brands Montecristo and H. Upmann. The other was General Cigar, which purchased Villazón in 1996, and in 1998 was with Cubatabaco in the courtroom over Cohíba cigars and in precedent-setting talks in Mexico City. The second category comprised smaller Tampa- and Miami-based Cuban American and American companies, such as the Fuente-Oliva-Newman consortium in Tampa and Padrón in Miami.[31] All were interlocked with production in the Dominican Republic, Honduras, Nicaragua, Jamaica, Mexico, Ecuador and Costa Rica.

Unsurprisingly, the more recent company is easier to piece together than labour history. There is no wealth of labour studies available for the earlier period.[32] Only now is a Cuban American labour history emerging for the post-1959 period,[33] and thus far it does include tobacco. Yet, consider the following from the 1 May 1977 *Miami Herald:*

> Experienced 'tabaqueros' roll lots of cigars daily for small shops. . . . Long Hours and Small Pay: Tobacco Business Keeps Rolling – Teodoro Santana learned as boy of 15 in Jovellanos, then Havana, and for the past seven years at Padrón, West Flagler. . . . Most of the tabaqueros working in dozens of small cigar shops sprinkled throughout Little Havana, and in four or five shops that produce several million cigars a year, like Santana, are products

of a time and place foreign to younger Cubans with American ideas of pay and work conditions. "It's slave-like work, and the young people don't want to do it," semi-retired Santana said. "Just as the rollers are of an era past, so are their employers, many of whom began amassing their knowledge by following their fathers through the fields in Cuba. . . . The rollers are all dying off," said Pérez-Carillo Sr. Many companies, he said, "already import many of the cigars they sell from Latin American countries, where poor people are still willing to labor all day long for a pittance."

Florida's minimum wage policy was often invoked by companies to explain why they had to go offshore. But this was lucrative business, transformed through technology, experimentation, litigation and labour practices, to the extent that much of today's cigar rolling bears little resemblance to that of a century ago.

What is striking about the offshore cigar sector is a pragmatism as regards the end of the embargo. The 1990s cigar hype was such that neither island nor offshore production could meet demand, though demand peaked in the late 1990s, and the bubble may soon burst. In the event of any normalisation of US-Cuba relations, the Florida-Havana cigar best-case scenario is to be able to import the island's leaf while limiting the import of island-manufactured cigars, but in all probability this would be resisted by Cuba and non-US Havana cigar importers, especially those in Europe. Arguably, some US/non-US importers are now so interlocked that they are already able to sidestep the embargo.

¿Habano o no?

The cigar advertisements featured in the 1992-founded New York glossy *Cigar Aficionado* were key to the 1990s US cigar boom. They ranged from a suggestive Carmen rolling cigars on her thighs to "Agnes, have you seen my Don Diegos? A word of warning, don't let your Don Diegos out of your sight," with Agnes in pre-Lewinsky-type image.[34] Don Diegos, handmade in the Dominican Republic for Consolidated Cigar, were now owned by Tabacalera Española. Some were more explicit: "The only thing sexier than sex is a cigar. . . . On one end, the fire. On the other, a Lady. In between, the ultimate pleasure. Let your senses take over, enjoy La Diva Cigars." La Diva was being made in the Dominican Republic with a Connecticut wrapper. Or "You never forget the first time," accompanied Don Sixta cigars, made in the Cuban tradition of generations of the Plascencia family.[35]

In the late 1990s, Tabacalera de García, a subsidiary of the Fort Lauderdale Consolidated Cigar, ran a two-page ad for Montecristo La Corona: "Born in Cuba. Perfected in the Dominican Republic."[36] Theirs was but one in an aggressive marketing campaign meant to bolster the real quality *Habanos* as those made outside Cuba. By the 1990s, counterfeit cigars had become big business, as brand battles in trade disputes centered around the leaf and the Havana seed that has been taken, licitly and illicitly, for growing trials.[37] There were also two epicenters of Havana seed leaf production: the Partido/Vuelta Abajo region of western Pinar del Río and the central Vuelta Arriba in Cuba, and the central Cibao in the Dominican Republic. There were also growing areas in Mexico, Nicaragua, Honduras, Ecuador and Brazil, replacing the earlier Florida-Georgia area in the United States, though Connecticut remained.

The Dominican Republic was not historically considered a producer of quality cigar leaf. In 1962, however, an émigré Cuban tobacco agronomist, Napoleón Padilla, who was part of the Washington reconstruction plan after the fall of Trujillo, helped found the Instituto del Tabaco in Santiago de los Caballeros in the Cibao.[38] Thirty years later, when Cuba was facing the depths of its post-1989 crisis and dislocation, Cuban-American family businesses such as the Fuentes saw long years of hard investment and effort in the Cibao bear quality Havana seed leaf and cigars, and that is what their advertising drew on: "Chateau de la Fuente: Birthplace of a Dream"; "Never Before Was There Such a Cigar. . . . The Most Sought After Cigar on Earth" (October 1999). With close ties to Tampa (Newman) and Ecuador (Oliva),[39] their family business was producing cigars in the early 1990s that arguably surpassed the quality of many from Havana, and it continues to come close to this day.

Cigar advertising and cigar labels constitute a telling iconography.[40] The 1990s US cigar imagery was a far cry from that of the nineteenth century. One only has to see the finely embossed romantic imagery of labels of old: Royal Palm-lined plantations where the leaf was grown and, for the London market, House of Lords or Buckingham Palace, equalled almost by the size and elegance of palatial buildings in Havana, such as that of Aldama, where the cigars were made. There was classical romance, as in Romeo y Julieta, and humour as in Punch, who was surrounded by depictions of white, male cigar workers, all rather dapper young Hispanics, at a time when the workforce included children, convicts, soldiers, enslaved Africans and indentured Chinese immigrants. More politically, in 1897, a year before the end of Cuba's Second War of Independence, one label celebrated three of Cuba's great generals in the war: Calixto García, Máximo Gómez and Antonio Maceo. Idyllic images were painted of Cuba's relationship with the neighbouring United States, far removed from the reality of today, a century later, after forty years of hostilities, broken diplomatic relations and embargo. Perhaps more in tune with history, an omen of what was to come, the American eagle could also be seen 'embracing' the Cuban flag.'

Key West, the southernmost of the Florida Keys, located only ninety miles from Cuba, was the first port of call for émigré manufacturers and workers to develop a Cuban cigar industry, and was also home to Cuban émigré nationalist and labour unrest.[41] In the 1890s, Spanish manufacturers undercut national and class strife by moving to Tampa, whose town patricians were working aggressively to attract the industry. West Tampa and Ybor City became resplendent,[42] as symbolised by Ybor City's Cuban Club from its early twentieth-century heyday.[43] Cuban traditions continued, such as that of the reader in the factories, paid by the workers to read to them while they laboured; news in the morning, novels in the afternoon.[44] By 1930, however, the industry was headed for decline due to the Depression, mechanisation, and relocation. The advent of the cigar machine cemented a process of feminisation and deskilling of mechanised cigar rolling, which had started with the introduction of the *bonches,* or bunching molds, in hand rolling.[45] The big losers in the Tampa story were the Afro-Cubans, who gradually fell foul of US South-style segregation, driving a wedge into the community that had fought together on a nationalist and worker ticket.[46] In the 1960s, local historians rescued Ybor City from developers and opened a museum, complete with cigar makers' cottages, but the commercialised attraction was almost entirely Hispanic in its re-creation of the past.[47] Only a lowly building on the outskirts of the renovated center boasted a plaque to the Martí-Maceo Society, founded in 1904 by Afro-Cubans holding on to the dream of a united Cuba.[48]

José Martí visited the Ybor factory in 1892 to fund-raise for his newly created Cuban Revolutionary Party.[49] Descendants of Cubans proudly recall how their worker forebears donated their day's wages to the cause for independence. Martí also went to Jamaica to raise support among the Cuban émigré community of tobacco manufacturers, workers and growers, visiting Temple Hall Cuban tobacco-growing colony not far from Kingston, the capital.[50] Jamaica was the refuge for a number of Cuba's more famous independence leaders, including Maceo.

The 1990s cigar revival included the brand Temple Hall Estates, whose label bears the founding date of 1876, during Cuba's first War of Independence, from 1868 to 1878, when the first Cubans founded the Jamaican cigar economy. There was also Macanudo, among the best Jamaican cigars, made under the supervision of Benjamín Menéndez,[51] a master cigar maker who also once made Partagás. In the late nineteenth century, there was Partagás in Havana and Partagás in Key West. In Havana at the time of the Revolution, Partagás was made by Cifuentes, who then left Cuba in 1960. A photo of Cifuentes Jr., much used in 1990s ads, claimed "Fidel Castro thought I had left with only the shirt on his back. But my secrets were locked in my heart." Cifuentes took his tobacco knowledge to the General Cigar Company in Jamaica and the Dominican Republic, along with some clever marketing of Partagás, "the cigar that knew Cuba when: Made in the Dominican Republic under the supervision of Ramón Cifuentes, the same master cigar-maker who made those legendary cigars over 30 years ago in Cuba" (Summer 1994). Behind Macanudo and Partagás was Ed Cullman and his Cullbro Tobacco,[52] the parent company of General Cigar and a leading producer of the Connecticut wrapper. Cifuentes and Menéndez joined the company in the early 1960s, and in the 1970s, the company launched Partagás, claiming the brand name was theirs.

Fidel Castro gave up smoking in the early 1980s, in a drive to encourage the smoking Cuban population to smoke less on health grounds, but in the early days of the Revolution he could always be seen smoking a cigar. So could Che Guevara who, while Argentine, developed a taste for Cuban cigars. Castro was the target of several CIA assassination attempts, one of which was to have him smoke an exploding cigar, and another to make him look foolish by injecting substances into the cigar that would cause his beard to fall out, or LSD, which would make him speak gibberish. So serious were these attempts that an elegant Miramar mansion became a top-security cigar factory, whose workforce was composed of the women of his male security guards. That was the origin of the now famous Cohíba cigar, later marketed commercially, a story much retold in the cigar press. The present manager of the Cohíba factory, Emilia Tamayo, is one of four women cigar factory managers today. Cohíba is now big outside Cuba, too: made in the Dominican Republic and marketed in the United States by Cullbro, who registered Cohíba in the United States before the Cubans had gone commercial with the brand.

No post-1959 émigré Cuban story would be complete without Miami. However, Miami was not a major cigar player. Initially, small concerns catered to little more than the local Cuban émigré community. One exception was Padrón, who, out of his small Miami business, went on to grow tobacco in Nicaragua. The Nicaraguan economy is a post-1963 phenomenon, thanks to a generous offer made to émigré Cubans by Anastasio Somoza on land around northern Estelí. After the 1979 Sandinista Revolution, the area became a battlefield for the contras, and much of the tobacco moved north, to southern Honduras, around Danlí. Padrón and son, however, are among the few still there. A recent ad campaign of theirs ran, "Seeds of Survival. Despite wars in Nicaragua and bombings in Miami."[53] Padrón took a beating for going public against the embargo and for normalisation of US-Cuba relations.

The more the cigar revival gained in momentum, and the more island Cuba featured in this, the more the old-time Miami Cuban American Lobby was prone to become incensed with *Cigar Aficionado*. The issue carrying editor Marvin Shanken's cover feature interview with "el jefe" Fidel Castro[54] – an issue that also covered counterfeit cigars – so enraged parts of the Cuban community that it was de facto barred from sale in Miami. Five years later, an issue was given over largely to Cuba, including interviews with key Cuban figures and a feature on Cuba's cigar summit, as well as general reportage. Its cover highlighted precisely what the lobby did not want: an end to the embargo and the opening up of travel to Cuba.[55] To this, the response of the Miami-based Cuban American National Foundation came in the form of a page ad reading, "Lift the smoke screen, not the embargo."[56] It came in an issue that also carried a debate about Cuba generated around the time of John F. Kennedy's presidency.

By the late 1990s, *Cigar Aficionado* circulation had risen to half a million, with sell-out issues whose glossy covers and inside pages featured cigar-smoking stars (Arnold Schwarzenegger, Tom Selleck, Alfred Hitchcock, Groucho Marx, Charlie Chaplin, Jack Nicholson, Bill Cosby, Whoopi Goldberg, Demi Moore, Madonna, Janet Jones, Susan Lucci, to name but a few); sportsmen, including a very elegantly attired El Duque, one of Cuba's leading baseball players who had recently crossed over to the United States;[57] and politicians such as Britain's Winston Churchill, who has *Habanos* named after him.[58] The theme of cigar-smoking famous people had, of course, been cleverly taken up earlier by the London-based Cuban writer Guillermo Cabrera Infante[59] and in other works: one amusing caption ran, "The psychoanalyst Jacques Lacan, famous for the meanderings of his thought, smoked only twisted cigars of the *culebras* type."[60]

Cigar World is London's less big-time glossy answer to *Cigar Aficionado*, and it is edited by London-based Hunters & Frankau's Simon Chase. The caption to a photo of Chase at the Avelina plantation in Cuba ran as follows: "Any resemblance between this photo and pictures of the Fuente family in their plantations is entirely intentional."[61] The US market is for the Fuentes' H. Upmann, with some clever advertising: "When a cigar can make you forget about Havana . . . that's One-Upmannship";[62] and "Ever wonder what those cigar makers did after leaving Cuba? One upmannship?"[63] Hunters & Frankau, who once owned H. Upmann in Havana, and in 1994 celebrated with the Cubans its 150th anniversary,[64] continued to handle its London market. Chase is Britain's man in Havana and has been one of the masterminds behind the now yearly *Habano* Festival, which in 1999 raised $750,000 in a cigar auction for the Cuban health system. One of the items auctioned was a Vegas Robaina humidor. Alejandro Robaina is one of the Pinar del Río smallholders to have benefited from the 1990s tobacco recuperation programme, with an incentive package including part-dollar payments. In 1999, he was declared *Habano* man of the year for the quality of his leaf, which included the successful new strain Habana 2000,[65] and Vegas Robaina was a new brand of *Habanos* named after the tobacco from this family farm.[66]

A New Counterpoint?

What would Don Fernando have made of all this? The reader will by now have recognised how the new Cuban counterpoint within my on- and off-island cigar story resonates with Ortiz revisited, whether Pérez-Firmat's translational incessant *cocción*, Benítez-Rojo's transformative chaos and representational promiscuity, or Coronil's provisionality and counterfetishism of text. And so I set myself up as Doña Juana in counterpoint with Don Fernando. I haven't gone into the business, I don't smoke, but my thirty-year addiction to researching Havana cigar history and the 1990s Havana cigar revival put me on the fashion catwalk, and state of the art technology enabled me to create my own virtual cigar world with a cigar band in my very own image. In my story, there are no metanarratives, no cut-and-dried extremes, no unambiguous solutions or blueprints for the future; rather, within globalising capital, there is a transnationalising and reconfigured response of the 'proud cigar brand', a fluidity, a provisionality, an inconclusive *cubanía* that carries within it the possibility of a certain harmony rising against injustice. Robaina travels the world with his tobacco, just as Buena Vista's Compay Segundo, an inveterate smoker of *Habanos*, plays London, New York and Havana's *Habano* Festival 2000 Gala Dinner. The economics of transnational mergers and the slick advertising images, plus the culture associated with enjoying cigars (as with music, dance, and sport), might just harmonise erstwhile hostile politics. I take pleasure in thinking Don Fernando would have been drawn to such a latter-day allegory of that Cuban commodity par excellence, the Havana cigar.

Notes

1. A companion article linking offshore developments with the 1990s tobacco reforms can be found in Jean Stubbs, 'Turning Over a New Leaf? The Havana Cigar Revisited', *New West Indian Guide*, 74:3 & 4 (2000), p.4 – Chapter 8 in the present volume.
2. Fernando Ortiz, *Cuban Counterpoint: Tobacco and Sugar*, Durham and London: Duke University Press, 1995 [1940].
3. Jean Stubbs, *Tobacco on the Periphery* (London: Amaurea Press, 2023 [1985]), pp.235-55.
4. Gustavo Pérez-Firmat, *The Cuban Condition: Translation and Identity in Cuban Literature* (Cambridge: Cambridge University Press, 1989); Antonio Benítez-Rojo, *The Repeating Island: The Caribbean and the Postmodern Perspective* (Durham: Duke University Press, 1992).
5. Ortiz, *Cuban Counterpoint* (1995 [1940]), p.xi.
6. Ibid.
7. Ibid.
8. Coronil in Ortiz, *Cuban Counterpoint* (1995 [1940]), pp.xi-xii.
9. Coronil in Ortiz, *Cuban Counterpoint* (1995 [1940]), p.xii.
10. Pedro Pérez Sarduy & Jean Stubbs (eds), *Afro-Cuban Voices: On Race and Identity in Contemporary Cuba* (Gainesville: University Press of Florida, 2000). See also Pérez Sarduy & Stubbs, *AFROCUBA: An Anthology of Cuban Writing on Race, Politics and Culture* (Melbourne: Ocean Press/Latin America Bureau/Center for Cuban Studies, 1993).
11. Pérez-Firmat, *The Cuban Condition* (1989), p.47.

12 The quote is taken from Francis Ewald & Jean-Jacques Brochler, 'Una vie pour l'histoire', *Magazine Littéraire* 212 (1984), p.22.
13 Benítez-Rojo, *The Repeating Island* (1992), p.152.
14 Ortiz, *Cuban Counterpoint* (1995 [1940]), p.13. Benítez-Rojo takes this and subsequent quotes from the Caracas edition: Ortiz, *Contrapunteo Cubano del tabaco y el azúcar* (Caracas: Biblioteca Ayacucho, 1978).
15 Benítez-Rojo, *The Repeating Island* (1992), p.158.
16 Coronil in Ortiz, *Cuban Counterpoint* (1995 [1940]), p.xxi; Ortiz, *Cuban Counterpoint* (1995 [1940]), p.7; Espino Marrero, *Cuban Cigar Tobacco: Why Cuban Cigars are the World's Best* (Neptune City: TFH Publications, 1996).
17 Coronil in Ortiz, *Cuban Counterpoint* (1995 [1940]), p.xxvii.
18 Stubbs, 'Turning over a New Leaf?' (2000), p.v.
19 Ortiz, *Cuban Counterpoint* (1995 [1940]), p.4.
20 Interestingly, a later general text on tobacco in history took as its subtitle 'The Cultures of Dependence'. Jordan Goodman, *Tobacco in History: The Cultures of Dependence* (London: Routledge, 1993). For tobacco history, see also V. G. Kiernan, *Tobacco: A History* (London: Hutchinson Radius, 1991).
21 We know relatively little about these histories. For Jamaica, see Jean Stubbs, 'Political Idealism and Commodity Production: Cuban Tobacco in Jamaica, 1870-1930', *Cuban Studies*, 25 (1995), pp.51-81 – Chapter 7 in the present volume. For Mexico, see José González Sierra, *Monopolio del humano: elementos de la historia del tabaco en México y algunos conflictos de tabaqueros veracruzanos: 1915-1930* (Xalapa, Mexico: Veracruz University, 1987). The United States will be discussed later.
22 *The Tobacco Leaf* (4 August 1897); press cuttings taken from the Tony Pizzo Collection, University of South Florida, Tampa; *The Tobacco Leaf* (18 May 1898); M. F. Hetherington, *History of Polk County, Florida* (Chulmota: Mickler House Publishers, 1971), p.79.
23 Michael Bure & Mary Ellen Moore, *Tampa: Yesterday & Tomorrow* (Tampa: Mishler King, 1981); A. Stuart Campbell, *The Cigar Industry of Tampa, Florida* (Tampa: University of Tampa, 1939); Karl H. Grismer *Tampa: A History of the City of Tampa and the Tampa Bay Region of Florida* (St Petersburg: St Petersburg Printing, 1950); Charles F. Harner, *A Pictorial History of Ybor City* (Tampa: Trend Publications, 1975); Glenn L. Westfall, *Don Vicente Martínez Ybor: the Man and His Empire: Development of the Clear Havana Industry in Cuba and Florida in the Nineteenth Century* (New York: Garland, 1987), *Key West: Cigar City USA* (Key West: Historic Key West Preservation Board, 1984).
24 Swisher and Havana Tampa.
25 Hampton Dunn, *Yesterday's Tallahassee* (Miami: E A Seeman, 1974); Armando Méndez, *Ciudad de Cigars: West Tampa* (Tampa: Florida Historical Society, 1994).
26 The University of Florida, Gainesville, became the state agricultural flagship college. Florida Agricultural Experiment Station booklets held at University of Florida range from 1892 to 1972 and covered tobacco culture, strains, and disease.
27 US Department of Agriculture, *1961 Special Study on Cigar Tobacco*, 2. I am indebted to colleagues at the University of Florida for facilitating access to departmental agricultural holdings that contain a copy of the report.
28 *Tampa Tribune* (27 May 1962).
29 Ibid.
30 *Tampa Tribune-Times* (4 April 1982).
31 The broader émigré cigar success story is reflected in James S. Olsen & Judith E. Olsen, *Cuban Americans: From Trauma to Triumph* (New York: Twane; London: Prentice Hall International, 1995). It is, however, a story yet to be pieced together in its entirety. I was surprised to find scant reference to cigar or tobacco in the University of Miami Special Cuba Collection on the post-1959 period. The collection is, however, a unique and invaluable source of press clippings and ephemera for the period as a whole.

32　Nancy A. Hewitt, 'Varieties of Voluntarism: Class, Ethnicity, and Women's Activism in Tampa', in Louise Tilly & Patricia Gurin (eds), *Women, Politics, and Change* (New York: Russell Sage Foundation, 1990), pp.63-86, '"The Voice of Virile Labor": Labor Militancy, Community Solidarity, and Gender Identity among Tampa's Latin Workers, 1880-1921', in Ava Baron (ed.), *Work Engendered: Toward a New History of American Labor* (Ithaca: Cornell University Press, 1991), pp.142-67; Durward Long, 'La Resistencia: Tampa's Immigrant Labor Union', *Labor History* 6:3 (1965), pp.193-213, 'The Historical Beginnings of Ybor City and Modern Tampa', *Florida Historical Quarterly* 45:1 (1966), pp.31-44, 'The Open-Closed Shop Battle in Tampa's Cigar Industry, 1919-21', *Florida Historical Quarterly* 47:2 (1968), pp.101-21, 'Labor Relations in the Tampa Cigar Industry, 1885-1911', *Labor History* 12:4 (1971), pp.551-9, 'The Making of Modern Tampa: A City in the New South', *Florida Historical Quarterly* 49:4 (1971), pp.333-45; Robert Ingalls, *Urban Vigilantes in the New South: Tampa, 1882-1936* (Knoxville: University of Tennessee Press, 1988); Gary Mormino & George E. Pozetta, '"The Reader Lights the Candle": Cuban and Florida Cigar Workers' Oral Tradition', *Labor's Heritage* (Spring 1993); Louis A. Pérez, Jr., 'Reminiscences of a *Lector.* Cuban Cigar Makers in Tampa', *Florida Historical Quarterly* 53:4 (1975), pp.443-9, 'Cubans in Tampa: From Exiles to Immigrants, 1892-1901', *Florida Historical Quarterly* 47:2 (1978); Gerald E. Poyo, 'Key West and the Cuban Ten Years War', *Florida Historical Quarterly*, 57:3 (1979), pp.289-307, 'The Anarchist Challenge to the Cuban Independence Movement, 1885-1890', *Cuban Studies/Estudios Cubanos* 15:1 (1986), pp.29-42, 'Evolution of Cuban Separatist Thought in the Emigré communities of the United States, 1848-1895', *Hispanic American Historical Review* 66:3 (1986), pp.485-507, *With All and for the Good of All* (1989).

33　Louise Lamphere, Alex Stephick & Guillermo Grenier, *Newcomers in the Workplace: Immigrants and the Restructuring of the US Economy* (Philadelphia: Temple University Press, 1994).

34　*Cigar Aficionado* (Autumn 1993).

35　*Cigar Aficionado* (August 1997).

36　*Cigar Aficionado* (October 1999).

37　The brand battle was mirrored by the even more aggressive marketing of Bacardí against the island's Havana Club rum, winning in US courts the right to sell their own identically named Havana Club brand. Significantly, Bacardí ads pandered to a lifestyle that went hand in hand with the new trendy cigars.

38　Napoleón S. Padilla, *Memorias de un cubano sin importancia* (Hialeah: A C Graphics, 1988), *Cultivo del tabaco negro: sol y tapado* (Santo Domingo: Instituto del Tabaco de la República Dominicana, 1982).

39　The Newmans had long ago bought the Cuban cigar Cuesta Rey. A lengthy interview with Stanley Newman can be found in *Cigar Aficionado* (August 1997). Oliva was featured in *Cigar Aficionado* (Spring 1993).

40　For an earlier treatise on cigar iconography, especially with reference to film, see Guillermo Cabrera Infante, *Holy Smoke* (London: Faber & Faber, 1985). In the 1990s, a spate of coffee table and museum-piece books were brought out on the Havana cigar: Eric Deschodt & Philippe Morane, *The Cigar* (Cologne: Konemann Verlagsgesellschaft, 1998); Eumelio Espino Marrero, *Cuban Cigar Tobacco: Why Cuban Cigars Are the World's Best* (Neptune City: T.F.H. Publications 1996); Enzo A. Infante Urivazo, *Havana Cigars 1817-1960* (Neptune City: T.F.H. Publications, 1997); Narciso Menocal, *The Tobacco Industry in Cuba and Florida: Its Golden Age in Lithography and Architecture* (Coral Gables: Cuban National Heritage, 1995); Antonio Núñez Jiménez, *The Journey of the Havana Cigar* (Neptune City: ,T. F. H. Publications 1998); Iain Scarlet, *A Puff of Smoke* (London: Robert Lewis, n.d.). For the history of Florida cigar lithography, see Narciso Menocal, *Cuban Cigar Labels: The Tobacco Industry in Cuba and Florida: Its Golden Age in Lithography and Architecture* (Coral Gables: Cuban National Heritage, 1995).

41 Poyo, 'Key West and the Cuban Ten Years War' (1979); Westfall, *Key West* (1984).
42 Bure & Moore, *Tampa* (1981); Campbell, *The Cigar Industry* (1939); Grismer, *Tampa* (1950); Harner, *A Pictorial History* (1975); Westfall, *Don Vicente Martínez Ybor* (1987).
43 This was reflected in Tampa publications: *Tampa, Florida's Greatest City, Tampa's Hillsborough County, 1918-19*.
44 Mormino & Pozetta, 'The Reader Lights the Candle' (1993); Pérez, 'Reminiscences of a Lector' (1975). The reader was found internationally among cigar workers. For Puerto Rico, see Angel Quintero Rivera, 'Socialist and Cigarmaker: Artisan's Proletarianization in the Making of the Puerto Rican Working Class', *Latin American Perspectives* 10:2 (1983), pp.19-38. The fortunes of the Puerto Rican cigar industry were almost inverse to those of Cuba in timing, and generated their own struggles. See Juan José Baldrich, *Los que sembraron la no siembra: Los cosecheros de tabaco puertoriqueños frente a la corporaciones tabacaleras, 1920-1934* (Río Piedras: Huracán, 1988).
45 Hewitt, 'Voice of Virile Labor' (1991), 'Varieties of Voluntarism' (1990).
46 Susan Greenbaum, 'Afro-Cubans in Exile: Tampa, Florida, 1886-1984', *Cuban Studies* 15:1 (1985); Winston James, *Holding Aloft the Banner of Ethiopia: Caribbean Radicalism in Early Twentieth-Century America* (London: Verso, 1998); Nancy Raquel Mirabal, 'Telling Silences and Making Community: Afro-Cubans in Ybor City and Tampa, 1899-1915', in Lisa Brock & Digna Castañeda Fuentes (eds), *Between Race and Empire: Afro-Americans and Cubans before the Cuban Revolution* (Philadelphia: Temple University Press, 1998).
47 This is reflected in *Florida's Cuban Heritage Trail/Herencia cubana en la Florida* (Tallahassee: Florida Department of State, n.d.).
48 We have little reference to Afro-Cubans in the earlier Key West period. It is interesting to note, however, that Mario Sánchez's paintings *'The Reader and the Cigar Makers'* and *'Manungo's Diablito Dancers'* depict Afro-Cubans. See Kathryn Hall Proby, *Mario Sánchez: Painter of Key West Memories* (Key West: Southernmost Press, 1981).
49 Poyo, *With All and for the Good of All* (1989), 'Evolution of Cuban Separatist Thought' (1986), 'The Anarchist Challenge' (1986); Westfall, *Don Vicente Martínez Ybor* (1987).
50 Stubbs, 'Political Idealism' (1995).
51 Behind Menéndez was an earlier history of Canary Islander migration into tobacco in Cuba.
52 Cullman and Cullbro were featured in *Cigar Aficionado* (Spring 1993 & Autumn 1994).
53 *Cigar Aficionado* (August 1997).
54 *Cigar Aficionado* (Summer 1994).
55 *Cigar Aficionado* (June 1999).
56 *Cigar Aficionado* (October 1999).
57 *Cigar Aficionado* (April 1999).
58 *Cigar Aficionado* (Autumn 1993).
59 Cabrera Infante took up this theme in 1985.
60 Deschodt & Morane, *The Cigar* (1998), p.161.
61 *Cigar World* (Winter 1998/1999).
62 *Cigar Aficionado* (Spring 1993).
63 *Cigar Aficionado* (Summer 1994).
64 *Cigar World* (Winter 1994/1995).
65 Habana 2000, along with its earlier strain Habana '92, were both featured in Espino Marrero, *Cuban Cigar Tobacco* (1996). An earlier work on tobacco agronomy is Eumelio Espino Marrero & Torrecilla Guerra, *El tabaco cubano: recursos fitogenéticos* (Madrid: Instituto Cubano del Libro, Editorial Científico-Técnica, 1999).
66 *Cigar World 2000* (Winter 1999/2000).

10

HAVANA CIGARS AND THE WEST'S IMAGINATION[*]

> 'Smoking a Havana is universally recognised as a supreme
> form of pleasurable indulgence . . .'[1]

IN 1997, at the height of the 1990s cigar hype, the US magazine *Newsweek* ran two cigar features entitled 'Blowing Smoke' and 'Cool Fools'.[2] The latter addressed the Gen X market for hip imagery, designer clothes, drinks, coffee and cigars. The former read:

> Cigars are smelly, expensive, and bad for you. They're also the hottest things going, as celebs, models and just plain folks-with-smokes fire up the trend. How could this happen? . . . You'd never guess it, but there are actually a few Americans left who've never smoked a cigar. Maybe you're even one of them.[3]

Well, I'm not an American, but I was one who had never smoked a cigar, until, that is, January 2001 in Cuba, down on the farm, in Vuelta Abajo, a mecca for any cigar connoisseur. Harvest in full swing, octogenarian grower Alejandro Robaina – who now has his own Vegas Robaina cigars and was voted Havana Cigar Man of the Year[4] – offered me a cigar rolled with his leaf. As we talked and rocked on his veranda, he autographed another in silver for me – the cigar historian – to keep. Later I purchased a metal canister (my own

---

[*] Originally published in Sander L. Gilman & Zhou Xun (eds), *Smoke: A Global History of Smoking* (London: Reaktion Books, 2004), pp.134-9.

special humidor) from the *Casa del Habano* (Havana cigar shop) adjacent to the cigar factory in the neighbouring town of Pinar del Río, and now display it proudly on the bookshelf in my study at home. I haven't smoked since, but my addiction to researching and writing about Cuban tobacco continues unabated.

The supreme cigar experience is a visit to Cuba in January or February, to the green rolling fields of sun-grown tobacco or the sea of white cheesecloth over shade-grown tobacco in Vuelta Abajo. Havana, however, is the city of the cigar, bringing in special cigar-lover trips and coveted revenue from tourists avid to buy at a fraction of the cost abroad. The 1990s cigar hype brought the paradox of quantity versus quality, since cigar tobacco was grown in less well-suited areas; young workers were crash-trained; and quality export brands – Cohíba Siglo III, Hoyo de Monterrey Double Corona, Montecristo A, Partagás, Ramón Allones Gigantes or the new Trinidad and Cuaba – were made in non-export factories outside Havana. This has now abated, and connoisseurs and neophtyes alike whiff the past at the old Partagás factory by the Capitol building in Havana or the recently refurbished cigar hotel, Conde de Villanueva Hostal del Habano, which are caught up in what one recently retired Cuban cigar expert has described as belonging to:

> the world of MAGICAL REALISM, as defined by the great Cuban and universal writer Alejo Carpentier to speak of Latin American cultures in which the Havana cigar is inscribed. The REALISM is that of the agricultural and industrial workers who fashion the leaf of Vuelta Abajo, Partido and other parts of Cuba in combination with the climate, winds and sun characteristic of these, the island's tobacco regions. . . . The MAGICAL is in its hedonism, its sublime gift to the smoker's palate. . . .[5]

Havana Magic

The Cubans know cigars. When they spin a long yarn, they are said to be *contando la historia del tabaco en dos tomos*, telling the two-volume story of tobacco. Tobacco is clearly that important to the island and its people, and, of all its tobacco products, the cigar has reached mythical proportions: long considered the best in the world, and long imitated elsewhere.

The early cigar belonged to the Amerindians, but, from the conquest of Columbus in 1492, the story became one of swashbuckling piracy, contraband and uprisings against Spanish colonial monopoly.

Highly lucrative, the cigar was prey to German, British, French and North American capital, part of a nineteenth- and twentieth-century world cigar tobacco economy whose tobacco blends were produced as far afield as Cameroon, Turkey, Java and Sumatra, and whose main markets were London,

Amsterdam, Bremen and New York. The cigar was also at the heart of major political upheavals, exile communities and rival economies, from 1868 with the outbreak of Cuba's first War of Independence with Spain, through the Cuban Revolution of 1959 and the 1990s cigar hype.

The world mystique of the Havana cigar started more than five centuries ago, when Spanish envoys chronicled men with firebrands in their hands Columbus, his eyes set on gold, attached no importance to this, although the indigenous people clearly did, calling it *tabacco*. The Cuban ethnographer Fernando Ortiz[6] would later delight in tobacco as the Indian's inseparable companion, part of mythology, religion, magic, medicine, ceremonies, collective stimulation, public and private customs, as well as politics and wars. For slaves from Africa transported to Cuba as human cargo, it was both profane and sacred – and it is still important today in Afro-Cuban religions. Tobacco travelled from the New to the Old World and back as one of modern history's commodities. In the case of Cuba, the form observed by Columbus became *the* luxury smoke of the nineteenth and twentieth centuries: what in Cuba came to be popularly known in Spanish as a *tabaco* or *puro* (which literally translate as tobacco and pure), but more so *El Habano* (taking its name from Havana, home of the palatial factories producing cigars for the world's nobility) – the Havana cigar or simply Havana.

An iconography of cigar culture emerged and became fertile terrain for invented traditions, imagined communities and cultural contestations. Late nineteenth-century visual imagination was fired by tobacco art, from the cigar-smoking woman healer immortalised in Victor Patricio Landaluze's engravings to the splendid gold-embossed cigar labels on which chromolithography permitted the brilliant use of colours on an unprecedented scale.[7]

Writing on Florida's late nineteenth-century domestic 'clear Havana' industry, the historian L. Glenn Westfall commented: "Cigars became synonymous with status, a barometer of a male's success and affluence . . . sales were augmented with more sophisticated printing techniques . . . manufacturers promoted brands and pictorial themes of a Spanish nature."[8] The Spanish theme lost popularity in the 1920s in the United States with the rise of mass-produced, machine-made cigars, but made a comeback in the late twentieth century.

Counter-offensive

The cigar boom of the 1990s has been attributed in no small measure to the market-driven engineering of the New York-founded glossy *Cigar Aficionado*, first published in 1992 and edited by Marvin Shanken. The magazine has symbolised above all cigar smokers' anti-anti-smoking crusade. As one New Yorker expressed it in the very first issue:

Each evening after dinner, accompanied by my two dogs, I stroll into Park Avenue to walk my cigar. Too many of my friends . . . have been swayed in recent years by the insidious campaign against cigar smoking, and this . . . has made me defensive at times, argumentative, even an activist against America's anti-smoking lobby. . . .[9]

He went on to reminisce about Winston Churchill's waving to the crowds in the 1940s, with his "Havana cigar (he even has a type of cigar named after him), 1950s public tolerance and respect for the fashion of cigar smoking among male members of the power elite, and the early 1960s Kennedy puffing a favourite Havana." He ended: "When America is not fighting a war, the puritanical desire to punish people has to be let out at home."[10]

A year later, a Shanken editorial entitled 'Rise Up' clamoured: "Cigar smokers are being recognised for something more than a scorned, isolated minority. . . . Let the world understand how potent a force we can be."[11] It was accompanied by a cartoon strip on the stigma attached to cigar-smoking pariahs, the greatest pariah of all being a Castro-like figure. Castro might have given up smoking a decade earlier, but he was still the ultimate prohibition icon. He had, after all, been the target of failed CIA assassination attempts during the early 1960s that included a poisoned cigar, after which he had smoked only top-security Cohíba cigars rolled personally for him. Subsequent cover features, however, made it clear that the right to smoke included island Havanas, doubly attractive because they are illegal in the United States under Washington's 40-year trade embargo on Cuba. Despite issues over the years promoting cigar smoking among women, *Cigar Aficionado* is subtitled "the good life magazine for men" and carries sensual, if not to say overtly sexual, ads – including a modern-day Miami-vice Carmen suggestive of cigars still being rolled on young women's thighs. *Cigar Aficionado* circulation has soared, and the web-based revolution ushered in www.cigaraficionado.com, complete with its 'Hall of Fame' and 'Cigar Stars', which honoured those leading the industry through its 1990s boom.

Cigar Cool

A *Newsweek* feature in 1997 contained an inset:[12]

Will Cigars Stay Hot? How To Track the Trend.

The subheading ran: "All trends – cigars, Rollerblades, tattoos – move through predictable stages of cool, according to Lawrence Samuel of marketing consultants Iconoculture, Inc. Once mainstream, trends either die, mutate into microtrends or cement into national pastimes."[13] Four stages are identified, from Fringe (pre-cool), through Trendy (cool) and Mainstream (post-cool), to Mutation (neo-cool). The pre-cool bankers, investors and lawyers of pre-1995 flout political correctness at smoke-out cigar nights; the cool yuppies, gender-benders and college students of 1995 puff up circulation of *Cigar Aficionado* (for boomers) and smoke (Gen X) in cigar bars and smoke-friendly eateries; post-cool Corporate America of 1996 cashes in, and Joe and Jane in Dockers lure 'nice-vice' cigars into suburbia; and in 1997 neo-cool down-town kids and smugglers of illegal Cubans produce backlash variations. US cigar sales would recede the following year, but elsewhere cigars, especially those from Cuba, held their own.

In 1998 the UK journal *Economist* ran an article entitled: 'Cuban Cigars: Let the Good Times Roll':

> After Fidel Castro gave up smoking cigars in 1985, so did the rest of the world.... It looked as though the Cuban industry would be stubbed out.... But it has made a comeback. Cigars are an eloquent accessory for the rich, and there is a backlash against political correctness that has made smoking in public virtually impossible in America and increasingly so in Europe. Libertarians (and libertines) are uniting in bars the world over.[14]

Havana cigar events became *de rigeur*. As reported in the *Cuban Review* of April 1997, a 700-strong gathering, from more than 40 countries, including 137 Americans defying US restrictions, thronged the famous Tropicana Cabaret for a gala dinner attended by Fidel Castro.[15]

Cigar Cities

The processes that originated in Cuba are emulated in cigars crafted outside of the country. "A premium cigar," declared Mark Stucklin, "is one that is made entirely by hand using whole and intact leaves for filler – only in Cuba [is] that bunching of the filler done by hand as opposed to a bunching device.... To Cuba, more than anywhere we owe the development ... of the long-filler handmade cigar...."[16]

Beyond Cuba, standard practice required cheaper cigars – known as 'stogies' in the United States – to be stuffed with a short filler of shredded tobacco and wrapped in a paper binder made from tobacco scraps pressed into a homogenous roll. Nonetheless, the quest for Cuban-quality cigars and leaf had led émigrés from the war-torn Cuba of the late nineteenth century and the revolutionary country of the late twentieth century to the surrounding Caribbean and Central America, but most of all Florida – from Key West, Tampa and Ybor City, through what was once Marti City, where Ocala now stands, to Jacksonville,

Tallahassee and Panhandle Gadsden County towns aptly named Amsterdam, Sumatra and Havana.

If Havana Cuba was cigar city, so in its time Key West was 'Cigar City USA' and Tampa (more specifically West Tampa and Ybor City) the 'Smoke Capital of the World'.[17] So linked were they that in 1892 the exiled independence leader José Martí sought in Tampa support for his Cuban Revolutionary Party. The most famous cigar ever rolled in Ybor City was smuggled into Cuba containing his order of 1895 for insurrection. Ybor City and Tampa may be ghosts of what they once were, but workers record a past of idealism, radicalism and nationalism – and also, it is all too often forgotten, a culture of smoking. An issue of the *Floridian* in 1972 described a good cigar of Ybor City as a "burning brown torpedo full of history and romance and poetry," and wrote of one of the few remaining cigar makers, the 76-year-old Servando López:

> His eyes twinkle as he lights a cigar he's made. The sunlight filtering through the streaked windows bounces off his hair as he examines the even burn that is one of the signs of a fine cigar. He looks for the long ash, as would any connoisseur. López gets pleasure too from the old men who hobble in wearing shabby clothes, too poor to dress better but glad to hand over their centavos to buy the dignity of a fine cigar.[18]

Back in the mid-1980s – when cigar sales were at an all-time low and cigar mystique had become part of Hollywood nostalgia – local Tampa historians narrowly saved Ybor City from being razed to the ground by developers. Louis A. Pérez Jr interviewed José de la Cruz, who had left Cuba after a Havana cigar workers strike to arrive in Tampa in 1912 and later become an organiser of the great strike of 1931. To quote from an article that Pérez wrote, in which De la Cruz recounts the passions of the 1920s and '30s:

> a long silence came between us as Don José sent a billow of shapeless gray-white smoke rising to the ceiling. Moments passed as he proceeded to chase the lingering smoke away with the half-hearted pendulum swings of an arm heavy with age. . . . "We won, you know. I know what history is going to say . . . but I want *you* to know that it is not so."[19]

The post-1959 successes of émigré growers, manufacturers and, to a lesser extent, workers came to pose a serious 'offshore Havana' challenge to the island Havana of post-1989 crisis-ridden Cuba. As its backer, the Soviet Union, disintegrated, so its enemy, the United States, tightened the noose – just when the cigar revival was beginning. In 1995 the Cuban-American writer Gustavo Pérez-Firmat wrote:

Exiles live by substitution. If you can't have it in Havana, make it in Miami. . . . Life in exile; memory enhanced by imagination. Like Don Quijote, every exile is an apostle of the imagination, someone who invents a world more amenable to his ambitions and dreams. It is no accident that for every twenty years the most popular eatery in Little Havana . . . is all cigar smoke and mirrors.[20]

The media war heated up. In the Miami *El Nuevo Herald*, the aggrieved writer Martín Mendiola in his regular 'Puro Humo' column declared: "When asked which are the best cigars in the world, most, including *Cigar Aficionado*, tell us they're the Cuban cigars . . . but we find that many of the Dominican, Honduran, Nicaraguan, Jamaican and Canary Island cigars are much better quality . . . possibly created by or learned from Cuban forebears."[21] Young Miami Cuban Americans who launched the magazine *Generation ñ*, their version of Gen X, and who had grown up in anti-smoking Florida rediscovered the Cuban cigar. The cover of August 1997 shouted: "Cigars . . . finally 'Blood's thicker than water'."[22] They were to be seen frequenting the Biltmore Hotel, built in 1926 and resurrected in the 1990s, in Coral Gables, with its Cigar Salon, Friday night 'Cigars under the Stars' courtyard and black-tie cigar dinners. Cigar festivals sprang up anew in Key West; cigar-smoke shops linked arms with baseball; bric-a-brac memorabilia included Havana Roller Pens, Havana Choco Grande Cigars and Habaneros candles, accompanying the usual ash trays, mugs and baseball caps.[23]

And so, out of the parallel production and marketing of identical or similar brands – that of the island which is served by and serves primarily European markets, and that which is offshore and is integrally structured into the US cigar industry have grown economic, political and cultural contestations that are fertile terrain for invented traditions and imagined communities. Yet, to quote a Fort Lauderdale cigar bar entrepreneur: "American culture is coming of age. We smoke fine cigars. We drink fine wine. American culture is growing and maturing."[24] If this is the case, the chances are that there might be an end to the 40-year US embargo that has made smoking real Havanas an illicit pleasure.

Notes

1   Sergio Morera, Simon Chase & Bill Colbert, *Havanas: A Unique Blend of Sun, Soil and Skill* (London, 1993).
2   Kendall Hamilton, 'Blowing Smoke', *Newsweek* (21 July 1997), pp.54-61; and Mark Peyser et al., 'Cool Fools', *Newsweek* (21 July 1997), p.61.
3   Hamilton, 'Blowing Smoke' (1997), p.54.
4   See *Cigar World* (Winter 1998-99), p.2.
5   Adriano Martínez Rius, *Habano el Rey* (Barcelona: Epicur, 1998), p.11.

6 Fernando Ortiz, *Cuban Counterpoint: Tobacco and Sugar* (Durham and London: Duke University Press, 1995 [1940]). Ortiz posed the classic Cuban counterpoint between tobacco and sugar, on which see Fernando Coronil's introduction to the 1995 edition of *Cuban Counterpoint*; Antonio Benítez-Rojo, *The Repeating Island: The Caribbean and the Postmodern Perspective* (Durham: Duke University Press, 1992); and Gustavo Pérez-Firmat, *The Cuban Condition: Translation and Identity in Cuban Literature* (Cambridge: Cambridge University Press, 1989). I posit a new counterpoint between the offshore and the island Havana cigar: Jean Stubbs, 'Tobacco in the Contrapunteo: Ortiz and the Havana Cigar', in Mauricio A. Font and Alfonso W. Quiroz (eds), *Cuban Counterpoints: The Legacy of Fernando Ortiz* (Lanham: Lexington, 2004) pp.105-23 – Chapter 9 in the present volume.
7 For full-colour reproductions, see Antonio Nuñez Jiménez, *The Journey of the Havana Cigar* (Neptune City: TFH Publications, 1996 [1988]); Joe Davidson, *The Art of the Cigar Label* (Secaucus: Wellfleet Press, 1989); Florida Cuban Heritage Trail (Tallahassee, n.d.); and Narciso Menocal, *Cuban Cigar Labels: The Tobacco Industry in Cuba and Florida: Its Golden Age in Lithography and Architecture* (Coral Gables: Cuban National Heritage, 1995).
8 L. Glenn Westfall, 'The Cuban Cigar Industry and its Age', in *Ex Libris: The Special Collections in the University of South Florida Tampa Campus Library* (Tampa, n.d.).
9 Guy Talese, 'Walking my Cigar', *Cigar Aficionado* (Autumn 1992).
10 Ibid.
11 *Cigar Aficionado* (Winter 1993).
12 Feature article containing inset is Hamilton, 'Blowing Smoke' (1997) pp.54-61.
13 'Will Cigars Stay Hot? How to Track the Trend', *Newsweek* (21 July 1997), p.59.
14 'Cuban Cigars: Let the Good Times Roll', *Economist* (2 May 1998), pp.59-60.
15 Francisco Isla, 'The Cohíba Has the World at its Feet', *Cuban Review*, 11:23 (April 1997), p.13.
16 Mark Stücklin, *The Cigar Handbook: A Buyer's Guide to the World's Finest Cigar Brands* (New York: Barnes & Noble, 1997), p.8.
17 See Glenn L. Westfall, *Don Vicente Martínez Ybor: the Man and His Empire: Development of the Clear Havana Industry in Cuba and Florida in the Ninteenth Century* (New York: Garland, 1987), and *Key West: Cigar City USA* (Key West: Historic Key West Preservation Board, 1984); Armando Méndez, *Ciudad de Cigars: West Tampa* (Tampa: Florida Historical Society, 1994); José Rivero Muñiz, *The Ybor City Story: 1885-1954* (Tampa, 1976); and Gerald E. Poyo, *With All and for the Good of All: The Emergence of Popular Nationalism in the Cuban Communities of the United States, 1848-1898* (Durham: Duke University Press, 1989).
18 Allen Cowan, 'A Good Cigar is More than a Smoke', *Floridian* (26 November 1972), p.24.
19 Louis A. Pérez Jr., 'Ybor City Remembered', *Tampa Bay History*, 7:2 (Fall/Winter 1985), pp.170-1.
20 Gustavo Pérez-Firmat, *Next Year in Cuba: A Cubano's Coming-of-Age in America* (New York: Doubleday, 1994), p.82.
21 Martín Mendiola, 'Puro Humo', *El Nuevo Herald* (22 July 1997), p.8.
22 See *Generation ñ*, 11/13 (August 1997).
23 See *Generation ñ*, 11/16 (December 1997).
24 Stephen Schatzman, 'There's an Entire New Generation of Cigar Smokers', *South Florida Gourmet* (July 1998), p.14.

11

REFLECTIONS ON CLASS, RACE, GENDER AND NATION IN CUBAN TOBACCO, 1850-2000*

ALMOST 20 years since the publication of *Tobacco on the Periphery: A Case Study in Cuban Labour History*,[1] I find myself returning yet again to the theme of labour and Cuban tobacco. I do so as a social historian paying tribute to a historical sociologist, my fellow British scholar, O. Nigel Bolland. As scholars, we are all inescapably tied to place and time, and I thought it fitting to reflect on how my approach to labour history has evolved.

Growing up in the Manchester area, then the heartland of northern England textile manufacturing, undoubtedly contributed to my interest in labour history. When I embarked on my research, I was influenced greatly by the work of three British historians – Paul Thompson, E. P. Thompson and Eric Hobsbawm –[2] and subsequently two Cuban scholars – historian Manuel Moreno Fraginals and ethnographer Fernando Ortiz.[3] I adopted an approach for tobacco similar to that of Moreno Fraginals for sugar, and I opened my book with a quote from Ortiz. Yet it had already become apparent that the classic Ortiz counterpoint, of tobacco symbolising all that sugar was not, did not always hold.

Drawn by the class approach of the British Marxist school of history, I was also steeped in British empiricism. Documents of direct relevance, however, especially those relating to the twentieth century, were at the time not readily available in Cuba. This made for the laborious yet rewarding task of ploughing through much tangential documentation, as there was often a wealth of

---

* Originally published in Constance Sutton (ed.), *Revisiting Caribbean Labor: Essays in Honor of O. Nigel Bolland*, Kingston: Ian Randle, 2005, pp.118-36.

information to be gleaned from unlikely sources. Oral history rapidly assumed importance, and my research came to demand resourcefulness and flexibility, taking cues from the written to the oral sources and vice versa. Cross-checking contradictory statistics, confronting mainstream and trade press with worker journals and interviewing workers and their families, helped fill gaps and direct my thinking along new paths.

The research extended in time and scope. A more comprehensive study of the tobacco sector linked factory to non-factory work, urban industrial to rural and semi-rural labour, in the broader national and international context of tobacco growing and manufacturing. The study was still largely on socio-economic and political aspects of formal labour history, which meant a bias toward the more structured, better-documented, predominantly male sector of the cigar makers, but pointers were raised as to other less-documented sectors.

As my research neared conclusion, I found myself asking questions less of a class nature and more in tune with the new women's and black history, as well as of a national and international nature. The lie was given to 'accepted truths' permeating even the more serious tobacco historiography. Cigars conjured up an elite male world, and cigar makers were those Hispanic Cuban male aristocrats of labour fashioning their quality product from a strong, fragrant leaf. The legend surrounding the prestigious cigar export industry and master cigar maker had contributed to myths in history. Familiar male icons stood for solid labour, political idealism and militancy. The single most obvious iconography of women was the seductive embossed lady on the luxury cigar labels. These and other myths I was led to question further in subsequent work, historical and contemporary, and of an interdisciplinary nature, working with agronomists, anthropologists and sociologists. I draw heavily on this here, to nuance a class approach to labour with considerations of race and gender, as well as nation. My interest along these lines was bolstered by my incursions into Caribbean history and Cuban studies outside Cuba, and I am currently embarked on work that, through the prism of the Havana cigar, goes beyond island and émigré Cuba and is transregional in scope.

What follows traces that process. It first unravels the notion of a white male urban aristocracy of labour in an international division of labour which brought with it de-industrialisation and deskilling along race and gender lines in pre-1959 Cuba. It then shifts focus to agricultural labour and the post 1959 gendered transition from small household to cooperative farming. Finally, it moves offshore to the demise of Cuban labour history in Florida, USA, enmeshed in processes of globalisation. Brief concluding pointers lie in the realm of politico-cultural contestations intrinsic to an understanding of labour that transcends any narrow confines of class.

Aristocracy of Labour?

Around the 1850s, half the Cuban population was dependent on tobacco; by the 1890s one third; and in the twentieth century whole areas and towns in the provinces of Pinar del Río, Havana and what was Las Villas. The overall decrease in numbers, radically changing composition, and general worsening of salaries and working conditions further complicated the make-up of an already heterogeneous labour sector in the many processing stages from the leaf to the finished product.[4]

Nineteenth-century Cuba was primarily a sugar plantation economy based on slave labour. Tobacco was the one nineteenth-century industry to produce a significant class of urban industrial wage labourers, and on a scale unparalleled in the twentieth century. That tobacco workers remained one of the largest sectors of the Cuban working class up until the 1950s was more an indictment of the development of Cuban industry as a whole than a measure of the industry itself.

The decrease in the number of cigar makers was especially marked in Havana, where the large export factories were concentrated. While there are no reliable figures for home and outwork, anecdotal evidence and oral histories suggest this was considerable. What the figures do show, by the mid-twentieth century, is that over 50 percent of those in tobacco were in growing, a further 30 percent in sorting and 10 percent in stemming the leaf, compared with only 6 percent in cigar rolling and a tiny one percent in cigarette manufacturing.

That the 6 percent retained a particular importance merits attention. Cigar rolling is skilled work, but there is little to indicate it was originally considered as such in nineteenth-century Cuba. Cigar makers were found in barracks, prisons and homes; and African slaves, indentured Chinese and free coloureds were brought into rolling shops, often under quite appalling conditions. Early wage labourers lived in, side by side with slave and indentured labour in badly ventilated galleries over the rolling shops, receiving only part of their pay in money, having leave of absence only once a week, and having to hold down a cigar makers' *libreta* or identification card in which debts were recorded, restricting workers from freely transferring their labour from one factory to another. From this period dates the much-abused system of apprenticeship, as also the tradition of the reader, initially brought in to alleviate the monotony of the work rather than edify the mind or redress grievance.

Figures for the 1860s signal 60 percent of the work force in Havana and 55 percent throughout the island were slaves and free coloureds, that is, non-white. By 1899, the figures had dropped to 30 and 37 percent, respectively. Against the backdrop of 1880s abolition of slavery and 1890s depression and war turmoil, black workers were among the many who left Cuba for Key West and Tampa, in Florida, USA, and other surrounding territories.

There was also an entrenchment of white workers in the rolling and sorting of quality cigars, swelled in numbers by an influx of Spanish immigrants to the better Havana factory jobs. They succeeded in enforcing stringent requirements to become master cigar makers, sorters or box decorators, restricting entry along national and race lines. Correspondingly, this was when the 'skill' of cigar making most came into its own. With the twentieth-century decline of the industry, the quality rolling skill was maintained in theory but not always in practice; and its national and racial component broken down. Thus, the proportion of black Cuban cigar workers in Havana, for example, increased to 40 percent in 1943; this compared with only 11 percent of those in cigar sorting and box labelling, the cream of the trades.

There was little reference to women cigar rollers, although the preponderant home and outwork industry suggested they were not insubstantial in number. Women interviewed in the late 1960s spoke of being taught by their fathers to roll cigars in the home and of working in smaller local rolling shops. However, women were not brought into cigar rolling in the major factories, and even twentieth-century cigarette machinists in Cuba were an overwhelmingly white male work force, who, like cigar makers before them, hastened to ensure control over their 'skill'. In this, Cuba differed from other countries, especially with the advent of the machine.

Women were drawn into the factories as cigarette packers and to place the bands and cellophane and metal tubes on the cigars. The first signs of female factory labour on anything like a large scale, however, was in stemming and came after the 1868-78 War of Independence. The shortage of labour produced by the war and the exodus of cigar makers caused what was once a male preserve to be seen as a woman's job. Thus, Carmen may have immortalised Seville's women cigar rollers, but Cuba's Carmens were stemmers. Large export stemmeries in Havana, Las Villas and Pinar del Río, employed hundreds of women, many of them black, at the height of the stemming season. Interviews corroborated high figures for unemployment and underemployment and ways in which women shared outwork, only in extreme cases agreeing to lay-offs, and with strict respect for seniority. Nonetheless, the fact that they were women, and many of them black, compounded endemic seasonal and cyclical factors and helped 'deskill' stemming, causing stemmers to be one of the worst paid and least considered sectors.

Skill, what is recognised and treated as such, is relative; it is not only technically but socially defined.[5] What in Cuba went into defining master cigar rolling as skilled and stemming as unskilled falls as much into the latter as the former category. This did not, however, go unchallenged. The first major challenge to the exclusiveness and control of the trade came from cigar makers in the less prestigious and less well-paid factories working on inferior-type cigars who were not unionised. This was in the 1880s, a time when a large concentration of production and workers coincided with the abolition of slavery and an influx of newly freed as well as newly immigrant Spanish labour. The explosion of labour militancy and strikes displayed marked racial and nationalist overtones to straight class interests. Incipient labour movements divided along reformist, anarchist, anarchosyndicalist, socialist and nationalist lines.

A second major challenge came in the 1920s, when a semblance of national craft unions had been consolidated. As the 1930s Depression and mechanisation loomed over the industry, anti-labour repression increased. Militancy and strikes went far beyond the confines of existing unions, involving women stemmers for whom unionisation was in its infancy. There is reference to a short-lived Guild of *Despalilladores* (the original masculine word in Spanish for stemmers) in 1878 and no other recorded attempt until the 1917 Guild of *Despalilladoras* (the word by then feminine). Able to benefit from the cigar makers' tradition of the reader, worker education and militancy, stemmers displayed high rates of literacy, organisation, and strikes in the 1920s and 1930s.

The National Federation of Stemmers was set up in the late 1930s as a sister organisation to that of the cigar makers, under elected black communist leaders Inocencia Valdés and Lazaro Peña. Valdés, by then advanced in years, was a veteran of the nineteenth-century Florida émigré community and its support for labour and independence struggles. She led what was not only the sector with the highest unionisation rates in the industry but also Cuba's majority female labour sector (only domestics and textile workers compared). Women stemmers came to be a force to be reckoned with, leading one stemmery manager in the 1940s to angrily claim the need to put a stop to these 'nigger' women.

We are now much more familiar with the deskilling process associated with the racialisation and feminisation of labour described above than when I was grappling with these issues. However, the silences within Cuban labour are still there: the stemmers and their leader Inocencia Valdés, for example, are crying out for further study.[6]

Household and Farm Labour

In the market economy of twentieth-century pre-revolutionary Cuba, much traditional farming had been disrupted by large-scale foreign and local capital investment. This held to a lesser degree for tobacco: alongside modern farming units with salaried labourers, there was a particularly intensive form of small-scale, labour-intensive, small-tenant and subtenant farming and sharecropping. This produced a semi-peasantry/semi-proletariat which farmed small plots of land according to an intricate system of land tenure and rent-in-kind, was highly dependent on unpaid family labour, and was forced at times of the year to sell its labour. A visibly exploitative form of male labour in male-headed households was accompanied by intensified women's participation in subsistence production and family reproduction crucial to family survival, plus the seasonal harvesting and a sorting of tobacco.

With the agrarian reforms of the 1960s and subsequent rural development policies, the land peasants worked was made their own, the family wage was effectively upped, and children were sent to school. In the process, and despite government policies to the contrary, the old societal definition of women servicing the home and family was to a certain extent reinforced.

The all-out national effort for a record 1970 sugar harvest had a devastating effect on tobacco: the harvest that year was only 44 percent that of 1966. This led to a 1971-76 tobacco recuperation, with attention to crop costing and pricing and agrotechnology. In 1977, national policy was to encourage small farmers, who, since the 1960s, had been drawn into Credit and Service Cooperatives (Cooperativa de Credito y Servicio, CCS), to pool their land in Agricultural Production Cooperatives (Cooperativa de Producción Agrícola, CPA). Tobacco farmers were in the forefront to do so, and, by the early 1980s, CPAs accounted for 50 percent of private tobacco land. However, while output and yields had increased, tobacco CPAs were also among the first to run into difficulties.

The number of tobacco CPAs peaked in 1981, and then fell back to the 1979 level by 1985, though the land area more than quadrupled. Membership was at a peak in 1983 but then fell, such that in 1985, on four times the land area, there were only twice as many farmers. Those reporting financial losses were the more tobacco-intensive: thus, 1983-84 CPA as opposed to CCS end-of year balances were in the ratio of 1:10 in tobacco, as compared with ratios of 9:10 in sugar and 1:12 in coffee. Cost of labour was cited as a major problem – having to bring in seasonal labour, provide transport and accommodation, and pay the higher salaries of nonagricultural workers. One key aspect overlooked was the impact of collective farming in effecting a separation of productive from reproductive labour in a sector that had moved from smallholding, which was heavily dependent on family labour. This was not so marked in sugar, as sugar had been a plantation crop economy with considerable agricultural wage labour, but it was very much so in tobacco, as also in coffee, the two prime smallholder crops.

This came out very clearly in 1980s field work, which was conducted in two predominantly tobacco-growing areas – San Luis (Vuelta Abajo) in Pinar del Río province and Cabaiguán (Vuelta Arriba) in Sancti Spíritus province.[7] Given the almost total absence of any gender breakdown by crop (beyond cane/non-cane agriculture), it was essential to build up good local disaggregated data, complemented by local history, participatory action research, and life-story techniques.[8]

The two areas were chosen because they presented differences in terms of history, land structure and organisation, and type of tobacco grown. In San Luis, farms were smaller than in Cabaiguán, but land yields and the superior quality of the export tobacco grown made for farms of double the value and income, and the greater crop intensity made for a larger proportion of unpaid labour. In San Luis in particular, dealers and landowning foreign companies and local families operated on a patriarchal system of benefits, turning the National Tobacco Growers' Association (founded 1942) into a powerful instrument, against which the Sharecroppers' and Tenant Farmers' Association (1952) attempted to protect its members.

Where little else was grown, as in San Luis, tobacco families were highly susceptible to market changes; and wage labourers, at peak harvest times, faced an influx of migrant labour from surrounding areas, which undercut already low casual wage rates. In Cabaiguán, there was a greater chance of other agricultural and non-agricultural work, but the area as a whole was less prosperous. After the 1959 Revolution and 1960s land reforms, in San Luis, a substantial part of quality leaf production under company and landowner family hands was continued by the state; in Cabaiguán, state tobacco land was more by default than because it had been farmed by any large enterprise before and the state farms were never very successful.

In the 1980s, in both San Luis and Cabaiguán, it became clear that women had, indeed, been central to tobacco production. The domestic division of labour was almost complete: men oversaw agricultural production in the broader sense and rarely took part in servicing the family and household, whether it be washing, cooking, cleaning, caring for the children, fetching and carrying water, picking tubers, grinding corn, or feeding the chickens and pigs. If this had not been considered work by the census enumerators, it certainly was by farming families, men and women alike. The same applied to pre-1959 child labour, which helps explain why large families were prevalent. Boys and girls started work at seven, the boys in the fields with their fathers and the girls around the house with their mothers. At harvest, when extra labour was needed, girls and women cooked for the field hands. The poorer the family, the greater the need for family labour, and women and girls would be out in the fields planting, weeding, pruning and harvesting.

The type of tobacco helped determine the kind and extent of women's work. San Luis tobacco was harvested by the leaf which was then threaded by hand and hung on poles to dry – women's work. Harvesting in Cabaiguán was heavy men's work, as the tobacco was cut in stalks of four leaves at a time, strung over outstretched arm, and then transferred to poles. Women's CPA and CCS membership varied significantly: in 1983, 24 and 1.6 percent in San Luis, 38 and 25 percent in Cabaiguán. The lower figure for San Luis was also in part explained by the more urban setting providing other job opportunities, the higher figure for Cabaiguán by its more diverse agricultural economy and women's involvement in non-tobacco activities on the cooperatives.

In the early 1990s the CPAs might still have been described in Cuba as a 'superior form of collective production'. They were, however, being outperformed in terms of production, yields and profits by CCS smallholders. In the context of what was a difficult decade for the economy as a whole, and agriculture was no exception, a quiet reversal of policy took place in favour of smallholder farming.[9] The gender ramifications of this for household production and reproduction are far from clear. The situation in tobacco demonstrates that no simplistic conclusions can, or should, be reached. The 2003 figure for women's membership of the tobacco CPAs in Cabaiguán had dropped to 13 percent – a very clear signal of the need for follow-up study.

Such a study might also include an aspect unstudied in the 1980s, which is the impact Canary Islander identity might have had in terms of household. The Cabaiguán area had a strong Canary Islander presence, the cultural ramifications of which were seen to be strengthened in the 1990s. The substantial numbers of Canary Islanders who migrated to Cuba in the late nineteenth and early twentieth centuries to farm tobacco introduced a particular gender dynamic. Communities tended to display marked endogamy, such that it was not unknown for marriages to be arranged with women back in the Canary Islands, and endogamy among descendants has continued up until the present day.[10]

Émigré Labour

At the time of writing my book, dependency theory had given way to core/periphery thinking, and *Tobacco on the Periphery* seemed an obvious title for contextualising the labour history. I charted what now appears to me to have been an almost linear approach to the inevitability of foreign domination over a national industry in decline. That line was broken with the 1959 Revolution, but only now am I much more aware of just how fragmented it has been before and since.

When the manuscript of the book was read for publication, one reader's comment struck home: what was needed was the full story of the 'Havana Cigar universe'. The reader was Cuban American historian Louis Pérez, and his comment was grounded on knowledge of the Havana cigar history in Key West and Tampa, Florida.[11] His work, and that of others since,[12] suggested the need to integrate on and off-island cigar history.[13]

Cuba's tobacco product par excellence, the cigar, considered since the mid-nineteenth century to be the best in the world, has been long imitated elsewhere. This was a process fostered by Cuba's own political history of nineteenth- and twentieth-century political upheavals and out-migration, creating émigré communities and rival economies, of which the cigar was one, creating an 'offshore' as well as island Havana cigar.

After the 1959 Revolution, new émigré Cuban cigar tobacco communities joined older ones in the Caribbean, Central America, the United States and as far afield as the Canary Islands. Smaller manufacturers, dealers, growers and workers abroad profited from the upheaval in Cuba and the tight trade embargo that was the political response of the United States (for a while much of the Americas} to the Revolution. Eastern European bloc and Third World countries emerged as Havana cigar partners; Western European markets became a battleground for disputed Havana cigar brands.

Thirty years on, a new chapter opened when the demise of the Eastern European socialist bloc in 1989 ended Cuba's special trade and aid and the United States tightened and extra-territorialised its embargo. As external geopolitical realities compounded internal weaknesses, the Cuban revolutionary government devised a structural adjustment strategy, courting non-US trade and investment. The Havana cigar became a key player. Cuban production plummeted, and battles fought in international courts over market brand names were but the more visible tip of a cigar war. A US cigar revival gained momentum, involving two US cigar giants – Connecticut-based General Cigar and Fort Lauderdale-based Consolidated Cigar – and émigré Cuban tobacco interests, in all-out competition with island Cuba.

The 'offshore Havana cigar' story began in Key West, the southernmost of the Florida keys, only 90 miles from Cuba. First port of call for émigré manufacturers and workers, Key West was also home to Cuban émigré nationalist and labour unrest. In the 1890s Spanish manufacturers undercut Key West national and class strife by moving to Tampa and building Ybor City. Founding fathers of Cuban independence, Antonio Maceo and José Martí, both in exile for many years, visited Key West, Tampa and Ybor City in the 1890s, mustering support for the independence cause. Descendants today proudly recall how their worker forebears donated their day's wages to the independence cause.

Early twentieth-century West Tampa and Ybor City flourished and catapulted women workers to the fore.[14] By 1930, the industry was headed for decline, due to depression, mechanisation and relocation. The advent of the cigar machine cemented a process of feminisation and deskilling of mechanised cigar rolling. The big losers in the Tampa story were the Afro-Cubans, who gradually fell foul of US South-style segregation driving a wedge into this community that had fought together on a nationalist and worker ticket.[15] From the turn of the century on, they were forced to live their lives increasingly separate from Hispano-Cubans. A drift north to New Jersey was driven by the experiences of segregation, decline and mechanisation of the industry from the 1930s on.

From the 1890s to the 1990s, Florida tobacco might be seen as framed by two embargoes: a lesser-known embargo of the 1890s and the current 40-year embargo dating back to the early 1960s. The first helped establish Florida as a major Havana cigar state; the second culminated in the de-agriculturalisation and deindustrialisation of Florida's cigar sector. The century as a whole was one of successive boom-bust processes: in Gadsden county and northern Florida (1890s-1970s), the Tampa Bay area (1890s-1990s), and Miami (1960s-90s). Alongside the better-known histories of Key West, Tampa and Ybor City in their early twentieth-century heyday, little has been written about their history since. Less still is known about the rise and fall of the growing history of Gadsden county and its tobacco towns of Havana, Sumatra, Amsterdam and Quincy, linked to the machine manufacturing of Jacksonville and Tampa (Swisher and Havana Tampa).[16]

Before the United States declared its 1962 embargo on Cuba, steps were taken to prepare for such a contingency. In 1961, the US Department of Agriculture commissioned a study to determine the effect on the cigar industry and tobacco farmers if supplies of Cuban tobacco were no longer available. According to the findings, Cuba was the source of nearly a quarter of leaf tobacco for US cigars. Some two-thirds of the seven billion cigars sold in the United States in a typical year contained Cuban tobacco. Around 670 million 'clear Havanas' (made wholly of Cuban leaf) and 'Havana filler' cigars used 45 percent of Cuban tobacco imports; the other 55 percent was used in 'blended filler' cigars. If imports were to cease, 'clear Havana' manufacturers foresaw their problems as 'insurmountable' unless Cuban tobacco were to be replaced by some tropical or subtropical tobacco in order to obtain the aroma and flavour needed. This marked the start of a drive to grow Cuban seed tobacco and subsequently move cigar hand-rolling operations out of Florida to subtropical lands of the Caribbean and Central America.

In the 1950s, the Havana cigar industry was still the largest single employer in Tampa, with thousands working in cigar manufacturing and a source of overseas support for Cuban revolutionary organisations. After the 1960s, almost all that was left of the industry had relocated, and more than 6,000 cigar makers lost their jobs. Thus, Villazón opened two factories in Honduras for the manufacture of hand-made Havanas. The Armenia Avenue factory stayed in West Tampa, but to produce only machine-made cigars. By the 1980s, the introduction of homogenised leaf drove yet another nail in the coffin of the quality hand-made cigar and craft cigar maker.

The Dominican Republic was not historically considered a producer of quality cigar leaf. In 1962, however, an émigré Cuban tobacco agronomist was part of the Washington reconstruction plan after the fall of Trujillo and helped found the Tobacco Institute in Santiago de los Caballeros, in the central Cibao area. Among those who made their name in the Dominican Republic were the Fuente family. Four Fuente factories of pre-Dominican times were damaged by fire: two in Tampa – one in 1921 and another in 1948 – one in Nicaragua in 1977, and one in Honduras in 1979. After a failed effort in Tampa in 1979, with Cuban and Vietnamese labour, Fuente almost abandoned the business, but then took good advantage of the rapidly expanding free trade zones offering duty-free import and export and a plentiful pool of cheap labour. As Cuba was facing its post-1989 crisis, the Fuente family saw long years of hard investment and effort in the Cibao bear quality Havana seed leaf and cigars. With close ties to cigar interests in Tampa and Ecuador, the family business produced cigars that in the early 1990s surpassed the quality of many from Havana.

In 1992 Fuente claimed to have the largest handmade cigar factory in the world, with 400 rollers making 18 million cigars a year. The company's arrival coincided with a turning point in the Dominican cigar industry. In 1976, 5 million cigars were exported to the United States; in 1979, 11 million. Between 1979 and 1981, when US cigar giant Consolidated Cigar moved its operations from the Canary Islands to La Romana, exports tripled to 33 million. In 1990, 52 million cigars were shipped to the United States, accounting for 47 percent of the US premium cigar market. All wrapper leaf was imported, but filler was produced in the Cibao valley, where all but Consolidated Cigar were located. Nearly all export quality cigars were made in free-trade zones.

In 1992, Consolidated employed 400 workers producing 'Havana' cigars and had warehouses for 24 different kinds of tobacco leaf being blended to make them: filler from Brazil, Java and the Dominican Republic; binder from Indonesia and Mexico; wrapper from Cameroon, Connecticut, Mexico, Nicaragua and Brazil. In Santiago de los Caballeros's free trade zone, General Cigar, in 1992, employed 60 sorters and leaf graders and 120 rollers, and had warehouse inventories of leaf, including their own famed Connecticut shade wrapper.

No post-1959 émigré Cuban story would be complete without Miami. However, Miami was not a major cigar player. Initially, small concerns catered to little more than the local Cuban émigré community. One exception was Padrón who, out of his Miami business, went to grow tobacco in Nicaragua. The Nicaraguan economy was a post-1963 phenomenon, thanks to a generous offer made to émigré Cubans by Somoza on land around northern Estelí. After the 1979 Sandinista Revolution, the area became a *contra* battlefield, and much of the tobacco moved north, to southern Honduras, around Danlí. Padrón and son, however, remained, and the turn of the twenty-first century saw their cigars surpass in quality those from the Dominican Republic. Florida's minimum wage policy was often invoked by companies to explain why they 'had' to go offshore. But this was lucrative business, transformed through technology, experimentation, litigation and labour practices, to the extent that many of today's factories, and the workers in them, bear little or no resemblance to those of a century ago. Unsurprisingly, it is easier to piece together company than labour history,[17] and this I have only begun to do now through archival and oral history. What is clear is that offshore Havana cigar makers are today very different from their predecessors. In Florida, there are still older male cigar makers in small shops in places like Ybor City, Little Havana or Miami Beach, but for almost a tourist facade. The real labour is not in Florida but where poorer people, often indigenous and black women, are willing to labour long in return for little.

Political and Cultural Contestations

An iconography of cigar culture has accompanied the Cuban and Florida 'clear Havana' story. This can be seen in not only the history but also lithography, art, literature, music and popular culture – fertile terrain for the political and cultural contestations of 'invented traditions' and 'imagined communities'.[18] It is key to current work of my own, which has obliged me to revisit my previous work, which has included revisiting Ortiz to posit a new Cuban counterpoint, that of the on- and off-island tobacco, and also incursions into the imaginary.[19]

While post-1959 Miami, in tune with many other off-shore cigar settings, is associated with the forces of Hispanic-Cuban political conservatism, earlier periods in Key West, Tampa and Ybor City are identified with Hispanic and Afro-Cuban political romanticism, idealism, nationalism and radicalism, as they were on the island. In 1897, a year before the end of Cuba's Second War of Independence, a beautifully embossed cigar label celebrated three of Cuba's great generals: Calixto García, Máximo Gómez and Antonio Maceo. Idyllic images were also painted of Cuba's relationship with the neighbouring United States. More in tune with history – an omen of what was to come – might be another label on which the American eagle could be seen 'embracing' the Cuban flag.

New historical studies are suggestive of a more nuanced approach to this history where labour is concerned. It is argued that tobacco workers returning from Florida in the early twentieth century, many of them black, saw their nationalism and radicalism compromised by their class hostility to Cuban elites; this predisposed them to the US.[20] Parallels might be drawn with similar arguments that have been made regarding Puerto Rican cigar makers in the same period – one of the aspects under consideration in work of my own in progress.

In the 1960s, in the wake of the Cuban Revolution, Tampa historians employed archival and oral history to bring alive the past. They were successful in rescuing Ybor City from developers and a museum was opened, complete with cigar makers' cottages. The Ybor factory was, however, turned into boutiques and a tourist attraction that evolved commercially into one that was heavily Hispanic in its recreation of the past. A lowly building on the outskirts of the renovated centre boasts a plaque to the Martí-Maceo Society, founded in 1904 by Afro-Cubans wishing to hold on to the dream of a united Cuba.

At the turn of the twenty-first century, descendants of those same Afro-Cubans were instrumental in having the museum mount an exhibition which told their story, one that did not stop after the early decades of the twentieth century, but continued up to and after the 1959 Revolution. It is, as they say, very much the story of 'those who came before'. The post-1959 new waves of more conservative in-migration from Cuba sealed a silencing of the earlier radical labour movement. It is only now that some of those who left Florida are returning and reclaiming that history, one that contrasts with the view from Miami, predominantly that of wealthy, ultra-conservative, Hispano-Cuban elites.

What is clear is that working with local scholars and their communities has become collaborative participatory historical research, and this in turn has helped stimulate interest in what have been under-researched areas. In Cuba and selected case study sites – Florida, Jamaica, Puerto Rico, the Canary Islands and more recently Brazil and Connecticut – archival material, oral and ethnographic testimony, visual representation in art and lithography, plays, songs, and stories, together tell a narrative. The silences, however, are also telling, and often associated with what has been described to me as an 'awkward history'. The challenge now lies in addressing that awkward history, juxtaposing myth and reality in the politics of memory, as I move to a more discursive and representational approach to understanding transnational labour.

Notes

1 Jean Stubbs, *Tobacco on the Periphery* (London: Amaurea Press, 2023 [1985]).
2 Paul Thompson, The *Voice of the Past: Oral History* (New York: Oxford University Press, 2000); E. P. Thompson, *Making of the English Working Class* (2002); Eric Hobsbawm, *The Age of Revolution: Europe 1789-1848* (London: Weidenfeld & Nicolson, 1962).
3 Manuel Moreno Fraginals, *The Sugarmill: The Socioeconomic Complex of Sugar in Cuba, 1760-1860* (New York: Monthly Review, 1976); and Fernando Ortiz, *Cuban Counterpoint: Tobacco and Sugar* (Durham and London: Duke University Press, 1995 [1940]).
4 For further detail, see Jean Stubbs, 'Labour and Economy in Cuban Tobacco, 1860-1958', *Historical Perspectives*, 2:3 (1985), pp.449-67 – Chapter 2 in the present volume.
5 Skill was central to my thinking as my interest shifted from women to gender: Jean Stubbs, 'Gender Constructs of Labour in Prerevolutionary Cuban Tobacco', *Social and Economic Studies*, Institute of Social & Economic Research, University of the West Indies, 37:1 & 2 (1988), pp.241-69 – Chapter 5 in the present volume.
6 There are no equivalent studies to those on Puerto Rico: Amilcar Tirado Aviles, 'Notas sobre el desarrollo de la industria del tabaco en Puerto Rico y su impacto en

la mujer puertorriqueña, 1898-1920', *CENTRO*, 2:7 (1989); and N. Valle Ferrer, *Luisa Capetillo: Pioneer Puerto Rican Feminist* (New York: Peter Lang, 2006).

7   This was written up by me in a number of articles, including 'Gender Issues in Contemporary Cuban Tobacco Farming', *World Development*, 5:1 (1987), pp.41-65 – Chapter 4 in the present volume; and 'Women and Cuban Smallholder Agriculture in Transition', in Janet H. Momsen (ed.), *Women and Change in the Caribbean* (Kingston: Ian Randle; Bloomington: Indiana University Press; London: James Currey, 1993), pp.219-31 – Chapter 6 in the present volume. See also an article co-authored with Mavis Álvarez: 'Women on the Agenda: The Cooperative Movement in Rural Cuba', in Carmen Diana Deere & Magdalena Leon (eds), *Rural Women and State Policy: Feminist Perspectives on Latin American Agricultural Development*, Boulder: Westview Press, 1987, pp.142-61 – Chapter 3 in the present volume.

8   Reflections on methodology formed the basis for 'Some Thoughts on the Life Story Method', *IDS Bulletin*, 15:1 (1984), pp.34-7.

9   The most recent of these was Jean Stubbs, 'Turning Over a New Leaf? The Havana Cigar Revisited', *New West Indian Guide*, 74:3 & 4 (2000), pp.235-55 – Chapter 8 in the present volume.

10 Endogamy is brought out clearly in José Alberto Galván Tudela, 'Identidad, endogamia étnica y adaptación sociocultural del inmigrante canario en Cuba', *Guize* (1995). See also Galván Tudela, 'Canary Islanders in Cuban tobacco', in Mario Luis López Isla (ed.), *La aventura del tabaco* (Santa Cruz de Tenerife: Centro de la Cultura Popular Canaria, 1998).

11 An early article was Louis A. Pérez, Jr., 'Reminiscences of a *Lector*. Cuban Cigar Makers in Tampa', *Florida Historical Quarterly* 53:4 (1975), pp.443-9.

12 Studies of Florida include Glenn L. Westfall, *Key West: Cigar City USA (Key West:* Historic Key West Preservation Board, 1984); Gerald E. Poyo, *With All and for the Good of All: The Emergence of Popular Nationalism in the Cuban Communities of the United States, 1848-1898* (Durham: Duke University Press, 1989); Gary Mormino & George E. Pozetta, '"The Reader Lights the Candle": Cuban and Florida Cigar Workers' Oral Tradition', *Labor's Heritage* 15 (1993), pp.4-28. For key labour studies elsewhere in the region, on cigar makers see A. G. Quintero Rivera, 'Socialista y tabaquero: La proletarización de los artesanos', in *La danza de la insurrección: Para una sociología de la música latinoamericana* (Buenos Aires: CLACSO, 2020 [1978]), pp.29-84; and José González Sierra, *Monopolio del humo: elementos de la historia del tabaco en México y algunos conflictos de tabaqueros veracruzanos: 1915-1930* (Xalapa: Verezcruz University, 1987). For the agricultural sector see Juan José Baldrich, *Los que sembraron la no siembra: Los cosecheros de tabaco puertoriqueños frente a la corporaciones tabacaleras, 1920-1934* (Río Piedras: Huracán, 1988) and Michiel Baud, *Peasants and Tobacco in the Dominican Republic, 1870-1930* (Knoxville: University of Tennessee Press, 1996).

13 This I began to do in 'Political Idealism and Commodity Production: Cuban Tobacco in Jamaica, 1870-1930', *Cuban Studies*, 25 (1995), pp.51-81 – Chapter 7 in the present volume.

14 See Nancy A. Hewitt, '"The Voice of Virile Labor": Labor Militancy, Community Solidarity, and Gender Identity among Tampa's Latin Workers, 1880-1921', in Ava Baron (ed.), *Work Engendered: Toward a New History of American Labor* (Ithaca: Cornell University Press, 1991), pp.142-67.

15 The groundbreaking study of this was Susan D. Greenbaum, 'Afro-Cubans in Exile: Tampa, Florida, 1886-1984', *Cuban Studies* 15:1 (1985); see also her *More Than Black: Afro-Cubans in Tampa* (Gainesville: University Press of Florida, 2002).

16 I refer to aspects of this history in 'Tobacco in the Contrapunteo: Ortiz and the Havana Cigar', in Mauricio A. Font & Alfonso W. Quiroz (eds), *Cuban Counterpoints: The Legacy of Fernando Ortiz* (Lanham: Lexington, 2004), pp.105-23 – Chapter 9 in the present volume.

17 Also not unsurprisingly, in the voluminous studies of post-1959 Miami Cubans, labour rarely features. An exception is Louise Lamphere, Alex Stepick & Guillermo Grenier, *Newcomers* in *the Workplace: Immigrants and the Restructuring of the US Economy* (Philadelphia: Temple University Press, 1994), which includes work on Cuban workers in the construction, apparel and catering sectors.
18 I refer to the concepts in Eric Hobsbawm & Terence Ranger (eds), *The Invention of Tradition* (Cambridge: Cambridge University Press, 1993); and Benedict Anderson, *Imagined Communities* (New York & London: Verso, 1991).
19 Stubbs, 'Tobacco in the Contrapunteo' (2004), and 'Havana Cigars and the West's Imagination', in Sander L. Gilman & Zhou Xun (eds), *Smoke: A Global History of Smoking* (London: Reaktion Press, 2004), pp.134-9 – Chapter 10 in the present volume.
20 See Lillian Guerra, 'Perceiving Populism: US Imperialism and the Paradox of Labour Struggle in Cuba, 1906-1909', paper presented at Latin American Studies Association (2001), and 'From Revolution to Involution in the Early Cuban Republic', in Nancy P. Appelbaum, Anne S. Macpherson & Karin Alejandra Rosemblatt et al. (eds), *Race and Nation in Latin America* (Chapel Hill: University of North Carolina Press, 2003), pp.132-62.

12

Reinventing Mecca: Tobacco in the Dominican Republic, 1763-2007[*][1]

It was a crowning moment for Dominican tobacco when in 2003, in the city of Santiago de los Caballeros, regional capital of the Cibao central valley, Grupo León Jimenes celebrated the centenary of La Aurora cigar factory with the opening of the state-of-the-art Centro Cultural 'Eduardo León Jimenes' and publication of the book *Huella y memoria: E. León Jimenes: un siglo en el camino nacional, 1903-2003*.[2] The book divides company history in four periods, each of which coincides with an accepted periodisation of Dominican tobacco history during the century in question.

The first (1903-29) saw the rise of manufacturing, in cigars and then cigarettes, in tandem with agriculture and industry in the Cibao, and especially Santiago. It was in this period that León Jimenes oversaw the growth of La Aurora into one of the Dominican Republic's two largest tobacco companies, profiting from mechanised cigarette manufacturing for the regional and national market, while also continuing hand-rolled cigar production. The second (1930-61, and particularly after 1945) witnessed stagnation of the company and the region under the state monopoly of Compañía Anónima del Tabaco (CAT), better known as La Tabacalera, of General Rafael Leónidas Trujillo. Despite León's death in 1937, the business continued in family hands, but it was not until after Trujillo that La Aurora's fortunes improved. This post-Trujillo third period (1962-82) saw the renewed expansion of the company in primarily cigarettes (and the national beer, Presidente), with La Aurora successfully undercutting CAT. Such was León Jimenes's success that

---

[*] Originally published as *Commodities of Empire Working Paper* 3 (2007), at https://commoditiesofempire.org.uk/publications/working-papers/working-paper-3.

President Juan Bosch, during his ephemeral time in power (1962-63), celebrated the company as a model of progress. This expansion was strengthened in the fourth period (1982-2003). The renewed expansion in cigars, especially in the 1990s, accompanied the Cibao's new positioning in the global cigar export market – particularly in the United States. As the company grew, so also its banking and philanthropic interests – hence the new Cultural Centre, founded:

> to nourish creativity through research, conservation, exhibition and dissemination of all Dominican artistic and cultural manifestations, as well as all that may contribute to nurturing a society that is conscious of its most transcendental values, proud of itself, and capable of assuming an active role in impoving the quality of life in the country. [3].

Emblematic as it is of Dominican twentieth and early twenty-first century cigar tobacco, the León Jimenes story would be incomplete without reference to the little-explored connection between Dominican and Cuban tobacco history, which is the objective of this paper. The title 'Reinventing Mecca' refers to the period after the 1959 Cuban Revolution, when US and émigré Cuban tobacco interests combined to project the Dominican Republic as *the* home of quality tobacco, including famous Havana cigar brands. The US quest for alternative leaf tobacco sources after the 1960 US embargo on trade with Cuba, coupled with the exodus of Cuban tobacco families – a key number of whom found their way to the Cibao – produced a dramatic post-1959 shift in Dominican tobacco history. This was augmented with Cuba's post-1989 crisis, as the East European socialist bloc disintegrated and Cuba's tobacco plummeted in both quantity and quality, though both have recovered since.[4]

In exploring the full significance of the post-1959 Dominican shift, the paper first provides an overview of Havana cigar history by way of contextualising Dominican tobacco history. Turning to the Dominican Republic, the initial focus is on the 'long tobacco century' (1763-1930), in tandem with developments in Cuba. By the mid-nineteenth century, Cuba had become the international standard for premium cigars and cigar tobacco, but saw this severely undercut during the 1868-98 independence struggles and subsequent US occupation and investment. The 1930-61 dominance of Trujillo and La Tabalacera follows almost as an interlude prior to two key periods: 1962-92, during which the seeds were (literally) sown for Cuban-type Dominican leaf to replace embargoed Cuban leaf on the US market, overtaking Cuban production and export levels in leaf in the late 1970s and cigars by the late 1980s; and 1992-2007, when Cuban-Dominican cigars dominated on the US market, also competing aggressively with Cuban cigars on the global market. The whole post-1961 period is then re-examined in the context of the Cuban influx to the Cibao and the Dominican exodus from the Cibao to New York.

The paper concludes by revisiting Dominican tobacco history as interpreted by scholars, especially the longue durée approach to 'Dominican exceptionalism' and the peasantry, stemming from the late nineteenth-century vision of Dominican patriot Pedro Francisco Bonó.[5] The debate centres around the 'patriotic', 'democratic' Cibao, with its autonomous tobacco peasantry contrasting with the plight of the dispossessed in the expansion of oligarchic cacao and imperialist sugar – a vision formed during the period when Cuban leaf and cigars became the world standard and which predated by almost a century the contrapuntal vision of Cuban tobacco and sugar by Cuban ethnographer Fernando Ortiz.[6] The Dominican exodus from the Cibao to New York is an ending which resonates as a twenty-first century Bonó-type lament for the plight of the dispossessed, but this time in tobacco itself – Bonó's vision of tobacco having all but dissipated.

The Cuban-Dominican Tobacco Connection[7]

The Havana cigar is a commodity that for over a century and a half has been at the heart of political and economic rivalries, linked with foreign and local capital and labour, and with out-migration at key turning points in Cuban history. Late nineteenth-century independence and the 1959 Revolution created Cuban communities and economies abroad, centred on commodities like tobacco. These in turn came to constitute serious competition for, while also being interlocked with, island production. Today, as in the past, parallel production and marketing systems of identical or similar brands, and the cultural and labour practices associated with them, raise issues of identity and reconciliation, in the context of both political nationalism and economic pragmatism, and cut across imperial and neo-imperial boundaries.

Cuban tobacco was developed with Spanish, German, British and French capital, for European, North American and world markets. Vuelta Abajo, in Cuba's westernmost province of Pinar del Río, became known as the tobacco mecca for the Havana cigar, which in turn became the centre around which revolved a nineteenth-century world cigar tobacco economy whose key retail outlets were London, Amsterdam, Bremen and New York. The backdrop to Cuba's First and Second Wars of Independence from Spain (1868-78 and 1895-98) was an out-migration to the United States (notably Florida and New York), the Caribbean, Mexico and Central America, and across the Atlantic, notably Spain and its outlying Canary Islands, where there were bi-directional migration flows. In the overseas settler territories, Cuban tobacco interests came together, providing a familiar means of livelihood and an economic and political mainstay for the independence struggle at home. Over time, rival economic and political interests built up, often with trading and other advantages over the home country in turmoil. At the turn of the century, US capital investment in tobacco on the island came fast, swallowing up tracts of Cuban tobacco land and major manufacturing companies. There were 'independents' who held out, but the industry as a whole never regained its former glory, and the 1930s depression and labour unrest culminated a process whereby US-owned manufacturing withdrew from Cuba to the United States.

The migratory phenomenon re-emerged after the 1959 Revolution, and new Cuban tobacco 'host communities' grew up in Nicaragua, Honduras, Ecuador, Brazil and the Dominican Republic, as well as Florida and New Jersey in the United States and the Canary Islands in Spain. Smaller manufacturers, dealers, growers and workers proved to be as astute as larger monopoly capital in finding fertile ground for overseas business. They profited from the post-1959 internal economic upheaval in Cuba that was the product of insurrection, agrarian reform and nationalisation, plus the tight trade embargo that was the political response of the United States (and for a while the whole area) to the Cuban Revolution. Western European markets became a battleground for disputed Havana cigar brands. At the same time, the Eastern European bloc and key Third World countries emerged as strong Havana cigar partners.

A new chapter opened when the demise of the Eastern European socialist bloc in 1989 signalled the end of Cuba's special trade and aid. At the same time, the United States took steps to tighten and extraterritorialise the embargo in the form of the 1991 Torricelli and 1996 Helms-Burton Acts. As external geopolitical realities compounded internal weaknesses of both an economic and political nature, the Cuban revolutionary government devised a structural adjustment strategy, courting non-US trade and investment. The Havana cigar became a key player in the Cuban strategy for the 1990s, with international court battles over market brand names – the more visible tip of a cigar war. At the same time a US anti-anti-smoking cigar revival gained momentum, involving the two US cigar giants – Connecticut-based General Cigar and Fort Lauderdale-based Consolidated Cigar – along with émigré Cuban tobacco interests, in the Dominican Republic especially, followed by Honduras, Nicaragua, Ecuador and Brazil, in all-out competition with island Cuba.

As of the late 1980s, the state-owned Cuban tobacco sector blazed the internal adjustment trail with the disaggregation of tobacco land from cooperatives back into private smallholdings. In 1994, part-dollar payments were introduced as an incentives package for the tobacco sector, and a new holding company, Habanos SA, was set up to handle overseas marketing ventures. Both measures followed fast in the wake of two landmark 'credit for tobacco' deals struck between the Cuban state tobacco enterprise, Cubatabaco, and its French and Spanish parastatal tobacco counterparts – Societé Nationale des Tabacs (SEITA) and Tabacalera Española SA. A European cigar marketing deal was struck in Britain with Hunters & Frankau. By 1997, Cuba was investing heavily in tobacco to meet a world market demand in excess of supply. Heightened US-Europe rivalry was mirrored by that within the Havana cigar universe. A new twist came in 1999 when Tabacalera Española and SEITA formed Altadis (Alianza de Tabacos y Distribución), which bought 50 percent shares in Habanos SA. Tabacalera Española had earlier in the year bought Consolidated Cigar Co. and subsequently created Altadis USA. The company was thereby heavily involved in both the island and overseas Havana cigar business, especially in the Dominican Republic, where its subsidiary company is today Tabacalera García.

Parallel production and marketing systems of identical brand names, in and outside Cuba, involving island and émigré Cubans, for non-US and US markets, clearly pose economic and political challenges for any eventual normalisation of relations between Cuba and the United States and reconciliation between tobacco interests on and off the island. However, the historical interconnections among the various cigar economies are more far-reaching than might appear at first glance.

There are the tobacco histories of territories closely interlocked with Cuba, due to out- and in-migration at key moments in Cuban history. In the United States, the better known of these histories are those of Tampa and Key West, the lesser known that of Gadsden County, in Florida. Their tobacco history, which began with Cuba's 1868-78 War of Independence, was boosted by a first US embargo on Cuba in the 1890s and ended with the second embargo of the 1960s. Less known are the Cuban tobacco histories of Jamaica and, in Spain, the Canary Islands. Then there are the closely interconnected tobacco histories of Cuba, Puerto Rico and the United States. Cuban and Puerto Rican cigar makers populated New York in the nineteenth century; the 1898 US occupations of Cuba and Puerto Rico paved the way for massive inflows of tobacco capital; and Puerto Rican (following Jamaican) migrant labourers toiled in the fields of Connecticut in the latter part of the twentieth century, growing tobacco derived from Cuban seed. Today, there is virtually nothing left of cigar tobacco in the United States, Jamaica, the Canary Islands or Puerto Rico, as company investment has relocated growing and manufacture, part of the recent wave of globalisation, following a trail blazed by a catalyst group of Cuban émigrés to the Dominican Republic, Nicaragua, Honduras, Ecuador and Brazil.

It is a history I have come to conceptualise as a new counterpoint, no longer Ortiz's *Cuban Counterpoint of Tobacco and Sugar*, but rather a counterpoint between island and off-island Cuban tobacco.[8] There is a mirror image of this in the Dominican Republic and the work of Pedro Francisco Bonó, whose thinking, like that of Ortiz in the case of Cuba, permeated a renewed Dominican scholarly interest in tobacco and the Cibao, part of a wider flourishing of post-Trujillo scholarship. Such was the renewed interest in tobacco that Dominican historian Antonio Lluberes Navarro described it in 1984 as the most studied sector of the Dominican economy after sugar.[9] The Dominican Republic was equally under focus for the explosion of out-migration to the United States from the 1960s on, and especially during the 1980s and 1990s. This exodus – demonstrably linked to US-Dominican political events, economic and migration policies, and rural impoverishment – has only in a few studies been directly linked to tobacco.[10]

Strikingly, while there has been some comparative study of Cuba and the Dominican Republic, there has been none with a tobacco focus. Yet Napoleón Padilla's evocatively titled *Memorias de un cubano sin importancia* is highly suggestive regarding the centrality of Cuba to developments in post-1959 Dominican tobacco.[11] By then retired and living in Miami, Padilla recounted his life as a Cuban tobacco agronomist who left Cuba in 1960 in opposition to the revolutionary agrarian reforms, worked helping build up the Cibao's Instituto del Tabaco (INTABACO) in the early 1960s, and returned to the Dominican Republic in later life for the United Nations Food and Agriculture Organisation. Four years after publication of Padilla's book, *Cigar Aficionado* (a cigar lovers' glossy life-style magazine launched in New York in 1992) began to run informative feature articles on companies and personalities in the contemporary cigar world, involving, quite prominently, Cubans in the contemporary Dominican Republic. Hence this incursion into Cuban-Dominican tobacco history.

The Long Tobacco Century (1763-1930)

Raymundo González wrote of the Dominican *largo siglo campesino* (long peasant century), from 1763 to 1930, contrasting this with Cuba and Puerto Rico where plantations were fast expanding.[12] The long peasant century applied especially to the central Cibao, where tobacco predominated, in contrast to plantation sugar in the south and east.

Tobacco, of course, predated 1763. Indeed, a pioneering place in the history of tobacco growing by European settlers in the Americas has been claimed by Dominican historians for Hispaniola in 1531 (Cuba following in 1580, Brazil in 1600, Virginia in 1612, and Maryland in 1631), and tobacco from Hispaniola is recorded as having been the first to reach Spain after the Spanish Conquest. However, because of tobacco contraband with the English, French and Dutch on the north and east coasts, in 1605 Felipe III ordered settlements to be destroyed, and people and livestock to be moved to the centre and south. The colony went into further decline when Spanish interest turned more to the mines of Mexico and Peru, enabling the French to take the western part of the island. Tobacco developed despite Spanish mercantile control, as subsistence farmers traded with French St Domingue. By the early eighteenth century, there were also companies trading in tobacco, the Governor of Santiago in 1721 having requested royal permission to sell tobacco to St Domingue, accepting payment in slaves to increase production, given the labour shortage in the Cibao.

In the eighteenth century the Spanish introduced the Estanco del Tabaco, setting up subsidiaries of Reales Fábricas de Tabacos de Sevilla in Cuba, Mexico, Peru, Venezuela and the Philippines. It was 1763 when they did so in Santo Domingo, the year Havana was under British occupation, to buy leaf through funds located in the Reales Cajas de México. The Factoría was not functional until 1770 and had a short and chequered existence until its ending in 1796. There was also conflict. By 1771, growers were protesting about the low prices of Spanish official buyers, forcing a price increase in 1773, after which crop surpluses led to planting restrictions in 1778.[13] Such was the opposition that growers were again allowed to sell inferior quality tobacco to St Domingue in return for money or slaves.

After the end of the Factoría in 1796 and the Haitian Revolution of 1791-1804, when the Dominican colonial economy plunged into crisis, the Cibao tobacco economy might have been wiped out had it not been for the early policies of the Haitian occupying governments to free slaves, redistribute land, and allow free trade with new markets. The year 1805 saw the first Haitian invasion of the eastern part of the island, and many rich white *colonos* left when Haitian President Boyer incorporated the east into Haiti in 1822. As they abandoned the countryside, tobacco growing was left to former peons and slaves, and their families, and thus a tobacco peasantry of poor whites and coloureds formed. González cites evidence to suggest that the poor sympathised with the aims of the new black republic, but differences in language and religion, and Africanisation, were anathema to elites, who were primarily white, European and Catholic; and later, it is recorded, the masses themselves were inspired to rebellion and independence in 1844.

That year, tobacco was arguably the most stable and productive sector of the economy, from which derived the economic, social and political importance of the Cibao. Trade routes opened through the north coast ports of Monte Cristi and Puerto Plata to territories in the Caribbean (St Thomas, Puerto Rico, Curaçao, Martinique), the United States, Spain, France and Germany. As early as 1811, virtually all tobacco was being exported to Europe through Puerto Plata, with France and Spain being the main buyers, but with growing markets in Holland and Germany, especially the latter.

Quality Dominican tobacco is known to have been used as wrapper for Cuban cigars, causing a French diplomat to write in 1849: "The tobacco leaf of Santo Domingo has a better taste and looks more pleasant than other kinds, and offers a perfect elasticity and good strength".[14] The Cibao became a tobacco-growing and processing area, with small-scale manufacture of *andullo* (pressed or plug tobacco), cigars and cigarettes, *serones* (bags) and thread, and breeding of pack animals. According to Ferrán, Dominican tobacco competed successfully against Cuban tobacco in Spain in terms of quality. Thus, the Captain General of Santo Domingo wrote to the King of Spain praising Dominican tobacco and proclaiming it superior to that of Cuba. In 1860, the Spanish Consul, Mariano Álvarez, complained the Germans would buy Dominican tobacco and manufacture cigars that they sold like 'Habana cigars', but at very low prices.

By the early 1870s, tobacco exports were far greater than those of sugar, coffee, cacao and mahogany; and Germany had a virtual market monopoly, Dominican tobacco imports to Hamburg alone increasing twelve-fold over 1864-1972. Why Germany? Hamburg and Bremen had begun trading in the Caribbean through St Thomas and were well placed at the time of Dominican independence. In the case of tobacco, most European countries had either state monopolies, and/or were supplied through their own colonies in the Americas and Asia, while in Germany there was free trade.

During 1888-97, exports of sugar doubled, cacao and coffee quadrupled, but tobacco declined. This has been attributed to four determining factors: lack of agrotechnology; the economic development of the country with foreign capital as of 1870; the international market, especially Germany, which was the main buyer for tobacco; and Dominican state policy.

Much has been made of the deteriorating quality of Dominican leaf in the late-nineteenth century. Samuel Hazard noted that Dominican tobacco was poorer in quality than that of Cuba, not because of the quality of the land but the lack of attention and knowedge.[15] That year, eight importers in Hamburg and Altona wrote complaining about the lack of quality classification. Lluberes noted: "Since the colonial period, the quality of the Cibao leaf has been spoken of, and its natural similarity to the Cuban leaf, but it was not handled well".[16]

Attempts were made to rectify this, as evidenced in *El Eco del Pueblo* of 14 January 1883, which reported on La Sociedad 'El Progreso' de Santiago contracting Cubans to advise on seeds and new strains. Regulations were brought in for growing and exporting, export duties reduced, and franchises awarded to establish model tobacco farms – many of which failed and were withdrawn. Later:

> The Cuban War of Independence (1895-98) gave a small boost to Dominican tobacco, since it was thought it might replace Cuban tobacco on the American market. It was a passing illusion. The American occupation of Cuba and Puerto Rico following the Hispanic-American War meant the introduction of capitalist interests in the tobacco economies of these countries. Leaf varieties were improved, as were growing conditions; but

above all the respective tobacco economies became even more tied to the American market.¹⁷

According to a 1909 Secretaría de Agricultura report:

> in the Republic there is no lack of good tobacco seed, and certain farmers, cultivating and exploiting this well, have succeeded in selling their tobacco as though it were from Vuelta Abajo, and it has been consumed as though it came from there. But in general there has not been the same level of care.¹⁸

Tobacco production quadrupled between 1870 and 1930, albeit with a slowing down in 1880-1900 and some extreme year-to-year fluctuations linked to political events, inclement weather (in the absence of technology and irrigation), and the market. In 1879, a major crisis developed when the German government, in a protectionist move for home-grown tobacco, more than doubled tobacco import duties. Market-oriented growers switched to cacao, until cacao lost out in the twentieth century to competition from West Africa. Through the late-nineteenth century, however, small firms operated in rural areas; entire communities engaged in collecting and weaving palm fibre for the *serones*; and some 90,000 mules each carried two *serones*, before the decline in animal transport with the completion of the Cibao railroads – Santiago-Sánchez in 1881 (twenty years later extended to the capital) and Santiago-Puerto Plata in 1897. Along the railroads emerged important tobacco towns such as Villa González and Navarrete.

The German market continued to be predominant, but France, Holland, the French Antilles, Spain and other markets were also of significance. The First World War closed the German market completely, and with US occupation (1916-24) the United States paid special attention to agriculture in the form of experimental stations and technification, and took almost all the tobacco for its own consumption or re-export to Europe, at increased prices. After the war, Germany began to recover predominance, and prices and production dropped.

The late-nineteenth and early-twentieth centuries saw a huge increase in US investment, primarily in the south – in sugar and mining (aluminium and nickel) – and to a lesser extent in the north – in bananas, but also in tobacco. The First World War brought price increases between 1915 and 1919, and during the US occupation of 1916-24 there were US companies with buyers in Santiago, including Tropical Tobacco Co., and Cullman Bros, of New York. In this period, Cuba was also importing Dominican tobacco, with buyers including Alfredo F. Pellerano, for the Eminencia factory in Havana, and Francisco Lavandero y Cía, for Havana Tobacco Company brands La Legitimidad, Susini, Henry Clay, Pedro Murías, Fin de Siglo and others.

After the war, soaring profits were to be made by exporters in the short-lived 'Dance of the Millions' when high prices led to a *furia de tabaco* (tobacco mania), to the detriment of food-crop production. In the crisis of 1920, Cibao exporters tried to convince the US military government to grant Dominican tobacco preferential access to the US market, but the US intent to modernise a semicolony did not extend to favouring a competitor to American tobacco growers. The military government did, however, guarantee a minimum price for the 1920 and 1921 harvests.

The 1920s recovery of European economies stimulated the tobacco trade, and from 1923 Belgium, Germany, France and Holland were the four largest buyers of Dominican tobacco. Companies from those countries became established in the Cibao, alongside companies attracted from the United States under the occupation. The Tropical Tobacco Company was set up and expanded, acquiring interests in CAT and manufacturing their own cigarettes in Santiago. The Dutch Curaçaose Handelsmaatschappij (Curaçao Trading Company) started to buy large quantities, as did Dutch merchant Hugo Scheltema, representing Compañía Dominicana de Tabacos. The Spanish Tabacalera began to buy Dominican tobacco on a regular basis, through its own permanent representative in the Cibao, and the French Companie Générale des Tabacs, through Albert Oquets. Together with the Santiago firm of V. F. Thomen, they determined prices and set market trends, overshadowing the two remaining representatives of German importers: Schulze & Lembcke and G. A. Luening. In effect, the international market moved into the Cibao, buying, processing and shipping directly, with modern processing techniques and commercial practice. By 1930, however, tobacco exports were in fourth place, after sugar, cacao and coffee, representing only 6 percent of total exports; and exports were subsequently adversely affected by the Spanish Civil War and outbreak of the Second World War.

Internally, the demand for tobacco had led to an ever more complex trading system with several levels of intermediaries, often advancing credit, often under contract. This was even more marked in the early-twentieth century, with buoyant world market prices and the emergence of a regional tobacco industry, new technology facilitating mass cigarette production and leading to a vertical integration of agriculture and industry. The 1920s, under the Horacio Vasquez government, saw attempts to modernise agriculture, including experimentation with seed selection (including from Cuba), new tobacco-curing sheds, and irrigation, though large-scale irrigation for rice displaced much tobacco land. In 1923, the state intervened to buy tobacco; agricultural modernisation was again taken up under Horacio Vasquez in 1924, with the Escuela Agrícola de Moca being set up in 1926 with professionals contracted mainly from Italy; and in the 1930s there was experimentation with varieties such as Cuban Shade, or *tabaco cubano*, to compete on the international market.[19]

Two types of growing developed: the more established around La Vega and Santiago in central Cibao; and the more shifting on cleared woodland, in areas like Mao, where tobacco was grown in large quantities and sold to merchants in Santiago. Mao developed, as did many other tobacco areas, with two main groups linked to tobacco: one in leaf growing and commercialisation; and the other in cigar making based on family labour for local consumption.

Manufacturing, Trujillo and La Tabacalera (1930-61)

For the years 1870-1930, Baud identified three market-driven periods: 1870-1900, especially after the 1879 harvest, when little attention was paid to the quality of tobacco, as merchants were buying bulk at low prices and quality was sacrificed to quantity; 1900-20, when the market was more profitable and merchants and public officials tried to increase production, but the price to the growers remained low; and the post-First World War period, when the 'Dance of the Millions' sent prices to unprecedented heights, foreign importers came into the region and made efforts to improve quality, and a group of market-oriented growers emerged alongside a larger and increasing number of poor growers.

Broadly speaking, these coincided with Lluberes's earlier identification of three phases of manufacturing from the end of the nineteenth century, with small-scale cigar and cigarette production, some for export but mainly for Cibao regional consumption, to Trujillo's La Tabacalera monopoly, consolidated especially after 1934: first, the growing number of small concerns; second, their growth alongside larger new ones; and third, the consolidation of large companies with cigarette mechanisation.

A home industry had developed from the early-nineteenth century on, in Santiago and rural areas, producing cigars, plug and cigarettes primarily for the domestic market. Small-scale cigar rolling expanded rapidly in the late-nineteenth century, but by the early-twentieth century this was giving way to factories such as La Anacaona and La Matilde, of Simeón Mencía y Sucursales, as well as La Aurora and CAT – these last in particular symbolising the growing division in the industry. Small informal sweatshops found themselves in a weak financial position, threatened by the larger producers and central government.[20]

In the early 1900s, tobacco manufacturing was boosted by protectionist measures introduced by President Ramón Cáceres, including higher taxes on imported cigars and cigarettes. Exports of cigars peaked in 1911, cigarettes in 1927 – machines having been introduced in Santiago's La Anacaona and La Matilde factories and Santo Domingo's La Habanera. However, cigar and cigarette exports together accounted for less than half a percent of total exports, and were irregular, mainly for Caribbean markets, exported through Monte Cristi, Sánchez, Comendador, Macorís and Barahona.

By 1934, the manufacturing industry was predominantly mechanised production of cigarettes for domestic consumption. In contrast to one hundred registered manufacturers of cigars, there were only two for cigarettes: CAT and the Dominican Tobacco Company, one of two US buying companies, along with Cullman's Tropical Tobacco Co., which also had shares in CAT and Dominican Tobacco. When Trujillo moved to monopoly that year, Cullman cut secret deals but soon pulled out.

Trujillo came to power in 1930 with an economy in recession. Tobacco was particularly hard hit. From 1928 to 1930, the price for tobacco dropped by 44 percent (in comparison with cacao 41 percent, coffee 35 percent and sugar 12 percent). The ten million cigars produced by the major factories in 1929 dropped back to five million in 1930. The crisis was such that in 1931 the Santiago Chamber of Commerce, Industry and Agriculture penned a letter to Trujillo requesting government support and protection. Trujillo's response, despite business opposition, was to increase state taxes and establish a monopoly on major exports such as tobacco, coffee and cacao. The Trujillo plan was to oust the controlling group of companies and families, initially by the government buying and selling leaf at guaranteed minimum prices; and by increasing cigar and cigarette price controls and taxes on production and trade, and then by acquiring majority shares in CAT.[21]

From 1930 to 1945 Trujillo put through a radical development of infrastructure, in which the peasantry was forced to participate, building roads and irrigation channels. This was supported by a policy of *campesinización* (peasantisation), with new *colonias agrícolas* and land distribution of 30 *tareas*[22] to the impoverished, designed to strengthen minifundia and achieve food self-sufficiency, but these were on mainly poor land in marginal areas.[23] CAT modernised and expanded: sales agreements were signed with enterprises in Santo Domingo, San Pedro de Macorís, La Romana, Puerto Plata and Santiago; by the late 1930s, several small cigarette and other companies had been bought up; in the early 1940s, aid was given to growers as part of Trujillo's plan to Dominicanise the Haitian border; and the Second World War saw a growth in production as imports declined. After Copello's death in 1944, Trujillo took over his shares, thereby exercising complete control, and set up a new company, Comisiones en General, with exclusivity on the distribution and sale of Tabacalera's products. The 1940s Secretaría de Agricultura launched a tobacco-growing campaign, headed by Costa Rican-born agronomist Luis Carballo, who had come to the Dominican Republic in 1914. Carballo's genetic experiments led to the creation of what became the leading Dominican tobacco, Amarillo Parado, and he was followed by Joaquín (Quín) Díaz, who created Quín Díaz.

In 1946, CAT's daily output of 100 cigars was low in comparison with La Aurora's 350, and profits were down, but the new company strategy broadened to new types of contracts with national and foreign companies. In 1949, CAT signed an agreement with Central Romana, for the exclusive sale of cigars and cigarettes, and this was followed by others, as well as strong advertising campaigns in the press and on radio. Expansion was facilitated by repression of worker action, the regime appointing its own 'official' worker leaders; though unions were able to survive clandestinely, and 1940s 'liberalisation' recognised workers' right to strike, and a labour code was introduced in 1951.

In 1953, CAT (Santo Domingo) had an output of some 9 million cigars (37.72 percent of total production), while León Jimenes (Santiago) and Imperial, León del Rosario (Moca) each produced some 7.5 million (31.14 percent). In 1954, an agreement was signed between CAT, León Jimenes and Imperial to create a consortium controlling 65 percent of national production and sales. In 1955, CAT entered into negotiations with Phillip Morris and J. R. Reynolds for the production and sale of their products in the Dominican Republic, but Trujillo rejected their offer. The regime was by then facing ever greater opposition, and Trujillo was shot in 1961.

The end of the Trujillo dictatorship signalled a new economic and political opening that was both internal and external, and significantly so for tobacco, coming as it did when the US embargo on Cuba created a vacuum on the US tobacco market. The first increase was in the demand for Dominican leaf for cigar manufacturers in Tampa and New Jersey. Then, as production costs rose rapidly in the United States and factories that had established operations outside the United States – primarily in Central America and the Canary Islands – faced unrest, companies transferred operations to the Dominican Republic, attracted by the concessions provided by the new Dominican Free Trade Zones and low labour costs. Their success then attracted others.

The Seeds are Sown (1962-92)

At the time of his death, Trujillo is estimated to have controlled 60 percent of total cultivated land. This was the backdrop to the start of a land reform in 1962, and between 1962 and 1977 close to 200,000 hectares were distributed to some 37,000 farm families in 300 communities. In the late 1970s a policy of cooperative farming was linked to agro-industry, and since then the balance between the state and private sectors has oscillated, often in favour of the latter.

INTABACO, set up in 1962 under the directorship of Luis Carballo, shaped tobacco growing over the following years. It survived the politically turbulent years of 1962-64, with the ephemeral presidency and military ousting of Bosch, and the ensuing political vacuum. After the 1965 US occupation, it had the official support of Balaguer throughout his early years in power (1964-78), as well as Hector Guzmán (1978-82) and Jorge Blanco (1982-86). Initial steps were taken to improve Amarillo Parado and Quín Díaz and, with seed selection of Villa González grower Santiago Díaz, to create Chago Díaz. In 1963, Piloto Cubano was introduced, brought from Cuba; and 1964-65 saw the first experiments to produce San Vicente wrapper, also from Cuba, and US Dixie Shade, though these were not planted commercially until 1974.

INTABACO's tobacco censuses of 1963 and 1972[24] evidence that, while tobacco continued to be produced overwhelmingly on small farms (of less than 75 *tareas*), during the decade 1960-70 these declined in number, while the number of large farms increased. The tobacco grown by the latter was Virginia or Burley, locally called *tabaco cubano*, and often by Cubans. In the words of González:

> Many of the administrators and other employees of the largest estates are exiled Cubans, and their compatriots are also employees in the tobacco warehouses where processing and packing take place. These Cubans, with their experience and knowledge and their enterprising spirit, may very well help revolutionise the country's tobacco industry.[25]

This was echoed by Ferrán:

> The Cuban seed was introduced in the Dominican Republic in 1963 with the help of Cuban farmers and producers who transposed a technology that was relatively complex to the neighbouring republic after Castro took power in Cuba. It was in the interest of the Dominican government and the Fetab Inc. cooperative, which was then receiving a subsidy, to take over the market that the Cuban government had lost in the United States. . . .
> The principle exports are to the United States, since the buyers there cannot obtain Cuban tobacco, and the Canary Islands, where it is processed and re-exported to the United States.[26]

The United Kingdom and Switzerland were explored as possible markets, but they continued to buy from Cuba. Ferrán reported:

> There are those of the opinion that in the matter of quality and prices, the Dominican long filler can compete with the Cuban in these markets. But from the outset two difficulties are faced: i) the manufacturers do not like to break good, already established commercial relations; ii) and also, they do not like to change producers because of the risk they would run in receiving tobacco with a different aroma, which would affect the blends.[27]

While growers were financed for Cuban tobacco by a processing company guaranteeing a contract price, or Banco Agrícola through INTABACO, or commercial banks, there was practically no financial aid for *tabaco criollo*. In contrast to the increase in *tabaco cubano* in the 1960s, there was an overall decrease in tobacco production and export, Dominican tobacco being undercut on European markets by Philippine, Brazilian, Colombian and other tobaccos.[28]

For domestic consumption, it was mainly Chago Díaz and Quín Díaz, also known as *tabaco de olor*. For export, there were two varieties: *tabaco criollo*, with subvarieties Amarilla Parado, Punto de Lanza, Amarillo Planchado and Piloto Cubano. By 1970, the Cuban tobacco output of some 350 growers was in the region of 45,000 *quintales* on 35,000 *tareas* of land, whereas in 1963 it had only been 3,500 *quintales*, a mere 0.27 percent of national production, on 890 *tareas*. Tobacco exports doubled in value 1962-71, with the Cibao producing 70 percent of the country's tobacco.

In the early 1970s there were fifteen buying companies, each employing over 450 workers, and 35 local processing plants, each with some 150 workers, in addition to day labourers. In 1972 one company alone, INETAB, with Dutch and Dominican capital, was to employ 9,600 in production, and a further 14,000 in processing and packing. By the late 1970s some 300,000 depended on tobacco, which was the country's fourth agro-exporting sector (after sugar, coffee and cacao). In 1978 there were two cigarette factories and 35 small cigar factories registered, with a concentration of the latter in Tamboril, Santiago province; and there were other small 'factories' unregistered and without brands, producing mainly for domestic consumption but with some export of cigars to the United States. Registered export companies numbered eighteen. Piloto Cubano was produced by the medium to large grower and sold already selected.

In 1978, Tabacalera Española and SEITA, the strongest in Europe, were looking to Dominican leaf for mild cigarettes and cigar wrapper:

> now that we know the cost of North American manpower has made it impossible to produce in the US. At the moment, the Republic of Nicaragua, which had been attractive for wrapper production, is facing political difficulties, which is why the Dominican Republic offers great potential for growing this class of tobacco.[29]

Cuban émigré tobacco interests had operated in Nicaragua since 1963, with generous land grants and other concessions from Anastasio Somoza. The year 1978, however, was the build-up to the 1979 Nicaraguan Revolution, occasioning greater attention to the Dominican Republic. In December 1978, the National Council for Free Trade Zones (FTZs) was established to coordinate promotion, operation and development of FTZs as the foreign investment model, and the 1980s saw their marked expansion, foreign investors attracted by cheap labour and tax concessions.

This had its early beginnings in 1967, when the US conglomerate Gulf & Western took over the US-owned South Puerto Rico Sugar Company, and with it almost 300,000 acres of land around La Romana refinery, and then rapidly diversified. In 1969, with the backing of Balaguer's policy of industrial incentives, it entered into an agreement with the government to manage an industrial park outside La Romana. With generous tax concessions it built the installation for its own subsidiary companies and attracted 24 other businesses, such that by the 1980s turnover was greater than Dominican GDP. Then, in 1985, when the sugar industry was in crisis, and having profited greatly by speculating on Dominican sugar on the futures market, Gulf & Western sold its Dominican holdings to a Palm Beach-based consortium headed by the Fanjuls – émigrés from Cuba with major sugar holdings.

By the late 1970s, the food, beverage and tobacco industries were the most important in terms of output and numbers employed. While mainly small family-run plants, in the three main FTZs of La Romana, San Pedro de Macorís and Santiago there were over 40 tobacco plants employing over 4,000 workers and tobacco manufacturing was reported as the largest sector in GDP (18.6 percent in 1978).[30] There were 1.4 million hectares of tobacco under cultivation, an increase of over 100 percent since 1975, set to further increase when irrigation projects started to take effect, especially in the Cibao. Tobacco was fourth in export value, and production had overtaken that of Cuba. Disease and market setbacks caused exports to fall in 1982 and 1983; but the following year saw a slight recovery, by which time there were 60 tobacco plants in FTZs, again set to increase in size and number. Cigar production and exports grew with the FTZs, taking off especially in the late 1980s, when the Dominican Republic, as well as largest supplier of leaf to the United States, became the leading world cigar exporter: in 1988, over 50 million units, followed by Cuba with 49 million and Honduras with 32 million.

Concentration of production and trade in the 1980s Dominican Republic was such that by the early 1990s a small group of companies, headed by Kelner's Tabacos Dominicanos and cigarette monopolies E. León Jimenes and La Tabacalera, dominated the sector. León Asensio in Tamboril was one of the largest agro-industrial complexes. Trade was controlled by six major exporting companies, which were US, Dutch and Spanish, and their Dominican buying subsidiaries. The main exporting families were Espaillat, Thomén, Kelner-Tavares and Méndez-Bogaert. The main companies were Compañía de Tabacos Quisqueya, Panamericana de Tabacos, Compañía Dominicana de Tabacos, José Méndez and Compañía de Tabacos Dominicanos (TABADOM).

Cigar Hiatus (1992-2007)

The year 1992 was a landmark for Dominican-Cuban tobacco, as major US backing for a cigar come-back was launched with the publication of *Cigar Aficionado,* helping promote the Dominican Republic as the new cigar mecca, with Cuban and US companies producing some of the same brands made in Cuba before 1959. The 1992 autumn/winter inaugural issue carried three feature articles, two on Cuba, where tobacco had been hit hard in the crisis following the break-up of its partner East European socialist bloc, and one on the Dominican Republic.[31] Since then *Cigar Aficionado* has played a significant part in the boom-bust period of 1992-98, as well as the gradual recuperation and levelling out since.

Dominican exports grew from 73 million in 1994 to 320 million in 1998, predominantly to the US market. In 1997, tobacco moved into third place in domestic exports, after ferro-nickel and sugar. Such was the Dominican cigar success that in 1998 the *Miami Herald* took great pleasure in reporting a team of Cuban cigar experts had spent several weeks in the Dominican Republic in the winter of 1998 observing production and market techniques.[32]

While traditional companies strengthened their infrastructure, trained personnel, expanded growing areas, and financed growers to increase production, further concentrating production and trade, a multitude of smaller and newer companies were formed. Around a hundred new cigar factories were set up, with foreign and domestic capital, some by Cubans long in the business, but many had little or no knowledge of the business, which led to poor quality tobacco and cigars.

The Cibao capital of Santiago, having been relegated by Trujillo and Balaguer, grew chaotically, its population doubling, from some 300,000 in the early 1980s to 600,000 in the mid-1990s, by which time its Victor Espaillat Mera FTZ (established in 1975) was producing 80 percent of the country's cigars. In 1997, there were 130 registered cigar manufacturers, 18 in FTZs, employing 125,000, some 55,000 of whom in agriculture, on 400,000 *tareas*, and export value was over US$200 million.[33] Other cigar centres – Tamboril, Villa González, Licey, San José de Las Matas, Janico, Villa Bosono – witnessed a similar population increase. The growth of Villa González was mainly due to the CAT cigar and cigarette factory, and that of Tamboril to León Asensio.

One of the many newcomers in the mid-1990s was Spanish-born, Uruguayan-raised Litto Gómez, who switched from the jewellery trade in Miami to cigar manufacturing in Tamboril, acquiring 180 acres of land to grow Piloto Cubano and hiring an experienced agronomist to run the farm. According to Gómez, "A lot of people said, 'You're moving to Tamboril? You're crazy', because of all the labor problems they had years ago".[34] Cuban-American Carlos Fuente, who had moved there in 1980, was quoted as saying: "In 1980, Tamboril was

Vietnam. They were shooting machine guns in the streets . . . it was a war zone." A Santiago FTZ was eminently attractive by comparison, and most of the export factories clustered in Santiago, bussing in workers from Tamboril.[35]

This changed with the cigar boom, when newcomers set up in Tamboril, paying higher wages and offering the chance to work commute-free. The poaching began in earnest. "We woke up one January," Cuban-American Manuel Quesada declared in a *Cigar Aficionado* interview, "and between Fuente, Davidoff, ourselves and León Jimenes, we were missing 300 to 400 cigar-makers."[36] La Romana, in the east, was sheltered from the 'roller wars' that dominated Santiago, whereby Tabacalera de García Ltd., Consolidated's La Romana factory, appeared to have fared better than most.

Gómez was quick to insist he was not one of the new 'mavericks' but acknowledged:

> . . . a lot of new factories opened in Tamboril. The town went from two to 80 factories. Some were very small factories, with four to six rollers – but some had as many as 50 or 60 rollers! And with most of these factories, the operators had no idea what making a cigar was all about. They just opened the factories, put their equipment in and hired rollers from other factories. And they gave money away. They made large gifts to get the good and experienced rollers to work for them. A roller who was making anywhere from $50-70 a week was offered a salary four times that amount, of $200-250 a week.[37]

Gómez related how the mavericks had difficulty finding good leaf and keeping their factories open five days a week; how there was no quality control; and how, when 90 percent went out of business with the 1998 slump, the mavericks were the first to go. As many as 60 Tamboril factories went out of business between 1997 and 1999, leaving empty shells of factories and only three export factories: Gómez's Tabacalera La Flor, Tabacalera Real Felipe Gregorio SA and José A. Blanco's Tabacalera Palma SA. Rollers were left without jobs, and, while some of the established factories took back the good rollers, others would not. Tabacalera de García, General Cigar Dominicana and Fuente were the greats, each making tens of millions of cigars annually; and there were several mid-size companies, such as Cigars Davidoff (Swiss-based Davidoff withdrew cigar production from Cuba in the early 1990s), OK Cigars (Avos brand), Tabacalera El Crédito, Matasa, Tabacalera La Flor (La Flor Dominicana) and several others belonging to émigré Cubans.

By 1998, the Dominican Republic had 36 FTZs, home to 40.6 percent of enterprises and employing 171,000, of whom some 37,000 were in Santiago I & II, 7,000 in Esperanza and 6,063 in Moca. That year, seven new FTZs were approved, six in the Cibao – Laguna Prieta, Los Manantiales, Tamboril,

Pontezuela in Santiago, Salcedo and Montecristi. Twelve of the enterprises approved were for processing tobacco, employing some 5,000.[38] When the boom peaked, all were caught off-guard. At the start of 1998 there were more than 140 factories, by April only 100, and the prognosis was for no more than 24 by the end of the year.

The 1997-98 harvest of a record 940,000 *quintales* saw much tobacco grown poorly and on poor land. Such was the glut of tobacco that, pressured by the Cibao Tobacco Growers Association of Villa González and the Growers Union of Moca, the state paid out to each 40 million and 10 million pesos, respectively, to buy tobacco at above market prices and promised a further 200 million pesos. Warehouses were full, and the expectation was that the market would recover the following year. That was not to be, and in 1999 a state resolution was passed to restrict planting, allowing only 20,000 *tareas* by growers with finance and a buying contract from manufacturer, processor or exporter. A total of 60 factories closed their doors, while 20 that were more established continued to operate normally, some with double their 1994 sales, but with tobacco stockpiled.[39] Sandoval charted the events of 1998:

> The crisis in the Dominican tobacco sector that began in 1998 is the worst in memory, if not history. Never before has a price for tobacco gone unnegotiated, and therefore unpaid, for two years. Tobacco is prone to crisis, but even in the worst crises a price was always set.[40]

The crisis was so severe that Monsignor Juan Antonio Flores Santana, Archbishop of Santiago and other clergy signed the 'Declaration of Villa González' urging then President Leonel Fernández to find a solution to the crisis.

Small and medium producers were left unpaid, turning to other jobs where available, while a host of dependent industries also suffered. Producers staged large protests outside government offices. Secretary of Agriculture Amilcar Romero declared overproduction stemmed in no small measure from producers planting outside the dedicated tobacco zones:

> In Cibao during the boom, people began to plant tobacco everywhere: in their yards, in empty lots in Santiago and other cities and in other people's yards. . . . So much tobacco was harvested that in one instance, *sartas*, or braids of drying tobacco leaves, were even hung to dry in the carport of a car sales lot.[41]

Traditional tobacco growers held the Secretaría de Agricultura, Banco Agrícola and Asociación Dominicana de Exportadores de Tabaco (ADET) in part to blame for providing credit to non-traditional producers to plant tobacco on non-traditional lands. Agronomist Manuel Ureña argued this was exacerbated by new factories producing low-quality cigars, with a shortage of wrapper. Only one cigar, Fuente Fuente Opus X, launched in 1995, claimed at the time to be made completely with Dominican tobacco; and in 1997 wrapper in Connecticut, Ecuador and Indonesia was affected by weather, while Central African wrapper was of a high quality but only a small amount was produced.

In early 1998, more than 50 small factories closed, and in July 1998-June 1999 a further 75-100, leaving more than 20,000 unemployed. By June 1999, 75 percent of 129 Cibao cigar factories were closed and others were scaling back, occasioning major debate as to the solution: INTABACO should buy and market warehoused 1997-98 production; there should be long-term planning to avert overproduction; and a national council comprising representatives from the farming sector should be set up. Almost everyone was arguing that the government had to intervene in some form or another, buying excess tobacco and renegotiating loans, though INTABACO warned against creating a bail-out mentality, exonerating producers planting outside officially designated tobacco-producing zones.[42]

Gradually the sector picked up. According to INTABACO's *Boletín Estadístico 2004*, of the tobacco areas divided into north, northeast, central, and south, that year the north was producing almost 70 percent of Dominican *tabaco negro*, and the northeast a further 25 percent. Santiago province alone produced 65 percent, with some 70 percent of the crop for cigar manufacturing, the highest price being commanded by Piloto Cubano. The areas with the most planting were Valverde (over 12,000 *tareas*) and Navarrete and Villa González (each in the region of 8,000); and over 40 percent of cultivation was under irrigation. Leaf was exported mainly to the United States, Puerto Rico and Honduras (over 80 percent of total export value), contrasting with exports to the next largest markets of Switzerland and Spain (each barely 4 percent).[43] Tobacco imports for cigar blends included wrapper, especially Connecticut USA and Connecticut Ecuador, together with filler and binder from Honduras, El Salvador, Nicaragua, Indonesia, Java, Cameroon and Brazil.

However, it was major companies that had most strengthened their hand, including international conglomerates. In 1998, General Cigar relocated machine production from Alabama to Santiago's FTZ. In 1999, SEITA bought Consolidated; Swedish Match bought General Cigar's Santiago factory and Tabacalera El Crédito; and Tabacalera Española subsequently merged with SEITA to form Altadis, the world's largest cigar company, third largest cigarette company, and fourth in total tobacco trade, operating in Cuba for the European market and the Dominican Republic for the US market.

There were five main manufacturers of leading brands (some owned, some made under license for other companies) in 2002: Tabacalera Arturo Fuente (including the brands Arturo Fuente, Ashton, Bauzá, Cuesta Rey, Don Carlos, Fuente Fuente Opus X, Hemingway, La Única); Tabacalera de García, subsidiary of Altadis USA (Cabañas, H. Upmann, Don Diego, Flamenco Las Palmas, Henry Clay, La Corona, Montecristo, Por Larrañaga, Primo del Rey, Romeo y Julieta 1875, Santa Damiana); General Cigar, subsidiary of Swedish Match (Bolívar, Canaria D'Oro, Cifuentes, Cohíba, Macanudo, Partagás, Ramón Allones); MATASA (José Benito, Cubita, Fonseca, Licenciados); and Tabacos Dominicanos (Avo, Davidoff, Zino). That year, Tabacalera De García's La Romana factory was declared the largest factory under one roof in the world. While only employing half the number of workers as at the height of the cigar boom (2,500 in 2002 as against 5,000 in 1997-98), the factory was making more than 50 million cigars a year, of which 28-30 million were hand-made.

Cubans In

Cuban involvement in the Dominican Republic in the early post-1959 years was in agriculture and is perhaps best symbolised by Napoleón S. Padilla. Born in Havana in 1919, Padilla died in Miami in the late 1990s, having published his memoirs.[44] His father was the son of an immigrant Canary Islander, who settled in Cuba's Pinar del Río province in the late nineteenth century, at a time when large numbers of Canary Islanders were being encouraged to settle in Cuba. The family lost property in 1896 during the War of Independence and was then briefly in the tobacco business. Padilla trained as an agricultural engineer, first specialising in sugar. He moved to tobacco when the San Juan y Martínez Experimental Tobacco Station opened in 1945, developing flue-cured and Burley cigarette tobacco, and was involved in proposals to create the Tribunal de Cuentas, Banco Nacional and Banco de Fomento Agrícola e Industrial. He worked for Villaamil, Santalla y Cía (1948-57); and from 1954 to 58, by then a leading tobacco agronomist, he travelled regularly on tobacco business to the United States, especially North Carolina (Duke and North Carolina State Universities and the Oxford Tobacco Experimental Station).

Shortly after the 1959 Revolution, Padilla was involved in a tobacco deal to beat the impending US blockade, but he soon opposed the revolutionary government's proposals for land reform and nationalisation of industry and left Cuba in June 1960. In 1962 he was sent by the Interamerican Development Bank to work in the post-Trujillo Dominican Republic. Having met then Dominican President Juan Bosch earlier in Cuba, he was invited to attend the 1962 inauguration of the Estación Experimental Tabacalera del Pontón, La Vega. Bosch's new Secretary of Agriculture, Antonio Guzmán, supported the Institute and sent two young Dominican agronomists, one of whom was Hipólito Mejía, to study in North Carolina. Padilla helped draft Dominican tobacco legislation similar to that of pre-1959 Cuba, including Law 5961 to create INTABACO. His catalyst mission was to work with INTABACO to develop a tobacco sector that could fill the void created on the US market by the embargo on Cuba. He recommended Cuban growers and brought in Cuban technicians to introduce new tobaccos, carry out a census of tobacco farms, and conduct soil studies and training at Pontón.

In 1966, Padilla went to work for the United Nations Food and Agricultural Organisation, but in 1978 he was contacted by Mejía, then Secretario de Agricultura under the newly elected President Guzmán, and returned to the Dominican Republic in 1979, 1980 and 1982. He retired in 1982, but kept alive his tobacco interest by supporting the Cuban American National Foundation lobby against any US attempt to normalise relations with Cuba. This included new legislation to extend the extra-territoriality of the US embargo, and preparing cases for the US-based Asociación Cubana de la Industria del Tabaco against international tobacco companies involved in Cuba.[45]

The post-1959 Cuban presence in Dominican cigar manufacturing that followed in the 1970s was twofold. Cuban family firms began to relocate, beginning with the Quesadas in 1974, followed by the Fuentes, Olivas, Toraños and Pérez-Carillos in the 1980s and 1990s. Since its inception in 1992, *Cigar Aficionado* has regularly featured them and the Dominican Republic, comparing it favourably with Cuba. In 1996, at the height of the cigar boom, the central town of Villa González, with its cigar factories, was likened to Pinar del Río, in Vuelta Abajo. In the words of Emilio Reyes, of Tabaco Flor de los Reyes:

> I just spent four years in Cuba's Vuelta Abajo and Partido region and I can promise you that the Yaque Valley [in the Cibao] is growing some of the best tobacco in the world right now. In some cases, this valley may be growing better quality tobacco than even in Cuba.[46]

The Fuentes story is particularly salient. While Padilla's family story began with nineteenth century Spanish immigration to Cuba and post-1959 Cuban emigration to the United States, the US Cuban émigré story of the Fuente family began in the early twentieth century to Tampa, Florida, and in the 1980s and 1990s they became solidly grounded in the Dominican Republic. In the 1992 inaugural issue of *Cigar Aficionado*, Gordon Mott wrote of Arturo Fuente Sr. and the Dominican Republic:

> [H]e no longer feels like an outsider. . . . The Dominican Republic is as much at home to him as any of the three other countries where the family has made cigars before. In fact, the Caribbean island nation has become home to many of the world's major cigar makers outside of Cuba: General Cigar, Consolidated Cigar, Tabacos Dominicanos, Arturo Fuente and MATASA as well as others. These companies produce a range of premium brands, mainly for the American market, including Partagás, Macanudo, H. Upmann,

Don Diego, Arturo Fuente and Davidoff. For most, the journey was a simple choice based on business necessity – a place to make cigars after Fidel Castro took control of the Cuban cigar industry and the US trade embargo closed the doors on Cuba in 1962.[47]

As Fuente Sr. told the story, four of their factories had been damaged by fire – Tampa in 1921 and 1948, Nicaragua in 1977 and Honduras in early 1979. They had either rebuilt or moved on. After a failed attempt to produce hand-rolled cigars again in Tampa in 1979, with Cuban and Vietnamese labour, they had two choices, Carlos Fuente Jr explained:

> Sell out or go to a foreign country again . . . civil wars or political instability in Central America argued against returning there. Mexico's strict investment laws at the time dampened expectations of a reasonable profit. And Cuba was out of bounds. In a sense, the Dominican Republic was the only option left.[48]

The Fuentes had considered the Dominican Republic in the 1970s, but it wasn't until 1980 that they set up operations in Santiago's FTZ. By 1992, Fuente boasted the largest hand-made cigar factory in the world; and, when Dominican cigar exports topped 60 million cigars in 1993, an 18 percent increase over 1992, and the Dominican Republic ranked first in the world for handmade premium cigar production, Fuente was in the lead, producing over 20 million. None of the Dominican cigars made were *puros* (pure) – that is, made from 100 percent Dominican tobacco – but in 1992 Fuente harvested the first wrapper from what was to become Chateau de la Fuente, and in 1995 launched his new Fuente Fuente Opus X, a 100 percent Dominican cigar.

From their first factory in 1980, which was little more than four walls and a roof, with seven employees, the Fuentes rose to four factories, employing over 1,000 rollers, and their own leaf facility in the FTZ in Palmar Abajo, Villa González. The cigars manufactured were either owned totally or partially, or made under license. Some brands don't carry the Fuente name: like Ashton, a joint venture with Holt's Cigar Co.; Bauzá, marketed by Oscar Boruchin of Mike's Cigars in Miami; and brands such as Cuesta-Rey and La Única under license with the Tampa-based Newman family. Each of the four factories makes certain brands. Factory No. 1 in Santiago, the oldest, makes Arturo Fuente, Hemingway, Fuente Fuente Opus X, Ashton Cabinets, Savinellis, Diamond Crown and a couple other brands. Factory No. 2 in Moca manufactures most of the cigars for the Newman family – Cuesta-Rey, La Única. Factory No. 4, in Santiago, makes Sosa, Bauzá and Montesino, though some Montesino is made at Factory No. 1 and Factory No. 3.

It is Carlos Fuente Jr. who has become one of the most prominent figures in Dominican cigars. Time spent in Nicaragua on the tobacco farms of Angel Oliva and his son, Johnny, shaped his desire to grow Dominican wrapper, to create a cigar with 100 percent Dominican tobacco. His determination was even greater after being told in 1989 that cigar manufacturers in the Dominican Republic were not really making Dominican cigars, they were assembling them with tobacco from elsewhere. Knowing that there had been trials with Dominican wrapper in the late 1960s, Fuente approached Oliva to produce Cuban-seed wrapper on his Dominican farm. There, according to Oliva, the soil was just like that of San Luis in Cuba, where he had grown up. Oliva, also big in Ecuadorian wrapper, had left behind their Pinar del Río business in 1960 and moved into growing in Central and South America. Then, after the 1973 Sandinista Revolution in Nicaragua, Oliva turned to the Dominican Republic. Oliva later sold the Dominican farm on which they had conducted the trials to Fuente.

From one factory in 1990, eight years later the Fuentes had four, three in Santiago and one in Moca FTZs. As fast as they trained workers, Fuente complained, they would be poached by others: "that's when my father said the scene reminded him of when he used to watch the old cowboy movies with the California Gold Rush. The cigar business became like the Gold Rush." Fuente reminisced:

> It's unbelievable when I think back to being in Ybor City [Tampa] with my father and my grandfather, in a little wooden house that had a little cigar factory in the back . . . our heritage is Cuban. The way we make cigars, the way my father blends cigars, was taught by my grandfather. Before the embargo, we made cigars strictly of Cuban tobacco. Our heart was in Cuban tobacco. After the embargo, we were forced to look for other tobaccos, but it was always that love, that heritage . . . we make a cigar with that kind of complexity often found in Cuban cigars, yet always trying to achieve finesse and balance.
>
> We all have very strong emotional ties to Cuba. We always will have emotional ties to Cuba. When I was born and then raised in Tampa, I didn't speak English until I started first grade. My heritage is Cuban; I'm very proud to be a Cuban-American. When I was growing up, the conversation in my home was always that when there was an opportunity to go back to Cuba, we would visit. . . . I would like to go back to Cuba one day . . . and meet the great cigarmakers of Cuba and the great tobacco growers . . . but not necessarily to open a factory. I believe my responsibility is to the Dominican Republic and to our customers. I have a great love for the Dominican Republic and that is where my heart is. . . .[49]

Among the Cubans who moved into key positions in the two major US companies operating in the Dominican Republic (Consolidated Cigar and General Cigar), the story of Benjamín (Benji) Menéndez Toraño is worth recounting. Of Spanish-origin, son of the founder of H. Upmann and Montecristo brands in Cuba, who left in 1960 for Miami, where he worked for Philip Morris. He then went to the Canary Islands, where in 1961 he founded Compañía Insular Tabacalera (CIT) in Las Palmas, making Montecruz, a Montecristo look-alike. The company sold to Gulf & Western in 1972, and he stayed on until 1977, when he and his brother Felix opened a cigar factory in Brazil. Hired by General Cigar in 1983, he went to Jamaica and then the Dominican Republic to become General Cigar's vice-president for Dominican premium cigar manufacture, working for company director Ed Cullmann, who had earlier sold the family the US rights to Montecristo. A parallel history is that of Angel Daniel Nuñez, son of a Dominican tobacco farmer who, after training as an agronomist, started in INTABACO in 1972 and General Cigar in 1974. He worked under Cullman growing Havana-seed Connecticut wrapper leaf in the Dominican Republic for Dominican-made Partagás and Macanudo cigars, using Connecticut and Cameroon wrappers – part of a broader General Cigar strategy to develop new strains of tobacco grown in Connecticut, Honduras (San Agustín), Nicaragua (Ometepe) and the Dominican Republic. Nuñez rose to be President of General Cigar in late 2006. The company had by then been bought by Swedish Match AB of Stockholm and was reported to have 8,000 employees, with leaf growing and manufacturing in Honduras and the Dominican Republic, and whose brands included Macanudo, Partagás, Cohíba, Punch and Hoyo de Monterrey. Menéndez himself left General Cigar in 1997 to become director of Central American and Caribbean tobacco operations for Tabacalera Española, subsequently Altadis USA.

After Alonso Menéndez and Pepe García, makers of Montecristo cigars, left Cuba, García bought the Menéndez interest out and began making Montecruz, along with Don Diego and others, for the Canary Islands company Compañía Insular Tabacalera (CIT). Consolidated bought CIT in 1972, and in 1982-83 Gulf & Western moved Consolidated production from the Canaries to La Romana. In 1988, after Hurricane Gilbert tore the roof off the Gore family's Royal Jamaica factory in Kingston, Jamaica, Consolidated started to make cigars for them. Consolidated was soon to buy the trademark and relocate production to the Dominican Republic. In 1989, Consolidated acquired the American Cigar Company, complete with rights to Cuban trademarks owned by American Tobacco's pre-1959 subsidiary Tabacalera Cubaña.

The trademark issue became highly litigious, with manufacturers who had left Cuba claiming the right to their trademarks. García had been in litigation in the United States, and in the mid-1970s the US government decided he was the rightful owner of H. Upmann, Montecristo and Por Larrañaga in the United States. Cuban Cigar Brands was formed as a partnership between García and

Consolidated, which had a controlling interest. This was initially a holding operation. Then, in 1975, Consolidated started to produce H. Upmann for the United States, paying royalties to Cuban Cigar Brands. There was also litigation in other countries, especially France and Spain, involving Cifuentes over Partagás, Ramón Allones and La Gloria Cubana trademarks and Consolidated over H. Upmann and Montecristo (Montecristo accounting for 75 percent of the premium cigar business in Spain). One outcome was the trademark agreement between Tabacalera Española and Consolidated, the latter keeping the US and Dominican rights. By 1995, Consolidated was producing 45 million handmade cigars: 25 million from the Dominican Republic, 12 million from Honduras and 8 million from Mexico.

After the 1990s boom, the Dominican cigar factory run by Menéndez (TND) was closed and production moved to Tabacalera de García Ltd., run by José Seijas, with its massive factory in La Romana making all the Dominican brands for Altadis USA, including best-selling 'Cuban' brands Romeo y Julieta, H. Upmann and Montecristo. In effect, Cuban-Americans and international cigar capital positioned itself well around the US embargo on Cuba. But what of the Dominican tobacco sector?

Dominicans Out

Rosemary Vargas-Lundius was among those who documented 1980s rural poverty, a major cause of which was attributed to limited access to productive land and credit, reinforced by government price stabilisation not pegged to rural income. Vargas-Lundius argued the need for a Dominican rural development strategy to stem what by then had become a massive rural-urban-overseas drift.[50] The overseas drift was overwhelmingly to the United States and has been documented in a number of studies produced primarily by Dominican-Americans in the United States.[51] During the period 1961-86 over 400,000 Dominicans legally migrated to the United States. The annual average during 1962-72 was in the region of 11,500, increasing to 16,000 in the 1970s, over 30,000 in the 1980s, and 40,000 in 1991 and 1992. It was not until 1996 that a decline began, and in 1998 only 20,000 were admitted. By and large, scholars concur that such a massive exodus was not a spontaneous movement but an orchestrated event. Successive waves have been linked to political events, economic policies and US legislation favouring a chain of third world immigration, as well as specifics in the Dominican case.

Emigration was restricted by Trujillo to stem the mounting protest from outside and foment domestic population growth to fuel agricultural modernisation and expansion and industrialisation. After Trujillo, US policy favoured emigration to release rising social and political tension. Fear of a second Cuba, escalating unrest, the overthrow of the ephemeral presidency of Juan Bosch in 1963, and the US invasion of 1965 to pacify the revolutionary movement to reinstate Bosch, led many to migrate. Initially, it was a middle class fearful of the Bosch regime and then of popular unrest after Bosch's defeat. The US ambassador to the Dominican Republic requested new facilities and extra personnel for the Consulate in 1962, and advocated visas as a safety valve against political agitation and as a way to improve relations between the two countries. Many progressives, labour organisers and dissident students were given visas, and others were deported under the terms of agreement between the Dominican and US governments.

During the second half of the twentieth century, a momentous shift in American economic life took place, as US transnational firms searching for cheap labour and maximum profit shifted manufacturing to the Third World, especially Latin America. The US government campaigned to convince nations to lower their tariffs and adopt 'free trade' policies and FTZs, which have increased the gap between rich and poor and accelerated labour migration. US assessments of impending domestic unskilled labour shortages encouraged migration until the late 1960s, when there were changes in migration policy. By then, family-centred chain migration replaced US-initiated deterritorialisation, making emigration a self-sustaining process, benefiting a second wave of migrants and creating a safety net for a third massive wave of undocumented migrants from 1978 to 1994.

Out-migration was conditioned by the way the Dominican elite managed state-building and economic planning. The restructuring of the Dominican economy, agribusiness and especially the FTZs rendered US production five times more costly. The decade of the development of FTZs in the Dominican Republic (1982-92) was also the decade of most migration; FTZ profits were booming, but GDP was down and per capita consumption dropped by 22 percent. In 1988, the Dominican Republic was second only to Mexico for the number of FTZ firms in Latin America and the Caribbean, yet FTZs only employed 3 percent of the labour force, and many were internal migrants, women, non-unionised, earning less than the national minimum wage and with a high turnover.

Migrants were primarily from underprivileged sectors, but there were more professionals in the 1980s due to deteriorating conditions under an austerity plan in line with International Monetary Fund (IMF) conditions. A 1985 IMF loan allowed the Dominican government to reschedule the commercial bank and Paris Club debt. Repayments proved too onerous and were suspended a year later, occasioning civil disturbances. In 1989, President Joaquín Balaguer turned against the IMF, but in 1990, shortly before being sworn in for a sixth term, he announced the doubling of fuel and basic food prices as part of austerity measures for resuming IMF assistance. The real value of the minimum wage fell during 1980-85 by 20 percent, and there was little improvement in subsequent years as evidenced in the riots of 1988, 1989 and 1990, by which time unemployment was running at 29 percent.[52] By 1991, the purchasing power of the minimum wage was at half its 1970 value, and swathes of the middle class were affected.

Balaguer tackled economic development by easing US investment and emphasising industry, commerce and finance and political stability by dismembering opposition through incarceration, assassination and expatriation of political dissidents. During his first twelve years there were dichotomous tendencies: unprecedented economic growth, in the form of industry and business, alongside growing unemployment levels and urban drift. The 1980s were characterised as 'the lost decade', and, while the late 1990s were again economic boom years, poverty and unemployment rates remained consistently high. Balaguer had the support of the traditional landed elite and new entrepreneurial groups, and suppressed political opposition to modernising the state and economy. Unemployment rose from 15 percent in 1971 to 30 percent in 1991, and by 1992 per capita income was below that of the early 1970s. Ramona Hernández, Director of the Dominican Studies Institute in New York, has characterised this as US and Dominican state complicity in an "evil alliance" of capital and state, benefiting only the few, whereby large numbers opted to seek their fortunes abroad.[53]

The link between the peasantry and out-migration was early established in an article by Nancie González entitled 'Peasants' Progress: Dominicans in New York'.[54] In 1983, Sherri Grasmuck introduced the concept of 'stair-step migration' in enclave patterns of labour circulation, comparing Dominican labour in the United States and Haitian labour in the Dominican Republic. Studying the impact of emigration on three sender communities, two of which were Licey and Santiago, she highlighted the need for agrarian reform and agricultural investment to avert the Dominican Republic as a disarticulated economy,[55] with persistently high unemployment and depressed wages, provoking migration.

This was demonstrated in Fernando Ferrán and Patricia Pessar's study of seven communities linked with major export commodities – La Aldea, Juan Pablo, Los Pinos and San José de las Matas (coffee); Licey al Medio and Tamboril (tobacco); and La Amapola (cacao):

> The international demand for the cash crops grown in the seven communities has encouraged class differentiation and heirarchy as successful commercial farmers have used their profits and loans to buy additional land from small and middle-sized landowners. The latter have often descended into the ranks of the landless who search for paid agricultural work.[56]

For Them, Emigration Became a Strategy.

The links between tobacco and out-migration were closely documented by Max Castro in the case of Licey, whose fortunes for two centuries had revolved around tobacco.[57] Dominant to an extent unusual even for the region, tobacco was the chief cash crop by far and tobacco processing, the principal industry. In the late 1980s impoverished minifundism was at its maximum expression in Licey, as also migration to the United States, whose earliest origins date back to the 1930s but increased significantly from the early 1960s.[58] According to a 1974 national survey, 4.1 percent of Dominican households had at least one migrant member living abroad.[59] In 1980, the figure was 32.8 percent for urban Licey and 11.4 percent for rural Licey, and for Santiago 16.7 percent.[60]

Why was Licey such a high emigration community? By the fall of Trujillo, the economy had become increasingly unviable. In 1960, two years before the onset of large-scale migration, Licey had the second highest agricultural population per hectare, with a density of 3.86 times the national average and 2.85 denser than Santiago. A total of 81.4 percent agricultural land was under cultivation that year, but with a low level of productivity, as tobacco was grown with a low level of capital investment and technical input. *Tabaco criollo* was traditionally cultivated on tiny plots by peasants with little access to capital or modern techniques and relatively primitive methods, and rarely irrigated: 97.4 percent of Licey holdings were under 5 hectares, compared with 86.3 percent for the country, and 72.42 percent were under one fifth of the upper limit of a manifundio, compared with 49.9 percent for the country. The median holding was 5-10 *tareas*.

There was little evidence of any major change in land tenure or agricultural technology but rather manoeuvring for control at the top for substantial profit, while those lower in the chain were forced to adapt to less favourable terms. The capital accumulation and dynamism of the large international traders and manufacturers, and to a lesser extent local intermediaries, contrasted with the stagnation and low level of capitalisation in the producing areas. The six huge international tobacco leaf-buying firms, together controlling 90 percent of the world market, demonstrated tremendous gains in productivity from capitalisation and technology in the tobacco manufacturing industries, while producers in Licey were dependent on animal power for transporting their crop. A hierarchy of relatively large firms controlled packing and processing operations locally through middle-sized packers and warehouses; and wholesalers and small tobacco buyers provided direct financing for the crop, and bought from the producers themselves. Cheap tobacco was grown by virtue of the fact that it was articulated with subsistence farming, which supplemented the insufficient income derived by small producers from selling at low prices.

It was, in Castro's view, a highly skewed informal arrangement, allowing easy credit to producers but at a high cost. The changes of the twentieth century had produced an enormous concentration of economic power at one pole of the tobacco universe and an increasingly unviable and less independent producer at the other, which resulted in increasingly onerous sharecropping arrangements. In 1960, 15.3 percent of Licey land, compared with 3.7 percent for Santiago province, was *a media*,[61] favoured by growers because they lacked money to pay rent and needed to supplement their meagre income, though often only breaking even or ending up in debt. Where growers had carried out processing, there were now packing warehouses for fermenting, selecting and packing the leaf, drawing their labour force (80 percent female) from households in the area, hired on a daily basis, avoiding any benefit payments, at wage levels described as superexploitative. Remittances helped equalise sender communities and there was return migrant mobility, but emigration primarily functioned as an escape valve, helping maintain the status quo and conservatism rather than introduce new thinking.

Two Dominican worlds – that of the Cibao and New York – became integrally interconnected in more ways than remittances and returnees. From 1980-90, the New York Dominican population increased from 125,380 to 332,713, the fastest growing ethnic group in the city for that period. By 1990, there were over 300,000 Dominicans in New York; and in 2000, out of a total of over one million Dominicans in the United States, 53.2 percent lived in that city. Much like the Puerto Ricans of the 1950s, the Dominicans went largely unnoticed at first, but by the 1990s they comprised the second-largest Hispanic group in the North East. They form part of the 'latinisation' of the United States, in what has been described as the "harvest of empire".[62] Migration from the 'empire's backyard' – Mexico, the Caribbean, Central and South America – has been unparalleled since the Second World War, and has been escalating since the 1960s.

The Dominican migration fits the larger picture of contingents of workers shuttling between their national territories and the diaspora, such that many 'Dominican-Yorks' "live suspended between two worlds, developing survival strategies in competition for scarce resources and labour market incorporation".[63] While the vast majority went into the service sector and light manufacturing, especially the garment industry, a dynamic enclave economy of small businesses emerged.[64] In the 1990s, Dominicans were estimated to own over 20,000 such businesses, especially grocery stores, cabs, travel agencies, restaurants, and small sweatshops, such as cigar *chinchales*, known as buckeyes in the United States, often taken over from Cubans who came before them.

Today, in Manhattan and the Bronx can be found a handful of small storefront *tabaquerías*, hand-rolling cheap cigars for over-the-counter sales, which might have been bought from Cubans or started up by Dominicans. From those surveyed in 2006,[65] they are typically from Tamboril, employ only a few rollers and buy their tobacco from middlemen – some Miami-based, others in the Dominican Republic – or direct from family-farmed land in the Tamboril area. Thus, Martínez Cigars, today run by Jesús Martínez, opened for business in the Chelsea district of Manhattan in 1974 when his father Antonio left Tamboril, bringing with him skilled Tamboril rollers to hand roll premium cigars using blends of Dominican tobaccos with Connecticut, Cameroon and Sumatra wrappers. Others in Manhattan include La Rosa Cubana owned by Frank Almanzar, whose father Antonio was born in Santiago, worked for seventeen years at La Aurora, and founded the company in 1958; Q [Quisqueya] Cigars; and PB Cuban Cigars, which in response to the city's smoking ban introduced a legal smoking lounge. All use the word 'Cuban' to attract customers, deriving from their use of Dominican Cuban-seed tobacco filler. Rosario Dominican Cigars in the Bronx markets cigars hand rolled with leaf from the farm in the Tamboril area that has been in the family for generations. Reserva Dominicana began in 2001 when owner Israel Capellán imported cigars his family made in the Dominican Republic, and has a small retail outlet in Manhattan and five rollers in the Bronx making cigars for the Manhattan shop. In Union City, New Jersey, once a stronghold of the Cubans, there are now only a handful of *tabaquerías*, owned by Dominicans. One is Puros Indios, which no longer hand rolls there but maintains a retail outlet, along with one in Miami, for cigars made in the Dominican Republic. None have the quality or cost anywhere near as much as premium cigars, but these 'corner factories', Savona wrote in *Cigar Aficionado*, "afford the cigar lover an opportunity to get up close and personal with . . . something that's rare in twenty-first-century America: rolling cigars entirely by hand".[66]

Bonó and the End of 'Dominican Exceptionalism'

But let us return to Pedro Francisco Bonó's vision of Dominican tobacco 'exceptionalism' and the Dominican tobacco peasantry. Bonó was born in Santiago, in 1828, and died in 1906, his life spanning much of the turbulent nineteenth century. As a young man, he was drawn into the 1857 Revolution and Restoration. He epitomised what were identified as the nineteenth century patriotic, liberal, federalist views of the Partido Azul (Blue Party) of Cibao tobacco interests, in opposition to the Partido Rojo (Red Party) of the south. The Blues *(los Azules)* came to power in 1879 as the party of Cibao tobacco interests, with Puerto Plata oriented to Hamburg, Bremen and St Thomas, in contrast to the Reds *(los Rojos)* of southern cattle and lumber interests, with Santo Domingo oriented to England, Curaçao and St Thomas.

Rodríguez Demorizi is to be attributed with rescuing Bonó from oblivion,[67] and Bonó's thinking has permeated Dominican intellectual thinking ever since. Bonó introduced concepts of class, race, capitalism and inequality into Dominican history, and mounted a spirited defence of the Cibao peasantry, arguing that tobacco was 'democratic' in contrast to 'oligarchic' cacao. Sugar was less important at the time, but his anger was also directed against the encroaching sugar industry in the south and its impact on the dispossessed. This he saw as capitalist and foreign, whereas tobacco was nationalist, much as Ortiz later saw Cuban tobacco in counterpoint to sugar.

The patriotic liberalism of the Cibao, based on tobacco, was contrasted with the conservatism and foreignness of the south, based on cattle, forestry and then sugar. In the words of Vega: "tobacco has always been more Dominican than sugar, due to its birth, its spirit and its method of production, industrialisation and marketing".[68] Moya Pons elaborated on how Cibao tobacco:

> maintained the whole population occupied in the cyclical production of tobacco, putting in train the entire energy of the region. Tobacco was an industry that had a multiplier effect in terms of employment and income, and was therefore democratising in its social effects. . . . The whole process put in motion an enormous body of growers with their families . . . day labourers, thread and bag makers, packers, makers of plug tobacco, cigarette makers, traders, creditors and agents for selling the crop. It also created a dynamic economic cycle. . . . Because of this, the Cibao was a region . . . that was enterprising and hardworking.[69]

Since wealth was much less concentrated than in the south, Cibao people (*cibaeños*), argued Moya Pons, were open to nineteenth century liberal ideas. However, the Partido Azul came to power at precisely the moment new industry was to develop in the south with:

> a massive immigration of exiled Cubans who came to the country as a result of the first Cuban War of Independence. . . . From the outset of the war, many Cubans emigrated to the Dominican Republic, and in a few years some 5,000 exiles reached our country, many of whom had a hard time because they were persecuted by Buenaventura Baez and then by María González, whose governments wanted to maintain good relations with the Spanish colonial government. As soon as Baez was defeated and the Blues could act freely, Luperón and his political friends gave the best welcome and assistance to all Cuban and Puerto Rican patriots who arrived in the country, through Puerto Plata in particular, seeking refuge or help to liberate their countries.[70]

Two important outcomes were that Puerto Plata and Santiago benefitted from the influx of Cuban professionals, but Cubans were primarily a source of capital and technology to invest in sugar in the south. This sugar expansion coincided with tobacco losing out on overseas markets, leading Bonó to lament the "neglect of tobacco and the favour that was shown to sugar, cacao and coffee".[71] Gradually the Partido Azul itself gravitated to sugar and the south.

This, then, was the backdrop to Bonó's strident writing condemning foreign interference, as evidenced in his oft-quoted 1880 essay 'Privilegiomania':

> that foreign capitalists come and establish four or six sugar cane estates on fertile terrain almost at give-away prices . . . the owners find themselves surrounded by a population that used to have possession of the land, and are now labourers . . . while I see Santo Domingo's cane being increasingly protected, I see the blacks of Sabana Grande and Monte Adentro becoming ever poorer, and if this continues, the day is not far distant on which all the small owners who until now have been citizens will end up being labourers, or rather serfs, and Santo Domingo will be a small Cuba, or Puerto Rico, or Louisiana.[72]

He decried land concessions to Cubans to develop the sugar industry, and on them he again laid blame in his essay 'Una Suplica': "this development is due to the Cuban immigration".[73]

Two nineteenth-century waves of Cuban migration to the Dominican Republic were occasioned by the wars of independence of 1868-78 and 1895-98. Cubans are held to have revolutionised the Dominican sugar industry in 1875 by bringing steam technology to two mills in the Dominican Republic – La Caridad in San Carlos and La Angelita in San Pedro de Macorís. They were among an influx of Cubans, Puerto Ricans and Americans into sugar, but, it was argued, in comparison with Cuba and Puerto Rico, lack of capital and the predominance of the peasantry held back any Dominican transformation into a plantation economy.[74]

In the nineteenth century, the central valleys of the Cibao were likened in soils and climate to the tobacco areas of western Vuelta Abajo, central Villa Clara and Eastern Cuba around Holguín. While colonial Cuba's tobacco was considered as superior quality for export and premium cigar manufacture, by the late 1850s, the newly independent Dominican Republic occupied tenth place in the world tobacco trade, almost all the tobacco being exported as leaf to Germany. Cuban émigrés were recorded as primarily merchants and professionals, though there was also mention of artisans, especially in cigar rolling in Santiago, Puerto Plata and Santo Domingo. Roberto Marte contrasted this with the mass Cuban tobacco migration to the United States (Tampa, Key West, Ybor City, Mobile and Savannah), quoting figures of almost 16,000 Cuban émigrés in the years 1873-86, an estimated 40,000 by the end of the century, and 30,000 in tobacco in tobacco alone at the time Cuban independence leader

José Martí founded his Cuban Revolutionary Party in Key West in 1892, with the support of Florida's Cuban tobacco workers.[75]

Martí visited the Dominican Republic in 1892 and 1895, as he did Key West and Tampa and Jamaica in 1892 and 1894. He was close to Dominican-born Máximo Gómez, who, after supporting the Dominican annexation of Spain against Haitian occupation and arriving in Cuba as a soldier of Spain, had risen to become a general of Cuba's 1868-78 Liberation Army. Gómez's return to the Dominican Republic coincided with the Cibao elite's efforts to promote modern agricultural enterprise, and Gómez is on record as having undertaken a rare attempt to foster a large-scale model tobacco plantation: La Reforma, in the Monte Cristi region, during the years 1889-96.[76] The Montecristi Manifiesto for Cuban independence was printed in Santiago, and funds were raised for the cause through patriotic clubs in the city, as they were wherever Cubans had settled. It is well documented that Gómez remained in Cuba after the war, through the US occupation of Cuba, and into the early years of the fledgling Cuban Republic. The Cuban presence all but disappeared from early-twentieth century accounts of Dominican history. The majority, it is suggested, returned to Cuba, and their presence was not to be noted again until post-1959. The sugar / tobacco dichotomy, however, was firmly implanted.

González, in his 1994 monograph on Bonó, mapped the importance of a longue durée approach to understanding the resilience of the Cibao peasantry, the significant impact of Haitian domination being the historical block on the plantation economy and nineteenth-century expansion of the peasant economy. San Miguel took this further to capture how Dominican scholars and political leaders have fashioned an imagined colonial period out of foundational works, such as Bonó's nineteenth century progressive romanticism.[77] Thus, he argued, in the twentieth century Manuel Arturo Peña Battle and Joaquín Balaguer epitomised the paroxism in the relationship between historiography and power under Trujillo as 'persuasive fiction' in their elitistist and racist interpretations of the tragic loss of a golden age and bifurcation of the island.[78] Historian and ephemeral Dominican President Juan Bosch provided a progressive, yet still tragic, analysis of a deformed Dominican '*arrítmia histórica*' – that is, of Dominican history being 'out of rhythm', 'off-beat', or 'out of sinc' with mainstream Caribbean history, seen as that of the plantation.[79]

Are the Dominican Republic and Dominican tobacco now 'in sinc' with history? The country has clearly entered the contemporary mainstream of Caribbean development, not with the plantation but with FTZs, in the context of which it has risen to cigar prominence. If the 'exceptionalism' has gone, what, too, of the peasantry and 'democratic tobacco'?

I began this paper with the León Jimenes story, and I wish to end by way of that story. In the peak year of 1997, the Santiago daily *Listin Diario* brought out a new magazine, *Cigarro*. Its second issue featured congratulatory letters to the editor from José León and others for a publication that drew attention to the fact that:

> In this day and age of real globalisation and world integration, in which the comparative advantages of each nation need to be strongly promoted, the Dominican Republic must show the world that it is we who offer the best beaches, the best sun, the best *merengue*, and above all, the best cigar in the world.[80]

In 2000, the Dominican government released a stamp depicting a cigar, a tobacco leaf and the words *La Tierra del Tobaco* (The Land of Tobacco). David Savona, who has written feature articles on Dominican tobacco since the 1990s for *Cigar Aficionado*, concluded in 2004:

> It's hard to imagine a cigar world without the Dominican Republic, but the country hasn't been a market leader for long. Although its oldest cigarmaker, La Aurora SA has been in business for a century, most of the cigars it made in the past were for local consumption. In the 1970s the first free trade zones opened in the country, welcoming companies that would make cigars strictly for export. It took nearly a decade for the Dominican Republic to overtake the Canary Islands and Jamaica to become the leading cigar producer for the United States. The increases in cigar production here have been extraordinary.[81]

In the early 1990s, cigars were a secondary business for the León family. Then, in 1993, at the start of the boom, Guillermo León was named executive vice president of La Aurora SA. Charged with developing the US market, dividing his time between Santiago and the United States, he became a stalwart member of ProCigar, the Dominican cigar association. Asked about Cuba in a feature for *Cigar Aficionado*, his response was upbeat:

> People already prefer our cigars the way they are. The brands are already established. I can't say that using Cuban tobacco or whatever would never happen. I think Cuba has good tobacco. If some day that is what the consumer asks for, why not? There are people that like tobacco from Nicaragua, Honduras or Indonesia. Cuba is a good producer of tobacco, so why not contemplate all the possibilities. To speculate about whether we would create a factory in Cuba, I doubt it. First of all, our roots aren't Cuban; we are very traditional and very Dominican, and we have defended our national pride to the end. When the Dominican market was not appealing to anyone, we maintained it. Even when we had the chance to increase our profit margin by moving the production to somewhere else, we maintained

our tradition here, which is to give the people the cigars they wanted. We have good relationships with people from Havana. They have visited us at La Aurora. But that's it.[82]

León Jimenes is by far the most prominent Dominican cigar company of the twenty-first century, but its major competitors Tabalacera A. Fuente and Tabacalera de García create a different scenario as regards Cuba. The June 2007 issue of *Cigar Aficionado*, titled 'Cuba Tomorrow', featured articles on Cuba written by leading Cuban and Cuban-American political figures and analysts in Cuba and the United States, interspersed with an abundance of page and double-page ads for Dominican-Cuban cigars, taken out by Tabacalera García ("makers of the finest Dominican cigars," including Montecristo, Romeo y Julieta, Trinidad, Don Diego, Ashton, Vega Fina, La Aroma de Cuba), as well as General Cigar (Dunhill, Viva Bolívar, Macanudo), Arturo Fuente, Oliva, Toraño, and Pérez-Carrillo (La Gloria Cubana).

The success story of the cigar companies is undeniable. Yet the questions remain. At what cost Dominican success? What of the Dominican model when the dispossessed have poured out of the countryside and into the cities of Santiago, Santo Domingo and New York? Where is the Bonó vision for the twenty-first century? And what will happen when the US embargo on Cuba ends?

Notes

1 I am particularly grateful to the following colleagues for contributing to and facilitating this research: Roberto Cassá (National Archive, Santo Domingo), Rafael Emilio Yuñen and Iturbides Zaldivar Luna (Eduardo León Jimenes Cultural Centre, Santiago de los Caballeros), Ramona Hernández and Sarah Aponte (Dominican Studies Centre, New York), Humberto García (Caribbean Institute, University of Puerto Rico), Jorge Duany (Centre for Social Research, University of Puerto Rico), and Max Castro (formely of the North-South Centre, University of Miami). For their hospitality and stimulating thoughts, my special thanks to Lynne Guitart in Santiago de los Caballeros, Elsy Doñe Molina in Santo Domingo, Constance Sutton, Antonio Lauria and Pamela Scorn in New York.
2 José Alcántara Almánzar & Ida Hernández Caamaño, *Huella y memoria: E. León Jimenes: un siglo en el camino nacional, 1903-2003* (Santo Domingo: Grupo León, 2003).
3 Centro Cultural Eduardo León Jimenes, *Inaugural Brochure*, 2003, p.3. The Centre, with its galleries, multimedia library, 200-seat auditorium, creative arts workshop, and cigar heritage area, also projected a Caribbean heritage, such that when it opened it was described by CARIFORUM as a model institution for the Caribbean, as well as the Dominican Republic, furthering mutual knowledge and thereby contributing to Caribbean integration. See *Cariforum Cultural Review of the Caribbean*, Special Edition Centro León: a cultural space for the Caribbean, 11 (October 2003).
4 The 1990s developments are charted in Jean Stubbs, 'Turning Over a New Leaf?

The Havana Cigar Revisited', *New West Indian Guide*, 74:3 & 4 (2000), pp.235-55 – Chapter 8 in the present volume.

5   For Bonó, see Emilio Rodríguez Demorizi (ed.), *Papeles de Pedro Francisco Bonó: para la historia de la ideas en políticas en la República Dominicana* (Santo Domingo: Editorial del Caribe, 1964).

5   Fernando Ortiz, *Cuban Counterpoint: Tobacco and Sugar* (Durham & London: Duke University Press, 1995 [1940]).

7   The first five paragraphs of this section have been reproduced, with minor editorial changes, from Jean Stubbs, 'Tobacco in the Contrapunteo: Ortiz and the Havana Cigar', in Mauricio A. Font & Alfonso W. Quiroz (eds), *Cuban Counterpoints: The Legacy of Fernando Ortiz* (Lanham: Lexington, 2004), pp.105-23 – Chapter 9 in the present volume. See also, 'Reflections on Class, Race, Gender and Nation in Cuban Tobacco: 1850-2000', in Constance Sutton (ed.), *Revisting Caribbean Labor: Essays in Honour of O. Nigel Bolland* (Kingston, Jamaica: Ian Randle, 2005), pp.118-36 – Chapter 11 in the present volume; 'Political Idealism and Commodity Production: Cuban Tobacco in Jamaica, 1870-1930', *Cuban Studies*, 25 (1995), pp.51-81 – Chapter 7 in the present volume; and *Tobacco on the Periphery* (London: Amaurea Press, 2023 [1985]).

8   This is explored in Stubbs, 'Tobacco in the Contrapunteo' (2004).

9   Antonio Lluberes Navarro, 'La crisis del tabaco cibaeño 1879-1930', in Antonio Lluberes, José del Castillo & Ramón Albuquerque (eds), *Tabaco, azúcar y minería* (Santo Domingo: Banco de Desarrollo Interamericano, 1984). Lluberes wrote a series of articles on Dominican tobacco in *EME-EME Estudios Dominicanos*: 'La economía del tabaco en el Cibao en la segunda mitad del siglo XIX', 1:4 (Jan-Feb 1974), pp.35-60; 'Las rutas del tabaco dominicano', 4:21 (Nov-Dec 1975). pp.3-22; 'Tabaco y catalanes en Santo Domingo', 5:28 (Jan-Feb 1977), pp. 13-26; 'El tabaco dominicano: de la manufactura al monopolio industrial', 6:35 (Mar-Apr 1978), pp.3-27. See also: Paul Mutto, 'Desarrollo de la economía de exportación en la República Dominicana, 1900-1930', *EME-EME Estudios Dominicanos*, 25 (Nov-Dec 1974), pp.67-110; Nancie González 'El cultivo del tabaco en la República Dominicana', *Revista Ciencia*, 2:4 (Oct-Dec 1975), pp.19-50; Fernando I. Ferrán, *Tabaco y Sociedad: la organización del poder en el ecomercado de tabaco dominicano*, Santo Domingo: Fondo para el Avance de las Ciencias Sociales, 1976; Frank Moya Pons, 'La economía dominicana y el partido azul', *EME-EME Estudios Dominicanos*, 28 (Jan-Feb 1977), pp.3-12; Iturbídes Zaldívar Luna, *Producción y comercialización de tabaco negro en la República Dominicana* (Santiago de los Caballeros: Universidad Católica Madre y Maestra, 1979); Harry Hoetink, 'El Cibao, 1844-1900: Su aportación a la formación social de la República', *EME-EME Estudios Dominicanos*, 8:48 (May-June 1980), pp.3-20; Bernardo Vega, 'Tabaco e historia', *EME EME Estudios Dominicanos*, 10:57 (Nov-Dec 1981), pp.3-13; Baud, *Peasants and Tobacco in the Dominican Republic* (1996); Pedro L. San Miguel, *Los campesinos del Cibao: economía de mercado y transformación agraria en la República Dominicana, 1880-1960* (Río Piedras: Editorial de la Universidad de Puerto Rico, 1997); Esteban Rosario, *Trujillo y la tabacalera* (Santo Domingo: Amigo del Hogar, 2004). Of particular interest is Compañía Anónima Tabacalera Museo del Tabaco, 'Guión para la motivación y presentación del Museo', Mimeo (30 May 1982), a three-part study for a well-thought out little tobacco museum that functioned in Santiago in the 1990s, authored by Zaldívar, Rafael Emilio Yuñén (later to become director of the León Jimenes Cultural Centre) & Danilo de los Santos. More general historical works include Rafael Emilio Yuñén, *La isla como es: Hipótesis para su comprobación* (Santiago: Universidad Católica Madre y Maestra, 1985); Roberto Cassá, *Historia social y económica de la República Dominicana* (Santo Domingo: Punto y Aparte Editores, 1977-1983).

10 See Max Castro, 'Dominican Journey: Patterns, Context, and Consequences of Migration from the Dominican Republic to the United States', PhD dissertation, University of North Carolina at Chapel Hill, 1985; Fernando I. Ferrán & Patricia

Pessar, 'Dominican Agriculture and the Effects of International Migration', in Anthony Maingot (ed.), *Small Country Development and International Labor Flows* (Boulder: Westview Press, 1991); Gabriela Sandoval, '"Y en el campo se está respirando pobreza": Survival and Global Economic Integration of the Dominican Tobacco Sector', Paper presented to LASA, Washington (2001).

11 Napoleón S. Padilla, *Memorias de un cubano sin importancia* (Hialeah: A. C. Graphics, 1998).

12 Raymundo González, 'Ideología del progreso y campesinado en el siglo XIX", *Ecos*, 1:2 (1993), pp.25-43.

13 This was also the decade of the tobacco growers' revolt in Cuba, 1777.

14 Quoted in Michiel Baud, 'La gente del tabaco: Villa González en el siglo veinte', *Ciencia y Sociedad*, 9:1 (1984), p.11.

15 Samuel Hazard, *Santo Domingo: Past and Present with a glance at Hayti* (Santo Domingo: Editorial de Santo Domingo, 1982 [1873]).

16 Lluberes, 'La crisis del tabaco cibaeño' (1984), p.13. Editor's translation from the Spanish, as all other quotes that follow and were originally in Spanish.

17 Ibid., p.16.

18 'Memoria del Ministro de Agricultura e Inmigración, R, Tejera, al presidente R. Caceres', Santo Domingo (22 Feb 1909), *Gaceta Oficial 1991* (11 May 1909), p.20.

19 Emilio Armando Olivo Ponce De León, *Reflexiones sobre la agropecuaria dominicana* (Santo Domingo: El Nuevo Diario, 1999).

20 In 1907, there is record of 215 male and 4 female cigar workers, 8 male and 10 female cigarette workers, and 126 warehouse workers in 87 *tabaquerías* and 26 *cigarrerías*. These included 26 in Santiago, 11 in Santo Domingo and 5 in La Romana, but the remainder were scattered and much of the industry rested on home and outwork production. In 1900, for example, Anacaona reported 35 factory workers and 12 women home workers, while Matilde reported 18 men and 36 factory women, and 4 women home workers. This contrasted with CAT a decade and a half later, employing 200 cigar workers, and its major cigar competitor La Aurora half that number.

21 Eseteban Rosario, *Trujillo y la tabacalera* (Santo Domingo: Amigo del Hogar, 2004). The full story includes many intrigues, one of which concerned Amadeo Barletta (Dominican Tobacco). Traditionally Germany was the main exporter of tobacco, but in 1934 the volume of tobacco exported to France vastly exceeded the volume to any other European country. To pay for an arms deal with France, Trujillo had imposed controls on tobacco production and trade (Valentina Peguero, *The militarization of culture in the Dominican Republic, from the Captains General to General Trujillo*, Lincoln & London: University of Nebraska Press, 2004). Trujillo clashed with Barletta over this and landed him in jail, the Italian government demanded his release, and the US government also exerted pressure. After his release, Barletta moved to Cuba.

22 *Tarea* is a land measure: 0.625 hectare (16 *tareas* = 1 hectare).

23 Orlando Inoa, *Estado y campesinos al inicio de la era de Trujillo* (Santo Domingo: Librería la Trinitaria, 1994).

24 Instituto del Tabaco de la República Dominicana, *Primer censo tabacalera nacional, 1963: Datos preliminares* (Santiago, 1963); *Segundo censo tabacalera nacional, 1973* (Santiago, 1973). A third census was later conducted: *Tercer censo tabacalera nacional, 1977* (Santiago, 1977). INTABACO produced regular reports and studies on tobacco growing, such as *Cultivo del tabaco negro en República Dominicana* (Santiago, 2002).

25 González, 'El cultivo del tabaco' (1975), p.34.

26 Fernando I. Ferrán, *Tabaco y sociedad: la organización del poder en el ecomercado de tabaco dominicano* (Santo Domingo: Fondo para el Avance de las Ciencias Sociales, 1976), p.58.

27 Ibid., p.65.

28 In 1967, Brazilian and Philippine tobacco sold to Spain for an average US$32-35 and US$47-48, while the price of Dominican tobacco was US$45-55.
29 Iturbides Zaldívar Luna, *Producción y comercialización de tabaco negro en la República Dominicana* (Santiago de los Caballeros: Universidad Católica Madre y Maestra, 1979), pp.78-9.
30 Economist Intelligence Unit, *Dominican Republic: Annual Supplement, 1978* (London: EIU, 1978).
31 Gordon Mott, 'CigarLand: The Dominican Republic has Become one of the World's Largest Producers of Premium Cigars', *Cigar Aficionado* (Autumn 1992).
32 Juan O. Tamayo, 'Castro to firm up ties with Dominicans', *Miami Herald* (17 August 1998).
33 Olivo, *Reflexiones* (1999).
34 'Chat with Litto Gómez, Owner, La Flor Dominicana', Transcipt of Live Interview (19 August 1997), *Cigar Aficionado*.
35 Ibid.
36 Marvin R. Shanken, 'An Interview with Manuel Quesada: Owner, MATASA, Makers of Fonseca, Licenciados, Romeo y Julieta, José Benito, Cubita, Royal Dominicana, Credo and Casa Blanca cigars', *Cigar Aficionado* (February 1998).
37 'Chat with Litto Gómez' (1997).
38 Danilo de los Santos & Carlos Fernández Rocha (eds), *Este lado del país llamado el norte* (Santo Domingo: Comisión Permanente de la Feria Nacional del Libro, 1998).
39 Honduras, Nicaragua and Mexico, where production has also grown exponentially, found themselves in a similar situation with large stocks.
40 Sandoval, 'Y en el campo se está respirando pobreza' (2001), p.2.
41 Ibid., p.4.
42 Sandoval's study (2001) examines tobacco as one aspect of a complex livelihood strategy, involving networks that allow producers to continue when the sector is in crisis, homing in on segmented labour, gender and ethnic labour segmentation, as well as tobacco as symbolic for Ortiz and Bonó.
43 Rafael Taveras & Valerio Tineo, *Boletín Estadistico 2004* (Santiago: Instituto del Tabaco de la República Dominicana, 2005). The 2005 Santiago telephone directory listed 47 tobacco companies.
44 Padilla, *Memorias* (1998).
45 When I spoke with Padilla in Miami in 1988, he was working on these cases.
46 James Suckling, 'Tobacco Central. The Dominican Republic Has Some of the World's Best Growing Regions for Premium Cigar Tobacco', *Cigar Aficionado* (Autumn 1996). Suckling wrote regularly for *Cigar Aficionado*. Two years later he wrote: 'After the Gold Rush. Leading Dominican Cigar Companies Take Back the Retail Shelves as Newcomers Struggle', *Cigar Aficionado* (April 1998).
47 Mott, 'Cigarland' (1992), pp. 63-5.
48 Ibid., p.65.
49 Marvin R. Shanken, 'An Interview With Carlos Fuente Jr., President, Tabacalera A. Fuente y Cía.', *Cigar Aficionado* (December 1998). I visited the Fuente main factory in Santiago's free trade zone in 2006, which on the outside was a standard cement bloc building but inside had been refurbished in sections reminiscent of a nineteenth century Havana cigar factory. When I interviewed Fuente there, he exuded a pride in both his Cuban heritage and his Dominican factories and farm.
50 Rosemary Vargas-Lundius, *Peasants in Distress: Poverty and Unemployment in the Dominican Republic* (Boulder, San Francisco & Oxford: Westview Press, 1991).
51 The creation of the Dominican Studies Institute at City College, City University of New York, provided a significant impulse to this. Among the key general studies are, Sarah Aponte (ed.), *Dominican Migration to the United States, 1970-1997: An Annotated Bibliography* (New York: CUNY Dominican Studies Institute, n.d.); Sherri Grasmuck, 'International Stair-Step Migration: Dominican Labor in the United States and Haitian Labor in the Dominican Republic', in R. I. Harper Simpson (ed),

Research in the Sociology of Work: Peripheral Workers, Vol. 2 (London: JAI Press, 1983), pp.149-72; 'The impact of Emigration on National Development: Three Sending Communities in the Dominican Republic', *Development and Change*, 15 (1984), pp.381-413; Jorge Duany, *Quisqueya on the Hudson: The Transnational Identity of Dominicans in Washington Heights* (New York: CUNY Dominican Studies Institute, 1994); Silvio Torres-Saillant & Ramona Hernández, *The Dominican Americans* (Westport: Greenwood Press, 1998); Ramona Hernández, *The Mobility of Workers Under Advanced Capitalism: Dominican Migration to the United States* (New York: Columbia University Press, 2002); Silvio Torres-Saillant & Blas R. Jiménez, *Desde la Orilla: hacia una nacionalidad sin desalojos* (Santo Domingo: Editorial Manatí, Ediciones Librería La Trinitaria, 2004).

52 Economist Intelligence Unit, *Dominican Republic: Country Profile 1990-91* (London: EUI, 1991).
53 Hernández, *Mobility of Workers* (2002).
54 Nancie González, 'Peasants' Progress: Dominicans in New York', *Caribbean Studies*, 10:3 (1970), pp.154-71.
55 Grasmuck, 'International Stair-Step Migration' (1983), and 'Impact of Emigration' (1984).
56 Ferrán & Pessar, 'Dominican Agriculture' (1991).
57 Castro, 'Dominican Journey' (1985)
58 Ibid.
59 Antonio Ugalde, Frank D. Bean & Gilberto Cardenas, 'International Migration from the Dominican Republic: Findings from a National Survey', *International Migration Review* 13 (1979).
60 Grasmuck, 'Impact of Emigration' (1984).
61 A *media* is a sharecropping system whereby the grower turns over half the crop to the landowner/middleman.
62 Juan González, *Harvest of Empire: A history of Latinos in America* (New York & London: Viking, 2000).
63 Duany, *Quisqueya on the Hudson* (1994).
64 Alejandro Portes & Luis Guarnizo, 'Tropical Capitalists: US-Bound Immigration and Small-Enterprise Development in the DR', Working Papers, Commission for the Study of International Migration and Cooperative Development, 1990.
65 I conducted an informal survey in 2006 using a snowball approach to visit the shops and talk with the rollers.
66 David Savona, 'The Corner Cigar Factory: A Steadfast Group of Small-Output Factories Brings Cigar Making Back to New York', *Cigar Aficionado* (December 2004). Savona also published on Dominican tobacco. See, for example, 'The Calm. The Gold Rush Days of the Cigar Boom are Gone, and So Are Most of the Quick-Buck Artists Who Flocked to the Dominican Republic', *Cigar Aficionado* (October 1999).
67 Rodríguez, *Papeles de Pedro Francisco Bonó* (1964). Studies since then incude Freddy Peralta, 'La sociedad dominicana vista por Pedro Francisco Bonó', *EME-EME*, 5:29 (1977), pp.13-54; Raymundo González, *Bonó, un intelectual de los pobres* (Santo Domingo: Centro de Estudios Sociales P. Juan Montalvo, SJ, 1994).
68 Vega, 'Tabaco e historia' (1981).
69 Moya, 'Economía dominicana' (1977), p.5.
70 Ibid., p.7.
71 Ibid., p.9.
72 Quoted in Rodríguez, *Papeles de Pedro Francisco Bonó* (1964), p.251. This is also developed in Peralta, 'Sociedad dominicana' (1977).
73 Rodríguez, *Papeles de Pedro Francisco Bonó* (1964), p.253.
74 Roberto Marte, *Cuba y la República Dominicana: transición económica en el caribe del siglo XIX* (Santo Domingo: Universidad APEC, 1988). See also Emilio Rodríguez Demorizi (ed.), *Martí en Santo Domingo* (Barcelona: M. Pareja, 1978).
75 Evaristo Heres Hernández & Javier López Muñoz, 'La inmigración cubana y su

influencia en Santiago 1868-1908', *EME EME Estudios Dominicanos*, 5:29, (March-April 1977), pp.55-104.
76 Similarly, in 1889-92, a Dutch company attempted large-scale planting, based on the Dutch East Indian colonial experience, in connection with which the British Consul-General commented to the Home Office in 1893 that the cost of raising tobacco from Sumatra seed on Dominican soil was too high to allow remunerative speculation.
77 Pedro L. San Miguel, *La isla imaginada: historia, identidad y utopía en La Espanola* (San Juan & Santo Domingo: Editorial Isla Negra/Ediciones Librería La Trinitaria, 1997).
78 Manuel Arturo Peña Battle, *Ensayos históricos* (Santo Domingo: Fundación Peña Battle, 1988); Joaquín Balaguer, *La realidad dominicana* (Buenos Aires: Imprenta Ferrari Hermanos, 1947).
79 Juan Bosch, *Composición social dominicana. Historia e interpretación* (Santo Domingo: Alfa y Omega, 1979 [1970]).
80 *Cigarro*, magazine of *Listín Diario*, 2:24 (October 1997), p.4.
81 David Savona, 'Dominican Dominance', *Cigar Aficionado* (May/Jun 2004).
82 Gordon Mott, 'An Interview with Guillermo León: President, León Jimenes Cigars', *Cigar Aficionado* (July/August 1998)

Part Three

Transnation

13

EL HABANO AND THE WORLD IT HAS SHAPED: CUBA, CONNECTICUT AND INDONESIA*1

IN 2009, the two major international cigar conglomerates, Swedish Match and British Imperial Tobacco, were on opposite sides of the Washington lobby for maintaining and lifting the United States' fifty-year trade embargo on Cuba. Ten years earlier, in 1999, the US glossy *Cigar Aficionado* ran a feature by its European editor James Suckling on East Java, Indonesia, titled 'Tobacco Mecca'.² Suckling celebrated the quality of top cigar leaf from both Java and Sumatra and reported that, in 1996, Swedish Match had opened a premium cigar factory in Pandaan, near Surabaya, with the help of Cuban rollers from Havana's Partagás factory. Indonesian workers were described as meticulous by project manager Sander Van Hattem, who had previously run a small factory in the Dominican Republic. According to Suckling, "If you have ever wondered what a modern, well-financed Cuban factory would look like, the Swedish Match operation is it." What is the connection between these two developments? How are they to be framed in the broader tobacco histories of the United States (Connecticut, in particular) and Indonesia (Sumatra and Java) in connection with Cuba? And what are the contemporary implications for all three, given the major international shifts in tobacco in response to the growing international antismoking lobby?

Those are questions I seek to explore here, in the context of how, in the fifty years since the Cuban Revolution of 1959, *El Habano* has continued to be not only *the* world premium handmade cigar but also one much imitated

* *Originally published in Cuban Studies 41 (2010), pp.39-67.

the world over.³ Since the late nineteenth century, by which time *El Habano* had made its mark, the seed, agricultural and industrial know-how, and human capital have all been transplanted abroad in an attempt to replicate the quality product. The upheavals of two landmark political events in Cuba – the late-nineteenth-century wars of independence from Spain and the 1959 Revolution – exacerbated this process. Each brought waves of out-migration and growing overseas competition, involving Cuban agronomists, growers, manufacturers and workers.⁴

What follows first draws on earlier work to outline the broader island and offshore Havana cigar history as a backdrop to documenting the history that links Cuba with Connecticut and Indonesia. It moves on to the late-nineteenth-century development of tobacco, originally from the Americas, as a cash crop in Indonesia with Dutch capital in the latter part of the nineteenth century, which gave rise to the famed Sumatra wrapper leaf. It then traces Connecticut tobacco history and the development by US capital – and fleetingly British capital – of a leaf to undercut Sumatra, creating a hybrid out of Cuban and Sumatra seed: the equally famed Connecticut shade wrapper (shade tobacco also is grown across the Florida-Georgia border area). It subsequently turns to Java towering over Connecticut and Cuba in tobacco, leading up to the late-twentieth-century opening, with Swedish capital, of the Havana cigar factory in Pandaan. Finally, it signals how *El Habano* highlights the need to conceptualise a global historical approach, and it concludes by posing, though not answering, a key question as to the future of *El Habano* in the context of global antismoking and the growing popularity of smokeless Swedish *snus* (moist snuff). With or without the US embargo on Cuba, will the future lie with *El Habano* or *snus*?

Transnationalising the History of the Havana Cigar

Fernando Ortiz grounded his classic concept of transculturation in the *contrapunteo* of tobacco and sugar, fashioning the two commodities as metaphorical constructs and highlighting the fetish power of the commodities and a counter-fetish interpretation that challenged "essentialist understandings of Cuban history."⁵ Both the fetishism and the counterfetishism are of particular significance when it comes to understanding Havana cigar history. The cigar, more than any other product of Cuba, has come to symbolise Cuban nationalism and sovereignty, and yet the cigar equally lies at the heart of a highly interconnected island-offshore history.⁶

Crucial to 'de-essentialising' Havana's cigar history is documenting the transnational history of its agriculture and industry, agricultural science, and technology, peasantry and labour. Cigar leaf tobacco was grown and cigars manufactured in Cuba for marketing across the world, but in particular to Europe and to the United States until, in response to the 1959 Revolution, the United States imposed its trade embargo on Cuba. Over time, however, both before and since the Revolution, interlocking economies and communities have been created in neighboring Caribbean islands and surrounding mainland territories – Dominican Republic, Jamaica, Honduras, Mexico, Nicaragua and Puerto Rico, as well as Brazil (Bahía), the United States (Connecticut, Florida, Georgia, New York), Europe (the Canary Islands, in particular) and beyond (the Philippines and Indonesia).

The lifting of the Spanish monopoly on Cuban manufacture in 1817 heralded *El Habano*'s coming of age as the world's luxury tobacco product of the nineteenth century, taking over from pipe and snuff. With Spanish, German, British and French capital, it conquered European, North American, and world markets, notably London, Amsterdam, Bremen, Madrid, Paris, Lisbon and New York. Out-migration, mainly north to the United States but also to the Caribbean and Central America, as well as in-migration from the Canary Islands, marked Cuba's First and Second Wars of Independence from Spain (1868–78 and 1895–98). From the Florida-Georgia tobacco towns of Key West, Tampa, Marti City (today's Ocala), Quincy, Havana, Sumatra, and Amsterdam – to New York and Connecticut, as well as in Jamaica and Mexico, Cuban tobacco interests came together in the settler territories, providing a familiar means of livelihood for the displaced migrant community and an economic and political mainstay for the independence struggle at home.[7]

Early-twentieth-century US occupation opened Cuba to mass US investment in major leaf and manufacturing concerns, undercutting other foreign investment; in its carving up of the world, the cartel formed by the American Tobacco Company and British Imperial Tobacco agreed Cuba would be the former's domain.[8] Yet rival economic and political interests to Cuba built up abroad – with trading and other advantages over the home country in turmoil – and returnee Cuban cigar workers found themselves without jobs, only to leave again. A second wave of Canary Islander settler, return, cyclical and relief migration contributed to the Canary Islands' own emergent tobacco agriculture and industry, and the 1930s Depression and labour unrest culminated a process whereby US-owned manufacturing withdrew production from Cuba to the United States. By then, mass-mechanised cigarette production was fast overshadowing the cigar, and relocation north was to undermine successful Cuban opposition to the introduction of the cigar machine. The Cuban industry was not to regain its former glory, but independents held out – small family firms, producing the premium handmade Habano, which predominated right up until the 1959 Revolution.

The Revolution reaccentuated the migratory phenomenon. Smaller manufacturers, dealers, growers and workers sought fertile ground for overseas business, profiting from upheavals linked to insurrection, agrarian reform and nationalisation, plus the US trade embargo that – with US pressure – extended to most of the Americas, Canada and Mexico being the only early exceptions. Prior to the embargo, the US Department of Agriculture (USDA) commissioned a report to document the extent to which the US cigar industry relied on Cuban leaf imports and to advise on sourcing alternative supplies.[9] The report's recommendations were to seek these in neighboring Caribbean and Central American territories, whereby agronomists, growers and manufacturers would experiment in the Dominican Republic and Nicaragua in particular. Over time, Western markets became a battleground for disputed Havana cigar brands from island-offshore parallel production and marketing systems, and Eastern European socialist bloc and some third-world countries emerged as new Havana cigar partners.

Thirty years on, the fall of the Berlin Wall in 1989 signaled the beginning of the end of the special Soviet bloc trade and aid that had built up in the vacuum left by US hostility and embargo. At the same time as the US response to Cuba's ensuing crisis was to tighten and extraterritorialise the embargo in the 1991 Torricelli and 1996 Helms-Burton Acts, a US cigar revival was in full swing, engineered in part by the New York glossy *Cigar Aficionado*, created in 1992. The then two US cigar giants Consolidated Cigar and General Cigar and émigré Cuban tobacco interests were in all-out competition with island Cuba. Cuba, in turn, courted non-US trade and investment, and cigars became part of its crisis structural adjustment strategy. In 1994, landmark credit-for-tobacco deals were struck between the Cuban state tobacco enterprise, Cubatabaco, and its French and Spanish parastatal tobacco counterparts, Societé Nationale des Tabacs (SEITA) and Tabacalera Española; a new holding company, Habanos SA, was set up to handle overseas marketing ventures; and a European cigar-marketing deal was struck in Britain, with Hunters & Frankau.

In 1999, as the cigar revival peaked, Tabacalera Española and SEITA formed Alianza de Tabacos y Distribución (Altadis), which bought 50 percent shares in Habanos. Tabacalera Española had earlier that year bought Consolidated and was in both the Havana and the clone Havana cigar business through Altadis and Altadis USA. In 2007, Altadis was sold to the British Imperial/Gallaher group and General Cigar to Swedish Match, which was the backdrop to the lobbying efforts of each in Washington regarding the US embargo. In what ways do Connecticut and Indonesia fit into this larger picture?

Sumatra Wrapper and the Deli

"Horticulturalist's quest for perfect tobacco spans globe" was the lead for a 1988 article by Linda Hirsh in Connecticut's *Hartford Courant*,[10] featuring seventy-seven-year-old Henry Nienhuys, who had managed plantations in Indonesia, Cuba and the Connecticut Valley. His grandfather Jacobus Nienhuys was reported as having been the first to take Sumatra tobacco to Holland in 1860 and as having formed the Deli – Deli Maatschappij Company. Hirsh quoted *The Dictionary of Tobacco* on the Sumatra strain having first been imported to America in 1883, and from then until 1910, US cigar manufacturers used 4.5 million pounds a year.[11] In 1899, the USDA first experimented with nets, to simulate the natural cloud coverage of Sumatra; and by 1911, when Nienhys was born, their use for growing tobacco under cloth – shade tobacco – was gaining momentum.

Nienhuys grew up in Haarlem, in the Netherlands, and studied tobacco at the agricultural University of Wageningen, where he wrote his doctoral thesis comparing Sumatra wrapper and Connecticut shade. He traveled to Hartford, Connecticut, where he grew tobacco on the Brewer family farm in 1936, and he joined the Deli in 1937. In pre–Second World War years, the Nienhuys family belonged to a close-knit community of Dutch families, who then became prisoners of war. After the war, from 1946 to 1949, the Deli sent Nienhuys back to Connecticut to work on the tobacco farms and bring his experience and knowledge back to Indonesia to rehabilitate tobacco plantations from wartime neglect.

Allegedly disenchanted when the company began dictating from Amsterdam what kind of fertiliser to use on the crops, Nienhuys responded to a call from Henry Duys, the owner of Connecticut tobacco farms, telling him that blue mould had decimated his crop and asking whether he would return to work with him. He joined Duys in 1952, and Hirsh reported, "Between managing Duys' South Windsor farms and the Hartford warehouse, he would spend part of the season in Cuba. There he studied the climate to monitor when blue mould spores were in the air, then dusted the leaves to control the spots." At the time, local wrapper was harvested only by those whom Nienhuys called diehards, because "it is cheaper to grow the tobacco in Honduras and Guatemala, where labor is right around the corner." Nienhuys left tobacco in 1970, as did many others, to set up horticultural nurseries.

The Indonesia story as told by Hirsh is ratified in the official history of what later became Deli Universal Company.[12] Despite early efforts to grow tobacco in the mid-1850s on Java, which yielded only low grades, Dutch entrepreneurs firmly believed the region's climate could produce higher quality tobacco. The arrival of Nienhuys heralded the start of the colony's growth in tobacco. In 1867, Nienhuys and his partner P. W. Janssen secured financial backing, half of which came from the Nederlandsche Handel-Maatschappij, and in 1869, they established the Deli Maatschappij, with a concession to produce cigar tobacco along Sumatra's Deli River.

The initial Dutch commercial attention to East Sumatra is said to have derived from an 1863 delegation sent from Java, which included Nienhuys, who had already been growing tobacco in Java.[13] The delegation's report was unfavorable, yet Nienhuys stayed; arranged land concessions; and secured financing for the Deli, which within twenty years had increased cultivation tenfold on twenty-one estates. When Nienhuys returned to the Netherlands in 1871, Jacob Theodore Cremer took his place; and though other companies followed the Deli – such as Deli Batavia (1875), Tobacco Company Arendsburg (1877) and Senembah Company (1889) – by 1883, the year Cremer himself returned to the Netherlands, the Deli's exports had soared to nearly 7.6 million pounds. By 1900, the company had bought up most other plantations, and the Deli reigned supreme, controlling not only the Sumatra tobacco industry, with a monopoly on tobacco exports and acting as broker for tobacco growers, but also the East Sumatra rubber and palm oil plantation belt, all worked with Javanese, Chinese and other migrant labour.[14]

Sumatra leaf was by then renowned worldwide as cigar wrapper, as its thin central vein and thin flexible texture meant that it could be used to wrap up to four times as many cigars as other leaf. Growers in the United States lobbied hard for protectionist high duties to keep Sumatra imports down, but companies were to establish plantations in Sumatra for their own supply, and by the outbreak of the First World War, more than 90 percent of all US-imported wrapper came from Sumatra.

The US cigar history was to be fast overshadowed in the twentieth century by that of Indonesia, in the context of the different colonial and postcolonial systems that emerged.[15] London and Amsterdam had been established as European twin pillars of the international circulation of tobacco in the seventeenth century as the British and Dutch expanded their empires. Tobacco became big business, with Crown and state playing a central role. European states such as Spain, Portugal and France all established monopolies purchasing and processing tobacco, whereas German states enforced all-important taxation. There were no such monopolies in Britain, the Netherlands or the United States, but whether via monopoly or market, the state was heavily involved.

After 1800, the United States rose to preeminence, partly because its competitors were few – only Brazil and Cuba in the Western Hemisphere, and Holland and Germany in Europe – and partly because the colonial system ensured global segmentation. The Dutch Culture System of the 1830s and 1840s in the Netherlands East Indies was designed to foster export crops: sugar, coffee and indigo first, and then others, including tobacco. After 1866, when tobacco was allowed to be cultivated on a private basis, production grew, and it was the Deli that accounted in large part for Sumatra exports soaring from 17 million pounds in the late 1860s to nearly 170 million pounds by the First World War. The Deli region was by then producing one-third of the Sumatra crop, and East Sumatra was reputed to have Indonesia's greatest concentration of agricultural estates. Tobacco dominated the area around the capital Medan, beyond which were rubber and palm oil plantations.

By the outbreak of the First World War, the Dutch East Indies was the world's second-largest exporter of leaf, accounting for 18 percent of the market. Sumatra and Java supplied the international market via Amsterdam and Rotterdam in the Netherlands and Bremen in Germany, competing with Algeria, the Philippines, the United States and Cuba. After the First World War, France was second to the United States as a buyer of Sumatra tobacco, and Belgium and France joined Germany as main purchasers of Java tobacco, which continued to dominate the Netherlands market. There were also growing numbers of Chinese and Javanese traders. In contrast, whereas in 1840 the United States exported 87 percent of the world's leaf, with the breakup of the colonial system and the opening of new regions to the international market, especially the Dutch East Indies, Brazil and Cuba, the US share of world output had dropped to 30 percent by 1884 and, by 1984, a century later, to only 13 percent.

The Deli's enormous profits were invested in turn-of-the century railroad construction in Indonesia, the United States and elsewhere. By the 1920s, however, the company's fortunes began to decline. Cigar smoking had dominated the tobacco market, but in 1927, sales of cigarettes surpassed cigars, and in the 1930s, cigar sales plummeted during the Depression. The Second World War and Japanese occupation brought Sumatra's tobacco exports to a virtual standstill, and the Deli was cut off from its Dutch financial backers. The end of the war saw the Deli reenter a dramatically changed Dutch East Indies and a global market dominated by tobacco giants; and in Indonesia's subsequent struggle against the Dutch for sovereignty, which it attained in 1949, the Deli was in turmoil, from squatters' illegal land occupations, strikes and labour organising, to the so-called Indonesianising of estate personnel. In early 1958, when all Dutch economic interests were nationalised, the Deli, almost exclusively Dutch owned, lost its estates. Remaining Dutch personnel left soon thereafter, and the operation transferred to Indonesian nationals.

The Deli relocated greatly reduced operations to the Netherlands and took over the US American Sumatra Tobacco Corporation,[16] whose origins dated back to 1891, when A. Cohn and Company purchased fourteen thousand acres in the Florida-Georgia belt for tobacco cultivation. The company's tobacco plantation, named Amsterdam, claimed at the time to be the largest tobacco plantation in the world under single ownership. In 1907, seven of the larger growers and packers in the area merged to form the American Sumatra Tobacco Company, with a division in Amsterdam, by then a small company town. It became the

American Sumatra Tobacco Corporation in 1910 and grew during and after the Second World War into one of the world's largest sources of wrapper, linking New York–based financial partners with farmers in the South. The Deli bought American Sumatra in 1955 but shut down its leaf operations in 1965, continuing the production of only the new homogenised tobacco sheets (also known as reconstituted tobacco), in which it became a major player in Italy, Greece and the fast-growing Brazilian market.

The Deli's involvement in the import-export market for flue-cured and burley tobaccos brought partnership with the Universal Leaf Tobacco Company in the mid-1960s, followed by merger in 1986. Universal, which had been founded in 1918, had grown by the 1960s into one of the world's largest leaf tobacco distributors and had restructured after the merger, combining tobacco interests in Universal Leaf Tobacco and grouping diversified trading acquisitions under Deli Universal.[17]

Of significance here is that the Deli's advantage over competitors and enormous profits derived in no small part from what US and Dutch reports decried as coolie slave labour. The Deli may have been renowned among cigar smokers for growing and curing the world's most prized wrappers, but it was also reviled for making other Dutch colonial ventures look benevolent. Its labour and living conditions were infamously compared to those of slavery, and peasant labourers' burning of its barns became a constant worry for both the Deli and the colonial government.[18] The Deli legacy was what Ann Laura Stoler, in her late-twentieth-century fieldwork for *Capitalism and Confrontation in Sumatra's Plantation Belt, 1870–1979*, referred to as one of "brutalities alternatively whispered and shouted,"ever present in peasant-labourer discontent, which still saw the burning of tobacco barns, and in the postcolonial state's "maneuvers and menaces," open to foreign business and ruthless in stamping out oppositional political and labour organising.[19]

Connecticut and Shade

Contrary to Indonesia's contemporary tobacco preeminence, the history of Connecticut's Tobacco Valley – so intimately linked to that of Nienhuys, the Deli, American Sumatra, Universal Leaf and Cuba – is one little in evidence today. Margaret Buker Jay, in her 'Historical Perspective', in *Changing Landscape through People: Connecticut Valley Tobacco*, began thus:

> Anyone driving an automobile in the summertime through the fields and hills of the picturesque Connecticut Valley to the north of Hartford is struck by the great number of tobacco tents constantly coming into view, covering acres of land, running up the hillsides and stretching over the valleys. The

visual landscape of the Connecticut Valley has changed dramatically from the view which prompted this observation in 1917. Tobacco production dominated the landscape of many communities for most of this century. This *was* 'Tobacco Valley'.[20]

In and among suburban and small-town residential areas are now only small expanses of tent-covered shade tobacco land, alongside disused tobacco barns and derelict seasonal farmworker camps. Valley tobacco acreage was at its height in 1921, with almost thirty-one thousand acres, having grown from fewer than forty acres in 1839. Linked with Cuba's fortunes, the 1960s and the 1990s would witness ephemeral revival. However, neither revival was on a scale to stem the steady tide of long-term decline that had begun with the 1950s introduction of homogenised binder and wrapper, compounded by the US Report of the Surgeon General in 1964 on the hazards of smoking and sealed by offshore relocation.

Escalating costs – taxes, labour, fertiliser, fuel and interest rates – all reduced profit margins, and acreage fell as land was sold for industrial, commercial, and suburban residential development. Hartford County's population increased 28 percent over the decade from 1950 to 1960; many towns (e.g., East Granby, Granby, Windsor, East Windsor) grew by more than 50 percent; and four towns (Enfield, Simsbury, South Windsor and Windsor Locks) more than doubled in population.

In 1960, there had been some 9,000 acres under tobacco, and during the decade this stabilised to around 6,000 acres, but by 1979, it had declined to 3,000 acres and was at a low of 720 acres in 1992. Acreage increased only slightly to 910 in 1994 before dwindling again. At the turn of the twenty-first century, tobacco was still a cash crop for some, but many had given up the crop altogether. Companies had stopped buying from contract growers, had liquidated land holdings, and had gone out of business. What was once the heart of the old shade district are today's Buckland Mall, Bradley International Airport, technology business parks and suburban subdivisions.

James F. O'Gorman, in his 2002 *Connecticut Valley Vernacular: The Vanishing Landscape and Architecture of the New England Tobacco Fields*, describes how "tobacco sheds remain the most characteristic example of agricultural vernacular architecture in the Connecticut River Valley . . . common relics of a vanishing episode of Valley life."[21] Accompanying the text are the US– Puerto Rican photographer Jack Delano's haunting visual images of a fading way of life: the shade tents and wooden sheds; shifting immigrant populations; long, hot hours labouring in summer fields; the autumnal curing process and stripping rooms.

What was often recounted in its heyday as a proud New England story of twentieth-century tobacco family dynasties was, in O'Gorman's words, "a high risk, labour-intensive, controversial but potentially rewarding occupation for owners if not for labourers. Cultivation demands constant attention, backbreaking hard work in the fields and under the tents, and knowledgeable adherence to detail in the curing sheds and stripping and sorting rooms."[22] The story was also laced with cutthroat tobacco business and labour practices, as narrated in snapshot detail almost half a century earlier by the local writer Mildred Savage, whose 1958 best-selling novel *Parrish*, made into a 1961 Hollywood movie of the same name, was described at the time as a scenic, tobacco-road soap opera.[23]

The late-twentieth-century end of that heyday would see relocation to the Dominican Republic and Central America, Brazil and Ecuador in search of alternatives not only to outcast post-1959 Cuba but also – in a cost-cutting, profit-making drive – to outcast Connecticut itself.

From Havana 'Segars' and Seed ...

As related in *Connecticut and Tobacco: A Chapter in America's Industrial Growth*, "It is a curiosity of history that the original Dutch and English settlements in Connecticut were in the very areas that some two and half centuries later were to become the heart of Connecticut's valuable tobaccoland."[24] The first tobacco growers were Native Americans, but the tobacco was said to be bitter in taste, and early colonists replaced it with a West Indian variety brought to Connecticut from Virginia. By the early 1700s, tobacco, centered around Windsor, became an important article of trade between valley towns and the West Indies. It declined in the late 1700s, as a result of increased competition from Virginia and England's refusal to allow trade with the West Indian colonies, but it was to come into its own with cigars in the late 1700s and early 1800s with a Cuban connection:

> Colonel Israel Putnam is generally credited with the introduction of the cigar into Connecticut in 1762, on his return from an expedition against Havana. [W]ithin a generation of his time, there was a swing in the taste of Connecticut smokers to cigars. West Indian cigars were coming into the state by 1791, the year in which an advertisement offering 'segars' first appeared in the *Connecticut Courant*.[25]

These were Cuban-manufactured imports. The first advertisement for 'segars' of domestic manufacture was published in the *Connecticut Courant* of 1799.

As the story goes, farmers' wives began home rolling cigars for barter in Windsor, and this spread through the valley. The first cigar making on a commercial basis is also credited to a woman. Little attention was paid to quality, and the cigars were known as paste or barnyard segars, sold to storekeepers for a dollar or two per thousand and retailed at a cent a piece. The shortest – twofers – sold two for a cent. The Viets brothers set up the first cigar factories in Suffield and East Windsor in 1810: "Samuel Viets had by chance come upon a wandering Cuban who understood the art of cigar rolling. He engaged him to teach his craft to a dozen or more women in a newly opened factory at Suffield."[26]

Peddlers traveled the New England countryside selling short sixes and long nines – so named from the size and bundle – made with all-Connecticut leaf or Connecticut filler and Cuban or Maryland wrapper. After factory operations were well established, Havana filler with a Connecticut wrapper began to be used. What became known as the half-Spanish cigar had a favorable effect on local markets, and as manufacturers began to blend Cuban and Brazilian with native leaf, demand for quality Connecticut leaf created warehouses for packing and shipping to New York and other cigar-manufacturing centers.

Larger cigar manufacturers began to emerge after an experimental transplant of Maryland broadleaf resulted in 1830s Connecticut broadleaf, which had an elegant, light-bodied, fine finish, for binder and wrapper. Then:

> Sometime in the early 1870's, under the supervision of state and federal soil and plant specialists, experiments were again undertaken with carefully selected Havana seeds. . . . The leaf obtained after a few crops was not only excellent as a binder but was far superior to any of domestic growth as a wrapper. Seeds were imported for each new sowing and the plants obtained from them for the first three years were known as 'Spanish' or 'Havana.' After a necessary cultivation of four years in Connecticut soil the type acquired certain desired characteristics and was then called 'Havana Seed' [and later] became generally known as 'American' as distinct from 'Spanish'.[27]

Writing almost a century later, in the 1950s, P. J. Anderson, an agronomist with the Connecticut Agricultural Experiment Station, recorded that the name of the man who imported the seed was not known:

> [But p]robably he hoped to duplicate in Connecticut the aroma and other qualities for which the tobacco of Cuba is famous. Although the seed evidently came from Cuba, today there is no district in that island which grows tobacco like it. By generations of selection and acclimatization here, the size and shape of the leaf have so changed that we fail to recognise the Cuban ancestor.[28]

After the Civil War, competition from Pennsylvania and Wisconsin's dark leaf halted New England expansion, then the development of the new Havana seed tobacco and the return to light-coloured cigars restored the competitive advantage that Connecticut had over other US growers. However, they faced a strong new foreign competitor.

European manufacturers had, since the 1860s, been using Dutch East Indies Sumatra wrapper; a sample shipment reached New York manufacturers in 1876, and by the 1880s, it was being imported there. In 1883, alarmed farmers formed the New England Tobacco Growers Association, which petitioned Congress for tariff restrictions, as a result of which duties increased from $0.35 to $0.75 per pound, and again to $2 in 1890. They were reduced to $1.50 in 1894 for three years, after which they increased to $1.85, yet this did not stop imports increasing, as domestic cigar consumption rose, such that annual US purchases of Sumatra tobacco in the 1890s approached $6 million. In 1900, 5 million pounds of leaf were still being imported, and only the high tariff levels enabled Connecticut growers to survive economically. The long-term solution was to develop a leaf that could compete in quality with the Sumatra wrapper.

Experiments in 1898, supervised by the US Bureau of Plant Industry, resulted in just such a leaf, destined to become Connecticut shade: US Type 61. The first experiment, in 1900, in the small town of Poquonock, was carried out by Dr. E. H. Jenkins, director of the Connecticut Agricultural Experiment Station, with Marcus Floyd, of the USDA's Division of Soils, who had experience in Florida shade and chose soil comparable to that of Florida.[29] The story is recounted thus:

> From one field a superior crop developed from Cuban seeds. Unlike its richly flavoured parent, it was completely bland in taste. Experimentally, some of the wrappers were entered in an exhibition at St Louis in 1904 and won a prize. The seeds of numerous varieties continued to be planted, a specific seed to each separate acre. Of the many specimens that finally evolved, four types were found to have merit. Among these were Uncle Sam Sumatra and Hazlewood Cuban.
>
> It was the latter that received approval as best for growing under shade in Connecticut soil, and potentially the most profitable. Seed selection among Connecticut Valley farmers became so expert and so precise that experienced Cuban farmers turned to buy tobacco seeds from the Yankees.[30]

Anderson's 1950s account concurs:

> In the original tests, seed was imported from Sumatra. The experiment proved this variety was unsuited to shade culture and seed from Cuba was tried. After a few years of selection, the Cuban type became established and its culture spread until it reached about 9,000 acres. The variety is identical

to the tobacco grown generally in Cuba today but has been more carefully selected for uniformity. Its only competitor is the imported Sumatra wrapper. The common Cuban strain was for many years the only one grown under cloth but in recent years new higher-yielding strains have been developed and are rapidly replacing the old Cuban. Connecticut 15, Connecticut 49, and Fowler Special are now grown on more acres than common Cuban.[31]

After additional experiments with seed, curing and fertiliser, shade dramatically changed the Connecticut landscape.[32] Whereas thousands of small, independent farmers had grown broadleaf and Havana seed outside tobacco in combination with other crops, shade required substantial investment in poles, wires and netting beyond the resources of the average farmer. Because of the high initial investment required, increased production costs, and greater financial risks, shade was dominated by a small number of large companies, some owned outside the state with investments in other cigar leaf areas, cigar manufacture, or tobacco trading.

The Connecticut Tobacco Company, formed in 1901 by Marcus Floyd and a group of Connecticut growers, was one of the first. In 1917, it merged with American Sumatra, with its extensive holdings in Florida-Georgia, and by the mid-1930s, American Sumatra was the largest single producer of cigar tobacco in Connecticut, owning six thousand acres and sorting and packing facilities in Bloomfield and East Hartford. Other leading corporations were Cullman Brothers (subsequently Cullbro), Consolidated, General, Imperial and Hartman (formed in 1928 as a result of the consolidation of several smaller companies). Prominent growers included Windsor Shade, formed in 1937 by a group of independents, though shade land was mostly owned and rented out under a variety of leasing arrangements. Growers formed cooperatives in an attempt to maintain fair prices for their product, the first recorded being the warehouse system in Hartford in 1852, which was disbanded in 1862 and only briefly reorganised in 1870. In the early twentieth century, a major cooperative was the Connecticut Valley Tobacco Growers Association (CVTGA), and others followed.[33] After being hard hit in the 1920s and 1930s with the drop in cigar consumption, cigar mechanisation and the demand for smaller and cheaper cigars, the onset of the Second World War saw concerns that unfair competition from abroad was approaching crisis level:

> Tobacco is imported into this country that is grown and produced by indentured labor – coolies who received but a few cents a day and are forced to work for a given period of time or suffer the consequences. This ever-increasing tendency to use tobacco that is produced by almost slave labor, that employed foreign capital, foreign material and equipment, is slowly piling on the last few straws which tend to break the camel's back. Only in

the last few years under trade agreements, the import duty has been cut from $2.35 a pound to $1.50 a pound, on Sumatra tobacco.[34]

In 1940, Dr. Boyd, an economist at Storrs Agricultural Station, demonstrated that Connecticut alone could supply wrapper for the 2.5 billion cigars then wrapped with imported tobacco. He called for the state to foster this project and end the decreasing duties on imports from low-wage or no-wage countries – the last cut of nearly 40 percent having resulted in a drastic drop in acreage – and for a campaign to smoke valley-wrapped cigars.[35] Nothing, however, would stem the tide of late-twentieth-century decline.

To Homogenisation, Migration and Relocation

In 1954, homogenised binder was introduced, whereby scrap filler, stems and leaves that would otherwise be rejected were reduced to powder; mixed with water and cellulose adhesive; and formed into thin, paper-like sheets cut to the desired width. This reconstituted tobacco, classified as 'manufactured binder sheet' and fed automatically from a spool into cigar-making machines, with substantially reduced labour and raw materials manufacturing costs, was a technological development that salvaged up to 40 percent of what had before been scrap or at best converted to nonbinder use. As reported in a spate of articles in the local *Hartford Courant* and *Hartford Times*, this was to exacerbate a dramatically imposed reduction in acreage and was subsequently compounded with the introduction of processed cigar wrapper as well.[36]

By the early 1960s, the annual cost of equipment, maintenance, materials, supplies and services required in Connecticut tobacco production was estimated at around $23 million, and a visual cost-cutting change came when shade growers switched from white to orange cloth – the colour came from the lead chromate that impregnated the cloth to make it last longer.[37]

The local press reported more dramatic downturns in the late 1960s and 1970s, and more federal price-support policies, as well as the 1966 Federal Crop Land Adjustment Program, provided subsidies to growers while they experimented with new crops or found new jobs. The climate was one of downturn for even major companies such as Consolidated and Bayuk Cigars; and the Connecticut-Massachusetts Tobacco Cooperative, the receiving agency for tobacco under the government price-support programme, was taking about two-thirds of binder tobacco.[38]

By the 1940s, more than half the grading and sizing of wrapper was being done in Puerto Rico. Some of the wrapper went into cigars made on the island, but most returned for machine manufacture on the US mainland. During the Second World War, special wartime shade labour arrangements were made, and in 1942, the Shade Tobacco Growers Association (STGA) was set up to help underwrite the expense of housing, food, medical care and transportation for seasonal workers.

Growers had long met their labour requirements in various ways, some more savory than others. They employed child labour, until this was legislated against, and then local high school students during their summer holidays.[39] Many of those who worked the tobacco as students reminisced in *Windsor Storyteller* how hard and dirty the work was but also how welcome the money was for them and their families, and the fun they had in what for the community was almost a "rite of passage."[40]

Growers turned further afield for their main sources of labour, and the successive waves of migrant labour appear to have had less fun. In the 1920s and 1930s, students were bussed up from black colleges of the US South.[41] They, too, welcomed the work for the money but met with racial hostility, as did the Jamaicans subsequently brought up during the Second World War under agreement with the British colonial government.[42] From the 1950s to the 1970s, the growers flew in Puerto Ricans under agreement with the Puerto Rican Migration Division. Specially created to meet agricultural labour needs along the Eastern Seaboard, the division functioned as an escape valve in the areas of Puerto Rican tobacco that collapsed when US companies pulled out. The conditions Puerto Rican migrant workers faced came in for heavy criticism, and the programme was finally brought to an end in 1974.[43] Since then, reduced numbers of day labourers have been bussed in, many of them Central American, Mexican and Chicano, as well as Hartford-resident descendants of Jamaicans and Puerto Ricans.

Only Consolidated Cigar – then a subsidiary of Gulf & Western and the largest grower in the area, accounting for 45 percent of acres planted – and General Cigar's Cullbro division increased growing. Hartman, like many others, had switched to vegetable farming, reducing tobacco to 75 of its 1,289 acres and leasing its Windsor Tobacco Farm to Consolidated.[44]

Although the antismoking crusade following the 1964 Report of the Surgeon General was directed mainly against cigarettes, it did affect cigars: airlines, for example, while introducing smoking and no-smoking sections, banned cigar and pipe smoking. By 1979, US cigar sales had dropped 50 percent from the 9.1 billion units sold in 1964.[45] Two years later, in 1981, Consolidated launched a $5 million advertising campaign for Backwoods, a "wild 'n mild" cigar, in an attempt to lure younger smokers, but within months, it, too, had cut half of its 1,800 acres of tobacco land.[46]

By then, only half of the tobacco crop grown by Hartford County's eighty independent farmers was sold commercially, and farmers were forced to sell to the government at break-even prices.[47] As the *New York Times* reported, in Connecticut, "Shrinking markets, rising prices, a decrease in cigar smoking and an increase in foreign competition – as well as torrential rains and flooding in the wettest June in memory – have hastened the atrophy of the once muscular industry."[48]

Connecticut made a limited comeback in response to a new generation of cigar smokers as the late 1980s revalidated a get-rich, conspicuous-consumption culture of socialising with fine liquors and cigars. Then 1990s health research findings extended to mouth and throat cancer associated with cigar smoking as well as the lung cancer associated with cigarette smoking, and new health warnings were introduced on packaging. In the early 1960s, the Connecticut tobacco industry may have optimistically estimated that business would not suffer unduly from government findings on smoke and health, because cigarette smoking was the villain,[49] but by the 1990s, the anti-tobacco lobby had gained significant ground.

The Boston-based Tobacco Divestment Project targeted three Hartford-area insurance firms – AETNA, Travelers and Cigna – to divest their tobacco stocks: City University New York and Harvard were the first two universities to eliminate their stock holdings; in 1991, the Yale-New Haven Hospital announced it would sell its tobacco stocks, and Yale University was considering divestment; and in 1992, West Hartford Beth Israel Synagogue became the first Reform Jewish Congregation in North America to divest its stocks.[50]

When the early 1990s cigar revival came, with the newly founded New York glossy *Cigar Aficionado* embarking on its anti-antismoking quest, a Connecticut feature was prominent: "That tobacco is grown in Connecticut is certainly a surprise to the uninitiated," said Daniel Nuñez, director of Cullbro Tobacco's Connecticut and Dominican Republic operations.[51] Many top producers of cigars, especially from the Dominican Republic, fought to get best-quality Connecticut wrappers for their cigars, because they were among the best to buy, the article declared. Davidoff cigars, once made in Cuba, also used the best-available Connecticut wrapper on Dominican-produced cigars. "A nice Connecticut wrapper," declared Christophe Kull, president of Davidoff of Geneva's US operations, "is like the skin on a baby's bottom, very silky, very fine. From a marketing point of view, it is considered at the moment to be one of the best tasting and looking wrappers available."

The high price of Connecticut tobacco, it was explained, reflected high labour, land and other costs of running a US-based operation. "Connecticut wrapper is very expensive," agreed Carlos Fuente, president of Tabacalera A. Fuente y Compañía, the Tampa-based firm that relocated to the Dominican Republic to produce handmade premium cigars:

> But the producers of Connecticut wrapper run first-class operations, and, additionally, the sorting has been very good. You can always count on high quality, and aside from being expensive, it sells. Though wrapper leaf

tobacco seed varieties developed in the valley have been planted in Costa Rica, the Dominican Republic, Honduras, Mexico, Panama and other places, no one has yet been able to duplicate the color, flavour and texture of the Connecticut Valley leaf.

Yet by the early 1990s, Consolidated, General and other smaller companies had relocated operations offshore, and only a handful of farms remained. Cullbro, which a decade previously had operated seven farms on 1,300 acres, had only four farms on 400 acres in 1992 and only 200 acres planted with tobacco, having cut production by half in 1991. Cullbro's Ed Cullman explained:

> We are growing a lot less tobacco than we used to grow, but these things tend to go in waves. The valley as a whole is growing about 1,200 acres. In 1970, there were nine billion cigars being consumed; now there are just over two billion. That's a huge change that occurred in the cigar business, and it has to be reflected in the growing of wrappers in Connecticut.

The other remaining leaf processor was Windsor Shade, then a cooperative of twelve farmers, working about a thousand acres between them. In 1998, as the 1990s cigar boom peaked, Consolidated cultivated a modest 150 acres, while Enfield Shade farmed 400 acres supplying wrapper to Altadis USA.

Java and Besuki Leaf

Although Sumatra, Connecticut and Cuba may have attained preeminence for quality leaf, Java's central principalities and residency of Besuki overtook all of them in volume. In Besuki, George Birnie, a Dutch agricultural extension worker, was convinced that tobacco could grow well in Bondowoso and Jember. Together with C. Sandenberg and A. D. van Gennep, in 1859, he established De Landbouw-Maatschappij Oud-Djember (LMOD). Other pioneers were J. D. Franssen van de Putte (De Landbouw-Maatschappij Soekowono) and Ry van Beest Holle and Geertsema (De Cultuur Maaatschappij Djelboek). In the Klaten regency of the central principality of Surakarta, the Dorrepaal family, backed by strong financial connections, formed Cultuur Maatschappij, CM-Wedi-Birit (CM) and competed with Deli and Besuki.

Ratna Saptari's comparative work on tobacco regimes in Dutch-colonial Sumatra and Java links the emergence of Nienhuys in Sumatra with Birnie and Dorrepaal in Java to 1860s increased demand for leaf tobacco as the Dutch Culture System was reaching its end and state intervention was giving way to a larger and stronger role for private enterprise.[52] All formed estates according to different local arrangements. The *apanage* system, which was in Java unique to the central principalities, gave benefits to companies through local village heads, but the Dutch never applied it to the directly ruled parts. There, the 1856 Landrental Law enabled investors to hire land for twenty years. This was subsequently replaced by *erfpacht* for up to seventy years, later reduced to fifty years, but otherwise unchanged until nationalisation in 1958.

In Besuki, short-lease farmland was initially restricted to dry lands, but diminishing yields led to its extension to irrigated lands as well from the mid-1870s. After 1875, *erfpacht* was granted on extensive uncultivated areas of Jember, where tobacco became the primary crop. By 1883, LMOD leased 5,700 hectares (14,000 acres) of irrigated lands and 4,300 hectares (10,600 acres) of dry land. By 1908, the figures had risen to 16,000 hectares (40,000 acres) and 11,000 hectares (27,000 acres), respectively, and LMOD controlled 11,400 hectares (28,000 acres) of *erfpacht* land. In the early 1900s, Amsterdam-Besoeki Tabak Maatschappij (ABTM) established estates in Jember. Planters set up the Besoeki Immigration Bureau, bringing in mainly Madurese and later Javanese, from densely populated areas of Central and East Java, as a result of which Besuki had the highest migrant population.

Dutch companies also purchased cigar tobacco that local peasants grew under conditions that conceded peasants weak rights over the land they cultivated but exacted heavy labour obligations. In 1917, peasant rights were increased and company rental rights reduced, but the strong influence of companies over local rulers and the Dutch authorities enabled production with very low costs and very high profits, especially from 1890 to 1915 and in the 1920s. In the early twentieth century, there were two major types of tobacco – Kedu, for cigar binder and filler, and Deli, wrapper – grown primarily on lowland Jember. But in the 1920s, a hybrid of Deli and Kedu gradually expanded, such that hybrid and Kedu became the types grown. Tobacco exports through the main Besuki port of Panurukan accounted for 20 percent of total tobacco exports from Java, on par with Semarang, the main port for Central Java Province. In its heyday, from 1926 to 1930, Besuki supplied 25 percent of Java exports, exceeding any other region of Java.

Tobacco was grown on both dry and wet land leased from peasants on relatively short five-year leases and on *erfpacht* land, made possible because it was still relatively sparsely populated in comparison with other parts of Java, especially the hinterland of Besuki, the Bondowoso, Jember and Banyuwangi regencies. Smallholder farmers (*vrimantabak*) were also important, their share of exports and acreage often exceeding plantation tobacco.

Two regional studies by Indonesian scholars on Besuki Residency are illuminating. Writing in the 1990s, Soegijanto Padmo traced the transition from small-scale development from the 1860s to the 1890s, with several individually owned estates producing tobacco and other cash crops, to corporatisation in the 1880s, with more specialised production by fewer and larger companies from

1890 to 1920.⁵³ During the final years of Dutch rule, the degree of consolidation was such that the Klaten and Besuki regencies were each basically under the control of one major corporation, the Klaten Estate Company and LMOD, and after 1958, under the new state tobacco company regional groupings Pusat Perkebunan Negara Baru (PPN-Baru or PPN).

S. Nawiyanto critiqued what he saw as the negative bias of Dutch and Indonesian historiography on the devastating effects of Japanese occupation.⁵⁴ He documented how the Dutch, anticipating war in 1939, were already turning export cash-crop plantations over to food production, in effect starting what has been described as the Japanisation of rice farming in Indonesia. Besuki Residency, which had become the leading center of twentieth-century Indonesian agricultural production, was then targeted for the highest quota of forced rice delivery imposed by the Japanese, to feed the troops and for wartime self-sufficiency.

Tobacco was at the time the most important export crop, run by large-scale companies, on both farm and plantation, drawing in waves of Madurese and Javanese migration. Cultivation restriction policies – of up to 60 percent for large plantations – during the Depression had taken their toll, but there were signs of recovery in the years before the Japanese invaded. Under the occupation, however, producers lost their Dutch and other international markets, and tobacco fields were converted to meet each residency's quota of rice. In June 1943, it was decided that Hatabako Company buy all tobacco exclusively, buying was concentrated in six store houses, and farmers were allowed to produce tobacco only for domestic consumption and some export to the other Indonesian islands as part of mutual exchange for nonmilitary commodities.

The collapse of the plantation economy weighed heavily on the peasantry, whose income derived mainly from the plantation sector, and Jember was one area where parts of estate lands were redistributed to produce food. This was a time bomb when plantation owners came to reclaim their *erfpacht* rights and came into conflict with squatters, who were strongly supported among Indonesian nationalist circles. In effect, Nawiyanto argues, the profound reorientation of commodity production during the Japanese period helped cement the foundations for independence and nationalisation.⁵⁵

Fast-forward to 2009 and James Suckling's *Cigar Aficionado* article with which I opened: "Listen to the tobacco. The massive warehouse is silent except for the sound of tobacco leaves in motion. Hundreds of young women build and dismantle piles of tobacco that have just arrived from the fields located around the city of Jember, in Indonesia's East Java province."⁵⁶ They worked in silence. "We forbid our workers to speak while they work. Otherwise, they may make a mistake. They must work meticulously. The tobacco must be handled with respect," said Sin Teguh Wanamarta, a Dutch-trained physician working with his father, Eddy Dharsan Wanamarta, processing and trading tobacco at their company, PT Ledokombo. Chinese Indonesians, the Wanamartas were two of a handful of key tobacco men in and around Jember buying, processing, packing and shipping tobacco around the world in the boom 1990s.

Suckling celebrated the Sumatra wrapper leaf that had spawned the Sumatra-seed cigar tobacco grown in many regions of the Americas, mainly for use in machine-made cigars. However, he explained, Java tobacco was cheaper and more readily available; and although tobacco grown in East Java, particularly near Jember, was important to premium cigar makers, a lot of poor tobacco was also grown and shipped to manufacturers supplying the US cigar market. "People could see the money," said Jan Meskens of the Netherlands-based Indoco International, which marketed and sold tobacco from Indonesian processor PT Tempu Rejo. "You had just about anyone setting up and trading in tobacco. It was bananas. We just kept supplying our regular customers, but plenty of people wanted tobacco from us. We did not speculate; but others around us certainly did."

In the mid-1990s, Jember tobacco dealers were receiving visits from US buyers who had never set foot in Indonesia before. Although the boom lasted for only two or three harvests, companies took advantage of the situation and just about anything passing for cigar tobacco was sold, mostly to European manufacturers such as the French SEITA, Swedish Match, Dutch Agio and Swiss Burger Group, which together accounted for close to half the global cigar market. "No one could keep up with the demand," Meskens commented.

Wrapper was grown mostly south of Jember, and to the north filler, on which European manufacturers had a monopoly. One US company that maintained its supplies of quality tobacco from Java during the boom was Consolidated. In the early 1990s, Tempu Rejo and PT Perkebunan Nusantara had developed a premium version of *tembakau bawah naungan* (TBN, 'tobacco under sheet', or shade grown).[57] The TBN was a cross between what had come to be known as Besuki tobacco and Connecticut shade. A lot of tobacco sold as TBN, however, was either shade-grown Besuki or an inferior tobacco grown outside the region resembling TBN, called *vorstenlanden bawah naungan* (VBN), grown in central Java. Consolidated first used TBN on machine-made cigars for several years, before using it on some key handmade brands; and many cigar manufacturers today use Indonesian binder and wrapper.

Driving around Jember in 1999, Suckling reported that it was difficult to see a house without tobacco drying in the sun. Most was for cigarette production, as cigar production was small and of uneven quality. The only premium cigar factory was in Pandaan, near Surabaya, which Swedish Match had opened three years earlier. Heralding what a "modern, well-financed Cuban factory might look like," Suckling quoted the project manager Van Hattem celebrating its workers: "It's not just money here that motivates workers like it is in the Caribbean. They have pride in their work. They are slower than rollers in other countries, but their quality is excellent." Contrast this with a Jember tobacco worker who commented, "It's amazing that more people do not riot considering their situation." That worker also added that a few tobacco-drying barns had been burned that September in protest: "It is so difficult for us to survive."[58]

El Habano or Snus?

In 1995, four years before Suckling's Java article, as the US-engineered cigar boom of the 1990s was gathering momentum and Cuba was seeking ways out of the depths of its early 1990s crisis, Suckling reported for *Cigar Aficionado* on Connecticut-seed tobacco for shade wrapper being grown in the Partido tobacco district of Havana province.[59] Not as prestigious as El Corojo tobacco grown in the Vuelta Abajo tobacco district of Pinar del Río province, destined for the handmade *Habano*, the Connecticut seed was mostly destined for small, European, machine-made cigars. It was a Cuban joint venture with Lippoel Leaf BV in the Netherlands, which described the leaf as 'Cuban-grown shade tobacco of the Connecticut type', meeting the demand for light-coloured shade tobacco.

In the words of Adriano Martínez, of Habanos SA, "It has an important place in the market, and we want a part of the action. I can't see how any of the growers or manufacturers of cigars with Connecticut wrapper should care. Most of them have made a point of growing Cuban seed tobacco; so it's the same thing." The Cubans hoped to tap into the European market with better-quality Connecticut at a lower price. The small cigars could also be sold as 100 percent Havana leaf, which would be a plus in many European countries, especially France.

The Cubans did not expect to sell their Connecticut wrapper tobacco to makers of handmade cigars in the Dominican Republic or Honduras, because it would be illegal to sell cigars with Cuban-grown wrappers in the United States. Nor did they see Cuba as an option: "We could use the Connecticut wrapper grown here, but we won't," declared Martínez. "We will never do that, since it would change the character of the cigars. Our cigars have a unique character and this has not included Connecticut wrapper."

Suckling quoted a tobacco expert familiar with the Cuban project and the global market for tobacco as saying, "It doesn't taste like Cuban leaf and it doesn't taste like Connecticut. If you want to do Connecticut, why do it outside [the state]? There is so much land out there still to be planted in Connecticut, but everybody around the world is copying Connecticut. You can find it in Ecuador or wherever, even in Indonesia." He also reported General Cigar President Austin McNamara's comment: "The most generous thing I can say is that it is an honor and privilege having the Cubans recognise Connecticut as an important tobacco by planting it themselves."

Potentially, the Cubans could plant up to two thousand acres of Connecticut tobacco – nearly the total shade-leaf planting in the Connecticut Valley. But Cuban Partido's enterprise manager, Rafael Collazo, said, "It all depends on the demand in the market. It is a commodity. This whole thing is totally commercial. It is clear, given the economic situation that we are in, that we need to find new sources for hard currency."

Forward again to 1999, and *Cigar Aficionado* veteran reporter David Savona penned a feature on Connecticut shade.[60] Nothing, he wrote, seems to draw cigar smokers like oily, golden-brown Connecticut shade. Savona quoted Theo W. Folz, president and chief executive officer of Consolidated Cigar, as saying, "I would estimate that 50 percent of the handmade cigars sold [in the United States] are made with Connecticut-shade tobacco." He wrote of Connecticut growers proudly recounting Connecticut inventions, like the automated sewing machine stitching tobacco leaves together for hanging in the barns, which elsewhere is done slowly, by hand – and more cheaply, one might add. Tobacco barns elsewhere can be built for a fraction of the cost of those in Connecticut, which have to withstand the cold and snow of winter and need gas burners to create tropical conditions for curing.

In the drive to push down costs, the quest for cheap labour was clearly a prime determinant in the demise of Connecticut and the rise of Indonesia. Cuba's 1959 Revolution aimed to break with this, but Cuba's proud export product, *El Habano*, still had to navigate these international waters. Historians tend to study developments in a particular nation, but the nation-state is not always the logical unit of analysis, nor does the world consist solely of interacting national communities. Rather, by reason of commodity flows, migration, wars, and such, people create their own cross-national systems,[61] themselves "de-essentialising" national history, as Don Fernando Ortiz has so evocatively suggested.

But where and with what does the future lie? Swedish Match was the leading premium cigar manufacturer in the United States, with substantial machine-made cigars businesses in both the United States and Europe and main markets in the United States, France, Spain, Benelux, Germany and Australia. It had played an important role in the industrial and commercial sector in Sweden since the early twentieth century. Its tobacco operations began with AB Svenska Tobaksmonopolet, a monopoly founded in 1915, and Svenska Tändsticks AB, in 1917. The two merged in 1992 as the Procordia Group, and in 1994, they were joined under the company name Swedish Match, whose US and European foothold came through buying and selling acquisitions. In 2007, for example, the company acquired Bogaert Cigars, which had been producing machine-made cigars since 1937 in Jabbeke, Belgium, and in Pasuruan, for France, Germany, the Netherlands and Belgium, and PT Java cigar manufacturing in Indonesia. In 2009, it had ten production plants, the main ones in the United

States, Dominican Republic, Honduras, Belgium and Indonesia – the others were in Brazil, Bulgaria, the Netherlands, the Philippines and Sweden. The company distributed third parties' tobacco products on the Swedish market, and it derived more than half its sales and two-thirds of operating profits from cigars and from *snus*.[62]

Snus is the company's landmark product. It is claimed that when more than 1 million Swedes emigrated across the Atlantic from 1846 until 1930, they took with them their tradition of *snus*, such that it became an identity mark for Swedes, and main streets of Swedish American districts came to be called *snus* boulevards. *Snus* began to regain popularity in the late 1960s, after the documented health risks associated with smoking. By 2006, 220 million cans of *snus* were sold to about 1 million users in Sweden – nearly one-fifth of whom were women – and in 2010, Swedish Match promoted itself as the market leader in smoke-free tobacco, especially *snus*, its fastest-growing product in both Sweden and the United States.

In 2010, Indonesia, one of the world's largest tobacco producers, was the only Southeast Asian country not to have ratified the World Health Organisation's Framework Convention on Tobacco Control. Pressure on government not to sign came from the tobacco sector, the livelihood of whose 600,000 workers and 3.5 million farmers would be hit.[63] The fate of Connecticut, by contrast, appeared to be sealed, and that of Cuba, in the balance. Cuba had stepped up its health-related domestic antismoking campaign, and in late 2009, it announced a 30 percent reduction in growing, as international markets for both leaf and cigars were down. The 2009–10 harvest, however, was good, and sales were better than expected. That is a story beyond the confines of this article, but the question is whether, with or without the US embargo, *El Habano* will continue to hold its own. Or is *snus* the future?

Notes

1 This article is derived from a paper presented at the International Workshop of the Netherlands-funded Plants, People and Work Project, held in Yogyakarta, Java, Indonesia, in August 2009.
2 James Suckling, 'Tobacco Mecca: Indonesia's East Java Continues to Produce Fine Tobacco Despite Its Troubled Economy', *Cigar Aficionado* (January/February 1999). Since it was founded in 1992, *Cigar Aficionado* has been an invaluable source of feature articles, reportage and news on the Havana cigar and the global cigar world, and its entire archive is available online.
3 There is a considerable body of work on the significance of Cuban tobacco, especially the Havana cigar: the Cuban ethnographer Fernando Ortiz's classic *Cuban Counterpoint: Tobacco and Sugar* (Durham & London: Duke University Press, 1995 [1940]); former cigar maker Gaspar Jorge García Galló's *Biografía del tabaco habano* (Havana: Comisión Nacional del Tabaco Habano, 1961 [1959]); Cuban historian José Rivero Muñiz's *Tabaco: su historia en Cuba*, 2 vols. (Havana: Instituto de Historia,

1965), as well as studies such as Jean Stubbs, *Tobacco on the Periphery* (London: Amaurea Press, 2023 [1985]). Recent promotional publications include those by Cubans Eumelio Espino Marrero, *Cuban Cigar Tobacco: Why Cuban Cigars Are the World's Best* (Neptune City: TFH Publications, 1996); Enzo A. Infante Urivazo, *Havana Cigars, 1817–1960* (Neptune City: TFH Publications, 1997); and Antonio Núñez Jiménez, *The Journey of the Havana Cigar*, Neptune City: TFH Publications, 1996 [1988]. They all have a national focus but make reference to the many falsifications at home and abroad. See also Charles del Todesco, *The Havana Cigar: Cuba's Finest* (New York: Abbeville Press, 1997); Gerard Père et Fils, *Havana Cigars* (Paris: Seul, 1995).

4   Little work connects the various offshore economies and communities, but a recent landmark exception is Araceli Tinajero, *El lector de tabaquería: Historia de una tradición cubana* (Madrid: Editorial Verbum, 2007), which links the institution of reading in Cuba, New York, Tampa, Puerto Rico, Mexico and Spain. Evan M. Daniel is working on a transnational cigar worker history: 'Rolling for the Revolution: A Transnational History of Cuban Cigar Makers in Havana, South Florida and New York City, 1850s–1890s', paper presented at the 2006 Latin American Studies Association Congress, San Juan, Puerto Rico.

5   See the introduction by Coronil in Ortiz, *Cuban Counterpoint* (1995 [1940]), p.xxviii.

6   For a discussion, see Jean Stubbs, 'Tobacco in the Contrapunteo: Ortiz and the Havana Cigar', in Mauricio A. Font & Alfonso W. Quiroz (eds), *Cuban Counterpoints: The Legacy of Fernando Ortiz* (Lanham: Lexington, 2004), pp.105-23 – Chapter 9 in the present volume; 'Havana Cigars and the West's Imagination', in Sander L. Gilman & Zhou Xun (eds), *Smoke: A Global History of Smoking* (London: Reaktion Press, 2004), pp.134-9 – Chapter 10 in the present volume. Juan José Baldrich highlights the strong connections among Cuba, Puerto Rico, and the United States in 'From Handcrafted Tobacco Rolls to Machine-Made Cigarettes: The Transformation and Americanization of Puerto Rican Tobacco, 1847–1903', *Centro Journal* 17 (Fall 2005), pp.144–69, 'Cigars and Cigarettes in Nineteenth Century Cuba', *Revista/Review Interamericana* 24 (Spring/Winter 1994), pp.8-35.

7   The best-known Cuban émigré local histories are on Key West and Tampa: A. Stuart Campbell, *The Cigar Industry of Tampa* (Tampa: University of Tampa, 1939); Glenn L. Westfall, *Don Vicente Martínez Ybor: the Man and His Empire: Development of the Clear Havana Industry in Cuba and Florida in the Ninteenth Century* (New York: Garland, 1987), *Key West: Cigar City USA* (Key West: Historic Key West Preservation Board, 1984). Historical overviews include Gerald E. Poyo, 'The Cuban Experience in the United States, 1865-1940: Migration, Community and Identity', *Cuban Studies* 21 (1991), pp.19-36. Louis A. Pérez Jr. pioneered cigar-worker histories of Tampa in 'Reminiscences of a Lector. Cuban Cigar Makers in Tampa', *Florida Historical Quarterly* 53:4 (1975), pp.443-9. Others more recently include Nancy A. Hewitt's exploration of labour, gender, and race in *Southern Discomfort: Women's Activism in Tampa, Florida, 1800s–1920s* (Urbana: University of Illinois Press, 2001); Robert P. Ingalls & Louis A Pérez Jr., *Tampa Cigar Workers: A Pictorial History* (Gainesville: University Press of Florida, 2003). For the interconnections with race, see Susan D. Greenbaum, *Afro-Cubans in Ybor City: A Centennial History* (Tampa: Tampa Printing, 1986), and *More Than Black: Afro-Cubans in Tampa* (Gainesville: University Press of Florida, 2002); Evelio Grillo, *Black Cuban, Black American: A Memoir*, (Houston Arte Público Press, 2000); Winston James, 'From a Class for Itself to a Race on Its Own: The Strange Case of Afro-Cuban Radicalism and Afro-Cubans in Florida, 1870–1940', in Winston James (ed.), *Holding Aloft the Banner of Ethiopia: Caribbean Radicalism in Early Twentieth-Century America* (London: Verso, 1998), pp.232-57. There is a far more voluminous literature on Puerto Rican émigré communities in the United States, and there is reference to nineteenth-century Cuban cigar makers alongside Puerto Ricans in New York in the celebrated memoirs of Puerto Rican émigré cigar maker Bernardo Vega, in César Andreu Iglesias (ed.),

Memoirs of Bernardo Vega (New York: Monthly Review Press, 1984 [1977]). They also feature in Lisandro Pérez, *Sugar, Cigars, and Revolution: The Making of Cuban New York* (New York: New York University Press, 2018). For the lesser-known histories of Cuban tobacco in Jamaica and the Dominican Republic, see Jean Stubbs, 'Political Idealism and Commodity Production: Cuban Tobacco in Jamaica, 1870-1930', *Cuban Studies*, 25 (1995), pp.51-81 – Chapter 7 in the present volume; and 'Reinventing Mecca: Tobacco in the Dominican Republic, 1763-2007', Commodities of Empire Working Paper, 3 (2007), at https://commoditiesofempire.org.uk/publications/working-papers/working-paper-3 – Chapter 12 in the present volume.

8   For the broader picture, see Maurice Corina, *Trust in Tobacco: The Anglo-American Struggle for Power* (London: Michael Joseph, 1974); for Cuba, see Stubbs, *Tobacco on the Periphery* (2023 [1985]).

9   A copy of the 1960 USDA Report is housed in the Special Collections Library of the University of Florida and provides statistical and qualitative evidence on the history and juncture at the time of the US cigar industry, as well as the significant impact of the embargo on Cuban leaf imports. President John F. Kennedy famously ensured he had his supply of Havana cigars before signing the embargo into law.

10 Connecticut State Library, Hartford, holds a valuable Newspaper Clipping Files collection (CSL NCF) from which this and other features and reportage are taken.

11 Raymond Jahn, *The Dictionary of Tobacco* (New York: Philosophical Library, 1954).

12 Deli Universal N.V., available at http://www.deli-universal.nl.

13 See Lim Kim Liat, 'The Deli Tobacco Industry: Its History and Outlook', in Douglas S. Paauw (ed.), *Prospects for East Sumatran Plantation Industries: A Symposium*, South East Asian Studies Monograph Series 3 (New Haven: Yale University Press, 1962), pp.1-19.

14 For general Indonesian economic history, see P. Creutzberg (ed.), *Changing Economy in Indonesia: A Selection of Statistical Source Material from the Early 19th Century up to 1940*, 15 vols. (The Hague: M. Nijhoff, 1996 [1975]); J. Th. Lindblad (ed.), *Historical Foundations of a National Economy in Indonesia, 1890s–1990s* (North Holland: Koninkliijke Nederlands Akademie van Wetenschappen, 1996), *New Challenges in the Modern Economic History of Indonesia* (Leiden: Programme of Indonesian Studies, 1993). For Sumatra plantation history, see Thee Kian-Wie, *Plantation Agriculture and Export Growth: An Economic History of East Sumatra, 1863–1942* (Jakarta: Indonesian Institute of Sciences, 1977); and Ann Laura Stoler's excellent *Capitalism and Confrontation in Sumatra's Plantation Belt, 1870–1979* (Ann Arbor: University of Michigan Press, 1995).

15 For a discussion of the different colonial systems, see Jordan Goodman, *Tobacco in History: The Cultures of Dependence* (London: Routledge, 1993).

16 Julius Lichtenstein, then president of American Sumatra Tobacco Company, is credited with bringing together six independent cigar manufacturers competing for sales in local markets with regional brands in 1918. In 1921, Consolidated Cigar Corporation, later Altadis USA and then Imperial, officially formed. One of the original six manufactured a brand called Dutch Masters, which became the new corporation's flagship brand and one of the biggest-dollar-volume cigar brands in the United States. The signature brand today is Montecristo.

17 See Maurice Duke & Daniel P. Jordan (eds), *Tobacco Merchant: The Story of Universal Leaf Tobacco Company* (Lexington: University Press of Kentucky, 1995). All major tobacco companies were diversifying in response to the growing antismoking lobby. Deli Universal moved primarily into lumber from the 1980s and, from the 1990s, into wood products for the burgeoning do-it-yourself sector in the Netherlands, Belgium, and Germany.

18 Ratna Saptari, 'The Politics of Land, Labour and Leaf: Tobacco Regimes in Colonial Java and Sumatra (Late 19th–Early 20th Century)', paper presented at the workshop 'Plants, People, and Work', Yogyakarta, Java, Indonesia (2009). Saptari highlights early-twentieth-century debates regarding working conditions coming to a head

with a 1902 report and 1903 government-commissioned investigation of conditions in East Coast Sumatra plantations and the Labor Inspectorate established in 1908. Yet Deli expansion continued unabated, and by 1912, more than two hundred plantations had 150,000 workers and 35,000 to 50,000 new recruits arriving each year.

19 Stoler, *Capitalism and Confrontation (1995)*, refers to silences as the quiet menace of a colonial past casting its shadow over the present. See also K. L. Pelzer, *Planters against Peasants: The Agrarian Struggle in East Sumatra, 1947–1958* (Gravenhage: Martinus Nijhoff, 1982), *Planter and Peasant: Colonial Policy and the Agrarian Struggle in East Sumatra, 1863–1947* (The Hague: Martinus Nijhoff, 1978); and Jan Breman, *Taming the Coolie Beast* (New York: Oxford University Press, 1989).

20 Margaret Buker Jay, 'Historical Perspective', in Anadel Schnip & Katya Williamson (eds), *Changing Landscape through People: Connecticut Valley Tobacco, a Documentary of Photographs and Writing for the 1980s* (n.p.: n.d.). This volume is one of several nostalgic photographic books.

21 James F. O'Gorman, *Connecticut Valley Vernacular: The Vanishing Landscape and Architecture of the New England Tobacco Fields* (Philadelphia: University of Pennsylvania Press, 2002), p. 3.

22 Ibid., p.5.

23 Mildred Savage, *Parrish* (New York: Simon & Schuster, 1958).

24 *Connecticut and Tobacco: A Chapter in America's Industrial Growth* (Washington DC: Tobacco History, n.d.).

25 Ibid., p.26. Iain Gately, *La Diva Nicotiana* (New York: Simon & Schuster, 2001), p.172, in referring to Cuban tobacco flourishing with free trade after the end of the Spanish monopoly in 1817, states that although Havana cigars had a ready market in Europe, the main market was the United States. This dominance had existed ever since General Abe Putnam had participated in the British sack of Havana in 1762: "Putnam had loaded three donkeys with Havana cigars as his share of the plunder, which he sold singly to customers of a tavern he owned in Connecticut."

26 Ibid., p.30.

27 Ibid., pp.35–8.

28 P. J. Anderson, 'Growing Tobacco in Connecticut', *Connecticut Agricultural Experiment Station Bulletin* 564 (1953), p.10.

29 See Randall R. Kincaid, 'Shade Tobacco Growing in Florida',*Quincy North Florida Experimental Station Bulletin* 136 (1960). Shade wrapper was an important crop in the Florida-Georgia area in the first half of the twentieth century. According to Kincaid (p.4), "About 1898, tests conducted at Quincy showed that leaves grown under artificial shade were of fine quality comparable to wrapper tobacco imported from Sumatra". This was US Type 62, which increased in acreage in the area from three thousand in 1921 to six thousand in 1960 (though there was a drop in the 1930s). Some three-quarters of this was in Florida, with a concentration in Gadsden County, but also in Leon and Madison in Florida and Decatur and Grady in Georgia. Kincaid reports the major single production costs as by far labour and farm supervision, followed by shade cloth and maintenance, then fertilisers. Cigar manufacturing was important during that period in Florida, with factories from Quincy in the north to Key West in the south, but with most in Tampa. Kincaid also refers to wrapper produced elsewhere, principally Connecticut Valley, Cuba and Indonesia. In 1959, according to USDA figures, imports were principally from Cuba – 700,000 lbs in comparison with imports from Indonesia (the year after nationalisation of foreign companies there) of only 50,000 lbs. See also W. B. Tisdale, 'Tobacco Growing in Florida', *Florida Agricultural Experimental Station Bulletin* 198 (1928), pp.379–428.

30 *Connecticut and Tobacco* (n.d.), pp.43–6.

31 Anderson, 'Growing Tobacco', (1953), p.1. States came to be known for their different tobaccos: Ohio and Pennsylvania, filler; Wisconsin, filler and wrapper; Connecticut

Valley, binder and wrapper, especially Sumatra, deemed the finest wrapper with the exception of Cuba's, which was produced in small quantity and first exported in 1900. Tobacco was grown from imported or Florida-grown seed, in beds preferably heated by artificial means and heavily fertilised. Both Cuban and Sumatran tobaccos were grown in the Northwest and West and, mainly, Cuban on the Florida peninsula. Sumatra harvesting was from June to September, whereas Cuban, especially under irrigation further south in Florida, had two main crops: spring and autumn. See Milton Whitney, 'Methods of Curing Tobacco', *USDA Farmers' Bulletin* 6 (Washington DC: Government Printing Office, 1902).

32 From the 1890s, the Connecticut Tobacco Valley Experiment Company in Poquonock carried out fertiliser experiments in tandem with experiments in curing tobacco. In the early 1920s, the Experimental Tobacco Station, directed by Anderson, was the only one in New England and one of only four or five in the United States.

33 The Dodd Research Center holds CVTGA records and printed materials for 1920-49, as well as runs of the trade journals *Tobacco* (1920-49) and *Tobacco Leaf* (1930-44) and photocopies of *Connecticut Valley Tobacco Grower*, the official publication of CVTGA (1923-27).

34 Merrill Crawford, 'Tobacco Valley', *Connecticut Circle* (November 1940), p.24. This marked Tobacco Valley Centenary, with photos and text.

35 Ibid., p.29.

36 Examples of the many local press articles from the time are 'Farmers Vote for Federal Price Support', 'Referendum Vote Approves Quotas', 'Nu Way Tobacco Co. Starts Production of Processed Cigar Binder', 'Outdoor Acreage Reduced by 12.5%', and 'Connecticut-Massachusetts Tobacco Cooperative'. All from CSL NCF.

37 Synthetic fibers were also tested from time to time, but the preference remained for cotton. See 'Shade-Grown Tobacco Lends Color to Valley', *Hartford Courant* (26 May 1968). In Brazil, black petroleum-based synthetic nets would be used.

38 See Russ Harvard, 'Economics Shrinking State Tobacco Fields', *Hartford Courant* (7 February 1972); Harold Street, 'Consolidated Won't Buy Annual Broadleaf Crop', *Hartford Courant* (20 December 1960); 'Production of Valley Broadleaf Dropping This Year to New Low', *Hartford Courant* (1 March 1961).

39 Child labour is discussed in Jay, 'Historical Perspective'. For a press report, see John J. Egan, 'Tobacco Child Labor under Fire by Labor Commissioner', *Hartford Times* (31 December 1946).

40 *Windsor Storyteller: A Chronicle of 20th Century Life in Windsor* (Windsor: Windsor Historical Society, 1999).

41 A good discussion of this can be found in S. K. Close, 'The Ties That Bind: Southwest Georgians, Black College Students, and Migration to Hartford', *Journal of South Georgia History* 15 (2000), pp.19-27. See also Marcia Hinckley, '"We just went on with it": The Black Experience in Windsor, Connecticut, 1790-1950', master's thesis, Trinity College, Connecticut (1991). There was much local press coverage, as in 'Florida Teenagers Work on Tobacco Farms', *Hartford Courant* (21 July 1957).

42 Fay Clarke Johnson provides a moving account in *Soldiers of the Soil* (New York: Vantage Press, 1995).

43 Chapter 2 in Ruth Glasser, *'Aquí me quedo': Puerto Ricans in Connecticut* (Middletown: Connecticut Humanities Council, 1997) is titled 'Tobacco Valley' and provides an incisive overview. The rich collections in the Library of the Center for Puerto Rican Studies, Hunter College, City University of New York, hold records of the Farm Labor Program, 1948-93, including correspondence of the Hartford Office of the Puerto Rican Migrant Labour Division and the Shade Tobacco Growers Association (STGA). Trinity College Hartford Project has in its holdings two excellent videos: *Connecticut River Valley* (narrator Lowell Thomas) and *Puerto Rican Passages* (narrator José Feliciano).

44 Among the press articles, see Johanna Ball, 'Tobacco Grower to Switch Crops', *Hartford Courant* (17 November 1978).

45 'US Cigar Sales Left in Ashes', *Hartford Courant* (14 June 1979).
46 Kristina Goodnough, 'Summer Jobs Wither in Tobacco Cutback', *Hartford Courant* (8 December 1981).
47 Martin Kearns, 'Tobacco Demand Lessens: Pressure Put on County Growers by Profit Drop', *Hartford Courant* (14 December 1981).
48 Samuel G. Freedman, 'Connecticut's Tobacco: Gone with the Wind?' *New York Times* (6 July 1982).
49 Lee Grabar, 'State Tobacco Industry Not Expected to Suffer', *New Haven Register* (12 January 1964).
50 Insurance and health were big business in Connecticut, so this was big news. See Kevin Sack, 'Cuomo Weighs Move to Drop Tobacco Stocks', *New York Times* (9 June 1990); Robert S. Capers, 'Yale-New Haven Hospital to Sell Its Tobacco Stocks', *Hartford Courant* (15 August 1991); Robert S. Capers, 'Synagogue Sells Off Tobacco Investments', *Hartford Courant* (1 January 1992).
51 Dirk Vaughan, 'Wrapped Up: Some of the Best Cigars Use Connecticut's Tobacco Wrapper Leaves', *Cigar Aficionado* (Winter 1992).
52 See Saptari, 'Politics of Land, Labour and Leaf' (2009); T. S. Raffles, *History of Java* (Kuala Lumpur: Oxford University Press, 1978).
53 Soegijanto Padmo, *The Cultivation of Vorstenlands Tobacco and Besuki Tobacco in Besuki Residency and Its Impact on the Peasant Economy and Society, 1860-1960* (Yogyakarta: Additya Media, 1994). See also S. Nawiyanto, 'Growing "Golden Leaf": Tobacco Production in Besuki Residency, 1860-1970', *Historia* 4:2 (2009), pp.144-58.
54 S. Nawiyanto, *The Rising Sun in a Javanese Rice Granary: Change and the Impact of Japanese Occupation on the Agricultural Economy of Besuki Residency, 1942-1945* (Yogyakarta: Galangpress, 2005). See also Nawiyanto, 'The Economy of Besuki in the 1930s Depression', in I. Brown & P. Boomgard (eds), *Weathering the Storm: The Economies of Southeast Asia in the 1930s Depression* (Singapore: Institute of Southeast Asian Studies, 2000), pp.171-88.
55 The Dutch disputed Indonesian nationalisation in a landmark case over Indonesian tobacco, better known as the Bremen Tobacco Case, of 21 August 1959, in the Bremen Court of Appeal. The court ruled the expropriation and/or nationalisation of Dutch companies legal and gave the green light to Indonesia's decision to trade on the Bremen market in place of Amsterdam. See *The Bremen Tobacco Case 60* (special issue), Department of Information, Republic of Indonesia (1960).
56 Suckling, 'Tobacco Mecca' (2009). For a study of Jember, see A. C. Mackie, 'The Changing Political Economy of an Export Crop: The Case of Jember's Tobacco Industry', *Bulletin of Indonesian Economic Studies* 21 (1985), pp.113-38.
57 At the time, Central African wrapper supplies had declined in quality and quantity during the 1980s because of internal problems in the tobacco-producing nations of Cameroon and the Central African Republic, as well as poor relations between the African growers and their French backers.
58 Saptari, 'Politics of Land, Labour, and Leaf' (2009) refers to the reports of the burning of tobacco barns in the principalities and the Javanese protest of *pepe*, sitting down en masse, over company occupation of communal lands. Among the studies of conflict in Java, see M. L. Lyons, *Bases of Conflict in Rural Java* (Berkeley: Center for South & Southeast Asia Studies, 1970). See also Jan Breman, *Good Times and Bad Times in Rural Java: A Study of Socio-Economic Dynamics towards the End of the Twentieth Century* (Leiden: KITLV Press, 2002).
59 James Suckling, 'A Connecticut Leaf in Cuba', *Cigar Aficionado* (Autumn 1995).
60 David Savona, 'Made in the Shade: For a Century, Connecticut Farmers Have Grown Some of the World's Finest Cigar Wrapper Tobacco', *Cigar Aficionado* (November-December 1999).
61 Conceptualising the global history approach to commodity chains, migration and labour is beyond the scope of this article, but for a succinct discussion, see Marcel

van der Linden, *Transnational Labour History: Explorations* (Aldershot: Ashgate, 2003). Such an approach shapes, for example, the Commodities of Empire British Academy Research Project in the United Kingdom, the Anti-Commodities Project at Wageningen University, the International Institute of Social History (Amsterdam) in the Netherlands, and *Journal of Global History*.

62 The company's US premium brands include Macanudo, once produced in Jamaica, and Partagás, Punch, Hoyo de Monterrey, La Gloria Cubana and Cohíba – all Cuban – made in the Dominican Republic or Honduras.

63 The focus of this article has been on cigars, which constitute but one small sector of the global tobacco industry, dominated as it is by cigarettes and, in several parts of the world, by chewing tobacco. The 2010 dispute between the United States and Indonesia erupted over the United States' blocking of Indonesia's very popular local *kretek*, or clove, cigarettes. See 'WTO to Rule on US Clove Cigarette Ban', Reuters (20 July 2010). At the same time, in the context of US President Barack Obama's July 2010 visit to Indonesia, scientists there were calling for reopening the debate on the medicinal properties of tobacco. See 'Indonesia, President Obama and Tobacco', *Jakarta Post* (27 July 2010). Therein lies another story in the making.

14

Beyond the Black Atlantic: Understanding Race, Gender and Labour in the Global Havana Cigar[*1]

THE CARIBBEAN has long been part not only of an Atlantic but also a far more global political, economic and socio-cultural world. European empires that carved up the region they labelled the West Indies likewise staked their claim to territories in what in similar terms was for them their East Indies. Across networks of territories of the imperial west and east, and also through the interstices of empires, commodities, peoples and ideas flowed. In the nineteenth century, Cuba was a hub for such networks,[2] and the handmade Havana cigar established itself globally as *the* luxury tobacco product of the century.[3] Coveted and replicated across the world, *El Habano* lay at the heart of transnational processes of production, commerce and myth making, as travel facilitated transfers of knowledge and practice, whereby seed, agricultural and industrial know-how, and human capital were all transplanted. This was accentuated by the migratory flows accompanying landmark political upheavals in Cuba, such as the late nineteenth-century struggles for independence from Spain, early twentieth-century US occupations, and the 1959 Revolution.

The result was often-disputed identical brands, produced in Cuba and abroad, by island and émigré Cubans, and distributed through parallel chains, networks and circuits. In turn, this created a complex multi-tiered licit and illicit system that aimed to capitalise on the prestige of the 'authentic' product. Cuban cigar communities and economies were re-created abroad, often contested along class, race and gender lines, from both within and without.

* Originally published in *Comparativ* 5:21 (2012), pp.50-70.

Moreover, above and beyond these communities and economies lay a far wider 'Havana cigar universe', which involved competing economies; political, social and cultural worlds; and imaginaries.

What follows first charts the broader Havana cigar universe. It then draws on the late Cuban ethnographer Fernando Ortiz's now classic Cuban counterpoint of tobacco and sugar and British social theorist Paul Gilroy's critique of the moral economies of Black Atlantic cultures, to frame a global commodity and labour history approach. Subsequently, it travels geographical 'pathways' of this one commodity, the luxury handmade Havana cigar, and the leaf that goes into its making, painting four time-sequential vignettes. The focus moves from struggles around more readily understood hierarchies of class, race and gender in cigar manufacturing in Cuba and Florida to those accompanying less readily recognised emasculated hierarchies in leaf growing in Connecticut and Indonesia. A final section highlights how Indonesia's rise to global pre-eminence challenges us to think beyond the racialised and gendered hierarchies of the Western Hemisphere and Black Atlantic to more global configurations.

The Havana Cigar Universe

Understanding how the 'Havana' became the centre of a whole cigar universe can be documented through agricultural science and technology; management, land tenure, labour, migration and consumption; and also forms of communication. To give but a recent example, *Cigar Aficionado*, the up-market glossy magazine for 'the discerning male,' founded in New York in the early 1990s, was highly successful in engineering an anti-antismoking campaign to promote cigar consumption. It did so socially and culturally as well as commercially, nurturing a whole cult of cigar cool whose epitome was the Havana.[4] Written for the connoisseur and punctuated by aggressive marketing, *Cigar Aficionado* reportage and feature articles signalled where and by whom Havana seed leaf is today grown outside Cuba, as also who is manufacturing and marketing the off-island Havana, and where.

The history behind this is what I set out to trace, charting the formation, growth and decline of post-1868 and post-1959 Cuban cigar émigré communities; exploring economic, social and political processes in receiver territories as well as Cuba; and delving into the politics of historical myth and memory in émigré culture, associated as they are among Cubans in the United States with post-1868 political idealism and post-1959 political conservatism.[5] In the process, broader histories emerged, and these, for analytical purposes, I group into four categories.

First, there are closely interlocking cigar histories of territories with significant migratory flows out of and into Cuba. Most notable is that of Florida, boosted and eventually destroyed by two US trade embargoes on Cuba: one in the 1890s build-up to Cuba's final War of Independence from Spain; and the other in the 1960s on the heels of the 1959 Revolution. Over and beyond the better-known Cuban émigré southern Florida cigar histories of Key West, Tampa and Ybor City,[6] there are also lesser-known histories of the Florida-Georgia shade tobacco belt, and linked cigar centres such as Amsterdam, Havana, Jacksonville, Quincy and Thomasville.[7]

Equally in this first category would be nineteenth- and early twentieth-century New York, whose veritable explosion of cigar manufacturing involving many Cubans is only now being studied;[8] and Jamaica, with its little-known late nineteenth-century/early twentieth-century history of tobacco growers, workers and manufacturers who fled Cuba in the war-torn 1870s to found the once-thriving Jamaican tobacco economy.[9] Finally, looking across the Atlantic, the late nineteenth- and early twentieth-century mass migratory waves of Canary Islanders into Cuban tobacco – in the context of the Canaries' geo-strategic position on the route between Spain, Africa and the Americas – fuelled subsequent return migration into the Canaries' own tobacco growing and production, using a blend of tobaccos from various parts of the world.[10]

In a second category are the closely intertwined histories of Puerto Rican and Cuban tobacco with no significant tobacco migration but closely monitored trade networks and circuits of knowledge.[11] Puerto Rico's own turbulent tobacco history in the late nineteenth and early twentieth centuries, fostered by US capital with the US invasion of 1898 after the end of Spanish colonial rule, was in turn undercut in the mid-twentieth century in the US-blessed, Puerto Rican strategy of Operation Bootstrap. The early twentieth century saw considerable numbers of Puerto Rican cigar workers heading north to US centres of cigar manufacturing, especially New York, where they joined Cuban émigrés. State-engineered migrant farm labour programmes of the third quarter of the twentieth century then transported displaced farmers and agricultural labourers from what were once Puerto Rican tobacco areas to the shade tobacco fields of Connecticut.[12]

The third category are cigar histories that have seen small yet significant catalysts of Cuban cigar migration – those of late nineteenth-century Mexico[13] and late twentieth-century Nicaragua and Honduras, and also Ecuador and Brazil,[14] but most notably the Dominican Republic. Hitherto far behind in the Havana cigar stakes, the Dominican Republic was reinvented in the 1990s as home to the born-again Havana cigar for the US market, where the real Havana was forbidden fruit.[15]

Finally, there are African and Asian interconnections, linked to global and imperial cigar expansion involving the United Kingdom, the Netherlands, Germany and France. The French moved into territories such as Cameroon, whose leaf became part of the global cigar blend; while the tobacco history of the Philippines – the third last colony of Spain, along with Cuba and Puerto Rico, and a US colony until 1946 – mirrored that of its erstwhile colonial counterparts.[16] The shade tobacco of Cuba, Florida-Georgia and Connecticut was itself derived from, and in competition with, that of Sumatra (and Java), in turn originally derived from Cuban and American seed (tobacco being indigenous to the Americas).[17] Developed initially by the Dutch and marketed primarily in the Netherlands and Germany, the cheaper Indonesian leaf and ultimately cigar were destined to flood the global market.

Conceptualising Race, Gender and Labour in the Global Havana Cigar

Cuban ethnographer Fernando Ortiz blazed new ground in the Cuba of 1940 by publishing *Cuban Counterpoint: Tobacco and Sugar,* grounded on an analysis of these, Cuba's two major commodities. It was the seminal work in which he developed his concept of transculturation, using tobacco and sugar as metaphorical constructs, highlighting both their fetish power as commodities and a counter-fetish interpretation that challenged "essentialist understandings of Cuban history."[18]

Drawing on myth and culture, Ortiz began his counterpoint with an allegory to the dispute between *Don Carnal* (Carnival) and *Doña Cuaresma* (Lent) in the book *Libro de buen amor* (The Book of Good Love, 1330) by the medieval poet Juan Ruiz, known as the Archpriest of Hita (c.1283- c.1350). He thereby set the scene for a drama personifying masculine dark tobacco and feminine white sugar – *Don Tabaco* and *Doña Azúcar*. This was the literary precedent to enacting a long sequence of literal and figurative contrasts: sugar was a centripetal, centralising force reproducing the relationship between the exploitative metropolis and the exploited colonies, while tobacco was a centrifugal, decentralising force signifying autonomy, freedom and independence. Tobacco was quality and distinctiveness, 'the best', as opposed to 'the most' for sugar: the proud cigar band against the lowly sack. Sugar was black and unfree, in its slavery, contrasting with tobacco as white and free in its labour. Ortiz then unpicked these opposites in ways suggestive of new transculturations, akin to Cuba's emblematic culinary *ajiaco* (a stew of indigenous root vegetables), which was not so much *fusión* (a melting pot fusion) but *cocción* (an incessant simmering concoction), conflict and transformation, *mestizaje* (understood as both cultural and biological race mixing).

The 1990s revival of interest in the work of Ortiz[19] saw him as a thinker ahead of his times, writing in moments of international and domestic upheaval, which framed his concerns and help explain his work's allegorical character: a thinker very much in tune with the fluidity of the contemporary world. Ortiz's binary opposites were seen as tropes for events, ideas and interpretations that were in constant flux, and were the attraction of his work over half a century later, in the newly globalising world.[20]

The Ortiz revival coincided with the landmark 1990s work of Paul Gilroy conceptualising the hybridity of the Black Atlantic, and Ortiz's ideas resonate even more closely with the underlying thinking of Gilroy's *Darker than Blue: On the Moral Economies of Black Atlantic Culture* (2010).[21] The title, Gilroy explains, was taken from African American writer Ralph Ellison on Louis Armstrong: "What did I do to be so black and so blue?" (p.149) The subtitle is borrowed from British historian Edward Thompson's work on the moral economy of the English crowd in the eighteenth century;[22] and the book posits the need to interrogate Black Atlantic culture along the lines of morality and political culture, juxtaposing dissent and accommodation, in a society in which consumer citizenship has largely corroded moral citizenship.

Gilroy highlights unsustainable consumer culture, contestations of human rights and geopolitical conflicts, weaving through the ways in which consumerism of goods has undermined the political and social aspirations of African Americans – his main concern – by individualising what was once a collective spirit. This he demonstrates through a compelling analysis of the lost moral power of commodities such as the automobile (once the symbolic vehicle of freedom in the US civil rights movement), music (by Chuck Berry, Jimi Hendrix and Bob Marley) and writing (by Ralph Ellison and Frantz Fanon).

Gilroy depicts African American Studies as frozen at a critical juncture in its history. He argues that, whereas the colour line was once an overriding social and historical phenomenon, today we are beset by economic and ecological crises, neo-imperial warfare, and a fundamental questioning of broader human rights, all of which challenge established analytical comfort zones. He asserts the need to rethink how "the policies of race and racism, as well as the political and commercial value of blackness, have been altered decisively." He argues:

> The geo-political order is changing. Old inequalities persist and new varieties of unfreedom emerge. The racialised structuring of our world which was established during the nineteenth century is evolving too. . . . This situation requires new analytical tools and conceptual adjustments. . . . The teleological sequence that made the overdevelopment countries into the future and their formerly colonised territories into the past is being left behind. If the West now represents the past while the rest are to be the future, what does that change do to the assumptions about history and historicity that were required by racial hierarchy?[23]

What are the implications of this for my work on the global Havana cigar? For Ortiz the cigar, more than any other product of Cuba, symbolised freedom, independence, nationalism and sovereignty. Yet there are equally ways in which it lies at the heart of an on- and off-island history that has embedded within it not only challenges to nationalism and sovereignty but also new forms of unfreedoms, as suggested by Gilroy; and this takes us to the heart of global commodity and labour history.

Commodity chain analysis tends to focus on the substitution of a product or parts of a product by other such products that are cheaper to produce, different in quality, or new on the market; and on opportunities for traders to reorganise supply and create consumer alternatives, unbound by former dependencies and monopolies of suppliers.[24] The appearance of new products or varieties does not necessarily entail the collapse of the older chain because frequently parallel structures develop. The emergence of informal and/or illicit economies and their impact on a chain are more difficult to trace, yet these hidden parts of a global commodity chain may be essential to an undemanding of its entire functioning. Historians have frequently presented chains as linear connections between producers, traders and consumers. Extending the analysis to encompass networks and circuits of knowledge challenges us to understand the fragilities and disconnections of their political, social and cultural dimensions.[25]

There are multifaceted implications of this for understanding global labour history. Historians of the earlier era of the Black Atlantic have demonstrated the relationship between, on the one hand, the emergence of regions of 'freedom' in Western Europe, following the decline of serfdom and feudalism and the rise of market commerce and capitalism, that swelled the consumer markets for commodities previously produced under slave regimes, and, on the other, a commodity history nurturing colonial and post-colonial systems of migrant labour and forms of neo-slavery. Commodification in the Black Atlantic during the period after the formal end of African slavery in the Americas was when the line dividing freedom and unfreedom became even more blurred, and systems of control, often physical, violent and segregated, were put into place.[26]

Moreover, commodity production was not fixed in a single space but rather moved in a continual peripatetic movement of people, production and the final goods. Marketing and consumption of the commodity (and the meanings attached to advertising and consumption) were ever more divorced from the realities of the labour and production processes and the locales where the product originated. In the process, global labour historians today argue, forms of labour management and discipline practiced under slave regimes of the Americas were replicated in controlled migrant labour camps and the 'coolie' of the East is the slave of today.[27]

My Havana cigar traversed such a history, whereby – alongside island and émigré Cubans – Europeans, African Americans and Caribbeans in Connecticut as well as Sumatrans, Javanese, Madurese and Chinese in Indonesia all played a part in the production of a *Cuban* cigar. Strikingly, they did so without significantly changing associations of the cigar with an iconography of Hispano-Cuban white skilled masculine labourers and exotic white women in the marketing or the cultural meanings attached to the pleasure, desire and consumption of the luxury product.

Cuba: Those Militant Cigar Workers

Let us turn now to where my cigar story begins in Cuba: where, in Ortiz fashion, cigar making conjures up that elite white male world and cigar makers were those Hispanic Cuban male aristocrats of labour fashioning their quality product from a strong, fragrant leaf. The late nineteenth-century Cuban legend surrounding the prestigious cigar export industry and master cigar maker was one in which Hispanic white male icons symbolised labour, political idealism and militancy, while the single most obvious iconography of women was the seductive embossed Hispanic white lady on the luxury cigar labels. This was, of course, a highly circumscribed view, removed from reality.[28]

Hand cigar rolling is skilled work, but there is little to indicate it was originally considered as such. Nineteenth-century cigar makers were found in barracks, prisons and homes. African slaves, indentured Chinese and free coloureds were brought into rolling shops alongside white Spanish wage labour, often under appalling conditions. Early wage labourers lived side by side with slave and indentured labour, in badly ventilated galleries over the rolling shops, receiving only part of their pay in money, having leave of absence only once a week, and having to hold down a cigar maker's *libreta,* or identification card, in which debts were recorded, restricting workers from freely transferring their labour from one factory to another.

Figures for the 1860s signal 60 percent of the work force in Havana and 55 percent throughout the island were slaves and free coloureds. By 1899, the figures had fallen to 30 and 37 percent, respectively. Against the backdrop of 1880s abolition of slavery and 1890s depression and war turmoil, many 'non-whites' were among those who left Cuba; and there was an entrenchment of Hispanic white workers, with an influx of Spanish immigrants into the skilled jobs in Havana's premium export factories. With the twentieth-century relative decline of the industry, the quality rolling skill and its national and racial component broke down, and the proportion of black cigar workers in Havana increased to 40 percent in 1943, though stood at only 11 percent of those in cigar sorting and box labelling, the cream of the trades. There was little reference to women cigar rollers, although the preponderant home and outwork industry suggests the contrary, and women interviewed spoke of being taught by their fathers to roll cigars in the home and working in smaller local rolling shops. Women were excluded from rolling in the premium export factories.[29]

Thus, while in Spain Carmen may have immortalised the women cigar rollers of Seville, Cuba's Carmens were to be the stemmers, taking out the central vein of the cigar tobacco leaf. Even then, in the mid- to late nineteenth century, factory stemmers were Hispanic and male, and their pay and conditions on a par with the cigar makers. By the twentieth century, however, it was women stemmers who formed the majority work force. In addition to the stemming departments in the cigar factories, there were large stemmeries in the tobacco agricultural regions of Havana, Las Villas and Pinar del Río, many belonging to US export companies and each employing on a short seasonal basis hundreds of women, especially black women, who were among the worst paid and least considered sectors.

Through their guilds, late nineteenth-century master cigar makers, sorters or box decorators succeeded in restricting entry along national, race and gender lines, and that was when the skill of premium cigar making most came into its own. The first major challenge to the exclusiveness and control of the trade came in the 1880s, from cigar makers in the less prestigious and less well-paid factories working on inferior-type cigars, who were not unionised, at a time when a large concentration of production and workers coincided with the abolition of slavery and a potential influx of newly freed labour. The challenge came in the form of an explosion of labour militancy and strikes with marked racial and nationalist overtones to class interests, with incipient labour movements divided along reformist, anarchist, anarcho-syndicalist and nationalist lines.

A second major challenge came in the 1920s, when a semblance of national craft unions had been consolidated, again amidst hard economic times as the 1930s Depression loomed near. The question of mechanisation hovered over the industry, and there was stepped up anti-labour repression. Militancy and strikes went far beyond the confines of existing unions, involving women stemmers for whom unionisation was in its infancy.[30] Cuba's women stemmers – in effect Cuba's majority female labour sector (only domestics and textile workers compared) – displayed high rates of literacy and organisation, and mounted a strong labour challenge in the form of strikes in the 1920s and 1930s.

Workers across the cigar industry proved to be a force to be reckoned with on issues vital to the very fabric of Cuban economy and society, notably the two attempts to mechanise an industry seen to be cause for national pride. The issue was volatile and ensured solidarity among tobacco and non-tobacco workers alike. This came to a head in 1948, in the context of cold war policies, when manufacturers and government coincided in wanting an end to militant communist-led union opposition to the machine. One stemmery manager angrily declared "the need for a bloody purge, a need to put a stop to these nigger women."[31]

We know relatively little about the 'nigger' women stemmers, but one thing is clear: those women and men who left Cuba did not leave behind them a labour situation uncontested along class, race and gender lines.

South Florida: Those Radical Émigrés

Cuban émigré workers and their families in Florida in the late nineteenth and early twentieth centuries found themselves on newly divisive terrain of the reconstruction and Jim Crow US South. The initial wave left Cuba under Spanish rule and with slavery in place, and struggles that were by no means undivided. In Florida, their enclave community was then beset by new dimensions of racial segregation, violence and lynching, in addition to influxes of Italian and Spanish immigrants.

Florida's early offshore Havana cigar world of Key West had also been home to Cuban nationalist and labour unrest, such that by the 1890s Spanish manufacturers sought to undercut this by relocating to other Florida towns, whose patricians were aggressively attracting industry. Descendants today proudly recall how their worker forebears donated from their wages to the independence cause, and how the communication from New York for the 1895 landing signalling the outbreak of the second War of Independence was rolled in Florida into a cigar and smuggled into Cuba. They also speak with sorrow of a community divided.

The big losers in Tampa were 'non-white' Cuban cigar makers and their families, increasingly forced to live their lives separate from Hispano-Cubans and join the African American drift north. The advent of the cigar machine cemented this, with a process of feminisation and de-skilling in mechanised cigar rolling, which had started with the introduction of the bunching moulds in hand rolling. In Florida, labour struggles were undercut by vigilante violence and relocation north, notably to New Jersey.[32]

Even so, in the 1950s, Tampa's Havana cigar industry was still the city's largest single employer, with thousands working in cigar manufacturing and providing a source of overseas support for Cuban revolutionary organisations. It was after the 1960s embargo that this changed dramatically; as more than 6,000 cigar makers lost their jobs. A US Department of Agriculture (USDA) report prior to the embargo is illuminating as to why.[33] Cuba was the source of nearly a quarter of leaf tobacco for US cigars. Some two-thirds of the seven billion cigars sold in the United States in a typical year contained Cuban tobacco. Around 670 million 'clear Havanas' and 'Havana filler' cigars used 45 percent of Cuban tobacco imports; the other 55 percent was used in 'blended filler' cigars. If imports were to cease, 'clear Havana' manufacturers foresaw their problems as 'insurmountable' unless Cuban leaf was to be replaced by some subtropical tobacco to obtain the aroma and flavour needed. This marked the start of a quest to grow Cuban seed tobacco and move Havana cigar hand-rolling operations to the Caribbean and Central America. As a result, by the 1970s the cigar industry was fast disappearing as a factor in the economic life of Tampa Bay; by the 1980s, mechanised rolling using homogenised leaf[34] was yet another nail in the coffin for labour; and Florida's minimum wage policy was often invoked by companies to explain why they 'had' to go offshore.

The post-1959 new wave of Hispanic white migration from Cuba, primarily to Miami but also to Tampa, sealed a silencing of Afro-Cubans' earlier presence and activism in labour, mutual aid and community movements. The imagery bolstered was again the familiar Hispanic male cigar maker and seductive 'Latin' lady on cigar labels and bands; and a whole iconography of Hispanic Cuban cigar culture accompanied the retelling of the Florida 'clear Havana' story.[35] When Tampa's Ybor City and famed Vicente Martínez Ybor factory were rescued from demolition from developers in the 1980s, they became a tourist attraction complete with cigar museum, heavily Hispanic and male in their recreation of the past. One lowly building, on the outskirts of the renovated centre, remained as home to the Martí-Maceo Club founded in 1904 by those wishing to hold on to the dream of a united Cuba.[36] It wasn't until the turn of the twenty-first century that the museum was to mount an exhibition that bore testimony to Afro-Cuban families.

Their story is told in Susan Greenbaum's *More than Black: Afro-Cubans in Tampa* (2002), whose opening is particularly striking. In the early 1960s, an Afro-Cuban lawyer was defending, and having to translate for, a Mexican farm worker in the Tampa courthouse. Afterwards, the presiding judge asked the lawyer how he had learned to speak Spanish: "The lawyer replied: 'I always have known how. I was born in Cuba.' The judge's retort: 'Cuban? I didn't know you were a Cuban. I always thought you were a nigger.'"[37] For Greenbaum, the casual racism on the judge's part captured how, in the United States, media stereotypes and popular construction of Cuban-American identity, especially the (Hispanic) Cuban-American Miami 'success story' had silenced blackness.

Her ethno-historical study retraced the social and cultural adaptations of black Cuban cigar makers, charting their attempts to negotiate the multiethnic, multicultural industrial enclave of Tampa while also involved in the politics of Cuba, from independence through revolution. Theirs were shifting diasporic identities – Afro-Cuban, Afro-Cuban-American, African-American. Over the generations, there were periods when they identified more as African-American than Cuban-American, but, she argues, there was no linear progression nor can there be said to be an identifiable end-point.

It might be argued that such shifting racial identities were not all that dissimilar from identity politics among Cubans in Cuba, as well as the United States. Over time, the island experience itself uneasily traversed variants of race relations: the more archetypal bipolar US-type system of the black/white divide (especially during and after US occupation); the more three-tiered system of the kind erected for the non-Hispanic Caribbean (distinguishing black, brown – *mulato/a* – and white); and the fluid racial continuum of the Hispanic Caribbean and Ibero-America. There were historical moments in Cuba when one or other appeared uppermost. There were times that were more inclusionary, when the races came together, such as the late nineteenth-century independence struggles of 1868-98 and late twentieth-century revolutionary period of 1959-89, with a primacy of nation over race and class. There were other more exclusionary times, when the races were pushed apart (1899-1958 and 1989 to the present). Throughout, there have been struggles in which there has been a primacy of race over class, and vice versa.[38] Similar observations have been drawn for gender/class primacy, largely, it should be noted, in the context of processes of feminisation of labour.[39] However, it is to processes of emasculation of labour that I now wish to turn.

Connecticut: Those Seasonal Farm Hands

While Cubans in Cuba and Cuban émigrés in Florida were fighting their battles, a related story of shade tobacco leaf, developed from Cuban seed for Havana cigar binder and wrapper, was unfolding in what was once known as Connecticut Tobacco Valley. Today comprising only small expanses of tent-covered shade tobacco land, alongside disused tobacco barns and derelict farm worker camps, tobacco acreage was at its height in 1921. An ephemeral 1960s revival was not on a scale to stem the decline that began with the 1950s introduction of homogenised binder and wrapper, was compounded by the 1964 US Surgeon General's report on the hazards of smoking, and was sealed with offshore relocation.

What is often recounted in its heyday as a proud New England story of twentieth-century tobacco-growing dynasties was also laced with cut-throat tobacco business and labour practices. Growers met their high seasonal labour requirements in various ways, including child and high school summer labour,[40] but especially immigrant and migrant labour.

From the mid to late nineteenth century, waves of Irish and Eastern and Southern Europeans were met off the boats by middlemen and 'sold' to farmers, a practice described in 1911 as "a little nearer the slave trade than anything I had experienced."[41] Shortly thereafter, Southern planters, concerned about the lure of better pay in the North and with the aid of the Ku Klux Klan, went to great lengths to prevent black workers and their families from boarding trains and buses to head north.[42] Some did succeed in leaving, however, and, starting in 1916, African American students were recruited from black colleges in Georgia, Florida and Virginia for summer work.[43] Referred to in Connecticut as 'plantation darkies' or 'plantation negroes', Southern blacks, it was reported, "streamed into Hartford" hoping for a better life, safe from violence, and worked in tobacco warehouses after the harvest or in better-paid non-agricultural jobs. As a result, the black population of Hartford more than doubled from 1910 to 1920, occasioning a 1922 special report on 'The Negro in the Industries and Other Work of the State'.[44]

During the Second World War, the USDA and War Manpower Commission declared tobacco a crop essential to the war effort (smokes for the boys), and in 1943 the Farm Security Administration turned to the British West Indies, Jamaica in particular, for farm labour. Jamaican-born Fay Clarke Johnson documented oral histories of this all-but-forgotten interlude in *Soldiers of the Soil* (1995), its title borrowed from the Allied war effort.[45] Conditions were basic, and men tended to keep to camp, as they often met with hostility. In the words of George Christie, from Manchester, Jamaica, in a telegram sent to President Franklin D. Roosevelt: "Jamaicans dissatisfied of conditions ... driven as dumb cattle, work under intimidation. United Nations fight for freedom, justice and fair play. We should have same. Please investigate."[46]

After the war, growers turned to employ displaced Europeans, before bringing in waves of Puerto Rican migrant labour to the camps under agreements signed with the Puerto Rican Department of Labour Migration Division (DTDM). During the 1960s and early 1970s, Puerto Ricans accounted for most Connecticut farm labour.

The Puerto Rican agricultural migration to Connecticut paralleled the earlier Cuban manufacturing out-migration to Florida in being integrally linked to upheavals on the island. These ranged from the US occupation of Puerto Rico in 1898 and its subsequent incorporation into the United States, accompanied by the rise and decline of US investment in Puerto Rican tobacco and many struggles associated with it,[47] post-Second World War Operation Bootstrap, which resulting in an estimated 78 percent decline in the agricultural labour force in the years 1940-79.[48] The migrants were male and many came to Connecticut from Puerto Rico's own tobacco valley to work for the very same employers.[49]

Contracts stipulated they must be strong in physical stature, in good health, free from communicable diseases, accustomed to hard work, and with no police records or reputation as troublemakers. However, documents of the Shade Tobacco Growers Association and the DTDM Hartford Office from the mid-1950s to the mid-1970s, and Connecticut local press and other holdings from the 1950s,[50] detail many complaints lodged by migrant workers and battles fought by them and organisations active on their behalf, including the

Young Lords, the Puerto Rican Socialist Party and the Episcopal Church in Puerto Rico subsequently replaced by the Ecumenical Ministry of Agricultural Workers. The more growers tried to curb the work of organisations such as these, as well as access to farms and camps, the greater the protests; and the insults meted out to workers, as in 1973, were highly racialised: *"cerdos que se venden por unos centavos"* (pigs bought for a few cents), *"negros sucios"* (dirty niggers), *"esclavos de la colonia"* (slaves from the colony).[51]

In 1974, the attempt to have a farm workers bill passed in the Connecticut General Assembly was frustrated, and it was reported that farmer groups "insisted that an anti-strike clause must be included in the bill, or else their livelihoods would be in danger. The tobacco growers also threatened to move their operations to Latin America, where they hoped to find both good growing conditions and a docile labor force."[52] After failing to sign a further agreement with the Puerto Rican government and bussing in Mexican-American day labourers on a much smaller scale, companies and growers did, in effect, move their operations abroad.

Indonesia: That Coolie Slave Labour

The other side of the globe, Indonesia was fast cementing an advantage over competitors with enormous profits derived in no small part from what was decried as 'coolie slave labour'. Renowned among cigar smokers from the late nineteenth century for growing and curing the world's most prized wrapper leaf, Dutch Indonesia was also reviled for making other colonial ventures look benevolent. Its labour and living conditions were infamously compared to those of slavery, and unrest became a constant source of concern. It was what Ann Laura Stoler, in *Capitalism and Confrontation in Sumatra's Plantation Belt, 1870-1979* (1995) referred to as one of "brutalities alternatively whispered and shouted": ever present in peasant-labourer discontent and in the post-colonial state's "maneuvers and menaces," open to foreign business and ruthless in stamping out oppositional political and labour organising.[53]

It is not known for certain when tobacco, which is indigenous to the Americas, was taken across the world to Asia, but the first tobacco to be taken to Holland from Sumatra is reported to have been in 1860. Soon after, large-scale Dutch colonial investment followed in Indonesian tobacco, developed from Cuban seed and with the aid of Cuban agronomists. Sumatra leaf was favoured on the world market as cigar wrapper, since its thin central vein and thin flexible texture meant it could be used to wrap up to four times as many cigars as other leaf.[54]

While Sumatra first attained pre-eminence, lending its name to the quality cigar wrapper leaf, it was early overtaken in volume by Java. Estates emerged according to different local land tenure and labour arrangements. The *apanage* system, which was unique to the Central Principalities, gave benefits to companies through local village heads, but was never applied by the Dutch to the directly ruled parts. There, the 1856 Landrental Law enabled investors to hire land in *erfpacht,* initially for twenty years, subsequently replaced for up to seventy years, later reduced to fifty years, but otherwise unchanged until nationalisation in 1958.

In Besuki, in central Java, *erfpacht* was granted on extensive uncultivated areas around Jember, where tobacco became the primary crop. Estates required labour, and planters set up their Immigration Bureau, bringing in Madurese and later Javanese, from densely populated areas of Central and East Java, as a result of which Besuki had the highest migrant population. Dutch companies also purchased cigar tobacco grown by local peasants, under conditions that conceded peasants weak rights over the land they cultivated and exacted heavy labour obligations. In 1917, peasant rights were increased and company rental rights reduced, but the strong influence of companies over local rulers and the Dutch authorities enabled production with very low costs and very high profits, especially up until the 1920s, when Besuki supplied 25 perceent of Java's exports, exceeding any other region of Java.

This is highlighted in the work of Soegijanto Padmo, S. Nawiyanto and Ratna Saptari,[55] which traces the transition from small-scale development in the 1860s-90s, with a number of individually owned estates producing tobacco and other cash crops, to corporatisation in the 1880s and more specialised production by fewer and larger companies over 1890-1920. During the final years of Dutch rule, the degree of consolidation was such that whole regions came under the control of one major corporation, and, after 1958, under one state enterprise.

Japanese occupation during the Second World War had a devastating effect on tobacco, as export cash crop plantations were turned over to food production, to feed the troops and for wartime self-sufficiency. Producers lost their Dutch and other international markets as tobacco fields were converted to meet the quota of rice to be delivered; tobacco buying was concentrated in six store houses; and farmers were only allowed to produce tobacco for domestic consumption and some export to the other Indonesian islands as part of mutual exchange for non-military commodities.[56]

Jember was one area where parts of estate lands were redistributed to peasants to produce food. This was a 'time bomb' when plantation owners returned to reclaim their *erfpacht* rights and came into conflict with 'squatters', who were strongly supported among Indonesian nationalist circles.[57] In Indonesia's subsequent bitter armed and diplomatic struggle against the Dutch for sovereignty, attained in 1949, there were squatters' illegal land occupations, strikes and labour organising, and the 'Indonesianising' of estate personnel. In early

1958, all Dutch economic interests were nationalised, and Dutch personnel left soon thereafter, operations transferring to Indonesian nationals.[58]

Developments since fast undermined any hopes of a fairer deal for labour. An attempted coup in 1965 led to a violent army-led anti-communist purge in which over half a million people were killed. The 'New Order' administration courted Western investment, which was a major factor in the subsequent three decades of substantial economic growth. Then, in the late 1990s, Indonesia was the country hardest hit by the East Asian financial crisis, and reforms since then have not stemmed instability, unrest, corruption and violence, not least in the central Jember tobacco area.[59]

Thus, while over recent decades tobacco from Indonesia has been again celebrated the world over for its high quality and low price, the backdrop is dramatic. "We forbid our workers to speak while they work. Otherwise, they may make a mistake.... They must work meticulously. The tobacco must be handled with respect," it was reported in *Cigar Aficionado* in 2009. However, tobacco barns continue to be burned in protest, and, as one tobacco hand confessed, it is "so difficult for us to survive" and "amazing that more people do not riot considering their situation."[60]

New Geo-political Hierarchies

Where is this leading? Gilroy invites us to consider new analytical tools and make conceptual adjustments in face of the persistence of old inequalities alongside new varieties of unfreedom, questioning our assumptions about labour history, historicity and hierarchy. My Havana cigar journey is suggestive of ways in which we might do that.

London and Amsterdam had early become European twin pillars of the international circulation of tobacco, as the British and Dutch expanded their empires. Tobacco was big business, with crown and state playing a central role. European states such as Spain, Portugal and France all established monopolies purchasing and processing tobacco, while German states enforced all-important taxation. There were no such monopolies in Britain, the Netherlands or the United States, but, whether via monopoly or market, the state was heavily involved.[61]

After 1800, the United States rose to pre-eminence, partly because its competitors were few – only Brazil and Cuba in the Western Hemisphere and Holland and Germany in Europe – and partly because the colonial system ensured global segmentation. The Dutch Cultivation System was designed to foster export crops: sugar, coffee and indigo first; then others, including tobacco, and by the outbreak of the First World War, the Dutch East Indies was the world's second largest exporter of leaf grown on a concentration of plantations. Sumatra and Java supplied the international market via Amsterdam and Rotterdam in the Netherlands and Bremen in Germany, competing with the Philippines, the United States and Cuba. The outcome was that, whereas in 1840 the United States exported 87 percent of the world's leaf, the US share of world output dropped to 30 percent by 1884, and 13 percent by 1984, a century later, with the break-up of the colonial system and the opening of new regions to the international market, especially Brazil, Cuba and the Dutch East Indies.[62]

The Second World War and Japanese occupation brought Indonesia's tobacco exports to a virtual standstill, and the end of the war saw a dramatically changed Dutch East Indies with Indonesia's struggle for sovereignty. The subsequent suppression of political and labour mobilising, however, in the drive to control labour and push down costs, must be seen as a prime determinant in the contemporary global rise of Indonesian tobacco. Cuba's 1959 Revolution fought for the opposite, but those who worked before and since to make Ortiz's proud export produce, *El Habano*, still had to navigate these international waters – whether as émigrés in Florida or in the face of competition from Connecticut's migrant field hands and Indonesia's coolies, arguably the new emasculated slave labour of today.

In my analysis here, I have limited myself to the context of labour, but there is a racialised and gendered literary nostalgia associated with the Havana cigar and a far broader context of how the Havana cigar story fits into the body of work on white manhood and imperialism – the era of hyper-masculine imperial adventuring personified by Theodore Roosevelt in the US war with Spain over Cuba at the end of the nineteenth century or US presidents from 1959 to this day. These are beyond my scope for now, but they are challenges that lie ahead.

Notes

1 An earlier version of this article was given as a paper at the Conference 'Being on the Move: Transfers, Emancipation and formation of the Black Atlantic', held at Erfurt University, Germany, in July 2010. I thank Patricia Wiegmann and Nora Kreuzenbeck, the organisers of that conference, for hosting me and encouraging me to work on this further. A revised version was subsequently given as a paper at the 36th Annual Conference of the Caribbean Studies Association, in Curaçao, in June 2011.
2 This comes to the fore in the US-Caribbean context in Matthew Pratt Guterl, *American Mediterranean: Southern Slaveholders in the Age of Emancipation* (Cambridge: Harvard University Press, 2008).
3 Many publications highlight this, for example, Eumelio Espino Marrero, *Cuban Cigar Tobacco: Why Cuban Cigars Are the World's Best* (Neptune City: TFH publications, 1996); Charles Del Todesco, *The Havana Cigar: Cuba's Finest (*New York: Abbeville Press, 1997). See also my early monograph *Tobacco on the Periphery* (London: Amaurea Press, 2023 [1985]).
4 Having researched tobacco trade journals in the past, the striking levels of

sophistication in *Cigar Aficionado* feature articles and advertising caused me to re-evaluate the importance of cultural and consumer histories in connection with the highly informative cigar reportage. For my preliminary reflections on this, see: 'Havana Cigars and the West's Imagination, in Sander L. Gilman & Zhou Xun, *Smoke: A Global History of Smoking* (London: Reaktion Books, 2004), pp.134-9 – Chapter 10 in the present volume. For a broader discussion, see Arjun Appadurai, *Modernity at Large: Cultural Dimensions of Globalization* (Minneapolis: University of Minnesota Press, 1996).

5   Little work connects the various offshore economies and communities, but this is brought to the fore in the autobiography of tobacco agronomist Napoleón S. Padilla, *Memorias de un cubano sin importancia* (Hialeah: AC Graphics, 1998). See also Araceli Tinajero, *El lector de tabaquería: Historia de una tradición cubana* (Madrid: Verbum, 2007), which links the institution of reading in the cigar factories in Cuba, New York, Tampa, Puerto Rico, Mexico and Spain; Evan Matthew Daniel, 'Rolling for the Revolution: A Transnational History of Cuban Cigar Makers in Havana, South Florida and New York City, 1853-1895', PhD dissertation, The New School 2010.

6   Among the pioneers were Louis A. Pérez, 'Reminiscences of a *Lector*. Cuban Cigar Makers in Tampa', *Florida Historical Quarterly* 53:4 (1975), pp.443-9; Glenn L. Westfall, *Key West: Cigar City USA (Key West:* Historic Key West Preservation Board, 1984), and *Don Vicente Martínez Ybor: the Man and His Empire: Development of the Clear Havana Industry in Cuba and Florida in the Nineteenth Century* (New York: Garland, 1987); Gerald E. Poyo, 'The Cuban Experience in the United States, 1865-1940: Migration, Community and Identity', *Cuban Studies* 21 (1991), pp.19-36; and Gary Mormino & George E. Pozetta, '"The Reader Lights the Candle": Cuban and Florida Cigar Workers' Oral Tradition', *Labor's Heritage* 15 (1993), pp.4-28. More recently: Robert P. Ingalls & Louis A. Pérez Jr., *Tampa Cigar Workers: A Pictorial History* (Gainesville: University Press of Florida, 2003).

7   I explored the history of North Florida with the aid of Kyle Doherty during my 2011 spring semester at the University of Florida. I am indebted to Paul Losch, Assistant Head of the University's excellent Latin American and Caribbean Library, for alerting me to the footnote (p.300) in Gerardo Castellanos, *Motivos de Cayo Hueso*, (Havana: Ucar, García y Cía, 1935), on the existence of Cuban cigar factories and workers in late nineteenth- and early twentieth-century Gainesville; and to Head Librarian Richard Phillips for referring me to Daniel Bronstein, 'La Cubana City: A Cuban Manufacturing Community Near Thomasville, Georgia, During the 1890s', *Georgia Historical Quarterly* 90 (2006), p.3. Our research suggests an unexpectedly significant North Florida history.

8   There is reference to nineteenth- and twentieth-century Cuban cigar makers alongside Puerto Ricans in New York, in César Andreu Iglesias (ed.), *Memoirs of Bernardo Vega* (New York: Monthly Press, 1984 [1977]). See also Lisandro Pérez, *Sugar, Cigars, and Revolution: The Making of Cuban New York* (New York: New York University Press, 2018).

9   I documented the earlier Cuban-Jamaican history in 'Political Idealism and Commodity Production: Cuban Tobacco in Jamaica, 1870-1930', *Cuban Studies*, 25 (1995), pp.51-81 – Chapter 7 in the present volume.

10 The 1990s granting of autonomy to the regions of Spain, which coincided with the revitalisation of links abroad in Cuba's post-Soviet crisis 1990s, produced a spate of work on the Canaries, Cuba and tobacco, including Andrés Arnaldos Martínez & Jorge Arnaldos de Armas, *La industria tabaquera canaria, 1852-2002* (Gran Canarias: Lit Romero, 2003); Anelia Rodríguez Concepción, *Tradición insular del tabaco* (Santa Cruz de Tenerife, 2000); Mario Luis López Isla, *La Aventura del tabaco* (Santa Cruz de Tenerife, 1998); C. Legna Verna & J. L Rivero Cevellos, *La industria tabaquera en Canarias: Globalización y restauración*, Bilbao, 1997); Gregorio J. Cabrera Déniz, *Canarios en Cuba: Un capítulo en la historia del archipélago, 1875-1931* (Las Palmas de

Gran Canaria, 1996); and Manuel de Paz, *Wangüemert y Cuba*, 2 vols (Santa Cruz de Tenerife: Lit. Romero, 1991).

11 Juan José Baldrich makes this point in his work on Puerto Rican tobacco, see 'From the Origins of Industrial Capitalism in Puerto Rico to its Subordination to the US Tobacco Trust: Rucabado and Company, 1865-1901', *Revista Mexicana del Caribe* 3 (1998), p.5; see also M. Burgos Malave, 'El conflict tabacalero entre Cuba y Puerto Rico', *Revista de Estudios Generales* 4 (1989-1990), p.4.

12 Ruth Glasser makes this point in *Aquí me quedo: Puerto Ricans in Connecticut* (Hartford: Connecticut Humanities Council, 1997). I draw out the Connecticut history in '*El Habano* and the World It Has Shaped: Cuba, Connecticut and Indonesia', *Cuban Studies*, 41 (2010), pp.39-67 – Chapter 13 in the present volume. Connecticut's links with both Puerto Rico and Cuba find their way into the novel *Parrish*, written by local writer Mildred Savage (New York, 1958), and made into a 1961 Hollywood blockbuster tobacco 'soap opera' movie.

13 There is little in the way of comparative study, but for two studies on tobacco in Mexico see: Susan Deans-Smith, *Bureaucrats, Planters and Workers: The Making of the Tobacco Monopoly in Bourbon Mexico* (Austin: University of Texas Press, 1992); and José González Sierra, *Monopolio del humo: elementos de la historia del tabaco en México y algunos conflictos de tabaqueros veracruzanos, 1915-1930* (Xalapa: Universidad Veracruzana, 1987).

14 Little connects Brazil with Cuba, though there are excellent Brazilian tobacco studies, notably Bert Jude Barickman, *A Bahian Counterpoint: Sugar, Tobacco, Cassava, and Slavery in the Reconcavo, 1780-1860* (Stanford: Stanford University Press, 1998); Catherine Lugar, 'The Portuguese Tobacco Trade and Tobacco Growers of Bahía in the Late Colonial Period', in Dauril Alden & Warren Dean (eds), *Essays Concerning the Socioeconomic History of Brazil and Portuguese India* (Gainesville: University Press of Florida, 1977); and Jean-Baptiste Nardi, *O fumo brasileiro no periodo colonial* (Sao Paulo: Ed. Brasiliense, 1996). See also Michiel Baud & Kees Kooning, 'Germans and Tobacco in Bahía (Brazil), 1870-1940', *Jahrbuch fur Geschichte Lateinamerikas* 37 (2000).

15 See my detailed discussion in 'Reinventing Mecca: Tobacco in the Dominican Republic, 1763-2007', Commodities of Empire Working Paper, 3 (2007), at https://commoditiesofempire.org.uk/publications/working-papers/working-paper-3 – Chapter 12 in the present volume. For the most recent in a spate of tobacco studies in the Dominican Republic since the 1970s, see: José Chez Checo & Mu-Kien Adriana Sang, *El tabaco: historia general en República Dominicana* (Santo Domingo: Grupo León Jimenes, 2007).

16 The Philippines connection is one yet to be documented, but see: Edilberto C. de Jesús, *The Tobacco Monopoly in the Philippines: Bureaucratic Enterprise and Social Change, 1776-1880* (Quezon City: Ateneo de Manila University Press, 1980). For an excellent snapshot comparative representational study of the Philippines, Puerto Rico, Cuba, Hawai'i, and Guam, see Lanny Thompson, *Imperial Archipelago: Representation and Rule in the Insular Territories under US Dominion after 1898* (Honolulu: University of Hawai'i Press, 2010).

17 I explore this in '*El Habano* and the World it Has Shaped' (2010).

18 Fernando Coronil, 'Introduction', in Fernando Ortiz, *Cuban Counterpoint: Tobacco and Sugar* (Durham & London: Duke University Press, 1995 [1940]), p.xxviii.

19 Ibid.; Antonio Benítez Rojo, *The Repeating Island: The Caribbean and the Postmodern Perspective* (Durham & London: Duke University Press, 1992); Pérez-Firmat, *The Cuban Condition* (1989).

20 I elaborate on this in 'Tobacco in the Contrapunteo: Ortiz and the Havana Cigar', in Mauricio A. Font & Alfonso W. Quiroz (eds), *Cuban Counterpoints: The Legacy of Fernando Ortiz* (Lanham: Lexington, 2004) – Chapter 9 in the present volume.

21 Paul Gilroy, *Darker than Blue: On the Moral Economies of Black Atlantic Culture*

(Cambridge: Harvard University Press, 2010), and *The Black Atlantic: Modernity and Double-Consciousness* (Cambridge: Harvard University Press, 1993).

22 E. P. Thompson, 'The Moral Economy of the English Crowd during the Eighteenth Century', in Thompson, *Customs in Common: Studies in Traditional Popular Culture* (New York: The New Press, 1993), pp.185-258.

23 Gilroy, *Darker Than Blue* (2010), p.2.

24 A classic is Gary Gereffi & Miguel Korzeniewicz (eds), *Commodity Chains and Global Capitalism* (Westport: Praeger, 1994), which includes Terence Hopkins & Immanuel Wallerstein, 'Commodity Chains: Construct and Research'.

25 Appadurai's 'regimes of values' and 'concepts of commodification', for example, see A. Appadurai (ed.), *The Social Life of Things: Commodities in Cultural Perspective* (Cambridge: Cambridge University Press, 1986), and *Modernity at Large: Cultural Dimensions of Globalization* (Minneapolis: University of Minnesota Press, 1996); James Ferguson, 'Cultural Exchange: New Developments in the Anthropology of Commodities, *Cultural Anthropology* 3 (1988); Philip Raikes, et al., 'Global Commodity Chain Analysis and the French Filière approach: Comparison and Critique', *Economy and Society* 29 (Aug 2000), p.3; Peter Dicken et al., 'Chains and Networks, Territories and Scales: Towards a Relational Framework for Analysing the Global Economy', *Global Networks* 1 (2001), p.2; Alex Hughes & Suzanne Reimer (eds), *Geographies of Commodity Chains* (London & New York: Routledge, 2004).

26 For the earlier period, a classic is Eric Williams, *Capitalism and Slavery* (Chapel Hill: University of North Carolina Press, 1994 [1944]); and major work has been produced by, among others, Robin Blackburn, *The American Crucible: A Landmark History of the Rise, Abolition and Legacy of Slavery in the New World* (London: Verso, 2011), *The Making of New World Slavery From the Baroque to the Modern, 1492-1800* (London: Verso, 1997), and *The Overthrow of Colonial Slavery, 1776-1848* (London: Verso, 2011 [1988]). For the US post-slavery period, see Paul Ortiz, *Emancipation Betrayed: The Hidden History of Black Organizing and White Violence in Florida from Reconstruction to the Bloody Election of 1920* (Berkeley: University of California Press, 2005). See also Robin D. G. Kelley, *The Black Radical Imagination* (Boston: Beacon Press, 2002), and *Race Rebels: Culture, Politics, and the Black Working Class* (New York: Free Press, 1996).

27 Thought-provoking work in this respect is that of Marcel van der Linden, *Workers of the World: Essays toward a Global Labor History* (Leiden & Boston: Brill, 2008); van der Linden et al. (eds), *Transnational Networks in the Twentieth Century: Ideas and Practices, Individuals and Organizations* (Leipzig: Akademische Verlagsanstalt, 2008); and van der Linden & Rana P. Behal (eds), *Coolies, Capital and Colonialism: Studies in Indian Labour History* (Cambridge: Cambridge University Press, 2006).

28 I discuss this in 'Reflections on Class, Race, Gender and Nation in Cuban Tobacco, 1850-2000', in Constance Sutton (ed.), *Revisiting Caribbean Labor: Essays in Honour of O. Nigel Bolland*, Kingston, 2005, pp.118-36 – Chapter 11 in the present volume; 'Gender Constructs of Labour in Prerevolutionary Cuban Tobacco Farming', *Social and Economic Studies* 37: 1 & 2 (1988), pp.241-69 – Chapter 5 in the present volume; 'Gender Issues in Contemporary Cuban Tobacco Farming', *World Development* 5:1 (1987), pp.43-68 – Chapter 4 in the present volume. See also Andrew Zimbalist, *Cuba's Socialist Economy Toward the 1990s* (Boulder & London: 1987).

29 Ibid.

30 Interestingly, there is reference to a short-lived *Gremio de Despalilladores* (the original masculine word in Spanish for stemmers) in 1878, and no other recorded attempt until the 1917 Gremio de Despalilladoras (the word by then feminine).

31 A detailed study of the struggle waged against the cigar machine can be found in Martin Duarte Hurtado, *La máquina torcedora de tabaco y las luchas en torno a su implanatación en Cuba* (Havana: Ciencias Sociales, 1973).

32 See Susan D. Greenbaum, *More Than Black: Afro-Cubans in Tampa* (Gainesville:

University Press of Florida, 2002); Nancy A. Hewitt, *Southern Discomfort: Women's Activism in Tampa, Florida, 1800s–1920s* (Urbana: University of Illinois Press, 2001); Evelio Grillo, *Black Cuban, Black American: A Memoir* (Houston: Arte Público Press, 2000); Winston James, 'From a Class for Itself to a Race on Its Own: The Strange Case of Afro-Cuban Radicalism and Afro-Cubans in Florida, 1870-1940', in *Holding Aloft the Banner of Ethiopia: Caribbean Radicalism in Early Twentieth-Century America* (London: Verso, 1998), pp.232-57; and Nancy Raquel Mirabal, 'Telling Silences and Making Community: Afro-Cubans in Ybor City and Tampa, 1899-1915', in Lisa Brock & Digna Castañeda Fuertes (eds), *Between Race and Empire: African-Americans and Cubans Before the Cuban Revolution* (Philadelphia: Temple University Press, 1988). Also R. P. Ingalls, *Urban Vigilantes in the New South: Tampa, 1882-1936* (Knoxville: University of Tennessee Press, 1988).

33 A copy of the 1960 70-page USDA Report is housed in the Special Collections Library of the University of Florida and provides statistical and qualitative evidence on the history and juncture at the time of the US cigar industry, as well as the significant impact of the embargo on Cuban leaf imports. President John F. Kennedy famously ensured he had his supply of Havana cigars before signing the embargo into law.

34 Homogenised leaf, also known as reconstituted leaf was introduced in the United States in the 1950s. Comprising huge sheets made from tobacco scraps, it was used first as a binder and only later as a wrapper in mechanised production. This was not to characterise Tampa's 'clear Havana' industry, and its use spread later only.

35 See Kathryn Hall Proby, *Mario Sánchez: Painter of Key West Memories* (Key West: Banyan Books, 1981); Joe Davidson, *The Art of the Cigar Label* (Secaucus: Wellfleet, 1989); Narciso Menocal, *The Tobacco Industry in Cuba and Florida: Its Golden Age in Lithography and Architecture* (Coral Gables: Cuban National Heritage, 1995). Also, the image recreated in the Broadway hit play *Anna in the Tropics*, by Cuban-American Pulitzer-winning playwright Nilo Cruz (New York, 2003), and the melancholy for that age in Cuba and Tampa expressed in Pablo Medina, *The Cigar Roller* (New York: Grove Press, 2005), and in the earlier novels of Ybor City-born José Yglesias, *The Truth About Them* (New York: Pioneer, 1971), and *Down There* (New York & Cleveland: The World Publishing Company, 1970).

36 The Club was named after Cuba's two great independence leaders: José Martí, the political leader of Hispanic descent, and military General Antonio Maceo, of part African heritage.

37 Greenbaum, *More than Black* (2002), p.1.

38 Pedro Pérez Sarduy and I documented this in the introduction to our edited collections *Afro-Cuban Voices: On Race and Identity in Contemporary Cuba* (Gainesville: University Press of Florida, 2020 [2000]), and *AFROCUBA: An Anthology of Cuban Writing on Race, Politics and Culture* (London: Ocean Press, 1993). Our work was born of pressing concerns over growing racism in 1990s crisis Cuba and the need to articulate black Cuban experiences and perception.

39 This comes to the fore in Hewitt, *Southern Discomfort* (2001) and my 'Gender Constructs of Labour' (1988).

40 There were press reports on child labour – see, for example: John J. Egan, 'Tobacco Child Labor Under Fire by Labor Commissioner', *Hartford Times* (31 December 1946) – that contrast with the gentle nostalgia of 1990s personal testimonies of local people, see *Windsor Storytellers: A Chronicle of 20th-Century Life in Windsor*, 2 vols (Windsor: Windsor Historical Society, 1999).

41 This is recounted in James F. O'Gorman, *Connecticut Valley Vernacular: The Vanishing Landscape and Architecture of the New England Tobacco Fields* (Philadelphia: University of Pennsylvania Press, 2002), p.37.

42 This is a point made forcefully by Ortiz in *Emancipation Betrayed* (2005). For a graphic recounting of that history, see Stetson Kennedy, *Jim Crow Guide: The Way*

it Was (Boca Raton: University Press of Florida, 1990 [1959]), *The Klan Unmasked* (Boca Raton: University Press of Florida, 1990 [1954]), *Palmetto County* (Tallahassee: A & M University Press, 1989 [1942]).

43 Stacey Close, 'The Ties that Bind: Southwest Georgians, Black College Students, and Migration to Hartford', *Journal of South Georgia History* 15 (2000), p.19.

44 Quoted in Margaret Buker Jay, 'Historical Perspective', in Anadel Schnip & Katya Williamson (eds), *Changing Landscape through People: Connecticut Valley Tobacco, a Documentary of Photographs and Writing for the 1980s* (n.p., n.d.).

45 Fay Clarke Johnson, *Soldiers of the Soil* (New York: Vantage, 1995). The rallying cry was 'Keep the Boys in Smokes'. Thousands of Jamaican men signed up to contribute to the war effort, also seeking adventure and economic betterment.

46 Ibid., p.80, quoted from *The Hartford Courant* (29 July 1944), p.8.

47 During the first half of the twentieth century, tobacco was not only second in economic importance in Puerto Rico but also a scenario of struggle, on which there have been some excellent studies. A 1950s classic is Robert A. Manners, 'Tabara: Subcultures of a tobacco and mixed crops municipality', in Julian H. Steward et al. (eds), *The People of Puerto Rico* (Urbana: University of Illinois Press, 1956), pp.93-170. More recently, see Teresita A. Levy, 'The History of Tobacco Cultivation in Puerto Rico, 1899-1940', PhD dissertation, City University of New York (2007). The new historians of the 1970s and 1980s produced pioneering labour studies, notably Angel G. Quintero Rivera, 'Socialist and Cigarmaker: Artisans' Proletarianization in the Making of the Puerto Rican Working Class', *Latin American Perspectives* 10 (1983), pp.19-38; and Juan José Baldrich, *Sembraron la no siembra: Los cosecheros de tabaco puertoriqueños frente a la corporaciones tabacaleras, 1920-1934* (Río Piedras: Huracán, 1988). More recently, see: Erick J. Pérez Velasco & David Baronov, *Bibliografía sobre el movimiento obrero en Puerto Rico, 1873-1996* (San Juan: Cildes, 1996); and Arturo Bird Carmona, *Parejeros y desafiantes: la comunidad tabaquera de Puerta de Tierra a principios del siglo XX* (San Juan: Huracán, 2008). Fictional representations of 1920s and 1930s struggles can be found in Enrique Laguerre, *Los dedos de la mano* (Río Piedras: Ed. Cultural, 1978 [1951]).

48 After becoming US citizens in 1917, many Puerto Ricans went to the mainland in search of work. The Hawaii Sugar Planters Association recruited them to cut sugar alongside Japanese, Filipinos, Chinese and Portuguese. By 1926, hundreds of Puerto Rican families were picking cotton in Alabama, and by the 1940s thousands of Puerto Ricans were to be found in poorly paid agricultural work. For the 1950s and 1960s Great Migration to the US mainland, see: Jorge Duany, 'A Transnational Colonial Migration: Puerto Rican's Farm Labor Program', *New West Indian Guide* 84: 3&4 (2010), pp.225-51; and, for a comparative study of Cuba, Puerto Rico and the Dominican Republic, see Duany, *Blurred Borders: Transnational Migration between the Hispanic Caribbean and the United States* (Chapel Hill: University of North Carolina Press, 2011), pp.269-89. Also, Ismael García-Colón, 'Claiming Equality in Western New York', *Latino Studies* 6 (2008); Carmen Teresa Whalen, *From Puerto Rico to Philadelphia: Puerto Rican Workers and Postwar Economies* (Philadelphia: Temple University Press, 2001); Cindy Hahamovitch, *The Fruits of their Labor: Atlantic Coast Farmworkers and the Making of Migrant Poverty, 1879-1945* (Chapel Hill & London: University of North Carolina Press, 1997); Frank Bonilla, 'Manos que Sobran: Work, Migration and the Puerto Rican in the 1990s', in Carlos Alberto Torre et al. (eds), *The Commuter Nation: Perspectives on Puerto Rican Migration* (Río Piedras: University of Puerto Rico, 1994); and Gloria Bonilla-Santiago, *Organizing Puerto Rican Migrant Farmworkers: The Experience of Puerto Ricans in New Jersey* (New York: Peter Lang, 1988).

49 There has been no study as such of gender and migration in tobacco, in contrast with the many studies on women and migration in the garment industry and on women in the Puerto Rican tobacco industry: Fernando Pico, 'Las trabajadoras del tabaco en Utuado según el censo de 1910', in *Al filo del poder: subalternos y dominantes*

en Puerto Rico, 1739-1910 (Río Piedras: University of Puerto Rico, 1993), pp.173-94; Amilcar Tirado Avilés, 'Sobre el desarrollo de la industria del tabaco en Puerto Rico y su impacto en la mujer puertorriqueña, 1898-1920', *CENTRO: Journal of the Center for Puerto Rican Studies* (Winter 1989-90); and J. J. Baldrich, 'Gender and the Decomposition of the Cigar-making Craft, 1899-1931', in Félix Matos Rodríguez & Linda Delgado (eds), *Puerto Rican Women's History: New Perspectives* (Armonk: M. E. Sharpe, 1998), pp.105-25. See also two studies of the anarchist, feminist writer and activist Luisa Capetillo, who, exceptional for her times, was a cigar factory reader and not only in Puerto Rico but also in New York, Tampa and Havana, see Norma Valle Ferrer, *Luisa Capetillo: Historia de una mujer proscrita* (San Juan: Ed. Cultural, 1975); and Julio Ramos (ed.), *Amor y anarquía: Los escritos de Luisa Capetillo* (San Juan: Huracán, 1992).

50 Records housed in the Library of CENTRO, the Centre for Puerto Rican Studies, Hunter College, City University of New York, include the archives of the Farm Labor Program (1848-1993), Connecticut Shade Tobacco Growers' Agricultural Association Files (STGAA, 1955-76), Regional and Field Offices (1948-1993), Hartford Regional Office (1961-1984), and Regional Field Office Farm Labourer Files (1958-1983). Rich press collections for the same period are housed at the Hartford State Library; the Hartford Project, Trinity College, Hartford; University of Connecticut, Storrs; Windsor Tobacco Museum; and Windsor Historical Society, among others.

51 STGAA, CEPR, Windsor: File 30, Box 2526. There is no study of racialisation as such in the Connecticut case, but see: Ramón Grosfoguel & Ramón and Chloe S. Georas, 'The Racialization of Latino Caribbean migrants in the New York Metropolitan Area, *CENTRO: Journal of the Center for Puerto Rican Studies* 7 (1995). Suggestive of work that needs to be done, raising the issue of race/class primacy in struggle, is: W. James, 'Afro-Puerto Rican Radicalism in the United States: Reflections on the Political Trajectories of Arturo Schomburg and Jesús Colón', *CENTRO: Journal of the Center for Puerto Rican Studies* 7 (1995). Schomburg and Colón were cigar makers who left Puerto Rico for New York in the early twentieth century and opted for different trajectories of struggle: for Schomburg, race was uppermost, and for Colón, class.

52 STGAA, CEPR, Windsor: File 30, Box 2526.

53 Ann Laura Stoler, *Capitalism and Confrontation in Sumatra's Plantation Belt, 1870-1979* (Ann Arbor: University of Michigan Press, 1995); Stoler refers to contemporary silences as the quiet menace of a colonial past casting its shadow over the present. See also Karl L. Pelzer, *Planters against Peasants: Colonial Policy and the Agrarian Struggle in East Sumatra, 1863-1947* (Gravenhage: Brill, 1982); and Jan Breman, *Taming the Coolie Beast* (New York: Oxford University Press, 1989).

54 The late nineteenth- and early twentieth-century experiments with nets in territories of the Americas (Florida, Georgia, Connecticut and Cuba) were to simulate the natural cloud coverage of Sumatra in the hopes of producing a cigar wrapper leaf that was similarly thin and elastic. Growing tobacco under cloth was what was to become Shade, as opposed to sun-grown, tobacco, see Randall R. Kincaid, 'Shade Tobacco in Florida', *Quincy North Florida Experimental Station Bulletin* 136 (1960 [1956]). I discuss this in more detail in '*El Habano* and the World It Has Shaped: Cuba, Connecticut and Indonesia', *Cuban Studies*, 41 (2010), pp.39-67 – Chapter 13 in the present volume.

55 Soegijanto Padmo, *The Cultivation of Vorstenlands Tobacco and Besuki Tobacco in Besuki Residency and its Impact on the Peasant Economy and Society, 1860-1960* (Yogyakarta: Aditya Media, 1994); S. Nawiyanto, *The Rising Sun in a Javanese Rice Granary. Change and the Impact of Japanese Occupation on the Agricultural Economy of Besuki Residency, 1942-1945* (Yogyakarta: Galang Press, 2005); Ratna Saptari, 'The Politics of Land, Labour and Leaf: Tobacco Regimes in Colonial Java and Sumatra (Late 19th-Early 20th Century)', paper presented at the workshop on Plants, People and Work, Yogyakarta (2009). Saptari highlights early twentieth-

century debates regarding working conditions coming to a head with a 1902 report and 1903 government-commissioned investigation of conditions in East Coast Sumatra plantations and the Labour Inspectorate established in 1908. Yet Deli expansion continued unabated, and by 1912, more than two hundred plantations had 150,000 workers and 35,000 to 50,000 new recruits arriving each year. See also S. Nawiyanto, 'Growing "Golden Leaf: Tobacco Production in Besuki Residency, 1860-1970', *Historia* 4 (2009), pp.144-58, and 'The Economy of Besuki in the 1930s Depression', in Ian Brown & Peter Boomgard (eds), *Weathering the Storm: The Economies of Southeast Asia in the 1930s Depression* (Singapore: Institute of Southeast Asian Studies, 2000), pp.171-88.

56 See Nawiyanto, *Rising Sun* (2005).
57 The Dutch disputed Indonesian nationalisation in a landmark case over Indonesian tobacco, better known as 'The Bremen Tobacco Case', of 21 August 1959, in the Bremen Court of Appeal. The Court ruled the expropriation/nationalisation of Dutch companies legal and gave the green light to Indonesia's decision to trade on the Bremen market in place of Amsterdam, see: 'The Bremen Tobacco Case', Special issue 60, Department of Information, Republic of Indonesia, 1960.
58 Nawiyanto argues this convincingly in *Rising Sun* (2005).
59 See J. A. C. Mackie, 'The Changing Political Economy of an Export Crop: The Case of Jember's Tobacco Industry', *Bulletin of Indonesian Economic Studies* 21:3 (1985), pp.113-38; see also J. Breman, *Good Times and Bad Times in Rural Java: A Study of Socio-Economic Dynamics towards the End of the Twentieth Century* (Leiden: Brill, 2002); and Margo L. Lyons, *Bases of Conflict in Rural Java* (Berkeley: University of California, 1970).
60 James Suckling, 'Tobacco Mecca: Indonesia's East Java Continues to Produce Fine Tobacco Despite its Troubled Economy', *Cigar Aficionado* (January/February 1999).
61 A good discussion of this can be found in Jordan Goodman, *Tobacco in History: The Cultures of Dependence* (London & New York: Routledge, 1993).
62 Ibid.

15

EL HABANO: THE GLOBAL LUXURY SMOKE*1

> *As civil liberties triumphed and political constitutions were guaranteed, the cigar came into ascendancy once more, coinciding with the advent of economic liberalism in Cuba, which threw the port of Havana open to all nations. And in this atmosphere of free industrial and commercial enterprise Havana tobacco, by the unanimous plebiscite of the world, was awarded the imperial scepter of the tobacco world. Havana tobacco from then on became the symbol of the triumphant capitalistic bourgeoisie. The nineteenth century was the era of the cigar.*[2]

CUBAN ETHNOGRAPHER Fernando Ortiz blazed new ground in the Cuba of 1940 with the publication of his seminal work on transculturation, by fashioning a Cuban *contrapunteo* (counterpoint) out of Cuba's two major commodities: tobacco and sugar, encapsulated in the proud cigar band versus the lowly sugar sack. He used tobacco and sugar as metaphorical constructs,

---

*   Originally published in Jonathan Curry-Machado (ed.), *Global Histories, Imperial Connections, Local Interactions* (Basingstoke: Palgrave Macmillan, 2013), pp.248-76. A subsequent revised version was published in Italian and Spanish as 'Política e sapere: como si é globalizzato el sigaro avanza/Política y saber: cómo se globalizó el habano', in Laura Mariottini & Alessandro Oricchio (eds), *El Habano: Lingua, storia, societá di un prodotto transculturale/Lengua, historia, sociedad de un producto cultural* (Rome: Edizioni Efesto, 2017), pp.67-105.

highlighting the fetish power of the commodities and a counter-fetish interpretation that challenged essentialist understandings of Cuban history.

The fetishism and counter-fetishism are of particular significance when it comes to understanding the history of the Cuban cigar, which in Spanish came to be called simply *un tabaco* (a tobacco), *un puro* (pure in that it was made wholly with Cuban leaf), or *un habano* (a Havana, by virtue of the port city through which it made its entrée into the world). For Ortiz, tobacco and the cigar most 'transculturated' and most came to symbolise Cuba and Cubans' quest for freedom, independence and national sovereignty. By the same token, both lay at the heart of un-freedoms, dependence, and a highly contested island/offshore history, one that took on new dimensions with the nineteenth-century meteoric rise of *El Habano* (the Havana) as the world's luxury smoke, competing with pipe and ousting snuff.

The lifting of the Spanish monopoly on Cuban tobacco in 1817 heralded the Havana cigar's coming of age. Nineteenth-century Spanish, German, British, French and US capital backed the vertiginous expansion of cigar manufacturing for export in Havana and palatial Havana cigar factories,[3] and *the* Havana conquered European and North American markets. It became de rigueur in the male entrepreneurial world of the rapidly growing industrial, trading and financial conurbations of London, Amsterdam, Bremen, Hamburg, Madrid, Paris, Lisbon and New York. With its fine taste and aroma, and its smoke assuaging the senses, it was one of life's pleasurable luxuries that sent out a message of wealth, power and distinction across the world.

Its beginnings, however, were far different; and what follows explores how the Havana came to establish itself at a later and not earlier stage in life as the coveted luxury smoke, doing so amidst moral and mythical discourses, ranging from bodily and spiritual uplift to harbinger of death. It first traces cigar 'pre-history': the social life and discourse, changing values and meanings, surrounding tobacco and the cigar, which was but one of the forms in which tobacco was consumed, as their materiality was forged in a global commodity chain.[4] It then enters the nineteenth-century 'golden age' of the Havana and its aggrandised, mythicised and contested history. It ends with how this luxury handcrafted smoke, whose *non plus ultra* was *El Habano*, made a comeback in the fiercely competitive, highly mechanised and ultimately proscribed world of tobacco.

The analysis draws on a range of sources, which include my own work and that of Cuban scholars and writers, as well as academic and popular histories of tobacco,[5] and the glossy publications on the Havana cigar that proliferated in recent years.[6] It thus 'smokes' its way through a complex history of origin, production, transport, marketing and consumption of this luxury product as we have come to know it, as well as the myth and legend in which it is enveloped.

Tobacco Becomes a Commodity

Histories of tobacco often start with the caveat that much of what is 'known' is little more than accepted wisdom, shrouded in myth and legend. It is thus 'accepted' that tobacco is native to the Americas, where it was found some 18,000 years ago by humans of Asiatic origin who crossed the Bering Strait. Plant geneticists identify tobacco's 'centre of origin' – that is, the meeting place between the species' genetic origin and the area in which it was first cultivated – in the Peruvian-Bolivian-Ecuadorean Andes around 5000-3000 BC. Archaeologists and ethnographers concur that nomads and settlers incorporated it into their arsenal of plants with medicinal and spiritual properties.

There is also 'acceptance' that of the many species of tobacco, two – later known as *Nicotiana rustica* and *Nicotiana tabacum* – were destined to travel the world and become major global commodities, the latter in particular. Yet there was striking diversity in the ways in which tobacco was grown and used. Depending on time, place and people, it was sniffed (or 'snuffed'), chewed, eaten, drunk, smeared over body, inserted in enemas and smoked. It was offered to the gods in ritual, and it was an everyday narcotic, both pleasurable and healing. The oldest form was most likely chewing followed by snuffing (as among the Incas), but as it spread towards Central America smoking cigars (as among the Mayans) would seem to have taken precedence over other forms, whereas in the northern part of the continent smoking by pipe was most prevalent.

Thus, by 1492 – the landmark year when Christopher Columbus made landfall in the Caribbean, discovering the New World for Spain and paving the way for the conquest of the Americas – tobacco was widespread and diverse in uses, the pipe predominating in North America and the cigar in South and Central America and the Caribbean. Tobacco and smoking were unknown to Europeans, such that when Columbus went ashore on a small island that is today part of the Bahamas, seeking precious metals, he seemingly attached no importance to the dried leaves included in the islanders' gifts. Later arriving in Cuba, he was at least intrigued enough by islanders carrying firebrands of leaves to detail two of his expedition, Rodrigo de Xerez and Luis de Torres, to investigate in the interior and report back. They tried it for themselves, becoming the first Europeans to smoke tobacco, but none of this appears to have been recounted until almost twenty years later by Fray Bartolomé de las Casas.[7]

In Spain, the habit met with either indifference or opprobrium. Note was taken of its healing properties, but there were Spaniards who, in their crusading zeal, saw it as a vice of the infidel Indians: the Devil's weed. The earliest account of what it felt like to smoke, as opposed to what it looked like or did to the Indians, is thought to have been written by Breton seafarer Jacques Cartier in 1534. Around the same time, lapsed Carmelite friar André Thevet documented its use among Christians in Brazil, and Roman Catholic clergy in the Americas adopted snuff, resulting in what is thought to have been the first tobacco prohibition in the form of an ecclesiastical decree of 1588 issued in Lima. Rodrigo de Xerez himself faced the wrath of the Inquisition and was thrown into a dungeon for publicly smoking in Spain.

Accounts of the plant's medicinal properties began to outweigh spiritual misgivings, and as word spread, so did the plant. Its tiny seeds were carried to Spain and Portugal in the 1550s and grown as an exotic new addition to palace gardens, and the plant was studied by court physicians. Jean Nicot, sent from France to Lisbon in 1559 to arrange the marriage of Catherine de Medici, took an avid interest, and began experimenting medicinally; the French court began taking the 'Nicotian herb' as snuff; and its fame travelled back to Portugal and on to the Vatican, Italian states, Bohemia, Spain, the Lowlands and Switzerland.

Transmuted from Devil's herb to medical panacea, it was grown domestically, though small quantities of imported tobacco, especially from Cuba, were prized above all others. England was where it was seen to be most associated with pleasure and most commodified, thanks in no small part to the marauding ventures of Hawkins, Raleigh and Drake during the Elizabethan era. Sailors, corsairs and pirates popularised smoking, the English preference for pipe over cigar deriving from contact with and eventual colonisation of North as opposed to South America. At the English court, smoking symbolised that virile spirit of adventure, and even the Virgin Queen (after whom Virginia was named) is reputed to have inhaled, persuaded by her then favourite Raleigh.

Genoese and Venetian fleets carried tobacco to the Levant and Middle East, and the Spanish and the Portuguese to Africa and Asia. Arguably the greatest impact was on Africa, where the Portuguese had taken control of Arab trading posts, introducing tobacco from Brazil; and by the end of the sixteenth century, Africans had evolved their own practices and myths. When Africans began to be traded across the Atlantic as slaves, the enslaved would in part have been purchased with tobacco and would be familiar with its use.[8]

The seventeenth century witnessed both prohibition and expansion. The century opened in England with James I, who succeeded Elizabeth I, in 1606 blasting it as satanic and introducing taxation and an import duty; yet the Virginia Company was also set up. That same year, Phillip II of Spain introduced a ban on tobacco cultivation, which was lifted in 1614, but a special tax was introduced in addition to duty, depending on place of origin, the highest being on Cuban tobacco. Tobacco in Cuba had been *cosa de indios y negros* (a thing for Indians and blacks), but, as it worked its way up from the lower strata of society, so did whites develop a taste for it, forbidding the Negroes from selling or cultivating tobacco except for their own use. All tobacco had to be imported into Seville, and in 1620 the first Seville tobacco factory was opened producing snuff. In 1636, the Spanish monarchy founded La Tabacalera, reputed to be the world's first tobacco company, and introduced state tobacco shops called *estancos*, where its products were sold and further taxed.[9]

Governments became as addicted as their people, and within decades most European countries had established taxes and duties. Much of the continent was caught up in the Thirty Years War (1618-48), driven by religious and imperial conflict, and smoking was spread by the Dutch, described as a new nation of *tabagophiles*. Protestant allies of the Protestant English, the Dutch set up the West India Company that was later the model for the English and French, attacked the Spanish fleet, traded slaves and carried tobacco as a valuable instrument of exchange, earning it repute as the first globally available luxury commodity in their trading empire.

Prohibitions elsewhere – Russia, Islamic states such as the Ottoman Empire, Japan and China – proved short-lived, as tobacco spread like a seventeenth-century epidemic, dispersed as an article of maritime trade and a staple of the silk route, endemic in the world of smuggling and contraband. It was to counter this, especially the smuggling and contraband of tobacco, that the English passed the 1651 and 1660 Navigation Acts, to limit trade to English ships; and in their new North American colonies, it was tobacco that was at the heart of an infamous system of production (plantation slavery) and an intricate web of commerce (the trans-Atlantic triangular trade of goods and slaves), on the back of which fortunes were made and wars fought.[10]

Other major tobacco-producing countries in the Americas also relied on slave labour, notably Portuguese Brazil, destined to become the world's second-largest tobacco exporter after Virginia and largest importer of slaves. Among Spain's colonies, Venezuela and Cuba were Spain's largest and second-largest producers. In Cuba, *vegueros* (settler growers) rose up in arms on three successive occasions during the early eighteenth century against repressive regulation.[11] By then, the growing number of Spanish settlers, distanced from Spain, had adopted the habit of smoking cigars and many were involved in smuggling and contraband with those from other trading nations.

Most of the tobacco shipped legally to Spain was to Cadiz, to be rolled into cigars, or to be made into snuff in Seville, where a third new factory in 1758 was described as the largest industrial building of its time in the world.[12] Yet returning Spanish emigrants who had made their fortune "clung to the expensive and aristocratic vice of smoking Havana cigars, which they had sent to them from Cuba."[13] In Spain, it was never common to smoke Havanas!

The Havana Cigar Comes of Age

While Spain held on to Cuba and Spanish America, Britain's American colonies sparked the Seven Years' War (1756-63). George Washington, a lieutenant colonel son of a Virginia tobacco-farming family, killed Frenchmen building a fort, and war ensued on four continents: France declared war on Britain, which in turn declared war on Spain. According to another Virginia tobacco farmer, Thomas Jefferson, this was the backdrop to the 1776 declaration of independence of the thirteen British colonies, which were quick to forge alliances with France (1778) and Spain (1779) and negotiate peace with Britain (1782). Tobacco debts were negotiated as part of reparations and trade resumed.

In 1788, the Schlottmann factory was set up in Hamburg to manufacture leaf imported from Cuba, and Hamburg would become a major centre of the tobacco trade. Meantime, in France, the expenses of war and the court occasioned taxes deemed intolerable by a people of smokers who rose up in revolution in 1789, and snuff, the mark of aristocracy, fell firmly out of favour. It remained for Napoleon Bonaparte, having reinstated tobacco taxes to help finance his armies, to redraw the political map of Europe and profoundly change the continent's smoking habits.

Britain held firm, its navy having defeated the combined French and Spanish fleet at Trafalgar, and, while subject to continental blockade, found a weak spot in Spain. There Seville's factory had expanded to include three types of cigar and an early form of cigarette, marking a shift from snuff to smoking, which had become endemic among Spain's largely rural population. The smallest and cheapest smokes were made from *tabaco picado* (shredded tobacco), later dubbed *papelotes* (paper ones, from the paper around them); the largest and most expensive were the *puros* (pure ones), smoked by nobility, including King Fernando VII; and in between were the *papantes*.

Officers of the French army occupying Andalusia took to smoking *puros* and *papantes*; and contraband and smuggling boomed as *bandoleros* (bandits) operated in resistance to the French and were joined by a British expeditionary force in Spain in 1808, which also took to cigars. In England, the Regency period and its Romantic movement, as well as the cavalry, all extolled the cigar; and the Duke of Wellington's triumphal return from Waterloo was a triumph also for the cigar: from 1814 on, as a result of the Peninsular and American wars, the 'Spanish vice' was taking hold. In 1800, England imported 26lbs of cigars; in 1824, 15,000lbs; and by 1830, 250,000lbs, including a first direct shipment from Cuba. The House of Commons had a designated smoking chamber; the smoking jacket and cap made their entrée; and the growth of cigar smoking led to tobacconists specialising in the import of cigars, crowned by the Havana. Queen Victoria came to the throne in 1837 with a court prohibition, but to little avail.

Developments in the Americas combined with those in Europe. In 1803, Napoleon raised financing through the sale of Louisiana, doubling the size of the emergent United States and moving the frontier west. West coast Hispanics smoked cigars, and along the eastern seaboard the 'Spanish' cigar was gaining popularity due to the fast-growing trade with neighbouring Cuba. During the Seven Years War, the British occupied Havana in 1762 and the settlement with Spain traded Havana for Florida. Legend has it that the North American taste for Cuban cigars developed after General Putnam returned from the British occupation of Havana with three donkeys laden with Havana cigars as plunder and sold them in a tavern in Connecticut; shortly after, the Cuban seed was imported to grow cigar leaf and produce cigars there.[14]

The eleven-month British occupation of Havana broke the Spanish monopoly hold on Cuban tobacco, and, while reinstated in 1764, it was hard to enforce and finally ended in 1817. By then Spain had lost all its mainland territories in the Americas, leaving only Cuba, along with neighbouring Puerto Rico and Santo Domingo, and the Philippines in the Pacific. Cigar production boomed in Spain, and the women drafted into the factories would be later immortalised in Georges Bizet's opera *Carmen* (1875); but with free trade Cuban cigars gained in preference over those made in Spain, or elsewhere, with either imported Cuban or home-grown leaf.

In 1817, King Ferdinand VII of Spain restored absolute monarchy in Spain but was swayed by Cuban economist Francisco Arango y Parreño to abolish the Spanish monopoly there: "things had been set in motion, the epic story of the Havana had begun."[15] Shipping using the port of Havana increased, steam ships shortened crossings and commerce boomed, tobacco growing and cigar manufacturing flourished, and by 1840 the *puro* had become the *habano*.

At the same time, the wheels were in motion for competition for the Havana. The Netherlands was a case in point:

> From 1825 onward, while British and French elites, and all the others after them, devoted themselves to Havana, huge workshops were set up in the Netherlands to treat tobacco from their Indonesian possessions, mixed with tobacco from Brazil, Java, and Sumatra for the wrapper and binder leaf and Bahía for the filler. Their experts developed a 'special light' taste and matching prices which would make a fortune.[16]

Descendants of pipe smokers became cigar smokers, and the Netherlands exported countless more cigars per capita than any other nation except Denmark, overshadowing Spain and Cuba.

Havana factories continued to supply the elite luxury market, but the upheavals of the latter part of the century took their toll. The history of *El Habano* would be marked by in- and out-migration of growers, manufacturers and workers, along with circulation and transfer of seed and know-how. Spain, the United States, the Caribbean and Central America, but also territories across the Atlantic and far further afield, all formed part of an increasingly globalised phenomenon of 'Cuban' tobacco growing and cigar manufacturing and marketing.

Early twentieth-century US occupation opened Cuba to mass US investment, and the American Tobacco Company, or Trust as it was known, bought up major leaf and manufacturing concerns. By then more interested in profits deriving from mass-mechanised cigarette production and unable to undermine successful Cuban opposition to standardisation and the introduction of the cigar machine, the Trust ultimately transferred much of its cigar production to the United States. Smaller family firms, however, known as 'independents', fought back against foreign standardisation and affirmed their agricultural and industrial expertise.[17] They were able to hold out, many of them producing the premium handmade *Habano* right up until the 1959 Revolution.

US hostility to Cuba's revolution led to a US trade embargo that – with US pressure – extended to most of the Americas (Canada and Mexico being the only early exceptions). Prior to the embargo, the US Department of Agriculture commissioned a report to document the extent to which the US cigar industry was reliant on Cuban leaf imports and advise on sourcing alternative supplies. The report's recommendation was to seek these in neighbouring Caribbean and Central American territories, whereby agronomists, growers and manufacturers would experiment in the Dominican Republic and Nicaragua in particular. Western markets became a battleground for disputed Havana cigar brands from island/offshore parallel production and marketing systems, while Eastern European socialist bloc and 'Third World' countries emerged as new Havana cigar partners.

Thirty years on, the fall of the Berlin Wall in 1989 signalled the end of Soviet bloc trade and aid that had developed in the vacuum left by US hostility and embargo, and the US response to Cuba's ensuing crisis was to tighten and extra-territorialise the embargo. Yet at the same time, the US anti-antismoking cigar revival was in full swing, engineered in no small part by the New York glossy *Cigar Aficionado*, created in 1992. US Cuban tobacco interests were in all-out competition with island Cuba, which courted non-US trade and investment, making cigars part of its crisis structural adjustment strategy and striking landmark credit deals in 1994 between the Cuban state tobacco enterprise and its French and Spanish parastatal tobacco counterparts. The US cigar bubble burst in 1999, but the luxury market for premium handmade cigars held around the world, most notably for the island-produced *Habano* in Europe and newly emerging Asian economies such as China, such that Cuba reported a 9 percent increase in profits in 2011.

Quality, Skill and Terroir

What is it about the Havana that makes it so special? Ask those in the trade and they will speak of the quality and skill of growing and manufacturing in Cuba – what the French, in protecting their champagne, coined as *terroir*. The very special quality of the Cuban cigar is attributed in particular to the leaf grown in the Vuelta Abajo region of western Cuba, today's Pinar del Río province, and to a lesser extent in Vuelta Arriba, in central Cuba, and to the handcrafting of the cigar itself.[18]

In 1940, José Perdomo, at the time occupying a key role in Cuba's Comisión Nacional por la Propaganda y Defensa del Tabaco Habano (founded in 1927), wrote:

> The Cuban cigar is a luxury article. As such, it goes to market without the intention of competing with any other cigar. Rather, it is designed for the minority who can afford such luxuries.

According to Perdomo, there were certain conditions which a cigar must fulfill to be considered a genuine Havana: it must be made with only leaf grown in Cuba, and leaf of only the highest quality, and it must be manufactured in Cuba, entirely handmade, using long filler, and bearing the official Seal of Warranty of National Origin. In the words of Perdomo:

> The entire industrial process of this cigar is carried on in Cuba in a special climatic situation where there is not the slightest suggestion of artificiality. It is only necessary to locate each department of work in the factory in the proper place. The sunshine, average temperature, and humidity of the atmosphere in Cuba are closely linked with the quality of the Havana cigar. These factors, plus the composition of the soil and subsoil, in harmonious combination, are what make it possible for Cuba to produce tobacco with both the agricultural and industrial qualities of the Havana.[19]

These claims have been echoed by many others before and since. According to Cuban expert in the trade Enzo Infante Urivazo:

> The name *habano*, used to designate cigars made in Cuba, was not chosen by the Cubans. It emerged somewhat spontaneously in the international tobacco markets when certain features of undisputed quality led consumers to regard as best the products that came from Havana or were exported out of Havana harbor.

Once the Havana was acknowledged the best, some said it was because of the leaf, others the cigar makers' skill, yet others the growers' skill, but, Infante Urivazo declared: "The factors that have contributed to the prestige of Cuba tobacco are found first and foremost in the soils." After that, the Havana cigar "is both an art and a science."[20]

According to Cuban geographer Antonio Nuñez Jiménez:

> Havana tobacco is the favoured child of Cuban agriculture, thanks to the combination of extraordinary geographical factors and the expert, painstaking efforts of our agricultural and industrial workers, which have favoured our unparalleled leaf.[21]

Cuban cigar maker-historian-educator Gaspar Jorge García Galló placed more emphasis on the skills involved in the cigar's making, and wrote extensively on the psychology of the cigar maker as well as writing a biography of the cigar itself. Towards the end of the latter, he declared: "The intention of this book has been to celebrate creative work."[22]

Seeds, people, skills and know-how can all be transferred, but *terroir* cannot. Hence the power of the concept, which means, as expressed by Vahé Gérard: "Cuba is still the promised land for the cigar lover."[23] However *terroir* has to be defended, not least by seals of approval and branding. Ortiz himself wrote that Havana tobacco:

> can display crowns, sceptres, the emblems of royalty, and even an emperor's title. Tobacco proudly wears until the moment of its death the band of its brand; only in the sacrificial fire does it burn its individuality and convert its ashes as it ascends to glory.[24]

Curiously, nonetheless, in accounting for the rise of *El Habano*, relatively little explanatory attention has been given to royal favour, stamps of warranty and sumptuous labelling. This is somewhat intriguing when manufacturers such as Bernardo Rencurrel and Hija De Cabañas y Carvajal early curried royal dispensation (in 1810) for being purveyors to the Spanish crown, and the latter (making cigars since 1797) is attributed with having introduced the first Havana 'segar' on the London market, before Spain lifted its monopoly on Cuban tobacco in 1817 and predating the Office of Patents and Brand Names of Havana set up that same year.

By the 1830s there were voices calling for protective measures to guarantee the quality and prestige of the Havana cigar, and in 1839 the Real Sociedad Económica de Amigos del País founded a school for apprentices in tobacco. In 1842, the Spanish Captain General issued a decree forbidding the use of all brands other than those approved by the Civil Government and warning engravers not to print seals for manufacturers without approval. In 1843, two German brothers, Herman and August Upmann, travelled from Bremen to Cuba looking for a business opportunity, and in 1844 opened a cigar store in Havana. Said to be the first foreigners to be authorised, they went on to become merchants in cigars and banking, solidly established in both by the 1860s.

In 1847 the Real Sociedad Económica de Amigos del País sponsored Havana's First Public Exhibit of Products of the Industry, awarding medals to local manufacturers for their products. At the time, in the words of Narciso Menocal in his book on the glory days of Cuban cigar labels, the Cuban cigar "was enjoying a moment of supreme international predominance."[25] Cabañas took the Gold Medal at the 1851 Queen Victoria's Great Exhibition in London, and in 1867 Partagás took gold at the Paris World Fair.

Cigar brands had to be registered under Municipal Ordinances, but there was such concern over brand profusion that in 1889 the Union of Cigar Manufacturers of Havana was authorised to vet members placing a seal on boxes as a guarantee of origin. The seal bore the royal crown and the coats of arms of Spain and City of Havana on the left and on the right Columbus. In the centre it read:

> The Union of Cigar Manufacturers guarantees the origin and legitimacy of the cigars bearing this seal and will, pursuant to the law, prosecute anyone attempting to falsify or amend it.[26]

Significantly, the age of the cigar was also the age of the lithographic industry. Invented in the late eighteenth century in Germany, lithography was developed in the early nineteenth century in France as chromolithography, which, from 1840 on, became the "art form of the middle class" and was also adopted for advertising. Cuban scholar Zoila Lapique Becali documents how lithography was available in Cuba three years before it was in the United States and four before Spain. In 1822, a first French shop was opened in Havana for printing music sheets, known as La Litografía de Música or La Litografía de La Habana. In 1840 two lithographic shops were set up, almost in unison, one French and the other Spanish, initially to reproduce engravings of Cuba but soon used by manufacturers to print labels. Demand was such that within five years new lithographic shops were opened involving Cubans and Europeans.[27]

The iconography on Cuban cigar labels for export assured an international clientele that they were buying a Cuban product, and not an imitation: "Like all exceptional quality and expensive products, cigars are counterfeited. Havana cigars are the most affected, including boxes, packaging and certification labels."[28] They were also, however, incredibly richly embossed gold and coloured labels, designed to denote a quality product that stood out. They were, in the words of Cuban expert Adriano Martínez Rius:

... expressions of luxury and power ... of the brands with magnificent lithography that further empowered and consolidated the universal grandeur of the *Habano*. From that moment on, the *Habano* had a presentation in accordance with its lineage.

Martínez Rius continued:

From a purely informative phase it moved into what in the present-day we would call MARKETING, aimed at attracting potential consumers and promoting the various manufacturers' trade marks.[29]

Taste and 'Cubanicity'

Ask smokers today what makes a Havana cigar so special, and they'll celebrate its taste, feel and aroma, and the experience of the smoke. Again in the words of Martínez Rius:

In the contemporary world, the cigar is known as a genuine symbol of pleasure, and if it's a Havana, it's the NON PLUS ULTRA of its kind, the preference of those who know how to enjoy an excellent smoke.[30]

Ortiz opened *Cuban Counterpoint* with the statement: "Tobacco is born, sugar is made. Tobacco is born pure, is processed pure and smoked pure." He continued:

In the same box there are no two cigars alike; each one has a different taste ... the merit of tobacco lies in ... the exquisite aroma of the pure Havana cigar, which is intoxicating ... tobacco affords satisfaction to the touch and sight.... What smoker has not passed his hand caressingly over the rich brevas or regalías of a freshly opened box of Havanas? ... catharsis for nervous tension to the smoker who handles them and holds them delicately between lips and fingers? (. . .) Poets who have been smokers have sung of the rapt ecstasy that comes over them as they follow with eyes and imagination the bluish smoke rising upward.... Whereas sugar appeals to only one of the senses, that of taste, tobacco appeals not only to the palate, but to the smell, touch, and sight.[31]

Ortiz singled out the Havana cigar as an article of pleasure and vice, a luxury article like champagne, something unique that cannot be surpassed or substituted.[32] Tobacco's enduring appeal, he argued, derived from natural and social factors whose effects can be reduced to two: hedonism and utilitarianism. First feared and regarded with suspicion, contempt, repulsion, "a thing for the savages," it then spread among the lower ranks of new settlers before those of higher social standing. In Cuba, in the cleansing rituals of Afro-Cuban religions, cigar smoke was to ward off evil; in England, Chaucer upbraided cigar smokers of London as "English Moors," having fallen into the "Negro's introduced fashion." It was not long, however, before the partisans of tobacco divided into two groups, hedonists and panaceists, the former were the real victors while the latter provided the rationale:

> Pleasure sought tobacco, the dislike of new things and austerity opposed it; but medicine justified it for reasons of its own, and sensuality was able to hide behind the cloak of curative science.[33]

Smoking a Havana became not only a symbol of position and wealth but an exotic luxury consumed and reduced to ashes, a high cost for wasteful and fleeting pleasure, making this a luxury of rare distinction: "People smoked ostentatiously, the same way they displayed a little Negro slave, a cage of talking parrots, a mahogany coach, or a tortoise-shell cane."[34] The 'Ortizian' approach would be echoed in two contemporary studies, one by Jarrett Rudy in his 2005 book on smoking in nineteenth-century Montreal and the other by Matthew Hilton in 2000 on smoking in nineteenth-century Britain. Each, however, took the analysis a stage further.

Rudy rehearsed some of the same arguments:

> The cultural categories of tobacco connoisseurship were most clearly exemplified in the cigar. It was a symbol of wealth and power, and its smokers were criticized for their extravagance. The most expensive and most prized cigar was the Cuban.

The St James Club, one of Montreal's elite men's clubs, imported Cuban cigars specifically for its members. "They pointed to the skilled labour of the cigar maker and the *terroir* of the tobacco as the cultural categories that accounted for the value of the cigar."[35] Connoisseurs were "men of taste," theirs was the acquired taste of "men of culture," and the cigar was made by skilled labour in a male-dominated cigar rolling process, learned through long apprenticeship and control of entry into trade:

> As with grapes used to make champagne and French wine, it was the experience of the cultivator and his relationship to the soil and climate that determined the quality of the tobacco leaf.[36]

However, Rudy makes an acute observation: "While the quality of Cuban tobacco probably fluctuated, the suggestion of tobacco being Cuban was more important than the actual quality of the tobacco." The appearance of being Cuban was a priority for cigar manufacturers and "Through advertising, they evoked a sense of 'Cubanicity' that could be attached to any cigar to raise its value."[37] What was important was not its origins but its perceived origins.

Thus, from 1900 to 1940 the Montreal firm Granda Hermanos y Cía made 'authentic' Cuban cigars in Canada. The Granda brothers learnt cigar making in Cuba and acquired the special skills of 'Spanish' as opposed to 'German' hand work, using long filler instead of the short filler of cheaper cigars and sorting into many more shades than the German three or four. Granda's advertising was extensive compared with other cigar advertising and their Spanish name captured the cachet of Cubanicity.

Hilton subsequently argued that the mass phenomenon of smoking that has remained central to individual and group identity is rooted in the bourgeois liberal context of smoking, involving that specific liberal notion of the self, especially promoted by gentlemen smokers of pipe and cigar in the mid to late nineteenth century:

> It is bourgeois because the culture of smoking was promoted by a specific cohort of the male population which had sufficient economic and cultural capital to buy expensive pipes, cigars and tobacco mixtures.... The context is liberal because the understanding of smoking ... stressed the central tenets of this national political, economic and cultural creed: individuality and independence.[38]

Hilton pursues this idea further to argue for an understanding of how a particular section of the male population legitimated their activity in the perceived feminine world of consumption by first emphasising the rational, pointing to the intellectual, the skilful and the purposeful aspects of smoking. They then used this as a solid base from which to explore the more irrational or ephemeral, demonstrating aspects of their individuality through knowledge of figures such as Columbus, Nicot and Raleigh, as well as the more masculine domains of production and manufacture, including descriptions of Cuba's growing regions and Havana factories. Theirs was "a freemasonry of smokers" and a camaraderie based on a shared command of the tobacco experience.

Where if not in the cigar establishment would that knowledge and that 'freemasonry of smokers' and camaraderie be forged, and Iain Scarlet's *A Puff of Smoke* paints a very clear picture of one such London cigar establishment that has endured to this day as James J. Fox & Rupert Lewis on St James's, Piccadilly. Scarlet opens: "London is arguably the cigar capital of the world and Robert Lewis is certainly the longest established cigar merchant in London and probably the United Kingdom." His book marked the bicentenary of the firm in the part of central London, close to the royal palace, which to this day "has a worldwide reputation not only for pomp, pageantry and gentlemen's clubs" but also exclusive shops (hatters, tailors, gunmakers and the like).[39]

When the troops returned home after fighting with Wellington in the Peninsular wars, Scarlet recounts:

> the craze for cigars swept London with much the same enthusiasm as the hula-hoop 150 years later. . . . The shop in Great Newport Street began to resemble a club. Gentlemen came not only to buy their cigars and tobacco, but to relax and (seated on nothing much more comfortable than a tobacco tub) enjoy a chat and a smoke and, perhaps, a glass of sherry.

In 1834-35, the lease was taken on St James's Street and "It was a wise move. The street which had once been famous for its coffee and chocolate houses was now the centre of gentlemen's clubland and a fashionable shopping district."[40]

The owners travelled to hotels all over the country by rail with sample cases, including Havana cigars, laying them out in private rooms of the best hotels, inviting tobacconists, hoteliers and innkeepers to view and place their orders, and at the end of the day wining and dining on a grand scale. Mr Churchill opened his account at the shop in 1900, after being introduced to the Havana cigar while serving as a soldier in Cuba in the 1890s. He purchased fifty Bock Giraldías and would repeat his order for many years to come. Later, during the Second World War, Havana cigar manufacturers combined together to send him 5,000 cigars, and the gift was repeated annually until after the war.

The Ultimate Smoke

Sander Gilman and Zhou Xun in their 'Introduction' to *Smoke* wrote of Europeans' encounter with smoke on arriving in the New World:

> Smoke, ineffable yet perceivable; real yet illusionary; present yet transient; breathable yet intoxicating. It was smoke that captured the world's imagination. It was an experience for which they had initially no vocabulary and to which they sought (and continue to seek) to give meaning. Smoke was a cure, but it soon became a passion.[41]

They continued:

> The cigar is a prime example of how tobacco continued to re-invent itself, enchanting the world once more – and at its roots was one of the original ways of consumption. The cigar became fashionable first in Spain, then

in Britain and other parts of Europe. It was first conceived of in Cuba and was launched into full swing in the Philippines. A not-too-distant cousin of the way that the Cubans had smoked when they met Colombus's sailors, it was pure smoke.[42]

While the eighteenth century was the century of snuff, the early nineteenth century appeal was that of Lord Byron in 1823: "Thy naked beauty – Give me a cigar!" Cigars became the mark of status for aristocrats, the privileged, wealthy and social elites. With the twentieth-century rise of the cigarette, the tobacco industry created a product that could be virtually all things to all people. In the words of Gilman and Xun, "Its promotional strategies demonstrated 'a sophisticated notion of culture and its operative mechanisms' representing innovative notions of social and cultural 'engineering'."[43] Where cultural norms and expectations proved an obstacle, the answer was to change the culture.

By the twentieth century, across the globe, humankind had a tobacco habit. In the four centuries since Rodrigo de Jerez and Luis de Torres smoked a Cuban cigar, tobacco production, trade and consumption had soared. The First and Second World Wars, and the intervening and initial post-war years, were a smoker's paradise, as the cigarette rode supreme – in reality and on screen. The cigarette, however, with its monopolies, global corporations and immense profits, was also to be tobacco's downfall. Its addictive dangers ushered in health prohibitions throughout the western world, though fostering new booms in the non-western world where there were no such prohibitions.

It was counter to this that the cigar made a 1990s comeback. The new rich were to be seen frequenting newly created cigar divans of London and New York. In the words of Iain Gately, they were:

> ... dedicated to the pleasures of owning and smoking the most expensive and flamboyant of smoking devices. . . . The cigar revival is explained in part by the spirit of conspicuous consumption which permeated the age. . . . Cigars were a field in which discrimination and purchasing power could be exercised with equal freedom, and smoking a cigar was a perfect demonstration of both.[44]

Aaron Sigmond, founding director of *Smoke* magazine, wrote in 1997, at the height of the 1990s cigar boom:

> Each cigar is a new and sensual experience which instantly distinguishes a smoker from those around him. When two cigar enthusiasts meet, a bond is created that words can do little to convey. Cigars embody a certain sense of fraternity which spans generations, diminishes political differences, and somehow makes all quarrelling suddenly seem petty.[45]

Yet the new answer to 'why smoke?' was really power-smoking, in the same fashion as power-dressing; and the most sought-after 'power smoke' of them all was Fidel Castro's erstwhile specially hand-rolled Cohíba, which takes us to a different kind of *terroir*, one which has political and cultural caché.

When Cuban writer Reynaldo González published *El Bello Habano* (The Fine Havana) in 2004, it read as a modern-day ode to the Havana cigar, with evocative chapter headings: '*Una caja de recuerdos magicos*' (A Box of Magical Memories), '*El Diablo es buen negocio*' (The Devil is Good Business), '*Caballo medieval, montura renacentista*' (Medieval Horse, Renaissance Trappings), '*Los piratas también fuman*' (Pirates Smoke Too), '*Don Habano, caballero ilustrado*' (Don Habano, Educated Gent), and '*Incendios libertarios: humo de tabaco*' (Libertarian Fire: Cigar Smoke). He covered traditional ground:

> The secret of the exquisite legitimate Havana lies in the privileged land where it is grown, the virtuosity of the plant and the care that goes into it, and it's exclusively handmade by women and men jealously guarding their craft.[46]

In the more heady years of the late 1960s, however, a young Swiss by the name of Zino Davidoff wrote in a more personal vein: "When I was twenty, I fell in love with the great tobacco plantations in Cuba. This passion of my youth has never been spent." His father encouraged him to travel to the Americas to learn about the tobacco trade: "'I am not able to give you much money,' he said, 'only some letters of introduction to tobacco merchants. But if you use them correctly, these letters are worth gold. In our business, friendship is not a vain word.'" He went to Buenos Aires and then Bahía, where one day an old planter said, "Son, you love tobacco. Go to Cuba – to the land of the red clay soil. There you will discover the *puro*, the pure cigar. Then, nothing else will exist for you." He left for Cuba "in the state of anticipation a young archaeologist might for Greece or a seminarian for Rome." For two years he stayed there wrapped in "a veritable state of excitement which affected all the senses." He worked on a farm, was curious about everything, and in his words:

> I learned very quickly that just as there are no two great wines which are the same, no two cigars are identical.... Eventually I knew which were the best cigars in the world – and why.[47]

Davidoff was captivated by Cuba's cigars and they would dominate his life for the next thirty years:

> When I returned to Europe, I decided to dedicate my talents to the tobacco business. The *puro* of Cuba is not a cigar like any other.... It is the king of

tobacco products and should be treated according to its rank. . . . Irreplaceable virtues of this magic island: its geology, wind, water, its miraculous soil. . . . For Cubans, and for me, the puro can be nothing other than Cuba, nothing other than a Havana.

He wrote at the time (1969):

> Neither war nor politics has altered the cigar. Great cigars still come from the same precious land. Surviving every vicissitude, a good Havana with a gold or purple band, in its wooden box with cedar shavings, encased in its baroque splendour, is still the master of the cigar world. It cannot be cut off from its glorious past or its obscure origins. Of noble lineage, it will never be a simple manufactured object. . . . It is something that commands respect. . . . A good cigar contains the promise of a totally pleasurable experience. . . . If there is a secret to the cigar, it is to be found in the slow movements, the dignified measured smoking. The movements are more than mannerisms; they are ceremonial acts. . . . The conversation of cigar smoking ought to be slow and majestic. . . .[48]

He continued:

> A cigar cannot be truly enjoyed without contemplation, without thinking. You cannot smoke anything at any time, in any place. A cigar should fit your mood, habits, personality, surroundings. . . . There is an occasion for each cigar and a cigar for each occasion.[49]

Davidoff acknowledged that in the early years of revolution, when cigar manufacturing was nationalised, "the great names, the best Havanas – vestiges of decadent capitalism and the power of money – were condemned without appeal."[50] Sales plummeted, some dispossessed owners sued in The Hague, others established themselves in Virginia, Florida, Philippines, the Canary Islands and the Middle East. In the 1970s and 1980s, he saw himself as part of reviving the quality and brands in Cuba, and for many in Europe Davidoff would become synonymous almost with Cuban cigars. That was until his falling out with Cuba, thirty years later, and his move to the Dominican Republic, where his cigars are produced to this day.

By the late 1990s, Cuban cigars were again on the ascendancy, so much as to occasion claims such as that by Nancy Stout in *Habanos*:

> Throughout the history of the cigar, the *habano* has been unequivocally considered the pinnacle of smoking pleasure. The unparalleled quality of the

Havana cigar has bound the idea of Cuba with its most coveted export, and has held the imagination of aficionados around the world for 500 years.[51]

She continued:

> Throughout the world and throughout the history of the existence of cigars there has been one, and one only, that has been recognised by the true connoisseur as the ultimate cigar, the legendary and peerless one, the non plus ultra, and that is the *habano*. *Habanos* are cigars produced only in Cuba, shipped only from the port of Havana, made entirely of special varieties of Cuban-grown tobacco, and marketed only by the designated name *habano*.... They are smoked by the most famous people, and sold for the highest prices, They are imitated and counterfeited. And, always, as the true sign of a rare luxury item, supply sometimes cannot meet demand.[52]

Nevertheless, the imitations and the counterfeits are not always what they seem, as they might be made with Cuban leaf by Cubans and in very similar climes. At the height of the boom, all kinds of new arrangements surfaced, one of which was the Graycliff story in the Bahamas. As recounted by Jean Edmond in a 1996 Graycliff brochure, there Avelino Lara, "King of Torcedores (cigar rollers)" was "like a fine XO cognac" deploying "forty years of wisdom to create a new masterpiece cigar that will surpass even his greatest accomplishments." His tobacco blends remained "as secretive as a CIA operation" and "with Avelino's background, the Graycliff line will be nothing short of sensational":

> Flamboyant entrepreneur and proprietor of Graycliff, Enrico Garzaroli, is in ecstasy for he knows the demand will far surpass what can be produced and at a price tag only for the very affluent. Graycliff also has the largest selection and collection of authentic Cuban cigars than any other restaurant in the world.

Lara had been head of Cuba's El Laguito factory that makes Cohíba, and, in Lara's words: "the Cohíba is to Cuba as Dom Perignon is to France. It represents something very special to the country." Having Lara there, Garzaroli said: "it's almost like having Picasso come to your home and create five years of art which you make available to the public." Edmond himself wrote while staying at Graycliff: "As I sat in the parlor with a snifter of Delamain Reserve De Familie Rare, a cognac as superb as the cigar I was about to light, I felt like the Czar of Russia in the days of extreme elegance."[53]

If ever a story could encapsulate the many contemporary twists and turns to the luxury *Habano*'s history, this must surely be one!

Notes

1. My special thanks go to Karin Hofmeester and Bernd-Stefan Grewe for facilitating my participation in the 2011 commodity-chain workshop in Konstanz and encouraging me to frame my work on the luxury Havana cigar in the context of global histories, imperial commodities and local interactions.
2. Fernando Ortiz, *Cuban Counterpoint: Tobacco and Sugar* (Durham and London: Duke University Press, 1995 [1940]), p.309.
3. As beautifully illustrated in Adriano Martínez Rius, *The Great Habano Factories* (Barcelona: Select Publications, 2005), pp.30-3. See also Carlos Venegas Fornias, 'La Habana: ¿ciudad industrial?, *Catauro* 7:12 (2005), a special issue of the journal published by the Fundación Fernando Ortiz, which was given over to tobacco.
4. Classics linking materiality and regimes of value remain Arjun Appadurai (ed.), *The Social Life of Things: Commodities in Cultural Perspective* (Cambridge: Cambridge University Press, 1986), and *Modernity at Large: Cultural Dimensions of Globalization* (Minneapolis: University of Minnesota Press, 1996); and Gary Gereffi & Miguel Korzeniewicz (eds), *Commodity Chains and Global Capitalism* (Westport: Praeger, 1994), which includes Hopkins & Wallerstein, 'Commodity Chains'. See also Daniel Miller, 'Consumption and Commodities', *Annual Review of Anthropology*, 24 (1995), pp.141-61; James G. Carrier & Josiah McC. Heyman, 'Consumption and Political Economy', *Journal of the Royal Anthropological Institute* 3:2 (1997), pp.355-73; Mark Tungate, *Luxury World: The Past, Present and Future of Luxury Brands* (London & Philadelphia: Kogan Page, 2009); Maxine Berg & Elizabeth Eger (eds), *Luxury in the Eighteenth Century: Debates, Desires and Delectable Goods* (Basingstoke: Palgrave Macmillan, 2003); and Christopher J. Berry, *The Idea of Luxury: A Conceptual and Historical Investigation* (Cambridge: Cambridge University Press, 1994)
5. Jean Stubbs, *Tobacco on the Periphery* (London: Amaurea Press, 2023 [1985]), 'Havana Cigars and the West's Imagination', in Sander L. Gilman and Zhou Xun (eds), *Smoke: A Global History of Smoking* (London: Reaktion Press, 2004), pp.134-9 – Chapter 10 in the present volume; and 'El Habano and the World It Has Shaped: Cuba, Connecticut and Indonesia', *Cuban Studies*, 41 (2010), pp.39-67 – Chapter 13 in the present volume. Cuban 'classics' are those by José Rivero Muñiz (*Tabaco: su historia en Cuba*, 2 vols., Havana: Instituto de Historia, 1965) and Gaspar Jorge García Galló (*El tabaquero cubano: psicología de las profesiones*, Havana: Imprenta El Siglo XX, 1936, and, with Wilfredo Correa García, *The Story of Havana Cigars*, Havana: Editorial José Martí, 2001). A cultural studies approach can be found in Reynaldo González, *El Bello Habano: Biografía íntima del tabaco* (Havana: Editorial Letras Cubanas, 2004), akin to the earlier Guillermo Cabrera Infante, *Holy Smoke: A Literary Romp Through the History of the Cigar* (London: Faber & Faber, 1985). Examples of more general studies are Sander L. Gilman & Zhou Xun (eds), *Smoke: A Global History of Smoking* (London: Reaktion Books, 2004); Iain Gately, *Tobacco: A Cultural History of How an Exotic Plant Seduced Civilization* (New York: Grove Press, 2002); Jordan Goodman, *Tobacco in History: The Cultures of Dependence* (London & New York: Routledge, 1993); and V. G. Kiernan, *Tobacco: A History* (London: Hutchinson Radius, 1991). See also Wolfgang Schivelbusch, *Tastes of Paradise: A Social History of Spices, Stimulants, and Intoxicants* (New York: Vintage, 1993 [1980]) and James Walvin, *Fruits of Empire: Exotic Produce and Western Taste* (New York: New York University Press and Palgrave Macmillan, 1997).
6. The early 1990s saw the New York launch of the glossy magazine *Cigar Aficionado*, which was instrumental in engineering the 1990s cigar revival, and the late 1990s saw the publication of a spate of coffee table books by both Cuban and non-Cuban authors. These included Antonio Nuñez Jiménez, *The Journey of the Havana Cigar* (Neptune City: TFH Publications, 1996 [1988]); Gérard Père et Fils, *Havana Cigars*,

Edison: Wellfleet Press 1997 [1995]; Eric Deschodt & Philippe Morane, *The Cigar* (Cologne: Könemann Verlagsgesellschaft, 1998); Enzo A. Infante Urivazo, *Havana Cigars 1817-1960* (Neptune City: TFH Publications, 1997); Eumelio Espino Marrero, *Cuban Cigar Tobacco: Why Cuban Cigars are the World's Best* (Neptune City: TFH Publications, 1997); Charles Del Todesco, *The Havana Cigar: Cuba's Finest* (New York, London, Paris: Abbeville Press Publishers, 1997); Nancy Stout, *Habanos: The Story of the Havana Cigar* (New York: Rizzoli, 1997); and Adriano Martínez Ruis, *Habano el Rey* (Barcelona: Epicur Publicaciones, 1999). A later volume, most impressive of all for its sheer size, was Min Ron Nee, *An Illustrated Encyclopaedia of Post-Revolution Havana Cigars* (Sankt Augustin: AWM-Verlag, 2003).

7 Bartolomé de las Casas, *Obras Completas* (Madrid: Alianza Editorial, 1992). This was revisited in Armando Rangel Rivero 'El tabaco en Cuba ¿único desde 1492?' and Reynaldo González 'La estela que dejó el tabaco en la cultura internacional', *Catauro* (2005).

8 Kiernan, *Tobacco* (1991) among others, writes of how tobacco spread so quickly round the world by trade, possessing, as French historian Fernand Braudel expressed it, the supreme asset of flexibility in adapting itself to the most diverse climates and soils.

9 This is recounted in the classic works on Spanish tobacco history by José Pérez Vidal, *España en la historia del tabaco* (Madrid: Consejo Superior de Investigaciones Científicas, 1959), and *Historia del cultivo del tabaco en España* (Madrid: Servicio Nacional de Cultivo y Fermentación del Tabaco, 1956). See also José M. Rodríguez Gordillo, *Un archivo para la historia del tabaco* (Madrid: Jacaryan, 1984).

10 Among other works, see Allan Kulikoff, *Tobacco & Slaves: The Development of Southern Cultures in the Chesapeake, 1680-1800* (Chapel Hill & London: University of North Carolina Press, 1986).

11 See José Rivero Muñiz, *Las tres sediciones de los vegueros en el siglo XVIII* (Havana: Academia de la Historia de Cuba, 1951). Also Charlotte A. Cosner, 'Rich and Poor, Black and White, Slave and Free: A Social History of Cuba's Tobacco Farmer's 1718-1817', PhD thesis, Florida International University (2010), and 'Vegueros and Tabaqueros: Rebellion, Revolution and "The Devil's Plant": Challenges to State Control in Colonial Cuba', *Cuban Studies Association Occasional Paper* 9 (1998).

12 See Pérez, *Historia del cultivo del tabaco* (1956), and *España en la historia del tabaco* (1959). Also Santiago de Luxán Meléndez et al. (eds), *El mercado del tabaco en España durante el siglo XVIII: fiscalidad y consumo* (Las Palmas de Gran Canaria: Universidad de Las Palmas de Gran Canaria, 2000), on state finances, contraband and consumption.

13 Ortiz, *Cuban Counterpoint* (1995 [1940]), pp.76-7.

14 Ibid., p.77, recounts this thus: "It was well on in the second half of the eighteenth century, after the conquest of Havana by the English in 1762, that Havana cigars set out to conquer the world. It was then that Havana cigars traveled to England in the red coats of the British officials and to North America with the Yankee officers who had been in charge of the colonial regiments that helped occupy Havana and not long afterwards, in 1776, were to win the independence of their own country. After this momentous episode in Cuba's history the taste for cigars began to spread beyond Spain. In 1788 the first factory manufacturing cigars was set up in Hamburg by H. H. Schlottmann, and by 1793 they were in wide use in all Germany. . . . In the nineteenth century it was the invasion of Spain by Napoleon's armies and Lord Wellington's troops. . . ."

15 Deschodt & Morane, *The Cigar* (1998), p.55.

16 Ibid., p.169.

17 The dispute was encapsulated in a volley between Gustavo Bock, *The Truth about Havana Cigars* (New York: Havana Tobacco Company, 1904), and the counter-attack on behalf of the 'independents' by journalist and cigar maker José González Aguirre, *La verdad sobre la industria del tabaco habano* (Havana, 1905).

18 Interestingly, in 1772, Felipe de Fondesviela, Marques de la Torre, in recognition of the quality of its tobacco, decided the area should be separate from Havana and have a municipal government of its own, at the time called New Philippines. An excellent 'pocket' analysis of *terroir* can be found in Becky Sue Epstein, *Champagne: A Global History* (London: Reaktion Books, 2011).
19 José E. Perdomo, *Léxico tabacalero cubano* (Miami: Ediciones Universal, 1998 [1940]), p.193.
20 Infante, *Havana Cigars* (1997), pp.11 & 13.
21 Núñez, *Journey of the Havana Cigar* (1996), p.57.
22 García, *Biografía* (1961), p.271.
23 Gérard, *Cigars* (2002), p.8.
24 Ortiz, *Cuban Counterpoint* (1995), p.43.
25 Menocal, *Cuban Cigar Labels* (1995), p.25.
26 Ibid., p.37.
27 Zoila Lapique Becali, *La memoria en las piedras* (Havana: Editorial Boloña, 2003), and 'Los sucesos de la historia de España y Cuba en las etiquetas de los cigarrillos y habanos cubanos', in Consuelo Naranjo Orovio & Carlos Serrano (eds), *Imágenes e Imaginarios Nacionales en el Ultramar Español* (Madrid: Consejo Superior de Investigaciones Científicas, 1999), pp.103-16; also 'La litografía en el siglo XIX', *Catauro*, 7:12 (2005), pp.18-20. Frédéric Miahle and Edouard Laplante were particularly famous for their engravings of Cuba at the time (Emilio Cueto, *Frédéric Mialhe, Mialhe's Colonial Cuba: The Prints that Shaped the World's View of Cuba*, Miami: Historical Association of Southern Florida, 1994).
28 Gérard, *Cigars* (2002), p.68.
29 Martínez, *Habano el Rey* (1999), pp.24 & 69.
30 Ibid., p.28.
31 Ortiz, *Cuban Counterpoint* (1995), pp.8-9.
32 Ibid., p.71.
33 Ibid., p.201.
34 Ibid., p.213.
35 Jarrett Rudy, *The Freedom to Smoke: Tobacco Consumption and Identity* (Montreal: McGill-Queens University Press, 2005), p.47.
36 Ibid., p.60.
37 Ibid., pp.62-3.
38 Matthew Hilton, *Smoking in British Popular Culture 1800-2000* (Manchester & New York: Manchester University Press, 2000), p.3.
39 Iain Scarlet, *A Puff of Smoke* (London: Robert Lewis, n.d.), pp.1, 3.
40 Ibid., p.13.
41 Gilman & Xun, *Smoke* (2004), p.9.
42 Ibid., p.17.
43 Ibid., p.343.
44 Gately, *Tobacco* (2002), p.342.
45 Aaron Sigmon in Mark Stücklin, *The Cigar Handbook: A Buyer's Guide to the World's Finest Cigar Brands* (New York: Barnes & Noble Books, 1997).
46 González, *El Bello Habano* (2004), p.125.
47 Zino Davidoff, *The Connoisseur's Book of the Cigar* (New York: McGraw Hill, 1969), p.3.
48 Ibid., pp.7-8.
49 Ibid., pp.29-30.
50 Ibid., p.44.
51 Stout, *Habanos* (1997), inside cover.
52 Ibid., p.9.
53 Jean M. Emond, 'Avelino Lara King of the Torcedores', in *Smoke Affair: Where Every Day's a Holiday*, Brochure for Graycliff Hotel, Restaurant, and Cigar Establishment, Nassau, Bahamas (n.d., c.1996).

16

TRANSNATIONALISM AND THE HAVANA CIGAR: COMMODITY CHAINS, NETWORKS, AND KNOWLEDGE CIRCULATION*1

AFTER THE 1959 Cuban Revolution, when the United States declared its trade embargo on Cuba, the race was on to produce a quality 'Havana cigar' and leaf elsewhere in the Caribbean. This was a new twist to a long history. By the mid-nineteenth century the handmade 'Havana' had become world famous as *the* luxury cigar, and while by the mid-twentieth century, in Cuba and the world over, cigarettes far out-shadowed cigars in terms of production and sales, the Havana still held its own niche luxury market. It also lay at the heart of transnational processes linked to commodity chains, networks and knowledge circulation. Seed, agricultural and industrial know-how and human capital were all transplanted for its replication, a process accentuated by major migratory waves linked to such landmark political upheavals as Cuba's late nineteenth-century struggles for independence from Spain, early twentieth-century US occupation and the mid-century revolution. This led to often-disputed identical brands, produced in Cuba and abroad, by island and émigré Cubans; distributed through parallel chains, networks and circuits; and promoted through high-profile cigar conferences and events, both in Cuba and abroad. In turn, this phenomenon created a complex multi-tiered licit and

---

* Originally published in Catherine Krull (ed.), *Cuba in Global Context: International Relations, Internationalism, and Transnationalism* (Gainesville: University Press of Florida, 2014), pp.227-42.

illicit system that aimed to capitalise on the prestige of the 'authentic' product. A similar phenomenon is to be observed in brand disputes and international court cases regarding other products of Cuba, most notably rum – Bacardi and Havana Club being a case in point. The Havana cigar, however, has been elevated to almost iconic status, which makes it of particular interest as a prism to explore broader issues. Here I have chosen three Caribbean island territories – Jamaica, Puerto Rico and the Dominican Republic – to illustrate this. Each played a major part in Havana cigar history, and the fortunes of all three have waxed and waned in tandem with not only Cuba but also their own transnational commodity and migration histories.

A Framework for Understanding the Global Havana Cigar

Global commodity chain analysis[2] tends to focus on the substitution of a product or parts of a product by other such products that are cheaper to produce, different in quality, or new on the market; and on opportunities for traders to reorganise supply and create consumer alternatives, unbound by former dependencies and monopolies of suppliers. The appearance of new products or varieties does not necessarily entail the collapse of the older chain because parallel structures frequently develop. The emergence of informal or illicit economies and their impact on a chain are more difficult to trace, yet these hidden parts of a global commodity chain may be essential to an understanding of its entire functioning. Historians have frequently presented chains as linear connections among producers, traders and consumers. Extending the analysis to encompass networks and circuits of knowledge challenges us to understand the fragilities and disconnections of their political, social and cultural dimensions.[3]

The Havana cigar as a global commodity cannot be understood as an element in a primarily economic chain but, rather, as an article shaped by markers whose political, social, cultural and migratory ramifications not only create parallel, substitute, informal and illicit commodity networks but also whole competing social and cultural worlds and imaginaries. In this process neighbouring Caribbean islands and surrounding mainland territories – the Dominican Republic, Jamaica, Honduras, Mexico, Nicaragua and Puerto Rico – feature prominently. They are, however, part of a far wider network of territories, ranging from the Americas – Brazil (Bahía), Colombia (El Carmen), Ecuador (close to Quito) and the United States (Connecticut, Florida-Georgia, New York) – to Europe (the Canary Islands), Africa (Cameroon) and Asia (the Philippines and Indonesia).[4]

Agricultural science and technology (that is, management, land tenure, labour, migration and consumption patterns) and forms of communication all play a part in this complex. Thus the publication *Cigar Aficionado*, from its founding in the early 1990s, was highly successful in engineering – socially and culturally as well as commercially – an anti-antismoking campaign to promote the consumption of cigars, nurturing a cult of 'cigar cool' whose epitome was the Havana.[5] Written for the connoisseur and punctuated by aggressive marketing, its articles signal where Havana seed leaf is being grown outside of Cuba, and by whom, and also who is manufacturing and marketing off-island Havanas, and where. This, then, is the world of the 'offshore Havana cigar'; or what those in the trade in Cuba refer to as *dobles marcas* – the term replacing the older *imitaciones* and *falsificaciones* long lamented by the Cuban industry. Today, as in the past, these competing brands raise issues of ownership and sovereignty, economic pragmatism and political nationalism.

In twenty years of research on the 'global Havana cigar', my own conceptual questions initially centered around such issues, with the Havana as my prism. My approach was threefold. First, I traced the formation, growth, and decline of post-1868 and post-1959 Cuban cigar émigré communities, exploring economic, social and political processes in receiver territories as well as in Cuba. Second, I charted the response to those communities from political and corporate tobacco and political interests abroad, especially the extent to which they were co-opted and the ways in which they subsequently had an impact on the broader tobacco and political history. Third, I delved into the politics of historical myth and memory in émigré culture, associated in the United States with post-1868 political idealism and post-1959 political conservatism.

A more sweeping global history began to emerge, however. By the mid-nineteenth century the Havana cigar had become the yardstick by which other cigar economies were measured: if the Cuban cigar economy was depressed, other cigar economies tended to ride high, and vice versa.[6] Several of the histories of these other economies are today all but forgotten, while others have been reinvented; but a fourfold typology linked to Cuba can be posited.

Thus, there are firstly the closely interlocking cigar-manufacturing histories of territories with significant migratory flows out of and into Cuba. This would apply to the Florida-Cuban cigar history, whose product was boosted and eventually destroyed by two US trade embargoes on Cuba: 1890, in the buildup to Cuba's final War of Independence from Spain; and 1960, after the Revolution. Over and beyond the better-known Cuban émigré South Florida cigar histories of Key West, Tampa and Ybor City, the history encompasses the lesser-known histories of the Florida-Georgia shade-tobacco belt, and links the aptly named cigar centres of Amsterdam and Havana, as well as Jacksonville, Quincy, Thomasville and others.[7] There are also the little-known nineteenth and early twentieth-century histories of the tobacco workers, manufacturers and growers who left Cuba to work in New York cigar manufacturing and the Jamaican tobacco economy. Across the Atlantic the travelling cigar is integral to Canary Islands history, from the late nineteenth- and early twentieth-century mass migratory waves of Canary Islanders into Cuban tobacco, in the context of the Canaries' geostrategic position on the route between Spain, Europe, Africa and the Americas. Subsequent return migration was to fuel the Canaries' own tobacco-growing and production, using a blend of tobaccos from different parts of the world.

The closely intertwined histories of Puerto Rican and Cuban tobacco show no significant tobacco migration, but do reveal closely monitored trade networks and circuits of knowledge. Puerto Rico's turbulent tobacco history in the late nineteenth and early twentieth centuries, fostered by US capital with the US occupation of 1898 after the end of Spanish colonial rule, in turn was undercut in the mid-twentieth century in the US-blessed, Puerto Rican strategy of Operation Bootstrap. The early twentieth century saw considerable numbers of Puerto Rican cigar workers heading north to US centres of cigar manufacturing, especially New York, where they joined Cuban émigré cigar workers. State-engineered migrant farm labour programmes of the third quarter of the twentieth century then transported displaced farmers and agricultural labourers from what were once Puerto Rican tobacco areas to Connecticut, whose shade tobacco can be traced back to Cuban leaf and cigars.

Still other cigar histories have seen small yet significant catalysts of Cuban cigar migration – including those of late nineteenth-century Mexico and late twentieth-century Nicaragua and Honduras, and also Ecuador and Brazil. Most notably these also include the Dominican Republic, which was hitherto far behind in the Havana cigar stakes but during the 1990s was reinvented as home to the born-again Havana cigar for the US market, where the real Havana was forbidden fruit.

Finally, the history shows Asian and African interconnections, linked to global and imperial cigar expansion involving the United Kingdom, the Netherlands, Germany and France. The shade tobacco of Cuba, Florida-Georgia and Connecticut was derived from, and in competition with, that of Sumatra (and Java), itself derived from Cuban and US seed (tobacco being indigenous to the Americas). Developed initially by the Dutch and marketed primarily in the Netherlands and Germany, the cheaper Indonesian leaf and ultimately cigar were destined to flood the global market. Likewise, the French moved into territories such as Cameroon, whose leaf also became part of the global cigar blend; while the tobacco history of the Philippines – the third-last colony of Spain, along with Cuba and Puerto Rico, and a US colony until 1946 – mirrored that of its erstwhile colonial counterparts.

What follows traces the commodity and migration histories linked to the cigar of one Caribbean territory drawn from each of the first three groupings. First is Jamaica, which witnessed foundational Cuban cigar migration, followed by Puerto Rico, with insignificant migration but significant trade and knowledge transfer. Both islands' flourishing late nineteenth-century and early twentieth-century tobacco economies have today all but disappeared. Finally is the Dominican Republic, where post-1959 Cuban migration catalysed its contemporary positioning as an offshore cigar production epicenter.

Jamaica: From Cuban Émigrés to 'Soldiers of War'

Tobacco was grown and manufactured in Jamaica by Cubans fleeing from Cuba's First War of Independence from Spain. A half century later, what initially developed as an economic mainstay of the émigré community and became a springboard for support of Cuba's independence effort had evolved into a Jamaican sector, employing British and US capital.[8]

Strategically close to Cuba, Jamaica was an important route for late nineteenth-century gunrunning and expeditions to the island, and provided refuge for some of Cuba's leading independence leaders, activists and their families. Among them were tobacco growers and cigar workers, dealers and manufacturers, notably Benito and Juan Machado, whose factory heralded Kingston's early industrialisation. Predating this, in 1873, a treatise on the growth, culture and manufacture of tobacco was published in Kingston by Guillermo González, "in grateful idea towards a country in which his compatriots have found congenial shelter." This was a time when it was declared "a scandal that with the East and West Indies in our possession we [the British] had not a good cigar from either."[9]

Efforts were made to support Cuban refugees by combining Cuban seed with technical knowledge, and by 1883-84 the *Blue Book Departmental Report* could cite former Cuban General Villegas as "an extensive cultivator of Havana tobacco at Colbeck's plantation."[10] The quality of the leaf was upgraded using the best Cuban Vuelta Abajo seed brought in through the offices of the British consul in Havana and Hope Gardens in Kingston, and with improved methods of cultivation. By 1891-92 the Governor's Report claimed that an increase in cigar exports indicated a taste for quality Jamaican-made cigars, and the Machado Company took a London Chamber of Commerce prize for its product.[11]

After the introduction of the cigar machine in the late 1920s and 1930s, handmade cigar operations wound down. They ended in 1954, when the then B. & J. B. Machado Tobacco Company became the Cigarette Company of Jamaica Ltd., later to be bought by British-owned Carreras, subsequently part of Imperial Tobacco. A new chapter opened in Cuban-Jamaican cigar manufacturing in 1965, when exiled Havana cigar manufacturer Ramón Cifuentes established the General Cigar Company of Jamaica, renamed Cifuentes y Cía in 1976, and produced brands such as Partagás. There was a renewed spurt in Jamaican growing and manufacturing in the 1990s, but both sectors have since relocated to the Dominican Republic.

What is of interest here, however, is a little-known offshore interlude to Jamaica's cigar history during the Second World War, linked to another Havana cigar story in what was once known as Connecticut Tobacco Valley. At its height in the early 1920s, the famous shade wrapper was grown from a leaf that agronomists perfected from Cuban seed.[12] A 1960s revival was not on a scale to stem the steady tide of long-term decline that had started with competition from the Sumatra leaf and was compounded with the 1950s introduction of a homogenised binder and wrapper and the 1964 US Surgeon General's report on the hazards of smoking; the failure was sealed with offshore relocation, again primarily to the Dominican Republic.

Often recounted as a proud New England story of family dynasties, shade-tobacco growing was, according to writer James O'Gorman, "a high risk, labour intensive, controversial but potentially rewarding occupation for owners if not for labourers. Cultivation demands constant attention, backbreaking hard work in the fields and under the tents, and knowledgeable adherence to detail in the curing sheds and stripping and sorting rooms."[13] Laced with cutthroat business and labour practices, the Connecticut tobacco story was narrated in snapshot detail by local writer Mildred Savage, whose best-selling 1958 novel *Parrish,* made into a 1961 Hollywood movie of the same name, was described at the time as a scenic, tobacco-road soap opera.[14]

Growers met seasonal labour requirements with immigrant and migrant workers – Irish in the nineteenth century, followed by eastern and southern Europeans of peasant stock-often met off the boats by middlemen and sold to farmers, a practice described in 1911 as "a little nearer the slave trade than anything I had experienced."[15] The growers employed child labour until legislation prevented that; they then turned to local high school students and southern black college students from Florida, Georgia and Virginia, disparagingly referred to locally as "plantation darkies or plantation negroes."[16]

During the Second World War, with tobacco having been declared essential to the Allied war effort, growers recruited men from the British West Indies. Invariably referred to as 'Jamaicans', these labourers came primarily from Jamaica but also from the Bahamas, Barbados, Grenada, Antigua and British Honduras. Fay Clarke Johnson, a Jamaican who in the early 1970s relocated with her family from Montreal to Hartford, worked with the West Indian Social Club in Connecticut to document testimonies of their all but lost history in her 1995 book *Soldiers of the Soil.*[17] They told her of their US points of entry in Florida, of Louisiana holding barracks, and of then being sent to Michigan, Ohio, New York and Connecticut; of sailing on the SS *Shank,* with 4,000 to 5,000 of them packed together in a ship made to hold only 1,900;

and subhuman conditions with little food and water. The camps they lived in were basic, and men kept to camp or moved in groups, because they met with hostility even while being praised for conducting themselves "as gentlemen and as good British subjects." There were nonetheless those who demanded their rights, as expressed, for example, in a telegram sent to President Franklin Roosevelt from George Christie, of Manchester, Jamaica: "Jamaicans dissatisfied of conditions on General Cigar Farm, driven as dumb cattle, work under intimidation. United Nations fight for freedom, justice and fair play. We should have same. Please investigate."[18]

The war's end in 1945 signaled the end of the 'Jamaican' programme, and more than thirty thousand Jamaicans, Bahamians, other West Indians and Hondurans working on farms were to be sent home at the end of the season. Few who had been there for six years had plans to return home – those who worked for seven were entitled to stay permanently – and Hartford's West Indian Social Club was instrumental in helping them settle and find work. Hence, in Savage's novel, Parrish and his mother are greeted when they arrive on the tobacco farm by Gladstone, "one of the Colored *boys*," who speaks in what Parrish describes as "a strange Calypso rhythm."[19] The 'boy' is from Jamaica, Parrish is told, one of those who stayed.

Puerto Rico:
From Factories and Fields to New York and New England

By the 1940s more than half of the grading of Connecticut shade tobacco was done in Puerto Rico, with some of the tobacco going into cigars made on the island, but most returning for machine manufacture on the US mainland. After the war, in 1948, the Puerto Rican Department of Labor Migration Division (Departamento de Trabajo División de Migración, DTDM) was set up, and one-quarter of the Puerto Rican migrants sent to the mainland United States went to work in tobacco. Many of them were recruited from what were once tobacco areas: San Lorenzo, Barranquitas, Caguas, Comerío, Cayey.

Ruth Glasser charted the link between island and mainland in *Aquí me quedo* [Here I stay]: *Puerto Ricans in Connecticut* (1997). She documented the agricultural and industrial upheavals behind migration, from US occupation in 1898 to the decline of small farming and displaced rural families pouring into San Juan. Most significantly, the post-Second World War Operation Bootstrap was designed to attract manufacturing, but companies failed to provide sufficient jobs to compensate for the loss of agricultural land to industrialisation, which displaced more rural families and workers, and resulted in an estimated 78 percent decline in the agricultural labour force in the years 1940-79. Island officials concluded that at least sixty thousand workers a year would have to leave in order for unemployment not to rise. Years earlier, Connecticut tobacco concerns had gone to Puerto Rico and there employed many who later became migrants from Puerto Rico's own tobacco valley to Connecticut. "Ironically," Glasser commented, "they came to the mainland to try to get a living wage from the very same employers."[20]

Puerto Rican historians have documented the late nineteenth- and early twentieth-century heyday of Puerto Rican tobacco, and its paradigmatic relationship with the United States and Cuba; and the life stories of feminist writer and cigar factory *lectora* (reader) Luisa Capetillo and of New York-based cigar maker Bernardo Vega provide glimpses into the Cuban-Puerto Rican-US cigar connection.[21] By the mid-1960s, the story was very different: 20 percent of the Puerto Rican migration to the United States was to Connecticut, second only to New Jersey. The records of the Connecticut Shade Tobacco Growers Agricultural Association, the DTDM Hartford Office and Connecticut local press and other holdings from the mid-1950s to the mid-1970s all extensively detail the use, and abuse, of Puerto Rican migrant labour.[22]

Signed annual contracts stipulated that labourers had to be strong in physique, in good health, free from communicable diseases and accustomed to hard work; they must have no police records or reputation as troublemakers, and be willing to work and live in the same boardinghouses with domestic workers and British West Indian workers. At least one in ten must have a working knowledge of English.

Most telling was how the battle to improve wages and conditions contributed to the suspension of the programme. By the late 1960s, the churches, the Young Lords activists, the Hartford branch of the Puerto Rican Socialist Party and lawyers from Legal Services offices all worked in support of the farm workers, as did the Industrial Mission of the Episcopal Church in Puerto Rico, which hired a staff of organisers for the Puerto Rican Migrant Support Committee, replaced in 1972 by the Ecumenical Ministry of Agricultural Workers. Incoming workers in 1973 might have been met with jostling and insults: "*cerdos que se venden por unos centavos*" (pigs bought for a few cents), "*negros sucios*" (dirty niggers), "*esclavos de la colonia*" (slaves from the colony),[23] but the more that growers tried to curb access to farms and camps, the greater the protests.

In summer 1974, United Farm Workers' leader Cesar Chávez lent support to the struggle, but the attempt to have a farmworkers bill passed in the Connecticut General Assembly was frustrated. Growers, it was reported, "insisted that an anti-strike clause must be included in the bill, or else their livelihoods would be in danger. The tobacco growers also threatened to move their operations to Latin America, where they hoped to find both good growing conditions and a docile labor force."[24] Newspaper articles, protests and court cases had focused a great deal of attention on the Puerto Rican migrant farmworker programme, which shrank from some twelve thousand workers in

1974 to less than two thousand in 1984 as farms mechanised and operations relocated abroad; Puerto Ricans still in the state sought to settle in nearby cities and find other work.[25]

The Dominican Republic: From Connecticut to Cibao to New York

The late twentieth-century Cuban-Dominican connection directly follows from this Puerto Rican history, as companies headed south.[26] In the accepted twentieth-century periodisation of Dominican tobacco history, 1903-29 saw the rise of manufacturing in cigars and then cigarettes, in tandem with the growth of the central Cibao region's agriculture and industry and of its capital, Santiago de los Caballeros, home to León Jimenes's La Aurora cigar factory.[27] From 1930 to 1961 the Cibao stagnated under General Rafael Leónidas Trujillo's state monopoly Compañía Anónima del Tabaco (CAT). The post-Trujillo years, 1962-82, saw renewed expansion, with León Jimenes undercutting CAT, and post-1982 witnessed the rise of the Cibao's global cigar positioning.

After the 1959 Cuban Revolution, the seeds were (literally) sown for the Cuban-type Dominican leaf to replace the embargoed Cuban leaf on the US market, and Dominican overtook Cuban production and export levels by the late 1980s. In 1962 Washington sent the exiled Cuban tobacco agronomist Napoleón Padilla to help set up the Dominican Tobacco Institute (INTABACO).[28] In 1963 Cuban cigar leaf seed was introduced; 1964-65 saw the first experiments in producing the San Vicente wrapper, also from Cuba, although it was not planted commercially until 1974. By now administrators and other employees of tobacco estates and processing and packing plants were exiled Cubans. Thus, Fernando Ferrán refers to "the help of Cuban farmers and producers who transposed a technology that was relatively complex . . . after Castro took power in Cuba. It was in the interest of the Dominican government . . . to take over the market that the Cuban government had lost in the United States."[29] Tobacco exports doubled in value from 1962 to 1971, with the Cibao region producing 70 percent of the country's tobacco.

Cuban émigré tobacco interests operated in Nicaragua after 1963, with land grants and concessions from President Anastasio Somoza, but the 1979 Nicaraguan Revolution ushered in a shift to Honduras and the Dominican Republic, where free trade zones (FTZs) offered cheap labour and tax concessions for foreign investors.[30] In 1978, in the three main FTZs of La Romana, San Pedro de Macorís and Santiago, some forty FTZ tobacco plants employed more than four thousand workers.[31] By 1984 the country had sixty such plants, and by 1988 it was the largest supplier of leaf to the United States and the leading world cigar exporter (more than 50 million units), followed by Cuba

(49 million) and Honduras (32 million). By the early 1990s a small group of companies dominated the sector – León Asensio in Tamboril was one of the largest agro-industrial complexes – and trade was controlled by six US, Dutch and Spanish exporting companies, and their Dominican subsidiaries.

The time was ripe for the engineered comeback of *Cigar Aficionado*, whose 1992 inaugural issue carried three features: two on Cuba, in crisis following the breakup of the Eastern European socialist bloc, and one on the burgeoning Dominican Republic.[32] Dominican exports grew from 73 million in 1991 to 320 million in 1998, predominantly to the United States, and tobacco was third in exports (after ferro-nickel and sugar). The *Miami Herald* delightedly reported that Cuban cigar experts would be spending several weeks in the Dominican Republic in the winter of 1998, observing production and marketing techniques.[33] There were by then 130 registered cigar manufacturers in the Dominican Republic, 18 in FTZs, employing 125,000, with some 55,000 in agriculture. Santiago's Victor Espaillat Mera FTZ (established 1975) produced 80 percent of the country's cigars, and Santiago's population had doubled from the early 1980s to the mid-1990s, as had other cigar centers (Villa González, Licey, San José de las Matas, Janico, Villa Bosono and Tamboril).

Yet all was not well. While traditional companies strengthened, a multitude of smaller companies formed. Some of these were operated by Cubans long in the business, but many others had little or no knowledge, which led to poor quality leaf and cigars. According to Cuban American Carlos Fuente, who relocated from Tampa in 1980, Tamboril was a Vietnam, a war zone – they were shooting machine guns in the streets. A Santiago FTZ was attractive by comparison, and export factories clustered there, bussing in workers from Tamboril. This changed with the boom, when newcomers in Tamboril began poaching in earnest. "We woke up one January," Cuban American Manuel Quesada declared, "and between Fuente, Davidoff, ourselves and León Jimenes, we were missing 300 to 400 cigar workers."[34] La Romana, in the east, was sheltered from the 'roller wars', whereby Tabacalera de García fared better than most. Tamboril, however, which went from two to eighty factories, saw sixty of these 'mavericks' go out of business in 1997-99. Such was the tobacco glut that, pressured by growers, the state intervened to buy tobacco at above-market prices and restrict planting; and President Leonel Fernández was urged to find a solution to the worst tobacco crisis in memory.

It was the major companies that subsequently picked up the business, such that in 2002 five main manufacturers were in place: Tabacalera Arturo Fuente; Tabacalera de García (subsidiary of Altadis USA, whose brands included H. Upmann, La Corona, Montecristo and Romeo y Julieta); General Cigar (including Cohíba, Macanudo – for which Jamaica was once famous – and Partagás); MATASA; and Tabacos Dominicanos (including Davidoff). Tabacalera de

García's La Romana factory was declared the largest factory under one roof in the world.

Nothing, however, could stem a rural-urban-overseas drift. In the 1980s Fernando Ferrán and Patricia Pessar studied seven communities linked with major export commodities, including, for tobacco, Licey and Tamboril, and Max Castro also studied Licey.[35] These researchers documented small farmers driven into the ranks of the landless searching for agricultural work, for whom emigration became a strategy. From 1980 to 1990 the 'Dominican York' population doubled, becoming the fastest-growing ethnic group in a city that by 2000 was home to more than half the million-plus Dominicans in the United States. A dynamic enclave small-business economy emerged, including small storefront *tabaquerías* that hand-rolled cigars, some bought from Cubans, others started up by Dominicans but playing on Cuba's name – as in Rosa Cubana. Typically these entrepreneurs came from Tamboril, Licey and Santiago.[36]

At What Cost and Whither the Future?

In the peak year of 1997, the Santiago de Caballeros daily *Listín Diario* brought out a new supplement, *Cigarro*, whose second issue featured a congratulatory letter to the editor from José León: "In this day and age of real globalisation and world integration, in which the comparative advantages of each nation need to be strongly promoted, the Dominican Republic must show the world that it is we who offer the best beaches, the best sun, the best *merengue*, and above all, the best cigar in the world."[37]

David Savona, writing in 2004 in *Cigar Aficionado*, was more circumspect: "It is hard to imagine a cigar world without the Dominican Republic, but the country hasn't been a market for long. Although its oldest cigar maker, La Aurora SA, has been in business for a century, most of the cigars it made in the past were for local consumption. In the 1970s the first free trade zones opened in the country, welcoming companies that would make cigars strictly for export. It took nearly a decade for the Dominican Republic to overtake the Canary Islands and Jamaica to become the leading cigar producer for the United States."[38]

At the start of the Dominican boom, Guillermo León was named executive vice-president of La Aurora. Charged with developing the US market, he became a stalwart of ProCigar, the Dominican cigar association. Questioned by *Cigar Aficionado*, he doubted that they would establish a factory in Cuba – not only were their roots not Cuban, but they were also very traditional and very Dominican, defending their national pride to the end. "We have good relationships with people from Havana. They have visited us at La Aurora. But that's it."[39]

Dominican cigar 'success' is undeniable. Yet at what cost, with the loss of Jamaican and Puerto Rican tobacco, and with a Dominican model whereby the dispossessed have poured out of the countryside and into the cities of Santiago, Santo Domingo and New York? And what might happen when the US embargo on Cuba does finally end? Will the Dominican-produced cigar hold its own or will the inevitable delight of the forbidden fruit of Cuba oust it from favor, notwithstanding the higher price of the 'authentic' Havana? The intrepid US cigar smoker already acquires Cuban cigars through various channels – buying them when traveling abroad in third countries or over the Internet or through distant friends. More importantly perhaps, in the fast-changing global economy in which China has already emerged as Cuba's principal cigar market, the real question to be asked is whether the US market might be destined to remain marginal, with or without the embargo.

Notes

1   For the ideas expressed in this chapter I am indebted to my colleagues in the Commodities of Empire British Academy Research Project, and in our sister collaborative projects Plants, People and Work (International Institute of Social History, Amsterdam) and Global Commodity Chains (University of Konstanz). The research underpinning this chapter was facilitated through semesters spent as a Rockefeller Scholar at the University of Florida (1993) and at Florida International University and the University of Puerto Rico (1998), and by funding from the British Academy and London Metropolitan University's Caribbean Studies Centre. I owe a special debt of gratitude to the Center for Latin American Studies, University of Florida, for having me as their 2011 Spring Semester Barcardi Scholar, enabling me to further my Florida research and to benefit not only from their excellent Latin American and Caribbean Library Special Collections, but also from the knowledge and ideas of colleagues who have helped inform my thinking.
2   A classic on this subject is Gary Gereffi & Miguel Korzeniewicz (eds), *Commodity Chains and Global Capitalism* (Westport: Praeger, 1994), which includes Terence Hopkins & Immanuel Wallerstein, 'Commodity Chains: Construct and Research'.
3   I am thinking here of Appadurai's regimes of values and concepts of commodification. See Arjun Appadurai (ed.), *The Social Life of Things: Commodities in Cultural Perspective* (Cambridge: Cambridge University Press, 1986), and *Modernity at Large: Cultural Dimensions of Globalization* (Minneapolis: University of Minnesota Press, 1996). See also James Ferguson, 'Cultural Exchange: New Developments in the Anthropology of Commodities', *Cultural Anthropology* 3 (1988), pp.488-513; Philip Raikes, Michael Friis Jensen & Stefano Ponte, 'Global Commodity Chain Analysis and the French *Filière* Approach: Comparison and Critique', *Economy and Society* 29:3 (Aug 2000), pp.390-417; Peter Dicken, Philip F. Kelly, Kris Olds & Henry Wai-Chung Yeung, 'Chains and Networks, Territories and Scales: Towards a Relational Framework for Analysing the Global Economy', *Global Networks* 1:2 (2001), pp.89-112; Alex Hughes & Suzanne Reimer (eds), *Geographies of Commodity Chains* (London & New York: Routledge, 2004).
4   This is detailed in my '*El Habano* and the World It Has Shaped: Cuba, Connecticut

and Indonesia', *Cuban Studies*, 41 (2010), pp.39-67 – Chapter 13 in the present volume.
5   I discuss this in 'Havana Cigars and the West's Imagination', in Sander L. Gilman and Zhou Xun (eds), *Smoke: A Global History of Smoking* (London: Reaktion Press, 2004), pp.134-9 – Chapter 10 in the present volume.
6   I concur with Juan José Baldrich's analysis of 'the Cuba paradigm', derived from his work on Puerto Rican tobacco. See, for instance, Baldrich, *Sembraron la no siembra: Los cosecheros de tabaco puertoriqueños frente a la corporaciones tabacaleras, 1920-1934* (Río Piedras: Huracán, 1988).
7   I am indebted to Paul Losch, assistant head of the Latin American and Caribbean Library at the University of Florida, for initially dropping the comment that there had been Cuban cigar factories in Gainesville and pointing out the footnote in Gerardo Castellanos, *Motivos de Cayo Hueso* (Havana: Ucar, García y Cia, 1935), p.300. Both he and head librarian Richard Phillips have since plied me with references and articles, and Kyle Doherty has been conducting research with me that suggests a more significant North Florida history than previously thought, spanning Gainesville, Fernandina, Lake City, Live Oak, St Augustine and Waldo.
8   I documented the earlier Cuban-Jamaican history in 'Political Idealism and Commodity Production: Cuban Tobacco in Jamaica, 1870-1930', *Cuban Studies*, 25 (1995), pp.51-81 – Chapter 7 in the present volume.
9   Guillermo P. González, *Tobacco Culture: As Practiced in Cuba* (Port Royal: De Cordova, McDougal, 1873). For the British declaration, see Hon. W. Fawcett, 'Tobacco in Jamaica', *West Indian Bulletin* 8:2 (1907), 209. See also *The Machado Story: A Pioneer Industry in Jamaica, 1874-1962* (Kingston: B. & J. B. Machado Co. Ltd., n.d.). They began importing leaf from Cuba and employing some twenty-five Cuban cigar makers in 1874. Within a few years they had three hundred workers, and they registered their first trademarks: Fantasía Habanera Cigarros Superiores and La Tropical.
10 'Governor's Report on Blue Book of 1881', *Jamaica Departmental Reports* (Kingston, Jamaica: Government Printing Establishment), xxv. In the report the general's name was given as "Vijegas".
11 'Governor's Report on Blue Book of 1891-92' and 'Director of Public Gardens and Plantations', *Jamaica Departmental Reports* (Kingston, Jamaica: Government Printing Establishment), xvii.
12 See P. J. Anderson, 'Growing Tobacco in Connecticut;' *Connecticut Agricultural Experiment Station Bulletin* 564 (January 1953); and Randall R. Kincaid, 'Shade Tobacco Growing in Florida;' *Quincy North Florida Experimental Station Bulletin* 136 (May 1960 [1956]). Anadel Schnip and Katya Williamson (eds), *Changing Landscape through People: Connecticut Valley Tobacco, a Documentary of Photographs and Writing for the 1980s* (n.p., n.d.), is one of several nostalgic photographic books capturing Connecticut's shade past.
13 James E. O'Gorman, *Connecticut Valley Vernacular: The Vanishing Landscape and Architecture of the New England Tobacco Fields*, with photographs by Jack Delano (Philadelphia: University of Pennsylvania Press, 2002), p.5.
14 Mildred Savage, *Parrish* (New York: Simon & Shuster, 1958).
15 Quoted in O'Gorman, *Connecticut Valley Vernacular* (2002), p.37.
16 S. K. Close, 'The Ties That Bind: Southwest Georgians, Black College Students, and Migration to Hartford', *Journal of South Georgia History* 15 (2000), p.19. For employment of high school students, see *Windsor Storytellers: A Chronicle of 20th Century Life in Windsor* (Windsor: Windsor Historical Society, 1999).
17 Fay Clarke Johnson, *Soldiers of the Soil* (New York: Vantage Press, 1995). She recalls "Fifty years ago, around the Second World War years, there was no talk about the hazards of tobacco. Rather, tobacco was considered to be the savior of the day . . . almost as important as bullets" (p. 3). Smoking promised contentment, satisfaction,

consolation. The rallying cry was "Keep the Boys in Smokes": Thousands of Jamaican men signed up to contribute to the war effort while also seeking adventure and economic betterment.
18 Ibid., pp.70 & 80; quotations are from Jamaica's *Daily Gleaner* (11 October 1943), and *Hartford Courant* (29 July 1944).
19 Savage, *Parrish* (1958), p.12.
20 Ruth Glasser, *Aquí me quedo: Puerto Ricans in Connecticut* (Middletown: Connecticut Humanities Council, 1997), pp.54-5.
21 See Juan José Baldrich, 'From the Origins of Capitalism in Puerto Rico to its subordination to the US Tobacco Trust: Rucabado and Company, 1865-1901', *Revista Mexicana del Caribe* 3:5 (1998), pp.80-106; M. Burgos Malave, 'El conflicto tabacalero entre Cuba y Puerto Rico', *Revista de Estudios Generales* 4:4 (1989-90), pp.181-91; Teresita A. Levy, 'The History of Tobacco Cultivation in Puerto Rico, 1899-1940', PhD dissertation, City University of New York (2007). See also N. Valle Ferrer, *Luisa Capetillo: Historia de una mujer proscrita* (Río Piedras: Editorial Cultural, 1990 [1975]); Julio Ramos (ed.), *Amor y anarquía: Los escritos de Luisa Capetillo* (Río Piedras: Ediciones Huracán, 1992); and Cesar Andreu Iglesias (ed.), *Memoirs of Bernardo Vega* (New York: Monthly Review Press, 1984 [1977]).
22 Records housed in the Library of CENTRO, the Center for Puerto Rican Studies, Hunter College, City University of New York, were catalogued and made available for public consultation in late 2004. They include the archives of the Farm Labor Program (1848-1993), Connecticut Shade Tobacco Growers Agricultural Association Files (STGAA) (1955-76), Regional and Field Offices (1948-93), Hartford Regional Office (1961-84), and Regional Field Office Farm Laborer Files (1958-83). Rich collections are also housed at Hartford State Library; the Hartford Project, Trinity College, Hartford; University of Connecticut, Storrs; Windsor Tobacco Museum; and the Windsor Historical Society.
23 STGAA, CEPR, Windsor, File 30, Box 2526.
24 Ibid.
25 The Trinity College Hartford Project holds video copies of two excellent documentaries on the Connecticut Puerto Rican and tobacco history: *Puerto Rican Passages* (1995) and *Connecticut's Tobacco Valley* (2001).
26 I draw here on my more detailed discussion in 'Reinventing Mecca: Tobacco in the Dominican Republic, 1763-2007', Commodities of Empire Working Paper, 3 (2007), at https://commoditiesofempire.org.uk/publications/working-papers/working-paper-3) – Chapter 12 in the present volume.
27 Grupo León Jimenes celebrated the centenary of La Aurora by opening the state-of-the-art Eduardo León Jimenes Centro Cultural and publishing José AlcantaraAlmánazar & Ida Hernández Caamaño, *Huella y memoria: E. Leoón Jimenes: un siglo en el camino nacional, 1903-2003* (Santo Domingo: Grupo León, 2003). For the most recent of a spate of tobacco studies since the 1970s, see José Chez Checo & Mu-Kien Adriana Sang, *El tabaco: historia general en República Dominicana* (Santo Domingo: Grupo León Jimenes, 2007).
28 Napoleón S. Padilla, *Memorias de un cubano sin importancia* (Hialeah: AC Graphics, 1998).
29 Fernando I. Ferrán, *Tabaco y sociedad: la organización del poder en el ecomercado de tabaco dominicano* (Santo Domingo: Fondo para el Avance de las Ciencias Sociales, 1976), p.58.
30 The FTZ explosion had its early beginnings in 1967, when the US conglomerate Gulf & Western took over the US-owned South Puerto Rico Sugar Company, and with it almost 300,000 acres of land around La Romana refinery, and then rapidly diversified. In 1985, when the sugar industry was in crisis, and having profited greatly by speculating on Dominican sugar on the futures market, Gulf & Western sold its Dominican holdings to a Palm Beach-based consortium headed by the Fanjul family – émigrés from Cuba with major sugar holdings, which is a whole other story.

31 Economist Intelligence Unit, *Dominican Republic: Annual Supplement, 1978* (London: EIU, 1978).
32 Gordon Mott, 'Cigar Land: The Dominican Republic Has Become One of the World's Largest Producers of Premium Cigars', *Cigar Aficionado* (Autumn 1992).
33 Juan O. Tamayo, 'Castro to Firm up Ties with Dominicans', *Miami Herald* (17 August 1998).
34 Marvin R. Shanken, 'An Interview with Manuel Quesada: Owner, MATASA, Makers of Fonseca, Licenciados, Romeo y Julieta, José Benito, Cubita, Royal Dominicans, Credo and Casa Blanca Cigars', *Cigar Aficionado* (January-February 1998).
35 Fernando Ferrán & Patricia Pessar, 'Dominican Agriculture and the Effects of International Migration', in Anthony Maingot (ed.), *Small Country Development and International Labor Flows* (Boulder: Westview Press, 1991); Max Castro, 'Dominican Journey: Patterns, Context, and Consequences of Migration from the Dominican Republic to the United States', PhD dissertation, University of North Carolina (1985). The creation of the Dominican Studies Institute at City College, City University of New York, provided an impulse to Dominican migration studies; an early entry was Sherri Grasmuck, 'International Stair-Step Migration: Dominican Labor in the United States and Haitian Labor in the Dominican Republic', in R. I. Harper Simpson (ed), *Research in the Sociology of Work: Peripheral Workers*, Vol. 2 (London: JAI Press, 1983), pp.149-72.
36 This I gleaned from an informal survey I conducted in 2006, using a snowball approach, to visit the shops and talk with the rollers.
37 *Cigarro*, magazine of *Listín Diario*, 2 (24 October 1997), p.4.
38 David Savona, 'Dominican Dominance', *Cigar Aficionado* (May-June 2004).
39 Gordon Mott, 'An Interview with Guillermo León: President, León Jimenes Cigars', *Cigar Aficionado* (July-August 1998).

17

Beyond Iberian Atlantic spaces: Trans-imperial and Trans-territorial Entanglements in Havana Cigar History (1756-1924)[*][1]

As the Spanish Empire waned, the impact of momentous developments elsewhere in Europe and across the Americas was to open up markets for Cuba's tobacco, especially the Havana cigar. In Europe, cigars were the predominant smoke in Holland and Germany, as well as Spain; the cigar, along with pipe smoking, grew in popularity in Britain and, along with snuff, in France and Italy. Cigars also rapidly gained ground, alongside plug tobacco, in the United States. In all these countries, there was a growing home industry for such commodities and large quantities were also imported. To satisfy export markets as well as domestic demand, manufacturing industries developed in many tobacco-growing countries, especially when unfettered by colonial restrictions.

However, manufacturing, protected by tariff barriers, developed at such a rapid pace in countries like Britain, France, Germany, Holland, Italy, Spain and the United States that these once major importers became more self-reliant and also major exporters. Cigarettes were also produced, but on nothing like the scale as when mechanisation would later revolutionise the industry, heralding the end of what had been 'the age of the cigar'.

---

[*] Originally published in Santiago de Luxán Meléndez & João Figueiro-Rego (eds), *El tabaco y la esclavitud en la rearticulación imperial ibérica (s.XVI-XX)* (Evora: Universidade de Evora, 2018), pp.389-426.

The history behind the Havana cigar's rise to fame was, from the outset, one of diverse trans-imperial and trans-territorial entanglements both within and ranging beyond the Iberian transatlantic world.[2] It was shaped by political and trade wars between imperial and newly independent nation states across the Americas, and Cuba's own burgeoning nationalism, insurrection against and independence from Spain, subsequent US dominance and revolution. Competing political, economic and social interests combined with in- and out-migration and resettlement to facilitate not only trade but also the spread and appropriation of knowledge and practice. Just as Spain would experiment 'back home' across the Atlantic, starting in the Canary Islands, so also the race was on among other imperial powers and their colonies, and in independent nations, to recreate in their territories the quality of the Havana cigar and its tobacco leaf.

To contextualise this history, I begin here by revisiting broader historiography to interrogate the temporality of the hand-crafted Havana cigar's entrée onto the world stage in a 'long nineteenth century' and 'British cycle' in world history,[3] that would see Spain's decline, resurgent Dutch competition, and British and US involvement in Cuba's tortuous path to frustrated sovereignty. I then draw on a range of sources, including my own earlier work,[4] that of Cuban scholars and writers[5] and Spanish historians who have worked on tobacco in Spain and the Spanish Empire,[6] other academic and popular histories of tobacco,[7] and glossy publications on the Havana cigar that have proliferated over recent years,[8] to chart the Havana cigar's rise to iconic status and the challenges this then posed. The stage is thus set for spatially mapping trans-imperial entanglements, which were already present in Cuba, in other territories near and far. This is then illustrated by two transnational counterpoints,[9] each nurtured on several levels, from the state to the subaltern, to cultivate 'Cuban-seed' cigar tobacco leaf, craft clone 'Cuban' cigars, and compete in the trade and consumption of both. The focus of the first counterpoint is more narrowly on British colonial Jamaica, Cuba's neighbouring island and part of the British West Indies. The second is broader, linking the far-distant Dutch East Indies, specifically the Indonesian island of Sumatra, with the closer United States, in particular northern New England and New York and southern Florida and Georgia. A brief concluding section signals the significance of origins and perceived origins in how Havana cigar history became quite so 'entangled'.

A Long Nineteenth Century

From a European perspective, the long nineteenth century as a historical concept is attributed perhaps most to Hobsbawm and his three classic volumes on the *The Age of Revolution: Europe 1789-1848*, *The Age of Capital: 1848-1875* and *The Age of Empire: 1875-1914*.[10] Hobsbawm's underlying argument was that the political and economic dual revolution, the political being the French and the economic being the (primarily British) industrial revolution, challenged old elite power structures and enabled subsequent capital and imperial ventures that fundamentally changed the world. The outbreak of the First World War marked the waning of the European nineteenth-century power balance. The title to his sequel *The Age of Extremes: The Short Twentieth Century, 1914-1991* speaks for itself, its endpoint being the fall of the Soviet Union.

The concept of the long century has earlier and later parallels, from Braudel's acclaimed earlier notion of the long sixteenth century for the Mediterranean world (1450-1640) to Stearns' later quest for extending the global long nineteenth century (1750-1914). For Stearns, the explanatory power of world history depended heavily on periodisation decisions regarding significant shifts in a range of factors, from trading patterns and technology to the challenges of empire formation, the impact of which varied according to time and place. Thus, Russia, Japan, China and the Ottoman Empire did not sit well with Hobsbawm's periodisation, nor did the Americas, where anti-colonial movements dating back earlier than 1789 were the backdrop to trans-Atlantic wars.

The rise of the modern world economy, it was argued, should be viewed in a more global frame that situates European powers as one set of competitors among many. Bayly, for example, contended that a prolonged global crisis profoundly changed the late eighteenth-century world. When the crisis ended, France had lost its first empire (Haiti, Canada and India) and been transformed by revolution. Britain had emerged with a power base in South Asia. The old Asian empires had entered a period of political and economic transformation, and the United States and most of Spain's colonies had become independent.

Arrighi, in what was for him a long twentieth century, succinctly recaps the development of capitalism's longue durée as a world system having four systemic cycles of accumulation, each with a certain overlap: a Genoese cycle, from the fifteenth to the early seventeenth centuries; a Dutch cycle, from the late sixteenth through most of the eighteenth century; a British cycle, from the latter half of the eighteenth through the early twentieth century; and a US cycle beginning in the late nineteenth century and continuing in the early 1990s, when he was writing. These cycles were associated with inter-state competition and the formation of political and organisational structures through imitation as well as innovation: to borrow Braudel's words, "Amsterdam copied Venice, as London would subsequently copy Amsterdam, and as New York would one day copy London."[11] In the cycle of hegemonic British 'free-trade' imperialism, Arrighi argued, colonialism, capitalist slavery and economic nationalism would all play their part, as also the rebelliousness that would ultimately be its downfall.

Bulmer-Thomas, in his recent economic history of the Caribbean since the Napoleonic Wars, likewise argued the case for the "age of free trade" along the British liberal model but in a short nineteenth-century, lasting from the end of the Napoleonic Wars in 1815 to the Spanish-American War of 1898. This was the period witnessing the end of mercantilism and rise of economic liberalism, when transfers of sovereignty among European colonial powers were coming to an end in the region. After the British ending of the slave trade in 1807, restrictions and monopolistic practices gave way to a new orthodoxy based on imperial preference. Spain (which, along with Portugal, was conspicuously absent from Arrighi's cycles) gave its colonies the right to trade with all countries while imposing tariffs favouring Spanish goods in Spanish ships, much along the lines of England's earlier Navigation Acts; and France similarly introduced its own tariffs. By the final emancipation from slavery in the Caribbean (conceded by Spain in Cuba in 1886), orthodoxy had changed again. Britain and Holland had eliminated imperial preferences, independent territories had adopted tariff systems, and the door was open for US encroachment in the region. Basing his notion of 'long' or 'short' century on cycles of growth or depression, Bulmer-Thomas saw the end of the nineteenth century as coinciding with the Spanish-American War in 1898, which marked the end of Spain as a colonial power in the Caribbean and the rise of the US empire with its colonies and neo-colonies.

In his previous economic history of Latin America since independence, Bulmer-Thomas chose as his start date that of Napoleon's 1808 invasion of the Iberian Peninsula. This undermined Spanish authority in Latin America and provided the hitherto weak independence movement with impetus it desperately needed. He did, however, signal how Spain's Bourbon reforms, which started in 1759, while not formally abandoning monopoly of external trade in Spanish America, had attempted to overhaul the external and internal trading systems, making the business of exporting and importing easier. With the exception of a handful of royal monopolies, such as tobacco, most productive activities were in private hands, and after independence tobacco also benefited from greater free trade and access to international capital markets. Spanish America, in effect, became Britain's 'informal empire'.[12]

In the case of Cuba and its iconic Havana cigar, an argument might well be made for Bulmer-Thomas's Caribbean short nineteenth century: 1817, after all, marked the lifting of the Spanish tobacco monopoly and 1898 the end of Spanish rule. However, a compelling argument can be made for the long century corresponding to Arrighi's 'British cycle', starting earlier than the date Bulmer-Thomas adopted in his Latin American history and also ending later.

In recent work of my own,[13] I began to question that it was the lifting of the Spanish monopoly that heralded the Havana cigar's coming of age, and I set the clock back to the outbreak of the Seven Years' War.[14] I am now drawn to develop this further and argue that international political events, starting with the Seven Years' War (1756-63), which saw the British occupation of Havana (1762-3), followed by the American Revolutionary War (1765-83), the French Revolution and French Revolutionary Wars (1789-99), the Haitian Revolution (1791-1804), and finally the Napoleonic Wars (1803-15), were all instrumental in weakening the already tenuous Spanish hold over Cuban tobacco.

Salient among Spanish historiography, for my purposes here, are the longue-durée studies by Fradera. In his most recent work on the imperial nation, Fradera signals the great revolutionary wave deriving from imperial wars in the Atlantic and Indian Oceans. Decolonisation in the Americas – French (1763-1803), British (1776-83), Spanish (1810-24), and Portuguese (1822) – put in crisis the Atlantic monarchies and empires of the 'Old Regime' compared with (imperial) nations and states developing in 'the liberal era' over the period 1750-1918. In his earlier work on Spain's 'post-imperial' colonies – Cuba, Puerto Rico and the Philippines – Fradera held that all were marked by transition, which enabled the colonial relationship to endure a cycle starting with the Seven Years' War up until the institutional 'colonial pact' began to break down. The Seven Years' War, which saw the British occupation of Manila and Havana, coincided with the emergence of the Second British Empire in Asia (and later Africa)[15] and the incipient Monroe Doctrine as applied by the nascent United States to the Caribbean. According to Fradera, the Spanish empire in decline managed to recompose with a new colonial model for its three territories, each with its similarities and differences. Tropical agriculture was one, whereby Cuba would prioritise sugar, Puerto Rico coffee and the Philippines tobacco. In the Cuban case, the Spanish 'colonial pact' was primarily with the saccarocracy and their large slave plantations. As we shall see, however, and on Fradera's own admission, this left room for maneuver in tobacco.

More specifically, on the Spanish Atlantic tobacco complex and Cuba's role within it, Spain's weak monopoly hold has been examined by, among others, Luxán, Gárate Ojanguren, Sanz Rozalén and Bergasa Perdomo in Spain, Cosner in the United States, and Náter in Mexico.[16] They all attach importance to late eighteenth-century events in repositioning Cuban tobacco in the Atlantic world. In defense of a commodity approach that takes into account territorial temporal specificity, I might highlight here the later start dates chosen for analysis in the case of Canary Island tobacco by Luxán (1827-1936) and Arnaldos Martínez and Arnaldos de Armas (1852-2002):[17] the year 1827 was when the crown authorised tobacco-growing trials in the Canaries and 1852 saw the introduction of the Canary Islands as a free port, a date which Luxán also recognised as a subsequent turning point. Free ports, it must be said, were at the time very much in tune with the British, who themselves made their mark in the Canaries. Here I have chosen not to focus on the Cuba-Canary Islands connection, by no means to downplay the integral role this has played in Havana cigar history, rather to highlight other trans-imperial/trans-territorial connections.

In effect, the Seven Years' War cemented a process of opening Cuban tobacco to British, French, German and US, as well as Spanish, capital and trade, paving the way for the Havana cigar to conquer European and North American markets. Thereafter, the Havana would become *de rigueur* in the male entrepreneurial world of the rapidly growing industrial, trading and financial conurbations such as London, Amsterdam, Bremen, Hamburg, Paris, Montreal and New York. With its fine taste and aroma, and its smoke assuaging the senses, the Havana made its mark as one of life's pleasurable luxuries, sending out a message of wealth, power and distinction across the world. This it retained, though taking serious knocks in Cuba's turbulent times and in the face of technological change. It was the First World War and its aftermath that marked the cigarette becoming the smoke of choice, by which time the threat of cigar mechanisation also loomed ominously over the hand-rolled cigar, leaving the Havana's fate hanging perilously in the balance.

The Havana's Long Century

Intrinsic to Hobsbawm's analysis was that the great revolution was the triumph not of industry as such but of capitalist industry, not of liberty and equality in general but of middle class or bourgeois liberal society, not of the modern economy and state but those of a particular geographical region of the world (parts of Europe and North America). The neighbouring and rival states of Great Britain and France were, in his words, twin craters of a larger volcano, simultaneous eruptions that reverberated around the world. The sequel periods of capital and empire saw the rise of bourgeois liberal regimes, nation states, industrial economies, world trading and financial systems, and European domination of the rest of the world. Capitalist enterprise, the engine of change, the agency of the transformation of the world, however, also contained within itself the seeds of its own decay. The bourgeoisie sought protection for their commercial interests through the pursuit of empire, only to see capitalism and imperialism slide into a major conflagration of global impact.

Curiously, in Hobsbawm's texts there is scant reference to the rise and demise of commodities, the quest for which fuelled the developments he so eloquently described. Yet his description of the rise of bourgeois liberal society was so classically mirrored by that of Ortiz in accounting for the rise of the Havana cigar:

> As civil liberties triumphed and political constitutions were guaranteed, the cigar came into ascendancy once more, coinciding with the advent

of economic liberalism in Cuba, which threw the port of Havana open to all nations. And in this atmosphere of free industrial and commercial enterprise Havana tobacco, by the unanimous plebiscite of the world, was awarded the imperial scepter of the tobacco world. Havana tobacco from then on became the symbol of the triumphant capitalistic bourgeoisie.[18]

Ortiz fashioned a counterpoint out of Cuba's two major commodities, encapsulated in the lowly sugar sack and the proud cigar band. In Cuba, the cigar came to be called simply *un tabaco* (a tobacco), *un puro* (pure in that it was made wholly with Cuban leaf), or *un habano* (a Havana, by virtue of the port city through which it made its entrée into the world). For Ortiz, sugar signified slavery and dependence while tobacco symbolised freedom and independence.

The Ortiz counterpoint was one turned on its head in earlier times, as argued by Moreno Fraginals. Boldly asserting "Cuba was the island most coveted by British interests,"[19] he attributed the success of the 1761 British attack on Havana to the wider context of the birth of the industrial revolution generating stronger, precision artillery that rendered obsolete the concept of a city's defenses. He also argued the British occupation made more transparent the breach between the power of the metropolitan Spanish Peninsula and the creole Havana oligarchy, when tobacco had been the peninsular monopoly and sugar an essentially local activity. The British occupying force suppressed Spanish central government yet retained local political structures, allowing the Havana oligarchy to benefit from British naval and trade superiority and expand sugar and plantation slavery. In his words:

> This reframes the old counterpoint of sugar and tobacco, which, aside from its economic significance, had exceptional political connotations. It was the battle between sugar dominated by creole social forces, produced in units of private property, and sold on the free market, and tobacco under Spanish colonial interests, grown by labour organised under a state institution, and its sale subject to monopoly controls. What is in counterpoint was not two commodities and two sets of interests, but rather two economic systems, and, up to a point, two nationalities, the peninsular Spanish and the nascent Cuban-Spanish.[20]

Such a politics of sugar and tobacco sits at odds with Spain's 'colonial pact', as formulated by Fradera, and also Ortiz's counterpoint. In the rapidly changing landscape, however, Moreno Fraginals conceded tobacco was one of the few plants that survived and multiplied at the hands of new settlers. A case in point, in the push for late eighteenth-century sugar expansion, was the emergence of western Vuelta Abajo, a region whose soils and climate would prove particularly suitable for cultivating cigar wrapper leaf, which became a fine complement to the mainly filler tobacco of central Vuelta Arriba.

Moreno Fraginals also pointed to how the United States emerged well positioned:

> After 1763, the English Thirteen Colonies began to trade broadly with Cuba, and this increased in an unforeseen way when the colonies became the United States of America and with the changing economic and political status of the Caribbean when the French Revolution triggered a period of continuous wars which accelerated the decline of the Spanish empire, breaking the fluid communication between Cuba and the metropolis and upturning world trade.[21]

As the revolution in Saint Domingue catapulted Cuba into world primacy, "Havana lived through an absurd millionaire orgy,"[22] with a free-for-all of trade in ships of many nations. During the years when Spain was at war with France and Britain, the United States became the neutrals controlling much of the trade in Cuban sugar and all that was connected with it, presaging how they would also later seek to control much of Cuban tobacco.

There is a certain historical inevitability to macro and micro tobacco histories sparking the Seven Years' War and shaping subsequent developments.[23] Washington, the lieutenant colonel son of a Virginia tobacco-farming family (later first US President, 1789-97), triggered France declaring war on Britain, which in turn declared war on Spain. According to Jefferson (third US President 1801-09), himself a Virginia tobacco farmer, this was the backdrop to the 1776 Declaration of Independence of Britain's Thirteen Colonies, which forged alliances with France (1778) and Spain (1779) and ultimately peace with Britain (1782). Tobacco debts were negotiated as part of reparations, and trade resumed. In France, the expenses of war and the court occasioned taxes deemed intolerable by a people (of smokers) who rose up in revolution in 1789, and snuff (the mark of aristocracy) fell out of favour. Napoleon raised tobacco taxes to finance his armies and redraw the political map of Europe, in the process profoundly changing the continent's smoking habits. Having defeated the combined French and Spanish fleet at Trafalgar and with Britain subject to continental blockade, an 1808 British expeditionary force was sent to Spain and took to smoking cigars, as had the French occupying Andalusia. Britain's triumph at Waterloo was a triumph for the cigar, whose virtues were extolled by the Romantics. The House of Commons introduced a designated smoking chamber, and smoking jacket and cap were donned. Tobacconists specialised in cigar imports, as cigar imports skyrocketed.

Across the Atlantic, Napoleon's 1803 Louisiana sale doubled the size of the emergent United States and moved the frontier west, where Hispanics already smoked cigars. Along the eastern seaboard, the growing popularity of the 'Spanish' cigar was attributed to General Putnam's return from the British occupation of Havana with three donkeys laden with Havana cigars, which he sold in a tavern in Connecticut. Cuban seed was imported to grow cigar leaf and produce cigars there, and, by the 1820s, the likes of Adams (sixth US President 1825-29) were inveterate cigar smokers.

With free trade, Cuban cigars gained in preference. Shipping using the port of Havana increased, steam ships shortened crossings, commerce boomed, and Cuban tobacco growing and cigar manufacturing flourished. The earliest rolling shop of importance was said to be Hija de Cabañas y Carvajal, founded in 1810 by Francisco Cabañas, who had been rolling cigars since 1797. It was his *segar*, which would first hit the London market, where, by the 1820s, hand-rolled Havanas had a solid reputation. Among those consolidating Havana rolling shops were Jaime Partagás (1827) and Ambrosio de Larrañaga (1834) and Havana, with some 400 shops, was fast becoming 'tobacco city'. London prices for Havanas doubled and trebled, according to size and class, from 1828 to 1847. Catering to this growing demand in Britain, as well as Germany, Denmark and France, and to a lesser extent the United States and Spain, Cuban cigar rolling shops would multiple to over 1,200 throughout the island, 516 in Havana, with 158 registered as first class (with 50 workers or more). The Cabañas factory was recorded as having 300, and other major cigar factories included new ones such as H. Upmann's La Madama (1844), followed by Gustav Bock's Aguila de Oro, both early signs of direct German investment, and La Corona (1845). International accolades accrued: Cabañas took the Gold Medal at the 1851 Queen Victoria's Great Exhibition in London, and Partagás took Gold at the 1867 Paris World Fair.

A turning point had been reached, however, with the 1850s European trade depression. While the British market remained buoyant, German and French imports dropped by two thirds and one half, respectively. By the 1870s, the United States was Cuba's only fast-growing market, handling virtually all Cuba's cigar exports; and, by the 1890s, total cigar export figures were at half the 1850s level. Over that same period, leaf exports to those same countries increased by one third. Whereas in 1859, the value of cigar exports had been twice that of leaf, in 1890 the value of leaf exports was twice that of cigars.[24]

By the 1850s, US manufacturers were producing 'clear Havanas' made with Cuban leaf and retailing them at four to five times the price of the domestic cigar, and 'half-Spanish' had become literally true of the US industry as a whole. The amount of Cuban leaf imported – mainly through New York – was about equal to the domestic leaf produced in the whole of New England, and the Havana leaf was well established as the *sine qua non* of a good cigar.

A strong Havana tobacco oligarchy expressed growing concern over the future of Cuban manufacturing and the extent to which tariffs, especially US tariffs, could hit the industry. The 1856 US tariff, brought in to protect the domestic tobacco industry, was a case in point: Cuba's tobacco exports dropped by one-third overnight. Foreign competition, overseas tariffs and heavy Spanish-imposed taxes and export duties made for Cuba's anomalous position of political dependence on Spain – whose interests lay in protecting its own manufacturing interests – and economic dependence on non-Spanish markets, especially the United States – which had its own incipient industry embarking along the same protectionist paths as its earlier European counterparts.

The upheavals of the Cuban wars for independence from Spain – the Ten Years' War (1868-78), the Little War (1879-80) and the Great War (1895-98) – then took their toll.[25] *Habano* history was marked by out-migration of growers, manufacturers and workers, who took with them their trade and know-how. Conversely, British and US direct investment would consolidate in Cuba. In 1888, Henry Clay and Bock, and Partagás, were both set up as London companies under their same names, with Bock and Bances as their Havana managing directors. The British consul in Havana at the time commented how this would be regarded favourably by the Spanish and Cubans, because they understood that British interests were of a purely commercial character. The interests in Partagás, which had been largely directed to its leaf operations, were liquidated in 1896, but two years later the Havana Cigar and Tobacco Factories Ltd. was set up, subsuming Henry Clay and Bock and Co., with Bock as Havana managing director. The company came to control some of the largest factories in Havana, including 35 cigar and 18 cigarette brands.

Until this point, relations between the United States and Cuba as regards tobacco had been almost exclusively mercantile. Direct US investment came in 1899, when the Havana Commercial Company bought up one cigarette and twelve cigar factories in Havana, along with the important leaf operation of F. García Bros. and Company. It would massively increase when, in 1901, the American Tobacco Company (ATC), or Trust as it was known, combined some twenty factories under the newly created American Cigar Company. In 1902, after absorbing Havana Commercial, the Trust set up a new subsidiary, the Havana Tobacco Company (later to become Cuban Tobacco), to consolidate all its Cuban manufacturing and leaf holdings. Henry Clay and Bock and the Havana Cigar and Tobacco Factories Ltd. remained officially registered British companies but financial control passed to the Trust, which that year accounted for 90 percent of Cuba's cigar exports. A new subsidiary set up in 1903 was the Cuban Land & Leaf Tobacco Company, which came to control supplies of the much-sought-after Vuelta Abajo leaf.

Significantly, British capital had moved into a newly expanding Havana export industry of the 1880s. This was cut short when US protectionism reached a new height in the form of the McKinley Tariff-Law of 1890, almost doubling duties on imported cigars, leading to a new wave of out-migration from the sector and the growth of existing and new US manufacturing centres, undercutting the Cuban industry. Leading tobacco manufacturers in Cuba would plead with Spain:

> Before the rigours of the new US tariff, which places the tobacco of the island in the most precarious circumstances, and having moreover almost completely closed to it the market of the Peninsula, help should be given to this most important source of wealth.[26]

Their recommendations that there be an immediate end to export duties and a new trade treaty with the United States met with a stony response from Madrid:

> The criteria of the Government would be based on the necessity of harmonising the interests of Cuba with those of the regions of the Peninsula, largely favoured by the trade legislation in force in such a way that the former are producing as little as possible.[27]

The Compañia Arrendataria de España was at the time buying only half the stipulated amount of leaf and the entry of manufactured tobacco into the Peninsula was strictly limited. Taxes on tobacco manufacturing in Cuba were raised so much that in 1893 manufacturers in Cuba again appealed to Madrid, declaring that soon they would be unable to continue; and a year later they decried the export of leaf and closing down of manufacturing concerns, since a cigar made abroad with exclusively Cuban raw material was cheaper than that exported from Havana.

The Great War was devastating for tobacco, and in its aftermath US occupation would facilitate US investment, poised to sap its last strength with buy-out offers. After fierce competition between two cigar- and cigarette-manufacturing US and British giants, ATC and Imperial Tobacco Company (ITC) – each of which had grown out of cut-throat competition and the merger of former companies – the two had formed a new cartel, British American Tobacco (BAT). This would trade outside Britain and the United States, except for Cuba, which, like Puerto Rico, would be ATC domain. With Cuba under US occupation, Spain classified Cuban cigars as foreign and more than doubled imported duties. Cuba also lost markets in other countries, such that the British market was about the only important one left, and there duties were rapidly increasing. The 1903 Cuba-US Reciprocal Trade Treaty only served to exacerbate the Cuban trend of exporting leaf more than cigars.

There was, all the same, an element of restored prosperity, with some new injections of Spanish capital and companies changing hands: Ramón

Cifuentes y Llano was one who bought the Partagás factory in 1900. A bitter rivalry developed, however, between the Trust, represented by Bock, and the smaller family firms, known as 'independents', struggling to hold their own, honouring long-standing traditions and conditions, which, they claimed, the Trust didn't.[28] Unrest rocked the industry, and Bock himself resigned in 1909, a year before his death. By then the Trust was already transferring production to the United States, and its share of Cuba's cigar exports dropped from an initial 90 percent to only 52 percent in 1904. Under the 1911 US anti-trust Sherman Act, the company would be broken up into smaller companies, and, faced with opposition in Cuba, much of what was left of US-owned Cuban cigar manufacturing later wound up in the United States.

Cuban manufacturing shifted more into cigarette production, while most new capital over the decade 1910-20 went into leaf handling companies. The full long-term effects on Cuba's cigar industry would not be felt until the 1920s, by which time cigar exports had fallen by almost two thirds and the value of leaf exports was almost triple that of cigars. The cigar hand-rolling industry would tip into a critical period, when, in 1925, Por Larrañaga attempted to introduce the cigar machine in Cuba, setting up a new subsidiary, Cía Tabacalera Internacional, under special contract with the American Machine and Foundry Company. The company and its backers underestimated the opposition this would arouse. The machine's introduction was seen as suicidal to the nation's prestigious hand-rolling industry. A nation-wide battle to ban the machine ensued and was won. A far greater threat, however, was the 1920s cigarette boom and competition from the cheaper machine-made cigar elsewhere, and the onset of the 1929 world depression would bring the Cuban industry to a virtual standstill. That, and how it would rebound after is, of course, is another story.

Mapping Trans-imperial/Trans-territorial Arrangements

Tracing the transnational connections in Havana cigar history, some much further field than I initially thought, I found myself delving into systems of land tenure and labour, cultivation and manufacture, as well as realms of science and technology, knowledge and communication, patterns of consumption, brand advertising, legend and mystique.[29] I started out along this road thanks to the 1990s New York launch of the glossy *Cigar Aficionado*, which was highly successful in engineering – socially and culturally as well as commercially – an anti-antismoking cigar campaign.[30] Written for the cigar connoisseur and punctuated by aggressive marketing, it nurtured a contemporary cult of 'cigar cool', featuring articles on Cuba and a whole universe of where and by whom Havana cigar seed leaf was being grown outside the island and of what I came to call the 'offshore Havana cigar'. Some offshore cigars boasted identical brand names to those in Cuba, today referred to in Cuba as *dobles marcas* (dual brands), a modern-day rerun of the long-lamented older *imitaciones* (imitations) and *falsificaciones* (falsifications).

Behind the brands were global and local histories of leaf cultivation and cigar manufacturing, some more longue durée than others. For analytical purposes, I grouped these into four categories. First, there are closely interlocking histories of territories with significant migratory flows into and out of Cuba. Across the Atlantic, there was Spain, and especially the Canary Islands, geostrategically positioned on the route between Spain, Europe, Africa and the Americas. This fuelled mass migratory waves of Canary Islanders into Cuban tobacco as well as subsequent return migration into the Canary Islands' own tobacco growing and production, using a blend of tobaccos from various parts of the world.[31] Geographically closer to Cuba, in the neighbouring United States, there was Florida, best known for its nineteenth-century Cuban émigré southern Florida cigar histories of Key West, Tampa and Ybor City.[32] There was also, however, the lesser-known North Florida-South Georgia Cuban-cigar-tobacco-growing belt with its cigar centres such as Amsterdam, Gainesville, Havana, Jacksonville, Quincy and Thomasville.[33] Agronomists worked to locate soils and climatic areas for growing a Cuban-type cigar leaf and develop hybrid strains resistant to pests and blight. Earlier, migrant Cuban growers, workers and manufacturers had taken their skills and knowledge north, to New England and New York, whose explosion of cigar manufacturing would see an influx of cigar rollers from depressed regions of Europe, such as Bavaria, and also Cuba.[34] Finally, there was neighbouring British colonial Jamaica, with its little-known history of tobacco growers, workers and manufacturers who fled war-torn nineteenth-century Cuba to found the once-thriving Jamaican tobacco economy.[35]

In a second category are the closely intertwined histories of Puerto Rican and Cuban tobacco with no significant tobacco migration but closely monitored trade networks and circuits of knowledge.[36] Puerto Rico's own turbulent tobacco history of the late nineteenth and early twentieth centuries saw Puerto Rican cigar workers heading north to US manufacturing centres, especially but by no means exclusively New York, working alongside Cubans.[37] After 1898, tobacco was fostered on the island by US capital, and not without incurring opposition, subsequently to be undercut mid-century in the US-sanctioned, Puerto Rican strategy of Operation Bootstrap. State-engineered migrant farm labour programmes then transported displaced farmers and agricultural labourers from what were once tobacco areas in Puerto Rico to work in New England tobacco, especially the shade-tobacco fields of Connecticut.[38]

In the third category are cigar histories that have seen small yet significant catalysts of Cuban cigar migration over varying time frames – those of

Mexico, Costa Rica, the Dominican Republic, Ecuador, Honduras, Nicaragua, and also Brazil. Mexico was in the frame in the late nineteenth-century, while the Dominican Republic, Nicaragua and others would rise to prominence a century later as new epicentres of the offshore Havana cigar destined for the US market, where – under the US embargo on Cuba that had been in place since 1960 – the real Havana was forbidden fruit.[39]

Finally, further afield, there are Asian and African interconnections, linked to global cigar expansion. As descendants of pipe smokers became cigar smokers, the Netherlands exported more cigars per capita than any other nation except Denmark, overshadowing Spain and Cuba. By the latter part of the nineteenth century, it was the Dutch in their East Indies who would develop a cheaper Sumatra wrapper leaf that would ultimately flood the global market. The later wrapper leaf of Cuba, Connecticut and Florida-Georgia would itself be developed with hybrids and nets, deriving from that of the Dutch East Indies.[40] The tobacco history of the Philippines – a US colony until 1946 – in many ways developed in tandem with that of Cuba and Puerto Rico.[41] In Africa, while the British moved into territories such as Rhodesia growing Virginia tobacco leaf for cigarettes, in territories such as erstwhile French Cameroon, it was the Dutch who would develop Cameroon wrapper leaf. Today, Indonesian and Cameroon leaf are found in most blends used in cigars made outside Cuba.[42]

What follows delves into two histories in our long century under consideration here, one from the first and the other from the last of my four categories: British colonial Jamaica and Dutch Indonesia in tandem with the United States. In each, we shall see in operation, what McCook calls the neo-Colombian exchange, or second conquest of the Greater Caribbean and the 'global turn' in science.[43] McCook's argument is that new models of commodity-led economic development drove, directly or indirectly, neo-Colombian exchanges of the long nineteenth-century (roughly 1720-1930). They differed from the Colombian exchanges of the sixteenth and seventeenth centuries[44] in that they were increasingly mediated by imperial and transnational scientific knowledge on a far greater geographical scale. In his words, "Elite faith in commodity exports as the engine of economic growth proved surprisingly robust, even as liberalism supplanted mercantilism as the dominant ideology."[45] It survived the rise and decline of European imperialism, revolutionary nationalism, abolition of slave trade and slaver, and the advent of North American neo-colonialism. New agricultural frontiers replaced older exhausted ones, and new forms of coercive labour replaced slavery.

Driven by boom-bust cycles and the dramatic expansion of the agricultural export economy, new scientific networks were what for McCook shaped the global movement of plants, animals and new technologies.[46] By the end of the eighteenth century, all European imperialist powers had botanical gardens that collected and disseminated especially plants of scientific and economic value. The British Royal Botanic Gardens at Kew emerged as the most important nineteenth-century centre for global plant transfer,[47] and botanical gardens and agricultural experimental stations became instrumental locally around the world – as, for example, Hope Gardens in the Jamaican case we consider first below. Also, and importantly, by the mid-nineteenth century, the binary divide between Western/non-Western, European/non-European, coloniser/colonised could no longer be solely applied, such that there were revealing exchanges between producers and agricultural stations, as evidenced in Cuba, Indonesia and the United States in the second of our cases.[48]

British Colonial Jamaica

Jamaica, close to Cuba's southeast coast, was strategically located for those fleeing late nineteenth-century war-torn Cuba. There British colonial authorities would offer them sanctuary, including some of Cuba's leading military independence fighters, deported, along with their families, by Spain.[49] British interest in doing so, however, was not solely political. Among the economic interests was tobacco, and Cubans would give a crucial boost to the Jamaican economy.

In the early 1890s, Cuban independence leader José Martí, himself in exile in the United States, visited Jamaica to rally support for the newly founded Cuban Revolutionary Party. He spoke of Cubans such as Don Benito Machado, founder-owner of Kingston's Machado cigar factory, "respected for their moral standing and public service," and "the grey-haired veteran of the Ten Years War, his children around him, rolling cigars on his Sunday of rest to further the contribution to the homeland."[50] He spent time in Kingston and travelled to meet with Cubans who were growing tobacco on Temple Hall Estate, north of Kingston.

At the time of Martí's visit, the Temple Hall community was estimated as comprising 20 families, about 100 people in all, on part of what had been a much larger sugar estate that had been divided up and auctioned off mid-century. A substantial part had been rented and then bought, along with other properties, by Middle-East-born, American-naturalised Simon Soutar, who had been in Havana before travelling to Jamaica.[51] Soutar left an account of how, in Havana, he was "struck with the great prosperity of the tobacco industry and the influence it had on the commerce and prosperity of that port."[52] In Jamaica, he sourced Cuban seed through Hope Gardens and, with Vuelta Abajo planter José Pita, cultivated a leaf similar to the celebrated Vega Pilotos of Vuelta Abajo, belonging to Partagás. Soutar also began making cigars. As he recalled:

> I got about twenty of the best Havana cigar makers, revolutionists who came

to Jamaica as refugees – Sestrero, Badell, Pino, and others, all celebrated workers from the factories of Partagás, Cabanas [sic], and 'La Honradez'. They made the cigars I exhibited at the Vienna exhibition in 1873, which gained the highest Medal and Diploma and secured orders from Prince Milan (afterwards King of Serbia), the Sultan of Turkey, and a number of other notables who considered them better than the usual run of the Havanas of that day.[53]

In 1873, Cuban émigré Guillermo González wrote and published in Kingston a treatise on growing and manufacturing Cuban tobacco, in his words for no personal gain. This he prefaced:

Since his residence in the Island of Jamaica, the writer of it has seen large quantities of native Tobacco of admirable quality and equal in their original state to any grown in Cuba. But through ignorance of the manner of planting it, in the first instance and by reason of even less experience in its proper treatment while growing, and subsequent process of curing, the value of the product was essentially diminished, while the labour bestowed on it, if it had but been properly directed, would have made it in every respect most valuable to the producer, and fully equal to plant of Cuban growth.

He therefore, as matter of instruction to the Island at large, and in grateful idea towards a country in which his compatriots have found genial shelter, has written the work.[54]

At the time, tobacco in Jamaica was sold in the form of rope, lengths of which were cut for a modest price in markets and by the roadside. This changed with the advent of Cuban leaf and cigars, though Soutar himself would later abandon tobacco, complaining:

A number of people had by this time gone in for cultivation of tobacco and manufacture of cigars and were flooding the foreign markets with questionable Jamaican cigars to my prejudice, so I gave up my factory in favour of the Machados, renting the lands to Cubans.

The system of cultivation pursued now is that of Vuelta Arriba, which can never produce a high-class tobacco.[55]

Benito and Juan Machado, according to Machado company history,[56] arrived in Jamaica in 1874. They came from a Santa Clara landowning family. Caught up in the Ten Years' War against Spain, they fled in their early twenties to the United States, where they learned the cigar business. There is no mention of whether the family land in Cuba was given over to tobacco, though this would have been quite possible since Santa Clara lay at the heart of Vuelta Arriba.

They were in contact with Martí in New York; and, since their health was not good, Martí suggested they go to Jamaica, which was climatically more akin to Cuba, and take up tobacco. Their Cuban property confiscated, they had left with money and in Jamaica married two Cuban sisters, each of independent means.

The Machados imported tobacco from Cuba's Vuelta Abajo; contracted experts at Temple Hall, in the parish of St Andrew, and Colbeck, in Clarendon, whose land, soil and climate were similar to Vuelta Abajo and which were within fairly easy reach of the capital city and port of Kingston; and employed refugee tobacco growers and cigar makers from Cuba. They travelled throughout Jamaica encouraging farmers to grow the tobacco leaf, advising on the best methods of cultivation and curing, and advancing money, and set up their initial firm, "a small affair, no larger than a reasonable sized drawing room, and employing only about twenty-five workers, who were all ex-Cubans skilled in the art of making fine cigars."[57] Within a few years, they had gone from 25 to 300 workers, moved to new premises and registered their first trademarks, the first ever in Jamaica: Trademark No.1 'Fantasía Habanera Cigarros Superiores' and No.2 'La Tropical'.

Less affluent family histories, handed down through the generations, are those of Lorenzo Palomino and José Blanchet.[58] Palomino escaped wounded from fighting in the Ten Years' War and arrived in Jamaica penniless in a 14-foot rowboat. He and a fellow Cuban worked their way across the island, heading for Spanish Town, where they had heard there was a community of Cubans. There, he married a Jamaican and settled, growing tobacco in Colbeck for the Machados. Blanchet, thought to have grown tobacco in central Cuba, married another Cuban refugee, Margarita Rojas, and also grew tobacco for the Machados.

Among the more prominent military and political figures with links to tobacco was veteran Dominican-born General Máximo Gómez, who, having risen in the ranks in the Ten Years' War, in 1878 left Cuba to join his family in Jamaica and was offered money to grow tobacco in Corbet.[59] In 1883, after a project with Maceo for a tobacco-growing colony in Honduras and at Monte Cristi in the Dominican Republic, Gómez was back in Jamaica in the late 1880s to farm La Reforma. In 1891, he would then found with Maceo and others a settler colony of some 100 Cubans farming sugar, tobacco and coffee in Nicoya, Costa Rica.

The timing of the Cubans' arrival in Jamaica was fortuitous. Tobacco had been cultivated in Jamaica from the time of the Spanish conquest. After the British took the island in 1655, when there was stiff competition from tobacco in the North American colonies, slave-based plantation sugar gained primacy, until it in turn could not compete with neighbouring Cuba. In his study of late nineteenth-century Jamaican rural land transactions, Satchell characterises the 1860s as a period of disintegration of the large sugar estates, with small settlers acquiring private and public land, and the 1870s as being marked by government and private repossessions and purchasing by foreigners.[60]

Cubans were welcomed for their growing and cigar expertise, and, while in the late 1860s domestic growing and manufacturing were of little importance, already in the 1870s, Jamaica was transformed from a net importer to net exporter of cigars and began to be self-sufficient in leaf. By the 1880s, Jamaica was established in both,[61] having the advantage of local backing and preferential status with Britain, when London was a major European cigar market of the time, and by extension other British colonies also.

Census figures indicate a generally growing Cuban population in Jamaica 1861-81.[62] Their numbers halved by 1891 and halved yet again by 1911, though they would redouble in the 1920s. This would correspond with an influx during Cuba's first independence war, followed by a falling off during the interwar years, the period of arms shipments and insurgent expeditions being organised back to Cuba, and Cuba's post-independence era, and a 1920s boom-cycle reversal. It is difficult to gauge how accurately census figures reflect actual numbers, and whether falling numbers were due to return or onward migration or acquired citizenship in Jamaica.[63] Figures were also most likely underestimated – the 1881 census peak falls far short of the 5,000 quoted in Machado company history. It is likewise difficult to say how many were connected with tobacco. However, while scattered over the island parishes, Cubans were concentrated most in St Catherine, Clarendon and St Andrew, as well as Kingston, where tobacco was predominant.

British Jamaica Handbooks, *Blue Book Departmental Reports* and *Governor's Reports* commented favourably on tobacco. The 1880-81 *Governor's Report* referred to increasing tobacco cultivation and export, asserting:

> The Jamaican cigars of certain brands have now made a name for themselves in the English market. In the Colony, they are almost universally smoked and their manufacture in Kingston alone gives employment to a large number of men, foreigners and natives.[64]

In the 1883-84 *Departmental Report*, there is reference to General Villegas, formerly of Cuba, an extensive cultivator of Havana tobacco at Colbeck's plantation, in whose judgement there were in Jamaica many thousands of acres well adapted for the cultivation of Havana tobacco. It was also commented that:

> tobacco growing in small patches is being extended and new applications are made for the best qualities of Havana Tobacco Seed. . . . The Cubans settled on the island are apparently the only persons who can cure tobacco properly but unfortunately their numbers are decreasing and in many cases

they take up other industries which appear to them to offer better returns for their labours.⁶⁵

Almost a decade later, the 1892-93 *Customs and Internal Revenue Report* would again attribute falling tobacco acreage to the withdrawal of many Cubans who had been growing tobacco;⁶⁶ and an 1893-94 entry lamented cultivation being practically confined to St Andrew and St Catherine, in the hands of the Cubans.

In an attempt to remedy this, quantities of the best Cuban seed were brought in through the offices of the British Consul in Havana and Hope Gardens in Kingston and offered free of charge to potential growers, along with visiting expertise. The aim was to obviate the need for imported leaf and export any surplus at a good price on the European market. Hopes were fired by Jamaica (in the form of the Machado Company) sharing a London Chamber of Commerce prize for tobacco with British North Borneo; and, as stated in the 1896-97 *Agricultural Society Report* on new settlers on the island:

> The Board recognises the advantages that have accrued to the island and will continue to accrue from the settlement here of large numbers ... of tobacco planters from Cuba and further views the recent introduction of a considerable amount of capital for the development of our agricultural industries as a matter for cordial congratulations.⁶⁷

In 1898-99, the *Collector of Taxes Report* was in "hopeful anticipation of the results to accrue from the establishment of a fast steam service between the Colony and the UK,"⁶⁸ and the *Public Gardens and Plantations Report* celebrated the Hon. Evelyn Ellis estate, where 60 acres were planted with Vuelta Abajo seed and the tobacco, which was cured on the spot, "was sold to a New York buyer, realizing high prices."⁶⁹

Cuban companies were all early entries in the official *Jamaican Register of Incorporated Companies and Societies*, which was kept after 1889.⁷⁰ Their presence was also evidenced by 1890s advertisements in the *Jamaica Post* and *Daily Gleaner*: for Leonte Quesada, G. J. Cordova, M. Delgado, Lascelles de Mercado, L. Chacón, S. V. Durán and C. A. López. Brand names for their cigars included 'Elegantes', 'La Flor de Habana', 'Especiales de Quesada' and 'La Amalia'.

Over time, however, they would face strong rivals: Colbeck's Cigar Company, the Cooperative Tobacco Company Ltd., Desnoes & Geddes, Jamaica Tobacco Company (JTC), El Caribbean Cigar & Tobacco Company (successors to S. V. Durán), Black Horse Tobacco Co. Ltd. and Gore Ltd. Likewise, large tobacco plantations would be consolidated by Ellis and JTC, with British and US capital.

A Cuban presence nonetheless remained, such that at London's 1907

Crystal Palace Tobacco Exhibition, Machado's award-winning 'La Tropical' cigars were a firm favourite, along with 'Flor de Machado', 'Exquisitos' and others. An article written on the occasion of the exhibition lamented Jamaica being lightly considered in the world's tobacco markets, notwithstanding the cigars of Machado, JTC and El Caribbean having the 'body' and 'bouquet' of better-class Havanas:

> It was the judgment of this expert that tobacco similar in quality could be marketed in England in quantity at remunerative prices – in face, too, of the fact that Cuba had one of its recurring rebellions on the tapis seriously affecting its tobacco crop. Why this island should not supply the United Kingdom with leaf tobacco and cigars is inexplicable.[71]

The cigar department of JTC – which already had ties to British (mainly cigarette) companies such as Wills & Wills, Lambert & Butler, John Player & Sons – still had a Cuban-born manager, Miguel Founaris [sic], and skilled Cuban cigar makers in its employ.

That same year, 1907, the director of public gardens and plantations in Jamaica articulated two crucial points: that the Cubans provided the expertise and the British, through Kew Gardens in London and Hope Gardens in Kingston, guaranteed the quality seed from Cuba. In his words:

> The history of economic plants in Jamaica is part of the history of the efforts made by the British Government to aid the colonies. . . . The history of the tobacco industry in Jamaica is a good illustration. [In the time of Jamaica's Governor Grant (1866-74), it was] a scandal that with the East and West Indies in our possession we had not a good cigar from either [and he suggested Jamaica should be] getting seeds, together with histories of their manufacture, of various kinds from Cuba, Manila, etc., though our consuls, and . . . some enlightened Jamaican proprietors to commence the cultivation.[72]

Among the Cubans he commended as having contributed to the dramatic transformation of the late nineteenth-century Jamaican tobacco economy were Soutar, Count José Duaney [sic], owner of the Hall Head Estate; O. M. Fuertado [sic], owner of Bellevue; Pedro Cisneros, a grower at Cherry Garden; General Vijegas [sic], an extensive grower at Colbeck's; J. C. Espín, who published a treatise on tobacco in the 1889 *Jamaica Bulletin*; and Antonio León, a planter who advised Hope Gardens on cutting and curing.

If the early Machados were reputed to have had benign paternalistic relations with their farmers, JTC was not. A possibly overstated case in this regard was made by the Machado Company:

When the crop failed or when, for some other reason, farmers could not pay back what they owed, the Machados were patient and waiting. There is no record of the Machados ever foreclosing or seizing a farmer's land because he owed money and could not pay. Thus, the relationship between the farmers and the Company and its officials flourished in an atmosphere of friendship, trust and co-operation.[73]

However, the Spanish Town Island Register Office recorded cases of planters trapped into mortgaging their livestock and other property to the Jamaica Tobacco Company in the event of crop failure.[74] For some, this was a first step in a downward direction from planter to labourer.

A 1914 traveller, who stopped to talk (in Spanish) with an elderly man on a Temple Hall tobacco farm, described him as

> evidently the family of one of those Cuban refugees who have introduced this industry so successfully that the best brands . . . such as those of Machado, can hardly be distinguished from Cuban production, and are largely exported into the other British islands.[75]

Long before then, however, ATC and ITC had formed BAT, which bought into JTC. JTC became the largest company, followed by Machado. The two were on a par in terms of cigar production, but JTC was poised for the twentieth century as a major cigarette producer. The two would merge in 1922, retaining the Machado name, but cigar operations dwindled thereafter and Jamaica's Cuban cigar history was destined to be all but forgotten.[76]

Dutch Indonesia and the United States

If Jamaica would become a forgotten player, this was not to be the case with Dutch Indonesia and the United States. As the Dutch and British had expanded their seventeenth-century empires, Amsterdam and London established themselves as European twin pillars for the international circulation of tobacco. Tobacco was big business, with Crown and state playing a central role. Spain, Portugal and France all had their monopolies purchasing and processing tobacco, and German states enforced all-important taxation. While there were no such monopolies in Britain and the Netherlands, the state was still heavily involved. The United States rose to pre-eminence as an independent nation with an advantage over colonial systems built on global segmentation, but not without stiff competition from the British and the Dutch.

Tobacco was not, of course, indigenous to Indonesia. The betel nut was to Indonesia what tobacco was to the Americas, and betel chewing only ceded to tobacco smoking when, from the start of the sixteenth century, successive waves of Portuguese, Spanish, Dutch and British had sought to dominate the spice trade in India and Indonesia.[77] In the early seventeenth century, the Dutch parliament granted a monopoly on trade and activities in the region to the Dutch East India Company; and the Dutch went on to become the dominant European power in the eighteenth century.

After the fall of the Netherlands to the First French Empire and the dissolution of the Dutch East India Company in 1800, the company's assets were nationalised as the Dutch East Indies colony. During the Napoleonic Wars, the French treated it as a proxy colony, administered through a Dutch intermediary. In 1811, Java fell to a British East India Company force and was returned to the Netherlands following the end of the Napoleonic Wars, under the terms of the 1824 Anglo-Dutch Treaty.

Tobacco had been early introduced to the royal courts in Java, such that the practice of mixing betel and tobacco was commonplace by the eighteenth century. In the late nineteenth century, the mixing of clove and tobacco would produce *kretek* cigarettes, a popular antidote to the 'white' tobacco cigarette that was being introduced.[78] Before then, however, the tobacco leaf was already destined for the Dutch manufacture of cigars. As Deschodt and Morane recount:

> From 1825 onward, while British and French elites, and all the others after them, devoted themselves to Havana, huge workshops were set up in the Netherlands to treat tobacco from their Indonesian possessions, mixed with tobacco from Brazil, Java, and Sumatra for the wrapper and binder leaf and Bahía for the filler. Their experts developed a 'special light' taste and matching prices which would make a fortune.[79]

Tobacco was, thus, well established when, in 1843, compulsory intensive planting was mandated as part of the Dutch Cultivation System, designed to foster export crops – sugar, coffee and indigo first, and then others, including tobacco.[80] This tied peasants to their land and forced them to work on government-owned plantations as indentured labour. When the System was ended, in 1870, and restrictions on small-scale production were finally lifted, smallholders would account for only a tiny share of the tobacco market. What emerged with liberalisation was a privatised plantation economy with Dutch, British and American corporate entities and associated trade and banking institutions, the beginning of an Indonesian tobacco industry fuelled by large capital.[81]

Indonesia, like Cuba, was strategically located for global trade and, while half way round the globe from Cuba, had climatic and soil conditions similarly suited for sugar and tobacco, such that by the late nineteenth century Indonesia and Cuba would share the peak of world trade in both. Knowledge and practice would be sought and shared regarding their cultivation,[82] and it was the plantation system that would come to dominate both in Indonesia. The Sumatra 'plantation belt' in particular developed into a multinational site with a variety of European plantation owners, operating with little interference from the Dutch colonial regime in Java, but with a harsh contract system of 'coolie' labour that would generate opposition from workers themselves.[83]

It was the island of Java that had seen early tobacco growing, yielding in the main a lower-grade leaf. However, in 1863, a delegation of Dutch entrepreneurs went from Java to East Sumatra, believing the region's climate and soils could produce a leaf of higher quality. The delegation's report was unfavorable, yet in that delegation was Jacobus Nienhuys, who had been growing tobacco in Java. Nienhuys stayed; arranged land concessions; and, in 1867, with his partner P. W. Janssen, secured financial backing, half of which came from the Nederlandsche Handel-Maatschappij. In 1869, they established the Deli Maatschappij, with a concession to produce cigar tobacco along Sumatra's Deli River.[84]

Within twenty years, the Deli had increased cultivation tenfold on twenty-one estates. When Nienhuys himself returned to the Netherlands in 1871, Jacob Theodore Cremer took his place; and, though other companies followed the Deli – such as Deli Batavia (1875), Tobacco Company Arendsburg (1877) and Senembah Company (1889) – by 1883, the year Cremer himself returned to the Netherlands, the Deli's exports had soared. By 1900, the company had bought up most other plantations, and the Deli reigned supreme, controlling not only the Sumatra tobacco industry, with a monopoly on tobacco exports and acting as broker for tobacco growers, but also the East Sumatra rubber and palm oil plantation belt, all worked with Javanese, Chinese and other migrant labour.[85] It was the Deli that accounted in large part for Sumatra exports soaring tenfold between the late 1860s and the First World War. The Deli was by then producing one-third of the Sumatra crop, and Sumatra had Indonesia's greatest concentration of agricultural estates, with tobacco dominating the area around the capital Medan.

Thus it was that in the latter part of the century, with the ending of the Dutch East Indies state-controlled Cultivation System, that Dutch Indonesia broke out of its colonial segmentation and emerged as a strong global competitor. By the outbreak of the First World War, the Dutch East Indies was the world's second-largest exporter of leaf, accounting for 18 percent of the world market. Sumatra and Java supplied the international market via Amsterdam and Rotterdam in the Netherlands and Bremen in Germany, in strong competition with other producer countries. Conversely, the breakup of the colonial system and opening of new regions to the international market – especially the Dutch East Indies, Brazil and Cuba – saw the US share of the world's leaf market drop from 87 percent in 1840 to 30 percent by 1884 (and it would be only 13 percent a century later).

Sumatra leaf gained particular fame as cigar wrapper, since, grown under natural cloud cover, it proved more elastic and thinner than sun-grown tobacco. This made it easier to handle and also lighter and thereby cheaper by weight in transportation costs and duties in international trade, such that Sumatra came to supply more than 90 percent of all US-imported wrapper. This led growers in the United States to lobby hard for protectionist high duties to keep Sumatra imports down, and US companies to establish plantations in Sumatra for their own supply.

US cigar history had itself taken off through the Cuban connection. Within a generation of Colonel Putnam returning to New England from the British occupation of Havana with plundered cigars, there was a reported swing in the taste of Connecticut smokers. A first advertisement offering 'segars' from Cuba appeared in the *Connecticut Courant* in 1791, and the first advertisement for 'segars' of domestic manufacture in 1799. It was later recounted that, in 1810, "Samuel Viets had by chance come upon a wandering Cuban who understood the art of cigar rolling. He engaged him to teach his craft to a dozen or more women in a newly opened factory at Suffield."[86] Havana filler with a Connecticut wrapper began to be used. Then, in the early 1870s, experiments conducted with carefully selected Havana seeds under the supervision of state and federal soil and plant specialists produced a hybrid binder and wrapper. In the first three years these were known as 'Spanish' or 'Havana', then 'Havana Seed' and eventually 'American' as distinct from 'Spanish'.[87] In the words of an agronomist at the Connecticut Agricultural Experiment Station, writing a century later:

> Although the seed evidently came from Cuba, today there is no district in that island which grows tobacco like it.... By generations of selection and acclimatization here, the size and shape of the leaf have so changed that we fail to recognise the Cuban ancestor.[88]

After the Civil War, competition from Pennsylvania and Wisconsin's dark leaf halted New England expansion, but the development of the new Havana seed tobacco and a return to lighter cigars restored the competitive advantage of Connecticut over other US growers. However, in Sumatra they faced a strong new foreign competitor.

Other European manufacturers had, since the 1860s, been using Sumatra wrapper. A sample shipment reached New York manufacturers in 1876, and by the 1880s, it was being imported there. In 1883, alarmed farmers formed the New England Tobacco Growers Association, which lobbied for high tariff restrictions. These enabled Connecticut growers to survive economically in the short term, but they saw their only long-term solution was to develop a leaf that could compete in price and quality with Sumatra.

Experiments in 1898, supervised by the US Bureau of Plant Industry, resulted in a hybrid leaf developed from Cuban and Sumatra seed. Again, as recounted later:

> From one field a superior crop developed from Cuban seeds. . . . The seeds of numerous varieties continued to be planted. . . . Of the many specimens that finally evolved, four types were found to have merit. Among these were Uncle Sam Sumatra and Hazlewood Cuban.
>
> It was the latter that received approval as best for growing under shade in Connecticut soil, and potentially the most profitable. . . . Seed selection among Connecticut Valley farmers became so expert and so precise that experienced Cuban farmers turned to buy tobacco seeds from the Yankees.[89]

In 1899, the USDA first experimented with nets, to simulate the natural cloud coverage of Sumatra; and, by 1911, growing tobacco under cloth was gaining momentum, thus creating what would become the famed Connecticut Shade.[90]

After additional experiments with seed, curing and fertiliser,[91] shade tobacco grown under cloth tents dramatically changed the Connecticut landscape. Whereas thousands of small, independent farmers had sun-grown Broadleaf and Havana seed tobacco in combination with other crops, Shade required intensive farming with substantial investment in poles, wires and netting beyond the resources of the average farmer. Because of the high initial investment required, increased production costs, and greater financial risks, Shade was dominated by a small number of large companies, some owned outside the state with investments in other cigar leaf areas, cigar manufacture, or tobacco trading. The largest of all was the Connecticut Tobacco Company, formed in 1901, which, in 1910, merged with the American Sumatra Tobacco Corporation, itself created out of the merger of seven of the larger growers and packers in the southern Florida-Georgia tobacco belt, to grow tobacco under tents, or nets. The Company's largest plantation, named Amsterdam, claimed at the time to be the largest tobacco plantation in the world under single ownership, would become infamous for its tied sharecropping system with child and family labour. Time, however, would also claim its demise.

Tents, or nets, would be introduced in Cuba;[92] other parts of the Americas, notably Brazil; and back on the island of Java, which didn't have the same cloud cover as Sumatra. Of significance here, however, is the raw competitive edge of companies like Connecticut Tobacco, American Sumatra and the Deli. This was owed in large part to their reconfigured plantation system and forms of coercive labour. In this, the Indonesian industry would win out. By the 1920s Sumatra leaf was used almost exclusively by US corporations. It proved more suited for machine-made cigars, which by then dominated the US industry, and thus had a longer lease of life than others. The Deli would ultimately take over American Sumatra, of which nothing remains today. Many hundreds of cigar-rolling shops in Indonesia were forced to close down, leaving the only substantial manufacturing industry centred around modern cigarette factories, competing – and by no means altogether successfully – with local kretek production and consumption.

Origins and Perceived Origins

The lowly Indonesian kretek couldn't be further removed from the proud Havana cigar. Yet the history of the two have in common that each in its own way found a way to fight back. Kretek history is well beyond our scope here, but in our reflections on Havana cigar history we might end by reflecting on origins and perceived origins.

In the words of Gilman and Xun, "The cigar is a prime example of how tobacco continued to re-invent itself."[93] In what became the 'age of the cigar', the Havana, more than any other, became the hallmark of status, privilege and wealth. The First World War and its aftermath cemented a smoker's paradise in which the cigarette not the cigar rode supreme. The cigarette, however, with its monopolies, global corporations and immense profits, would also be tobacco's ultimate downfall. Its addictive dangers ushered in health prohibitions throughout the western world, while fostering new booms in the non-Western world, where there were no such prohibitions. The cigar, especially the hand-rolled Havana cigar and its contenders, claimed to be less toxic to health and experienced a latter-day revival. The explanation for how this was engineered lies in what was achieved and fought over during its long nineteenth century.

A die had been cast. Much of mainland South America, especially after the break with Spain and Portugal, was turned into a raw-material-producing area for primarily Britain and then the United States. As a prime producer of sugar and tobacco, Cuba, while still a Spanish colony and then as a US neo-colony, was caught up in this maelstrom. The buck didn't stop there, however. Cuba's very primacy would also be a shackle for its people and a source of political and economic interests around which many actors would spin their intricate web of history.

With the advent of the 'British cycle' of 'liberal free trade', the relationship between manufacturing centres and primary producers was largely mercantile, tariff barriers playing a major part in protecting home industry. When capital accumulation and concentration of production morphed into a new age of monopoly corporations, these began to play a decisive role in economic and political life. In country after country, especially smaller ones, the strength of the monopolies and the protectionism and adverse terms of trade that accompanied them produced an imbalance toward the export of leaf and away from manufacturing. Any increase in manufacturing was largely in the area of inferior tobacco products for the home market, often considered of such secondary importance as to be left to smaller local concerns. The shift to mild cigarettes, moreover, began to produce a falling back of world demand for, and drop in the price of, their leaf. The new, cheaper, machine-made cigars, blended with cheaper tobaccos, commandeered much of what was left of the market.

In this, the hand-rolled Havana cigar was something of an exception. Its markets might have been down, yet fame it retained as a niche luxury product. What had made it so unique? The French, in protecting their champagne, coined the term *terroir*.[94] Similarly, Cubans would claim *terroir* for their cigar, its special quality being that it was wholly Cuban: made in Cuba with Cuban expertise and with leaf grown in Cuba, especially Vuelta Abajo. In the words of Vahé Gérard as late as 2002: "Cuba is still the promised land for the cigar lover."[95] Seeds, people, skills and know-how can all be transferred, but grounded *terroir* cannot. This Cuba would capitalise on, fashioning around it an aura that others would try to capture.

The age of the cigar was also the age of the lithographic industry, invented in the late-eighteen century in Germany and subsequently developed in France as chromolithography. In 1822 a first French shop opened in Havana for printing music sheets, and a further two opened in 1840, one French and the other Spanish, initially to reproduce engravings of Cuba. Used by manufacturers, French lithography soon replaced Spanish Royal Seals as signs of distinction on richly embossed cigar bands and labels for crafted cedar cigar boxes. New lithographic shops opened involving Cubans and other Europeans,[96] and the sumptuous iconography assured an international clientele they were buying an authentic Cuban product, not an imitation. This was an early form of brand advertising, which, in the words of Martínez Rius, "further empowered and consolidated the universal grandeur of the *Habano*. From that moment on, the *Habano* had a presentation in accordance with its lineage." [97]

Documenting the history of the Montreal firm Granda Hermanos y Cía, Rudy likewise emphasised the importance of their brand advertising, in which they used their 'Spanish' name to lay claim to making 'authentic' Cuban cigars in Canada. He observed: "the suggestion of tobacco being Cuban was more important than the actual quality of the tobacco.... Through advertising, they evoked a sense of 'Cubanicity' that could be attached to any cigar to raise its value."[98] What was important was not origins but perceived origins.

This would hold for the 'offshore' advertising in Jamaica, and in the United States, with its 'Spanish' and half 'Spanish' cigar. Similar considerations were also behind Jamaica and the United States seeking to replicate the leaf, which Sumatra would then undercut, ushering in innovations such as the tents, or nets, and hybrids that Connecticut, Florida-Georgia, Cuba and Java would in return introduce.

These are just some of the many angles to the diverse trans-imperial and trans-territorial entanglements that characterise Havana cigar history beyond Iberian Atlantic confines. When studied in tandem, as they are here, they raise questions broader than the scope of this one luxury commodity in our long nineteenth-century 'age of the cigar'. They signal, no less, the need to revisit, empirically and conceptually, the interconnectedness of imperial and national histories.

Notes

1 This paper is rooted in a project that has been ongoing over the past twenty years, linking transnational migration and commodity production through the prism of what I have come to call the 'Havana cigar universe'. The spatial and temporal frame of this has extended over the years from an initial study, whose focus was to compare the periods of Cuba's late nineteenth-century independence struggles and late twentieth-century revolution, and now embraces the period 1756-2016. I extend my special gratitude to the Iberian tobacco historians' group for embracing me in their fold and nudging me toward find-honing my understanding of the earlier part of my extended period. I draw inspiration from their recent volumes: Santiago de Luxán Meléndez, João Figueiroa-Rego and Vicent Sanz Rozalén (eds), *Tabaco y esclavos en los imperios ibericos* (Lisbon: Universidade Nova de Lisboa, 2015), and Santiago de Luxán (ed.), *Política y hacienda del tabaco en los imperios ibéricos (siglos XVII-XIX)* (Madrid: Centro de Estudios Políticos y Constitucionales, 2014). The responsibility remains mine, however, in the face of any factual or conceptual misgivings they, or other readers, may have.

2 Cf. Eliga H. Gould, 'Entangled Histories, Entangled Worlds: The English-Speaking Atlantic as a Spanish Periphery', *American Historical Review* 112:3 (2007), pp.764-99. Since writing this chapter, I have been alerted to such entanglements having more recently been conceptualised by Richard Drayton as "masked condominia", referring to connectedness and collaboration, rather than competition and rivalry, at various levels from the state to the subaltern. See Drayton, 'Trans-European Collaboration in the History of Imperialism, 1500-2000', in Drayton, *Masks of Empire* (2018). The extent to which Havana cigar history can be explained in this light calls for future exploration.

3 In my discussion I forefront a select range of work. My point of departure is 'the long nineteenth century' of 1789-1914, as elucidated by Eric Hobsbawm, *The Age of Revolution: Europe 1789-1848* (London: Weidenfeld & Nicolson, 1962), *The Age of Capital: 1848-1875* (London: Weidenfeld & Nicolson, 1975), and *The Age of Empire: 1875-1914* (London: Weidenfeld, 1987), and the sequel *The Age of Extremes: The Short Twentieth Century, 1914- 1991* (London & New York: Penguin & Vintage, 1994). Other works referenced are: Peter Stearns, 'Rethinking the Long Nineteenth Century in World History: Assessments and Alternatives', in *World History Connected*, 9:3 (2012); Christopher Alan Bayly, *Imperial Meridian: The British Empire and the World, 1780-1830* (London: Longman, 1989); Giovanni Arrighi, *The Long Twentieth Century: Money, Power, and the Origins of Our Times* (London & New York: Verso, 1994); Victor Bulmer-Thomas, *The Economic History of the Caribbean since the Napoleonic Wars* (New York: Cambridge University Press, 2012), and *The Economic History*

of Latin America since Independence (Cambridge: Cambridge University Press, 1995); Josep M. Fradera, *La nación imperial (1750-1918)* (Barcelona: Edhasa, 2015), *Colonias para después de un Imperio* (Barcelona: Bellaterra, 2005), and *Gobernar colonias* (Barcelona: Peninsula, 1999); Alfred W. McCoy, Josep M. Fradera & Stephen Jacobson (eds), *Endless Empire: Spain's Retreat, Europe's Eclipse, America's Decline* (Madison: University of Wisconsin, 2012).

4 My work dates back to my early monograph *Tobacco on the Periphery* (London: Amaurea Press, 2023 [1985]). I reference that monograph and work published since at relevant points in the text.

5 Cuban 'classics' are Fernando Ortiz, *Cuban Counterpoint: Tobacco and Sugar* (Durham & London: Duke University Press, 1995 [1940]) and José Rivero Muñiz, *Tabaco: su historia en Cuba*, 2 vols. (Havana: Instituto de Historia, 1965). See also, Gaspar Jorge García Galló & Wilfredo Correa García, *The Story of Havana Cigars* (Havana: Editorial José Martí, 2001); Reynaldo González, *El Bello Habano: Biografía íntima del tabaco* (Havana: Editorial Letras Cubanas, 2004); and Guillermo Cabrera Infante, *Holy Smoke: A Literary Romp Through the History of the Cigar* (London: Faber & Faber, 1985).

6 More specifically for my arguments here, I draw on Santiago de Luxán Meléndez (ed.), *Política y hacienda del tabaco en los imperios ibéricos (siglos XVII-XIX) (Madrid: Centro de Estudios Políticos y Constitucionales, 2014)*: 'Introducción general', pp.9-20, and 'La defensa global del imperio y la creación de los monopolios fiscales del tabaco americanos en la segunda mitad del siglo XVIII', pp.177-229; José Manuel Rodríguez Gordillo, 'El mercantilismo español en la encrucijada: el tabaco de Virginia en el estanco español en el siglo XVII (1791-1760)', pp.47-89; Monserrat Gárate Ojanguren, 'La quiebra del sistema imperial del tabaco hispánico. Un proceso en el largo plaza: 1717- 1817', pp.231-82; Vicent Sanz Rozalen, 'Las vegas de tabaco en el occidente cubano a comienzos del siglo XIX', pp.283-309; Oscar Bergasa Perdomo, 'Soñaban los déspotas con monopolios perfectos? Una visión a la luz de la teoría económica', pp.341-65. Also, Santiago de Luxán & Montserrat Gárate, 'La segunda factoría de la Habana antes de la Guerra de la Independencia de las Trece Colonias 1760-1779. Una lectura desde el estanco español', in *Studia Historica. Historia Moderna*, 37 (2015), pp.291-321; Vicent Sanz Rozalen, 'De la concesión de mercedes a los usos privados: propiedad y conflictividad agraria en Cuba (1816-1819)', in José A. Piqueras (ed.), Las Antillas en la era de las luces y la revolución (Madrid: Siglo XXI, 2005), pp.247-73, 'El estanco del tabaco y la expansión azucarera a comienzos del siglo XIX', in Josef Opartny (ed.), *Nación y cultura nacional en el Caribe hispano* (Prague: Universidad Carolina, 2006), pp.249-60, and 'Arango y el mundo del tabaco: estanco, reforma y abolición', in María Dolores González-Ripoll & Izaskun Álvarez (eds), *Francisco Arango y la invención de la Cuba azucarera* (Salamanca: Universidad de Salamanca, 2009), pp. 277-87. More broadly on Spain's tobacco history, see José Pérez Vidal, *España en la historia del tabaco* (Madrid: Consejo Superior de Investigaciones Científicas, 1959), and *Historia del cultivo del tabaco en España* (Madrid: Servicio Nacional de Cultivo y Fermentación del Tabaco, 1956); and José M. Rodríguez Gordillo, *Un archivo para la historia del tabaco* (Madrid: Jacaryan, 1984).

7 Relevant studies are Charlotte A. Cosner, *The Golden Leaf: How Tobacco Shaped Cuba and the Atlantic World* (Nashville: Vanderbilt University Press, 2015); and Laura Náter, 'Colonial Tobacco: Key Commodity of the Spanish Empire, 1500-1800', in Steven Topik, Carlos Marichal & Zephyr Frank (eds), *From Silver to Cocaine: Latin American Commodity Chains and the Building of the World Economy, 1500-2000* (Durham & London, Duke University Press, 2006), pp.93-117. For tobacco more broadly, see Iain Gately, *Tobacco: A Cultural History of How an Exotic Plant Seduced Civilization* (New York: Grove Press, 2002); Jordan Goodman, *Tobacco in History: The Cultures of Dependence* (London & New York: Routledge, 1993); and V. G.

Kiernan, *Tobacco: A History* (London: Hutchinson Radius, 1991). Also see tobacco in Wolfgang Schivelbusch, *Tastes of Paradise: A Social History of Spices, Stimulants, and Intoxicants* (New York: Vintage, 1993 [1980]); and James Walvin, *Fruits of Empire: Exotic Produce and Western Taste* (New York: New York University Press & Palgrave Macmillan, 1997).

8   In the context of a 1990s cigar revival, *Cigar Aficionado* was an early 1990s successor to the 1980s *Wine Spectator*, and after it came a spate of coffee table books by Cuban and non-Cuban authors. These included a reprint of Antonio Núñez Jiménez, *The Journey of the Havana Cigar* (Neptune City: TFH Publications, 1996 [1988]); Gérard Père & Fils, *Havana Cigars* (Edison: Wellfleet Press 1997 [1995]); Eric Deschodt & Philippe Morane, *The Cigar* (Cologne: Könemann Verlagsgesellschaft, 1998); Enzo A. Infante Urivazo, *Havana Cigars 1817-1960* (Neptune City: TFH Publications, 1997); Eumelio Espino Marrero, *Cuban Cuban Cigar Tobacco: Why Cuban Cigars are the World's Best* (Neptune City: TFH Publications, 1997); Charles Del Todesco, *The Havana Cigar: Cuba's Finest* (New York, London, Paris: Abbeville Press Publishers, 1997); Nancy Stout, *Habanos: Book of the Havana Cigar* (New York: Rizzoli International Publications, 1997); and Adriano Martínez Ruis, *Habano el Rey* (Barcelona: Epicur Publicaciones, 1999).

9   For my initial refashioning of Cuba's national counterpoint between tobacco and sugar, as constructed by Ortiz, into a transnational counterpoint between the island and offshore cigar, see Jean Stubbs, 'Tobacco in the Contrapunteo: Ortiz and the Havana Cigar', in Mauricio A. Font and Alfonso W. Quiroz (eds), *Cuban Counterpoints: The Legacy of Fernando Ortiz* (Lanham: Lexington, 2004), pp.105-23 – Chapter 9 in the present volume.

10 See footnote 3 for full bibliographical references of the works by Hobsbawm, Braudel, Stearns, Bayly, Arrighi, Bulmer-Thomas, and Fradera discussed here.

11 Quoted in Arrighi, *The Long Twentieth Century* (1994), p.14. The earlier history of New York symbolises this well. Having first been discovered by the French in 1524, New York was named Nieuw (New) Amsterdam, when claimed by the Dutch in 1609, and in 1624 designated capital of New Netherland, with Fort Amsterdam designed to protect the Dutch West India Company's Hudson River fur trade. It was renamed New York when taken by the British in 1664, and, after being named New Orange during the Third Anglo-Dutch War, reverted to the English and again became New York in 1764 in exchange for Suriname becoming a Dutch possession.

12 Among other studies, see Matthew Brown (ed.), *Informal Empire in Latin America: Culture, Commerce, and Capital* (Oxford: Wiley-Blackwell, 2008); and Rory Miller, 'Informal Empire in Latin America', in Robert Winks (ed.), *The Oxford History of the British Empire: Vol. V: Historiography* (Oxford: Oxford University Press, 1999), pp.437-49.

13 Jean Stubbs, 'Política e sapere: come si e globalizzato el sigaro avana?/Política y saber: cómo se globalizó el habano', in Laura Mariottini & Alessandro Oricchio (eds), *El Habano: Lingua, storia, societa di un prodotto transculturale. Lengua, historia, sociedad de un producto transcultural* (Rome: Edizioni Efesto, 2017), pp.67-105, and '*El Habano* and the World It Has Shaped: Cuba, Connecticut and Indonesia', *Cuban Studies*, 41 (2010), pp. 248-76 – Chapter 13 in the present volume.

14 For broader studies of the impact of the war, see Fred Anderson, *Crucible of War: The Seven Years' War and the Fate of Empire in British North America, 1754-1766* (New York: Knopf, 2000). Jacques A. Barbier & Allan J. Kuethe (eds), *The North American Role in the Spanish Imperial Economy, 1760-1819* (Manchester: Manchester University Press, 1984). Nikolaus Bottcher, 'Cuba and the Thirteen Colonies during the North American War of Independence', in Horst Pietschmann (ed.), *Atlantic History: History of the Atlantic System, 1580-1830* (Gottingen: Vandenhoeck and Ruprecht, 2002).

15 For an early argument attributing the Second British Empire as not having started

after the Napoleonic Wars but rather following a pattern developed since the Seven Years' War, in which 'trade not dominion' was the dominant British objective, see G. C. Bolton, 'The Founding of the Second British Empire', in *The Economic History Review*, 19:1 (1966), pp.195-200.

16 See footnote 6 for full bibliographical references of their work. For a broader analysis of the changes wrought in the late eighteenth century, see Sherry Johnson, *The Social Transformation of Eighteenth-Century Cuba* (Gainesville: University Press of Florida, 2001). Also, Celia María Parcero Torre, *La pérdida de la Habana y las reformas borbónicas en Cuba, 1760-1773* (Madrid, Consejo de Castilla y León, 1998).

17 Santiago de Luxán Meléndez, *La opción agrícola e industrial del tabaco en Canarias. Una perspectiva institucional. Los orígenes, 1827-1936* (Las Palmas: Universidad Las Palmas, 2006); Andrés Arnaldos Martínez & Jorge Arnaldos de Armas, *La industria tabaquera canaria: (1852-2002)* (Gobierno de Canarias/Cámaras de Canarias/Asociación Canaria de Industriales Tabaqueros, 2003).

18 Ortiz, *Cuban Counterpoint* (1995 [1940]), p.309.

19 Manuel Moreno Fraginals, *Cuba/España, España/Cuba: Historia Común* (Barcelona: Grijalbo Mondadori, 1995), p.128.

20 Ibid., p.145.

21 Ibid., p.146.

22 Ibid., p.146.

23 I refer to these in Stubbs, 'Política e sapere' (2017) and 'El Habano' (2010).

24 For an analysis of Cuba's cigar heyday and subsequent mid-nineteenth-century turning point, see Jean Stubbs, *Tobacco on the periphery* (London: Amaurea Press, 2023 [1985]).

25 For in-depth studies of developments in Cuba in this period, see Doria C. González Fernández, 'La manufactura tabacalera cubana en la segunda mitad del siglo XIX', in *Revista de Indias*, 194 (1992), pp.129-56, and 'La guerra económica y sus efectos en la economía tabacalera', in Consuelo Naranjo, Miguel Angel Puig-Samper & Luis Miguel García Mora (eds), *La nación soñada: Cuba, Puerto Rico y Filipinas ante el 98* (Aranjuez, Doce Calles, 1996), pp.305-16. Also, Joan Casanovas, Bread or Bullets: *Urban Labor and Spanish Colonialism in Cuba, 1850-1898* (Pittsburgh, University of Pittsburgh Press, 1998).

26 Quoted in Stubbs, *Tobacco on the Periphery* (2023 [1985]), p.24. The full texts of the report and government response are included in Vidal Morales y Morales 'Documentos relativos a la información económica de Madrid y al Comité Central de Propoganda de La Habana (1890)', Colección Facticia, Vol. 18. A good source of reference for these years is Julio Le Riverend, 'Años terribles para la economía tabacalera', *Habano*, 3:1 & 2 (1941).

27 Stubbs, *Tobacco on the Periphery* (2023 [1985]), p.24

28 For the dispute, see Gustavo Bock, *The Truth about Havana Cigars* (New York: Havana Tobacco Company, 1904), and the counter-attack on behalf of the 'independents' by journalist and cigar maker José González Aguirre, *La verdad sobre la industria del tabaco habano* (Havana, 1905). See Stubbs, *Tobacco on the Periphery* (2023 [1985]), pp.31-2.

29 See Jean Stubbs, 'Transnationalism and the Havana Cigar: Commodity Chain Transfers, Networks, and Circuits of Knowledge', in Catherine Krull (ed.), *Cuba in a Global Context: International Re- lations, Internationalism, and Transnationalism* (Gainesville: University Press of Florida, 2014), pp. 227-42 – Chapter 16 in the present volume. For the latter part of the period, I concur with the analysis of Leida Fernández Prieto, *Cuba agrícola: Mito y tradición, 1878-1920* (Madrid: Consejo Superior de Investigaciones Científicas, 2005), pp.209-54, *Espacio de poder, ciencia y agricultura en Cuba: El Círculo de Hacendados, 1878–1917* (Madrid: Consejo Superior de Investigaciones Científicas, 2009), 'Modernización y cambio tecnológico' (2009), pp.175-218, and 'Islands of Knowledge: Science and Agriculture in the History of Latin America and the Caribbean', *Isis*, 104:4 (2013), pp.788-97.

30 For a discussion of this, see Stubbs, 'Havana Cigars and the West's Imagination', in Sander L. Gilman and Zhou Xun (eds), *Smoke: A Global History of Smoking* (London: Reaktion Press, 2004), pp.134-9 – Chapter 10 in the present volume.
31 See Luxán, *La opción agrícola* (2006); Arnaldos & Arnaldos, *Industria tabaquera* (2003). See also, Anelio Rodríguez Concepción, *Tradición insular del tabaco* (Santa Cruz de Tenerife: Consejería de Agricultura, Ganadería, Pesca y Alimentación, 2000); Mario Luis López Isla, *La aventura del tabaco* (Santa Cruz de Tenerife: Centro de la Cultura Popular Canaria, 1998); Gregorio J. Cabrera Deniz, *Canarios en Cuba: Un capítulo en la historia del archipiélago (1875-1931)*, Las Palmas de Gran Canaria: Cabildo Insular de Gran Canaria, 1996; and Manuel de Paz, *Wangüemert y Cuba*, 2 vols (Santa Cruz de Tenerife: Centro de la Cultura Popular Canaria, 1991).
32 Among the pioneers were Louis A. Pérez Jr., 'Reminiscences of a *Lector*. Cuban Cigar Makers in Tampa', *Florida Historical Quarterly* 53:4 (1975), pp.443-9; Glenn L. Westfall, *Key West: Cigar City USA* (Key West: Historic Key West Preservation Board, 1984), and *Don Vicente Martínez Ybor: the Man and His Empire: Development of the Clear Havana Industry in Cuba and Florida in the Ninteenth Century* (New York: Garland, 1987); Gerald E. Poyo, 'The Cuban Experience in the United States, 1865-1940: Migration, Community and Identity', *Cuban Studies* 21 (1991), pp.19-36; Gary Mormino & George E. Pozetta, '"The Reader Lights the Candle": Cuban and Florida Cigar Workers' Oral Tradition', *Labor's Heritage* (1993), pp.4-28; and Winston James, 'From a Class for Itself to a Race on Its Own: The Strange Case of Afro-Cuban Radicalism and Afro-Cubans in Florida, 1870-1940', in *Holding Aloft the Banner of Ethiopia: Caribbean Radicalism in Early Twentieth-Century America* (London: Verso, 1998), pp.232-57. More recent work includes Consuelo E. Stebbins, *City of Intrigue, Nest of Revolution: A documentary history of Key West in the Nineteenth Century* (Gainesville: University Press of Florida, 2007); Robert P. Ingalls & Louis A. Pérez, *Tampa Cigar Workers: A Pictorial History* (Gainesville: University Press of Florida, 2003); Susan D. Greenbaum, *More Than Black: Afro-Cubans in Tampa* (Gainesville: University Press of Florida, 2002); Nancy A. Hewitt, *Southern Discomfort: Women's Activism in Tampa, Florida, 1800s–1920s* (Urbana: University of Illinois Press, 2001); Evelio Grillo, *Black Cuban, Black American: A Memoir* (Houston: Arte Público Press, 2000); Evan Matthew Daniel, 'Cuban Cigar Makers in Havana, Key West, and Ybor City, 1850s-1890s', in Geoffroy De Laforcade & Kirwin Shaffer (eds), *In Defiance of Boundaries: Anarchism in Latin American History* (Gainesville: University Press of Florida, 2015), pp.25-47, 'Rolling for the Revolution: A Transnational History of Cigar Makers in Havana, Florida, and New York', PhD dissertation, New School University (2010), and 'A Single Universe: Cuban Cigar Makers in Havana and South Florida, 1853-1899', in *Florida's Labor and Working-Class Past: Three Centuries of Work in the Sunshine State* (Gainesville: University Press of Florida, 2006).
33 The North Florida history is one I researched with the aid of Kyle Doherty during spring 2011 at the University of Florida. I thank Paul Losch, now Head Librarian of the University's Latin American and Caribbean Library, who alerted me to the footnote in Gerardo Castellanos, *Motivos de Cayo Hueso* (Havana: Ucar, García y Cía, 1935), p.300, on the existence of Cuban cigar factories and workers in late nineteenth- and early twentieth-century Gainesville; and then Head Librarian Richard Phillips, who referred me to Daniel Bronstein, 'La Cubana City: A Cuban Cigar Manufacturing Community Near Thomasville Georgia, During the 1890s', *Georgia Historical Quarterly* 90:3 (2006), pp.391-417. Our research suggests an unexpectedly significant North Florida-South Georgia Cuban cigar history, which I have yet to write up in detail.
34 See Lisandro Pérez, *Sugar, Cigars, and Revolution: The Making of Cuban New York* (New York: New York University Press, 2018), 'Cubans in Nineteenth-Century New York: A Story of Sugar, War, and Revolution', in Edward J. Sullivan (ed.), *Nueva York, 1613-1945* (New York: New York Historical Society, 2010), and 'Sugar, Slavery, and the

Rise of Cuban New York', in John Thorn (ed.), *New York at 400* (New York: Running Press/Museum of the City of New York, 2009).

35 Jean Stubbs, 'Political Idealism and Commodity Production: Cuban Tobacco in Jamaica, 1870-1930', *Cuban Studies*, 25 (1995), pp.51-81 – Chapter 7 in the present volume; abridged Spanish-language version: 'Cuba y Jamaica en el camino del tabaco', *Del Caribe* 26 (1997), pp.81-93.

36 Juan José Baldrich makes this point in his work on Puerto Rican tobacco: 'From the Origins of Industrial Capitalism in Puerto Rico to Its Subordination to the US Tobacco Trust: Rucabado and Company, 1865–1901', *Revista Mexicana del Caribe*, 3:5 (1998), pp.60-106. See also M. Burgos Malave, 'El conflicto tabacalero entre Cuba y Puerto Rico', *Revista de Estudios Generales*, 4:4 (1989–90).

37 There is reference to nineteenth- and twentieth-century Cuban cigar makers alongside Puerto Ricans in New York in C. A. Iglesias, *Memoirs of Bernardo Vega: A Contribution to the History of the Puerto Rican Community in New York* (New York: Monthly Review Press, 1984).

38 See Stubbs, 'Transnationalism and the Havana Cigar (2014), and 'Beyond the Black Atlantic: Understanding Race, Gender and Labour in the Global Havana Cigar', *Comparativ*, 5:21 (2012), pp. 50-70 – Chapter 14 in the present volume. Also, Ruth Glasser, *Aquí me quedo: Puerto Ricans in Connecticut* (Middletown: Connecticut Humanities Council, 1997).

39 See Jean Stubbs, 'Reinventing Mecca: Tobacco in the Dominican Republic, 1763-2007', Commodities of Empire Working Paper, 3 (2007), at https://commoditiesofempire.org.uk/publications/working-papers/working-paper-3 – Chapter 12 in the present volume. Instrumental in following through the USDA recommendation with the new Institute of Tobacco in the Dominican Republic's Cibao area was Napoleón Padilla, who had been chief tobacco agronomist in Cuba until he left after the Revolution in opposition to the agrarian reform. Early issues of *Cigar Aficionado* ran an ad with a photo of Cifuentes, of Partagás fame – who went first to Jamaica and later the Dominican Republic, there rebirthing his own Partagás brand for the US market – with a caption that conjures up shades of past exile and migration: "Fidel Castro thought I left with only the shirt on my back, but I took my knowledge with me." For the earlier and later periods of Mexican tobacco history, see Susan Deans-Smith, *Bureaucrats, planters and workers: The making of the tobacco monopoly in Bourbon Mexico* (Austin: University of Texas Press, 1992), and José González Sierra, *Monopolio del humo: Elementos de la historia del tabaco en México y algunos conflictos de tabaqueros veracruzanos: 1915-1930* (Xalapa: Veracruz University, 1987). There has been little published to date that connects the other territories with Cuba, though there are some excellent Brazilian tobacco studies, including B. J. Barickman, *A Bahían Counterpoint: Sugar, Tobacco, Cassava, and Slavery in the Recôncavo, 1780-1860* (Stanford: Stanford University Press, 1998); Catherine Lugar, 'The Portuguese Tobacco Trade and Tobacco Growers of Bahía in the Late Colonial Period', in Dauril Alden & Warren Dean (eds), *Essays Concerning the Socioeconomic History of Brazil and Portuguese India* (Gainesville: University Press of Florida, 1977); and Jean-Baptiste Nardi, *Fumo brasileiro no periodo colonial* (Sao Paulo: Editora Brasilense, 1996). See also Michiel Baud & Kees Kooning, 'Germans and Tobacco in Bahía (Brazil), 1870-1940', in *Jahrbuch für Geschichte Lateinamerikas*, 37 (2000), pp.149-76. See also José Chez Checo & Mu-Kien Adriana Sang, *El tabaco: Historia general en la República Dominicana*, 3 vols (Santo Domingo: Grupo León Jimenes, 2008).

40 Jean Stubbs, '*El Habano* and the World It Has Shaped: Cuba, Connecticut and Indonesia', *Cuban Studies*, 41 (2010), pp.49-67 – Chapter 13 in the present volume. Also Stubbs, 'Transnationalism and the Havana cigar' (2014), and 'Beyond the Black Atlantic' (2012).

41 See Edilberto C. De Jesús, *The Tobacco Monopoly in the Philippines: Bureaucratic Enterprise and Social Change, 1776-1880* (Manila: Ateneo de Manila University Press,

1980). For an early twentieth-century comparative US representational snapshot of the Philippines, Puerto Rico, Cuba, Hawai'i and Guam, see Lanny Thompson, *Imperial Archipelago: Representation and Rule in the Insular Territories under US Dominion after 1898* (Honolulu: University of Hawai'i Press, 2010).
42 For this contemporary twist, see Gabriela Greess, 'Meerapfel Tobacco Group: Excellent Wrappers from Cameroon', *Cigar Journal* (15 July 2013).
43 See Stuart McCook, 'The Neo-Colombian Exchange: The Second Conquest of the Greater Caribbean, 1720-1930, *Latin American Research Review*, Special Issue (2011), pp.11-31, 'Global Currents in National Histories of Science: The "Global Turn" and the History of Science in Latin America', *Isis*, 104:4 (2013), pp.773-6, and *States of Nature: Science, Agriculture, and Environment in the Spanish Caribbean, 1760-1940* (Austin: University of Texas Press, 2002). See also McCook, '"Squares of Tropic Summer": The Wardian Case, Victorian Horticulture, and the Logistics of Global Plant Transfers, 1770-1910', in Patrick Manning & Daniel Rood (eds), *Global Scientific Practice in an Age of Revolutions, 1750-1850* (Pittsburgh: University of Pittsburgh Press, 2016), pp.199–215, and '"The World Was My Garden": Tropical Botany and Cosmopolitanism in American Science, 1898-1935', in Alfred McCoy & Francisco Scarno (eds), *Colonial Crucible: Empire in the Making of the Modern American State* (Madison: University of Wisconsin Press, 2009), pp.499-507.
44 See Alfred W. Crosby, *The Columbian Exchange: Biological and Cultural Consequences of 1492* (Westport: Greenwood Publishing, 1972), and *Ecological Imperialism: The Biological Expansion of Europe, 900–1900* (Cambridge, Cambridge University Press, 1986).
45 McCook, 'Neo-Colombian Exchange', p.14.
46 Similar arguments are made in the Cuban context by Leida Fernández Prieto, *Cuba agrícola: Mito y tradición, 1878-1920* (Madrid: CSIC, 2005), pp.209-54, *Espacio de poder, ciencia y agricultura en Cuba: El Círculo de Hacendados, 1878-2917* (Madrid: CSIC, 2009), 'Modernización y cambio tecnológico en la agricultura de Cuba, 1878-1920', in Antonio Santamaría & Consuelo Naranjo Orovio (eds), *Más allá del azúcar: política, diversificación y prácticas económicas en Cuba, 1878-1930* (Madrid: Doce Calles, 2009), and 'Islands of Knowledge: Science and Agriculture in the History of Latin America and the Caribbean', *Isis* 104:4 (2013), pp.788-97.
47 Among the work highlighting the role of British policy toward its Caribbean colonies creating and disseminating science, see Lucile H. Brockway, *Science and Colonial Expansion: The Role of the British Royal Botanic Garden* (New York, Academic, 1979); David N. Livingstone, *Putting Science in Its Place: Geographies of Scientific Knowledge* (Chicago, University of Chicago Press, 2003); Richard Drayton, *Nature's Government: Science, Imperial Britain, and the 'Improvement' of the World* (New Haven: Yale University Press, 2000); Richard H. Grove, *Green Imperialism: Colonial Expansion, Tropical Island Edens, and the Origins of Environmentalism* (Cambridge: Cambridge University Press, 1995).
48 I concur with McCook and Fernández Prieto in calling for further study of multiple knowledge centres and their global interactions, thus decentering analysis from the centre/periphery hierarchy.
49 Notable among them was General Antonio Maceo, who operated in and out of Jamaica after being deported there at the end of the Ten Years' War, with other family members, including his mother Mariana Grajales. See Jean Stubbs, 'Social and Political Motherhood of Cuba: Mariana Grajales Cuello', in Verene Shepherd, Bridget Brereton & Barbara Bailey (eds), *Engendering History: Caribbean, Women in Historical Perspective* (London & Kingston: Ian Randle & James Currey, 1995), pp. 296-317, 'Mariana Grajales Cuello: madre política y social de Cuba', *Historia y Sociedad*, 11 (1999), pp.31-56, also 'En busca de Mariana: raza y género en la nación', in Damaris Amparo Torres Elers & Israel Escalona Chadez (eds), *Mariana Grajales Cuello: Doscientos años en la historia y la memoria* (Santiago de Cuba: Ediciones Santiago, 2015).

50 Guillermo de Zéndegui, *Ambito de Martí* (Havana: Fernández y Cía, 1954).
51 As recounted in an oral history interview the author conducted in 1993 with Dudley Soutar, Simon Soutar's great-grandson.
52 Quoted in Hon. W. Fawcett, 'Tobacco in Jamaica', *West Indian Bulletin* 8:2 (1907), p.214.
53 Ibid., p.215.
54 Guillermo P. González, *Tobacco Culture: As Practiced in Cuba* (Port Royal: DeCordova, McDougal, 1873).
55 Fawcett, 'Tobacco in Jamaica' (1907), p.215. Soutar was later recorded in the 1882 *Blue Book for Jamaica* serving from September 1880 as consul to Denmark and acting consul to Sweden and Norway.
56 *The Machado Story: A Pioneer Industry in Jamaica, 1874–1962* (Kingston: B. & J.B. Machado Co., Ltd., n.d.).
57 Ibid.
58 These were recounted to the author in oral history interviews conducted in Kingston, Jamaica, in 1993 with Sister Eloise-Marie and Sister Imelda Palomino, daughters of Lorenzo Palomino, and Blanca Blanchet, daughter of José Blanchet and Margarita Rojas.
59 See Severo Rijo, 'Máximo Gómez, veguero', *Revista Tabaco* 9 (1941).
60 Veront M. Satchell, *From Plots to Plantations: Land Transactions in Jamaica, 1866-1900* (Mona: University of the West Indies, 1990).
61 Ibid.
62 Stubbs, 'Political idealism' (1995), pp.69-70.
63 Naturalisation of Cubans is mentioned in the *Handbook of Jamaica* 1884-85 (Kingston: Government Printing Establishment), p.265.
64 'Governor's Report on Blue Book of 1881', *Jamaica Departmental Reports* (Kingston: Government Printing Establishment), p. xxv.
65 'Departmental Reports: Public Gardens and Plantations 1883-84', *Jamaica Departmental Reports* (Kingston: Government Printing Establishment), pp.43-4.
66 'Collector-General's Customs and Internal Revenue Report 1892-93', *Jamaica Departmental Reports* (Kingston: Government Printing Establishment), p.143.
67 'Agricultural Society Reports for 1897', *Jamaica Departmental Reports* (Kingston: Government Printing Establishment), p.341.
68 'Collector of Taxes 1898-99', *Jamaica Departmental Reports* (Kingston: Government Printing Establishment), p.152.
69 'Public Gardens and Plantations 1898-99', *Jamaica Departmental Reports* (Kingston: Government Printing Establishment), p.319.
70 *Register of Incorporated Companies and Societies*, no.1. Cigar entries also featured prominently in the early years of the *Register of Trademarks* (Tobacco 45) and *Register of Letters Patent for Investors under Law 51 of 1891*. See also Gisela Eisner, *Jamaica, 1830-1930* (Manchester: Manchester University Press, 1961).
71 Alexander Gray, 'Jamaica's Tobacco', in *Jamaica in 1907. Supplement to the African World* (9 March 1907), p.43.
72 Fawcett, 'Tobacco in Jamaica', p.209.
73 *The Machado Story*.
74 For examples of mortgage on livestock, see Jamaican Archives, Spanish Town, Island Record Office: Jamaica Tobacco Company, Liber 227, 107 (Marcelino Muñoz), 108, 109 (Miguel Muñoz), 112,114 (Joseph Blanchet), 385, 386 (Lorenzo Palomino). The names of the livestock are telling: Clarín, Rosado, Arogante, Chiquito, Benado, Pajarito, Marinero, Negrito, Valiente...
75 Vaquero, *Life and Adventure in the West Indies* (London: Bale & Danielson, 1914).
76 Cigar manufacturing ceased entirely in 1954, when it became the Cigarette Company of Jamaica Ltd. The company did mark Jamaica's independence from Britain in 1962 by describing itself in company publicity as "a part of Jamaica and a memorial to its founders who came seeking a home where they could live in peace

and freedom and who in exchange gave Jamaica its modern tobacco industry". Until the 1940s, Temple Hall was one estate, growing tobacco for Machado's Churchill cigars and also Virginia cigarette tobacco. Later subdivided, it no longer supported tobacco cultivation, the only hint of its past being the part still called Cuba Mount and a Cuban-Jamaican cigar brand called Temple Hall Estates resurrected in the 1990s cigar revival.

77 See Anthony Reid, 'From Betel-Chewing to Tobacco-Smoking in Indonesia', *Journal of Asian Studies*, 44:3 (1985), pp.529-47.
78 For the history of the kretek, see Mark Hanusz, *Kretek: The Culture and Heritage of Indonesia's Clove Cigarettes* (Jakarta: Equinox Publishing, 2000), and 'A Century of Kretek', in Gilman & Xun, *Smoke* (2004), pp.140-3.
79 Eric Deschodt & Philippe Morane, *The Cigar* (Cologne: Könemann Verlagsgesellschaft, 1998), p.169.
80 See Cornelius Fasseur, *The Politics of Colonial Exploitation: Java, the Dutch, and the Cultivation System*, (Ithaca: Cornell University), 1992.
81 Viz Peter Boomgarde, 'Maize and tobacco in Upland Indonesia', in Tania Li (ed.), *Transforming the Indonesian Uplands: Marginality, Power and Production*, Vol. 4: Studies in Environmental Anthropology (Oxford: Taylor & Francis, 1999), pp.47-80.
82 This has been documented in the case of sugar by Ulbe Bosma & Jonathan Curry-Machado, 'Turning Javanese: The Domination of Cuba's Sugar Industry by Java Cane Varieties (1880-1950)', *Itinerario*, 37:2 (2013), pp.101-20, and 'Two Islands, One Commodity: Cuba, Java and the Global Sugar Trade (1790-1930)', *New West Indian Guide*, 86:3-4 (2012), pp.237-62.
83 Among other studies, see Ann Laura Stoler, *Capitalism and Confrontation in Sumatra's Plantation Belt, 1870-1979* (Ann Arbor: University of Michigan Press, 1995); K. L. Pelzer, *Planter and Peasant: Colonial Policy and the Agrarian Struggle in East Sumatra, 1863-1947* (The Hague: Martinus Nijhoff, 1978); and Jan Breman, *Taming the Coolie Beast* (New York: Oxford University Press, 1989). Also, Thee Kian-wie, *Plantation Agriculture and Export Growth: An Economic History of East Sumatra, 1863-1942* (Jakarta: Leknas LIPI, 1977).
84 See Lim Kim Liat, 'Deli Tobacco Industry: Its History and Outlook', in Douglas S. Paauw (ed.), *Prospects for East Sumatran Plantation Industries: A Symposium* (1962), pp.1-19. Also, the company history of what would later become Deli Universal NV, available online, http://www.deli-universal.nl. For a latter-day feature on the life story of Jacobus Nienhuys' grandson Henry, who would continue the family tobacco tradition, straddling Indonesia, the Netherlands, Connecticut and Cuba, see Linda Hirsch, 'Horticulturalist's Quest for Perfect Tobacco Spans Globe', *Hartford Courant* (1988).
85 For general Indonesian economic history, see P. Creutzberg, *Changing Economy in Indonesia: A Selection of Statistical Source Material from the Early 19th Century up to 1940*, 15 vols (The Hague: M. Nijhoff, 1996[1975]); J. Th. Lindblad (ed.), *Historical Foundations of a National Economy in Indonesia, 1890s-1990s* (North Holland: Koninkliijke Nederlands Akadmie van Wetenschappen, 1996), and *New Challenges in the Modern Economic History of Indonesia* (Leiden: Programme of Indonesian Studies, 1993).
86 See Gately, *Tobacco* (2002), p.30.
87 Ibid., pp.35-8.
88 P. J. Anderson, 'Growing Tobacco in Connecticut', *Connecticut Agricultural Experiment Station Bulletin* 564 (1953), p.10.
89 *Connecticut and Tobacco: A Chapter in America's Industrial Growth* (Washington DC: Tobacco History, n.d.), pp.43-6.
90 See Randall R. Kincaid, 'Shade Tobacco Growing in Florida', *Quincy North Florida Experimental Station Bulletin* 136 (1960), pp.3-43. According to Kincaid (p.4), "About 1898, tests conducted at Quincy showed that leaves grown under artificial shade were of fine quality comparable to wrapper tobacco imported from Sumatra". See

also, W. B. Tisdale, 'Tobacco Growing in Florida', *Florida Agricultural Experimental Station Bulletin* 198 (1928), pp.379-428.

91 From the 1890s, the Connecticut Tobacco Valley Experiment Company in Poquonock carried out fertiliser experiments in tandem with experiments in curing tobacco. In the early 1920s, the Experimental Tobacco Station was the only one in New England and one of only four or five in the United States.

92 The net was originally a form of cheesecloth, similar to that used as mosquito netting. Today other materials are used – in Brazil notably a petroleum derivative, which has a bluish-grey tinge. For the introduction of the nets in Cuba, see Fernández, *Cuba agrícola* (2005), pp.209-54, 'Modernización y cambio tecnológico' (2009), and 'Islands of knowledge' (2013). She also attributes the practice to Sumatra and the United States, prior to its introduction in Cuba in 1901-02.

93 Gilman & Xun, *Smoke* (2004), p.17.

94 An excellent 'pocket' analysis of *terroir* can be found in Becky Sue Epstein, *Champagne: A Global History* (London, Reaktion Books, 2011).

95 Gérard Père et Fils, *Cigars: The Art of Cigars, The World's Finest Cigars*, 2 vols. (Paris: Flammarion, 2002), p.8.

96 See Zoila Lapique Becali, *La memoria en las piedras* (Havana: Editorial Boloña, 2003), and 'Los sucesos de la historia de España y Cuba en las etiquetas de los cigarillos y habanos cubanos', in Consuelo Naranjo Orovio & Carlos Serrano (eds), *Imágenes e Imaginarios Nacionales en el Ultramar Español* (Madrid: CSIC, 1999); also 'La litografía en el siglo XIX', *Catauro* (2005), pp.18-20. See also, Emilio Cueto, *Frédéric Mialhe, Mialhe's Colonial Cuba: The Prints that Shaped the World's View of Cuba* (Miami: Historical Association of Southern Florida, 1994).

97 Martínez, *Habano el rey* (1999), p.24.

98 Jarrett Rudy, *The Freedom to Smoke: Tobacco Consumption and Identity* (Montreal & Kingston: McGill-Queens University Press, 2005), pp.60-3. The Granda brothers' advertising was extensive and they made a point of saying how they had learnt their cigar making in Cuba and acquired the special skills of 'Spanish' as opposed to 'German' handwork, using long filler instead of the short filler of cheaper cigars, and sorting into many more shades than the German three or four.

18

Cuba-Canaries Havana Cigar Connections: A Hemispheric, Transatlantic and Global History[*][1]

THE HAVANA cigar, known simply as *El Habano*, took its name from the port-city of Havana though which it made its grand entrée onto the world stage in the long nineteenth-century 'age of the cigar'.[2] It was fitting, thus, that the 2019 annual Habanos Festival, attended by 1,200 cigar aficionados from over 60 countries, should have opened in the Antiguo Almacén de la Madera y el Tabaco in the city's port, paying tribute to the 500th anniversary of the founding of Havana as well as the 20th anniversary of its cigar brand San Cristobal de La Habana. At the closing gala, celebrating the 50th anniversary of the Trinidad brand, an auction of humidors was held that raised 1,505,000 euros, proceeds going, as in previous years, to the Cuban public health system.

The irony of this should not be lost in today's age when the serious health warnings associated with smoking are widely known. And yet, since the 1990s, in a veritable cigar revival, *El Habano* has catapulted back into its own as the world's most coveted handmade luxury smoke. Habanos SA, Cuba's state-owned cigar company, boasted a 2018 turnover of 537 million dollars (7 percent up over the previous year), marketing its 27 world-famous brands – including Cohíba, Romeo y Julieta, Partagás, Hoyo de Monterrey, H. Upmann and, perhaps most

---

[*] Originally published in Santiago de Luxán Meléndez, João Figueiro-Rego & Vicent Sanz Rozalén (eds), *Grandes vicios, grandes ingresos: el monopolio del tabaco en los imperios ibéricos, siglos XVII-XX* (Madrid: Centro de Estudios Políticos y Constitucionales, 2019), pp.253-92.

famous of all, Montecristo – through an exclusive sales distribution network in 150 countries across five continents.³

Included in this network are the Canary Islands, whose own tobacco history has been intricately bound up with that of Cuba since well before *El Habano*'s 'coming of age'. After the Spanish conquest and under Spanish state tobacco monopoly prohibition, the Canaries had served as an entrepôt for tobacco from Spain's colonies in the Americas, notably Cuba, and smuggling and contraband had been rife. The early nineteenth century, however, ushered in landmark change. While Cuba remained under Spanish colonial rule (until 1898), the Spanish state conceded an end to its monopoly on Cuban tobacco (1817), opening up the sector to not only private Spanish capital but also British, French, German and other investment interests, providing a firm foundation for *El Habano*'s growing international fame. Spain sought to make good its lost monopoly position in Cuba by authorising its own tobacco-growing trials, including in the Canary Islands (1828),⁴ as well as promoting tobacco in its two other remaining colonies, the Philippines and Puerto Rico. Tobacco remains important in the Philippines, yet little is left today of tobacco agriculture or industry in either Puerto Rico, or the Canaries, the scope of which lies beyond our confines here.⁵

What follows charts the rise and demise of Canary Islands tobacco from the early nineteenth century to the present in tandem with that of Cuba and with a special focus on the Havana cigar. It does so in the context of what has been seen as the nineteenth-century 'British cycle' in world history, with its ethos of 'free trade',⁶ or, as argued by some, "the imperialism of free trade".⁷ A preferred British strategy after the end of the Napoleonic Wars was to engage in many parts of the world, not least Ibero-American, establishing 'informal' commercial and diplomatic dominance rather than incorporating territories into the 'formal' British Empire. This was a strategy in which other powers, such as the Dutch and the French, also engaged, and which the United States, itself a diasporic offshoot, would aggressively carry forward in its globalising twentieth-century 'American cycle'.⁸ Drayton has challenged us to conceptualise scenarios such as these as "masked condominia", whereby an empire or nation may appear to rule, yet power is actually masked in multiple ways. Imperial, national and local connectivity and collaboration operate alongside competition and rivalry, with agency at various levels, from the state to the subaltern.⁹

In an attempt to rise to that challenge, what follows here takes into account three interlocking subtexts in cigar history. The first is that of nations with a history of state and parastatal tobacco monopolies (Spain, Portugal and France are cases in point) and others where private capital, in conjunction with state fiscal control, held sway (such as Britain, Holland, Germany and the United States). Notably, however, between the two models – of state monopoly vs private capital and state fiscal controls – there are instances of fewer differences in practice than in theory.[10]

The second is that of technological advances enabling cheaper mechanised mass-production of cigarettes, thereby revolutionising the industry. By the early twentieth century, cigarettes dominated the market and ruthless company takeovers had created monopolies and international cartels, swallowing up much of cigar as well as cigarette production. A prime example was when, in 1902, the two giants American Tobacco Company (ATC) in the United States and Imperial Tobacco Company (ITC) in Britain founded British-American Tobacco (BAT). This directly impacted on Cuba,[11] which (along with Puerto Rico) was earmarked for ATC, while the Canaries would fall within the BAT remit. By the late twentieth century, ATC would be long gone from Cuba, any lingering foreign presence having been wiped out by the agrarian reforms, nationalisations and US trade embargo that came fast in the aftermath of the 1959 Cuban Revolution. It would not be until the 1990s, when Cuba plunged into the depths of a devastating crisis with the disintegration of its by then major trading partner, the Soviet socialist bloc, and with the tightening of the US embargo, that Cuba would start courting non-US foreign capital investment. Habanos, set up in 1990, entered into a succession of deals, the most recent of which was in 2007, whereby Imperial Brands, successor to ITC and its successor Imperial Group, acquired 50 percent shares in Habanos. Imperial acquired the shares having bought Alianza de Tabacos y Distribución (Altadis, Spain) and Altadis USA, companies created after the 1999 merger of Spanish and French parastatals Tabacalera and Societé d'Explotación Industrielle des Tabacs et des Alumettes (SEITA); and in 2015 Imperial formed Tabacalera USA. In effect, companies such as these had multinational cigar investments in Cuba, Spain, France, Britain, the United States and across the globe. By the same token, BAT and other transnational tobacco corporations, which, as we shall see, had once moved into the Canaries, relocated to countries such as the Dominican Republic, competing from there to fill the vacuum of Cuban cigars on the US market created by the embargo, and thus contributing in no small measure to the Canaries demise.[12]

The third important point is that tobacco growing was early seen as a 'settler' or 'poor man's' crop,[13] and the cigar sector as a whole has continued to this day to be shaped by many small actors – in agriculture (growers, ranging from smallholders, rentier farmers and sharecroppers through to day labourers), industry (from owners of small businesses to their workers, and many outworkers), trade, and brand marketing – and their agency counts in this history.

Seen through this lens, a first section charts the Havana cigar universe alongside which to situate Canaries history. A brief macro-historical overview then highlights the Canaries-Cuba geostrategic positioning on the route to and from the Indies, migration, linkages with the central Spanish state and Britain, and the 'Cuban-style' Canaries export model. Pivotal economic and political junctures are subsequently brought into play, linking the commodity with mobilities of people, circuits of knowledge, and capital and labour. Special attention is paid to the post-1959/post-1989 periods, and a closing section returns full circle to Cuba, with a discussion of revitalised Canaries identities in a 1990s central Cuban setting that serves to further nuance our understanding of hemispheric, transatlantic and global drivers in Cuba-Canaries Havana cigar history.

The Havana Cigar Universe

Cuba's famed Havana cigar has long been shaped by political and economic developments tied to foreign and local capital and labour, accompanied by in- and out-migration at key turning points in Cuban history. The nineteenth-century Cuban cigar economy was developed primarily with Spanish, German, British and French capital, for European, North American and world markets, whose key retail outlets were Amsterdam, Bremen, London and New York, as well as Seville. It formed part of a growing world economy for cigars produced with tobacco as far afield as Cameroon, Java, Sumatra and Turkey, as well as closer to home in Brazil, the Dominican Republic, Jamaica, Mexico and Puerto Rico – and with imitation Havana cigars boasting brand names similar to those in Cuba.

The period before and after Cuba's wars of independence from Spain (1868-78, 1879-80, and 1895-98) and the intervening 1880s saw expansion and immigration, attracting manufacturers, workers and farmhands and their families, not least Canary Islanders, known simply as *isleños*.[14] They were recruited to bolster a white smallholder, rentier and sharecropping class in a heavily slave-based economy, slavery not being abolished until 1886.[15] However, economic conditions, labour and political unrest – marked by transatlantic reformist, anarchist, anarcho-syndicalist, annexationist and nationalist leanings – and the independence wars themselves, were the backdrop to outmigration. This was primarily to the neighbouring United States (especially Florida and the Eastern seaboard, up to New York and Connecticut) and the Caribbean (particularly Mexico, Jamaica and the Dominican Republic), as well as across the Atlantic to Spain and the Canaries. Cuban tobacco interests came together outside Cuba, providing a familiar means of livelihood for migrant communities and, in some instances, economic and political mainstay for the independence struggle itself. Over time, overseas economic and political interests built up, some fuelled by mobilities of people, others by catalyst circuits of knowledge, with trading and other advantages over the home country in turmoil, though not without their own turmoil as well.

Charting some of these overseas histories,[16] it became clear how many had been forgotten, and how few connections had been made with Cuba, much less the Canaries, when many were part of a Canaries-Americas migratory network. Florida history is an exception in having been well documented for its links with Cuba, pioneered by local historians, many interested in social and political histories 'from below', through the lens of class, gender, race and nation.[17] Connecticut and New York connections with Cuba (linked with Puerto Rico) have also been documented.[18]

Turn-of-the-century US capital investment came fast in Cuban tobacco, bolstered by US occupations (1898-1902, 1906-09), swallowing up tracts of Cuban tobacco land and major leaf and manufacturing companies and causing smaller concerns to relocate elsewhere, including the Canary Islands. At the same time, some smaller family businesses, declared 'independents', were able to hold their own, and there was a further wave of migration to Cuba from Spain, notably the Canary Islands. And yet, cigar manufacturing was challenged to regain its former glory as mechanised cigarette manufacturing came to dominate the industry. In the 1920s and 1930s, economic depression coupled with labour and political unrest, saw a successful battle of national proportions to stave off mechanisation of the cigar, and with it the essentially male craft of luxury cigar handrolling. This culminated a process whereby much of US-owned cigar manufacturing withdrew from Cuba to the United States; and the 1933 passing of Cuba's Nationality Act saw mass deportations, which included *isleños*, though the latter part of the decade would see large numbers recruited back, often on a seasonal migratory circuit. Cigar rolling languished through the 1940s and 1950s, when limited mechanisation was finally allowed. Outside the prestigious export factories, themselves facing a shrinking market and overseas competition, a diverse labour force that crossed race, ethnic and gender lines was to be found in agriculture and industry, rocked by militancy and strife, with significant communist-led union activism, and with a precarious cigar-rolling outwork sector, in small *chinchales* and individual homes dotted across poor neighbourhoods.[19]

The 1950s insurrection and 1959 Revolution, in the wake of which came agrarian reform and nationalisation, plus the embargo of the United States (and for a while the whole hemisphere, with the exception of Mexico and Canada), caused great internal upheaval; and tobacco in particular suffered in the late 1960s as a result of state prioritisation of sugar. It wasn't until the 1970s that a concerted tobacco recuperation programme was launched, drawing women, who had long been predominant in the sector as a whole, into the prestigious hand-rolling export sector. By then, smaller manufacturers, dealers, growers and workers were proving as astute as larger monopoly capital in finding fertile ground overseas, such that out-migration from Cuba gave rise to newer Cuban tobacco 'host comunities'. In the Americas, these were to be found in Brazil, the Dominican Republic, Costa Rica, Ecuador, Honduras and Nicaragua, the Caribbean and the United States.[20] Overseas markets fast became a battleground for disputed Havana cigar brands, fuelled in part by Spanish-Cuban émigré manufacturers in the Canary Islands, soon linked to US cigar companies.

Alongside older Western European markets for Havana cigars, Third World and Eastern European bloc countries emerged as new partners. Thirty years on, however, a new chapter opened when the 1989 fall of the Berlin Wall and demise of the Soviet bloc in 1991 signalled the end of the bloc's special trade and aid with Cuba. The United States took steps to tighten and extra-territorialise its embargo with the 1991 Torricelli and 1996 Helms-Burton Acts and pressured the European Union to introduce a stringent Common Position on Cuba, which would remain in place for the next two decades. At the same time, a 1990s US-engineered cigar revival was in train.[21] As external geopolitical realities compounded internal weaknesses, the Cuban revolutionary government devised a structural adjustment strategy, courting non-US trade and investment, in which the Havana cigar became a key player. The state-owned Cuban tobacco sector blazed an internal adjustment trail with the disaggregation of tobacco land from state farms to cooperatives and back into private smallholdings.[22]

The new holding company, Habanos SA, set up to handle overseas marketing ventures, struck overseas cigar marketing deals giving exclusive rights over the import and distribution of Havana cigars in return for advance payment. Credit-for-tobacco joint-venture deals were struck between the Cuban state tobacco enterprise and its Spanish and French parastatal tobacco counterparts, Tabacalera – which by then included the Canaries-based Centro Industrial de Tabaqueros Asociados (CITA) – and SEITA, and hard currency incentives were paid to tobacco growers and workers in Cuba.

The path was rocky, however. In 1993, Tabacalera and Cuba's then state tobacco enterprise Cubatabaco were locked in tense meetings to discuss the future of Montecristo and a host of other Havana cigar brands. In 1991 Tabacalera bought the world rights – excluding Cuba, the United States and the Dominican Republic – for Havana cigar trademarks that had been acquired from manufacturers who had left Cuba by Cuban Cigar Brands, a partnership formed by US tobacco giant Consolidated Cigar and Spain's Internacional Cifuentes. This led to international marketing problems for Cuba in third countries, not least France, where SEITA, along with Tabacalera, was a prime market; and in both countries court cases supported Tabacalera's ownership of the brands. It was soon dubbed the Montecristo War, since, in the words of

SEITA director Bruno Vouaille, "Montecristo is considered a reference point for all Cuban cigars."[23] Cubatabaco understood that Tabacalera would sell it the brands once it had control, while Tabacalera had in its sights becoming the brands' European distributor. Tabacalera had the trademarks, but not the cigars. Cuba had the cigars but couldn't sell them because Tabacalera had the trademarks. It was a no-win situation until the parties finally entered into agreement and created Altadis.

This came after Cuba had been investing heavily in tobacco to meet a newly revived world market demand in excess of supply and battles had intensified in US and international courts over market brand names. Major players in this were the then two US cigar giants – General Cigar and Consolidated Cigar – along with émigré Cuban tobacco interests, in Florida and the Dominican Republic especially, followed by Honduras, Nicaragua, Mexico, Connecticut and Brazil. The 1990s US cigar bubble burst in 1999, yet the market held, especially the luxury market for 'pure' Havana cigars (the Havana cigar is called a *puro*, since it is made entirely in Cuba with leaf grown in Cuba) in European and newly emerging Asian economies such as China. In 1999, Tabacalera and SEITA, which had acquired Consolidated Cigar in the United States, formed Altadis. Altadis then bought 50 percent shares in its joint venture with Habanos in Cuba, thereby managing both island and offshore brands. Imperial would later acquire Altadis, situating Havana cigars in the global market place in competition with global cigar giant, Swedish Match, itself a product of various mergers, including US General Cigar.

The Spanish State, 'Informal Empire', and 'Cuban-style' Development

Let us now situate this history from a Canaries optic. The buildup to and aftermath of the quincentennial of the Spanish conquest of the Americas (1492) and the Canaries (1496) ushered in new studies of Canaries-Americas/Canaries-Cuba shared histories of trade and migration.[24] The Canaries and Cuba were geostrategically situated on the route to and from the Indies, such that the early phase of Canaries migration was characterised as having been born of and shaped by the trauma of two synchronic processes of conquest. The pattern to emerge from the late seventeenth century was linked primarily to economic cycles, though also fuelled by political upheavals.

The migratory flow to Cuba increased especially after 1830. During the years 1835-51, some 45 percent of *isleños* entering Cuba came from Tenerife, 33 percent from Gran Canaria, and 10 percent from La Palma.[25] While the Canaries population was small in comparison to that of the Spanish peninsula, it accounted for 42 percent of the total Spanish migration to Cuba in 1846; and the 1846 figure of 20,000 *isleños* in Cuba had risen to almost 49,000 by 1862.[26] Migration peaked 1875-1930, linked to the displacement of much traditional peasant economy in the Canaries' post-1852 'free-trade' era. Cuba, for its part, became a prime destination, in its own 'free-trade' take-off, notwithstanding political unrest, wars of independence from Spain and US occupation.

The composition of the migration varied, with a significant proportion of families and extended kinship networks, but also, especially in the case of Cuba, with large numbers of young male contract labour. Seasonal, cyclical and return migration serviced the sugar and tobacco sectors in particular, in Cuba and the Canaries, as *isleños* became *golondrinos*, evidencing a close articulation between their two economies and a transatlantic labour market.[27] In the words of migrant José Antonio Brito Pérez:

> Both my grandfather Santos, now deceased, and my grandfather Antonio Fermín, would do a harvest here and another in Cuba; that happened very often. In Cuba, they'd finish (harvesting) more or less in March and then come here to plant. And when they harvested, they'd go back again. They were completely immersed in the world of tobacco and would see through the crops here and there. They used to say the quality here was the same, as good, as in Cuba.[28]

The First World War saw the paralysis of Canaries exports and a 10,000-strong emigration from the port of Santa Cruz de Tenerife alone.[29] Of these, 5,000 were destined for Cuba, whose wartime economy was booming and attracting migrants. Total official emigration (excluding illegals and stowaways) was recorded as 25,000, with a prevalence of men aged 20-59, from agricultural backgrounds, travelling primarily to Cuba. The emigration peaked in the months of October-January, preceding Cuba's sugar and tobacco harvests. There were those who would return at the end of the harvest, and remittances from those who stayed proved crucial to families back home.[30] After the war, this cycle was broken with the late 1920s economic depression and 1930s revolution in Cuba, which gave rise to the mass deportations of foreign labour, including *isleños*.

The migration continued through the Spanish Civil War years (1936-39), and again after the Second World War, whereby the period 1945-60 saw some 80,000 Canary Islanders leave for the Americas, especially in the 1950s, primarily to Venezuela. The trend slowed and reversed after the 1960s, and especially by the 1980s, with return migration from Cuba, Venezuela and Argentina in particular. By then, economically and politically, conditions in the Canary Islands, especially with the expanding tourism economy, were proving more attractive than those in the Americas. By the 1990s, the Canary

Islands, once a frontier for the Americas, had joined the ranks of frontier middle-income economies and societies serving as an entry point into richer countries of continental Europe. The tide had turned.

In this scenario, the relationship between Spain and the Americas, forged in conquest, commerce, smuggling, piracy, slave trade and war, was one in which Cuba, the largest of the Caribbean islands and under Spanish control, was early coveted by Britain.[31] During the Seven Years War (1756-63), the British occupation of Havana in 1762 might have only lasted 11 months, yet it heralded an ultimately unstoppable opening of Cuba to trade and commerce beyond Spanish control, from which other powers, including the United States, would benefit enormously.

From the mid-nineteenth century through to the 1920s and 1930s, the Canaries (along with Portuguese Madeira and the Azores) would also increasingly, like Cuba, become part of Britain's 'free-trade' 'informal' empire, at times sanctioned and at others contested by the central Spanish state.[32] The latter part of the nineteenth century saw the British-Canary Islands trading relationship strengthened with the Canaries free-port model. There was progressive concentration in primary export products (no longer wine but cochineal, subsequently sugar and tobacco, and then bananas and tomatoes, along with onions and potatoes); the import of manufactured products, raw materials (such as coal) and foodstuffs; and a predominance of British interests (alongside German, French, Belgian and later US) relative to those of Spain. It was an agro-commercial model closely linked to foreign, not least British, interests. This swept the island into a strategy of new crops, involving foreign and local capital, the latter often drawing on the savings of migrants. As an agro-export, non-industrial model, however, it was viewed as having consigned the Canaries to the periphery of the Spanish economy and Europe.[33]

A protracted process of declining British interests started after the First World War, by which time the export model faced increasing competition on the British market. By way of example, production costs of West Indian, especially Jamaican, bananas, were half those in the Canaries, and Jamaica, Costa Rica, Honduras and Colombia would become the world's prime banana producers. The 1930s economic depression, the buildup to the Second World War with the Spanish Civil War, and subsequent imposition of peninsular and German interests all signalled the coming withdrawal of the British presence, British officials in the Canaries being among the first to counsel this.[34] It would only turn around again later, with the growth of tourism.

The agro-export, non-industrial Canaries model of development has been characterised as Cuban-style, linked to cycles of products imitative of Cuba, such as sugar and tobacco. For tobacco, this began with the early experimentation of tobacco growing and was later advantaged by the free-port system, and *isleños* who had been involved in tobacco in Cuba gravitated to tobacco in the Canaries. The industrial development of Canaries tobacco, and within this of cigars, also proved to be an exception in the Canaries model, thereby occupying a special place in Canaries history, albeit in the process a prime source of revenue for, and recurrent source of tension with, the Spanish state and open to other foreign interests.[35]

Canaries Tobacco in the Frame

In the 1950s, José Pérez Vidal delineated four periods in Spanish tobacco history.[36] The first spanned the sixteenth and early seventeenth centuries, when tobacco was grown as a medicinal and ornamental plant. Tobacco supplies, part legal, but especially contraband, came from Spain's possessions in the Americas – especially Cuba and Venezuela – and also from Portuguese Brazil and British Virginia. The second extended from the late seventeenth to the end of the eighteenth century, when tobacco, under crown prohibition, was grown clandestinely at home. The third spanned the nineteenth century, after a partial lifting of prohibition, with growing trials in several provinces on the peninsula and especially in the Balearic and Canary Islands. The first half of the twentieth century was Pérez Vidal's fourth and final period, when there was no prohibition and a notable increase in growing and manufacture. Of interest to us here are his third and fourth periods, extended to the present day, as they pertain to the Canaries.

Writing two decades later on Canaries tobacco, Oswaldo Brito González referred to *vegueros* (especially *palmeros*) early returning from Cuba "sociologically cloaked with 'Indian' behavioural patterns", growing tobacco and making their own cigars or *chinguitos*.[37] Monopoly control generated patterns of evasion and resistance in the Canaries as it had in Cuba, exemplified by Cuba's *veguero* uprisings of 1717, 1718 and 1723 and the Canaries *Motín de Cevallos* (1720). At the same time, tobacco transported from Havana, while overseen and financially controlled in the Canaries, had given rise to a penchant for smoking Havana cigars. As later documented by Juan Manuel Santana Pérez, "The men of good taste do not savour the Seville tobacco, rather they prefer the cigar from Havana or those from Caracas in the Registry Ships."[38]

These were the beginnings of a singular history of Canaries tobacco, whose rise and demise has since been well documented. Andrés Arnaldos Martínez and Jorge Arnaldos de Armas opened their study with an overview chapter on the early Cuba-Canaries connection, before periodising this after 1852, when the Canaries were accorded free-port status, up until 2002, the end year of their study.[39] The first of their four periods, 1852-1921, was when tobacco was projected to take the place of the failing cochineal trade (due to the introduction of artificial colourings), but stymied by opposition from the

Spanish state monopoly Compañía Arrendataria de Tabacos (CAT) to allowing Canaries leaf or manufactured products into the peninsula:[40]

> [In 1887, CAT stipulated:] The quantities of tobacco acquired by the contractor from the Philippines, Cuba, Puerto Rico and the Canaries in relation to the total amount acquired are to be no less than the proportion of 6 million kilos from the Philippines, 3 million from Cuba, 1.5 million from Puerto Rico and 0.4 million from the Canaries.[41]

Complaints escalated that limited state buying was highly unfavourable to the Canaries; and towards the end of the century, coinciding with the independence of Cuba and the Philippines, even tighter price and fiscal controls were put into force that fuelled arguments for an opening within Spain. By 1914 cigar manufacturers were demanding free-trade zones in Santa Cruz de Tenerife, Las Palmas de Gran Canaria, Santa Cruz de La Palma and Arrecife "in imitation of those mentioned abroad, and then both for the price of raw materials and for labour, these modest factories in Gran Canaria will be able to compete with those in Holland, Belgium and Germany, which only for the benefits of the free zon flood the world with their products."[42] In 1921 CAT modified its contract with the Canary Islands, whereby prices paid for cigars were more favourable in comparison with those paid to Cuba. By then, only a small part of the leaf used in cigar production was grown domestically, as most was imported, mainly from the Philippines, Cuba and the United States.

The second and third periods were take-off (1922-59) and consolidation (1960-86). This was initially facilitated by agreements signed in the 1920s for Canaries tobacco on the peninsula and leaf imports, primarily from Cuba and the Philippines, and to a lesser extent Brazil and the Dominican Republic. However, there were continuing difficulties for Canaries production on the Spanish national market, due to the ambivalence, at best, of CAT and, after 1945, its successor Tabacalera; and 1950s mechanisation led a number of manufacturers to join forces in 1956 to form CITA. Fiscal legislation subsequently privileged manufacturing, which saw a major concentration of production and expansion of CITA, especially in the cigarette sector. This, however, pitted the Canaries against Tabacalera, culminating in the late 1970s with the restructuring of Canaries production and two joint ventures, Tabacanaria and Cigarcanaria, involving Tabacalera and a number of key local family concerns such as Zamorano and Fuentes. During the 1970s, major tobacco multinationals – US-based Philip Morris and R. J. Reynolds, British-based Gallaher, and Dutch-based Reemtsma – invested in locally established concerns, thus gaining access to Spanish tobacco monopoly markets.[43]

The fourth period, 1986-2002, was one of decline as Spain joined the European Community and common fiscal and labour policies applied to the islands increased costs. These, in tandem with broader forces of globalisation, had dramatic consequences for Canaries production as major factories closed and relocated. In 1991, a strategy was devised whereby Tabacanaria, Cigarcanaria and CITA fused to become CITA Tabacos de Canarias SA in Santa Cruz de Tenerife, interlocked with Philip Morris, BAT and R. J. Reynolds, and later Japan Tobacco International (which by then owned Gallaher). All, with the exception of CITA, would subsequently relocate out of the Canary Islands.[44]

A detailed institutional study by Santiago de Luxán (2006) opened in 1827, when tobacco-growing trials were first authorised, and ended in 1936, when the industry tipped into a decline. He periodised Canaries tobacco history in two main phases: 1636-1852, when the Canaries were a receiver area subject to the Spanish state monopoly, with tobacco coming in, especially from Cuba, and with much contraband; and 1852-1936, as an important tobacco economy, producing leaf and manufactured tobacco, on the margin of, while also subject to, the Spanish state monopoly. In the second period, tobacco was one of the strategic products for economic growth, protagonised by the Real Sociedad Económica del País de Gran Canaria, Reales Sociedades Económicas and Juntas de Fomento. The intractable problem of tobacco contraband, along with the "the watchful gaze of his British majesty,"[45] were key factors leading to the 1852 free-port status, which was reformed in 1870 and 1900. After that, there was little real further change until the 1959 stabilisation plan and then extensive free-port status under the 1972 *Regimen Económico y Fiscal*, enabling trade and industry, until Spain's entry into the European Community and the overall end of the Spanish monopoly in 1985-86.

Luxán delineated three periods during his timeframe: 1827-52, 1852-75, and 1875-1936. A salient point he made for the first period was that the level of tobacco contraband from the United States and Brazil to the Spanish peninsula after the 1817 end of prohibition on Cuba was a strong factor leading the Spanish Government to authorise tobacco-growing trials in the Canaries. This created a favourable climate for when the 1852 free-port status came into effect, though the 'tobacco option' for the Canaries did not really become a reality until after the 1870s, with the cochineal crisis. The comparative advantage of the Canaries' close relationship with Cuba would constantly be highlighted alongside the equally constant preoccupation with quality and not lagging behind Cuba (and Puerto Rico), and there would be constant complaints about Spain's more favourable treatment of its Caribbean colonies.

Luxán's third period was characterised by the failure of the 'agricultural option', as diagnosed in British consular reports throughout the latter part of the nineteenth century;[46] the latent contradiction between the free-port model and tobacco interests; and tobacco's minor importance for the Spanish state monopoly. Luxán concluded that the agro-industrial complex of tobacco, plausible as it was in the last third of the century, failed for lack of state support.

Hopes for a *Fábrica del Estado en Canarias*, with capital, technology, guarantees for growers and industry, and free-port status in theory could have benefitted tobacco but cochineal was the favoured export product until the 1880s. The subsequent consolidation of the Cía Arrendataria del Monopolio Nacional de Tabacos, after 1887, paved the way for tobacco manufacturing expansion, by then primarily in cigarette production, though cigar manufacturing also made its mark. A conclusión reached by Luxán, pertinent here, was that, in contrast to earlier overly pessimistic Canaries tobacco historiography, Canaries tobacco had been able to develop as a Canaries regional specialisation within the national economy. Running counter to this, as of the 1890s, was the alternative trilogy of bananas, tomatoes and potatoes backed by Britain. After the 1930s, the end-point of Luxán's study, several other countervailing forces would take their toll, as we shall see below.

Circuits of Knowledge and Experience

Throughout the Americas, early *isleño* migrants added their knowledge and experience of the lands of the Canaries to those of the indigenous peoples.[47] They became merchants, traders and the small peasant *colono* or rentier/sharecropper and agricultural labouring classes, recruited to supplant indigenous and later black slave labour, often under conditions that led them to be described as the white slaves of the Americas.[48] In his work, Manuel de Paz Sánchez refers to the 1820 Comisión de Población Blanca de Cuba signing contracts with two Canarians – Sebastian Ortega for 300+ persons to Bahía Honda via Mariel and Damaso Baudet for Guantánamo. He also makes Canaries connections between Cuba, Puerto Rico and Santo Domingo:

> A migration closely linked to subsistence crops such as tobacco and coffee, and also in the sugar plantation economy. A population settled in agricultural areas of the mountainous interior of Puerto Rico that gave rise to one of the sociocultural types most characteristic of the island, and also the Spanish Caribbean: the *jíbaro* or white peasant, similar in way of life to the Cuban *guajiro* or the Dominican *montero*.[49]

In Cuba, the *veguero* came to be identified with *isleño*, and *veguero* uprisings also known as *isleño* uprisings. The *veguero/isleño* conflict with the Spanish state has been signalled as forerunner to Cuba's late nineteenth-century *bandoleros* and the *mambises* (among whom were *isleños*) fighting for Cuba's independence from Spain. Foremost among them was *isleño* descendant José Martí, remembered by a statue in La Laguna, hometown of his mother Leonor Pérez.[50]

Publications and migrant testimonies bear testimony to the packed holds of boats plying the transatlantic voyage and the conditions under which many laboured in the tobacco fields.[51] Testimonies such as that of 87-year-old Francisco Pérez González in the 1990s were not unusual:

> I did 70 *vegas* in Cabaiguán, I came in 1915 with my mother, because my father was already here since 1905 and sent for us with the last *vega* he did for Alfredo Hidalgo and Pepe Paz, over in Arroyo Lajas. There they gave Dad an area in return for a fourth of the crop, we were there as sharecroppers for three years, I say we because although I was just a lad I had to work hard. Then we rented land in Guajen, near Cuatro Esquinas, and were there until 1923, when we sold for the years left on our rental and bought a little farm in La Fragua; we were able to do that with what we saved growing tobacco.[52]

While publications such as *El Guanche* (1924-25), *Patria Isleña* (1926-27) and *Tierra Canaria* (1930-31) were all too-often ephemeral, mutual aid societies were around longer. The Asociación Canaria de Beneficencia y Protección Agrícola was founded in 1872 and merged with the Asociación Protectora de la Inmigración Canaria y de Beneficencia de Matanzas in 1878. The Asociación Canaria de La Habana was founded in 1906, with priorities for health, education and recreation; acquired a ward in the Quinta del Rey opened in 1907; and built the Casa de Salud Nuestra Señora de la Candelaria in 1922. Altogether, another 70 delegations and associations were founded up until the mid-twentieth century, though after decades of inactivity, many, including the Havana Association, were dissolved. It wouldn't be until 1992 that the Asociación Canaria de Cuba Leonor Pérez Cabrera would recreate this mutual aid tradition, with delegations throughout the country.

As return migrants took back knowledge and experience for the Canaries tobacco sector, the migration, it was said, "hadn't been for free" and growers and rollers brought "West Indian airs."[53] As argued by Rodríguez Brito:

> Human factors motivated growing tobacco on the island, albeit physical factors have also been important. Growing began because some peasants, the majority of whom had worked in tobacco in their youth on the island of Cuba, on their return to La Palma tried to grow it first for family consumption and then commercially.[54]

They would also bring with them traditions, such as that of the *lector* in the factory, labour militancy and conflict with the Spanish state over taxes and controls, seen to set them at a disadvantage to the peninsula and Cuba.

Seeds were taken from the best *vegas* in Cuba, and manuals and reports were published. An 1851 report published in Madrid was *El tabaco habano*, by

Miguel Rodríguez Ferrer,[55] and the following year Francisco María de León y Falcón, Comisionado Regio de Agricultura, reported:

> The Canaries have comparative advantages due to our close relations with Cuba. In addition to the conditions of our soil, we have growers trained on the plantations of that island.... The trials that have been carried out have demonstrated that the tobacco is similar, if not superior, to the Cuban.[56]

These served to strengthen the lived experience of return migrants themselves. In the words of Luxán:

> Various generations of growers had travelled there and back. Reference should be made not only to the passing on of written information, or the exchanges on the part of patriotic societies such as the Sociedades Económicas de Amigos del País, but above all the emigration and in-situ learning about tobacco culture.[57]

Other manuals and reports followed in Santa Cruz de Tenerife and Gran Canaria.[58]

Anelio Rodríguez Concepción narrates how, in 1863, in La Palma, Juan Nepomuceno Déniz first received instruction to grow tobacco similar to that of the Partido area in Cuba.[59] A decade later, in 1876, the Madrid Fábrica Nacional accepted samples from Tenerife and La Palma; and by the late 1870s and 1880s the Canaries Sociedad de Amigos del País was comparing Canaries tobacco favourably with that of Cuba and Puerto Rico, demanding the Spanish government buy more from the Canaries. In 1885 the Liga de Cosecheros y Fabricantes was founded in La Palma, Tenerife and Gran Canaria, and that same year, Eufemiano Fuentes Cabrera's La Favorita factory had 100 workers, including Cuban-trained master cigar maker Lorenzo Arbelo Pérez. On the back of tobacco expansion from the 1870s to the 1890s, exports grew ninefold between 1885 and 1891 alone.

In the early twentieth century, with the future looking promising, key cigar tobacco-growing areas on La Palma were Breña Alta, Breña Baja, Mazo and El Paso. However, 1901 saw a 50 percent increase in taxes when the Spanish government decreed parity with the Americas and elsewhere. This was partly, it was alleged, as a result of *tinerfeños, grancanarios* and *palmeros* sending coveted Sumatra tobacco to the peninsula as Canaries tobacco, and partly due to competition from North Africa and the peninsula. That year, there were 16 tobacco firms officially registered in the Canary Islands, with a total of 397 workers, whose numbers swelled by 1914 to 1,000 in Tenerife, 900 in Gran Canaria and 340 in La Palma, where the Santa Cruz de La Palma factories of Luis Felipe Gómez Wangüemert's Flor de Palma and Africana (the latter along with Juan Cabrera Marín) and Francisco Cabrera Hernández' La Palmera cigars gained fame. The London-based La Palma Tobacco Company Ltd. also began operations, exporting at its peak 170,000 cigars.

Gómez Wangüemert illustrates well the Cuba-Canaries cigar connection in these years.[60] He migrated to Cuba, living there during Cuba's interwar years 1882-89 and again from 1914 to his death in 1942. During his return to La Palma, he employed his tobacco skills to good gain. In addition to entering the business, in 1906 he promoted tobacco at a major exhibition and founded two journals, short-lived yet important in their time: *Germinal* and *El Tabaco*. He extolled Canaries quality growing and manufacture, albeit also berating the lack thereof. In the 1906 first issue of *El Tabaco* (30 March 1906), he wrote:

> We tried to impress on the Government of the Mother Country, the Congress of Deputies and the press of Madrid ... the importance of the cultivation and manufacture of tobacco for this island ... that as the source of public wealth, the emigration that is causing depopulation can be stopped, that the Peninsula of Spain does not produce tobacco and this island is at present the only part of Spain where it is grown and manufactured following the practices of Cuba.[61]

In 1908, shortly after the Santa Cruz de La Palma Cámara Agrícola was set up, Wangüemert pushed for a subsidiary Estación Agronómica Provincial for experimentation in tobacco growing and drying on La Palma. An example in reverse was Juan Martín Lesmes, born in Cabaiguán, Cuba, in 1890, who went to the Canaries in 1930, producing La Fuma and La Verdad cigars. In 1940, he launched Peñamil in Santa Cruz de Tenerife, subsequently setting up Lorenzo Peñamil SA, which would be bought 40 years later by Tabacalera.

Capital and Labour

As the Canaries cigar industry developed, there were, in effect, two tobacco subsectors: one that was registered officially, comprising small to medium-sized factories mainly in La Palma, Tenerife and Gran Canaria, worked by hand until part mechanised, and supplying Tabacalera; and another which was more precarious, dominated by home and outwork, catering to the local market, with a large percentage of women, many of whom were poorly paid home workers in *barrios periféricos*.[62] Twentieth-century tobacco expansion did not go unaccompanied by struggle, in opposition to both Canaries manufacturers and the Spanish monopoly.[63] Strikes and other action reflected a growing consolidation of the labour movement from the early guilds and mutual aid societies of the late nineteenth century, especially among dock, transport and tobacco workers, though organisations remained weak and fragmented along political and other lines. Agustín Millares Cantero provides a glimpse of this, and also the mobility behind early ideologies, in the person of *tinerfeño* Secundino Delgado Rodríguez.[64] Described as having become an anarchist migrating from Cuba to Florida, he edited *El Esclavo* in Tampa, was involved in the Cuban independence struggle, and co-founded the Caracas journal *El Guanche* in 1897-98. He returned to Tenerife in late 1900 and in Santa Cruz was connected with *El Obrero*, strongly critical of foreign capital in the Canaries.

A 1901 tax increase was fiercely opposed by the Unión de Torcedores de Santa Cruz de La Palma and Confederación de Tabaqueros de Santa Cruz de La Palma. There were strikes in 1908 in Santa Cruz de La Palma and 1914 in Santa Cruz de Tenerife, and in the peak year of 1919 six strikes: in Las Palmas (one in El Crédito, two in Eufemiano Fuente's La Favorita, and one in La Flor Isleña), Santa Cruz de Tenerife and Santa Cruz de La Palma. Poor pay and conditions in the sector were constant cause for complaint: in 1919, in Santa Cruz de La Palma factories El Trabajo, Africana and Golondrina over pay, the sacking of a worker delegate in Africana, and a reduction in Tabacalera leaf buying; and in 1922, in Africana over the behaviour of the *capataz*, the mutual benefit society (providing health, education and a library), and the *lector*. There were strikes in the Severino Viera Martín factory to reinstate two women workers, in the Bartoto Apolinario factory over abuses of the *capataz* and day rates, and in Eufemio Fuentes' El Crédito and La Favorita for increased wages and union recognition. In a 1931 suspension of contracts between Tabacalera and Canarias, over 1,000 workers were laid off, and worker organisations declared a common front. In 1933, both the Congreso Tabaquero de Santa Cruz de La Palma and the Sindicato de Obreros/as Tabaqueros de Gran Canaria came out on strike. In 1935, a tobacco workers' strike was declared on the three tobacco islands when CAT threatened a 25 percent drop in production – handmade cigar production being the hardest hit.

Miguel Suárez Bosa, in his analysis of the labour movement in the Eastern Canaries (Gran Canaria, Fuerteventura and Lanzarote) for the period 1930-36, viewed the years 1900-19 as an attempted transition from early guilds to sectoral and federative labour organisations, followed by a 1919-30 lull in the labour movement.[65] The movement recovered during the Second Republic (1930-36) and was repressed during the 1936-39 Civil War period, as also under Franco. He detailed 1930-32 reorganisation, 1933-34 expansion and radicalisation, and 1935-36 reorganisation and popular front, punctuated by a 1933 general strike in support of tobacco workers. In 1932, with the majority of tobacco workers only working three days a week, there was mounting opposition to mechanisation, and in 1931 and 1933 there were strikes over Tabacalera reducing the quota. In 1935, the tobacco congress in Santa Cruz de Tenerife included the Unión de Torcedores de Santa Cruz de La Palma and

Confederación de Tabaqueros El Trabajo; and the Comisión Pro Defensa del Tabaco made demands for a 48-hour general strike and set up the Federación Tabaquera Regional and Regional Committee Pro Defensa del Tabaco Canario. Tabacalera's response was to increase the quota.

Manufacturers, grouped initially under the Sindicato de Fabricantes de Tabaco (set up in 1920) and then the Asociación Patronal de Fabricantes de Tabaco (as of 1929), found themselves pitted against a radicalisation of the labour movement with strong socialist and communist influences. Political divisions, however, remained in the major general unions, and the overall panorama of the cigar sector in the 1940s, as documented by Pilar Domínguez,[66] was one of dislocation caused by the war years. Given the much-lamented dependence on leaf imports, the main producers were also the main importers of leaf, some 40 percent of which was brought in through Puerto de La Luz, hence the location of several concerns close by. Production was mainly for the local market, with small exports to Guinea and African Atlantic coastal countries, as well as Spain, through CAT and Tabacalera. The sector was characterised most as one of fragmentation in small family businesses, piecework and a large family outwork sector in *chinchales*, with a marked gender division of labour and a prevalence of women workers on the fringes of fragile labour organisations.[67]

Post-1959/Post-1989

Fast forward to the 1990s, and, while a lifeline was being extended to Habanos in Cuba, the fate of Canaries cigars was being sealed. As reported by the glossy New York magazine *Cigar Aficionado*, Canaries cigar makers tried unsuccessfully to rekindle past glories.[68] While some eight to nine million cigars were produced annually in the Canaries at the time, close to six million by the largest manufacturer, CITA, with brands such as Peñamil, Condal and Goya making inroads into the US market, cigars were reported to be inconsistent in quality and overpriced. A strong US following for Canaries cigars in the 1960s and 1970s had been mainly due to the Menéndez and García families, who in the early twentieth century had established the reputation of Havana's H. Upmann factory and the brand Montecristo. They left after the 1959 Cuban Revolution and their Montecruz cigar made in Gran Canaria became the leading premium cigar brand sold in the United States in the 1970s, accounting for a third of Canaries cigars on the US market, which in turn accounted for over a third of total US consumption.

Cuban tobacco leaf was proving difficult to source from 1990s Cuba. However, because of the US embargo, Cuban leaf couldn't be included in blends for the US market. As Fernando Wangüemert, general manager for CITA cigars, explained at the time: "Our cigars for the US market are admittedly lighter than our normal ones produced here. We changed over the Cuban tobacco for other tobaccos. We had to."[69] Filler blends were mainly sourced from the Dominican Republic, with some from Brazil and Nicaragua; binders from the Dominican Republic and Indonesia; and wrappers from Connecticut and Indonesia. As a result, many cigars from the Canaries on the US market had little to distinguish them from others, except for where they were rolled. The popularity of Canaries cigars continued until the 1980s increased duties and labour costs after Spain entered the European Common Market. Consolidated Cigar, which bought out the Menéndez & García factory Insular Tabacalera SA (INTASA) in the early 1970s, averaging about 15 million cigars a year, moved operations to a massive factory in the Dominican Republic's La Romana free-trade zone. In the words of factory manager José Seijas, who had helped run the company's operations in the Canary Islands until they were shut down in the early 1980s: "It was an impossible situation. Labor costs simply became too much. We had to move our operations to the Dominican Republic."[70] By the 1990s, very little quality tobacco was grown in the Canaries, though the Vargas small family cigar business in La Palma still defended the best blend as that of La Palma and Cuban tobacco. CITA, meanwhile, had slowly built a beachhead in Miami, opening an office as well as a cigar bar and shop, as well as running a joint-venture cigar factory in the Dominican Republic with Swisher and MATASA.

Rodríguez Concepción narrates developments of the post-1959 years in La Palma. There, blue mould blights of the late 1960s caused manufacturers to turn more to importing tobacco throughout the 1970s, and blends with cheaper tobaccos, imported from Africa, Asia and the Americas, became the norm thereafter. Subsequent projects to revitalise tobacco growing in La Palma were to little avail. In the years 1982-88, the Junta Superior Coordinadora de la Política Tabaquera and Consejo Tabaquero de Canarias, set up by the Instituto de Desarrollo Agrario to strengthen relations with the Agencia General de Tabaco Nacional, raised hopes that tobacco growers and producers would expand production and put a brake on increased imports. Mercocanarias, the public insurance company under the Consejo Agrícola for buying and drying operations of the Taburiente Corporation, was the conduit for European Union funding, with quotas, to veteran growers. In the 1990s, the Canaries Government supported a La Palma tobacco-grower recuperation plan, with credit, price controls and a central curing shed, but this was small in scale. The most hectares brought under cultivation (in Breña Alta, Breña Baja, El Paso, Villa de Mazo and Los Llanos de Ariadne) for any one year were in 1998, and only 6.5. At the turn of the twenty-first century, alongside a handful of surviving *chinchales* on La Palma, only Tabacos Vargas had been able to carve out a niche for itself in Santa Cruz de La Palma, while Tabacalera strengthened its presence in Tenerife and Gran Canaria.

Cuba-Canaries connections are well illustrated by two examples from different periods of post-1959 Canaries tobacco: expansion (1960-86) and decline (1986-2000). The first is that of INTASA. Alonso Menéndez was the creator of the famous Montecristo brand in Cuba in 1935, having bought up the Havana factories of H. Upmann and Por Larrañaga. It was his sons, Benjamín and Felipe Menéndez, who relocated to the Canaries and began production of their earlier famous Cuban brands, such as Partagás and Gener, in 1964 under the rubric of General de Tabacos SA, and, in 1965, the Canaries Cigar & Tobacco Company. Their Montecruz, Don Miguel, Don Diego, Don Marcos and Flamenco cigar brands, made with leaf blends that included no Cuban tobacco, all met with success in the United States, where the embargo on Cuba gave them a niche market. In the early 1970s, they employed 700 workers in the Canaries, with an annual output of 22 million handmade cigars. When INTASA was bought up in 1974 by Consolidated Cigar, Benjamín Menéndez moved to oversee company production of Macanudo cigars in Jamaica. After a brief cigar sojourn with his brother Felipe in Brazil, he relocated again, along with the production of Macanudos, to Consolidated in the Dominican Republic. When Tabacalera bought up Consolidated, Menéndez was appointed Director of Central American and Caribbean operations for Tabacalera, also overseeing premium cigar business for the US market.[71] His brother Felipe became established in São Gonçalo, in the Recôncavo area of Bahía, in Brazil, growing tobacco and manufacturing Dona Flor and other brands for the Brazilian and international market.[72] The Canaries cigar rise and decline in the 1960s-80s was, thus, in no small part tied to the Menéndez's arrival and departure, and integrally related to the fortunes of Jamaica, Brazil and the Dominican Republic as well as the United States.

The second example is that of CITA, which, in 1991, took over Cigarcanaria SA, created by Tabacalera, after purchasing Lorenzo Peñamil in 1981, almost a decade after the death (in 1973) of Peñamil's Cuban founder Lesmes. This came on the heels of the mid-1980s fiscal incentives for foreign companies, which had attracted multinationals such as BAT, Gallaher, Reemtsma, Swisher and Dunhill alongside Tabacalera. BAT merged with Tabacanaria and Cigarcanaria, with 50 percent holdings by Tabacalera and initially Álvaro González SA and Lorenzo Peñamil SA. Over the years 1984-2000, during which the Canaries became part of the European Customs Union and companies such as Philip Morris, Reynolds and BAT relocated, tobacco shipments to mainland Spain were halved and employment in the sector was down by two thirds.[73] By then, in the global cigar market, China was the biggest producer, with 21 percent of the world market in cigars, all made by the China National Tobacco Corporation. Second was the United States with 18 percent, followed by France (7.4 percent), Germany (7 percent), the United Kingdom (6.2 percent) and Spain (3.8 percent). Only in Spain because of Farias, Italy because of Toscanos, and Cuba was consumption of cigars higher than that of cigarettes, while consumption in France, Belgium, the United Kingdom, Denmark and Sweden was over 90 percent cigarettes. After China Corp., Swisher International had become the major cigar company with 6.8 percent of world production and supplying one third of the US market. Ebas group (leader in Germany with A. André, in Sweden with Frans Suell, and in Holland) and Consolidated Cigar, second in the US market, were the only other companies with over 5 percent of the world market. BAT group (H. Wintermans, Skandinavisk Tabakskompagni and Imperial Tobacco), Swiss group Burger (Danneman, Canariense de Tabaco, Ritmeester) and SEITA in France had over 4 percent. Together, these companies represented 76 percent of the world market.[74]

Demand for Canaries cigars on the US market peaked at 27 million handmade cigars, until Consolidated's mid-1980s move to the Dominican Republic, closing two plants in Gran Canaria and one in La Palma. In 1995-99, Canaries exports to the United States halved, and, though they doubled to the rest of world, this was not enough to make up a shortfall of one third. With the exception of CITA, Guajiro and Canariense, there were only small concerns left (35 officially registered) and over 200 home workers. Tobacco was imported from the Dominican Republic, Cameroon, Sumatra and Java, and Cuba, though much Cuban wrapper was substituted by wrapper of Connecticut seed produced in Dominican Republic. In La Palma, a small sector used only a small amount of leaf from some five hectares in Breña and Caldera.

The strategy whereby Tabacanaria, Cigarcanaria and CITA fused to become CITA Tabacos de Canarios SA paved the way for operations in Las Palmas and Tenerife, and warehouses in La Laguna, counting on the expertise of, among others, Fernando and Luis Wangüemert. This brought revitalised links with Cuba, by then in the depths of its early 1990s crisis. CITA, subsidiary to Tabacalera, merged with the SEITA to form Altadis, and having bought up Consolidated, had also become part of a conglomerate producing in the La Romana free-trade zone of the Dominican Republic. In 2001, Francisco Javier Zamorano became President of CITA, with a 50 percent holding by Altadis and 50 percent Agrupación Tabaquera Insular Canaria (ATIC), the latter divided equally between four Zamorano brothers.[75] In the early 1990s, CITA speaheaded two developments in Cuba: the joint venture Compañía de Tabacos Isleños SA (COTAIS) for a modernised factory in Havana, for Punch and Hoyo de Monterrey cigarettes, and prefinancing tobacco growers – many of them *isleños* – in the central Ciego de Ávila region of Vuelta Arriba.

Shifting Identities in a Globalised Cigar World

In the heart of Cuba's central Vuelta Arriba tobacco region, not far from Ciego de Ávila, lies the small town of Cabaiguán. It couldn't be more Cuban. And yet, according to the 2001 Cuban census, it was also home to a quarter of Cuba's *isleño* descendants. The town's Reparto Canarias, built in 1957 by *palmero* descendant Eulogio Crespo Guerra, boasts nine streets bearing the names of the seven Canary Islands, plus El Teide for the one most inclined and Leonor Pérez for part of the Central Highway. In 2002, the town was witness to a celebratory explosion of Canaries culture and identity as 30 May was declared *Día de Canarias*, and a monument erected to the *Emigrante Canario* en Cuba – an initiative of the Viceconsejería de Acción Exterior y Relaciones Exteriores del Gobierno de Canarias and la Presidencia de la Delegación Provincial de Sancti-Spíritus de la Asociación Canaria de Cuba.[76] Located in the Reparto Canarias, the monolith is a bust of a mother sobbing, below which there is a couple with two children, inspired by a poem of the late *palmero decimista* Cuquillo, who lived in the munipality.[77] Also on the monolith are the shields of the seven islands.

Under the Constitution of 1978, the Spanish unitary state guaranteed autonomy for the regions that made up Spain, and, in this context, there was a reaffirmation of Canaries identity. This developed through the 1980s from a position of Canaries autonomy or self-determination to a sense of Canaries nationhood, accompanied by a process of identification with diaspora emigrants.[78] The period was one of increasing return migration from the Americas, not least Cuba, such that Canaries identity itself was shifting terrain. The period was also one in which tobacco played its part, and, across the water, back in Cuba, a new chapter was unfolding, which would be documented by both Canaries and Cuban scholars and aficionados.[79]

Integrally linked as Cabaiguán is to Cuba's tobacco history, it is an area where I conducted research in the early 1980s.[80] At the time, Canaries identity was not to the fore in the ways it was to become in the late 1980s and especially the early 1990s, when the twinning of the island of La Palma and Cabaiguán was but one of many between the Canaries and Cuba – a total of 37 between 1986 and 1996, with 90 percent of them between 1993 and 1996. There were 15 alone in 1994, in the depths of Cuba's 1990s crisis, or *Período Especial* as it was called. The subtext to '*hermanos de sangre y sudor*' was that Cuba took in *isleños* in their times of need, now it was the turn of the Canaries to help Cuba.

Cabaiguán *isleño* tobacco history has its origins in a smallholder tobacco and mixed agricultural and subsistence economy that enabled settler as much as seasonal labour, especially with the twentieth-century agricultural expansion of central Cuba. Whole families cleared land for tobacco and worked in the selecting and stemming sheds in Cabaiguán, Guayos, Neiva, Santa Lucía, Macaguabo, Guasimal, Bijabo, Manacas, Taguasco and Sancti Spíritus.[81] While many left under the deportations after the 1930s Nationalisation Law, many also stayed. Smallholders and rentier farmers had *isleño* sharecroppers, also often from their own places of origin with an agricultural background.[82] They formed part of a circular movement of tobacco and labour between the Canaries and Cuba, more likely than not intermarrying with other *isleños*. Women were central to household production, tending livestock and harvesting tobacco, and endogamy became an adaptive strategy.

José Alberto Galván Tudela linked these developments to the diasporic "historical imaginary" of migrants and their descendants in the context of Cuba's 1990s crisis, political events in the Canaries, Canaries' economic and cultural interests in Cuba, and Canaries cultural practices kept alive (as in Cabaiguán's Museo de la Cultura Canaria). The narrative, he argued, was not a reinvention but the lived-identity experience based on a *cubano/isleño* reading of key figures and events: the *veguero* uprisings as precursor to Cuba's independence struggles, the *bandolerismo* of Manuel García, Martí's mother Leonor Pérez, and Cuban Communist Party founder José Miguel Pérez, through to participants in Cuba's 1959 Revolution. Initiatives in the early 1960s included a restructured Canaries dance group, by art instructor José Ovidio Padrón together with José Garcés, the original creator of the group along with Juan 'Chimijo' Hernández in the 1930s. The group was further developed in the 1970s by Víctor Cruz and in the 1980s by Felicia Estrepa. The 1980s mapping of a Cuban ethnographic atlas, which involved the study of Canaries cultural traditions, both reflected and contributed to ethnic identification.[83] It was in this context that Galván Tudela concluded in the 1990s:

> To understand the phenomena of ethnicity that are occurring in Cuba, especially in the case of Cuban isleños, a systematic transnational perspective is needed. What I mean is to understand not only what is happening in Cuba but also in Spain and the Canary islands in particular, as also the economic and cultural globalisation permeating the world-system.

He continued:

> ... although there is no identification between the Canaries and Cuban immigrants in Miami, among whom are many descendants of isleños, the situation of Cubans in the state of Florida is well known to those who remain in Cuba, to the point that many aspects of their lives are to a large extent cushioned by the personal and family aid and support from those living there. Cubans are not only those who live on the island but also those who

are abroad, in America, and in many cities of Europe and in the Canaries, which is why without a shadow of doubt this cannot be overlooked in understanding the phenomena we are looking at here.[84]

As this chapter has set out to demonstrate, Cuba-Canaries cigar history provides a clear manifestation of this. Framed by the nineteenth-century British and twentieth-century American cycles of free trade and globalisation, that history is replete with examples of transnational and local connectivity and collaboration alongside competition and contestation, permeated by agency operating at all levels – Drayton's "masked condominia". Only by exploring broad hemispheric, transatlantic and global, as well as local, parameters can we begin to nuance more fully the pivotal formative changes that over time have shaped Cuban and Canaries economies, politics, societies and cultures.

A cursory glimpse at the Imperial company time-line bears testimony to the many sales, mergers and acquisitions in the company's history.[85] The most recent, at the time of writing in late April 2019, was Imperial's announced intention to sell its premium cigar business. This included two major cigar factories, one of the world's largest cigar retail chains, 50 percent of Cuba's Habanos SA, Altadis USA, and a "treasure trove of cigar brands such as Montecristo, Romeo y Julieta and H. Upmann."[86] In a context such as this, whither the future of the proud Havana cigar band and Cuba-Canaries Havana cigar connections remains to be seen.

Notes

1 This chapter is part of an ongoing study of a global universe shaped by attempts across the world to replicate the quality and fame of the Havana cigar. My early incursion into the Canaries part of this history was research conducted in 2002 in the three islands most linked to tobacco (Tenerife, La Palma and Gran Canaria). I am indebted to colleagues who generously hosted me and gave me my first grounding in Canaries tobacco, especially Manuel de Paz Sánchez and José Alberto Galván Tudela in La Laguna, Juan Manuel Santana Pérez in Las Palmas de Gran Canaria, and Anelio Rodríguez Concepción in Santa Cruz de La Palma. I presented my early findings at the 2004 conference of the Cuba Research Forum (University of Nottingham, UK) and the 2005 Habana Habanos conference (hosted by the Museo del Tabaco in Havana, Cuba). At the 2005 conference were Miguel Suárez Bosa, Pilar Domínguez Prats, Santiago de Luxán Meléndez and the late José Manuel Rodríguez Gordillo, to whom I owe a further debt of gratitude. In recent years I have been privileged to be part of the Ibero-Atlantic tobacco historians group headed by Santiago de Luxán and João Figueroa-Rego. I thank them and other colleagues in the group, notably Vicent Sanz Rozalén and Montserrat Gárate Ojanguren, for challenging me to conceptualise my work further, most recently at the 2018 XIII Coloquio de Historia Canario-Americano in Las Palmas de Gran Canaria. I draw on their work, and that of many others, in formulating my argument here.
2 Jean Stubbs, 'El Habano and the World It Has Shaped: Cuba, Connecticut and

Indonesia', *Cuban Studies*, 41 (2010), pp.39-67 – Chapter 13 in the present volume; 'Política e sapere: come si e globalizzato el sigaro avana? / Política y saber: cómo se globalizó el habano', in Laura Mariottini and Alessandro Oricchio (eds), *El Habano: Lingua, storia, societa di un prodotto transculturale. Lengua, historia, sociedad de un producto transcultural* (Rome: Edizioni Efesto, 2017), pp. 67-105; 'Beyond Iberian Atlantic Spaces: Trans-imperial and Trans-Territorial Entanglements in Havana Cigar History (1756- 1924)', in Luxán & João Figueiro-Rego (eds), *El tabaco y la esclavitud. en la rearticulación imperial ibérica (Evora:* Universidade de Evora, Evora, 2018), pp. 389-426 – Chapter 17 in the present volume.

3 For coverage of the Festival on the Habanos website, see http://www.habanos.com/en/noticias/el-festival-del-habano-cierra-su-xxi-edicion-con-la-noche-de-gala-dedicada-al-50-aniversario-de-trinidad/.

4 Santiago de Luxán Meléndez, *La opción agrícola e industrial del tabaco en Canarias: una perspectiva institucional: Los orígenes 1827-1936* (Las Palmas de Gran Canaria: Sociedad Canaria de Fomento, Económico SA (PROEXCA), Consejería de Economía y Haciendad del Gobierno de Canarias, 2006), and 'Cultivo, abastecimiento y estanco del tabaco en España en el tránsito del Antiguo Régimen al Estado Liberal', in Luxán Meléndez & João Figueiro-Rego, *El tabaco y la esclavitud en la rearticulación imperial ibérica* (Evora: Universidade de Evora, 2018); Andrés Arnaldos Martínez & Jorge Arnaldos de Armas, *La industria tabaquera canaria (1852-2002)* (Las Palmas de Gran Canaria: Gobierno de Canarias/Cámaras de Canarias/Asociación Canaria de Industriales Tabaqueros, 2003); Anelio Rodríguez Concepción, *La tradición insular del tabaco* (Santa Cruz de Tenerife: Consejería de Agricultura, Ganadería, Pesca y Alimentación, 2000).

5 Luxán & Figueiroa-Rego, *El tabaco y la esclavitud* (2018); Santiago de Luxán Meléndez (ed.), *Política y Hacienda del Tabaco en los Imperios Ibéricos (siglos XVII-XIX)* (Madrid: Centro de Estudios Políticos y Constitucionales, 2014); Santiago de Luxán Meléndez, Joao Figueiroa-Rego & Vicent Sanz Rozalén (eds), *Tabaco y esclavos en los imperios ibéricos* (Lisbon: Universidade Nova de Lisboa, 2015); Josep María Fradera, *Colonias para después de un imperio* (Barcelona: Bellaterra, 2005).

6 Stubbs, 'Beyond Iberian Atlantic Spaces' (2018); J. H. Elliott, *Empires of the Atlantic World: Britain and Spain in America 1492-1830* (New Haven: Yale University Press, 2006).

7 J. Gallagher & R. Robinson, 'The Imperialism of Free Trade', *Economic History Review* 6:1 (1953), pp.1-15.

8 Giovanni Arrighi, *The Long Twentieth Century: Money, Power, and the Origins of Our Times* (London & New York, Verso, 1994); Alfredo McCoy, Josep María Fradera & Stephen Jacobson (eds), *Endless Empire: Spain's Retreat, Europe's Eclipse, America's Decline* (Madison: University of Wisconsin Press, 2012); Victor Bulmer-Thomas, *Empire in Retreat: The Past, Present, and Future of the United States* (New Haven: Yale University Press, 2018).

9 Richard Drayton, 'Masked Condominia: Pan European Collaboration in the History of Imperialism, 1500 to the present', *Global History Review* (2012), pp.308-31, and *Masks of Empire: The World History Underneath Modern Empires and Nations, c.1500 to the present* (London: Palgrave, 2018).

10 Luis Álvarez Alonso, Lina Gálvez Muñoz & Santiago de Luxán Meléndez (eds), *Tabaco e historia económica: estudios sobre fiscalidad, consumo y empresa (siglos XVII-XX)* (Madrid: Ediciones del Umbral, 2006); Santiago de Luxán Meléndez, Monserrat Gárate Ojangurén & José Manuel Rodríguez Gordillo, *Cuba-Canarias-Sevilla. El estanco español del tabaco y las Antillas (1717-1817)* (Las Palmas de Gran Canaria: Cabildo de Gran Canaria, 2012); Santiago de Luxán Meléndez (ed.), *Política y Hacienda del Tabaco en los Imperios Ibéricos (siglos XVII-XIX)* (Madrid: Centro de Estudios Políticos y Constitucionales, 2014), and 'Cultivo, abastecimiento y estanco del tabaco en España en el tránsito del Antiguo Régimen al Estado Liberal', in Luxán & Figueiroa-Rego, *El trabajo y la esclavitud* (2018).

11 Jean Stubbs, *Tobacco on the Periphery* (London: Amaurea Press, 2023 [1985]), and *Tabaco en la periferia* (London: Amaurea Press, 2023 [1989])
12 For further detail, see company websites: https://www.bat.com/, https://www.imperial- brandsplc.com/index.html, https://www.imperialbrandsplc.com/About-us/Our-companies/ Tabacalera.html, http://www.altadis.com/ https://www.altadisusa.com/age-gate.
13 Jordan Goodman, *Tobacco in History: The Cultures of Dependence* (London & New York: Routledge, 1993).
14 Doria C. González Fernández, 'La manufactura tabacalera cubana en la segunda mitad del siglo XIX', *Revista de Indias*, 194 (1992), pp.129-156, 'La guerra económica y sus efectos en la economía tabacalera', in Consuelo Naranjo, Miguel-Ángel Puig-Samper & Luis Miguel García Mora (eds), *La nación soñada: Cuba, Puerto Rico y Filipinas ante el 98* (Aranjuez, Doce Calles, 1996), pp.305-16; Joan Casanovas, *Bread, or Bullets! Urban Labor and Spanish Colonialism in Cuba, 1850-1898* (Pittsburgh: University of Pittsburgh Press, 1998).
15 Vicent Sanz Rozalén, 'Los negros del rey. Tabaco y esclavitud en Cuba a comienzos del siglo XIX', in José Piqueras (ed.), *Trabajo libre y coactivo en sociedades de plantación* (Madrid: Siglo XXI, 2009), pp.151-76; Michael Zeuske, 'Postemancipación y trabajo en Cuba', *Boletín Americanista* LXIV, 1/68 (2014), pp.77-99, 'Sklaven und Tabak in der atlantischen Weltgeschichte', *Historische Zeitschrift* 303:2 (2016), pp.315-48.
16 Jean Stubbs, 'Political Idealism and Commodity Production: Cuban Tobacco in Jamaica, 1870-1930', *Cuban Studies*, 25 (1995), pp.51-81 – Chapter 7 in the present volume; 'Cuba y Jamaica en el camino del tabaco', *Del Caribe* 26 (1997), pp.81-93, 'Reinventing Mecca: Tobacco in the Dominican Republic, 1763-2007', Commodities of Empire Working Paper, 3 (2007), at https://commoditiesofempire.org.uk/publications/working-papers/working-paper-3 – Chapter 12 in the present volume; and 'El Habano' (2010).
17 Glenn L. Westfall, *Key West: Cigar City USA* (Key West: Historic Key West Preservation Board, 1984), *Martí City: Florida's Cigar Ghost Town* (Key West: Key West Cigar City USA, 200), *Tampa Bay, Cradle of Cuban Liberty* (Key West, Key West Cigar City USA, 2000); Gerald E. Poyo, *With All and for the Good of All: The Emergence of Popular Nationalism in the Cuban Communities of the United States, 1848-1898* (Durham: Duke University Press, 1989), and *Exile and Revolution: José D. Poyo, Key West and Cuban Independence* (Gainesville: University Press of Florida, 2014); Robert P. Ingalls & Louis A. Pérez Jr., *Tampa Cigar Workers: A Pictorial History* (Gainesville: University Press of Florida, 2003); Susan D. Greenbaum, *More Than Black: Afro-Cubans in Tampa* (Gainesville: University Press of Florida, 2002); Nancy A. Hewitt, *Southern Discomfort: Women's Activism in Tampa, Florida, 1800s–1920s* (Urbana: University of Illinois Press, 2001); Jean Stubbs, 'Havana Cigars and the West's Imagination', in Sander L. Gilman & Zhou Xun (eds), *Smoke: A Global History of Smoking* (London: Reaktion Press, 2004), pp.134-9 – Chapter 10 in the present volume; and 'Tobacco in the Contrapunteo: Ortiz and the Havana Cigar', in Mauricio A. Font and Alfonso W. Quiroz (eds), *Cuban Counterpoints: The Legacy of Fernando Ortiz*, Lanham: Lexington, 2004), pp.105-23 – Chapter 9 in the present volume.
18 Evan Matthew Daniel, 'Rolling for the Revolution: A Transnational History of Cuban Cigar Makers in Havana, Florida, and New York City', PhD dissertation, New York, The New School (2010); Lisandro Pérez, *Sugar, Cigars, and Revolution: The Making of Cuban New York* (New York: New York University Press, 2018); Jean Stubbs, 'Transnationalism and the Havana Cigar: Commodity Chain Transfers, Networks, and Circuits of Knowledge', in Catherine Krull (ed.), *Cuba in a Global Context: International Relations, Internationalism, and Transnationalism*, Gainesville: University Press of Florida, 2014, pp. 227-42 – Chapter 16 in the present volume; and 'Beyond Iberian Atlantic Spaces' (2018).
19 Jean Stubbs, 'Reflections on Race, Class, Gender and Nation', in Constance Sutton

(ed.), *Revisiting Caribbean Labor: Essays in Honor of O. Nigel Bolland* (Kingston: Ian Randle, 2005), pp.118-36 – Chapter 11 in the present volume.
20 Luigi Ferri, *Storia del cigaro. Mitología, tradizione e cultura* (Bologna: Odoya, 2014); Stubbs, 'Política e sapere' (2017), 'Beyond Iberian Atlantic Spaces' (2018).
21 Jean Stubbs, 'Turning Over a New Leaf? The Havana Cigar Revisited', *New West Indian Guide*, 74:3 & 4 (2000), pp.235-55 – Chapter 8 in the present volume; 'Havana Cigars' (2004), 'Tobacco in the contrapunteo' (2004).
22 Stubbs 'Turning Over a New Leaf' (2000).
23 Quoted in James Suckling, 'The Montecristo War', *Cigar Aficionado* (Summer 1993) p.63.
24 Julio Hernández García, *La emigración de las Islas Canarias en el siglo XIX* (Las Palmas de Gran Canaria: Cabildo Insular de Gran Canaria, 1981), *Canarias: la emigración* (Santa Cruz de Tenerife: Centro de la Cultura Popular Canaria, 1995); Antonio M. Macías Hernández, *Migración canaria, 1500-1980* (Gijón: Ediciones Jucar, 1992); Joan Maluquer de Motes, *Nación e inmigración: los españoles en Cuba* (Gijón: Ediciones Jucar, 1992); Raul García Medina, *La inmigración canaria en Cuba* (La Laguna: Editorial Globo, 1994); Gregorio J. Cabrera Déniz, *Canarios en Cuba: Un capítulo en la historia del archipiélago (1875-1931)* (Las Palmas de Gran Canaria: Cabildo Insular de Gran Canaria, 1996); Rafael Santana Rodríguez, *Influencia de la emigración en los factores económicos sociales en Cuba y Canarias* (Las Palmas de Gran Canaria: Sanro, 1999); Juan Manuel Santana Pérez, 'Isleños en la Cuba colonial', *Revista Tebeto* V (1993), pp.278-309; Consuleo Naranjo Orovio, 'Canarios en Cuba en el siglo XX', *Coloquio de Historia Canario-Americana* (1986) (Las Palmas: Cabildo de Gran Canaria, 1990), pp.515-36, 'La población española en Cuba, 1880-1953', in C. Naranjo Orovio & T. Mallo Gutiérrez (eds), *Cuba: la perla de las Antillas* (Madrid: Doce Calles, 1994), pp.121-36; Manuel de Paz Sánchez (ed.), *El 98 Canario-Americano: Estudios y documentos* (San Cristóbal de La Laguna: Ayuntamiento de La Laguna, Gobierno de Canarias, Caja General de Ahorros de Canarias, Cabildo Insular de Tenerife, 1999).
25 Jesús Guanche Pérez, *España en la savia de Cuba* (Havana: Ciencias Sociales, 1999).
26 Maluquer, *Nación e inmigración* (1992).
27 Macías, *Migración canarias* (1992), p.12.
28 Quoted in Rodríguez, *Tradición insular* (2000), p.136.
29 Julio Yanes, *Crisis económica y emigración en Canarias: el Puerto de Santa Cruz de Tenerife durante la guerra europea, 1914-1918* (Santa Cruz de Tenerife: Centro de la Cultura Popular Canaria, 1997), *La gran depresión en Canarias* (Tenerife: Centro de la Cultura Popular, 1997).
30 José Ramón García López, *Las remesas de los emigrantes españoles en América. Siglos XIX y XX* (Gijón: Ediciones Jucar, 1992).
31 Manuel Moreno Fraginals, *Cuba/España. España/Cuba. Historia común* (Barcelona: Ed. Crítica, 2020).
32 Francisco Quintana Navarro, 'Los intereses británicos en Canarias en los años treinta: una aproximación', *Vegueta* (1992), pp.149-72; Antonio M. Macías Hernández, 'Aproximación a la historia económica contemporánea de Canarias (1800-1960)', *Geografía de Canarias*, Vol.VI (Santa Cruz de Tenerife: Interinsular, 1999); Juan Manuel Santana Pérez, 'Comercio canario-americano a fines del Antiguo Régimen', *Presente y Pasado* 6:8 (1999), pp.101-22.
33 Ulises Martín, *El comercio exterior canario (1880-1920)* (Santa Cruz de Tenerife: Centro de la Cultura Popular Canaria, 1992).
34 Ibid.; Luxán, *Opción agrícola* (2006).
35 Fátima Melián Pacheco, *Aproximación a la renta del tabaco en Canarias* (Santa Cruz de Tenerife: Tabacanarias, 1986); Oscar Bergasa, Pedro González de la Fe & Santiago de Luxán Meléndez, 'Efectos sobre la industria del establecimiento de un impuesto específico sobre el tabaco en Canarias', *Economía Canaria 1999* (Las Palmas de Gran Canaria: Universidad de Las Palmas de Gran Canaria, 2000).

36　José Pérez Vidal, *Historia del cultivo del tabaco en España* (Madrid: Servicio Nacional de Cultivo y Fermentación del Tabaco, 1956), and *España en la historia del tabaco* (Madrid: Consejo Superior de Investigaciones Científicas, 1959).
37　Oswaldo Brito González, 'La industria tabaquera', *Rumbos*, 3-5 (1979), pp.7-20.
38　British Museum, Manuscripts Dept. Additional Fund, File 25,090. Quoted in Santana, 'Isleños' (1993), p.108; José Luis Cruz Hernández, 'El isleño ante el tabaco. Espacialización y determinación', *Guize* 3 (1996), pp.9-20.
39　Arnaldos & Arnaldos, *Industria tabaquera* (2003).
40　Eugenio Torres Villanueva, *La fundación de la Compañía Arrendataria de Tabacos*, Working Paper 9808 (Madrid: FundaciónEmpresa Pública, 1998); Lina Galvez Muñoz, *La Cia Arrendataria del Tabaco 1887-1945 – cambio tecnológico y empleo femenino* (Madrid: LID Editora, 2003).
41　Arnaldos & Arnaldos, *Industria tabaquera* (2003), p.53.
42　Ibid., p.62.
43　S. García Armenter, 'Informe sobre el tabaco canario y su repercusión en el mercado de los Estados Unidos', *La Provincia* (9 January 1985); José Luis Rivero Ceballos, 'La industria tabaquera en las Islas Canarias: una perspectiva de principios del siglo XXI', in Fernando Carnero Lorenzo & Luis Sebastián Nuez Yanez (eds), *Empresa e historia en Canarias* (Santa Cruz de Tenerife: Fyde Canarias, 2001).
44　C. Legna Verna & José Luis Rivero Ceballos, *La industria tabaquera en Canarias. Globalización y reestructuración* (Bilbao: Serie Estudios Regionales del Banco Bilbao, 1997).
45　As highlighted by Oscar Bergasa Perdomo in his prologue to Luxán, *Opción agrícola* (2006).
46　Luxán, *Opción agrícola* (2006), p.112; Quintana, 'Intereses británicos' (1992).
47　Jesús Guanche Pérez, *Procesos etnoculturales en Cuba* (Havana: Letras Cubanas, 1983), 'Aportes canarios a la cultura campesina', *Revista de la Biblioteca Nacional José Martí* 3:26 (1985), pp.46-74, and *Significación canaria en el poblamiento hispanico de Cuba* (Santa Cruz de Tenerife: Centro de la Cultura Popular Canaria, 1992).
48　Manuel de Paz Sánchez, *La esclavitud blanca: contribución a la historia del immigrante canario en América, siglo XIX* (Santa Cruz de Tenerife: Centro de la Cultura Popular Canaria, 1992).
49　Ibid., p.31.
50　José Fernández Fernández & José María Castellano Gil, *Mambises isleños* (Santa Cruz de Tenerife: Caja Canarias, 1999); Fernández Fernández, Castellano Gil & Nelson López Novegil, *El bandolerismo en Cuba* (Gran Canaria: Cabildo Insular de Tenerife, Cabildo Insular de Fuerteventura, Centro de la Cultura Popular Canaria, 1993-94).
51　Manuel de Paz Sánchez & Francisco Guerra de Paz, *Cuba y Canarias: Imágenes de una ausencia* (Islas Canarias: Gobierno de Canarias, 1998).
52　Quoted in Mario Luis López Isla, *La aventura del tabaco* (Santa Cruz de Tenerife: Centro de la Cultura Popular Canaria, 1998), p.62.
53　Rodríguez, *Tradición insular* (2000), p.69.
54　Wladimiro Rodríguez Brito, *La agricultura en la isla de La Palma* (La Laguna: Instituto de Estudios Canarios, 1982), pp.131-2.
55　Miguel Rodríguez Ferrer, *El tabaco habano: historia, su cultivo, sus vicisitudes, sus más afamadas vegas en Cuba . . .* (Madrid: Colegio Nacional de Sordomudos, 1851).
56　Quoted in Luxán, *Opción agrícola* (2006), p.63.
57　Ibid., p.81.
58　*Manual del cultivo del tabaco* (1859), *Memoria Redactada por las clases de agricultura y comercio de la Sociedad de Amigos del País de Las Palmas de Gran Canaria sobre el cultivo del tabaco* (1861), *Memoria sobre el cultivo de tabaco en Islas Canarias* (1862), *Instrucción para el cultivo del tabaco arreglada a hechos prácticos obtenidos de la Isla de Gran Canaria* (Juan Nepomuceno Déniz, 1863), *Guía del cultivo del tabaco* (1870), and *Memoria sobre el tabaco de la Isla de Cuba, en la que se indican algunas mejoras*

de que es susceptible su cultivo (Bartolomé Mitjans, 1872) (Luxán, *Opción agrícola*, 2006).
59 Rodríguez, *Tradición insular* (2000).
60 Manuel de Paz Sánchez, *Wangüemert y Cuba*, 2 vols. (Santa Cruz de Tenerife, Centro de la Cultura Popular Canaria, 1991); Rodríguez, *Tradición insular* (2000).
61 Quoted in Rodríguez, *Tradición insular* (2000), p.91.
62 Oswaldo Brito González, *Historia del movimiento obrero canario* (Madrid: Editorial Popular, 1980).
63 Miguel Suárez Bosa, *El movimiento obrero en las canarias orientales (1930-1936)* (Las Palmas de Gran Canaria: Caja Insular de Ahorros de Canarias, 1990), and *Economía, sociedad y relaciones laborales en Canarias en el período de entreguerras: una aproximación a la situación de los trabajadores en Gran Canaria, Lanzarote y Fuerteventura* (Las Palmas: Universidad de Las Palmas de Gran Canaria, 1995); A. de Terán, 'La industria tabaquera tiene su mayor incidencia social en Tenerife', *Dinámica, Revista de la Ingeniería Canaria*, 8 (1990), pp.18-21; Rodríguez, *Tradición insular* (2000).
64 Agustín Millares Cantero, 'Trabajadores y republicanos en Las Palmas (1900-1908)', *Vegueta* (1992), pp.121-36.
65 Suárez, *Movimiento obrero* (1990).
66 Pilar Domínguez Prats, 'El trabajo en las empresas tabaqueras de Las Palmas durante el primer franquismo, 1940-1955', in Álvarez et al., *Tabaco e historia* (2006), pp.547-76.
67 For the similarities with Cuba, see Stubbs, *Tobacco on the Periphery* (2023 [1985]), *Tabaco en la periferia* (2023 [1989]), 'Reflections' (2005).
68 James Suckling, 'The Canary Island Connections', *Cigar Aficionado* (July/August 1998).
69 Ibid.
70 Ibid.
71 S. García Armenter, 'Informe sobre el tabaco canario y su repercusión en el mercado de los Estados Unidos', *La Provincia* (9 January, 1985).
72 I have yet to write up this chapter of Bahía cigar history, but, for the late-nineteenth and early-twentieth centuries, a period itself interrelated with the Canaries, Madeira and the Azores, see Jean-Baptiste Nardi, *Fumo brasileiro no periodo colonial* (Sao Paulo: Editora Brasiliense, 1985); B. J. Barickman, *A Bahían Counterpoint: Sugar, Tobacco, Cassava, and Slavery in the Recôncavo, 1780-1860* (Stanford: Stanford University Press, 1998); and Michiel Baud & Kees Kooning, 'Germans and Tobacco in Bahía (Brazil), 1870-1940', in *Jahrbuch für Geschichte Lateinamerikas*, 37 (2000), pp.149-76.
73 Rivero, 'Industria tabaquera' (2001).
74 Ibid.
75 CITA, *La familia Zamorano a través de la vitofilia desde 1850* (Santa Cruz de Tenerife: CITA Tabacos de Canarios, 1999); Julián Huerta Galván, 'Marcas tabaqueras de la Isla de La Palma', *Coleccionable de la AVE* (La Coruña: Asociación Vitofílica Española, 2000); Cruz, 'El isleño' (1996).
76 Nestor Rodríguez Martín, 'Sobre la Asociación Canaria de Cuba', *El Día de Santa Cruz de Tenerife* (September 1986).
77 J. L. Martín Teixe & Mario Luis López Isla, *La leyenda de Cuquillo, el poeta isleño de Mazo y Cabaiguán* (Santa Cruz de Tenerife: Centro de la Cultura Popular Canaria 1994).
78 José Alberto Galván Tudela, 'La construcción de la identidad cultural en regionales insulares: Islas Canarias, España' in R. Avila Palafox & Tomás Calvo Buezas (eds), *Identidades, nacionalismos y regiones* (Madrid: Universidad Complutense de Madrid/ Universidad de Guadalajara, 1993); Manuel Hernández González, 'Reflexiones sobre la identidad canaria en América', *En el camino (Canarias entre Europa y América)* (Las Palmas: Ed. Edirca, 1992), pp.73-91.

79 Galván Tudela, *Canarios en Cuba: una mirada desde la antropología* (Santa Cruz de Tenerife: Museo de Antropología, 1997), 'Inmigración y construcción nacional en Cuba (a propósito de la obra de Fernando Ortiz)', *Areas, Revista de Ciencias Sociales* 19 (1999), pp.227-44; Mario Luis López Isla, 'El tabaco: cordón umbilical del naciente poblado de Cabaiguán', *Canariguán, Cabaiguán: Actas del 1 Coloquio de la Cultura Canario-Cubana* (1995), *Festividades de origen canario en Cabaiguan* (Gran Canaria: Ayuntamiento de Los Realejos, 1996); López Isla & E. L. Vázquez Seara, *Isleños en Cuba: episodios de la emigración canaria en Cabaiguán* (Santa Cruz de Tenerife: Editorial Ideas, 1997); Cruz, 'El isleño' (1996); Luis Fajardo et al., 'Presencia isleña en el cultivo del tabaco en la Cooperativa de Producción Agropecuaria "La Nueva Cuba"', *Guize* 3 (1996), pp.21-33; Guillermo Sierra Torres & Juan Carlos Rosario Molina, *Los canarios en Cuba: juntos pero no revueltos* (Tenerife: Centro de la Cultura Popular Canaria, 2001); Manuel de Paz Sánchez & José Abreu Cardet, 'Del Oriente profundo. Acerca de la presencia canaria en la comarca de Holguín (zona noriental de Cuba) durante el siglo XIX', *Anuario de Estudios Atlánticos* 42 (1996), pp.885-910; María Magdalena Pérez Álvarez, 'Aspectos históricos y etnoculturales de la integración social de los inmigrantes canarios en la zona rural de Pinar del Río, Havana, Asociación Canaria de Cuba Leonor Pérez Cabrera', unpublished manuscript (n.d.).

80 Jean Stubbs & Mavis Álvarez, 'Women on the Agenda: The Cooperative Movement in Rural Cuba', in Carmen Diana Deere & Magdalena Leon (eds), *Rural Women and State Policy: Feminist Perspectives on Latin American Agricultural Development* (Boulder: Westview Press, 1987), pp.142-61 – Chapter 3 in the present volume; Jean Stubbs, 'Gender Issues in Contemporary Cuban Tobacco Farming', *World Development* 5:1 (1987), pp.43-68 – Chapter 4 in the present volume.

81 Perdomo, José E., *Léxico tabacalero cubano* (Miami: Ediciones Universal, 1998 [1940]).

82 José Alberto Galván Tudela, 'La figura del partidario isleño', *Canarias en América/América en Canarias*, Entrega 19, *La Prensa* (11 July 1998), and 'El Sitio: La explotación agrícola de los isleños en Cuba (La aparcería en la producción tabacalera cubana)', *Canarias en América/América en Canarias*, Entrega 10, *La Prensa* (9 May 1998); María del Carmen Mateo López, 'Emigración canaria: endogamía y género', *Guize* 2 (1996), pp.35-43.

83 Colectivo de autores, *Atlas Etnográfico de Cuba* (Havana: Centro de Investigación y Desarrollo de la Música Cubana, 1999).

84 José Alberto Galván Tudela, 'Construyendo identidad: el pasado en el presente de los isleños cubanos', unpublished manuscript (n.d.).

85 Andrew Nagy, 'A Timeline Of How Imperial Brands Came To Be', *Cigar Aficionado* (1 May 2019).

86 David Savona, 'Imperial Brands Selling its Premium Cigar Business', *Cigar Aficionado* (30 April 2019).

19

Dominican, Puerto Rican and Cuban tobacco in the Long Shadow of Monopoly (1717-1930)*

THE COMPARATIVE history of Dominican, Puerto Rican and Cuban tobacco has travelled along divergent and entwined paths revolving around the long shadow of monopoly. The point of departure for my purposes here is the eighteenth-century creation of the Spanish imperial tobacco Real Factorías, seen in the context of the Iberian crown monopoly system, distinct from the trading companies of other nations, and the colonial counter-economy, as argued respectively by Dutch historians Pieter Emmer and Michiel Baud.[1]

The Spanish crown tobacco monopoly, created in 1636, centralised manufacture in the Real Fábrica de Sevilla (established earlier in 1620) supplied by tobacco leaf from the colonies, and it was in the eighteenth century that the imperial network of Factorías was created. Now well documented in its national and imperial framework by Spanish historians José Manuel Rodríguez Gordillo, Antonio González Enciso, Santiago de Luxán Meléndez, Montserrat Gárate Ojanguren and Vicent Sanz Rozalén, among others,[2] this comprised a centralised pricing mechanism designed to maximise fiscal revenue, with a powerful coercive instrument of control in the form of advance credit through the *situado* from the Vice Royalty of New Spain. By the end of the eighteenth

---

* Originally published in Santiago de Luxán Meléndez (ed.), *La transición del monopolio al libre mercado del tabaco en Cuba, Canarias y Filipinas y otros espacios americanos. Experiencias comparadas* (Las Palmas de Gran Canaria: Servicio de Publicaciones del Cabildo de Gran Canaria, 2024). I thank my Iberian historian colleagues for inviting me to reflect on this comparative history.

century, tobacco had become a fundamental bulwark of colonial rule and underwrote capital and loans taken on by the crown to meet state demands.

In the Spanish Caribbean, it was the Cuban leaf that was most valued by Spain, and the Cuban Factoría was created much earlier in the century than the Dominican and the Puerto Rican Factorías and outlasted them both. The first Factoría in Cuba was established in 1717, while the Dominican Factoría was not until 1763 – three years after the 1760 creation of the second Factoria *de La Habana* and in response to the British occupation of Havana of 1762-63, which cut off supplies of Cuban leaf to Spain. The Dominican Factoría was not really functional until 1770, and, while it succeeded in incentivising leaf exports to Seville, had a chequered existence until it came to an end in 1796. It struggled in what Baud epitomised as a strong colonial tobacco counter-economy underpinning what Dominican historian Raymundo González coined as the Dominican *largo siglo campesino* (long peasant century) of 1763-1930 in the north-central region of the Cibao,[3] where tobacco predominated, in contrast to plantation sugar in the south and east, and in Cuba and Puerto Rico. An early counter-economy was also predominant in Puerto Rico, where tobacco, as in the Dominican case, remained largely beyond Spanish interest or control and where the Factoría was not created until even later, in 1785. From the outset, the Puerto Rican Factoría was managed by a Dutch-based, Franco-Spanish, private company, which, as characterised by Puerto Rico's leading tobacco scholar Juan José Baldrich, was largely to give a legal character to what had up until then been mostly Dutch contraband.[4] The Puerto Rican Factoría lasted less than a decade, terminating in 1794.

By contrast, Cuban tobacco, which had by no means been exempt from a counter-economy with long-established growing and selling of tobacco, contraband and early grower opposition to the new state monopoly control, was both privileged and more controlled for a century by Spain until the Factoría's demise in 1817. After being freed from monopoly control, Cuban tobacco then rose to nineteenth-century global pre-eminence and became especially renowned for its luxury hand-rolled Havana cigars. The most celebrated study by far of this rise to fame is that by Cuban anthropologist Fernando Ortiz in his 1940 Cuban counterpoint of tobacco and sugar. This was followed by a spate of work on tobacco by José Rivero Muñiz, culminating in his two-volume overview history of Cuban tobacco, published in 1964-65, and, among other new work produced after the 1959 Cuban Revolution, the biography of Cuban tobacco by Cuban cigar roller and cigar factory reader turned historian Gaspar Jorge García Galló.[5] Others since, including myself, have explored Cuban tobacco's wider economic, political and socio-cultural ramifications in terms of race, class, gender and nation, and broader global contexts.[6]

Impetus was also given to Dominican tobacco history in the wake of Cuba's Revolution with the re-invigorated Cibao tobacco economy and the US embargo on trade with Cuba, part of a wider new Dominican scholarship in the opening after the Trujillo dictatorship of 1930-61. The 1970s saw a succession of articles in the Dominican journal *EME EME Dominican Studies*,[7] which included those by Dominican tobacco historian Antonio Lluberes Navarro, who in 1984 described tobacco as the most studied sector of the Dominican economy after sugar.[8] In the 1990s Baud and Pedro San Miguel, himself Puerto Rican, published their major studies of the Cibao peasant tobacco economy, and Spanish historian Antonio Gutiérrez Escudero subsequently contributed two informative articles. In 2003 and 2004, respectively, histories were published of the two largest tobacco companies to emerge in the early twentieth century – Cibao-based León Jimenes, by José Alcántara Almánzar and Ida Hernández Caamaño, and the Compañía Anónima de Tabaco (CAT) in the south, by Esteban Rosario; and in 2008 Grupo León Jimenes also published the three-volume history of Dominican tobacco by José Chez Checo and Mu-Kien Adriana Sang, arguably the most comprehensive single study of the three territories under consideration.[9]

Puerto Rican tobacco history has been less studied than Cuban and Dominican tobacco. Research conducted by US anthropologists in the 1940s and 1950s included comparative work on tobacco and sugar by John Augelli and on tobacco by Robert Manners, the latter part of a broader study of crop cultures, which included coffee and sugar, and this was revisited in 2021 by historians César Ayala and Laird Bergad.[10] Jorge Luis Chinea delved into the micro history of problems faced by the Puerto Rican Factoría, and other historians documented the early tobacco trade, while the later militancy of tobacco workers was a recurring theme in labour and gender history.[11] Three book-length publications that focus exclusively on tobacco history, however, are those by Teresita Levy in 2014, on growers in the early twentieth-century US period, and by Baldrich, himself a sociologist – his first in 1988 on the growers' refusal to harvest the tobacco for the big corporations in the 1920s and early 1930s and his second, long-awaited, overview of Puerto Rican tobacco history published in 2022, culminating decades of work.[12]

What follows draws on these and other sources to signal salient aspects of the tobacco trajectories across the three territories. It takes its cue from Emmer's argument regarding the Iberian monopolies in the early Atlantic trade and Baud's characterisation of the Dominican tobacco counter-economy, and then delves into micro-history in the Factoría's fleeting attempt to control the Puerto Rican counter-economy. It charts the rise of nineteenth-century Cuban tobacco to global fame and the dramatic impact of the 'Cuban model' on tobacco in Puerto Rico, and how this was transformed again after the political turmoil of the last decades of the century, US occupation and monopoly incursions in both Cuba and Puerto Rico, and the emergence of strong US tobacco sectors, involving Cubans and Puerto Ricans with trade and other advantages over the

Cuban and Puerto Rican home island territories. In the Dominican case, the full impact of Cuba came much later, when Cibao tobacco was catapulted into direct competition with post-1959 revolutionary Cuba, whereby final reflections on visions and counterpoints of tobacco help clarify the longue-durée of Cuban and Dominican tobacco, while Puerto Rican tobacco has been left as only a shadow of its former self.

The Iberian Monopoly System

Writing on global trade and monopolies from the sixteenth to the eighteenth centuries, Emmer made a convincing case for the pivotal role of the rise of new financial and commercial institutions such as the large joint-stock companies in intercontinental trade and shipping in early modern history. In the case of the Atlantic economy, he made four important points that are relevant here: there was a marked difference between the organisation of intercontinental trade on the Iberian Peninsula and in North-Western Europe; intercontinental trade made up a small proportion of total commercial activities; small companies and individual merchants remained dominant; and privateers played an important role, especially in times of war, when piracy and smuggling could flourish, and where Iberian trade circuits bordered on those of the French, English and Dutch.

The Iberian first expansion circuit was one in which the crown was paramount, with state officials collecting as much bullion as possible; no state-sanctioned incentive for individual profit; a large part of shipping in English, French and Dutch vessels; and Spanish merchants outnumbered by foreign and local merchants. As a result, the later second expansion circuit was one in which non-Iberian merchants dominated, creating mercantile elites in England, France and the Netherlands and joint-stock companies. Dutch merchants early formed the United East India Company for trading with Asia, backed by government but without state intervention, with large joint-stock capital offsetting risk, and obtaining a near monopoly on several commodities. The English East India Company followed suit, as also the French Compagnie del Indes Orientales, which floundered due to overly heavy state intervention; and by the end of the eighteenth century the Dutch and English companies were also weakened by the international political situation and internal problems.

Large-scale joint-stock companies were also created for the Dutch trade in the Atlantic, and the British and French trade to Africa, especially the slave trade. All were granted a monopoly but met with only temporary success and by around 1700 most had disappeared. The Dutch West India Company did quite well at first because of its privateering against Spain and Portugal but soon had to abandon its monopoly in most commodities, and by 1750 its monopoly on the slave trade was also crumbling. Similarly, England's Royal African Company lost its trade function after 1698, and the South Sea Company, with a monopoly on the slave trade to Spanish America, stopped trading around 1760.

During the eighteenth century it was private sole or company traders, with local resident partners, who were dominant. By the end of the century national mercantilist partitions of trade and shipping between the metropolis and the colonies exclusively reserved for national commercial groups began to give way. The Iberian system remained, albeit British, Dutch and French merchants made inroads and even specialised in illegal trade, investing heavily in privateering and piracy. Privateers were licensed by their governments in war to capture enemy ships, and this provided money to invest in profitable illegal trade contacts with Iberian America in times of peace. Early pirates of the seventeenth century also over time established themselves as legitimate traders, investing their gains in the region. This was to have ramifications during the nineteenth century as the old Iberian Empires in the Americas came to an end and impacted in different ways on Spain's three Caribbean island colonies under scrutiny here.

The Dominican Counter-Economy

The paradox of Spanish colonisation in the Americas, as Baud argued, was having a centralist ideology yet being unable to prevent a great deal of uncontrolled economic activity. This was especially marked in the colonial counter-economy that emerged in Hispaniola, which, Dominican historians claim, has a pioneering place in the history of tobacco. Native to the Americas, tobacco is recorded as first being grown there in 1531 by European settlers who learned growing techniques from the indigenous population (Cuba following in 1580, Brazil in 1600, Virginia in 1612 and Maryland in 1631). Tobacco from Hispaniola is said to have been the first to reach Spain after the Spanish Conquest, and tobacco played an important role in Dutch and French incursions into Spanish territory. Attempts were made by the Dutch to establish a legitimate trade, but in the face of Spanish mercantilism they, along with the French and the English, moved into contraband and piracy, and small tobacco farmers continued to resist Spanish intervention. It was because of endemic tobacco contraband with the English, French and Dutch on the north and east coasts that in 1605 Felipe III ordered settlements to be destroyed and people and livestock to be moved to the centre and south. When Spanish interest turned more to the mines of Mexico and Peru, the colony went into decline, enabling the French in 1659 to take the western part of the island, which became Saint-Domingue.

Tobacco, however, continued to develop in Spanish Santo Domingo and, while sugar and cattle came to predominate in the south, small-scale farming of food crops and tobacco predominated in the Cibao. There the tobacco contraband trade became an important mainstay for the northern Dominican economy, especially by the end of the seventeenth century, when French Saint-Domingue shifted to sugar, coffee, cacao and indigo. The Cibao became Saint-Domingue's chief supplier of tobacco; it was the Dominican *andullo*, pressed tobacco roll, or plug, from which small pieces were cut, that was consumed on French plantations; French settlers moved into tobacco in northern Spanish Santo Domingo; and the Spanish northern port of Monte Cristi was a prime meeting point for French, Dutch and Spanish traders. By the early eighteenth century, there were also companies trading in tobacco. In 1721 the Governor of Santiago requested royal permission to sell tobacco to Saint-Domingue, accepting payment in slaves to increase production, given the labour shortage in the Cibao.

When the second half of the eighteenth century witnessed fresh determination on the part of Spain to regain control of its Spanish American colonies, some liberalisation of the Spanish trade was accompanied by a drive for greater state intervention and control to increase revenues. This was the context in which the 1763 Factoría was designed to further legal trade in Cibao leaf to Seville. By 1771, however, growers were protesting against the low prices of Spanish official buyers, forcing a price increase in 1773, after which crop surpluses led to planting restrictions in 1778.[13] Such was the Dominican opposition that tobacco again expanded, catering to the local market, exported illegally to Saint-Domingue and other Caribbean territories, and used for buying slaves in Cuba and Puerto Rico, as well as being sold on the Spanish market through the Factoría.

After the end of the Factoría in 1796, in the wake of the 1791 slave uprising in Saint-Domingue and the revolution that led to the creation of the independent state of Haiti in 1804, and the volatile changing political scenarios under French (1795-1809), Spanish (1809-22), and Haitian (1822-44) rule, the Dominican colonial economy was again in crisis. The Cibao tobacco economy might have been wiped out had it not been for the early policies of the Haitian occupying governments to free slaves, redistribute land and allow free trade with new markets. As richer white *colonos* left, tobacco was grown by former peons and slaves, and their families, creating a tobacco peasantry of poor whites and coloureds, many of whom, it has been claimed, sympathised with the aims of the new black Haitian Republic, though differences in language, religion and Africanisation were anathema to Santo Domingo's primarily European and Catholic southern elites.

By 1844, tobacco was arguably the most stable and productive sector of the economy, from which derived the economic, social and political importance of the Cibao. Trade routes through the north coast ports of Monte Cristi and especially Puerto Plata to the Caribbean islands of St Thomas, Puerto Rico, Martinique and Curaçao supplied France and Spain, the main buyers, and growing markets in Holland and Germany, especially the latter. The Cibao tobacco counter-economy was then pitted against the increasingly powerful economy and state in the south during the nascent independent Dominican Republic of 1844-61 and Spanish re-annexation (1861-65) and through the restored Republic, to which I return later.

The Short-Lived Puerto Rican Factoría

A parallel counter-economy operated in Puerto Rico, where tobacco was generally eschewed by the Spanish, prized by the Dutch, and the mainstay of intense contraband until after the Napoleonic Wars of 1804-15, when it was traded freely. Of the small proportion consumed locally, it was chewed as quids (*mascaúra*) by the rural peasant farmers (*jíbaros*), while smoking cigars (*jumazos*) was favoured by the elites, and there was little use for the pipe (*cachimba*). Exports consisted of pressed tobacco, and the bulk went overseas by contraband with little destined for the Spanish market. On the receiving end of contraband were some well-reputed firms that freighted ships in Amsterdam and also served as purveyors for the Spanish navy.

The Franco-Spanish private company chosen by the Spanish monarchy to manage the Puerto Rican Factoría had been involved in a wide range of operations, which included loans to the crown and serving as consultants in the tobacco trade, and it had earlier requested authorisation to establish export warehouses in Puerto Rico. The director chosen for the Factoría was an Irishman known as Jaime (or Jayme) O'Daly. The period was one in which Spain was authorising the settlement of foreigners with skills from friendly Catholic nations and was also one in which slave revolts and intra-European warfare were creating an influx of foreign merchants from neighbouring Danish, French and Dutch islands. This coincided, moreover, with a revival of Spanish immigration into the region. Chartered companies ferried Spanish colonists as part of their operations, and, after the British occupation of Havana, Spain dispatched additional troops to revamp its military defenses.

Spanish immigrants soon found themselves in competition with enterprising foreigners, which was the case with the fledgling Puerto Rican Factoría, when Joseph Martín de Fuentes waged a battle against O'Daly. As documented by Chinea,[14] O'Daly had relocated to Puerto Rico in 1776 from the Dutch colony of St Eustatius and had been instrumental in the planning stages of the Factoría, documenting the feasibility of legal trade between the Puerto Rican capital of San Juan and Amsterdam. At O'Daly's request, a merchant in Cadiz recommended Juan Sayus, a native of France resident in Spain since 1768 and a naturalised Spanish citizen in 1786, for the position of *contador* (bookkeeper), and Sayus departed for Puerto Rico in 1787. Fuentes wanted the position, but O'Daly was informed he was not qualified. Fuentes persisted and arrived in 1789, accompanied by the Inspector of the Factoría de La Habana and a former official of the Cadiz treasury.

Fuentes criticised O'Daly's commercial operations and outlined changes to put the Factoría on a sound economic footing, setting the stage for bitter confrontation. Fuentes painted O'Daly as inept, corrupt and disloyal: holding back tobacco; cheating local producers; and encouraging illegal trading with merchants from St Thomas, Curaçao, St Eustatius, Dominica and Jamaica. He attributed this to O'Daly being a foreigner, with ties to Jews, Protestants and other non-Spaniards in nearby colonies, where he could easily escape at short notice. Only by placing a Spaniard such as himself in charge of the Factoría's accounts could an end be put to such underhand practices. O'Daly reacted swiftly to discredit Fuentes' allegations; Fuentes was charged with defamation of character, then went on the counter-offensive, and later died in prison under suspicious circumstances.

Fuentes underestimated O'Daly's support. O'Daly's brother Tomas was a protégé of Field Marshall Alexander O'Reilly, who the Spanish Crown had commissioned to report on conditions in Cuba and Puerto Rico after the British occupation of Havana. O'Reilly recruited Tomas to direct the massive defense projects of San Juan, and Tomas later established a sugar plantation with the son of an Irish nobleman and Spanish mother who came to Puerto Rico. While residing in St Eustatius in 1772, Jayme put up some 30,000 pesos to assist a Spanish fleet that had run aground in Anguilla. In return, he requested and was granted a license to settle in Puerto Rico for a two-year period with the right to export its products to cover the funds advanced. He remained in Puerto Rico to manage his brother's plantation before becoming director of the Factoría, and in 1786 was issued his *carta de tolerancia* as a Spanish subject. Fuentes' criticism of the Factoría, however, was probably not far off the mark. The Factoría received tobacco from the growers in warehouses in San Juan, San Germán and Arecibo, storing it until a frigate arrived. In 1786, a frigate was bought for the firm, and tobacco and coffee were the most valuable cargo on its first return voyage to Amsterdam in 1787, but coffee soon proved more profitable and displaced tobacco. Frustration over the Factoría's operations also turned violent in 1790 and 1792, when the San Germán and Arecibo warehouses were torched.

Prior to the establishment of the Factoría, merchants in St Eustatius claimed to have purchased annually from Puerto Rico between 48,000 and 68,000 *arrobas* of tobacco (1 *arroba* = 25 lbs), whereas between 1787 and 1792 their annual average to Amsterdam was 19,136 *arrobas*. When legal tobacco exports were directed to Cadiz, the illegal flow was channeled toward St Thomas, where several Dutch merchants had settled after the 1781 British attack on St Eustatius. Strong opposition to the Factoría, however, from growers, merchants and some treasury officials, and renewed war in 1793 between the French revolutionary government and the Spanish monarchy created a new opening for contraband. The Factoría itself traded tobacco in the non-Hispanic Caribbean, whereby in 1794 merchants in Hamburg, Bremen and Magdeburg bought the island's tobacco from importers in Copenhagen, Amsterdam and London, who purchased it as contraband in St Thomas and St Eustatius.

The privateering and contraband during the Napoleonic Wars and the wars for Spanish-American independence (1803-33) only really began to recede after peace was restored, but the Spanish crown also allowed a greater opening to foreign commerce well before the Cédula de Gracias of 1815 codified it into practice. The *situado* from the Viceroyalty of New Spain, which had subsidised colonial government and the *factoría*'s operations, came to an end with Mexican independence in 1821 (which Spain only finally recognised in 1836) and was eclipsed in the 1830s and 1840s with the arrival of German merchants and firms such as the Shrøder Bros., using St Thomas as the main port of departure for tobacco bound for Hamburg and Bremen. Puerto Rican leaf was used in manufacturing in Magdeburg and the Grand Duchy of Brunswick; London buyers of the leaf supplied German manufacturers; and, with direct shipping to European ports such as Altona, Bremen, Hamburg and London, ports on St Thomas, St Eustatius and Curaçao lost their dominance in the tobacco export trade.

The Global Ascendance of Cuba

The Factoría in Cuba was, by contrast, a major source of supply for Spain. It was, nonetheless, challenged at the outset by three major uprisings of the *vegueros* (tobacco growers) – in 1717, 1720 and 1723 – with demands for an end to the new state monopoly and fairer prices, and threatened refusal to plant unless prices were raised.[15] After the British occupation of Havana, the second Factoría was bolstered with increased financing in the form of the *situado* from New Spain, but grappled with contraband and was beset with internal problems, such that its supplies of tobacco to Spain declined over its latter decades, as documented in detail by Gárate.[16] The reconfiguration of European colonial powers throughout the eighteenth century created a greater and greater need for defenses against the French and the British, whereby Spain increased its mechanisms of domination and extraction of tobacco revenue to underwrite loans taken on by the crown. This further undermined the Factoría's legitimacy, and attacks on the tobacco monopoly at the end of the century coincided with the expansion of sugar in Cuba in the void left by France after the revolution in Saint-Domingue.

The Factoría, which at best had never been able to control contraband, became so mismanaged as to be selling off stocks to individual manufacturers operating illegally, contributing to its own downfall. Spain needed to hold onto Cuba as a source of revenue for its disintegrating empire, and, as Sanz has convincingly shown,[17] this meant meeting the demands of the Cuban elites tied to sugar and the slave trade. Francisco Arango, a leading proponent in attacking the Spanish tobacco monopoly, argued that the control of the Factoría meant, among other things, not having sufficient tobacco, without the threat of sanctions against the smuggling that went with it, to defray the necessary costs of acquiring slave labour. It fell to Intendente José Pablo Valiente, a close associate of Arango in La Ninfa sugarmill, to decree the abolition of the tobacco monopoly, freeing leaf cultivation and manufacture from monopoly constraints.

Freed from the Spanish monopoly, Cuban tobacco was developed with British, French, German and later US, as well as Spanish, capital to produce quality cigar tobacco leaf and luxury hand-rolled cigars, which became *de rigueur* on the overseas markets opening up with the technological and industrial transformation of Europe, North America and further afield. Particularly coveted was the leaf from the Vuelta Abajo region of western Pinar del Río, which was grown by smallholder *vegueros* and also, as now documented by Cuban historian Enrique López Mesa and US historian William Morgan, with slave labour and in Pinar del Río on large plantations in what was a 'second slavery' akin, albeit on a smaller scale, to that in sugar,[18] while the capital city of Havana produced the famed Havana cigar, or *puro*, as it came to be known, for using only pure Cuban leaf.

Paradoxically, since the cigar and cigar leaf became the driving force behind Cuba's subsequent tobacco development, it was the cigarette that was cause for early innovation and *the* Cuban local smoke. By the mid-1860s, there were sizeable cigarette factories supplying the royal houses of Europe with fine lithography, and possibly the world's first cigarette machine, which was demonstrated at the 1867 Paris Trade Exhibition and heralded as the symbol of industrial progress on the island. Hand-rolled cigar manufacturing was, however, Cuba's nineteenth-century industry *par excellence*. By the time the Havana *segar* first hit the London market in the 1820s, Havana was reputed to have some 400 rolling shops and well on the way to becoming the 'tobacco city'. Subject to yearly fluctuations, exports rose from just over 140 million cigars in 1840 to nearly 360 million by 1855, with growing demand in Germany, Denmark and France, as well as Britain, and to a lesser extent the United States and Spain.

At the same time, from the 1830s on, there were recurring problems of imitation Havana cigar brands made elsewhere with Cuban imported leaf, and, by the mid century, despite having gained a reputation for manufacturing the finest-quality and most sought-after cigars in the world, the long-term export market began to recede, oscillating for most of the latter part of the century between 100 and 200 million cigars a year. From German bankers in 1844 backing manufacturing in Cuba (H. Upmann is a case in point),[19] between 1859 and 1870 Germany, along with France, by then Cuba's major markets, cut imports by two thirds and a half, respectively, as they developed their own manufacturing. Only Britain continued systematically to import, rather than manufacture, cigars.

The trends were somewhat obscured by the fast-growing US market, which by the 1870s was Cuba largest single importer and by the 1880s was handling virtually all Havana cigar exports. In the period 1855-90, there was a 30 percent increase in leaf exports to Germany, other European countries and the United States, but by the 1870s Germany had been priced out of the market. The value of exports had also been inverted: in 1859 the value of cigar exports was twice that of leaf, in 1890 leaf twice that of cigar, and the amount of Cuban leaf imported was such that 'half-Spanish' became true of the US industry as a whole. When US imports began to fall in the 1890s, Havana might have boasted palatial cigar factories,[20] but Cuba's total cigar exports were around half their 1850s level. Cuban manufacturers found themselves in a position of political dependence on Spain, whose interests lay in protecting its own manufacturing and economic dependence on the United States, whose industry was on the same protectionist path.

The extent to which tariffs, especially US tariffs, could hit Cuban tobacco cannot be over-estimated, with US factories springing up to take advantage of this to import the leaf and manufacture cigars and agents for foreign firms setting up stemming shops in Cuba to reduce the dutiable weight of the exported leaf. This was especially accelerated in the aftermath of Cuba's first War of Independence from Spain (1868-78), when there was also an unprecedented concentration of manufacture in Havana factories as smaller concerns were unable to hold out. The 1890 US McKinley Tariff Law and the independence war of 1895-98, which culminated with US intervention, the defeat of Spain, and the devastation of tobacco in war-ravaged Vuelta Abajo, paved the way for US occupation and a new monopoly presence, that of the American Tobacco Company (ATC). After protracted warring, ATC and the British Imperial Tobacco Company (ITC) had come to an agreement that Cuba and Puerto Rico were part of ATC domain, and they created the British American Tobacco Company for operations elsewhere in the world. Buying up a significant part of the Cuban tobacco sector, ATC created two subsidiaries: Cuban Land & Leaf, and Havana Tobacco. The strategy of the former was geared to guaranteeing leaf exports to the United States, while the latter, in the face of strong opposition, especially to the 1920s attempt to introduce the cigar machine, transferred much of its cigar production to the United States. Militancy and unrest in the sector notwithstanding, with unprecedented strikes in the cigar sector through the 1920s, some 'independent' cigar manufacturers were able to hold out, but it was mechanised cigarette production that dominated for the local market.

The Impact of the 'Cuban Model'

The success of Cuban tobacco fast became a model to be emulated. As cigars, and only later cigarettes, displaced snuff, pipe and chewing tobacco as the dominant form of consumption in Europe and the Americas, and as the Cuban leaf and cigar increasingly became the standard by which to judge tobacco, flows of seed, knowledge, growers, manufacturers and workers enabled attempts to reproduce them elsewhere, in the region and globally. This was compounded during the upheavals of thirty years of Cuba's struggle for independence from Spain, which saw considerable Cuban out-migration to the United States, the surrounding region and beyond, where tobacco provided a familiar means of livelihood, and over time rival economic and political interests built up. Parallel production and marketing systems of similar and sometimes identical brand names evolved inside and outside Cuba, such that from Florida, Jamaica and Mexico, as well as the Dominican Republic and Puerto Rico under scrutiny here, to Spain's Canary Islands, France, Germany, and as far afield as Dutch Indonesia, connections among the various cigar economies became even more closely intertwined.[21]

In this context, from the mid nineteenth century, the Puerto Rican tobacco sector was radically transformed into one that operated very much in tandem with that of Cuba, cultivating a Cuban-type leaf and hand rolling a Cuban-type cigar. Tobacco agriculture changed from cultivating inexpensive filler and cut tobacco for Britain, the Netherlands, Germany and France to specialising in superior cigar filler for export, including to Cuba when needed, alongside the more inferior *boliche* for Spanish cigarettes. New areas opened up in the highlands around Aibonito, Cayey and Comerío, more suitable for the Cuban-style leaf than the older growing areas of the northwest near Isabela and southwest around Yauco.

During the last quarter of the century, small craft cigar shops catering to the local market gave way to factories, some of which employed up to a hundred workers, and to large companies in agriculture, manufacture and export. Spanish immigrant José Rodríguez Fuentes in 1870 established his aptly named Las Dos Antillas, which, along with others such as La Ultramarina and La Flor de Cayey, gained sufficient acceptance to become providers for the Spanish royal house.[22] Most small farmers continued to be financed by middlemen, but there were also specialised leaf dealers and larger-scale leaf growers catering to the Cuban, Spanish and increasingly US market, while cigar and increasingly mechanised cigarette manufacturing was almost exclusively for the local market. Rucabado y Portela and Sánchez y Hermano established factories in Cayey and Comerío, respectively, and in 1890 Mamerto Infanzón established La Habanera, a large cigar and cigarette factory in Mayagüez.

As sumarised by Baldrich, there were three overarching dimensions to the impact of Cuba. The first was in agriculture, with the Vuelta Abajo-type leaf bonanza and increasing cigar leaf exports. The second was the transformation of cigar and cigarette manufacturing, spread over many locations, from small-scale hand rolling to larger factories combining cigar and mechanised cigarette production, contributing to the substitution of Havana cigars and Cuban cigarettes with domestic ones. The third came after the US intervention in the war with Spain, Spain's defeat, and the US occupation and subsequent absorption of Puerto Rico.

This led to the complete loss of Puerto Rico's Cuban and Spanish tobacco markets, and an avalanche of US investment included ATC, which bought up manufacturers including Rucabado y Portela to create the Porto Rican-American Tobacco Company (PRATCO) and a subsidiary Porto Rican Leaf Tobacco Company, and brought in experts for growing cigar leaf for the US market. It was the cigar leaf for export that predominated, as independent leaf dealers and merchants also consolidated in a handful of companies, such that thousands worked on family patches, haciendas and corporate plantations, and tobacco expanded at the expense of coffee, which had earlier predominated. In the hands of smaller independent manufacturers, the cigar that became known as the 'Porto Rico' gained some popularity on the US market, though less so than the Havana. As in Cuba, however, militancy and unrest characterised the sector, with unprecedented strikes through the 1920s and apocalyptical social movements such as Los Hermanos Cheo gaining a foothold in tobacco-growing areas.[23] Also, even more markedly so than in the case of Cuba, growers, manufacturers and workers left the island for the US mainland.

The Cibao Goes Its Own Way

The direct impact of the Cuban model on the Dominican tobacco sector was less palpable. By the late 1850s, the newly independent Dominican Republic occupied tenth place in the world tobacco trade, and by the early 1870s, tobacco exports were far greater than those of sugar, coffee and cacao. While most European countries had state monopolies and/or were supplied through their own colonies in the Americas and Asia, Germany at the time had neither but had a virtual market monopoly on Dominican tobacco, such that imports to Hamburg alone increased twelve-fold over the years 1864-72. The Cibao had become a tobacco-growing and processing region in its own right, with small-scale manufacture of *andullo,* cigars and cigarettes, bags (*serones*) and thread and breeding of pack animals.

Tobacco production quadrupled between 1870 and 1930, albeit with a slowing down during 1880-1900 and some extreme year-to-year fluctuations linked to political events, inclement weather and the overseas market. In 1879, a major crisis developed when the German government, in a protectionist thrust for home-grown tobacco leaf, more than doubled tobacco import duties. This led Dominican growers to switch to cacao, until cacao lost out to twentieth-century competition from West Africa; but small firms continued to operate in rural areas, and entire communities engaged in collecting and weaving palm fibre for the tobacco *serones.* These were carried overland by some 90,000 mules, until the decline in animal transport with the completion of the Cibao railroads, including one from Santiago to Puerto Plata in 1897, along which emerged important tobacco towns.

The central valleys of the Cibao had early been likened in soils and climate to the tobacco areas of Cuba's western Vuelta Abajo, with the Dominican leaf competing successfully with Cuban tobacco, causing a French diplomat to write in 1849, "The tobacco leaf of Santo Domingo has a better taste and looks more pleasant, and offers a perfect elasticity and good strength."[24] Later, according to Ferrán, the Spanish Consul in 1860 complained that the Germans would buy Dominican tobacco and manufacture cigars that they then sold like "Habana cigars" at very low prices. The Dominican leaf, however, was much lamented as poorer in quality than that of Cuba due to a lack of attention and knowledge. Lluberes noted: "Since the colonial period, the quality of the Cibao leaf has been spoken of, and its natural similarity to the Cuban leaf, but it was not handled well."[25] Attempts were made to rectify this, by contracting Cubans to advise on seeds and new strains, introducing regulations for growing and exporting, reducing export duties, and awarding franchises to establish model tobacco farms – many of which failed.

The Cuban wars of independence gave a small boost to Dominican tobacco, which it was thought might replace Cuban tobacco on the US market. The German market, however, continued to be predominant, while France, Holland, the French Antilles, Spain and other markets were also of significance. The First World War then closed the German market completely, causing price increases, although after the war Germany began to recover predominance and prices dropped. The US occupation of 1916-24 brought with it a huge increase in US investment, as it had in Cuba and Puerto Rico, but this was primarily in the south in sugar and mining, and only to a lesser extent in the north in bananas and tobacco.

Special attention was, however, paid to agriculture in the form of experimental stations and technification, and US companies took almost all the tobacco for US consumption or re-export to Europe, at increased prices. Cuba was also importing Dominican tobacco at this time. Soaring profits were made by exporters in a short-lived *furia de tabaco* (tobacco mania), to the detriment of food-crop production, and exporters tried to convince the US military government to grant Dominican tobacco preferential access to the US market. The US aim to modernise a semi-colony did not, however, extend to favouring a competitor to US tobacco growers, although the military government did guarantee a minimum price for the 1920 and 1921 harvests.

The 1920s recovery of European economies stimulated the tobacco trade, and from 1923 Belgium, Germany, France and Holland were the four largest buyers of Dominican tobacco. Companies from those countries became established in the Cibao, alongside companies attracted from the United States. The Spanish Tabacalera, successor to the earlier state monopoly, and the French Compagnie Génèrale des Tabacs also began to buy Dominican tobacco on a regular basis, together determining prices, setting market trends, and overshadowing the remaining German importers. In effect, the international market moved into the Cibao, buying, processing and shipping directly, with modern processing techniques and commercial practice. By 1930, however, tobacco exports were in fourth place, after sugar, cacao and coffee, representing only 6 percent of total exports.

Some manufacturing had developed in the Cibao from the early-nineteenth century on, producing cigars, plug and cigarettes primarily for the domestic market. By the early twentieth century, small-scale cigar rolling was giving way to larger factories, such as La Aurora, precursor to León Jimenes, and CAT. Tobacco manufacturing was boosted by protectionist government measures, including higher taxes on imported cigars and cigarettes. Exports of cigars peaked in 1911 and of machine-made cigarettes in 1927, and the manufacturing industry was predominantly mechanised production of cigarettes for domestic consumption. Trujillo came to power in 1930, with the economy in recession and tobacco particularly hard hit, and, after acquiring majority shares in CAT, effectively brought to a close the Cibao's 'long peasant century' by operating CAT as a state monopoly on tobacco, in tandem with a monopoly on major exports such as coffee and cacao.

On Visions and Counterpoints

The renewed interest in Dominican tobacco history in the post-Trujillo period, alluded to earlier, included revisiting the nineteenth-century vision of Pedro Francisco Bonó (1828-1909). Writing in the 1880s, Bonó attacked class, race, capitalism and inequality in Dominican history and mounted a spirited defense of the Cibao peasantry. His anger was directed against the encroaching sugar industry in the south, driven by land concessions to exiled Cubans and Puerto Ricans, and the impact of this on the dispossessed. He saw sugar as capitalist and foreign and tobacco as nationalist, and contrasted the patriotic liberalism of the Cibao and its autonomous tobacco peasantry with the plight of the dispossessed in the expansion of oligarchic cacao and imperialist sugar and cattle in the conservatism and foreignness of the south.

Bonó epitomised the nineteenth-century patriotic, liberal, federalist views of the Partido Azul (Blue Party) of the Cibao capital city of Santiago, in opposition to the Partido Rojo (Red Party) of the South and the national capital city of Santo Domingo. *Los Azules* (the Blues) came to power in 1879 as the party of Cibao tobacco interests in opposition to *Los Rojos* (the Reds) of the South. Puerto Plata and Santiago benefited from an influx of Cuban and Puerto Rican patriots, but Cubans were primarily a source of capital and technology to invest in sugar in the South, and the sugar expansion coincided with tobacco losing ground. This led Bonó to lament the "neglect of tobacco and the favour that was shown to sugar, cacao and coffee".[26] The Partido Azul itself came to gravitate to sugar and the South, and this was the backdrop to his strident writing condemning foreign interference in his oft-quoted essay 'Privilegiomanía':

> foreign capitalists come and establish four or six sugar cane estates on fertile terrain almost at give-away prices ... the owners find themselves surrounded by a population that used to have possession of the land, and are now labourers ... while I see Santo Domingo's cane being increasingly protected, I see the blacks of Sabana Grande and Monte Adentro becoming ever poorer, and if this continues, the day is not far distant on which all the small owners who until now have been citizens will end up being labourers, or rather serfs, and Santo Domingo will be a small Cuba, or Puerto Rico, or Louisiana.[27]

While Cubans revolutionised the Dominican sugar industry by bringing steam technology, in comparison with Cuba and Puerto Rico it was the lack of capital and the predominance of the peasantry that was seen as holding back any Dominican transformation into a plantation economy. González, in his 1994 monograph on Bonó, celebrated this in his longue-durée approach to understanding the resilience of the Cibao peasantry, attributing the significant impact of Haitian domination as a block on the plantation economy enabling the nineteenth-century expansion of the peasant economy.[28] Bonó's thinking permeated that of Dominican historians, who celebrated his vision of Dominican society and tobacco as "more Dominican" than sugar, due to its birth, its spirit and its method of production, industrialisation and marketing, and as "democratising" in its social effects.[29] San Miguel, however, argued that Dominican scholars and political leaders had fashioned an imagined colonial period out of foundational works such as Bonó's nineteenth-century progressive romanticism to create a "persuasive fiction" based on interpretations of the tragic loss of a golden age and bifurcation of the island.[30] Historian and ephemeral Dominican President Juan Bosch further depicted a progressive, yet still tragic, analysis of a Dominican "*arrítmia histórica*", of Dominican history being out of rhythm, off-beat, or out of sinchronisation with mainstream Caribbean history, seen as that of the plantation.[31]

Bonó's work predated by over half a century the far wider known vision of Ortiz (1881-1969) for whom tobacco similarly signified freedom and independence in contrast to sugar, slavery and dependence. As Ortiz affirmed in his celebrated *Cuban Counterpoint: Tobacco and Sugar*:

> Out of the agricultural and industrial development of these amazing plants were to come those economic interests, which foreign traders would twist and weave for centuries to form the web of our country's history, the motives of its leaders, and at one and the same time, the shackles and the support of its people. Tobacco and sugar are the two most important figures in the history of Cuba.[32]

Ortiz's counterpoint fashioned striking contrasts between dark tobacco and white sugar, intensive versus extensive cultivation, the immigration of whites on the one hand and the slave trade on the other, liberty and slavery, skilled and unskilled labour, delicate work versus brute force. In similar vein to Bonó, he wrote:

> The cultivation of tobacco gave rise to the smallholding; that of sugar brought about the great land grants. In their industrial aspects tobacco belongs to the city, sugar to the country. Commercially the whole world is the market for our tobacco, while our sugar has only a single market. Centripetence and centrifugence. The native versus the foreigner. National sovereignty as against colonial status. The proud cigar band as against the lowly sack.[33]

Ortiz lived the transition between the nineteenth and twentieth centuries, caught up in the intellectual shifts of his time. He studied law, served as a diplomat, ran for office for the Liberal Party, and was then drawn to progressive cultural movements such as the Grupo Minorista and Afro-Cubanism. He shared many Cuban intellectuals' concern about the situation of Cuba since the end of Spanish colonial rule in 1898, and especially the crisis-ridden 1930s. Having studied a range of disciplines, including anthropology, sociology, history and music, he critiqued the concept of acculturation and developed that of transculturation.

The relative silence surrounding *Counterpoint* after its publication has been attributed to its criticism of the United States in Cuba, and the revival of Cuban interest in Ortiz with re-editions of his work came after the Cuban Revolution, as had the Bonó revival after Trujillo in the Dominican Republic. Subsequently, in Cuba's crisis 1990s, when tobacco again played a strategic role, Fernando Coronil, in his lengthy introduction to the 1995 new English edition of *Counterpoint* saw it as a foundational text of binaries in constant flux for understanding not only Cuban history, culture and identity but also more broadly our contemporary globalised world.[34] For his part, Enrico Mario Santí, in his 1992 Spanish new edition,[35] broadened the counterpoint, comparing the work of Ortiz in which tobacco was "good" and sugar "bad" with that of Luis Eduardo Nieto Arteta (1913-56) in Colombia, for whom tobacco was "bad" and coffee "good", and Celso Furtado (1960-2004) in Brazil, for whom coffee was "good" and sugar "bad"; and later, in 1998, Bert Barickman published his counterpoint of three commodities – sugar, tobacco and cassava – in the Bahían Reconcavo region of nineteenth-century Brazil.[36]

In Puerto Rico, there has been no idealised vision of tobacco, which expanded greatly during the ambiguities of Puerto Rico's status within the new US empire. The 'patriotic' vision there was that of coffee, a vision no less bound up in the ambiguities of the nineteenth-century Spanish colonial period, when, as Catalan historian Josep Fradera has convincingly argued, Spain attached special importance in Puerto Rico to coffee.[37] There have, however, been strands in common with the thinking of Bonó and Ortiz. This resonates in Augelli's comparison of sugar and tobacco as agricultural types in the Highlands of Eastern Puerto Rico, and Manners' study of the subcultures of a tobacco and mixed-crop municipality alongside other studies on sugar and coffee in *The People of Puerto Rico*,[38] and in Ayala and Bergad's nuancing of this in their work on early twentieth-century tobacco, coffee, sugar and mixed-crop areas.[39] Arcadio Diaz Quiñones, in his 1993 edited collection *La Memoria Rota*,[40] drew parallels with Ortiz, to critique the destruction wrought by colonialism, plantation and US intervention and call for a project of national regeneration. There is little, however, in Puerto Rico that is similar to how the contrapuntal role of these key commodities has been developed in the national history and the national psyche.

Old and New Counterpoints

In 1892 and 1895, Cuban independence leader José Martí visited the Dominican Republic, as he did many other parts of the Caribbean region, mustering support for his Cuban Revolutionary Party. He was close to Dominican-born Máximo Gómez, who, after supporting the Dominican re-annexation by Spain and arriving in Cuba as a soldier of Spain, rose to become a general of Cuba's

1868-78 Liberation Army. Gómez's return to the Dominican Republic coincided with the Cibao elite's efforts to promote modern agriculture, and Gómez is on record as having undertaken a rare attempt to foster a large-scale model tobacco plantation in the Monte Cristi region, during the years 1889-96.[41] The Montecristi Manifiesto for Cuban independence was printed in Santiago, and funds were raised for the cause through patriotic clubs in the city. It is well documented that Gómez remained in Cuba after the war, through the US occupation of Cuba and into the nascent Cuban Republic. Cubans, however, all but disappeared from early twentieth-century accounts of Dominican history. The majority, it is suggested, returned to Cuba, and their presence was not to be noted again until the 1960s and even more so after the 1990s.

The context for this is what I have fashioned elsewhere in the form of new counterpoints of Cuban tobacco on and off the island.[42] Nowhere has this been more competitively so, especially since the 1990s, than between Cuba and the Dominican Republic, where US tobacco interests, including General Cigar and Consolidated Cigar, directed attention to growing tobacco and manufacturing cigars, involving émigré Cubans, and new companies were created in special free trade zones in both the Cibao and the South. Also in the 1990s the Spanish and French parastatals *Tabacalera* and SEITA, successor to the *Compagnie Générale des Tabacs*, became involved in both Cuba and the Dominican Republic, and their successor merged company Altadis in turn created Altadis USA, positioned for marketing often identical cigar brand names, some made in Cuba and others in the Dominican Republic. The British Imperial Group, successor to ITC, subsequently took over the Cuban operations of Altadis, until selling its interest to a Hong Kong-based conglomerate. In both Cuba and the Dominican Republic cigar tobacco leaf and hand-made cigars continued to dominate the lucrative export market, although in each there was also mechanised production, and cigarettes continued to predominate on the home market.

By contrast, the Puerto Rican tobacco sector is now almost non-existent. Under the 1911 US anti-monopoly Sherman Act, ATC and PRATCO became independent corporations and engaged in a cigarette price war, and after the bankruptcy of PRATCO in 1939, eight large US companies, including Consolidated Cigar and General Cigar, took over operations of what was by then almost exclusively mechanised cigar as well as cigarette production. By the 1960s, most of Puerto Rican agriculture and industry and many of those who had worked in them had gone stateside. By the 1970s most of the companies had closed their operations and only the Consolidated Cigar's factory in Cayey remained. As Baldrich summed this up:

> Puerto Rican tobacco farming and manufacture have morphed beyond recognition from the start of their transculturation, centuries ago to the

present. Both have reinvented themselves several times over. (...) However, the current industry is but a shadow of its former self. Gone are the thousands employed in farming and manufacture; gone are the rich working class culture, trade unions, and other organizations that revolved around tobacco manufacture; gone is the apocalyptical sermon of the Hermanos Cheos. No return to the centrality of times past seems to be looming on the horizon.'[43]

How this will play out in the future is hard to tell. Few could have predicted that the hand-rolled Havana cigar – itself a counter-economy of a different kind to the global monopoly world of the machine-made cigarette – would again play a key role in Cuba's strategy to rise above the crisis 1990s and triumphantly travel the world, with the Dominican in strong competition, though it was clear by then it would be hard for the Porto Rican to make any comeback. Nothing in the tobacco history of these three territories, however, suggests that any path should be seen as set in stone.

Notes

1   Pieter Emmer, 'The Organisation of Global Trade: The Monopoly Companies, 1600-1800', *European Review* 22:1 (2014), pp.106-15; Michiel Baud, 'A colonial counter economy: tobacco production on Española, 1500-1870', *New West Indian Guide* 65:1-2 (1991), pp.27-49.
2   José Manuel Rodríguez Gordillo, *La creación del estanco en España* (Madrid: Fundación Altadis, 2002), *Historia de la Real Fábrica de Tabacos de Sevilla* (Seville: Fundación Focus-Abengoa, 2005); Agustín González Enciso (ed.), *Política económica y gestión de la Renta del Tabaco en el siglo XVIII* (Madrid: Fundación Altadis/ El Umbral, 2008); Santiago de Luxán Meléndez (ed.), *Política y Hacienda del Tabaco en los Imperios Ibéricos (siglos XVII-XIX)* (Madrid: Centro de Estudios Políticos y Constitucionales, 2014); Santiago de Luxán Meléndez & Montserrat Gárate Ojanguren, 'La creación de un sistema Atlántico del tabaco (siglos XVII-XVIII): El papel de los monopolios tabaqueros, una lectura desde la perspectiva español', *Anais de História de Além-Mar* 11 (2010), pp.145-75, 'La segunda factoría de la Habana antes de la Guerra de la Independencia de las trece colonias 1760-1779. Una lectura desde el estanco español', *Studia Historica. Historia Moderna* 37 (2015), pp.291-321; Laura Náter, 'Colonial tobacco: key commodity of the Spanish empire, 1500-1800', in Steven Topik, Carlos Marichal & Zephyr Frank (eds), *From Silver to Cocaine: Latin American Commodity Chains and the Building of the World Economy, 1500–2000* (Durham: Duke University Press, 2006), pp.93-117, *Redes del Imperio: Análisis de gobernabilidad a partir del sistema de monopolios de tabaco en la monarquía española (siglos VII y XVIII)* (Santo Domingo: Archivo General de la Nación, 2018); Santiago de Luxán, João Figueiroa-Rego & Vicent Sanz (eds), *Grandes vícios, grandes ingresos. El monopolio del tabaco en los imperios ibéricos, siglos XVII-XX* (Madrid: Centro de Estudios Políticos y Constitucionales, 2019); Santiago de Luxán Meléndez, Jean Stubbs & João Figueiroa-Rego, 'Los monopolios ibéricos del tabaco (ss.XVI-XIX)', Special Issue of *Millars*, 49:2 (2020); Santiago de Luxán Meléndez, João Figueiroa-Rego, Vicent Sanz Rozalén & Jean Stubbs, 'Tobacco in the Iberian Empires', in J.

Curry-Machado et al. (eds), *Handbook of Commodity History* (New York: Oxford University Press, 2024).
3   Raymundo González, 'Ideología del progreso y campesinado en el siglo XIX', *Ecos* 1:2 (1993), pp.25-43.
4   Juan José Baldrich, *Smoker Beyond the Sea: The Story of Puerto Rican Tobacco* (Jackson: University Press of Mississippi, 2022), p.6.
5   Fernando Ortiz, *Cuban Counterpoint: Tobacco and Sugar* (Durham and London: Duke University Press, 1995 [1940]); José Rivero Muñiz, *Las tres sediciones de los vegueros en el siglo XVIII* (Havana: Academia de la Historia de Cuba, 1951), *Tabaco: su historia en Cuba*, 2 vols. (Havana: Instituto de Historia, 1965); Gaspar Jorge García Galló, *Biografía del tabaco habano* (Havana: Comisión Nacional del Tabaco Habano, 1959).
6   Jean Stubbs, *Tobacco on the Periphery* (London: Amaurea Press, 2023 [1985]), '*El Habano* and the World It Has Shaped: Cuba, Connecticut and Indonesia', *Cuban Studies* 41 (2010) – Chapter 13 in the present volume; 'Beyond Iberian Atlantic Spaces: Trans-imperial and Trans-Territorial Entanglements in Havana Cigar History (1756- 1924)', in Santiago de Luxán Meléndez & João Figueiro-Rego (eds), *El tabaco y la esclavitud. en la rearticulación imperial ibérica (Evora:* Universidade de Evora, Evora, 2018), pp. 389-426 – Chapter 17 in the present volume; Gregorio J. Cabrera Déniz, *Holy Smoke: A Literary Romp Through the History of the Cigar* (London: Faber and Faber, 1985); Joan Casanovas, *Bread, or Bullets! Urban Labor and Spanish Colonialism in Cuba, 1850-1898* (Pittsburgh: University of Pittsburgh Press, 1998); Antonio Núñez Jiménez, *The Journey of the Havana Cigar* (Neptune City: TFH Publications, 1996 [1988]); Doria C. González Fernández, 'La manufactura tabacalera cubana en la segunda mitad del siglo XIX', *Revista de Indias*, 194 (1992), pp.129-156, 'La guerra económica y sus efectos en la economía tabacalera', in Consuelo Naranjo, Miguel-Ángel Puig-Samper & Luis Miguel García Mora (eds), *La nación soñada: Cuba, Puerto Rico y Filipinas ante el 98*, Aranjuez (Doce Calles, 1996), pp.305-16; Juan José Baldrich, 'Cigars and cigarettes in nineteenth-century Cuba', *Revista/Review Interamericana* 24:1-4 (1994), pp.8-35; Reynaldo González, *El Bello Habano: Biografía íntima del tabaco* (Havana: Editorial Letras Cubanas, 2004); Vicent Sanz Rozalén, 'Arango y el mundo del tabaco. Estanco, reforma y abolición', in Mara Dolores González-Ripoll & Izaskun Álvarez (eds), *Francisco Arango y la invención de la Cuba azucarera* (Salamanca: Universidad de Salamanca, 2009), pp. 277-88; Charlotte A. Cosner, *The Golden Leaf: How Tobacco Shaped Cuba and the Atlantic World* (Nashville: Vanderbilt University Press, 2015).
7   Antonio Lluberes Navarro, 'La economía del tabaco en el Cibao en la segunda mitad del siglo XIX', *EME-EME Estudios Dominicanos* 1:4 (1974), pp.35-60; 'Las rutas del tabaco dominicano', *EME-EME Estudios Dominicanos* 4:21 (1975), pp.3-22 'Tabaco y catalanes en Santo Domingo', *EME-EME Estudios Dominicanos* 5:28 (1977), pp.13-26, 'El tabaco dominicano: de la manufactura al monopolio industrial', *EME-EME Estudios Dominicanos* 6:35 (1978), pp.2-27; Fernando I. Ferrán, *Tabaco y sociedad: la organización del poder en el ecomercado de tabaco dominicano* (Santo Domingo: Fondo para el Avance de las Ciencias Sociales, 1976), 'La articulación del proceso de producción de tabaco en el Cibao', *Estudios Sociales* 10:37 (1977), pp.3-38; Freddy Peralta, 'La sociedad dominicana vista por Pedro Francisco Bonó', *EME-EME Estudios Dominicanos* 5:29 (1977), pp.13-54; Bernardo Vega, 'Tabaco e historia', *EME-EME Estudios Dominicanos* 10:57 (1981), pp.3-13.
8   Antonio Lluberes, 'La crisis del tabaco cibaeño, 1879-1930', in Antonio Lluberes, José del Castillo & Ramón Albuquerque, *Tabaco, Azúcar y Minería* (Santo Domingo: Banco de Desarrollo Interamérica/Museo Nacional de Historia y Geografía, 1984).
9   Michiel Baud, *Peasants and Tobacco in the Dominican Republic, 1870-1930* (Knoxville: University of Tennessee Press, 1996); Pedro L. San Miguel, *Los campesinos del Cibao: economía de mercado y transformación agraria en la República Dominicana, 1880-1960* (Río Piedras: Editorial de la Universidad de Puerto Rico, 1997); Antonio

Gútierrez Escudero, 'El tabaco en Santo Domingo y su exportación a Sevilla (época colonial)', in Enriqueta Vila Vilar & Allan J. Kuethe (eds.), *Relaciones de poder y commercial colonial. Nuevas perspectivas* (Sevilla & Lubbock: Escuela de Estudios Hispanoamericanos & Texas-Tech. University, 1999), 'Tabaco y desarrollo económico en Santo Domingo (siglo XVIII)', *Anuario de Estudios Hispanoamericanos* 58:2 (2001); José Alcántara Almánzar & Ida Hernández Caamaño, *Huella y memoria: E. León Jimenes: un siglo en el camino nacional, 1903-2003* (Santo Domingo: Grupo León, 2003); Esteban Rosario, *Trujillo y la tabacalera* (Santo Domingo: Amigo del Hogar, 2004); José Chez Checo & Mu-Kien A. Sang, *El tabaco: Historia general en la República Dominicana*, 3 vols (Santo Domingo: Grupo León Jimenes, 2008).

10   John P. Augelli, 'Sugar Cane and Tobacco: A Comparison of Agricultural Types in the Highlands of Eastern Puerto Rico', *Economic Geography* 29:1 (1953), pp.63-73; Robert A. Manners, 'Tabara: Subcultures of a Tobacco and Mixed Crops Municipality', in Julian Haynes Steward (ed.), *The People of Puerto Rico* (Urbana: University of Illinois Press, 1956), pp.93-170; César J. Ayala & Laird W. Bergad, *Agrarian Puerto Rico: Reconsidering Rural Economy and Society, 1889-1940* (Cambridge: Cambridge University Press, 2020).

11   J. A. Gaztambide Baez, 'La historia del tabaco en Puerto Rico', *Agricultura al Día* 15:1-2 (1968), pp.6-13; Celestino Andrés. Araúz Monfante, 'La acción ilegal de los holandeses en el Caribe y su impacto en las Antillas y Puerto Rico en la primera mitad del siglo XVIII', *Review Interamericana* 14:1-4 (1984), pp.67-79; Ana Crespo Solano, 'Reflections on Monopolies and Free Trade at the End of the 18th Century: A Tobacco Trading Company between Puerto Rico and Amsterdam in 1784', *Itinerario* 29:2 (2005), pp.73-90; Jorge L. Chinea, 'The Spanish Immigrant Joseph Martín de Fuentes: A Self-Styled Reformer, Imperial Watchdog and Nativist in Puerto Rico at the end of the eighteenth century', *Revista Mexicana del Caribe* 6:12 (2001), pp.85-109; Argelia P. Pacheco Díaz, *Relaciones comerciales entre Hamburgo, Puerto Rico y St Thomas: 1814-1867* (Morelia: Universidad Michoacana de San Nicolás de Hidalgo, 2012); Ángel. G. Quintero Rivero, 'Socialista y tabaquero: La proletarianización de los artesanos', in *La danza de la insurrección: Para una sociología de la música latinoamericana* (Buenos Aires: CLACSO, 2020 [1978]), pp.29-84; Norma Valle Ferrer, *Luisa Capetillo: Pioneer Puerto Rican Feminist*, New York: Peter Lang, 2006); Wilson Torres Rosario, *Juana Colón: Combatiente en el tabacal puertorriqueño* (Comerío: self-published, 2011); Amilcar Tirado, 'Cigar Workers and the History of the Labor Movement in Puerto Rico, 1890-1920', PhD dissertation, City University of New York (2012).

12   Teresita Levy, *Puerto Ricans in the Empire: Tobacco Growers and US Colonialism* (New Brunswick: Rutgers University Press, 2014); Juan José Baldrich, *Sembraron la no siembra: Los cosecheros de tabaco puertoriqueños frente a la corporaciones tabacaleras, 1920-1934* (Río Piedras: Huracán, 1988), 'From the Origins of Capitalism in Puerto Rico to its subordination to the US Tobacco Trust: Rucabado and Company, 1865-1901', *Revista Mexicana del Caribe* 3:5 (1998), pp.80-106, 'Tobacco Leaf Dealers in the Twilight of the Colony with Spain, 1860-1898', in *Actas del XXIII Coloquio de Historia Canario-Americana* (Las Palmas de Gran Canaria: Cabildo de Gran Canaria, 2020), *Smoker Beyond the Sea* (2022).

13   González, 'Ideología del progreso' (1993), pp.25-43.

14   Chinea, 'Spanish Immigrant Joseph Martín de Fuentes'.

15   Rivero, *Tres sediciones* (1951); C. A. Cosner, 'Vegueros and Tabaqueros: Rebellion, Revolution and "The Devil's Plant": Challenges to State Control in Colonial Cuba', *Cuban Studies Association Occasional Paper* 9 (1998).

16   Montserrat Gárate Ojanguren, *Cuba: tabaco y hacienda imperial, 1717-1817. Un siglo de gestión del estanco: funcionarios, ilustrados y militares* (Las Palmas de Gran

Canaria/San Sebastián: Universidad de Las Palmas de Gran Canaria/Real Sociedad Bascongada de Amigos del País (2019).
17 Sanz, 'Arango' (2009).
18 Enrique López Mesa, *Tabaco, mito y esclavos: apuntes cubanos de historia agraria* (Havana: Ciencias Sociales, 2016); William A. Morgan, 'The Internal Economy of Cuban Tobacco Slavery', *Slavery & Abolition* 37:2 (2016), pp.284-306, 'Tobacco in the Age of Cuba's Second Slavery', in Richard E. Morris (ed.), *Social Struggle and Civil Society in Nineteenth-Century Cuba* (New York: Routledge, 2023).
19 R. Martell Álvarez, Manuel Torres Gemeil & Mathias Franz, *Der kubanische Tabak und die Deutschen* (Stuttgart: Schoellkopf, 2013); Martell, *Fumando en La Habana. Los Upmann: una familia alemana-cubana* (Havana: Ediciones Cubanas, 2016).
20 Adriano Martínez Rius, *The Great Habano Factories* (Barcelona: Select Publications, 2005).
21 Jean Stubbs, 'Political Idealism and Commodity Production: Cuban Tobacco in Jamaica, 1870-1930', *Cuban Studies*, 25 (1995), pp.51-81 – Chapter 7 in the present volume; 'Reinventing Mecca: Tobacco in the Dominican Republic, 1763-2007', Commodities of Empire Working Paper, 3 (2007), at https://commoditiesofempire.org.uk/publications/working-papers/working-paper-3 – Chapter 12 in the present volume; '*El Habano*: The Global Luxury Smoke', in Jonathan Curry-Machado, (ed.), *Global Histories, Imperial Commodities, Local Interactions* (New York: Palgrave Macmillan, 2013), pp.248-76 – Chapter 15 in the present volume; 'Cuba-Canaries Havana Cigar Connections: A Hemispheric, Transatlantic and Global History', in Santiago de Luxán Meléndez, João Figueiroa-Rego & Vicent Sanz Rozalén (eds), *Grandes vícios, grandes ingresos. El monopolio del tabaco en los imperios ibéricos, siglos XVII-XX* (Madrid: Centro de Estudios Políticos y Constitucionales, 2019), pp. 253-92 – Chapter 18 in the present volume.
22 Baldrich, *Smoker Beyond the Sea* (2022), p.23.
23 Ibid., pp.143-64
24 Quoted in Michiel Baud, 'La gente del tabaco: Villa González en el siglo veinte', *Ciencia y Sociedad*, 9:1 (1984), p.11.
25 Lluberes, 'La crisis del tabaco' (1984), p.13.
26 Frank Moya Pons, 'La economía dominicana y el partido azul', *EME-EME* 28 (1977), p.9.
27 Quoted in Emilio Rodríguez Demorizi (ed.), *Papeles de Pedro Francisco Bonó: para la historia de la ideas en políticas en la República Dominicana* (Santo Domingo: Editorial del Caribe, 1964), p.251.
28 Raymundo González, *Bonó, un intelectual de los pobres* (Santo Domingo: Centro de Estudios Sociales P. Juan Montalvo, 1994).
29 Peralta, 'Sociedad dominicana' (1977); Moya, 'Economía dominicana' (1977); Vega, 'Tabaco e historia' (1981).
30 San Miguel, *La isla imaginada: historia, identidad y utopía en La Espanola* (San Juan & Santo Domingo: Editorial Isla Negra/Ediciones Librería La Trinitaria, 1997).
31 Juan Bosch, *Composición social dominicana. Historia e interpretación* (Santo Domingo: Alfa y Omega, 1979 [1970]).
32 Ortiz, *Cuban Counterpoint* (1995 [1940]), p.4.
33 Ibid., pp.6-7.
34 Ibid.
35 E. M. Santí, *Fernando Ortiz. Contrapunteo cubano del azúcar y el tabaco* (Madrid: Ediciones Cátedra, 1992).
36 Barickman, *Bahían Counterpoint* (1998).
37 Fradera, *Colonias* (2005).
38 John P. Augelli, 'Sugar Cane and Tobacco: A Comparison of Agricultural Types in the Highlands of Eastern Puerto Rico', *Economic Geography*, 29:1 (1953), pp.63-73; Manners, 'Tabara' (1956).

39 Ayala & Bergad, *Agrarian Puerto Rico* (2020).
40 Arcadio Díaz Quiñones, *La memoria rota: ensayos sobre cultura y política* (San Juan: Huracán, 1993).
41 Evaristo Heres Hernández & Javier López Muñoz, 'La inmigración cubana y su influencia en Santiago 1868-1908', *EME EME Estudios Dominicanos*, 5:29, (March-April 1977), pp.55-104.
42 Jean Stubbs, 'Tobacco in the Contrapunteo: Ortiz and the Havana Cigar', in Mauricio A. Font & Alfonso W. Quiroz (eds), *Cuban Counterpoints: The Legacy of Fernando Ortiz* (Lanham: Lexington, 2004), pp.105-23 – Chapter 9 in the present volume.
43 Baldrich, *Smoker Beyond the Sea* (2022), pp.192-3.

Select Bibliography

Acosta, José, 'La estructura agraria y el sector agropecuario al triunfo de la revolución', *Economía y Desarrollo*, 9 (January-February 1972)
— 'La revolución agraria en Cuba y el desarrollo económico', *Economía y Desarrollo*, 17 (May-June 1973)
Alcántara Almánzar, José; and Hernández Caamaño, Ida, *Huella y memoria: E. León Jimenes: un siglo en el camino nacional, 1903-2003*, Santo Domingo: Grupo León, 2003
Alonso Álvarez, Luis; Gálvez Muñoz, Lina; and Luxán Meléndez, Santiago de (eds), *Tabaco e historia económica: estudios sobre fiscalidad, consumo y empresa (siglos XVII-XX)*, Madrid: Ediciones del Umbral, 2006
Álvarez, Mavis; and Stubbs, Jean, 'La mujer campesina y la cooperativización agraria en Cuba', in Carmen Diana Deere and Magdalena León de Leal (eds), *La situación de la mujer rural en América Latina y el Caribe y sus políticas del estado*, Mexico City: Siglo XXI-ACEP, 1986, pp.83-100
Appadurai, Arjun (ed.), *The Social Life of Things: Commodities in Cultural Perspective*, Cambridge: Cambridge University Press, 1986
— *Modernity at Large: Cultural Dimensions of Globalization*, Minneapolis: University of Minnesota Press, 1996
Aranda, Sergio, *La revolución agraria en Cuba*, Mexico City: Siglo XXI, 1968
Arnaldos Martínez, Andrés; and Arnaldos de Armas, Jorge, *La industria tabaquera canaria (1852-2002)*, Gobierno de Canarias/Cámaras de Canarias/Asociación Canaria de Industriales Tabaqueros, 2003
Arredondo, Alberto, *Cuba: tierra indefensa*, Havana: Editorial Lex, 1945
Arrighi, Giovanni, *The Long Twentieth Century: Money, Power, and the Origins of Our Times*, London and New York, Verso, 1994
Augelli, John P., 'Sugar Cane and Tobacco: A Comparison of Agricultural Types in the Highlands of Eastern Puerto Rico', *Economic Geography*, 29:1 (1953), pp.63-73
Ayala, César J.; and Bergad, Laird W., *Agrarian Puerto Rico: Reconsidering Rural Economy and Society, 1889-1940*, Cambridge: Cambridge University Press, 2020

Baldrich, Juan José, *Sembraron la no siembra: Los cosecheros de tabaco puertoriqueños frente a la corporaciones tabacaleras, 1920-1934*, Río Piedras: Huracán, 1988
— 'Cigars and cigarettes in nineteenth-century Cuba', *Revista/Review Interamericana*, 24:1-4 (1994), pp.8-35
— 'From the Origins of Capitalism in Puerto Rico to its subordination to the US Tobacco Trust: Rucabado and Company, 1865-1901', *Revista Mexicana del Caribe*, 3:5 (1998), pp.60-106
— 'Tobacco Leaf Dealers in the Twilight of the Colony with Spain, 1860-1898', in *Actas del XXIII Coloquio de Historia Canario-Americana*, Las Palmas de Gran Canaria: El Cabildo de Gran Canaria, 2020, pp.1-11
— *Smoker Beyond the Sea: The Story of Puerto Rican Tobacco*, Jackson: University Press of Mississippi, 2022
Barickman, B. J., *A Bahian Counterpoint: Sugar, Tobacco, Cassava, and Slavery in the Recôncavo, 1780-1860*, Stanford: Stanford University Press, 1998
Baud, Michiel, 'La gente del tabaco: Villa González en el siglo veinte', *Ciencia y Sociedad*, 9:1 (1984), pp.101-37
— 'A colonial counter economy: tobacco production on Española, 1500-1870', *New West Indian Guide*, 65:1-2 (1991), pp.27-49
— *Peasants and Tobacco in the Dominican Republic, 1870-1930*, Knoxville: University of Tennessee Press, 1996
— ; and Kooning, Kees, 'Germans and Tobacco in Bahía (Brazil), 1870-1940', in *Jahrbuch für Geschichte Lateinamerikas*, 37 (2000), pp.149-76
Benjamin, Medea; Collins, Joseph; and Scott, Michael, *No Free Lunch: Food and Revolution in Cuba Today*, San Francisco: Food First, 1984
Bergasa, Oscar; González de la Fe, Pedro; and Luxán Meléndez, Santiago, 'Efectos sobre la industria del establecimiento de un impuesto específico sobre el tabaco en Canarias', *Economía Canaria 1999*, Palmas de Gran Canaria: Universidad de Las Palmas de Gran Canaria, 2000, pp.184-94
Bock, Gustavo, *The Truth about Havana Cigars*, New York: Havana Tobacco Company, 1904
Brito González, Oswaldo, 'La industria tabaquera', *Rumbos*, 3-5 (1979)
— *Historia del movimiento obrero canario*, Madrid: Editorial Popular, 1980

Cabrera Déniz, Gregorio J., *Canarios en Cuba: Un capítulo en la historia del archipiélago (1875-1931)*, Las Palmas de Gran Canaria: Cabildo Insular de Gran Canaria, 1996
Cabrera Infante, Guillermo, *Holy Smoke: A Literary Romp Through the History of the Cigar*, London: Faber and Faber, 1985
Casanovas, Joan, *Bread, or Bullets! Urban Labor and Spanish Colonialism in Cuba, 1850-1898*, Pittsburgh: University of Pittsburgh Press, 1998

Catasús, Sonia, 'Características de los núcleos familiares en dos áreas de estudio: Plaza de la Revolución y Yateras', *Serie Monografica* 2, Centro de Estudios Demográficos, Universidad de la Habana, 1984

Chez Checo, J.; and Sang, Mu-K. A., *El tabaco: Historia general en la República Dominicana*, 3 vols, Santo Domingo: Grupo León Jimenes, 2008

Chinea, Jorge L., 'The Spanish Immigrant Joseph Martín de Fuentes: A Self-Styled Reformer, Imperial Watchdog and Nativist in Puerto Rico at the End of the Eighteenth Century', *Revista Mexicana del Caribe*, 6:12 (2001), pp.85-109

Cosner, Charlotte A., *The Golden Leaf: How Tobacco Shaped Cuba and the Atlantic World*, Nashville: Vanderbilt University Press, 2015

Crespo Solano, Ana, 'Reflections on Monopolies and Free Trade at the End of the Eighteenth Century: A Tobacco Trading Company between Puerto Rico and Amsterdam in 1784', *Itinerario*, 29:2 (2005), pp.73-90

Cueto, Emilio, *Frédéric Mialhe, Mialhe's Colonial Cuba: The Prints that Shaped the World's View of Cuba*, Miami: Historical Association of Southern Florida, 1994

Davidoff, Zino (with Gilles Lambert), *The Connoisseur's Book of the Cigar*, New York: McGraw Hill, 1969

De los Santos, Danilo; and Fernández Rocha, Carlos (eds), *Este lado del país llamado el norte*, Santo Domingo: Comisión Permanente de la Feria Nacional del Libro, 1998

De Paz Sánchez, Manuel de, *Wangüemert y Cuba*, 2 vols., Santa Cruz de Tenerife, Centro de la Cultura Popular Canaria, 1991

— *La esclavitud blanca; contribución a la historia del immigrante canario en América, siglo XIX*, Santa Cruz de Tenerife: Centro de la Cultura Popular Canaria, 1992

— (ed.), *El 98 Canario-Americano: Estudios y documentos*, San Cristóbal de La Laguna: Ayuntamiento de San Cristóbal de La Laguna, Gobierno de Canarias, Caja General de Ahorros de Canarias, Cabildo Insular de Tenerife, 1999

Deere, Carmen Diana, 'Rural women and state policy: The Latin American agrarian reform experience', *World Development*, 13:9 (1985), pp.1037-53

— 'Cuba's National Food Program and its Prospects for Food Security', *Agricultural and Human Values*, 20:3 (1993), pp.35-51

— *The Evolution of Cuba's Agricultural Sector: Debates, Controversies and Research*, Gainesville: University of Florida, 1996

— et al., *An Annotated Bibliography on Post-1959 Cuban Agriculture*, Gainesville: University of Florida, 1996

— ; and León de Leal, Magdalena, 'Medicion del trabajo de la mujer rural y su posición de clase', *Estudios de Población,* 5 (1980)
— ; and Meurs, Mieke, 'Markets, Markets Everywhere? Understanding the Cuban Anomaly', *World Development,* 20:6 (1992), pp.825-39
Del Todesco, Charles, *The Havana Cigar: Cuba's Finest,* New York, London, Paris: Abbeville Press Publishers, 1997
Deschodt, Eric; and Morane, Philippe, *The Cigar,* Cologne: Könemann Verlagsgesellschaft, 1998
Drayton, Richard (ed.), *Masks of Empire: The World History Underneath Modern Empires and Nations, c.1500 to the present,* London: Palgrave, 2018
Duany, Jorge, *Quisqueya on the Hudson: The Transnational Identity of Dominicans in Washington Heights,* New York: CUNY Dominican Studies Institute, 1994

Espino Marrero, Eumelio, *Cuban Cigar Tobacco: Why Cuban Cigars are the World's Best,* Neptune City: TFH Publications, 1997

Ferrán, Fernando I., *Tabaco y sociedad: la organización del poder en el ecomercado de tabaco dominicano,* Santo Domingo: Fondo para el Avance de las Ciencias Sociales, 1976
— ; and Pessar, Patricia, 'Dominican Agriculture and the Effects of International Migration', in Anthony Maingot (ed.), *Small Country Development and International Labor Flows,* Boulder: Westview Press, 1991
Ferri, Luigi, *Storia del cigaro. Mitologia, tradizione e cultura,* Bologna: Odoya, 2014
Fradera, Josep María, *Colonias para después de un Imperio,* Barcelona: Bellaterra, 2005
Friedländer, Heinrich, *Historia económica de Cuba,* Havana: Jesús Montero, 1944

Galván Tudela, José Alberto (ed.), *Canarios en Cuba: una mirada desde la antropología,* Santa Cruz de Tenerife: Museo de Antropología, 1997
Gálvez Muñoz, Lina, *La Cia Arrendataria del Tabaco 1887-1945 – cambio tecnológico y empleo femenino,* Madrid: LID, 2000
Gárate Ojanguren, M., *Cuba: tabaco y hacienda imperial, 1717-1817. Un siglo de gestión del estanco: funcionarios, ilustrados y militares,* Las Palmas de Gran Canaria & San Sebastián: Universidad de Las Palmas de Gran Canaria & Real Sociedad Bascongada de Amigos del País, 2019
García Galló, Gaspar Jorge, *El tabaquero cubano: psicología de las profesiones,* Havana: Imprenta El Siglo XX, 1936

— *Biografía del tabaco habano*, Havana: Comisión Nacional del Tabaco Habano, 1961 [1959]
— ; and Correa García, Wilfredo, *The Story of Havana Cigars*, Havana: Editorial José Martí, 2001
Gately, Iain, *Tobacco: A Cultural History of How an Exotic Plant Seduced Civilization*, New York: Grove Press, 2002
Gaztambide Baez, J. A., 'La historia del tabaco en Puerto Rico', *Agricultura al Día*, 15:1-2 (1968), pp.6-13
Gérard, Père and Fils, *Havana Cigars*, Edison: Wellfleet Press 1997 [1995]
— , photographs by Matthieu Prier, *Cigars: The Art of Cigars, The World's Finest Cigars*, 2 vols., Paris: Flammarion, 2002
Gereffi, Gary; and Korzeniewicz, Miguel (eds), *Commodity Chains and Global Capitalism*, Westport: Praeger, 1994
Ghai, Dharam; Kay, Cristobal; and Peek, Peter, *Labour and Development in Rural Cuba*, London: Macmillan, 1988
Gilman, Sander L.; and Xun, Zhou (eds), *Smoke: A Global History of Smoking*, London: Reaktion Books, 2004
Gómez, Orlando, *De la finca individual a la cooperativa agropecuaria*, Havana: Editora Politica, 1983
González Aguirre, José, *La verdad sobre la industria del tabaco habano*, Havana: Imprenta P. Fernández y Cía, 1905
González, Nancie, 'Peasants' Progress: Dominicans in New York', *Caribbean Studies*, 10:3 (1970), pp.154-71
— 'El cultivo del tabaco en la República Dominicana', *Revista Ciencia*, 2:4 (1975)
González, Raymundo, 'Ideología del progreso y campesinado en el siglo XIX', *Ecos*, 1:2 (1993), pp.25-43
— *Bonó, un intelectual de los pobres*, Santo Domingo: Centro de Estudios Sociales P. Juan Montalvo, 1994
González, Reynaldo, *El Bello Habano: Biografía íntima del tabaco*, Havana: Editorial Letras Cubanas, 2004
— 'La estela que dejó el tabaco en la cultura internacional', *Catauro*, 7:12 (2005), pp.9-17
González Enciso, A. (ed.), *Política económica y gestión de la Renta del Tabaco en el siglo XVIII*, Madrid: Fundación Altadis/El Umbral, 2008
González Fernández, Doria C., 'La manufactura tabacalera cubana en la segunda mitad del siglo XIX', *Revista de Indias*, 194 (1992), pp.129-56
— 'La guerra económica y sus efectos en la economía tabacalera', in Consuelo Naranjo, Miguel-Ángel Puig-Samper and Luis Miguel García Mora (eds), *La nación soñada: Cuba, Puerto Rico y Filipinas ante el 98*, Aranjuez, Doce Calles, 1996, pp.305-16
González Sierra, José, *Monopolio del humo: Elementos de la historia del*

tabaco en México y algunos conflictos de tabaqueros veracruzanos: 1915-1930, Xalapa: Veracruz University, 1987

Goodman, Jordan, *Tobacco in History: The Cultures of Dependence*, London & New York: Routledge, 1993

Grasmuck, Sherri, 'International Stair-Step Migration: Dominican Labor in the United States and Haitian Labor in the Dominican Republic', in R. I. Harper Simpson (ed), *Research in the Sociology of Work: Peripheral Workers*, Vol. 2, London: JAI Press, 1983, pp.149-72

— 'The impact of Emigration on National Development: Three Sending Communities in the Dominican Republic', *Development and Change*, 15 (1984), pp.381-403

Greenbaum, Susan D., 'Afro-Cubans in Exile: Tampa, Florida, 1886-1984', *Cuban Studies*, 15:1 (1985)

— *Afro-Cubans in Ybor City: a centennial history*, Tampa: University of South Florida, 1986

— *More Than Black: Afro-Cubans in Tampa*, Gainesville: University Press of Florida, 2002

Gútierrez Escudero, A., 'El tabaco en Santo Domingo y su exportación a Sevilla (época colonial)', in E. Vila Vilar and A. J. Kuethe (eds.), *Relaciones de poder y commercial colonial. Nuevas perspectivas*, Sevilla & Lubbock: Escuela de Estudios Hispanoamericanos & Texas-Tech. University, 1999

— 'Tabaco y desarrollo económico en Santo Domingo (siglo XVIII)', *Anuario de Estudios Hispanoamericanos*, 58:2 (2001), pp.713-36

Hernández, Ramona, *The Mobility of Workers Under Advanced Capitalism: Dominican Migration to the United States*, New York: Columbia University Press, 2002

Hewitt, Nancy A., '"The Voice of Virile Labor": Labor Militancy, Community Solidarity, and Gender Identity among Tampa's Latin Workers, 1880-1921', in Ava Baron (ed.), *Work Engendered: Toward a New History of American Labor*, Ithaca: Cornell University Press, 1991, pp.142-67

— *Southern Discomfort: Women's Activism in Tampa, Florida, 1800s–1920s*, Urbana: University of Illinois Press, 2001

Hilton, Matthew, *Smoking in British Popular Culture 1800-2000*, Manchester & New York: Manchester University Press, 2000

Huerta Galván, Julián, 'Marcas tabaqueras de la Isla de La Palma", *Coleccionable de la AVE*, La Coruña: Asociación Vitofílica Española, 2000

Iglesias, César A. (ed.), *Memoirs of Bernardo Vega: A Contribution to the History of the Puerto Rican Community in New York*, New York: Monthly Review Press, 1984

Infante Urivazo, Enzo A., *Havana Cigars 1817-1960*, Neptune City: TFH Publications, 1997
Ingalls, Robert P.; and Pérez Jr., Louis A., *Tampa Cigar Workers: A Pictorial History*, Gainesville: University Press of Florida, 2003

Kay, Cristobal, 'New Developments in Cuban Agriculture: Economic Reforms and Collectivisation', *Occasional Paper* 1, University of Glasgow, Centre for Development Studies, 1987
Kiernan, Victor Gordon, *Tobacco: A History*, London: Hutchinson Radius, 1991
Kulikoff, Allan, *Tobacco and Slaves: The Development of Southern Cultures in the Chesapeake, 1680-1800*, Chapel Hill & London: University of North Carolina Press, 1986

Lamphere, Louise; Stepick, Alex; and Grenier, Guillermo, *Newcomers in the Workplace: Immigrants and the Restructuring of the US Economy*, Philadelphia: Temple University Press, 1994
Lapique Becali, Zoila, 'Los sucesos de la historia de España y Cuba en las etiquetas de los cigarillos y habanos cubanos', in Consuelo Naranjo Orovio and Carlos Serrano (eds), *Imágenes e Imaginarios Nacionales en el Ultramar Español*, Madrid: Consejo Superior de Investigaciones Cientificas, 1999
— *La memoria en las piedras*, Havana: Editorial Boloña, 2003
— 'La litografía en el siglo XIX', *Catauro*, 7:12 (2005)
Larguía, Isabel; and Dumoulin, John, *Hacia una ciencia de la liberación de la mujer*, Havana: Ciencias Sociales, 1984
— 'La mujer en el desarrollo: estrategia y experiencia de la Revolucion cubana', *Casa*, 149 (1985)
Legna Verna, C.; and Rivero Ceballos, José Luis (1997), *La industria tabaquera en Canarias. Globalización y reestructuración*, Bilbao: Serie Estudios Regionales del Banco Bilbao, 1997
Lehmann, David, 'Smallholding Agriculture in Revolutionary Cuba: A Case of Under-Exploitation?' *Development and Change*, 16:2 (1985), pp.251-70
— 'Agrarian Structure, Migration and the State in Cuba', in P. Peek and G. Standing (eds), *State Policies and Migration in Latin America and the Caribbean,* London: Croom Helm, 1982
Levy, Teresita A., *Puerto Ricans in the Empire: Tobacco Growers and US Colonialism.* New Brunswick: Rutgers University Press, 2014
Lluberes Navarro, Antonio. 'La economía del tabaco en el Cibao en la segunda mitad del siglo XIX', *EME-EME Estudios Dominicanos*, 1:4 (1974), pp.35-60

— 'Las rutas del tabaco dominicano', *EME-EME Estudios Dominicanos*, 4:21 (1975), pp.3-22
— 'Tabaco y catalanes en Santo Domingo', *EME-EME Estudios Dominicanos*, 5:28 (1977), pp.13-26
— 'El tabaco dominicano: de la manufactura al monopolio industrial', *EME-EME Estudios Dominicanos*, 6:35 (1978), pp.3-27
— 'La crisis del tabaco cibaeño 1879-1930', in Antonio Lluberes, José del Castillo and Ramón Albuquerque (eds), *Tabaco, azúcar y minería*, Santo Domingo: Banco de Desarrollo Interamericano, 1984
López Isla, Mario Luis (ed.), *La aventura del tabaco*, Santa Cruz de Tenerife: Centro de la Cultura Popular Canaria, 1998
López Mesa, E., *Tabaco, mito y esclavos: apuntes cubanos de historia agraria*. Havana: Editorial de Ciencias Sociales, 2015
Luxán Meléndez, Santiago de, *La opción agrícola e industrial del tabaco en Canarias: una perspectiva institucional: Los orígenes 1827-1936*, Las Palmas de Gran Canaria: PROEXCA/Gobierno de Canarias, 2006
— (ed.) *Política y Hacienda del Tabaco en los Imperios Ibéricos (siglos XVII-XIX)*, Madrid: Centro de Estudios Políticos y Constitucionales, 2014
— ; and Figueiroa-Rego, João (eds) (2018), *El tabaco y la esclavitud. en la rearticulación imperial ibérica*, Evora: Universidade de Evora, Evora, 2018
— ; Figueiroa-Rego, João; and Sanz Rozalén, Vicent (eds), *Tabaco y esclavos en los Imperios Ibéricos*, Lisbon:, Universidade Nova de Lisboa, 2015
— ; Figueiroa-Rego, João; and Sanz Rozalén, Vicent (eds), *Grandes vícios, grandes ingresos. El monopolio del tabaco en los imperios ibéricos, siglos XVII-XX*, Madrid: Centro de Estudios Políticos y Constitucionales, 2019
— ; Figueiroa-Rego, João; Sanz Rozalén, Vicent; and Stubbs, Jean, 'Tobacco in the Iberian Empires', in Jonathan Curry-Machado, Jean Stubbs, William Gervase Clarence-Smith and Jelmer Vos (eds.), *Handbook of Commodity History*, New York: Oxford University Press, 2024, pp.145-66
— ; and Gárate Ojangurén, Monserrat, 'La creación de un sistema Atlántico del tabaco (siglos XVII-XVIII): El papel de los monopolios tabaqueros, una lectura desde la perspectiva española', *Anais de História de Além-Mar*, 11 (2011), pp.145-75
— ; and Gárate Ojangurén, Monserrat, 'La segunda factoría de la Habana antes de la Guerra de la Independencia de las trece colonias 1760-1779. Una lectura desde el estanco español', *Studia Historica. Historia Moderna*, 37 (2015), pp.291-321
— ; Gárate Ojangurén, Monserrat; and Rodríguez Gordillo, José Manuel, *Cuba-Canarias-Sevilla. El estanco español del tabaco y las Antillas (1717-1817)*, Las Palmas de Gran Canaria, Cabildo de Gran Canaria, 2012
— ; Stubbs, Jean; and Figueiroa-Rego, João (eds), 'Los monopolios ibéricos del tabaco (ss.XVI-XIX)', Special Issue of *Millars*, 49:2 (2020)

MacEwan, Arthur, 'Cuban Agriculture and Development: Contradictions and Progress', in D. Ghai, A. R. Khan, E. Lee and S. Radwan (eds), *Agrarian Systems and Rural Development*, London: Macmillan, 1979, pp.331-65

Macías Hernández, Antonio M., *Migración canaria 1500-1980*, Gijón: Ediciones Jucar, 1992

Maluquer de Motes, Joan, *Nación e inmigración: los españoles en Cuba*, Gijón: Ediciones Jucar, 1992

Manners, Robert A., 'Tabara: Subcultures of a Tobacco and Mixed Crops Municipality', in J. H. Steward (ed.), *People of Puerto Rico*, Urbana: University of Illinois Press, 1956, pp.93-170

Marte, Roberto, *Cuba y la República Dominicana: transición económica en el caribe del siglo XIX*, Santo Domingo: Universidad APEC, 1988

Martell Álvarez, R. *Fumando en La Habana. Los Upmann: una familia alemana-cubana*, Havana, Cuba: Ediciones Cubanas, 2016

— ; Torres Gemeil, M.; and Franz, M., *Der kubanische Tabak und die Deutschen*, Stuttgart: Schoellkopf, 2013

Martín Barrios, Adelfo, *La ANAP, 20 años de trabajo*, Havana: Editora Política, 1982

Martínez-Alier, Juan, 'The Peasantry and the Cuban Revolution from the Spring of 1959 to the End of 1960', *Latin American Affairs* (1970)

Martínez-Alier, Verena, *Marriage, Class and Colour in Nineteenth-Century Cuba*, Cambridge: Cambridge University Press, 1974

Martínez Rius, Adriano, *Habano el Rey*, Barcelona: Epicur Publicaciones, 1999

— *The Great Habano Factories*, Barcelona: Select Publications, 2005

Mayo, José, *Dos décadas de lucha contra el latifundismo*, Havana: Editora Política, 1980

McCoy, Alfred W.; Fradera, Josep María; and Jacobson, Stephen (eds), *Endless Empire: Spain's Retreat, Europe's Eclipse, America's Decline*, Madison: University of Wisconsin Press, 2012

Melián Pacheco, Fátima, *Aproximación a la Renta del Tabaco en Canarias*, Santa Cruz de Tenerife: Tabacanarias, 1986

Méndez, Armando, *Ciudad de Cigars: West Tampa*, Tampa: Florida Historical Society, 1994

Menocal, Narciso, *The Tobacco Industry in Cuba and Florida: Its Golden Age in Lithography and Architecture*, Coral Gables: Cuban National Heritage, 1995

Meurs, Mieke, 'Agricultural Production Cooperatives in Cuban Socialism: New Approaches to Agricultural Development', in Sandor Halebsky and John Kirk (eds), *Transformation and Struggle: Cuba Faces the 1990s*, New York: Praeger, 1990, pp.115-30

Moreno Fraginals, Manuel, *The Sugarmill: The Socioeconomic Complex of Sugar in Cuba, 1760-1860*, New York: Monthly Review, 1976
— *Cuba/España. España/Cuba. Historia común*, Barcelona: Ed. Crítica, 2020
Morgan, William A., (2016). 'The Internal Economy of Cuban Tobacco Slavery', *Slavery and Abolition*, 37:2 (2016), pp.284-306
— 'Tobacco in the Age of Cuba's Second Slavery', in R. E. Morris (ed.), *Social Struggle and Civil Society in Nineteenth-Century Cuba*, New York: Routledge (2023)
Mormino, Gary; and Pozetta, George E., '"The Reader Lights the Candle": Cuban and Florida Cigar Workers' Oral Tradition', *Labor's Heritage* 15 (1993), pp.4-28
Moya Pons, Frank, 'La economía dominicana y el partido azul', *EME-EME Estudios Dominicanos* 28 (1977), pp.3-12

Nardi, Jean-Baptiste, *Fumo brasileiro no periodo colonial*, São Paulo: Editora Brasiliense, 1985
Náter, L., 'Colonial tobacco: key commodity of the Spanish empire, 1500-1800', in S. Topik, C. Marichal and Z. Frank (eds), *From Silver to Cocaine: Latin American Commodity Chains and the Building of the World Economy, 1500–2000*, Durham: Duke University Press, 2006, pp.93-117
Nee, Min Ron (with Adriano Martínez Rius), *An Illustrated Encyclopaedia of Post-Revolution Havana Cigars*, Sankt Augustin: AWM-Verlag, 2003
Nelson, Lowry, *Rural Cuba*, Minneapolis: University of Minnesota Press, 1950
Núñez Jiménez, Antonio, *The Journey of the Havana Cigar*, Neptune City: TFH Publications, 1996 [1988]

O'Connor, James, 'Industrial organization in the old and the new Cuba', *Science and Society* (1966)
Ortiz, Fernando, *Cuban Counterpoint: Tobacco and Sugar*, Durham and London: Duke University Press, 1995 [1940]

Padilla, Napoleón S., *Cultivo del tabaco negro: sol y tapado*, Santo Domingo: Instituto del Tabaco de la República Dominicana, 1982
— *Memorias de un cubano sin importancia*, Hialeah: A. C. Graphics, 1998
Peralta, Freddy, 'La sociedad dominicana vista por Pedro Francisco Bonó', *EME-EME Estudios Dominicanos*, 5:29 (1977), pp.13-54
Perdomo, José E., *Léxico tabacalero cubano*, Miami: Ediciones Universal, 1998 [1940]
Pérez, Lisandro, *Sugar, Cigars, and Revolution: The Making of Cuban New York*, New York: New York University Press, 2018

Pérez, Jr., Louis A. 'Reminiscences of a *Lector*. Cuban Cigar Makers in Tampa', *Florida Historical Quarterly* 53:4 (1975), pp.443-9
— 'Cubans in Tampa: From Exiles to Immigrants, 1892-1901', *Florida Historical Quarterly* 57:2 (1978), pp.129-40
Pérez Rojas, Niurka; and Echeverría León, Dayma, 'Políticas diferenciales para la promoción campesina en Cuba: La vinculación del hombre al área en el cultivo del tabaco', in Niurka Pérez Rojas, Ernel González Mastrapa and Miriam García Aguiar (eds), *Campesinado y participación social*, Havana: Universidad de La Habana, 1998, pp.113-24
— ; González Mastrapa, Ernel; and García Aguiar, Miriam, *UBPC: Desarrollo rural y participación*, Havana: Universidad de la Habana, 1996
Pérez Vidal, José, *Historia del cultivo del tabaco en España*, Madrid: Servicio Nacional de Cultivo y Fermentación del Tabaco, 1956
— *España en la historia del tabaco*, Madrid: Consejo Superior de Investigaciones Científicas, 1959
Pollitt, Brian, 'Some problems in enumerating the "peasantry" in Cuba', *Journal of Peasant Studies*, 4:2 (1977), pp.1162-80
— 'Agrarian reform and the "agricultural proletariat" in Cuba, 1958-66: further notes and some second thoughts', *University of Glasgow, Institute of Latin American Studies, Occasional Paper* 30 (1980)
— 'Revolution and the mode of production in the sugar-cane sector of the Cuban economy, 1959-80: some preliminary findings', *University of Glasgow, Institute of Latin American Studies, Occasional Paper* 35 (1981)
— 'The Transition to Socialist Agriculture in Cuba: Some Salient Features', *IDS Bulletin* 13:4(1982), pp.12-22
— 'Sugar, "Dependency" and the Cuban Revolution', *Institute of Latin American Studies Occasional Paper* 43 (University of Glasgow, 1985)
Poyo, Gerald E., *With All and for the Good of All: The Emergence of Popular Nationalism in the Cuban Communities of the United States, 1848-1898*, Durham: Duke University Press, 1989
— *Exile and Revolution: José D. Poyo, Key West and Cuban Independence*, Gainesville: University Press of Florida, 2014

Quesada y Miranda, Gonzalo de, 'Martí en Jamaica', *Anuario Martiano* 5 (1974)
Quintero Rivera, A. G. 'Socialista y tabaquero: La proletarización de los artesanos', in *La danza de la insurrección: Para una sociología de la música latinaomericana*, Buenos Aires: CLACSO, 2020 [1978], pp.29-84

Rangel Rivero, Armando, 'El tabaco en Cuba: ¿único desde 1492?', *Catauro* 7:12 (2005)

Regalado, Antero, *La lucha campesina en Cuba*, Havana: Editora Política, 1979
Rivero Ceballos, José Luis, 'La industria tabaquera en las Islas Canarias: una perspectiva de principios del siglo XXI', in Fernando Carnero Lorenzo and Luis Sebastián Nuez Yánez (eds), *Empresa e historia en Canarias*, Santa Cruz de Tenerife: Fyde Canarias, 2001
Rivero Muñiz, José, *Las tres sediciones de los vegueros en el siglo XVIII*, Havana: Academia de la Historia de Cuba, 1951
— 'Los cubanos en Tampa', *Revista Cubana*, 74 (1958)
— *Tabaco: su historia en Cuba*, 2 vols., Havana: Instituto de Historia, 1965
Roca, Sergio G., 'Reflections on Economic Policy: Cuba's Food Program', in Jorge F. Perez-Lopez (ed.), *Cuba at a Crossroads: Politics and Economics after the Fourth Party Congress*, Gainesville: University Press of Florida, 1994, pp.94-117
Rodríguez, José Luis, 'Agricultural Policy and Development in Cuba', *World Development*, 15:1 (1987), pp.23-39
Rodríguez Concepción, Anelio, *La tradición insular del tabaco*, Santa Cruz de Tenerife: Consejería de Agricultura, Ganadería, Pesca y Alimentación, 2000
Rodríguez Demorizi, Emilio (ed.), *Papeles de Pedro Francisco Bonó: para la historia de la ideas en políticas en la República Dominicana*, Santo Domingo: Editorial del Caribe, 1964
Rodríguez Gordillo, José M., *Un archivo para la historia del tabaco*, Madrid: Jacaryan, 1984
— *La creación del estanco en España*, Madrid: Fundación Altadis, 2002
— *Historia de la Real Fábrica de Tabacos de Sevilla*, Seville: Fundación Focus-Abengoa, 2005
Rodríguez Ramos, Manuel, *Siembra, fabricación e historia de tabaco*, Havana: Librería e Imprenta, 1905
Rojas, Iliana; Ravanet, Mariana; and Hernández, Jorge, 'Desarrollo y relaciones de clases en la estructura agraria en Cuba', in *Estudios sobre la estructura de clases y el desarrollo rural en Cuba*, Havana: Universidad de la Habana, 1983
Rosario, Esteban, *Trujillo y la tabacalera*, Santo Domingo: Amigo del Hogar, 2004
Rudy, Jarrett, *The Freedom to Smoke: Tobacco Consumption and Identity*, Montreal and Kingston, London, Ithaca: McGill-Queens University Press, 2005

San Miguel, Pedro L., *Los campesinos del Cibao: economía de mercado y transformación agraria en la República Dominicana, 1880-1960*, Río Piedras: Editorial de la Universidad de Puerto Rico, 1997

— *La isla imaginada: historia, identidad y utopía en La Espanola*, San Juan & Santo Domingo: Editorial Isla Negra & Ediciones Librería La Trinitaria, 1997

Santí, E. M. (ed.), *Fernando Ortiz. Contrapunteo cubano del azúcar y el tabaco*, Madrid: Ediciones Cátedra, 1992

Sanz Rozalén, Vicent, 'Los negros del Rey. Tabaco y esclavitud en Cuba a comienzos del siglo XIX', in José Piqueras (ed.), *Trabajo libre y coactivo en sociedades de plantación*, Madrid: Siglo XXI, 2009

— 'Arango y el mundo del tabaco. Estanco, reforma y abolición', in M. D. González-Ripoll and I. Álvarez (eds), *Francisco Arango y la invención de la Cuba azucarera*, Salamanca: Universidad de Salamanca, 2009, pp. 277-88

Schivelbusch, Wolfgang, *Tastes of Paradise: A Social History of Spices, Stimulants, and Intoxicants*, New York: Vintage, 1993 [1980]

Stout, Nancy, *Habanos: The Story of the Havana Cigar*, New York: Rizzoli, 1997

Stubbs, Jean, 'Dandy or rake? Cigar makers in Cuba, 1860-1958', *Collected Seminar Papers* no.29, *Caribbean Societies* Vol 1, London: Institute of Commonwealth Studies, 1982, pp.17-25

— 'Some Thoughts on the Life Story Method', *IDS Bulletin*, 15:1 (1984), pp.34-7

— *Tobacco on the Periphery: A Case Study in Cuban Labour History, 1860-1958*, new edition, London: Amaurea Press, 2023 [originally published Cambridge: Cambridge University Press, 1985]

— 'Labour and Economy in Cuban Tobacco, 1860-1958', *Historical Perspectives*, 2:3 (1985), pp.449-67

— 'Gender Issues in Contemporary Cuban Tobacco Farming', *World Development*, 5:1 (1987), pp.41-65

— 'Gender Constructs of Labour in Prerevolutionary Cuban Tobacco', *Social and Economic Studies*, Institute of Social & Economic Research, University of the West Indies, 37:1 & 2 (1988), pp.241-69

— *Tobaco en la periferia: El complejo agro-industrial cubano y su movimiento obrereo, 1860-1959*, new edition, London: Amaurea Press, 2023 [originally published Havana: Editorial Ciencias Sociales, 1989]

— 'State versus Grass-Roots Strategies for Rural Democratization: Recent Developments among the Cuban peasantry', *Cuban Studies*, 21 (1993), pp.149-68

— 'Social Equity, Agrarian Transition and Development in Cuba, 1945-1988', in Christopher Abel and Colin Lewis (ed.), *Welfare, Equity and Development in Latin America*, Basingstoke: Macmillan, 1993, pp.281-95

— 'Women and Cuban Smallholder Agriculture in Transition', in Janet H. Momsen (ed.), *Women and Change in the Caribbean*, Kingston: Ian

Randle; Bloomington: Indiana University Press; London: James Currey, 1993, pp.219-31
— 'Political Idealism and Commodity Production: Cuban Tobacco in Jamaica, 1870-1930', *Cuban Studies*, 25 (1995), pp.51-81
— 'Cuba y Jamaica en el camino del tabaco', *Del Caribe*, 26 (1997), pp.81-93
— 'Turning Over a New Leaf? The Havana Cigar Revisited', *New West Indian Guide*, 74:3 & 4 (2000), pp.234-55
— 'Tobacco in the Contrapunteo: Ortiz and the Havana Cigar', in Mauricio A. Font and Alfonso W. Quiroz (eds), *Cuban Counterpoints: The Legacy of Fernando Ortiz*, Lanham: Lexington, 2004, pp.105-23
— 'Havana Cigars and the West's Imagination', in Sander L. Gilman and Zhou Xun (eds), *Smoke: A Global History of Smoking*, London: Reaktion Press, 2004, pp.134-9
— 'Reflections on Class, Race, Gender and Nation in Cuban Tobacco: 1850-2000', in Constance Sutton (ed.), *Revisting Caribbean Labor: Essays in Honour of O. Nigel Bolland*, Kingston: Ian Randle, 2005, pp.118-36
— 'Reinventing Mecca: Tobacco in the Dominican Republic, 1763-2007', Commodities of Empire Working Paper, 3 (2007), at https://commoditiesofempire.org.uk/publications/working-papers/working-paper-3
— '*El Habano* and the World It Has Shaped: Cuba, Connecticut and Indonesia', *Cuban Studies*, 41 (2010), pp.39-67
— 'Beyond the Black Atlantic: Understanding Race, Gender and Labour in the Global Havana Cigar', *Comparativ*, 5:21 (2012), pp. 50-70
— '*El Habano*: The Global Luxury Smoke', in Jonathan Curry-Machado, (ed.), *Global Histories, Imperial Commodities, Local Interactions*, New York: Palgrave Macmillan, 2013, pp.248-76
— 'Transnationalism and the Havana Cigar: Commodity Chain Transfers, Networks, and Circuits of Knowledge', in Catherine Krull (ed.), *Cuba in a Global Context: International Relations, Internationalism, and Transnationalism*, Gainesville: University Press of Florida, 2014, pp. 227-42
— 'Política e sapere: come si e globalizzato el sigaro avana? / Política y saber: cómo se globalizó el habano', in Laura Mariottini and Alessandro Oricchio (eds), *El Habano: Lingua, storia, societa di un prodotto transculturale. Lengua, historia, sociedad de un producto transcultural*, Rome: Edizioni Efesto, 2017, pp. 67-105
— 'Beyond Iberian Atlantic Spaces: Trans-imperial and Trans-Territorial Entanglements in Havana Cigar History (1756- 1924)', in Santiago de Luxán Meléndez & João Figueiro-Rego (eds), *El tabaco y la esclavitud* (2018), pp. 389-426
— 'Cuba-Canaries Havana Cigar Connections: A Hemispheric, Transatlantic

and Global History', in Luxán et al. (eds), *Grandes vicios, grandes ingresos* (2019) pp. 253-92
— 'Revisiting Caribbean Labour: The Challenges of Connie's Legacy', in David Sutton and Deborah A. Thomas (eds), *Changing Continuities and the Scholar-Activist Anthropology of Constance R. Sutton*, Kingston: Ian Randle, 2022, pp.24-31
— 'Dominican, Puerto Rican and Cuban Tobacco in the Long Shadow of Monopoly (1717-1930), in Santiago de Luxán Meléndez (ed.), *La transición del monopolio al libre mercado del tabaco en Cuba, Canarias y Filipinas y otros espacios americanos. Experiencias comparadas*, Las Palmas de Gran Canaria: Servicio de Publicaciones del Cabildo de Gran Canaria, 2024
— ; and Álvarez, Mavis, 'Women on the Agenda: The Cooperative Movement in Rural Cuba', in Carmen Diana Deere and Magdalena León de Leal (eds), *Rural Women and State Policy: Feminist Perspectives on Latin American Agricultural Development*, Boulder: Westview Press, 1987
— ; Curry-Machado, Jonathan; Clarence-Smith, William Gervase; and Vos, Jelmer (eds), *Oxford Handbook of Commodity History*, New York: Oxford University Press, 2024
— ; Luxán Meléndez, Santiago de; and Figueiroa-Rego, João (eds), 'Los monopolios ibéricos del tabaco (ss.XVI-XIX)', Special Issue of *Millars*, 49:2 (2020)
— ; Luxán Meléndez, Santiago de; Figueiroa-Rego, João; and Sanz Rozalén, Vicent, 'Tobacco in the Iberian Empires', in Jonathan Curry-Machado, Jean Stubbs, William Gervase Clarence-Smith and Jelmer Vos (eds.), *Handbook of Commodity History*, New York: Oxford University Press, 2024, pp.145-66
— ; Wickeren, Alexander van; and Clarence-Smith, William Gervase (eds), *Tobacco in Global Perspective: Trade, Knowledge and Labour, 1780-1960*, London: Palgrave Macmillan, 2024
Stücklin, Mark, *The Cigar Handbook: A Buyer's Guide to the World's Finest Cigar Brands*, New York: Barnes & Noble, 1997

Tinajero, Araceli, *El Lector: A History of the Cigar Factory Reader*, Austin: University of Texas Press, 2010
Tirado Aviles, Amilcar, 'Notas sobre el desarrollo de la industria del tabaco en Puerto Rico y su impacto en la mujer puertorriqueña, 1898-1920', *CENTRO*, 2:7 (1989)
Trinchet Vera, Oscar, *La cooperativa de la tierra en el agro cubano*, Havana: Editora Política, 1984

Valle Ferrer, N., *Luisa Capetillo: Pioneer Puerto Rican Feminist*, New York: Peter Lang, 2006

Vega, Bernardo, 'Tabaco e historia', *EME-EME Estudios Dominicanos*, 10:57 (1981), pp.3-13

Walvin, James, *Fruits of Empire: Exotic Produce and Western Taste*, New York: New York University Press and Palgrave Macmillan, 1997

Westfall, L. Glenn, *Key West: Cigar City USA*, Key West: Historic Key West Preservation Board, 1984

— *Don Vicente Martínez Ybor: the Man and His Empire: Development of the Clear Havana Industry in Cuba and Florida in the Nineteenth Century*, New York: Garland, 1987

— *Marti City: Florida's Cigar Ghost Town*, Key West: Cigar City USA, 2000

— *Tampa Bay, Cradle of Cuban Liberty*, Key West: Cigar City USA, 2000

Zaldívar Luna, Iturbides, *Producción y comercialización de tabaco negro en la República Dominicana*, Santiago de los Caballeros: Universidad Católica Madre y Maestra, 1979

Zapata, Felipe, 'Esquemas y notas para la historia de la organización obrera', *Unidad Gastronómica* (Havana, June 1948 – June 1951)

Zimbalist, Andrew (ed.), *Cuba's Socialist Economy Toward the 1990s*, Boulder: Westview Press, 1987

Index

Africa, 219, 230, 282-3, 286-7, 310, 330-1, 348, 356-7, 395, 399, 424; *see also* Black Atlantic, Cameroon
agricultural experimental stations, 35, 58-9, 177, 185, 219, 231-2, 265-6, 268, 281, 358, 367, 380, 396, 424; *see also* Connecticut
agricultural labourers, 36, 39, 60, 63, 286, 332, 356; *see also* peasantry
agronomists, 43, 59, 73, 155, 169, 180, 197, 205, 216, 222, 227, 231-2, 235, 256, 258, 265, 296, 300, 314, 334, 337, 367, 376
agrotechnology, 59, 109, 201, 218
Altadis (Alianza de Tabacos y Distribución), 153, 176, 215, 258, 383, 387, 401-02, 429
Altadis USA, 215, 231, 235-6, 258, 271, 338, 383, 404, 429
American Cigar Company, 83, 235, 353
American Sumatra Tobacco Corporation, 158, 261-2, 267, 368
American Tobacco Company (ATC), 5, 12-14, 16, 20-1, 50, 83-6, 101-02, 141, 159, 235, 257, 314, 353-5, 364, 383, 421, 423, 429, *see also* Trust
Amsterdam (Netherlands), 175, 190, 213, 257, 259-2, 282, 298-9, 308, 331, 346, 349, 364, 366, 368, 384, 417-9
anti-machine movement, 22, 101-02; *see also* cigar machines
anti-smoking, 78, 103, 191, 194, 255, 270, 277, 322; *see also* smoking
apprenticeship, 9, 22, 144, 198, 316, 319
Arango y Parreño, Francisco, 313, 420

aristocracy of labour, 8, 97, 197-200
aroma, 205, 224, 265, 293, 308, 318, 349; *see also* taste
Asian tobacco, 286, 310, 330-1, 346, 348, 357, 399; *see also* China, India, Indonesia, Japan, Philippines, Vietnam
Asociación Nacional de Agricultores Pequeños (ANAP), 35, 37, 39-40, 45-7, 56, 59, 63, 77, 105-06, 115; *see also* FMC-ANAP brigades
Atlantic world, 284-6, 314, 331, 344-78, 381-408, 414; *see also* Black Atlantic, ransatlantic history

Balaguer, Joaquín, 224, 226-7, 237, 244
banks, 76, 80, 114, 156, 192, 212, 225, 229-31, 237, 317, 365, 421
Belgium, 163, 220, 261, 276-7, 389, 391, 401, 425
Besuki (Java), 271-5, 297
betel nut, 364
Black Atlantic, 284-305; *see also* Atlantic world, transatlantic history
blue mould blight, 59, 259, 399
Bock, 4, 12, 158, 321, 327, 352, 352-5
Bonó, Pedro Francisco, 213, 215, 241-5, 425-6, 428
Bosch, Juan, 212, 223, 231, 237, 244, 427
botanical gardens, 133, 310, 358, 363-4; *see also* Hope Gardens, Kew Gardens
box decorators, 24, 26, 93-94, 199, 291
Brazil, 208, 260, 262, 298, 323, 330, 400, 428; companies, 153; Cuban émigrés, 214-16, 286,

332, 357, 386-7; factories, 235, 277; tobacco, 157, 159, 180, 206, 216, 225, 230, 257, 264-5, 310-11, 313, 365, 366, 368, 384, 390-2, 399-400, 415
Bremen (Germany), 175, 190, 213, 218, 241, 257, 261, 282, 299, 308, 317, 349, 366, 384, 419
British American Tobacco (BAT), 128, 141, 144, 153, 158, 354, 364, 383, 392, 400, 421
British Imperial Tobacco, 12, 14, 255, 257-8, 429
Burley tobacco, 72, 112, 224, 231, 262

Cabaiguán (Cuba), 23, 40-3, 49, 52-6, 57, 58-9, 64-7, 68-70, 73-4, 76, 78, 108-14, 166, 201-03, 396, 402-03
Cabañas (cigars), 4, 16, 130, 231, 316-17, 352, 359
Cabrales, María, 125-6, 129, 147
cacao, 218-20, 222, 225, 238, 242-3, 416, 423-6
Camagüey (Cuba), 89-91, 95-6, 100
Cameroon, 330; tobacco, 175, 189, 230, 282, 286, 332, 357, 384, 401; wrapper, 156-7, 162, 206, 235, 241, 357
Canada, 59, 155, 164, 258, 314, 319-20, 346, 385; see also Montreal
Canary Islands, 208, 257, 330, 345, 348, 381-408, 422; cigars, 157, 194, 206, 223, 235, 245, 339, 396-8, 400; Cuban émigrés, 204, 213-14, 235, 324; migration, 15, 156, 161, 203, 231, 286, 332, 356, 403; tobacco, 215, 224, 286, 382, 393, 397, 399-400, 400-01; trade unions, 397-8; see also Gran Canaria, La Palma, Tenerife
Caribbean, 117, 121, 126, 135-6, 141, 152, 159, 171, 173, 175-6, 192, 204-05, 213, 217, 222, 232, 237, 240, 244, 257-8, 284, 293, 295, 309, 314, 329-31, 332-3, 336, 345, 347-8, 384-5, 392, 412, 415-16, 427-8; see also Cuba, Curaçao, Dominican Republic, Haiti, Hispaniola, Jamaica, Puerto Rico, St Eustatius, St Thomas
cash crops, 16, 37, 49, 150, 256, 263, 297
Castro, Fidel, 155-6, 158, 162-3, 181-2, 191-2, 224, 233, 323, 337
Central America, 121, 160, 175-6, 192, 204-05, 213, 223, 233-4, 240, 257-8, 264, 269, 293, 309, 314; see also Costa Rica, Nicaragua, Panama
Centro Industrial de Tabaqueros Asociados (CITA), 386, 391-2, 398-401
chewing tobacco, 283, 422
child labour, 40, 58-9, 65, 86, 107, 180, 202, 269, 303, 334, 368
China, 311, 314, 340, 346, 387, 400
chinchales, 21, 159, 178, 240, 385, 398, 400
Chinese workers, 9, 13, 19, 25, 180, 198, 260-1, 267, 274, 289, 296-8, 366
Cibao (Dominican Republic), 156-7, 180, 205-06, 211-13, 215-20, 225-7, 228-9, 232, 240, 241, 243, 337-9, 412-13, 416, 417, 423-6, 429-30
Cifuentes, 145, 158-9, 162, 181-2, 231, 236, 333, 354, 386
Cigar Aficionado, 153, 162-4, 179, 182-3, 190-2, 194, 216, 227, 232-3, 255, 258, 270, 275-6, 285, 300, 314, 331, 338, 339, 355, 398
cigar boom, 153-5, 190, 228, 229-30, 245, 271, 274-5
cigar brands, 154, 161-5, 175-6, 178, 186, 204, 212-15, 219, 230, 235, 245, 258, 283, 284, 314, 316-17, 324, 329-30, 353, 356, 361, 362, 381, 384, 386-7, 396, 398, 400, 420, 422, 429; see also Cabañas, Cohíba, Don Diego, El Laguito, Flor de Machado, Hoyo de Monterrey, La Aurora, La Corona, Macanudo, Montecristo, Montecruz, Partagás, Punch, Quin Díaz, Ramón Allones, Romeo y Julieta
Cigarcanaria, 391, 400-01
Cigarette Company of Jamaica, 144-5, 333, 378
cigarettes, 218, 221, 261, 283, 322, 329, 344, 353, 369-70, 379, 383, 420,

422, 425, 429; factories, 20, 225, 227, 369, 420; machines, 4, 18, 122, 199, 211, 221, 420; production, 4, 14, 19, 24, 84-6, 122, 198, 211-12, 220-1, 257, 274, 337, 355, 385, 393; workers, 28, 86-7, 90-1, 92, 93, 100, 199; *see also* La Honradez, machine-made

cigar leaf, 151, 255, 256, 352, 420, 423

cigar machines, 4, 6, 12, 15, 84-5, 99-100, 124, 159, 181, 204, 221, 268, 291, 302, 314, 333, 355, 421; *see also* anti-machine movement, machine-made cigars

cigar makers, 9, 11, 25-7, 81-2, 93-4, 97-8, 123, 127-8, 142, 159, 162, 178-9, 181, 183, 197-200, 215, 223, 228, 274, 290-4, 316, 319, 338, 360, 363, 398

cigar revival, 158, 170, 174, 175, 193, 204, 258, 314, 322, 381, 386

cigar ringers, 24, 88, 90-1, 92, 93-4

cigar rollers, 6-8, 12, 21, 24, 26, 86, 88, 157, 159, 179, 206, 228, 233, 240, 241, 274, 290, 325, 356

cigars, 82, 218, 283, 288, 309-10, 321-4, 344, 350, 369, 390, 417, 422, 425; factories, 4, 225, 227-8, 230, 232, 291, 327, 352, 422; iconography, 180, 190-1, 207, 317; labels, 82, 207, 290-1, 317, 370; production, 14, 21, 85, 88, 124, 128, 133, 152, 157, 178, 199, 211-12, 221-3, 226, 227, 233, 274, 276, 280, 285-6, 290, 291, 308, 313, 320, 331-2, 337, 352, 356, 378, 385, 393, 397, 429; rolling, 4, 9, 11, 18, 21, 24-6, 82-3, 97, 127, 134, 155, 181, 198-9, 204-05, 211, 221, 241, 243, 265, 290, 293, 319, 352, 367, 369, 385, 420, 425; sorting, 24, 26-7, 93, 290; trade, 6, 11, 82-3, 87, 102, 109, 122, 132, 136, 153, 154, 157, 161, 193, 197, 212, 221, 225-6, 261, 290, 308, 333, 338-9, 352-3, 353-4, 361, 384, 400, 425; workers, 4, 86-7, 90-1, 92, 99, 123, 141, 286, 290-2, 332-3, 356; *see also* Cuban cigars, Dominican cigars, hand-rolled, Havana cigar, luxury smoke, machine-made, offshore

class, 49, 81, 196-209, 242, 284, 294, 385, 412, 425

clear Havana, 177, 205, 207, 293, 352

cochineal, 389, 390-2, 393-4

coffee, 35, 39-40, 43, 76, 106, 114, 121, 201, 218, 220, 222, 225, 238, 243, 260, 298, 321, 348, 360, 365, 413, 416, 418, 423, 425-6, 428

Cohíba (cigars), 155, 163, 178, 182, 189, 191, 231, 235, 283, 323, 325, 338, 381

Colbeck, 128-129, 333, 360, 361-2

Colombia, 116, 225, 330, 389, 428

commodities, 122, 213, 256, 273, 276, 284-5, 287, 289, 297, 307-10, 329-42, 344, 348-9, 357-8; *see also* cacao, cochineal, coffee, indigo, palm oil, rubber, sugar, tobacco

Compañía Anónima del Tabaco (CAT), 211, 220-3, 227, 337, 398, 413, 425

Connecticut Agricultural Experimental Station, 265-6, 367

Connecticut (United States), 180, 208, 255-83, 313, 330, 334-9, 352, 367, 384; Cuban émigrés, 152, 175, 387; migrant labour, 215, 289, 294-6, 299; tobacco, 156-159, 179, 182, 206, 230-1, 235, 241, 256, 259, 265-6, 270-1, 275-6, 285, 286, 305, 332, 356, 367-8, 371, 399, 401; tobacco companies, 176, 204, 214, 230, 267-8, 281, 336, 368-9; *see also* Hartford, Windsor

Consolidated Cigar Co., 152-3, 156-7, 160, 163, 176, 178-80, 204, 206, 214-15, 228, 230, 232, 235-6, 258, 267-9, 271, 274, 276, 386, 399-401, 429

consumption, 5, 31, 35, 39, 43, 60, 72, 106, 112, 135, 159, 219, 221-2, 225, 237, 245, 266-7, 270, 273, 285, 289, 297, 308, 320, 321, 330, 339, 345, 355, 369, 398, 401, 422, 425-6

contraband, 189, 216, 311-12, 382, 389, 392, 412, 414-7, 419-20
cooperatives, 31-47, 58, 60, 60-1, 64, 66-7, 73-4, 76-7, 105-06, 108-12, 114-15, 151, 160, 176, 197, 201, 214, 224, 267, 271; CCS (Cooperativa de Crédito y Servicios), 33, 35, 37-8, 41-2, 47, 56-7, 60-1, 64, 66, 69-71, 79, 106, 109, 150, 165, 166, 201-03; CPA (Cooperativa de Producción Agrícola), 31, 33, 38-9, 41-4, 47, 59-60, 60-1, 66-9, 74, 77, 79, 106, 108, 110-11, 150, 165-7, 201-03; *see also* UPBC
Costa Rica, 121, 152, 175, 176-7, 271, 356, 360, 386, 389
counterfeits, 6, 162, 180, 182, 317, 325
counterpoint, 170-187, 196, 207, 307, 318, 345, 350-1, 412, 414, 425-30; *see also* Ortiz
Cremer, Jacob Theodore, 260, 366
Cuba, 14, 52-5, 122-5, 159, 162-3, 179, 207, 214-16, 219, 224, 230-1, 234-5, 243, 255-83, 285-7, 290-2, 292-3, 298, 305, 309-14, 317, 320-3, 327, 331-3, 336, 337, 345, 347-9, 354-6, 366, 369-70, 381-408, 412-13, 415-21, 424, 426-7, 429-30; 19th century, 3-11, 14-30, 121-49, 198, 284; 20th century, 3-11, 14-30, 198; agrarian reform, 31, 34, 41, 56, 65, 105, 111, 122, 150, 152, 201, 214, 216, 258, 383, 385; agriculture, 17, 22, 32, 36, 49, 63, 66, 106, 109, 154, 316; cigarettes, 18-19, 423; economy, 5, 12, 14-30; labour, 14-30, 87-91, 95-6, 100-01, 206, 244, 255, 257; migration, 125-6, 128-31, 159, 164, 197, 205, 213-14, 243-4, 286; peasant associations, 33, 35, 37-8, 47, 56-7, 60, 64, 106, 109; post-revolution, 31-47, 48-79, 63, 102, 104, 122, 150, 161, 175, 202, 204, 207, 214, 329; pre-revolution, 40-1, 48, 56, 63, 81-103, 105-06, 200; production, 3-4, 6-8, 20-1, 23, 123, 166, 181, 192, 198, 204, 212, 255, 352-4, 421; rural, 31-47; Special Period, 104, 116, 150-68, 170, 180, 206, 383, 402; tobacco farming, 48-79; trade, 5-6, 14, 21, 123, 154, 164, 166-7, 212, 264, 340, 353, 419; trade unions, 83, 97, 200; wars of independence, 5, 16, 21, 28, 85-6, 97, 121, 123, 125-8, 134, 175, 180, 190, 192, 199, 207, 212-14, 218, 231, 242, 256-7, 286, 292, 331-2, 353, 359, 384, 421, 424; *see also* Cabaiguán, Camagüey, Havana, Las Villas, Matanzas, Oriente, Partido, Pinar del Río, Puerto Príncipe, Sancti Spíritus, Santa Clara, Vuelta Abajo, Vuelta Arriba
Cuban Cigar Brands, 153-4, 163, 235, 386
Cuban cigars, 3-4, 14, 26, 83, 154, 159-60, 162, 166, 189, 217, 233, 290, 313-14, 319-20, 332, 340, 345, 353-4, 359, 420-2; *see also* Havana cigar
Cuban-Dominican tobacco connection, 213-16, 227
Cuban émigrés, 121, 125-6, 129, 132, 133, 134, 152, 159-160, 170-1, 176, 180-1, 192-3, 200, 204, 206, 212, 214-16, 224, 225, 232, 234, 242-3, 257-8, 284-5, 289, 292-4, 299, 329-34, 337, 356, 358, 360, 361-2, 384-6, 429
cubanicity, 318-21, 370
Cuban Land & Leaf Tobacco Company, 5-6, 17-18, 50, 58, 353, 421
Cuban leaf, 14, 128, 154, 205, 212, 224, 258, 275, 293, 314-15, 325, 329, 332, 337, 350, 352, 359, 412-13, 420, 422, 424
Cuban Revolutionary Party, 121, 127, 181, 193, 244, 358, 428
Cuban seed, 132, 156, 158, 177, 215, 224, 256, 287, 294, 296, 313, 332-4, 352, 358, 362-3, 368; *see also* Havana seed
Cuban tobacco, 5, 14-30, 48-79, 81-103, 121-49, 160, 162, 175, 177, 196-209, 212, 213, 218, 220,

224-5, 227, 234, 257, 265, 275, 286, 292, 308, 310-11, 314, 316, 319, 323, 325, 332, 337, 344-5, 348-9, 351, 356-7, 359, 382, 384, 398, 401-02, 411, 422, 424, 429; *see also* Cuban-Dominican tobacco connection
Cubatabaco, 41-3, 66-7, 79, 111-12, 152-3, 163-4, 176, 178, 214, 258, 386
Cullbro, 158-159, 164, 182, 269-71
Cullman, 158, 164, 182, 219, 222, 235, 267, 271
Curaçao, 153, 217, 220, 241, 417, 418-19
curing, 58-9, 109, 177, 220, 263, 267, 281, 334, 368

Danlí (Honduras), 160-1, 182, 206
Davidoff, 155-7, 228-9, 231, 233, 270, 323-5, 338-9
Deli tobacco, 259-262, 271-2, 366, 368
Denmark, 130, 313, 352, 357, 401, 419-20
depression, 17, 83, 85, 87, 92, 97, 101, 122-3, 175, 181, 200, 214, 257, 261, 273, 290, 347, 385
diversification, 34, 58, 226
division of labour, 83-91, 97, 102, 110, 112-13, 202
Dominican cigars, 156, 159-60, 162, 224-5, 228, 231, 233, 246
Dominican leaf, 212, 218, 223, 225, 337, 424
Dominican Republic, 121, 152, 155-7, 157-62, 175-7, 178-80, 181, 194, 205-06, 211-50, 255, 257-8, 264, 270-1, 275, 277, 286, 314, 324, 330-4, 337-40, 356, 360, 383-6, 391, 399-402, 412-13, 415-17, 422-3, 426-30; Cuban involvement, 231-6; migration, 236; tobacco companies, 220, 222, 226, 235-6; trade, 222, 227, 233; *see also* Cibao, La Romana, Licey, Moca, Monte Cristi, Puerto Plata, San José de las Matas, San Pedro de Macorís, Santiago de los Caballeros, Santo Domingo, Tamboril, Villa González

Dominican tobacco, 211-50, 337, 411, 423, 425; *see also* Cuba-Dominican tobacco connection
Don Diego (cigars), 157, 231, 233, 235, 246, 400
Dutch Cultivation System, 260, 271, 298, 365-6

Eastern Europe, 104, 165, 175, 204, 212, 214, 227, 258, 314, 338
Ecuador, 159, 175, 176-7, 180, 206, 214-6, 230, 234, 264, 275, 286, 330-1, 356, 386
education, 32, 34-6, 43, 46, 59, 64, 66-7, 97, 105, 113, 115, 200, 220, 394; *see also* literacy
El Caribbean Cigar & Tobacco Company, 139, 362
El Corojo (San Luis), 50, 58, 275
El Laguito (cigars), 161, 164, 325
Europe, 4, 14, 19, 82, 122, 163, 257, 276, 323, 330-1, 344, 356; *see also* Belgium, Denmark, Eastern Europe, France, Germany, Great Britain, Italy, Netherlands, Portugal, Russia, Spain, Sweden, Switzerland, Turkey
European Union, 164, 230, 386, 391, 399-400
exports, 23-24, 50, 85-6, 104, 150, 260, 273, 344, 421, 429

Factorías, 217, 411-13, 416-20
family labour, 40, 107, 109-10, 112, 200-01, 221
farms, 34-6, 49-50, 56-7, 75, 200-03, 269; *see also* cooperatives, plantations, sharecropping, smallholding, squatters, state, subsistence, tenant
Federación de Mujeres Cubanas (FMC), 32, 37, 41, 47, 63, 74, 79, 105, 116, 117; *see also* FMC-ANAP brigades
fertiliser, 35, 59, 62, 110, 153-4, 259, 263, 267, 281, 368
filler leaf, 41, 43, 156-7, 177, 205-06, 224, 230, 268, 272, 274, 292-3, 313, 334, 365, 399, 422

Flor de Machado (cigars), 139, 140, 363
Florida-Georgia tobacco belt, 177, 256-7, 261, 267, 286-7, 330-1, 356-7, 368, 371
Florida (United States), 83, 100, 102, 121-5, 127, 131-2, 145, 152, 159, 164, 170, 175-81, 192, 194, 197-8, 200, 203-05, 207-08, 213-14, 232, 244, 256-7, 261, 266-7, 280-1, 285-6, 292-5, 299, 305, 313, 324, 331-2, 334-5, 345, 356, 384, 387, 397, 422; see also Fort Lauderdale, Gadsden County, Gainesville, Jacksonville, Key West, Marti City, Maryland, Miami, Ocala, Quincy, Tampa
FMC-ANAP brigades, 37, 41, 47, 66, 79, 107, 111
food crops, 34-5, 43, 62, 72, 78, 105-06, 112, 139, 220-1, 273-4, 287, 297-8, 389, 393, 416, 424-5, 428
foreign competition, 6, 21, 85, 123, 353
foreign investment, 16-17, 122, 175, 218, 257, 267, 308, 349, 382, 384, 420; see also under France, Germany, Great Britain, Netherlands, Spain, United States
Fort Lauderdale (Florida), 152, 176, 194, 204, 214
France, 5, 152-3, 163-4, 166, 176, 214, 216-19, 236, 258, 260-1, 274-7, 286, 298, 310, 312-14, 317, 332-3, 344-8, 351-2, 364, 370, 382, 401, 414-16, 420-3, 424-5; investment, 175, 189, 213, 257, 308, 349, 382, 384, 420; tobacco companies, 220, 425, 429; trade, 122, 389, 414, 416; see also Paris
free ports, 348, 389-90, 392-3
free trade, 237, 346-7, 352, 382, 388, 416
free trade zones, 157, 158, 206, 223, 225-8, 230, 233-4, 237-8, 244, 337-8, 342, 391, 399, 401, 429
Fuente family, 156, 159, 178, 180, 183, 205-06, 227-33, 246, 270, 338-9

Gadsden County (Florida), 177, 193, 205, 215, 280

Gainesville (Florida), 177, 356
García, Calixto, 126, 180, 207
gender, 24, 27-8, 40-5, 48-79, 63, 81-105, 109, 110-16, 166, 196-209, 284-305, 319, 385, 412; see also women
General Cigar Company, 17, 23, 96, 152, 156-9, 164-5, 176, 178, 181, 204, 206, 214, 230, 232, 235, 246, 258, 267, 269, 271, 275, 338, 387, 429
Georgia (United States), 180, 256-7, 261, 267, 280-1, 295, 305, 334, 345
Germany, 5, 163, 217-19, 243, 260-1, 276-277, 286, 298, 317, 320, 332, 344-345, 352, 364, 366, 370, 382-383, 391, 401, 417, 420, 422-425; investment, 4, 16, 122, 175, 189, 213, 257, 308, 349, 352, 384, 420-421; manufacturers, 312, 419; trade, 122, 389-390, 424; see also Bremen, Hamburg
global history, 381-408
Gómez, Máximo, 124, 180, 207, 244, 360-1, 428
González, Guillermo, 131, 333, 359
Grajales, Mariana, 103, 125-6, 129, 147
Gran Canaria (Canary Islands), 235, 387, 391, 395-401
Granda Hermanos, 320, 370, 380
Great Britain, 133, 135-6, 153, 164, 176, 214, 216, 224, 241, 258, 260, 286, 298-9, 310-12, 319, 322, 327, 332-3, 344-51, 353-4, 360, 364, 369, 382-3, 389, 393, 401, 414, 420-1; investment, 5, 12, 16, 122, 139, 175, 189, 213, 256-7, 308, 333, 349, 353-4, 382, 384, 420; occupation of Havana (1762), 217, 313, 327, 348, 350, 352, 367, 389, 412, 417-19; tobacco companies, 140; trade, 122, 131, 133, 155, 163, 389, 414; see also London
Great Exhibition (London), 317, 352
Gulf & Western, 226, 235-6, 269, 342

Habanos SA, 152-3, 165, 176, 214, 258, 275, 381-2, 386, 398, 404
Haiti, 127, 129, 136, 147, 217, 238, 244,

346, 348, 416, 426; *see also* Saint-Domingue
Hamburg (Germany), 218, 241, 308, 312, 327, 349, 419, 423
hand-rolled cigars, 274, 339, 349, 355, 369-70, 420, 423, 429-30
Hartford (Connecticut), 259, 262, 267, 269-70, 295, 334-5
Havana cigar, 83-5, 101, 122, 130, 150-68, 170-87, 188-95, 206, 213-14, 255-83, 284-305, 307-28, 329-42, 344-78, 381-408, 420-1, 423; *see also* offshore
Havana (Cuba), 7, 15, 22, 24, 26, 28, 99, 123, 130, 132, 158, 161-2, 189, 193, 198-9, 217, 219, 231, 246, 264, 286, 290-1, 313, 315-17, 331-2, 340, 348, 350, 352, 356, 358, 362, 381-2, 390-1, 394, 401, 420; factories, 4-5, 7-8, 19, 83, 85-6, 92, 96, 101, 161, 219, 290, 308, 313, 320, 352-3, 400, 421; manufacturing, 5, 16, 18, 85-6, 97, 178, 205, 292, 316, 321, 353-4; tobacco, 123, 205, 307, 367; workers, 4, 8, 10, 24, 83, 86-90, 95-6, 100, 141, 198
Havana seed, 151, 156, 177, 180, 206, 235, 264-6, 285, 331, 355, 367-8; *see also* Cuban seed
Havana Tobacco Company, 5, 17, 20, 219, 353, 421
health, 36, 64, 78, 155, 164, 182-3, 269-70, 277, 283, 294, 295, 310, 334, 336, 369, 381, 394; *see also* anti-smoking
Helms-Burton Act (1996), 164, 175, 214, 258, 386; *see also* Torricelli
Henry Clay & Bock, 4, 16, 19-20, 20, 83, 86, 157, 219, 231, 353-4
Hill, George W., 83, 101
Hispaniola, 216, 415
home production, 7, 19, 22, 85-6, 199-203, 264, 290, 396, 403
Honduras, 121, 152, 156, 159-62, 175-6, 178, 180, 182, 194, 205-06, 214-16, 226, 230-1, 233, 235-6, 245, 257, 259, 271, 277, 286, 330-1, 335, 337, 356, 360, 386-7, 389; *see also* Danlí

Hope Gardens (Jamaica), 130, 132-4, 333, 358-9, 362-3
Hoyo de Monterrey (cigars), 178, 189, 235, 283, 381, 401
Hunters & Frankau, 153, 155, 161, 176, 183, 214, 258
H. Upmann, 3-4, 7, 16, 82, 153, 155-7, 159-62, 178, 183, 231, 232, 235-6, 317, 338, 352, 381, 398-9, 404, 421
hurricanes, 35, 59, 153, 174, 235

iconography, 82, 197, 290, 293, 370
Imperial Tobacco Company (ITC), 141, 144, 223, 267, 333, 354, 364, 383, 401, 404, 421, 429
indentured labour, 13, 19, 22, 25, 180, 198, 267, 290, 365
independence struggle, 121, 125-6, 175, 200, 204, 213, 273, 284, 294, 329, 345, 384, 393, 397, 403, 422, 429
independent manufacturers, 6, 14, 17, 21, 85, 101, 175, 214, 267, 314, 355, 385, 422
India, 346, 365
indigo, 260, 298, 365, 416
Indonesia, 157, 161, 206, 230-1, 245, 255-83, 285, 289, 296-9, 313, 330, 345, 357, 364-8, 399, 422; *see also* Dutch Cultivation System, Java, Sumatra
Indonesian tobacco, 282, 296, 332, 357; *see also* kretek
informal empire, 347, 387-90
Instituto del Tabaco (INTABACO), 156, 180, 216, 223-4, 230, 231, 235
irrigation, 35, 58-9, 109, 220-1, 226
Italy, 220, 262, 292, 310, 344-5, 401

Jacksonville (Florida), 177, 192, 286, 331, 356
Jamaica, 121-49, 152, 156, 158-9, 175, 176-7, 181-2, 194, 208, 215-16, 235-6, 244-5, 257, 269, 283, 286, 295, 330-5, 338-9, 345, 356-64, 370, 384-5, 389, 400, 418, 422; cigars, 128, 131, 134-5, 145, 158,

333, 362; Cuban émigrés, 128-31, 137-8, 360-1; labour movement, 13, 142, 144; tobacco, 122, 128, 133-8; tobacco companies, 128, 138, 333, 362; see also Hope Gardens, Kingston, Temple Hall
Jamaica Tobacco Company (JTC), 128, 134, 139-45, 362-4
Japan, 273, 311, 346, 392
Java (Indonesia), 157, 175, 189, 206, 230, 255-6, 259-60, 271-5, 287, 289, 296, 299, 313, 332, 365-7, 368, 371, 384, 401; see also Besuki, Jember
Jember (Java), 271-2, 273-4, 297-8
Jimenes, León, 212, 223, 244-5, 337-8, 413, 425
John Player & Sons, 140, 363

Kew Gardens (London), 133, 357, 363
Key West (Florida), 27-8, 86, 100, 103, 123-4, 126, 156, 174, 177, 180, 192-3, 198, 203-04, 207, 215, 243, 257, 280, 286, 292, 331, 356
Kingston (Jamaica), 121, 125, 129-34, 134, 142, 148, 181, 235, 333, 358-62
knowledge circuits, 284-5, 289, 314, 329-42, 356, 393-6; see also technology
kretek, 283, 365, 369

La Aurora (cigars), 211-12, 221, 223, 241, 245-6, 337, 339-40, 425
labour, 7, 8, 10, 15, 18, 22-4, 39, 60, 81-103, 256, 284-305, 297, 330, 355, 357, 366, 384, 388, 396-7; and gender, 97-101; conditions, 9, 11, 25, 83, 101, 198, 262, 290, 295, 397; costs, 62, 110, 201, 223, 263, 276, 337, 399; history, 81, 197, 203, 206, 285, 289-90, 298, 413; migration, 87, 100, 121, 125, 174, 237, 297, 332, 335; movement, 97-9, 116, 200, 290-2, 297, 394, 396-7, 413; shortage, 16, 46, 78, 87, 199, 217; unrest, 200, 204, 214, 257, 292, 296, 336, 422-3; see also agricultural labourers, aristocracy of, child, Chinese, division of, family, indentured, migrant, outwork, slavery, strikes, trade unions, unemployment, wage
La Corona (cigars), 3-4, 9, 11, 13, 19-20, 82-4, 86, 94, 96, 101, 161, 231, 338, 352
La Honradez (cigarettes), 18, 130, 359; see also Susini
landless, 37, 39, 107, 339
land occupations, 261, 297
land reform, 35, 105, 109, 152, 165, 223, 416
land tenure, 17, 49, 52-3, 114, 150, 239, 285, 297, 330, 355
La Palma (Canary Islands), 387, 391, 395-7, 399-402
La Romana (Dominican Republic), 157, 206, 222-3, 226, 228, 231, 235, 337-8, 342, 399, 401
Las Villas (Cuba), 21-3, 28, 52-6, 78, 87-91, 92-3, 100, 108, 198-9, 291
La Tabacalera, 211-12, 221-3, 226, 311
leaf selection, 23, 93-4, 100, 157, 206
leaf trade, 6, 11, 16, 23, 84-6, 88, 122, 135-6, 230, 261, 352, 354, 391, 398, 412, 421
lector, see readers
León Asensio, 226, 227, 338
libreta, 8-9, 25, 198, 290
Licey (Dominican Republic), 227, 239-40, 338-9
literacy, 46, 99, 200, 291
lithography, 317-18, 370, 420
livestock, 16, 34, 37, 48-51, 49, 54, 61, 76, 105, 109, 112, 149, 218, 241, 403, 416, 426
London (Great Britain), 83, 139, 155, 175, 180, 183, 189, 213, 257, 260, 298, 308, 317, 319, 320-1, 333, 346, 349, 352-3, 361, 364, 384, 396, 419-20; see also Great Exhibition, Kew Gardens
Louisiana (United States), 243, 313, 334, 351
luxury smoke, 7, 82, 122, 190, 197, 257, 284-5, 307-28, 329, 349, 381, 385, 412, 420; see also cigars

Macanudo (cigar), 156, 158, 181-2, 231, 232, 235, 246, 283, 338, 400
Maceo, Antonio, 124-7, 129, 146-7, 180-1, 204, 207, 303, 360, 377
Machado Tobacco Company, 97, 101, 128-9, 132, 139, 139-41, 144-5, 333, 358, 359-61, 363
machine-made cigarettes, 314, 423-4, 425, 429-30
machine-made cigars, 178, 274-7, 368-9, 429; *see also* anti-machine movement, cigar machines
Madrid (Spain), 257, 308, 354, 395
Marti City (Florida), 124, 177, 192, 257
Martí, José, 82, 121, 124-5, 126-8, 147, 164, 181, 193, 204, 244, 303, 358-60, 393, 428
Martínez Ybor, Vicente, 121, 124
Maryland (United States), 216, 265, 415
Matanzas (Cuba), 89-91, 95-6, 99-100
MATASA, 156-7, 228, 231, 338, 399
mechanisation, 40, 63, 76, 97, 99, 107, 150, 181, 200, 204, 222, 267, 291-2, 344, 349, 385, 396-7, 429; *see also* machine-made, technology
Menéndez family, 156, 158, 181-2, 235, 398-9
merchants, 15, 414-15, 417-19, 423
Mexico, 59, 116, 121, 152, 156-9, 161, 164, 175-6, 178, 180, 206, 213, 216, 233, 236, 237, 240, 257-8, 269, 271, 286, 314, 330-1, 348, 356, 384-7, 415, 419, 422
Miami (Florida), 156, 159-60, 176, 178-9, 182-3, 194, 205-08, 216, 227, 231, 233-4, 241, 293-4
migrant labour, 50, 109, 202-03, 215, 260, 269, 272, 289, 294, 299, 304, 334, 336, 366
migration, 28, 85-86, 122-3, 152, 204, 213-16, 231, 235, 236-9, 256-8, 268-71, 277, 284-5, 290-2, 304, 311, 313, 317, 323, 329-30, 332, 335, 339, 345, 353-4, 356-7, 361, 384-8, 393, 395, 402-03, 417, 422-3, 427; *see also* Cuban émigrés
mining, 219, 227, 424

Moca (Dominican Republic), 223, 228, 233
modernisation, 20, 31, 37, 48, 59, 150, 220, 236
monopolies, 4, 14, 17, 88, 122, 175, 221-2, 257, 260, 308, 313, 322, 347-8, 364, 369-70, 382, 386, 392-3, 396, 411
Monte Cristi (Dominican Republic), 217, 222, 229, 244, 360, 416, 429
Montecristo (cigars), 3, 82, 153, 156, 158, 163, 178-9, 189, 231, 235-6, 246, 338, 382, 386, 398-9, 404
Montecruz (cigars), 235, 398-9
Montreal (Canada), 319-20, 334, 349, 370

nation, 171, 196-209, 385, 412
nationalisation, 34, 122, 152, 214, 258, 273, 282, 298, 306, 324, 383, 385
nationalism, 174-5, 256, 289, 345, 346, 357
natural disasters, 35, 59; *see also* hurricanes
Netherlands, 216-19, 259-1, 274-5, 276, 282, 286, 296-8, 310-11, 313, 332, 344-7, 357, 364, 366, 382, 391, 401, 414, 417, 424-5; investment, 225, 256, 296; tobacco, 161, 272, 274, 282; trade, 226, 414-16; *see also* Amsterdam, Dutch Cultivation System, Rotterdam
networks, 289, 329-42
New England (United States), 266, 345, 352, 356, 367
New Jersey (United States), 124, 152, 159-60, 164, 175, 204, 214, 223, 241, 292, 336; *see also* Trenton
New York (United States), 83, 128, 133, 175, 190, 212, 213, 215-16, 219, 238, 240, 257, 262, 265-6, 286, 292, 308, 322, 330-1, 334-40, 345-46, 349, 352, 356, 359, 362, 367, 384
Nicaragua, 116, 122, 152, 156-7, 159-61, 175-6, 178, 180, 182, 194, 206, 214-16, 225, 230, 233-5, 245, 257-8, 286, 314, 330-1, 337-8, 356, 386-7, 399

Nienhuys family, 259-60, 262, 271, 366

Ocala (Florida), 124, 192, 257
offshore Havana cigar, 151-3, 170, 193, 204, 207, 285, 289, 292, 314, 331, 333, 355-6
Oliva family, 160, 232, 234, 246
Operation Bootstrap, 286, 295, 332, 335, 356
oral history, 82, 86, 92, 125, 197-8, 201, 208, 295
Oriente (Cuba), 21, 89-91, 98-9, 100
Ortiz, Fernando, 15, 166, 170-87, 190, 196, 207, 213, 215, 242, 256, 276, 285, 287-90, 299, 307, 316, 318-19, 349-50, 412, 427-8; *see also* counterpoint
Ottoman Empire, 311, 346
outwork, 8, 18, 20, 22, 199, 290

Padilla, Napoleón, 155, 180, 216, 231, 337
Padrón family, 160, 163-4, 178-9, 182, 206
palm oil, 260-1, 366
Palomino, Lorenzo, 129, 360
Panama, 116, 271
Paris (France), 18, 257, 308, 317, 349, 352, 420
Partagás (cigars), 3-4, 16, 82, 130, 153, 156, 158, 159-60, 162, 181-2, 189, 231, 232, 235-6, 255, 283, 317, 334, 338, 352-4, 358, 381, 400
Partido (Cuba), 15-16, 180, 189, 232, 395
peasantry, 22-3, 33, 35, 37, 44-5, 150, 201, 213, 216-17, 222, 238, 241, 244-5, 256, 262, 272-3, 297, 365, 413, 416-17, 425-6
pesticides, 35, 59, 62, 110, 153-4
Philip Morris, 223, 235, 391, 400
Philippines, 133, 217, 225, 257, 261, 277, 287, 299, 313, 322, 324, 330, 332, 348, 357, 363, 382, 391
Pinar del Río (Cuba), 15-18, 21-3, 40, 49, 52-6, 61, 76-8, 87-91, 95-7, 99-100, 108, 151, 159, 180, 183, 189, 198-9, 201, 213, 231-2, 234, 275, 291, 315, 420; *see also* San Luis, Vuelta Abajo

pipe smoking, 257, 310, 313, 344, 357, 417, 422
plantations, 15-18, 23, 37, 48, 56-7, 133, 139, 180, 198, 216, 243, 260-1, 273, 297, 299, 311, 365, 412, 416, 418, 420, 426, 428
plug tobacco, 344, 416, 425
Por Larrañaga (cigars), 153, 159, 231, 235, 352, 355, 400
Portugal, 257, 260, 298, 308, 310, 347-8, 364, 369, 382, 414
pressed tobacco, 218, 417
prices, 17, 59-60, 219
protectionism, 20, 85, 221, 260, 353, 367, 369, 421, 424-5
Puerto Plata (Dominican Republic), 217, 222, 241-3, 417, 426
Puerto Príncipe (Cuba), 95, 99
Puerto Rican tobacco, 286, 336, 411, 429
Puerto Rico, 14, 122, 141, 152, 177, 207-08, 215-16, 217, 230, 240, 243, 257, 263, 268, 286, 295-6, 304, 313, 330-3, 335-7, 340, 348, 354-6, 382-5, 392, 412-13, 417-20, 421-4, 426, 428; tobacco areas, 335, 423; tobacco companies, 423-4; *see also* San Juan
Punch (cigars), 178, 180, 235, 283, 401

quality, 199, 315-18
Quesada family, 126, 156, 160, 228, 232, 338
Quincy (Florida), 177, 257, 280, 280-1, 286, 331, 356
Quín Díaz (cigars), 222-24

race, 8, 13, 16, 24-7, 81, 90-1, 93, 95-7, 126, 127-9, 147, 196-209, 217, 242, 269, 284-305, 310, 334, 336, 385, 412, 416, 425, 427; *see also* Black Atlantic, slavery
railroads, 219, 261, 424
Ramón Allones (cigars), 162, 189, 231, 236
readers, 82, 84, 97, 123, 128, 181, 200, 336, 394, 412
repression, 97, 200, 223, 291

ringers, *see* cigar ringers
Robaina, Alejandro, 151, 183-4, 188; *see also* Vegas Robaina
rollers, *see* cigar rollers
Romeo y Julieta (cigars), 12, 156, 161-2, 180, 231, 236, 246, 338, 381, 404
Rotterdam (Netherlands), 261, 299, 366
rubber, 260-1, 261, 366
rural development, 31, 34, 41, 65, 111, 201, 236
Russia, 105, 117, 193, 311, 346

Saint-Domingue, 217, 351, 415-16, 420; *see also* Haiti
Sancti Spíritus (Cuba), 40, 49, 61, 77-8, 86, 108, 159, 201, 402-03
San José de las Matas (Dominican Republic), 227, 238, 338
San Juan (Puerto Rico), 335, 417-18
San Luis (Pinar del Río), 18, 40-3, 49, 52-6, 57-8, 58-9, 64-8, 71, 75-6, 108-12, 201-02, 234; *see also* El Corojo
San Pedro de Macorís (Domincian Republic), 222, 226, 243, 337
Santa Clara (Cuba), 17, 77, 95-6, 99, 128-9, 243, 359
Santiago de los Caballeros (Dominican Republic), 156-7, 180, 205-06, 211, 219-22, 226-31, 233-4, 240, 241-3, 245, 337-40, 426, 429
Santo Domingo (Dominican Republic), 217, 221-2, 241, 243, 313, 340, 393, 416
seeds, 220, 224, 265, 284, 287, 316, 329, 368, 394, 424; *see also* Cuban seed, Havana seed
self-sufficiency, 34, 35, 60, 104, 116, 150, 165-6, 222, 297, 361
Sevilla (Spain), 88, 199, 291, 310-11, 384, 390, 412, 416
shade tobacco, 18, 41, 62, 110, 157, 177, 189, 256, 259, 262-4, 268-9, 274-6, 280, 286, 294, 295, 331, 334-5, 356, 368
sharecropping, 16-18, 22-3, 34-5, 37, 40, 48-49, 50-1, 52-3, 62, 105, 107, 109, 200, 202, 240, 368, 383, 393, 403

skills, 26, 82, 97, 199, 315-9, 396
slavery, 8-9, 12-13, 15-16, 19, 22, 25, 118, 174, 180, 190, 198, 217, 262, 267, 289-90, 292, 296-8, 310-11, 319, 347, 350, 357, 360, 384, 393, 416-17, 420, 427; abolition, 16, 97, 200, 290, 357; *see also* race
slave trade, 334, 347, 389, 414-15, 420, 427
smallholding, 104-18, 150-1, 176, 183, 201, 203, 214, 272, 365, 383, 403, 420
smoking, 83-4, 163, 190-1, 261-2, 270, 276, 296, 309, 311-13, 319, 320-1, 324-5, 340, 352, 357, 365, 367, 369; *see also* anti-smoking, pipe
snuff, 257, 309, 311-12, 322, 344, 422
snus, 256, 275-7
Societé d'Explotación Industrielle des Tabacs et des Alumettes (SEITA), 152, 155, 166, 176, 214, 225, 230, 258, 274, 383, 386-7, 401, 429
soil, 35, 59, 266, 366, 424
Soutar, Simon, 129-30, 133, 145, 148, 358
South America, 135-6, 216, 234, 240, 309, 323, 369, 388, 415; *see also* Brazil, Colombia, Ecuador, Venezuela
South Puerto Rico Sugar Company, 226, 342
Spain, 20, 85, 122-8, 152-3, 158, 161, 163-4, 166-7, 175-6, 181, 190, 204, 213-14, 216-19, 235-6, 244, 256-8, 260, 276, 284-6, 290-2, 298-9, 309-13, 316-17, 320, 321, 327-8, 329, 331-3, 344-8, 350-8, 364, 369, 382-5, 387-90, 393, 400-01, 411-12, 414-3, 428; investment, 4, 16, 122, 175, 213, 257, 308, 349, 382, 384, 420; migrant labour, 8, 26-7, 97, 199-200; tobacco companies, 88, 123, 354, 391; trade, 123, 226, 416; *see also* Canary Islands, Madrid, Sevilla
squatters, 52-3, 139, 273, 297
state farms, 46, 56-8, 63, 66, 79, 105, 109, 150, 165-6
stemming, 18, 23-4, 28, 86-7, 90-4,

92-3, 97-9, 103, 198-200, 263, 291, 302, 334, 403, 421
St Eustatius, 417-19
strikes, 92, 97-8, 101, 123, 128, 141-4, 193, 200, 223, 261, 291-2, 296-7, 336, 397-8, 422
St Thomas, 217, 241, 417-19
subsistence production, 16, 37, 49, 56, 63, 105, 107, 201, 216, 239
sugar, 15, 18, 34, 37, 39, 43, 48-52, 54, 61, 76, 80, 104-06, 114, 121, 129, 139, 153, 166, 170, 172-4, 196, 198, 201, 213, 215, 218-9, 222, 225-7, 242-4, 256, 260, 285, 287-8, 298, 307, 318, 348, 350-1, 358, 360, 365, 369, 385, 388-90, 412-13, 416-17, 420-1, 423-8
Sumatra (Indonesia), 175, 189, 255, 259, 260-1, 266, 271, 280, 287, 289, 296, 299, 305, 313, 332, 345, 357, 365-8, 370, 384, 395, 401
Sumatran tobacco, 159, 161, 241, 256, 259-62, 266, 268, 274, 296, 334, 367; see also American Sumatran Tobacco Corporation
Susini, 18-19, 25, 86, 122, 219; see also La Honradez
sweatshops, 6, 12, 18, 20-2, 85, 159, 221
Sweden, 130, 235, 256, 276-7, 401
Swedish Match, 230, 235, 255, 258, 274-7, 387
Switzerland, 163, 224, 230, 274, 310, 323, 401

Tabacalera Cubana, 13, 21, 235
Tabacalera de García, 157, 179, 228-9, 230, 236, 246, 338-9
Tabacalera Española, 152-4, 163, 166, 176, 179, 214, 220, 222, 225, 230, 235-6, 258, 383, 386-7, 391-2, 396-8, 400-01, 425, 429
Tabacanaria, 391, 400
Tabacos Dominicanos, 156-7, 226, 231, 232, 338
Tamboril (Dominican Republic), 225, 226-8, 238, 240, 338-9
Tampa (Florida), 27-8, 82-3, 86, 100, 121, 124, 156, 159-61, 174, 176-8, 181, 192-3, 198, 203-07, 215, 223, 232-4, 243, 257, 270, 280, 286, 292-4, 331, 338, 356, 397; see also Ybor City
tariffs, 4-5, 14, 20, 85, 123, 142, 219, 237, 260, 266, 268, 310, 344, 347, 352-4, 367-8, 369, 421, 424
taste, 155, 164, 217, 264, 266, 275, 308, 310, 313, 318-21, 349, 365, 424; see also aroma
technology, 20, 59, 62, 82, 85, 107, 179, 206, 219, 220, 224, 256, 330, 355; see also knowledge circuits, mechanisation
Temple Hall (Jamaica), 121, 126-9, 140, 145, 148, 158, 181, 358-60, 364, 379
tenant farmers, 16, 34-5, 48, 50-1, 52-5, 105, 107, 109, 200, 403
Tenerife (Canary Islands), 387, 391-2, 395-8, 400-01
terroir, 315-18, 323, 370
tobacco, 17, 49, 51-2, 54, 58, 77, 106, 108-09, 123, 125, 129, 139, 150, 172-4, 189-90, 201, 204, 215, 218-21, 238, 256, 260-2, 267, 273-4, 283, 285, 287-8, 295, 297-8, 304, 307-10, 316-20, 321-3, 347-8, 350-1, 360, 364-5, 369, 385, 388-93, 402-03, 412, 415, 418, 420, 422, 424, 427-8; agriculture, 15-18, 22-3, 41, 53, 55, 58, 65-7, 78, 81, 100, 114, 131-3, 151, 153-4, 157-8, 166, 176, 197, 201, 217-8, 226, 244, 260-1, 269, 286, 294, 310, 313, 316, 331-2, 336, 352, 356, 360, 362, 366, 368, 390, 392, 394-5, 399, 401, 415, 419-20, 427, 429; blends, 14, 40, 140, 159, 175, 189, 206, 224, 230, 234, 241, 265, 286-7, 325, 332-3, 356-7, 370, 399-400, 403; brokers, 9, 156, 260, 366; business, 16, 154, 239, 241, 261, 297, 331; leaf, 17, 49, 202, 206, 212, 271, 303, 328, 333, 356, 368, 400, 411, 429; manufacture, 7, 81, 97, 154, 197, 239, 331, 344, 353, 393, 430; monopoly, 6, 21, 85, 276, 298, 382, 391, 419; processing, 82, 132-3, 274,

361; production, 40, 43, 59, 65, 111, 219, 230, 263, 268, 356, 399, 424; seed, 129-30, 133, 219, 271; sorting, 18, 24, 41, 49-50, 63, 65, 74, 88, 90-2, 111, 157, 198-9, 201, 206, 270, 291, 334; trade, 88, 131, 135, 154, 218, 220, 225, 230, 243, 260, 272, 298, 311-12, 337, 366, 413, 418, 423, 425; workers, 80, 82, 87-90, 95-6, 207, 275, 331, 396-7; *see also* Burley, chewing, cigar leaf, clear Havana, Cuban, Deli, Dominican, filler leaf, plug, pressed, Puerto Rican, seeds, shade, snuff, snus, stemming, Virginia, wrapper

Torricelli Act (1991), 175, 214, 258, 386; *see also* Helms Burton

trade, 17, 217, 286, 332, 349, 356, 414; *see also* exports, free trade, leaf trade, merchants, prices, protectionism, tariffs

trade embargo, 105, 117, 122, 152, 156, 163-5, 175-9, 191, 194, 204-05, 212, 214-15, 223, 231-3, 236, 246, 255-9, 277, 286, 314, 331, 337, 340, 357, 383-4, 385, 398-9, 413; *see also* Helms Burton; Torricelli

trade unions, 30, 83, 97-100, 141, 144, 199-200, 291, 385, 397-8, 430; *see also* labour

transatlantic history, 381-408; *see also* Atlantic world, Black Atlantic

transculturation, 170-1, 256, 287-8, 307; *see also* Ortiz

trans-imperial connections, 344-78

transnationalism, 329-42

Trenton (New Jersey), 83-4, 102-03, 159

Trujillo, Rafael Leónidas, 156, 180, 205, 211-12, 221-4, 227, 236, 239, 337, 413, 425, 428

Trust, 6-8, 10, 12, 314, 353-5; *see also* American Tobacco Company (ATC)

Turkey, 175, 189, 384; *see also* Ottoman Empire

unemployment, 10, 87-8, 93-4, 230, 238, 257, 336

Unidad de Producción Básica Cooperativa (UPBC), 150-1, 165-7; *see also* cooperatives

United States, 97, 104-05, 116, 122-5, 127-9, 135-6, 145, 147, 152, 157, 163, 171, 175-6, 193, 204, 215-16, 217-18, 224-6, 230-1, 245, 255-6, 260-1, 266, 276, 284-5, 298, 313-14, 317, 329-30, 336, 339, 344-7, 351-7, 359, 364-70, 368, 382, 384-5, 389, 391-2, 400-01, 420-1, 423-4, 428-9; cigars, 82-3, 100, 162-3, 178-9, 292, 386; Cubans, 103, 122, 175, 314; investment, 16, 97, 139, 175, 189, 214, 219, 238, 256, 286, 308, 314, 333, 349, 353, 356, 385, 420, 423-4; manufacture, 4, 11, 19, 21, 84-5, 122, 157, 177, 194, 258-9, 276, 314, 332, 352-3, 356, 385, 421; market, 85, 154, 212, 218-19, 227, 230, 232-3, 332, 337, 339, 398, 421, 423-5; migration, 21, 87, 123; tobacco, 122, 160, 164, 224, 227, 260, 332, 367, 413, 425, 429; trade, 4-5, 14, 157, 160, 164, 177, 192, 205-06, 212, 223, 226, 269, 274, 286, 291, 299, 389, 400; workers, 27-8, 88, 141; *see also* Connecticut, Florida, Florida-Georgia tobacco belt, Georgia, Louisiana, New England, New Jersey, New York, Virginia

US Department of Agriculture (USDA), 258-9, 266, 280, 295, 314

Valdés, Inocencia, 101, 103, 200
Vegas Robaina, 151, 183, 188; *see also* Robaina
Venezuela, 217, 311, 388-9, 397
Vietnam, 156, 206, 228, 233
Villa González (Dominican Republic), 219, 224, 227-9, 232, 233, 338
Virginia tobacco, 4, 14, 145, 224, 357
Virginia (United States), 216, 264, 295, 311-12, 324, 334, 351, 379, 390, 415
Vuelta Abajo (Cuba), 16, 49, 83, 86, 108, 128-9, 133, 151, 155, 160-1, 163,

166, 180, 188-9, 201, 213, 219, 232, 243, 275, 315, 333, 350, 353, 358-9, 362, 370, 420-1, 423-4; *see also* Pinar del Río
Vuelta Arriba (Cuba), 49, 108, 128, 166, 180, 201, 315, 351, 359, 401

wage labour, 18, 25, 37, 40, 50-1, 290
wages, 8-10, 13, 83, 92-3, 143, 179, 198, 201, 206, 238, 240, 290, 293, 336, 397
Wangüemert family, 395, 399, 401
Windsor (Connecticut), 263-5, 267, 269, 271

women, 19, 27, 31-47, 48, 63-73, 81, 86, 104-18, 181, 197, 199-200, 204, 265, 273, 290-1, 294, 313, 367, 385, 396-7, 403; *see also* gender
wrapper leaf, 41, 50, 65, 109-11, 128, 157-8, 160-1, 177, 206, 217, 224-6, 230, 260, 268, 270-1, 274, 280, 294, 296-7, 305, 313, 334, 337, 357, 365, 367, 399

Ybor City (Tampa), 82, 100, 121, 124, 146, 159, 181, 192-3, 204, 207, 234, 243, 286, 293, 331, 356

Also published by Amaurea Press

A new expanded edition of the classic study of Cuban tobacco

Tobacco on the Periphery
A Case Study in Cuban Labour History, 1860-1958
Jean Stubbs

"A well-timed reprint of a masterful and highly readable historical account"
(Kathinka Sinha-Kerkhoff, IISG Amsterdam)

"A solid study, obligatory reading for understanding the history of tobacco."
(Joan Casanovas, Universitat Rovira i Virgili)

"A major investigation that gave tobacco its rightful place in Cuban history."
(Juan José Baldrich, Universidad de Puerto Rico)

"A skillfully written study of tobacco as a commodity."
(Ratna Saptari, Universiteit Leiden)

"A gem in the historiography on the Cuban tobacco industry."
(Zoe Nocedo Primo, Museo del Tabaco, Habana)

This is the story of Cuban tobacco, whose agricultural and industrial development was fashioned as deftly as a Havana cigar around overseas trading interests. It traces the nineteenth-century growth of a strong tobacco oligarchy, peasant grower class and urban salaried work force, alongside slave and indentured labour, and examines how a prestigious manufacturing country was transformed into an exporter of leaf. Visibly poor peasant agriculture concealed foreign and home capital which, while creating some large plantations, used and even propagated a most extreme form of sharecropping. Well into the twentieth century, an increasingly embattled industry catered to dwindling luxury markets and an unstable, fluctuating home market with but a few relatively large, on the whole family, concerns and a proliferation of small sweatshop and outwork production.

Jean Stubbs penetrates the finer socio-political aspects of the radically changing nature and composition of peasantry and proletariat, including the interlacing of race, gender and skill, to take a closer look at areas of class action and national and class consciousness, be it through reformism, anarcho-syndicalism, revolutionary nationalism, socialism or communism.

This new edition expands on the 1985 original, adding other source material, with a new Preface and a Foreword by Victor Bulmer-Thomas. Spanish edition (*Tabaco en la periferia: El complejo agro-industrial cubano y su movimiento obrero, 1860-1959*) also available with a new Preface and Foreword by Oscar Zanetti Lecuona.

ISBN 9781914278051 (paperback), 9781914278068 (hardback), 9781914278075 (ebook)